Dynasties

C000246750

For thousands of years, societies have fallen under the reign of a single leader, ruling as chief, king, or emperor. In this fascinating global history of medieval and early modern dynastic power, Jeroen Duindam charts the rise and fall of dynasties, the rituals of rulership, and the contested presence of women on the throne. From European, African, Mughal, Ming–Qing, and Safavid dynasties to the Ottoman empire, Tokugawa Japan, and Chosŏn Korea, he reveals the tension between the ideals of kingship and the lives of actual rulers, the rich variety of arrangements for succession, the households or courts which catered to rulers' daily needs, and the relationship between the court and the territories under its control. The book integrates numerous African examples, sets dynasties within longer-term developments such as the rise of the state, and examines whether the tensions inherent in dynastic power led inexorably to cycles of ascent and decline.

Jeroen Duindam is Professor of Early Modern History at the Department of History, Leiden University.

Dynasties

A Global History of Power, 1300–1800

Jeroen Duindam

Leiden University

CAMBRIDGE
UNIVERSITY PRESS

University Printing House, Cambridge CB2 8BS, United Kingdom

One Liberty Plaza, 20th Floor, New York, NY 10006, USA

477 Williamstown Road, Port Melbourne, VIC 3207, Australia

314-321, 3rd Floor, Plot 3, Splendor Forum, Jasola District Centre, New Delhi - 110025, India

79 Anson Road, #06-04/06, Singapore 079906

Cambridge University Press is part of the University of Cambridge.

It furthers the University's mission by disseminating knowledge in the pursuit of education, learning and research at the highest international levels of excellence.

www.cambridge.org
Information on this title: www.cambridge.org/9781107637580

© Jeroen Duindam 2016

First published 2016

A catalogue record for this publication is available from the British Library

ISBN 978-1-107-06068-5 Hardback
ISBN 978-1-107-63758-0 Paperback

Cambridge University Press has no responsibility for the persistence or accuracy of URLs for external or third-party internet websites referred to in this publication, and does not guarantee that any content on such websites is, or will remain, accurate or appropriate.

Contents

Plates

Section II

Every effort has been made to contact the relevant copyright holders for the images reproduced in this book. In the event of any error, the publisher will be pleased to make corrections in any reprints or future editions.

The colour plates can be found between pages 160 and 161 and pages 288 and 289.

Figures

Maps

Preface

The global scope and thematic layout of this book do not allow digressions: most academic debates are left aside or relegated to the footnotes. My previous publications offer extended discussions of models and concepts commonly used in the history of courts and elites. The rationale for my comparative approach, explained briefly in the Introduction, has been defended at some length in earlier publications.

Bringing together results of specialised literature in many areas, I chose to use the relevant local terms at least once in the text. The glossary lists these terms with short explanations. Comparison relies on general concepts, but cannot be precise and verifiable if it fails to specify the local variants. At the same time, the use of these regional terms introduces the problem of transliteration conventions. While I have consistently tried to adopt accepted systems of transliteration, I lack the language expertise of the specialist and hence cannot myself control the results. Precision in this respect, surely, is not the key ambition of this book.

Chronology throughout the book is given in CE dates: CE and BCE are added only in unclear cases. Other calendars are never used, nor is the connection between dynastic rule and the calendar, common in many areas, considered here. Three years are given in parentheses the first time any ruler is mentioned in the text: birth, start of rule, end of rule. The year for the end of rule is marked with an asterisk (*) in cases where it did not coincide with death, usually with an endnote explaining the circumstances (abdication, dethronement).

Paramount dynastic rulers were mostly men. This book discusses women in power and close to power at length, but it uses 'ruler', 'prince', or 'king' in general statements where princesses and queens are implicitly included.

Acknowledgements

Writing a book is a solitary activity. This comparative global book, however, could never have been written without the advice and assistance of many people.

Hamish Scott supported me from the book proposal to the final draft, helping this project through its various stages with detailed but invariably encouraging comments and corrections. Jérôme Kerlouégan's typically nuanced, precise, and thought-provoking answers to my unending queries added as much to my grasp of Chinese history as my perusal of the relevant literature. Anne Walthall, who stepped in to help me with Japanese history, not only gave essential advice, but also commented on the entire text during the writing process.

Others likewise showed remarkable learning, forbearance, and generosity, by reading and commenting on the typescript in one of its multiple stages: Maaike van Berkel, Wim Blockmans, Marie Favereau-Doumenjou, Liesbeth Geevers, Jos Gommans, Metin Kunt, Elsbeth Locher-Scholten, Maarten Prak, Kim Ragetli, David Robinson, Robert Ross, Geoffrey Symcox, Bonno Thoden van Velzen, and Harriet Zurndorfer. During the writing process, I directly approached colleagues around the world after reading their specialised works; they gave expert advice, liberally shared their publications with me, and helped me with illustrations: Jan Abbink, Elif Akcetin, Tülay Artan, Sussan Babaie, Kathryn Babayan, Edna Bay, Cumhur Bekar, Suzanne Preston Blier, Wim Boot, Günhan Börekci, Remco Breuker, Craig Clunas, David Durand-Guédy, Patricia Ebrey, Emine Fetvacı, Anne Gerritsen, R. Kent Guy, Georgios Halkias, Leonhard Horowski, Rieko Kamei-Dyche, Hani Khafipour, Paulina Lewicka, Elizabeth Lillehoj, Keith McMahon, Rhoads Murphey, Marinos Sariyannis, Miri Shefer, Richard Wang, Constanze Weise, Christopher Wheeler, Zhongnan Zhao.

The Netherlands Institute for Advanced Studies (NIAS) in Wassenaar offered an ideal site for writing. Distant from urban distractions and located close to the beach, it fosters writing as well as outdoor relaxation. The invariably gracious and effective staff, catering for daily as well as for academic needs, multiplied the number of hours I could spend on concentrated writing. Erwin Nolet and Dindy van Maanen, operating the NIAS library, swiftly satisfied my voracious appetite for books and articles. The fellows at the NIAS, following the same beneficial routines, were great company, for evening gatherings, walks, and conversations. My Leiden colleagues gracefully respected my sabbatical leave at the NIAS, even during a semester with particularly heavy demands on all leading staff members. At the NIAS, three research MA students, Quinten Somsen, Veronika Poier, and Michiel Lemmers, helped me by reading and commenting on the first versions of my chapters.

During the writing process several colleagues took the risk of inviting me to talk about my work in the early stages of its progress. Graeme Murdock and his group of students at Trinity College Dublin were hospitable as well as intellectually helpful. The same can be said about Christian Windler's Berne University seminar meeting at Gerschnialp, where colleagues and students engaged in discussions as well as in Alpine excursions.

Over the last decade, various projects and co-operations have helped expand my comparative horizon. A European project on 'Tributary Empires' (COST/ESF action A 36) brought me into contact with a wide pool of scholars studying different regions and ages. The co-operation with Metin Kunt and Tülay Artan, in particular, has been lasting and fruitful. A Dutch-German-Chinese (CO-Reach) project on the 'Structures and legacies of dynastic power', organised with Sabine Dabringhaus, strengthened my connection to specialists in Chinese history. The Netherlands Organisation for Scientific Research (NWO) at various stages generously supported my initiatives, for the projects cited as well as in the cadre of my more extensive 'Horizon' project on 'Eurasian Empires', co-organised with Jos Gommans, Maaike van Berkel, and Peter Rietbergen. The conversation with these colleagues, and the eight researchers in our team, Liesbeth Geevers, Marie Favereau-Doumenjou, Cumhur Bekar, Lennart Bes, Willem Flinterman, Barend Noordam, Kim Ragetli, and Hans Voeten, has proved a lasting source of inspiration. The efficacy and friendliness of our project manager Rebecca Wensma has been a precondition for the success of our project. Recently Josephine van der Bent, a researcher herself, stepped in to support our project's daily machinery.

Lectures and discussions with colleagues across the globe proved essential for the emergence of my comparative work. Thomas Maissen and Subrata Mitra invited me to Heidelberg several times; Eugenio Menegon and his colleagues to Boston, Mark Elliott to Harvard, Craig Clunas to Oxford, David Robinson to Colgate, and Kent Guy to Seattle.

In general the easy connection to numerous regional specialists, generously sharing their insights, proved indispensable for this book, which could not have been written on the basis of printed knowledge alone.

Reports by anonymous readers of several presses, and the positive response of editors, confirmed my initial plans for this book while suggesting some important improvements. At Cambridge University Press, Michael Watson proved a constant support, while Amanda George effectively organised the final stages of the publication process. From the writing of my dissertation in the early 1990s onwards, Kate Delaney's comments and corrections have allowed me to develop my writing in English – her friendship and support have been a continuing presence during my entire career. David Claszen provided invaluable assistance in proofreading, and in compiling the index and glossary.

My wife Mariella not only made possible my protracted absences, but also read and corrected the entire manuscript with painstaking accuracy. My eldest son Guus, studying in the US, read and commented on the first drafts of all chapters. My younger son Nol accepted my absence in person and mind with typical generosity and patiently listened to my digressions. More fundamentally, they all contributed to my ease and comfort.

Jeroen Duindam

Maps

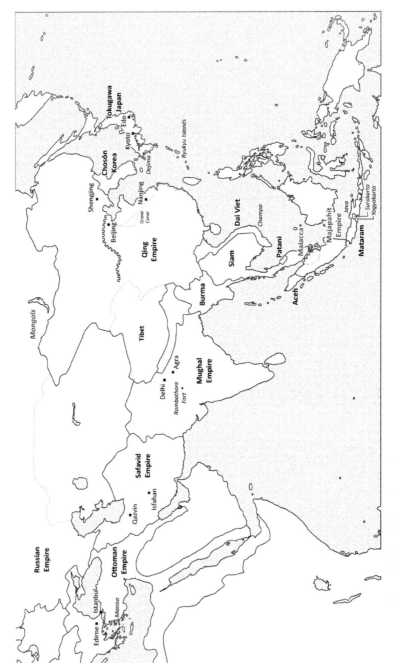

1 Map of Asia with main empires.

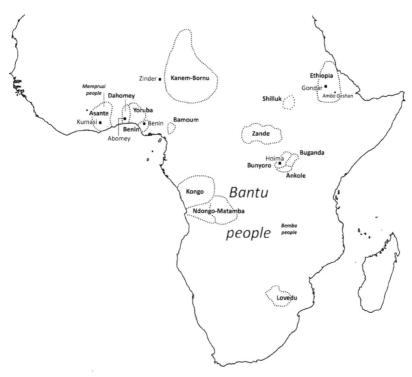

2 Map of Africa with kingdoms discussed in this book.

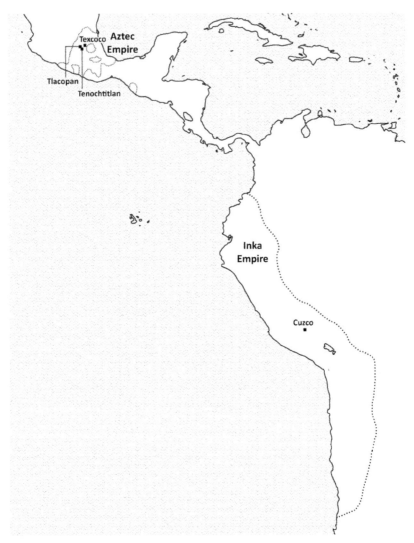

3 Map of Inka and Aztec empires.

Introduction

> One cannot imagine a dynasty without civilization, while a civilization without dynasty and royal authority is impossible, because human beings must by nature co-operate, and that calls for a restraining influence. Political leadership, based either on religious or royal authority, is obligatory ... This is what is meant by dynasty.
>
>   Ibn Khaldun, *The Muqaddimah*, ed. Franz Rosenthal, Book IV, chap. 20, 291.

Kinship to kingship?

Dynasty plays a marginal role in today's world. Most modern political systems define themselves as the antithesis of *ancien régime* monarchy, with election as the prime method of succession to high office and a strong bias against family-based networks of power. Royalty retains a surprising potential to attract crowds and generate veneration, but it is mostly seen as the relic of an earlier and darker age. Such reservations about kingship have a long history. Hippocrates (460–377 BCE) observed that 'where there are kings, there must be the greatest cowards. For [here] men's souls are enslaved, and refuse to run risks readily and recklessly to increase the power of somebody else.'[1] This connection between kingship and servitude has been noted many times since. The Englishman J. Alfred Skertchly, visiting the West African kingdom of Dahomey in the early 1870s, enjoyed the remarkable honour of being proclaimed a prince by the reigning king Glele (?–1858–1889).[2] Nevertheless, he ridiculed the obligatory ritual greeting performed by all who approached the king:

The ... salutation consists of a prostration before the monarch with the forehead touching the sand, and afterwards rubbing the cheeks on the earth, leaving a red patch of sand on either side ... Then follows the dirt bath ... a series of shovelling

---

[1] Hippocrates, *Airs, Waters, Places*, in *Hippocrates*, vol. I, trans. W.H.S. Jones, Loeb Classical Library (Cambridge, MA, 1923), 133.

[2] Following the first mention of all rulers in this book, three years are given in parentheses: birth, start of reign, end of reign. Question marks replace uncertain or unknown dates; where the end of the reign did not coincide with the death of the ruler, the last year is followed by an asterisk: *.

of the earth over the head ... when receiving or asking any particular favour, the saluter completely smothers himself with the red earth; rubbing it well into the arms and neck until it sticks to the perspiring skin like dough.[3]

The extreme elevation of one person over others does not conform to modern sensibilities. In 1786, one of Europe's leading monarchs, Habsburg emperor Joseph II (1741–1780–1790), abolished the reverence on bended knee at the Austrian court, arguing that this show of respect 'is unnecessary between humans, and should be reserved for God alone'.[4] The authority of hereditary princes strikes us as the inverse image of modern egalitarian society: it is often portrayed in contrast to modernity, as the undesirable situation from which we emancipated ourselves. However, almost all peoples across the globe until very recently accepted dynastic rule as a god-given and desirable form of power.

Throughout history, rule by a single male figure has predominated. These men rarely ruled without some guidance from mothers, spouses, and female relatives, yet women rulers holding supreme sovereign power remained the exception, even in societies where royalty was transferred through the female line.[5] Chiefs, kings, and emperors reigned over most

---

[3] J. Alfred Skertchly, *Dahomey As It Is: Being a Narrative of Eight Months' Residence in that Country* ... (London, 1874), 143.

[4] Jeroen Duindam, 'The Burgundian-Spanish legacy in European court life: a brief reassessment and the example of the Austrian Habsburgs', *Publication du Centre européen d'études bourguignonnes*, 46 (2006), 203–220, full quotation at 216 ('weil dieses zwischen Menschen und Menschen keine geziemende Handlung ist die Gott allein vorbehalten bleiben muß').

[5] On women and rule, see Chapter 2 below. On China, see Keith McMahon, *Women Shall Not Rule. Imperial Wives and Concubines in China from Han to Liao* (Lanham, MD, 2013). On Southeast Asia, see Barbara Watson Andaya, *The Flaming Womb: Repositioning Women in Early Modern Southeast Asia* (Honolulu, HI, 2006), 165–96. On Europe, see recently Matthias Schnettger, 'Weibliche Herrschaft in der Frühen Neuzeit: einige Beobachtungen aus verfassungs- und politikgeschichtlicher Sicht', *Zeitenblicke*, 8/2 (2009), www.zeiten-blicke.de/2009/2/schnettger/dippArticle.pdf; Ann Lyon, 'The place of women in European royal succession in the Middle Ages', *Liverpool Law Review*, 27/3 (2006), 361–93. On African matrilineal contexts, see Tarikhu Farrar, 'The queenmother, matriarchy, and the question of female political authority in precolonial West African monarchy', *Journal of Black Studies*, 27/5 (1997), 579–97. For a wider overview of female political roles, see Annie M.D. Lebeuf, 'La rôle de la femme dans l'organisation politique des sociétés africaines', in Denise Paulme (ed.), *Femmes d'Afrique noire*, (Paris, 1960), 93–120. For an example of sovereign female rule in southern Africa, see E. Jensen Krige and J.D. Krige, *The Realm of a Rain-Queen: A Study of the Pattern of Lovedu Society* (Oxford, 1943). On double descent or 'dual political systems' with matching leadership roles for women and men, see e.g. Beverly J. Stoeltje, 'Asante queen mothers', *Annals of the New York Academy of Sciences*, 810/1 (1997), 41–71; Isabel Yaya, *The Two Faces of Inca History: Dualism in the Narratives and Cosmology of Ancient Cuzco* (Leiden and Boston, MA, 2012). See also Joyce Marcus, 'Breaking the glass ceiling: the strategies of royal women in ancient states', in Cecelia F. Klein (ed.), *Gender in Pre-Hispanic America* (Washington, DC, 2001), 305–40. See in general the volume edited by Anne Walthall, *Servants of the Dynasty: Palace Women in World History* (Berkeley, CA, 2008).

polities across the globe for the last 10,000 years. Around 8000 BCE, the domestication of plant and animal life enabled the emergence of larger-scale settlements, a process which spread from different core areas to envelop the larger part of the world. Small and mobile kinship-based groups ruled by elders or chiefs will have arisen far earlier, but the expanding scale of sedentary settlements and the increased possibility of amassing surplus now stimulated social differentiation, hierarchy, and conquest. In many places 'stateless' societies persisted. Almost invariably though, dynastic leaders arose where hierarchy and differentiation developed. In the process, the scale of polities expanded: small groups led by chiefs were brought together under the authority of 'paramount chiefs' or kings. In the long run, kingdoms were sometimes absorbed by kings-of-kings or emperors. Royalty often presented itself as originating in conquest, with a stranger subduing the local population and founding a line of kings.[6] Ruling over an assemblage of groups previously unconnected or even hostile, kings were presented as standing above faction and as safeguarding harmony, both within society and between heaven and earth.

In whichever way royal leaders actually emerged or represented their origins, the dynastic organisation of power lasted. Dynasties could be short-lived or enduring; successful in creating a pacified and coherent polity or prone to violence and catastrophically inept. The dynastic set-up of power, however, proved to be remarkably persistent. The extended overarching polities which emerged in several continents were almost universally headed by dynastic leaders. The *pater familias* was head of his clan or family as well as leader of a polity; a simple mortal glorified as a demigod. The clash of these roles forms one of the themes of this book.

Dynasty persists into the modern world, but it has lost much of its aura during recent centuries. With the emergence of industrialised and urbanised societies in the nineteenth and twentieth centuries, alternative forms of power have become more prominent. Kingship evolved at a point where societies moved beyond kinship as the key principle of social organisation; it retreated in modern urban and industrial society. Kinship

---

[6] On strangers and conquerors in general, see Marshall Sahlins, 'The stranger-king or, Elementary forms of the politics of life', *Indonesia and the Malay World*, 36/105 (2008), 177–99; on the conquest nature of African kingdoms, see Jan Vansina, 'A comparison of African kingdoms', *Africa*, 32 (1962), 324–35, at 329. Specific explanations for the repeated story of migration and conquest in an African context can be found in Claude Tardits (ed.), *Princes & serviteurs du royaume: cinq études de monarchies africaines* (Paris, 1987), 20; Aidan Southall, 'The segmentary state in Africa and Asia', *Comparative Studies in Society and History*, 30/1 (1988), 52–82, at 61–3; and Lebeuf, 'La rôle de la femme', points to women as the mythic partners of stranger-kings, indicating the union of different peoples under one dynasty. See also Jeyamalar Kathirithamby-Wells, '"Strangers" and "stranger-kings": the Sayyid in eighteenth-century maritime Southeast Asia', *Journal of Southeast Asian Studies*, 40, Special Issue 3 (2009), 567–91.

and family, however, remain a force to be reckoned with. Personalised and enduring forms of leadership in politics and in business tend to acquire semi-dynastic traits even in the contemporary world. In autocratic states, the power of modern-day dynasts extends far beyond anything their predecessors could have imagined.[7]

Dynastic power throughout history shares some basic features. Kingship, emerging as an extension of kinship when a clan or lineage imposed its hierarchical supremacy on other descent groups, retains a powerful connection to family and genealogy. Deriving from the ancient Greek term for lordship and sovereignty, 'dynasty' is now commonly understood as a ruling family, a line of kings or princes.[8] While hereditary succession was never a universal aspect of polities governed by kings or emperors across the globe, the ruler's kin was close to power. The ruler and his relatives were served by a household of retainers and advisors. The material environment of these groups, whether a simple dwelling or a grand palace, structured access to the ruler. A focal point of redistribution and ritual, the dynastic centre interacted in various ways with society at large. This book examines these social patterns around dynastic rulers at four levels, beginning with and moving outwards from the figure in the centre: ruler, dynasty, court, and realm. At each of these levels, certain tensions arose; closer inspection reveals how quite distinct social patterns, which emerged around the world, can be understood as alternative solutions to these tensions (see Figure 1).

A single figure stood at the heart of the polity, governing as well as representing the realm as a mascot or totem. All kings, talented or inept, were subject to certain structural complications. The more the position of the ruler was elevated to omnipotence or sacrality, the more it tended to circumscribe the person on the throne. Hierarchical pre-eminence and ritual responsibilities severely limited the freedom of incumbent kings,

---

[7] Simon Sebag Montefiore, *Stalin: The Court of the Red Tsar* (London, 2007); Russ Baker, *Family of Secrets: The Bush Dynasty, America's Invisible Government, and the Hidden History of the Last Fifty Years* (New York, 2009); Bradley K. Martin, *Under the Loving Care of the Fatherly Leader: North Korea and the Kim Dynasty* (New York, 2006). Examples from the business world can be found in João de Pina-Cabral and Antónia Pedroso de Lima (eds.), *Elites: Choice, Leadership and Succession* (Oxford, 2000); see also the thirteen business dynasties in David S. Landes, *Dynasties: Fortunes and Misfortunes of the World's Great Family Businesses* (New York, 2006); for a typology mixing dynastic empires and modern totalitarian regimes, see Karl Wittfogel, *Oriental Despotism: A Comparative Study of Total Power* (New Haven, CT, and London, 1957).

[8] On dynasty and its various meanings in antiquity, see Cinzia Bearzot, 'Dynasteia, idea of, Greece', in Roger S. Bagnall et al. (eds.), *The Encyclopedia of Ancient History* (Oxford, 2012), 2240–1; Mischa Meier and Meret Strothmann, 'Dynasteia', in Hubert Cancik and Helmuth Schneider (eds.), *Brill's New Pauly: Encyclopedia of the Ancient World*, online edition (Leiden, 2002–) (accessed 9 October 2014); *OED Online* (accessed 6 March 2014).

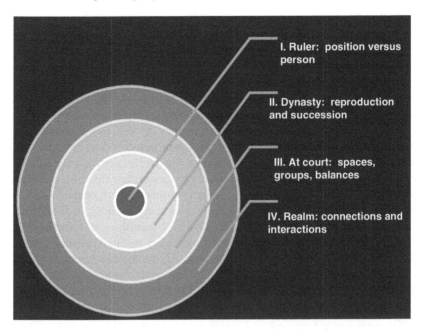

1 The layout of this book: concentric circles around the ruler.

complicated their personal relationships, and thwarted active political roles. The first chapter of this book examines the tension between position and person, between the ideals of kingship and the lives of the figures actually ruling. Do the expectations and ideas surrounding kingship contain shared or general elements globally? Do we find contrasting templates for rulership? How did youngsters learn to adopt such roles, and how did they cope with their elevated position from adolescence to maturity and old age? For long-living rulers in particular, this was a daunting challenge: where could they seek intimacy and support, whom could they trust without misgivings? Tensions between the unpredictable qualities of the persons ascending to the throne and the variable but consistently heavy demands of the position arose in many forms, and affected strong as well as weak rulers. These epithets – strong and weak, good and bad – need to be placed against the background of the tension between person and position. Strong-willed and intelligent figures, spurred by the demands of government but vexed by the restrictions placed on their shoulders, could respond by turning into archetypically 'bad' rulers resorting to violence or retreating into their palaces. Conversely, wholly undistinguished and pliable characters, lucky in their choice of advisors and passively following the latters' dictates, were likely to be remembered as good or wise rulers.

Moving one step away from the central figure, close relatives and the spouses or consorts come into view. The dynasty or royal clan around a ruler could be delimited in many ways, a process determined by traditions and choices regarding dynastic reproduction and succession. Women, only in exceptional cases themselves occupying the uppermost position of authority, were sometimes seen as the vehicles of royalty. In matrilineal polities, only sons of royal women could ascend to the throne, whereas the status of the father was irrelevant for succession. Female agency was determined not only by patterns of descent, but also by reproduction: harem-based polygyny dominated dynasties worldwide, whereas monogamous marriage was the rule only in Christian Europe. Numerous offspring safeguarded continuity, but foreboded rivalry. Siring only a few children made it easier to satisfy sibling ambitions, but increased the risk of extinction. All dynasties were concerned about the absence of direct successors and many were forced to seek alternative strategies such as adoption. The second chapter of this book examines the rich variety of arrangements for reproduction and succession – charting the agency of women and the place of royal relatives in dynastic settings. It challenges definitions of dynasty based exclusively on heredity, showing many alternatives to the concentration of power inherent in male primogeniture or eldest-son succession. Rights of succession invariably engendered tensions.[9] Relatives close to succession and sharing in dynastic prestige could act as powerful supporters, but they were liable to turn into dangerous rivals. How did dynastic rulers and their advisors deal with this challenge? What patterns can be found in the attitudes, functions, and locations of relatives eligible for succession?

Servants form the third concentric circle around the dynastic ruler: the household or court. Rulers and their relatives were served by an establishment catering for their daily needs as well as for the government of the realm. Who served the ruler in these different capacities? From which status groups in society were these servants drawn? Courts have traditionally been seen as arenas of conflict, the preservation of royal power as contingent upon exploiting rivalries among groups at court: *divide et impera*.[10] Some rulers were able to manipulate conflict, others were

---

[9] Jack Goody (ed.), *Succession to High Office* (Cambridge, 1966).

[10] Norbert Elias, *The Court Society* (Oxford, 1983), elaborates on Max Weber's typology of power, *Wirtschaft und Gesellschaft: Grundriss der verstehenden Soziologie* (Tübingen, 1972 [1921]); see the discussion and bibliography in Jeroen Duindam, *Myths of Power: Norbert Elias and the Early Modern European Court* (Amsterdam, 1995).

undermined by it, yet beyond these individual variations, some recurring patterns of conflict can be established. Tensions between 'inner' and 'outer' court staffs can be found in many places, pitting lesser-ranking confidants who were constantly in the ruler's proximity against prestigious state dignitaries whose connections with the ruler remained more distanced. Rulers themselves could seek support in inner court circles against overbearing relatives, nobles, or advisors. At most courts, as in most houses, some areas were easily accessible whereas others were more restricted. Palace layouts can be found for many courts in history. A comparative examination of these materials makes it possible to link status, functions, and gender to palace topography and to the issue of access to the ruler.

Finally, this aggregate of groups around the ruler as a whole was expected to engage in exchanges with its wider social environment. How did the dynastic court, a household inflated to extraordinary proportions, cultivate its relationship with the territories under its control? The court accumulated wealth through taxes, tribute, or gift-giving; it distributed offices, ranks, and honours. More often than not, it served as a centre of redistribution, as a source of rewards and punishments, as a locus of conspicuous hospitality, as the highest court of appeal, and as the key venue of ritual celebration. Courts connected numerous groups to their own expanded services, on a permanent or temporary basis, or through a system of ranks and rewards. In addition, they attracted state servants, soldiers, petitioners, litigants, purveyors, artists, and fortune-seekers in all guises. Great rituals drew participants and spectators to the court, to experience at first hand the spectacle of dynastic supremacy. Depending on individual temperament and regional traditions, rulers could adopt extroverted or withdrawn styles of representation. Whether or not rulers personally engaged with their subjects, all courts sought to convince wider audiences that their power could not be challenged. These audiences, however, were not always favourably impressed by the show of power at the centre. How did they view the principle of dynastic rule and its main protagonists?

Scope: time and place

A systematic and global examination of these four dimensions of dynastic rule demands a wide scope based on numerous examples. This can be achieved only by leaving aside the wider ecological, social, economic, and cultural contexts of the selected examples. Although regional traditions of rulership are discussed at some length in the first chapter, the historic roots, the ideals, and the sacral nature of kingship are given less prominence in this book than the social context of dynastic rule.[11] Rightly or wrongly, I assume that differences in the cultural representation and understanding of rulership do not diminish the universality of the four domains singled out here for further scrutiny. The impact of different traditions will become clear in the examination of dynastic practice. A focus on the breadth and variety of the examples uncovers patterns that remain hidden in detailed studies of single dynasties in their specific cultural settings. My comparison provides an open and dynamic model of dynastic power that cannot be obtained by concentration on any single case, or even by in-depth comparison of a few selected cases.

This examination of the social setting of dynastic rulers at the apex of society deserves a truly world-historical scale, accepting no limitations in time or place. Such an all-encompassing comparative effort, however, can hardly be achieved by a single individual. My examination is limited to the period between the end of the Mongol conquests and the rise of unchallenged European hegemony, from around 1300 to the early decades of the nineteenth century. It includes examples from the entire period, but focuses on the years after 1550.[12] In this phase of increasingly dense global contact, dynastic power and courtly splendour reached their apex in Europe as well as in Asia, from Versailles via Topkapı, Delhi, and Isfahan to the Forbidden City.[13] In Africa, too, spectacular examples of court culture appear in these centuries. Trade with Europe loomed large in the make-up of kingdoms along Africa's western coast: the growth of dynastic power and luxury here was contingent on slavery.[14] Only in the nineteenth century, however, did European colonial governance move

---

[11] See the classic works by J.G. Frazer, *The Golden Bough: A Study in Magic and Religion* (London, 1987 [1922]); Arthur M. Hocart, *Kingship* (London, 1927); and Hocart, *Kings and Councillors: An Essay in the Comparative Anatomy of Human Society* (Chicago, 1970 [1936]). For recent discussions and bibliographies, see Declan Quigley (ed.), *The Character of Kingship* (Oxford, 2005); W.M. Spellman, *Monarchies 1000–2000* (London, 2001); Francis Oakley, *Kingship: The Politics of Enchantment* (Oxford, 2008).

[12] On parallel developments in Europe and Asia, see Victor Lieberman, *Strange Parallels: Southeast Asia in Global Context, c. 800–1830*, 2 vols. (Cambridge, 2003–9), and Jack Goldstone's review of this work, 'New patterns in global history: a review essay on *Strange Parallels* by Victor Lieberman', *Cliodynamics*, 1/1 (2010), 92–102; and Goldstone, 'The problem of the "early modern" world', *Journal of the Economic and Social History of the Orient*, 41/3 (1998), 249–84.

[13] Japan seems to be the exception here, with the classic age of imperial court splendour in the Heian period (794–1185) outshining the military and political consolidation under the Tokugawa shoguns, at least in terms of the scholarly attention it has received. Possibly the same can be said about Majapahit in relation to the early modern sultanates in the archipelago, where the Dutch East India Company soon became a force to be reckoned with.

[14] John K. Thornton, *A Cultural History of the Atlantic World, 1250–1820* (Cambridge, 2012), 82, explicitly relates the rise of relatively centralised kingdoms in West Africa to their slavery-based income, which allowed the build-up of military power and courtly

older political structures into the margins. Change came more rapidly and destructively in the Americas after 1492. The Spanish conquest ended the relatively recent Aztec and Inka imperial ventures, instituting European-style viceregal regimes. My comparison necessarily ends where European hegemony became so consolidated that local regimes were subjugated or adopted European-style reforms.

Few dynasties lasted throughout the five centuries following 1300, and even in these cases continuity usually was a mixture of demographic reality, haphazard improvisation, and genealogical make-believe. The period roughly corresponds to the time-span of the Ottoman dynasty (1299–1922), the two 'Late Imperial' Chinese dynasties, Ming (1368–1644) and Qing (1644–1912), and the period of Muslim rule in northern India from the Delhi sultanate dynasties (1206–1526) to the Mughals (1526–1857). The Tokugawa *shoguns* ruled from 1600 onwards, while the imperial dynasty, thanks to several unobtrusive reparations of demographic mishaps, could boast a remarkable longevity from early into modern Japan. The Javanese sultans of Mataram, who started their rule in the late sixteenth and continued into the eighteenth century, claimed a link with the preceding house of Majapahit (1293–1527).[15] Other dynasties in the archipelago and on the Southeast Asian mainland likewise construed genealogical continuity, but none actually seems to have lasted throughout these centuries. In Europe, the same period comprises the rise and fall of numerous dynasties and the persistence of others, such as the Habsburgs. Only a few African dynasties lasted throughout this period. The Sefuwa dynasty of Kanem-Bornu around Lake Chad, which converted to Islam in the eleventh century, lasted into the nineteenth century. Its remarkable record was matched by the Christian 'Solomonic' dynasty in Ethiopia, which gained power in the thirteenth century while posing as successor to an earlier Solomonic tradition. The power of the Solomonids

splendour without increased taxation. The same point is made by Emmanuel Terray, 'L'économie politique du royaume Abron du Gyaman', *Cahiers d'études africaines*, 22 (1982), 251–75. More generally on the role of slavery in the rise of West African kingdoms, see Robin Law, 'Dahomey and the slave trade: reflections on the historiography of the rise of Dahomey', *Journal of African History*, 27 (1986), 237–67; Anne Caroline Bailey, *African Voices of the Atlantic Slave Trade: Beyond the Silence and the Shame* (Boston, MA, 2005), chap. 3, on African agency including Dahomey and Asante; and most recently, Sean Stilwell, *Slavery and Slaving in African History* (Cambridge, 2014).

[15] Soemarsaid Moertono, *State and Statecraft in Old Java: A Study of the Later Mataram Period, 16th to 19th Century* (Ithaca, NY, 1963), 7–9, also 53 on the Jogyakarta and Surakarta prolonging the Mataram legacy after 1755 under Dutch overlordship; see the genealogy in J.W. Winter, 'Beknopte beschrijving van het Hof Soerakarta in 1824', in G.P. Rouffaer (ed.), *Bijdragen tot de Taal-, Land- en Volkenkunde van Nederlandsch-Indië*, 54 (1902), 15–172, at 26–7.

was eroded in the later eighteenth century but re-emerged in the nine-teenth and twentieth centuries. It is more difficult to situate historically the Ogiso kings of Benin, who, according to early sources, ruled 'in the olden days before there was any Moon or Sun'. The precise starting point of their Eweka successors, who ruled Benin as 'Obas' (kings) from the early thirteenth century into the modern age, cannot be established with much accuracy.[16]

There is a sound practical reason for choosing this period, one which witnessed the emergence of global networks, the expansion of literacy, and the large-scale production of printed books. Numerous texts written by missionaries, diplomats, merchants, soldiers, and travellers make it possible to include regions that generated few indigenous written sources, notably Africa and the Americas. Lacking the abundant written records of polities in Asia and Europe, the history of these territories has been painstakingly reconstructed on the basis of archaeological finds, indigen-ous scripts, and oral traditions. European travellers' reports offer invalu-able supplementary material. The authors of these reports inevitably perceived the peoples and lands they encountered through the lens of European preoccupations. However, given that there are few alternative written sources, the problems involved in using them are outweighed by the benefit of including otherwise inaccessible territories in the following account. One of the questions raised by European sources of this period is that of 'commensurability': visitors straightforwardly translated their observations into European terminology. This draws attention to the way in which they recognised certain aspects, without necessarily proving actual similarities.[17] Modern researchers must therefore verify whether terms such as 'courtier' or 'noble' used in these texts correspond to the social categories of distant worlds. While I use sources generated by the global encounter, mutual perceptions and the transfer of peoples and artefacts between courts do not appear in my comparison.[18]

---

[16] See Dierk Lange, 'The kingdoms and peoples of Chad', in D.T. Niane (ed.), *General History of Africa*, vol. IV: *Africa from the Twelfth to the Sixteenth Century* (Berkeley, CA, 1984), 238–65; Donald E. Crummey, 'Ethiopia in the early modern period: Solomonic monarchy and Christianity', *Journal of Early Modern History*, 8/3 (2004), 191–209, and the literature cited there; Stefan Eisenhofer, 'The Benin kinglist/s: some questions of chronology', *History in Africa*, 24 (1997), 139–56.

[17] On encounters, translation, and 'commensurability', see Sanjay Subrahmanyam, *Courtly Encounters: Translating Courtliness and Violence in Early Modern Eurasia* (Cambridge, MA, 2012).

[18] I leave aside here the rich literature on the movement of people, ideas, artefacts, and germs, and the processes of cultural transfer; see e.g. Bhaswati Bhattacharya, Gita Dharampal-Frick, and Jos Gommans, 'Spatial and temporal continuities of merchant networks in South Asia and the Indian Ocean (1500–2000)', *Journal of the Economic and Social History of the Orient*, 50/2–3 (2007), 91–105;

This book does not provide an overview of dynastic histories; it examines a number of examples, some consistently present, others varying per chapter. Three criteria determine the choice of examples: the availability of specialised studies, the spread over several continents with diverging traditions, and the presence of practices not found elsewhere. Repetitions of familiar patterns in yet another region are not necessarily included: I do not aim to provide a comprehensive encyclopaedic panorama. The most thoroughly documented courts of Europe and Asia comprise a substantial part of the following chapters. Since the 1980s, an increasing number of works have dealt with European courts, a world with which I have familiarised myself through previous archival research into the courts of the Valois and Bourbons in Paris-Versailles and the Austrian Habsburgs in Vienna.[19] In the last two decades, numerous important studies have appeared on the major courts and dynasties of Asia, from the Ottoman, the Mughal, and the Safavid dynasties, to the Ming and Qing courts, to Japan, with its intriguing form of 'dual rulership' comprising the shogun and the emperor.[20] The availability of these specialised works enables a comparative examination that establishes detail and variation before seeking generalisation. As far as possible, the voices of contemporaries have been included. The written legacies of Asian empires, particularly rich on the dynastic centre, have been used only when they were available in translation or through the interpretations of modern authors. The literature on rulers and courts in other parts of the globe is more sparse, and hence these regions appear only sporadically in this book – where sufficient materials were available and when cases raise interesting comparative questions. Examples from Africa, the Americas, Southeast Asia, and Oceania will appear in particular where they cast doubt on common generalisations, and where they extend the variation in the patterns examined. Unexpected and divergent cases stretch and test the comparative framework of this book. Matrilineal succession, for example, problematises categories that seem self-evident within the patrilineal context dominant in Europe and Asia, and thus helps to reframe questions and definitions.

Sanjay Subrahmanyam, *From Tagus to the Ganges: Explorations in Connected History* (Oxford, 2011).

[19] Duindam, *Myths of Power*; Duindam, *Vienna and Versailles: The Courts of Europe's Dynastic Rivals, 1550–1780* (Cambridge, 2003); and Duindam, 'Royal courts', in Hamish Scott (ed.), *The Oxford Handbook of Early Modern European History, 1350–1750*, vol. II: *Cultures and Power* (forthcoming, 2015).

[20] See titles in the following chapters. While the literature on most European and Asian courts is concentrated on the centuries after around 1400, in Japan the phase before the rise of the shoguns in the twelfth century has attracted more attention.

Examples of African kingship complement European and Asian models of rulership in a significant way. The legacy of African kingship is rich and diverse, containing examples of matrilineal succession and female power, as well as notably sacralised forms of kingship. It also brings into focus the close relationship between kinship patterns and kingship, less easily discernible in more differentiated, larger-scale polities.[21] Finally, the inclusion of African kingship raises the question of whether scale and development are essential criteria.[22] Comparative political studies tend to examine polities they deem evenly matched in terms of population, surface, social stratification, modes of production, and political development. Alternatively, they rank the polities they study according to criteria related to scale and development. Scholars have labelled polities as empires, kingdoms, states, and chiefdoms. They elaborate typologies, differentiating 'ungoverned' and egalitarian societies from chiefdoms, chiefdoms from kingdoms or from early states, early states from mature states, and kingdoms from empires. These typologies and rankings do not enter into the criteria for my comparison. Any polity governed by a ruler surrounded by relatives and a body of servants qualifies. Only local chiefs nominated by or clearly subservient to a paramount chief do not fit into this picture; yet tributary polities paying homage to a more distant powerful leader do.

---

[21] See a critique of evolutionist typologies of kinship-based groups and states in David Sneath, *The Headless State: Aristocratic Orders, Kinship Society, and Misrepresentations of Nomadic Inner Asia* (New York, 2007); Sneath points to the persistence of kinship ties in states and to the 'continuities and similarities in power structures within a single analytical frame' (195).

[22] See Sneath, *Headless State*; George Peter Murdock, *Africa: Its Peoples and their Culture History* (New York, 1959), 33–9 and 144–5, presents a remarkable typology of 'African despotism' based on Karl Wittfogel's 1957 *Oriental Despotism*. Murdock denies the relevance of differences in scale (37); he presents a series of shared characteristics of 'African despotisms' (37–9), overstating the power of these kings but demonstrating the basis for comparison between African and Asian/European dynastic patterns. See further attempts at typology by Peter C. Lloyd, 'The political structure of African kingdoms: an explanatory model', in Michael Banton (ed.), *Political Systems and the Distribution of Power* (London, 1965), 63–112, and Aidan Southall, 'A critique of the typology of states and political systems' in the same volume, 113–40, including pertinent remarks about comparison. Related attempts at typology can be found in H.J. M. Claessen, *Van Vorsten en volken: een beschrijvende en functioneel-vergelijkende studie van de staatsorganisatie in vijf schriftloze vorstendommen* (Amsterdam, 1970), a comparison of scriptless societies; and H.J.M. Claessen and Peter Skalník (eds.), *The Early State* (The Hague, 1978), and several follow-up volumes. See also H.J.M. Claessen, 'Kings, chiefs and officials: the political organization of Dahomey and Buganda compared', *Journal of Legal Pluralism and Unofficial Law*, 19/25–6 (1987), 203–41, who at 204 suggests a three-tiered dimension of power (king–intermediaries–local chiefs) as the key difference between a chiefdom and a state. More recently, see Michał Tymowski, *Early Imperial Formations in Africa and the Segmentation of Power* (Basingstoke, 2011).

Populations may reach hundreds of millions or only thousands; royals may live in thatched mud huts, mobile tent encampments, or extended and luxurious palace complexes. Rulers can be companionable figures or distant and revered icons; government can be based on direct contact and verbal communication or rely on paperwork and intermediaries. The four dimensions chosen for this comparison are relevant for all dynastic environments.

Disregarding these commonly accepted criteria entails the comparison of very different polities, but it helps differentiate between timeless topoi of dynastic power and specific temporal or cultural characteristics. Why compare the sophisticated Chinese court, with its long-standing literary tradition, elaborate government apparatus, and exceptional scale, to a minor African polity such as the Mamprusi kingdom of northern Ghana, with its small non-literate population? In both polities, the ruler held a markedly ritualised responsibility for harvests and weather, for the harmony of heaven and earth.[23] Likewise, the troubled relationship between the ruler and his male relatives led to similar solutions in African kingdoms and in Tang, Ming, and Qing China.[24] How can these similarities between dynastic polities at the extremes of commonly accepted typologies of scale and development be explained? The inclusion of Africa not only helps to break down 'the false conceptual barriers dividing regions and cultures studied by separate groups of scholars', it also raises new questions.[25]

Powerful twentieth-century traditions of anthropological research relating to African kingship and succession rely on oral tradition and archaeology as well as on earlier Arabic and European written sources.[26] Research of the colonial or postcolonial periods

---

[23] See Susan Drucker-Brown, *Ritual Aspects of the Mamprusi Kingship* (Leiden and Cambridge, 1975); Evelyn S. Rawski, *The Last Emperors: A Social History of Qing Imperial Institutions* (Berkeley, CA, and London, 1998).

[24] Tardits (ed.), *Princes & serviteurs*; Denis Twitchett, 'The T'ang imperial family', *Asia Major*, 7/2 (1994), 1–61; David M. Robinson, 'Princely courts of the Ming dynasty', *Ming Studies*, 65 (2012), 1–12, and other contributions to this volume; Rawski, *Last Emperors*, 96–126.

[25] Southall, 'Segmentary state', 52–82 (quotation on 82), an article with many important ideas, which seeks explanations partly in 'modes of production' and levels of development.

[26] For Africa, this study relies in particular on the generation of anthropologists from E.E. Evans-Pritchard and M. Fortes to Jack Goody and Audrey Richards, with important later works by many historians and anthropologists, among them Jan Vansina and Claude Tardits. Rich specialised literature and sources explain the presence of examples from Asante, Dahomey, Benin, Zande, Ethiopia, Congo, and, towards the southeast, Buganda and Bunyoro.

reconstructing precolonial king-lists and royal traditions cannot always connect specific dynastic practices to specific periods: nineteenth-century practices are accepted as reflecting, to some extent, earlier variants. By including such examples from Africa, I push the boundaries of the period under analysis. However, as in the case of Asian polities, I stop before the European presence evidently became the dominant political factor.

Beyond great debates and grand narratives

The period 1300–1800 has convincingly been presented in terms of the gradual emergence of global networks and the concomitant ascendancy of European economic, military, and political hegemony. It witnessed the rise and fall of numerous imperial or royal houses across the globe. How does this book deal with the master narrative of the rise of the West, or, more broadly, with change over time? The following chapters, concerned with rulers, dynasties, courts, and realms, will not deal at length with any longer-term predefined historical developments. The common historical focus on the development of one region over time is replaced by a thematic, comparative, and anthropological perspective. It is not my intention to construct an unvarying model of dynastic power: I use the four dimensions of dynastic rule established here as a timeless framework that allows me to consider general patterns as well as variants in place and time. Specific changes in the ideals and practices of rulership, in the arrangements for succession and reproduction, in the treatment of dynastic kin, in the composition and functions of the court, and in the interaction with the population at large, will be registered and interpreted in a comparative context whenever possible. Where differences between regions appear to be consistent over time, a typology will be suggested. However, the main purpose of this study is to provide a framework that helps to understand dynastic rule in a global setting. This model of dynastic power moves comparison beyond the point of establishing similarities and differences. The overall framework suggests how divergent practices can be seen as part of the same pattern, while the detail brought together in each of the chapters underlines that striking similarities hide profound differences.

Only towards the end of the book, and as an afterthought rather than as a fundamental argument, shall I consider how this comparative framework fits longer-term developments, including the gradual consolidation of polities around the world as well as the changes related to modernisation and the rise of Europe. The conclusion will also consider cyclical views common among contemporaries. The prolific North African Arabic

writer Ibn Khaldun (1332–1406), numerous Chinese authors, and, argu-
ably, most other premodern political thinkers, viewed the gradual degeneration of dynastic power after the founding generation as inevitable,
usually as a consequence of increasing luxury and declining moral fibre.[27]
Their perception of repeated cycles of dynastic rise and decline, stripped
of its moral overtones, remains relevant for the understanding of dynastic
power. Can the tensions inherent in the dynastic set-up be understood as
structural causes of an alternating cycle of ascent and decline? Change
will thus be examined at three levels: within each of the four defined
themes, as a cyclical or recurring pattern inherent in dynastic power,
and as a long-term development.

Machiavelli, Montesquieu, and many other authors viewed the world
as divided into two categories: free peoples with limited government
and slave peoples subjected by all-powerful rulers. Despotic and capricious 'palace polities' in Asia served as a counterpoint to European-style
monarchy.[28] Indeed, at times charges of 'Oriental despotism' were
thrown at European princes to warn them against transgressing their
legitimate boundaries. For the general public in our contemporary age,
dynastic power in the East and the West first and foremost represents a
pre-enlightened and pre-democratic past, a previous stage of human
political development associated with privilege and suppression. These
understandable general attitudes have predisposed numerous scholars
to commence their research with anachronistic and prejudicial views of
ancien régime monarchy in general, and of Asian empires in particular.
This tendency can be detected in the choice of themes. While dynasty in
Europe, as elsewhere, was indisputably the dominant form of power,
republics have been studied eagerly as harbingers of a new age. The

---

[27] Ibn Khaldun, *The Muqaddimah: An Introduction to History*, ed. Franz Rosenthal
(Princeton, NJ, and Oxford, 1967). In the Chinese context, see Peter Kees Bol, 'The
"localist turn" and "local identity" in later imperial China', *Late Imperial China*, 24/2
(2003), 1–50; Frederic Wakeman, Jr, 'The dynastic cycle', in his *The Fall of Imperial
China* (New York, 1977), 55–70. In Greek and Roman contexts, see Polybius, *The
Histories*, ed. F.W. Walbank et al. (Cambridge, MA, 2011), III.5–8; G.W. Trompf, *The
Idea of Historical Recurrence in Western Thought: From Antiquity to the Reformation*
(Berkeley, CA, and London, 1979). See Arnold Toynbee's reinterpretation, *A Study of
History* (various editions), and a comment in Robert Irwin, 'Toynbee and Ibn Khaldun',
Middle Eastern Studies, 33/3 (1997), 461–79; and general observations in Southall,
'Segmentary state', 77.
[28] In his admirable overview, Samuel E. Finer, *The History of Government from the Earliest
Times*, 3 vols. (Oxford and New York, 1997–9), refers to palace polities in many places,
suggesting a structurally unstable pattern – a characteristic that Montesquieu and his
contemporaries likewise connected to 'oriental despotism'; see e.g. Thomas Kaiser, 'The
evil empire? The debate on Turkish despotism in eighteenth-century French political
culture', *Journal of Modern History*, 72/1 (2000), 6–34.

stepping-stones of democracy were carefully mapped, from Greek and Roman polities, via the rise of autonomous, urban centres in the European high middle ages, to the advent of representative institutions and popular sovereignty in the more recent European and American past. Even in monarchical settings, components surviving into present-day democracies such as representative assemblies, councils, and ministers, have received far more attention than the dynastic and courtly themes examined in this book.

In recent decades, historians have examined historic monarchies with more detachment, taking seriously the values of the period studied in addition to those of our own times. Two closely connected shifts engendered by this research are particularly important here for the way in which they open up comparative perspectives on European, African, and Asian forms of rulership: a new stress on the political relevance of the domestic environment of rulers, and a profound questioning of the 'absolute' power of rulers. In Europe, there has been a shift in attention from 'modern' state institutions and the sources generated by policy-making boards and councils to the social setting of dynastic power, the court. A closer look at state archives and private collections suggested that the domestic world around rulers stood at the heart of the early modern state. This was no 'gilded cage' captivating once powerful nobles through expensive luxury and endless squabbles, and allowing the state to develop without their interference.[29] In most European countries, high-placed nobles in domestic court offices retained political power, sometimes formalised and direct, sometimes through their proximity and intimacy with the ruler. While a role in the formalised part of the decision-making process was granted only to a small number of persons, numerous others could gain influence over the distribution of honours. Prominent noble courtiers were particularly well-placed here, but lesser-ranking staff might profit too. Anybody daily serving the prince or his relatives could hope to exert influence at some point; and many did so by carrying written petitions or verbally conveying requests. Repeated rulings against chamber servants acting as intermediaries suggest such actions were common and ineradicable. Nor was this often forgotten dimension of power necessarily male. Dynastic women, served by their own mixed female and male staffs, could formally rule in some or act as a regent in most countries. Outside of such conspicuous roles, they acted as patron

---

[29] See Duindam, *Myths of Power*; and Duindam, *Vienna and Versailles*. For a similar and definitive assessment of France, see Leonhard Horowski, *Die Belagerung des Thrones: Machtstrukturen und Karrieremechanismen am Hof von Frankreich 1661–1789* (Stuttgart, 2012). On Vienna, see Andreas Pečar, *Die Ökonomie der Ehre: der höfische Adel am Kaiserhof Karls VI. (1711–1740)* (Darmstadt, 2003).

for the women on their staffs and as intermediary with the male ruler – whether spouse or son.[30]

If European monarchy also depended in part on the manipulations of palace staff, then how exactly did it differ from Asian 'palace polities'? The presence of an expanding 'bureaucratic' state apparatus cannot be the answer. It has long since been accepted that in China administrative routines were particularly strong, and recent work underlines innovations introduced under the three successful 'high Qing' emperors Kangxi (1654–1661–1722), Yongzheng (1678–1722–1735), and Qianlong (1711–1735–1796*).[31] West and South Asian empires, notably the Ottomans and the Mughals, building on the Persian traditions of kingship and administration, likewise developed administrative routines.[32] In all major European kingdoms, as well as in the greater empires of Asia, domestic staffs catering for the rulers; clerks, administrators, and advisors responsible for the machinery of government; and, finally, military elites were present at the heart of power. There is no straightforward contrast between an 'East' governed by palace cliques and a 'West' based on orderly procedure and government by paper. At court, the changing balances between different elites took shape: this ubiquitous process needs to be placed in an open, comparative perspective, rather than in a model which first and foremost seeks to explain the rise of Europe.

From the 1980s onwards, scholarship has questioned the omnipotence of absolute rulers in Europe.[33] 'Absolutism', an echo of royal propaganda and revolutionary discourse, survived into modern scholarship because of

---

[30] Katrin Keller, *Hofdamen: Amtsträgerinnen im Wiener Hofstaat des 17. Jahrhunderts* (Vienna, 2005); Nadine Akkerman and Birgit Houben (eds.), *The Politics of Female Households: Ladies-in-Waiting across Early Modern Europe* (Leiden and Boston, MA, 2013); Jan Hirschbiegel and Werner Paravicini (eds.), *Das Frauenzimmer: Die Frau bei Hofe in Spätmittelalter und Früher Neuzeit* (Stuttgart, 2000).

[31] R. Kent Guy, *Qing Governors and their Provinces: The Evolution of Territorial Administration in China, 1644–1796* (Seattle, WA, 2010).

[32] Rhoads Murphey, *Exploring Ottoman Sovereignty: Tradition, Image and Practice in the Ottoman Imperial Household, 1400–1800* (London and New York, 2008); J.F. Richards, *The Mughal Empire* (Cambridge, 1995), 58–78; see also Stephen P. Blake, 'The patrimonial-bureaucratic empire of the Mughals', *Journal of Asian Studies*, 39 (1979), 77–94.

[33] See a parallel for Africa developed by John Beattie, 'Checks on the abuse of political power in some African states: a preliminary framework for analysis', in Ronald Cohen and John Middleton (eds.), *Comparative Political Systems: Studies in the Politics of Pre-Industrial Societies* (New York, 1967), 355–73, at 355: 'older writers about primitive states in Africa and elsewhere often spoke of chiefs and kings as possessing absolute power. But it is plain from the more thorough ethnography of the past half century or so that in fact the authority of such rulers is generally restricted by a wide range of social institutions.'

a narrow reading of high-handed state rhetoric and decrees: sources underlining the initiative of the centre. In the last two decades, regional and non-state sources have drawn attention to the agency of local elites. Notwithstanding a deferential attitude and polite formulae, their responses to the centre show a clear political agenda. The language of hierarchy, service, and loyalty did not preclude bargaining for and the protection of regional interests. Co-operation was beneficial for both parties, and elite interests were buttressed by the state as long as the elites fitted willingly into the framework of monarchy.[34] From the 1650s onwards, after a century of frequent conflict and spiralling costs of warfare caused by religious dissent, a mixed power elite of nobles and new men occupying state offices held power in most countries both in the centre and the provinces. They formed the core of a state machinery that expanded its grip on society as a whole. Only in the second half of the eighteenth century, when a new round of military competition over-strained the fiscal and financial capabilities of the European belligerents, was this arrangement challenged again. The reforms engendered by this financial crisis severely tested the compact between privileged elites and the state, leading to widespread contestation in France as well as in several other states.

These changes in the study of European 'absolute' rulership, a consequence of the uncovering of new sources and the reinterpretation of familiar materials, raise the question of whether a similar reconsideration is possible in the case of 'autocratic' Chinese emperors, Ottoman sultans, and their fellow rulers elsewhere.[35] Can we find Asian parallels to the actions and goals of men and women serving European rulers? The impact of high office-holders such as Ottoman viziers or Chinese grand secretaries has never been questioned, and increasing numbers of

[34] As shown by the example of Burgundy and the Condé: Julian Swann, *Provincial Power and Absolute Monarchy: The Estates General of Burgundy, 1661–1790* (Cambridge, 2003); Katia Béguin, *Les princes de Condé: rebelles, courtisans et mécènes dans la France du grand siècle* (Paris, 1999); see also her 'Louis XIV et l'aristocratie: coup de majesté ou retour à la tradition?', *Histoire, économie et société*, 19/4 (2000), 497–512.

[35] A stress on the agency of localities and their interaction with the centre can be found in many recent works on Asian polities: see e.g. Michael Szonyi, *Practicing Kinship: Lineage and Descent in Late Imperial China* (Stanford, CA, 2002); or Ramya Sreenivasan, 'A South Asianist's response to Lieberman's *Strange Parallels*', *Journal of Asian Studies*, 70/4 (2011), 983–93, notably at 986–7 underlining the impact of recent archival work on the local contexts of dynastic power. See also the work of Baki Tezcan, *The Second Ottoman Empire: Political and Social Transformation in the Early Modern World* (Cambridge, 2010), and numerous articles by the same author, bringing into line European and Ottoman early modern political experiences. Charles Tilly, *Trust and Rule* (Cambridge, 2005), presents a model of connections between rulers, elites, and the populace, with a series of top-down and bottom-up strategies, stressing the 'predatory' nature of rulership.

publications on Asian courts point to the agency of court women, servants, and eunuchs.[36] It is not justified to apply unquestioningly conclusions reached in a European context to other worlds, but there is a clear shared problem here: the long-standing preponderance of sources conveying an image of central power and order. Palace architecture functioned in this way in the past and continues to do so in the present. The most readily available and extensive written sources for the study of dynastic power were produced by scribal elites serving the ruler and hence rarely strayed far from official views. The rich variety of local and private sources as well as the reports generated by numerous mutual diplomatic missions available for early modern Europe make it relatively easy to find alternative viewpoints. In China, the officially approved histories ('veritable records' or *shilu*) created by Chinese literati administrators, describing many issues in great detail, stressed the power of the emperor and the dignity of literati ministers, while they reported on inner court agents mostly in the context of abuse and decline. The more diverse chronicles on Ottoman, Mughal, or Safavid history stay within the bounds dictated by the proximity of the authors to the court and its leading elites. Recent work suggests that the archival repositories of the Qing court and the Topkapı palace, as well as unofficial and regional sources, will help to reopen the debate on the nature of sultanic and imperial power.[37]

This book cannot provide an expert's view on every single dynasty, nor does it unearth sources unknown to specialists. It is neither a vindication nor an indictment of dynasty. It brings together numerous contemporary witnesses of dynastic power and examines specialised studies. My bird's-eye view demonstrates which questions are inextricably linked with

---

[36] On eunuchs, see Jane Hathaway, *Beshir Agha: Chief Eunuch of the Ottoman Imperial Harem* (London, 2005); Shaun Tougher, *Eunuchs in Antiquity and Beyond* (London, 2002); Tougher, *The Eunuch in Byzantine History and Society* (London, 2008); Kathryn M. Ringrose, *The Perfect Servant: Eunuchs and the Social Construction of Gender in Byzantium* (Chicago, IL, 2003); Shih-shan Henry Tsai, *The Eunuchs in the Ming Dynasty* (New York, 1996); Norman A. Kutcher, 'Unspoken collusions: the empowerment of Yuanming Yuan eunuchs in the Qianlong period', *Harvard Journal of Asiatic Studies*, 70/2 (2010), 449–95. On women, see the works cited in notes 5 and 30 above and in Chapter 2.

[37] See e.g. the recent revision of the role of the Mongol legacy at the Ming court and the position of Ming princes, based in part on a rereading of the *shilu*, combined with regional sources and archaeology, in David M. Robinson (ed.), *Culture, Courtiers, and Competition: The Ming Court (1368–1644)* (Cambridge, MA, 2008); Robinson, 'Princely courts of the Ming dynasty'; and Robinson, *Martial Spectacles of the Ming Court* (Cambridge, MA, 2013); or the combined reading of court and local sources in Michael G. Chang, 'Historical narratives of the Kangxi emperor's inaugural visit to Suzhou, 1684, in Jeroen Duindam and Sabine Dabringhaus (eds.), *The Dynastic Centre and the Provinces: Agents and Interactions* (Leiden and Boston, MA, 2014), 203–24.

dynastic power and suggests how diverging responses can be understood. Authorities in particular fields may find slips or omissions, but they will be compensated by the unexpected insights that come with comparison: this book allows them to see how the courts and rulers they know so well fit into the global framework of dynastic power. Novices will discover a fascinating world with its own logic, one remarkably consistent throughout history. In the end they may recognise in our own age mechanisms and attitudes familiar from the dynastic past.

1 Rulers: position versus person

Princes are like to heavenly bodies, which cause good or evil times, and which have much veneration, but no rest. All precepts concerning kings are in effect comprehended in those two remembrances: *Memento quod es homo*, and *Memento quod es Deus*, or *vice Dei*: the one bridleth their power, and the other their will.

> Francis Bacon, 'Of Empire', in *The Essays*, ed. John Pither (London, 1985), 119.

For even if I wear the purple, none the less I know this, that like unto all men, I am altogether clothed with frailty by nature.

> Ivan IV, in *The Correspondence between Prince A.M. Kurbsky and Tsar Ivan IV of Russia*, ed. J.L.I. Fennell (Cambridge, 1963), 122–3.

Do not disclose the secret to anyone. Indeed, we have strolled the earth and found no confidant.

> Muḥammad Bāqir Najm-i Sānī, *Advice on the Art of Governance*, ed. Sajida Sultana Alvi (New York, 1989), 56.

The ideal king

What traits characterise the good ruler? A rich contemporary literature discussed this question, admonishing rulers and presenting to them the lives of past paragons of rulership. An extension of the power of the *pater familias*, dominion by a single male person, was usually seen as the natural and most desirable form of power. Kingship was supported wholeheartedly, though nagging doubts about the wrongdoings of individual figures on the throne form a persistent part of this conviction. Distinct ideals of legitimate rulership have been outlined for Christian Europe, for Muslim West Asia, for Indic kingship in various religious guises, and for China's imperial tradition.[1] African kingship, itself at least as diverse as each of the

---

[1] Louise Marlow, 'Advice and advice literature', in Kate Fleet et al. (eds.), *Encyclopaedia of Islam, Three*, Brill Online Reference Works (Leiden, 2007–) (accessed 4 July 2014); Anthony Black, *Political Thought in Europe, 1250–1450* (Cambridge and New York, 1992); S.A.A. Rizvi, 'Kingship in Islam: a historical analysis', in A.L. Basham (ed.), *Kingship in Asia*

other traditions, had its own partly overlapping models. No single description of the ideal ruler holds universal validity. However, one prime responsibility seems to recur in most traditions: safeguarding harmony among the populations as well as between heaven (ancestors, spirits, deities, god) and earth. Likewise, one hazard inherent in kingship can be encountered in most traditions: the cruel and pleasure-loving ruler who pursues the interests only of his inner circle.

Numerous texts survive with advice to rulers: by ruling princes themselves preparing their sons for supreme office, by high-ranking advisors close to the practice of ruling, or by somewhat more distant clerics, religious scholars, and learned outsiders. In Europe and West Asia advice literature formed a literary genre, often called the 'princely mirror' or *speculum principis*. In South and East Asia, a variety of texts outlined the qualities and duties of the ruler, some of them adopting the familiar mirror metaphor.[2] Such texts reflect not only particular positions (ruler, vizier/minister, scholar/cleric/ monk) and political constellations (in power, threatened, retired, distant), but also position themselves in an ongoing literary discourse. Only by looking at the genre as a whole is it possible to differentiate between reiterated clichés and distinctive opinions. It is clear, however, that some authors adopted an outspoken didactic tone, admonishing rulers and underlining their religious and moral duties, whereas others were more willing to accept the daily realities of power, mixing moral precept with practical advice.

The first part of this chapter traces ideals of kingship in Europe, West Asia, and East Asia, showing how regional traditions and religions shaped views of the virtuous prince. At the same time, it introduces a miniature

---

and Early America (Mexico City, 1981), 29–82, and other shorter contributions in this book on Asian and pre-Columbian American kingship; Linda Darling, *A History of Social Justice and Political Power in the Middle East: The Circle of Justice from Mesopotamia to Globalization* (New York, 2013); Roger T. Ames, *The Art of Rulership: A Study in Ancient Chinese Political Thought* (Albany, NY, 1994). On Africa, see e.g. M. Fortes and E.E. Evans-Pritchard (eds.), *African Political Systems* (London, 1940); Tardits (ed.), *Princes & serviteurs*. On rulers themselves writing, see Pierre Monnet and Jean-Claude Schmitt (eds.), *Autobiographies souveraines* (Paris, 2012); some notable examples: Denis Twitchett, 'How to be an emperor: T'ang T'ai-tsung's vision of his role', *Asia Major*, 3rd series, 9 (1996), 1–102; Babur, *The Baburnama: Memoirs of Babur, Prince and Emperor*, trans. Wheeler M. Thackston (New York and Oxford, 1996); Louis IX, Saint Louis, *The Teachings of Saint Louis: A Critical Text*, ed. David O'Connell (Chapel Hill, NC, 1972); Louis XIV, *Mémoires, suivis de Manière de montrer les jardins de Versailles*, ed. Joël Cornette (Paris, 2007).

[2] Tang Taizong's 'Golden Mirror' (628) translated in Twitchett, 'How to be an emperor'; Sima Guang's (1019–86) *Comprehensive Mirror in Aid of Governance*; Zhang Juzeng's (1525– 82) *The Emperor's Mirror Illustrated and Discussed*; see quotations and comments in Patricia B. Ebrey, 'Remonstrating against royal extravagance in imperial China', in Duindam and Dabringhaus (eds.), *Dynastic Centre*, 127–49. On Islamic advice mirrors or *siyasetname*, see Jocelyne Dakhlia, 'Les miroirs des princes islamiques: une modernité sourde?', *Annales: histoire, sciences sociales*, 72/5 (2002), 1191–206; Suraiya Faroqhi, *Another Mirror for Princes: The Public Image of the Ottoman Sultans and its Reception* (London, 2008).

history of kingship in its various regional guises. Africa, America, and Polynesia, where traditions were not enshrined in equally extended literary heritages, are fitted into the framework more loosely. This overview of regional traditions provides the groundwork for the subsequent chapters which are based on questions rather than on areas.

Discussions of kingship in late medieval Europe from Aquinas to Erasmus stress the need for kings to be devout, honest, just, and merciful. They expect the populace to submit willingly, the king to reciprocate by showing grace and benevolence. Kings form part of a Christian community with its own ecclesiastical structures and leadership, exerting a powerful influence over the practices as well as the ideals of rulership. Nominally worldly rulers were bound in a hierarchy under pope and emperor, a notion never universally embraced and permanently challenged. All worldly rulers were in principle seen as instituted by God, a position often expounded by citing Paul's epistle to the Romans (13:1–7):

Let everyone be subject to the governing authorities, for there is no authority except that which God has established. The authorities that exist have been established by God. Consequently, whoever rebels against the authority is rebelling against what God has instituted, and those who do so will bring judgment on themselves. For rulers hold no terror for those who do right, but for those who do wrong. Do you want to be free from fear of the one in authority? Then do what is right and you will be commended. For the one in authority is God's servant for your good. But if you do wrong, be afraid, for rulers do not bear the sword for no reason. They are God's servants, agents of wrath to bring punishment on the wrongdoer. Therefore, it is necessary to submit to the authorities, not only because of possible punishment but also as a matter of conscience. This is also why you pay taxes, for the authorities are God's servants, who give their full time to governing. Give to everyone what you owe them: If you owe taxes, pay taxes; if revenue, then revenue; if respect, then respect; if honour, then honour.

Kings derive their authority from God, but need to defend the *bonum publicum*: protect the true religion, punish wrongdoers, listen to wise counsel, overcome faction in the country, and further the well-being of the people as a whole. Ruling demanded treating all groups equitably but not necessarily equally: ruling clans occupied privileged positions; priests, soldiers, peasants, and merchants could expect to be treated in different ways, as could regions or ethnicities.[3]

This harmonious ideal of kingship did develop a critical edge by integrating Aristotle's tripartite scheme of forms of government by one, few, and many (monarchy–aristocracy–polity) and more particularly by his criticism of the corrupted forms of these modes of government

---

[3] Black, *Political Thought in Europe*, 24–8, on the common good, chap. 5 on 'Kingship, law and counsel'.

(tyranny–oligarchy–democracy). Abusing their subjects and unduly enriching themselves along with their followers, kings turned into tyrants and forfeited popular support. Tyranny was attacked sharply, yet on the whole resistance by the population was not accepted as legitimate. Public welfare depended on the benevolence of the ruler and the fidelity of the people, and no easy solution was available when matters went awry on either side. Bad rulers were to be punished only by the divine power sanctioning their regimes.[4]

Justice appears both as a key value and as an important mechanism to maintain or restore the balance between the sovereign and his peoples. Jean de Joinville, companion to the French crusader-king Louis IX (1214–1226–1270; later Saint Louis), describes an instance of royal justice that has become iconic:

> During the summer he often went and sat in the woods of Vincennes after Mass. He would lean against an oak tree and have us sit down around him. All those who had matters to be dealt with came and talked to him, without the interference of the ushers or anyone else. He himself would ask 'Is there anyone here with a case to settle?' Those who did have a case stood up, and he said to them, 'Everyone be quiet and you will be given judgement, one after another' ... On some summer days I saw him go to the gardens in Paris to render justice to the people ... He had carpets laid out so that we could sit round him. Everyone who had a case to bring before him would gather around him at first, and then the king had judgement delivered in the same way as I said took place in the wood at Vincennes.[5]

It is not easy to verify whether this idealised scene was ever performed in practice, let alone to establish its frequency. Nevertheless, a stress on direct and personal royal justice can be found in many other places and times, in practice as well as in stylised representations. Kings allowed ordinary subjects to approach them and present their grievances, circumventing formal procedure and intermediary powers. They did so most often in the context of devotion, on their way to the chapel or after Mass: moments they themselves were publicly made aware of the humility of all in the face of God.

The just king, ostentatiously siding with his weaker subjects, occupied high moral ground and could more easily reprimand the mighty. Princely

---

[4] See similar statements in Barbara Watson Andaya, 'Political development between the sixteenth and eighteenth centuries', in Nicholas Tarling (ed.), *The Cambridge History of Southeast Asia*, vol. I: *From Early Times to c. 1800* (Cambridge, 1992), 402–59, at 421.

[5] Jean de Joinville and Geffroy de Villehardouin, *Chronicles of the Crusades*, ed. Caroline Smith (London and New York, 2009), 157; see Jacques Le Goff, *Saint Louis* (Paris, 1996), on Joinville and the king (481–7), on princely mirrors (402–31), and on the three roles of the ideal king (642–73): the just and peaceful king, the warrior, and the king providing for his peoples, citing George Dumézil's *L'idéologie tripartite des Indo-Européens* (Brussels, 1958).

adjudication confirmed to the populace the just and legitimate nature of their sovereign, while at the same time it helped to check the actions of notables or agents in the service of the king. The double-edged sword of supreme justice was dear to the heart of most kings; they were able to pardon subjects as well as to punish predatory elites.[6] In the declaration left in the Tuileries palace on the eve of his departure from Paris in June 1791, Louis XVI (1754–1774–1792*) emphatically stated his paternal vision of kingship, deploring the loss of: 'one of the fairest prerogatives everywhere attached to royal power, that of pardoning and commuting penalties'. Taking away this prerogative, he continued, the National Assembly 'diminishes the royal majesty in the eyes of the people so long accustomed to have recourse to the king in their needs and in their difficulties, and to see in him the common father who can relieve their afflictions'.[7] Traditional monarchs invariably left room for petitioning the king and his ministers, often through direct physical contact, gradually in more distant procedural form. Louis XIV (1638–1643–1715) somewhat overconfidently stated in his memoirs that his subjects, without exception, could address him at any time with their requests.[8] In the eighteenth century Frederick II of Prussia at times conspicuously supported lesser subjects against their powerful neighbours. His admirer Joseph II of Austria, reforming most traditional court practices, made a point of being accessible to simple Viennese, listening to their complaints at the servants' entry of the Hofburg palace as well as during his numerous travels.[9]

Niccolò Machiavelli (1469–1527) separated sharply the reputation the ruler needed to establish from his actual behaviour or dispositions, underlining the instrumental aspects of images of devotion, justice, and clemency. *Il Principe* famously subverted the highly idealised and static portrayal of rulership, arguing that force and fraud were necessary for rulers. Leadership guided solely by moral categories would end up making things worse for everybody. Exacerbated by the religious and political

---

[6] See Wittfogel, *Oriental Despotism*, 134–5, underlining the second aspect.

[7] Louis XVI's declaration of 20 June 1791, upon his flight from the Tuileries, in Frank Maloy Anderson (trans.), *The Constitutions and Other Select Documents Illustrative of the History of France, 1789–1907* (Minneapolis, MI, 1908), 47; see another translation in Paul Beik (ed.), *The French Revolution* (London, 1970), 158–67; the French original is available through Gallica: Louis XVI, *Mémoire du Roi, adressé à tous les François, à sa sortie de Paris* (Paris, 1791). On pardoning, see Neil Murphy, 'Royal grace, royal punishment: ceremonial entries and the pardoning of criminals in France, c. 1440–1560', in Jeroen Duindam et al. (eds.), *Law and Empire: Ideas, Practices, Actors* (Leiden and Boston, MA, 2013), 293–311.

[8] Louis XIV, *Mémoires*, ed. Cornette, 64.

[9] Derek Beales, *Joseph II*, 2 vols. (Cambridge, 1987–2009), 432–8.

crisis of the Reformation, Machiavelli's challenge triggered a sophisticated discussion which tried to establish a balance between moral ambitions and the daily requirements of rule – surely an unending quest. This
acknowledgement of the dilemmas inherent in political power did not, on
the whole, alter the ideals of kingship. High-handed statements of royal
power, such as those by Louis XIV's orator and bishop Jacques-Bénigne
Bossuet (1627–1704) or by the Sun King himself, reiterated the notion of
divine sanction, but consequently also accepted the moral strictures of the
king's role as paternal protector of his *peuples*.[10] The genre of the princely
mirror, however, seems to have dissolved into more differentiated and
specialised discourses on statecraft, sovereignty, and forms of government. At the same time, increasing numbers of rulers left 'political testaments' for their successors, only rarely made available to a wider public.
These works, too, pay homage to the moral-religious agenda of rulership,
but they mostly offer practical advice, on finances, on the selection of
advisors, and often on individual figures and families around the
throne.[11]

Not only was there an evident tension between the ideals and the
practices of rulership. The religious-moral categories of kingship never
entirely fitted the noble way of life usually shared by the king as *premier
gentilhomme* of his realm. A good king was not only devout and just, he was
also a valiant knight and a war leader. Protecting the realm against threats
was a necessary accomplishment. Yet the crucially important noble quality of valour could easily lead to military adventurism, causing the death of
numerous men and emptying the treasury. Likewise, hospitality and
generosity, key qualities for any high-placed nobleman, needed to remain
within bounds. A king valiantly fighting for military glory, lavishly entertaining his people, and liberally supporting the poor, could in the end turn
out to be a disaster, leading to forced loans and raised taxes. Conversely a
cowardly or miserly figure could never be accepted as the ideal ruler:
largesse and prowess surely ranked high among the popularly acclaimed
qualities of kingship. The key quality of moderation was necessary to
balance these contradictory requirements. Different advisors, moreover,
were pulling in different directions, with high noble soldiers, clerics, and
financial administrators often in opposed roles – a predicament familiar to
modern politicians.

[10] Jacques-Bénigne Bossuet, *Politique tirée des propres paroles de l'Écriture sainte* (Paris, 1709);
see Frederick II of Prussia's response to Machiavelli: *Anti-Machiavel, ou essai de critique
sur Le Prince de Machiavel* (Brussels, 1740).
[11] Heinz Duchhardt (ed.), *Politische Testamente und andere Quellen zum Fürstenethos der
Frühen Neuzeit* (Darmstadt, 1987); Georg Küntzel and Martin Hass (eds.), *Die politischen
Testamente der Hohenzollern nebst ergänzenden Aktenstücken* (Stuttgart, 1911).

Several of the contradictory ideals cited here were present in Muscovy, which combined Byzantine traditions conveyed through Kievan Rus' (882–1283) with influences arising from the Mongol Golden Horde over-lordship which lasted until 1480. The tsar was pictured as a strong auto-cratic ruler protecting his subjects against foreign powers and guarding the order of the realm. Defending the Orthodox Church and generously pro-tecting the weak were key obligations. The same works that praised the powerful autocrat endorsed another ideal: the meek and merciful tsar, more interested in piety than in worldly success. The son of Ivan IV 'the Terrible' (1530–1547–1584), Feodor Ivanovich (1557–1584–1598) was nicknamed the 'Bell Ringer' because of his unceasing church attendance. Although this tsar was feebleminded and took no part in government, he was applauded as a saviour:

For this cross-bearing tsar was very pious, merciful to all, meek, gentle, and compassionate; he loved the humble and accepted suffering, and moreover was generous to widows and orphans, had mercy on all who grieved and helped those in misfortune ... He conquered all the neighboring countries of unbelieving nations that rebelled against the pious Christian faith and his God-preserved royal state – not with military troops or with the sharpness of a sword, but with the all-night vigil and ceaseless prayers to God did he finally conquer them.[12]

At the same time, debauched tsars or erring tsars failing to listen to their advisors were frowned upon. Any tsar actively undermining the Orthodox Church was no longer regarded as a tsar, but as an anti-tsar or 'tormentor' who deserved to be overthrown. In this different context, we again encounter clashing images.[13] A major shift in the presentation and prac-tice of rule was initiated by Peter I (1672–1682–1725), who strengthened his position vis-à-vis the Orthodox Church and the high nobles or *boyars*. These changes formed a starting point for eighteenth-century tsaritsas who moved the Russian court, army, and administration closer to the European mainstream.[14]

West Asia between 1300 and 1800 cannot be subsumed under any single category, but the ideals of rulership reflect familiar ingredients mixed in differing proportions. West Asian and European advice litera-ture shared the influences of Greek exemplary stories and philosophy represented by, among others, Alexander the Great and Aristotle. The Persian tradition of kingship exerted a dominant influence throughout the

---

[12] Daniel Rowland, 'Did Muscovite literary ideology place limits on the power of the tsar (1540s–1660s)?', *Russian Review*, 49 (1990), 125–55, at 134–5.

[13] Ibid.

[14] On the changes at court, see Ernest A. Zitser, *The Transfigured Kingdom: Sacred Parody and Charismatic Authority at the Court of Peter the Great* (Ithaca, NY, 2004); and Paul Keenan, *St Petersburg and the Russian Court, 1703–1761* (Basingstoke, 2013).

region in political thinking and administrative practice as well as in the notion that true kings held a divine radiance (*farr*). Ferdowsi's *Shāhnāmeh* or *Book of Kings*, written around 1000 but reflecting the legendary history of pre-Islamic kings and heroes, ranks among the most powerful repositories of Persian tradition. Islam introduced a relatively egalitarian worldview and instituted a dominant position for the holy law or *sharīʿa*: a power above the reach of any ruler. The sharīʿa and the *ulema*, the legal scholars responsible for its interpretation, redefined the balance between religious and secular power and had a lasting influence on advice literature.[15] The position of the supreme religious and political leader of Islam, the caliph, proved less resilient. Rival claimants soon challenged the caliphate's pretensions of overlordship. The power of the caliphs waned with that of the Abbasids before succumbing to the Mongol onslaught on Baghdad (1258): caliphs now subsisted under Mamluk protection in Egypt, maintained largely as a source of legitimacy for the sultans.

Turkic slave-soldiers rising in the service of the Abbasid caliphs came to power in a series of independent dynastic polities. These Turkic steppe peoples added their share of practices to the mixture of Persian and Islamic models, including an outspokenly martial view of rulership and an ideal of sovereignty shared among clan leaders rather than monopolised in the hands of a single figure. From the thirteenth to the fifteenth century, this steppe impact would be reinvigorated in successive waves of conquest by Chinggisids and Timurids. On the whole, Persian and Islamic models remained dominant influences throughout West and South Asia, yet they were not necessarily adopted wholesale: the terms 'Persianate' and 'Islamicate' indicate the selective adoption of elements from Persia and Islam by dynasties also cultivating other styles. Islamicate dynasties in South Asia and Southeast Asia, for example, cultivated numerous habits that hardly fitted Islamic orthodoxy.[16]

Advice literature was written from different angles and social positions, roughly equivalent to those in Europe. Occasionally rulers wrote for their sons: Kaykāʾūs (d. 1083), king of a minor dynasty, expected his son to be subjected to the Seljuq Turks and advised him about government as well

---

[15] Saïd Amir Arjomand, *The Shadow of God and the Hidden Imam: Religion, Political Order, and Societal Change in Shiʾite Iran from the Beginning to 1890* (Chicago, IL, 1984), 85–100, stresses the relatively secular nature and continuity of Persian attitudes; see also Arjomand, 'The salience of political ethic in the spread of Persianate Islam', *Journal of Persianate Studies*, 1/1 (2008), 5–29; on the tension between religious attitudes and statements in books of political wisdom, see Antony Black, *The History of Islamic Political Thought: From the Prophet to the Present* (Edinburgh, 2001), 93.

[16] The term is frequently used in Marshall G.S. Hodgson, *The Venture of Islam: Conscience and History in a World Civilization* (Chicago, IL, 1974), followed by many other works.

as about alternative careers. More often men in government, such as Niẓām al-Mulk (1018–1092) serving the Seljuqs as vizier (*wazīr*), wrote tracts on rulership. Scholars, many of them from the ranks of the *ulema* (Muslim legal scholars), form the most important group. The prolific Persian writer Al-Ghazālī (*c.* 1058–1111), whose *Book of Counsel for Kings* occupies a minor position in the extended oeuvre of the author, ranks as a prime example of this group.[17] Although the ulema cannot be seen as priests in the Christian sense, they did contribute an outspoken religious-moral voice to the advice literature. Leaving aside the particulars of these numerous texts and concentrating on their shared ideas, a set of princely virtues can be detected that shows a more than superficial resemblance to the ideals outlined for Europe.[18] In addition, some familiar concerns emerge about men in power and their fickle temperaments. Piety is a precondition of good rulership; rulers are expected to defend the believers and help expand the community of Muslims or *umma*. Honesty, courage, wisdom, and justice appear as the key virtues, explained in different terms and with differing subcategories in individual texts. Honesty allows the ruler to rein in his passions, retain modesty, and act with generosity. Courage, valour, ambition, and perseverance help the ruler to attain high goals. Wisdom, good judgement, wit, and remembrance make for good government. Justice reflects the ruler's equity and affection for his people. Justice also engenders moderation and prevents the predominance of one virtue over the others. The balance among the virtues is of crucial importance; pursuing any of these virtues to its extremes would lead to corruption.[19]

Sultans were 'the shadow of god upon earth, with whom all creatures could seek shelter'.[20] From the Umayyads to the Ottomans, Islamic rulers ostensibly protected their subjects against injustice – *zulm* or *mazalim*.

---

[17] Ghazali, *Ghazali's Book of Counsel for Kings (Naṣīḥat al-mulūk)*, ed. Frank R.C. Bagley (New York, 1964).

[18] Bernard Lewis, *The Political Language of Islam* (Chicago, IL, and London, 1988), 17–18, notes the absence of the father metaphor for god as well as for rulers in the Islamic world – a marked contrast with Europe as well as with China, where the family metaphor was omnipresent. The shepherd and the flock were present in metaphors of ruling both in the Islamicate world and in Europe.

[19] Marinos Sariyannis, 'The princely virtues as presented in Ottoman political and moral literature', *Turcica*, 63 (2011), 121–44; see also Cornell H. Fleischer, *Bureaucrat and Intellectual in the Ottoman Empire: The Historian Mustafa Ali (1541–1600)* (Princeton, NJ, 1986).

[20] Lewis, *Political Language of Islam*, 21–2, note 48; Vasileios Syros, 'Shadows in heaven and clouds on earth: the emergence of social life and political authority in the early modern Islamic empires', *Viator*, 43/2 (2012), 377–406; Patricia Crone, *God's Rule – Government and Islam: Six Centuries of Medieval Islamic Political Thought* (New York, 2004); Anne K.S. Lambton, *State and Government in Medieval Islam: An Introduction to the Study of Islamic Political Theory: The Jurists* (Oxford, 1981).

Many dynasties organised their own law courts inviting complainants from the populace, personally judging their cases or referring them back to *qadi* courts applying *shari'a*. A description of the Ayyubid sultan Salah al-Din (1138–1171–1193) brings to mind Louis IX under the oak:

Everyone who had a grievance was admitted, great and small, aged women and feeble men ... and he always received with his own hand the petitions that were presented to him, and did his utmost to put an end to every form of oppression that was reported.[21]

The Mamluk Sultan Qalawun (1222–1279–1290), instructing his son al-Malik as-Salih on how to govern Egypt while he went on campaign, stressed justice, petitioning, and the *mazalim* court in his advice.[22] Princely accessibility and adjudication provided legitimacy as well as a check on the transgressions of office-holders. The topos of defence of the weak against the powerful was strongly present in Islamicate ideals of rulership. Following his accession, the first action of Mughal emperor Shah Jahan (1592–1628–1658; Plate 16) was to set up a 'chain of justice':

After my accession, the first order that I gave was for the fastening up of the Chain of Justice, so that if those engaged in the administration of justice should delay or practise hypocrisy in the matter of those seeking justice, the oppressed might come to this chain and shake it so that its noise might attract attention.[23]

Mughal court paintings represent this chain of justice alerting the sultan to injustice (Plate 1); the ruler's benevolent protection created order among men and beasts, bringing together predator and prey, lion and lamb.[24]

---

[21] Albrecht Fuess, '*Zulm* by *mazalim*? The political implications of the use of *mazalim* jurisdiction by the Mamluk sultans', *Mamluk Studies Review*, 13/1 (2009), 121–47, at 123; Nimrod Hurvitz, 'The contribution of early Islamic rulers to adjudication and legislation: the case of the *mazalim* tribunals', in Duindam et al. (eds.), *Law and Empire*, 135–56, and in the same volume Engin Akarli, 'The ruler and law making in the Ottoman empire', 87–109, stressing that Ottoman law was particularly severe for its own officers.

[22] Paulina Lewicka, 'What a king should care about: two memoranda of the Mamluk sultan on running the state's affairs', *Studia Arabistyczne i Islamistyczne*, 6 (1998), 5–45, on justice at 13, 15, 19, 37; see another example of advice in Axel Moberg, 'Regierungspromemoria eines ägyptischen Sultans', in Gotthold Weil (ed.), *Festschrift Eduard Sachau zum siebzigsten Geburtstage gewidmet von Freunden und Schülern* (Berlin, 1915), 406–21; and Léonor Fernandes, 'On conducting the affairs of the state: a guide-line of the fourteenth century', *Annales islamologiques*, 24 (1988), 81–91, with justice mentioned at 83. These texts were kindly made available to me by Paulina Lewicka.

[23] Jahangir, *The Tuzuk-i-Jahangiri; or, Memoirs of Jahangir*, ed. Henry Beveridge and Alexander Rogers (London, 1909), 7. Note that Shah Jahan was imprisoned by his son Aurangzeb in 1658, dying a few years later in 1666.

[24] See a brief reference to the delight princes took in 'showing themselves to be just', in Niccolao Manucci, *A Pepys of Mogul India, 1653–1708: Being an Abridged Edition of the*

Protection did not entail equality: a view of society prevailed in which the flock of food producers could live in order and harmony only through the intervention of soldiers and administrators operating under the aegis of the king, a thought often rendered in the 'circle of justice' or *daire-i 'adliye*:

> The world is a garden the fence of which is the dynasty,
> The dynasty is an authority through which life is given to proper behaviour.
> Proper behaviour is a policy directed by the ruler.
> The ruler is an institution supported by the soldiers.
> The soldiers are helpers, who are maintained by money.
> Money is sustenance brought together by the subjects.
> The subjects are servants who are protected by justice.
> Justice is something familiar [harmonious], and through it, the world persists.
> The world is a garden . . .[25]

This phrase, repeated in many variants throughout the Persianate-Islamicate world and sometimes attributed to Aristotle, stipulates a stable world based on agriculture, with peasants generating revenue for a ruler who with his administrators and soldiers establishes order and protects his peoples against predatory neighbours within and without.

Among the three major dynasties dominating West and South Asia in the early modern period, the Safavids (1501–1736) of Iran remained particularly close to the Persian legacy. Shah Ismail I (1487–1501–1524), starting out as the spiritual leader of a messianic movement, turned his 'redhead' Qizilbash supporters into a devoted fighting force, conquering Iran and Iraq. His personal brand of rulership was linked to the adoption of Shia Islam that would remain typical for Iran.[26] Successful conquest combined with proselytising in Anatolia caused sharp conflict with the Sunni Ottoman dynasty. The Ottomans, long since sedentary, had expanded and consolidated administrative routines in the wake of their conquest of Constantinople (1453). These developments would be matched by the Safavids and the Mughals in the reigns of respectively Abbas I (1571–1588–1629) and Akbar (1542–1556–1605). Around 1600 the Ottoman empire underwent a series of crises, necessitating a redefinition of power relations in the realm. The Mughals,

---

"*Storia do Mogor*" *of Niccolao Manucci*, ed. Margaret L. Irvine and William Irvine (New York, 1913), 207.

[25] Cited in Ibn Khaldun, *Muqaddimah*, 41; see also Linda T. Darling, 'Circle of justice', in Fleet et al. (eds.), *Encyclopaedia of Islam, Three*. Ibn Khaldun attributes the passage to Aristotle, who in any case was influential in the Arabic world as well as in Europe.

[26] Kathryn Babayan, 'The waning of the Qizilbash: The spiritual and the temporal in seventeenth century Iran', PhD thesis, Princeton University (1993); Babayan, 'The Safavid synthesis: From Qizilbash Islam to imamite Shi'ism', *Iranian Studies*, 27 (1994), 135–61.

moving southwards and almost coincidentally conquering a huge empire in India, showed great agility in adapting their specific blend of rulership to pre-existing traditions, allowing a relatively smooth connection with Hindu Rajput princes. Akbar in particular strayed far from the dictate of Islam, combining various religions in an eclectic blend of devotion tied to his personal style of rulership. Only with the advent of Aurangzeb (1618–1658–1707) did the Mughal dynasty revert to a more orthodox Muslim position. The Mughals, boasting descent in the female line from Chinggis Khan and in the male line from Timur Lenk, carefully cultivated their steppe genealogy, maintaining their mobile and martial style of rulership longer than the Ottomans or the Safavids.[27]

Conquering the north of the Indian subcontinent, the Mughals followed in the footsteps of several earlier Islamic conquest dynasties. Long before these conquests, Buddhism had lost ground in India while taking root in contiguous areas. In the mosaic dominated by Hindu and Muslim polities in South Asia, with an additional strong Buddhist presence in Southeast Asia, Persian and Islamic influences were becoming stronger.[28] What did earlier Indic traditions have to say about rulership?

Hindu kingship worked in tandem with Brahmin authority. The active king, governing his realm and waging war, needed the power of the Brahmins as interpreters of the Vedic tradition to affirm his authority. The world-renouncing Brahmin 'held the key to religious values' and to the all-important sacred rites.[29] An ideal ruler who successfully ascended to the status of world-renouncer would in the end necessarily give up kingship itself. Kingship, in practice and in theory, was stuck between the sacral and the secular, between 'divinity and mortal humanity, legitimate authority and arbitrary power, *dharma* and *adharma*'.[30] The equivocal character of kingship, shifting between moral, pragmatic, and even capricious or violent modes of behaviour, could be made to work in various ways. A seasonal bifurcation allowed the coexistence of the styles in one person, leading troops into war in the cold season, engaging in ritual interaction during the hot season, and finally retreating during the rainy

---

[27] Lisa Balabanlilar, 'The Begims of the mystic feast: Turco-Mongol tradition in the Mughal harem', *Journal of Asian Studies*, 69/1 (2010), 123–47.

[28] See Basham, 'Ideas of kingship in Hinduism and Buddhism', in Basham (ed.), *Kingship in Asia and Early America,* 115–32; on their mingling in Southeast Asia and on the impact of Theravada Buddhism there, see M.C. Subhadradis Diskul, 'Ancient kingship in mainland Southeast Asia', ibid., 133–59; on the same process plus the impact of Islam in the archipelago, see S. Supomo, 'Some aspects of kingship in ancient Java', ibid., 161–77.

[29] Richards (ed.), *Kingship and Authority in South Asia* (Madison, WI, 1978), iv–v.

[30] J.C. Heesterman, 'The conundrum of the king's authority', in Richards (ed.), *Kingship and Authority*, 1–27, at 3–4; James A. Santucci, 'Aspects of the nature and functions of Vedic kingship', in Basham (ed.), *Kingship in Asia and Early America*, 83–113.

season. Alternatively, the Brahmin's role as moral and ritual guardian made it possible for the king to engage in aggressive or frivolous behaviour without undermining his elevated position. A south Indian oral epic, probably reaching back to a dynasty ruling the Kongu region around 1000 CE, reports another solution: the joint rule of two brothers, the elder performing the ceremonial and moral aspects of monarchy, the younger displaying the fierceness and impetuosity expected of a warrior-king.[31] Interestingly, these variants all underline that the combined roles of kingship were seen as too much for most individuals to handle competently.

Chandragupta Maurya (*c.* 317–293 BCE), the founder of the Mauryan empire, brought most of northern India under his authority. Tradition attributes the authorship of an extended pragmatic manual of rulership, the *Arthashastra,* to one of Chandragupta Maurya's advisors, Kautilya. The book was probably compiled later, on the basis of several sources, yet it speaks with a clear voice. The *Arthashastra* puts the maintenance of order first on the list of the ruler's duties, understanding this requirement not only as the preservation of the caste system, but also as the protection of the weak against their stronger neighbours.[32] In addition it underscores that a policy of social justice usually worked best. On the whole, however, the *Arthashastra* deals with the threats to the power of the ruler far more than with the ideals of rulership. Chandragupta Maurya's grandson, Asoka (304–268–232 BCE), embraced Buddhism and widely broadcast his elevated view of rulership. Asoka's moral standards reflected the 'ten royal virtues' that can be found in texts from the earliest Buddhist sources to statements by the current king of Thailand:

> Liberality, generosity, and charisma;
> A high sense of morality;
> Self-sacrifice for the good of the people;
> Honesty and integrity;
> Kindness and gentleness;
> Austerity and self-control;
> To possess no ill-will and enmity;
> To promote peace and non-violence;

---

[31] Richards (ed.), *Kingship and Authority,* vii–viii, referring to Brenda Beck, 'The authority of the king: prerogatives and dilemmas of kingship as portrayed in a contemporary oral epic from south India', in the same volume at 168–91.

[32] On compilation and authorship, see Basham (ed.), *Kingship in Asia and Early America,* 116; for a comparison of Kautilya's *Arthashastra* and Han Feizi, see Roger Boesche, 'Han Feizi's legalism versus Kautilya's Arthashastra', *Asian Philosophy,* 15/2 (2005), 157–72, esp. 159–60 and 169–70.

Forbearance, patience, and tolerance, and
To rule in harmony without giving offence and opposing the will of his
people.[33]

The exemplary ruler embodying these virtues would inspire ministers and servants to be righteous; their example would not only comfort the people, but also bring celestial harmony:

This being so, moon and sun go right in their courses. This being so, constellations and stars do likewise; days and nights, moons and fortnights, seasons and years go on their courses regularly: winds blow regularly and in due season. Thus the devas (gods) are not annoyed and the sky-deva bestows sufficient rain. Rains falling seasonably, the crops ripen in due season ... when crops ripen in due season, men who live on those crops are long-lived, well-favoured, strong and free from sickness.[34]

The trickling down of the ruler's good example implies that his misbehaviour, too, could have far-reaching consequences: natural disasters, deformed animals or humans, or other ominous occurrences were habitually read as divine displeasure provoked by royal ineptitude.[35]

Kings stood outside of the regular order: they held powers unavailable to others. Extraordinary beings, singled out through special signs and physical marks, could choose between two paths: become a world-conquering 'wheel-turning monarch' (*chakravartin* or *cakkavatti*), or renounce the world and follow in the footsteps of Buddha.[36] Once they had chosen the way of the ruler, their personal rectitude remained of prime importance. At the heart of good rulership stood *dharma* or *dhamma*: the righteous path of social order and justice. The true victory of the ruler was to be found not primarily in military success, but in leading others to follow the path of dhamma. This necessitated not only maintaining justice and punishing injustice, but first and foremost cultivating the governance of the self.[37] The rise of Buddhism exacerbated the demands on rulers' morality, as it now became impossible to lay the burden of moral world-renouncing on the shoulders of the Brahmin.[38]

---

[33] Given here as cited in Georgios T. Halkias, 'The enlightened sovereign: Buddhism and kingship in India and Tibet', in Steven M. Emmanuel (ed.), *A Companion to Buddhist Philosophy* (Malden, MA, and Oxford, 2013), 491–510, at 496.

[34] The Buddha speaking to monks in 'The Book of the Fours', cited by Halkias, 'Enlightened sovereign', 496.

[35] On Southeast Asia, see Andaya, 'Political development', 420.

[36] Halkias, 'Enlightened sovereign', 499–500.

[37] Upinder Singh, 'Governing the state and the self: political philosophy and practice in the edicts of Aśoka', *South Asian Studies*, 28/2 (2012), 131–45, on non-violence (136–8), on justice (140–1), and on governance of the self (141–3).

[38] The same statement holds true with even greater force for ascetic and non-violent Jainism: see Lawrence A. Babb, *Absent Lord: Ascetics and Kings in a Jain Ritual Culture* (Berkeley, CA, 1996). Halkias, 'Enlightened sovereign', 502, underlines the impact of

Buddhist monks or *sangha* could still function as 'conscience-keeper of the state', but the ruler himself remained responsible.[39] In practice the highly idealised standards of Asokan kingship must have functioned largely as an aspiration 'for measuring reality – to praise those who approximate them and condemn those who do not'.[40]

The mixture of influences in the discourse on rulership changed over time and space: between the Indian heartland and the mainland polities towards the Southeast that embraced Indic examples; between the mainland and the Southeast Asian archipelago which itself contained endless variety. The Hindu–Buddhist legacy persisted while Islamic influence became dominant in the course of the fifteenth and sixteenth centuries. A Javanese variant of the 'circle of justice' evokes this mixture of influences, with the sage added to the king, soldiers, peasants, and merchants: 'The soldier is the fortress of the king, the peasant the food of the state, the merchant the clothing of the land and the sage provides the benefaction of prayers.'[41] A wajang play describes the ideal Javanese king, who:

is generous in giving alms, gives clothes to those who have none, gives a cane to those who slip, shelter to those scorched by the sun, food to those in hunger, consolation to the heavy of heart, a torch to those in darkness; he clears the thicket where it grows dense.[42]

These lofty ideals are also present in the 'eight life-rules' (*Asta-brata*) presented in a Javanese rendering of the Indic epic story *Ramayana*. Two of the guidelines, 'ruthless intelligence' and 'fiery courage', underline the need for political acumen, punishing wrongdoers, and military valour. Here as elsewhere, the ideals were superhuman as well as contradictory.[43] Complaints against wrongdoers in government service could be expressed in collective processions (*nggogol*); individuals could manifest their exasperation by doing *pepe*, to sit unprotected in the full sunlight on

---

Buddhism on the Brahmanical caste system and the vested power of the higher status groups.

[39] Halkias, 'Enlightened sovereign', 501.

[40] Gananath Obeyesekere, 'Religion and polity in Theravada Buddhism: continuity and change in a great tradition. A review article', *Comparative Studies in Society and History*, 21/4 (1979), 626–39, quotation at 635 in the context of criticism of Stanley Tambiah's *World Renouncer and World Conqueror*.

[41] Moertono, *State and Statecraft in Old Java*, 136; see another variant in Timothy Behrend, 'Kraton and cosmos in traditional Java', *Archipel*, 37 (1989), 173–87, at 179.

[42] Moertono, *State and Statecraft in Old Java*, 38; on Majapahit, see Theodore Gauthier Th. Pigeaud, *Java in the 14th Century: A Study in Cultural History. The Nagara-Kertagama by Rakawi Prapanca of Majapahit, 1365 A.D. III translations*, Koninklijk Instituut voor Taal-, Land-, en Volkenkunde 4/3 (The Hague, 1960), 3, citing as title of the prince: 'protector of the protectorless'.

[43] Moertono, *State and Statecraft in Old Java*, 43–4, full text at 152–5.

the square in front of the ruler's palace (*kraton*). Jesters and clowns were allowed some licence in voicing their critique.[44]

The interconnected worlds of mainland and archipelago in Southeast Asia can be portrayed as a set of interacting centres of dynastic power with unclear outer boundaries and overlapping spheres of influence, sometimes integrated into an overall hierarchy dominated by one conspicuous centre, sometimes breaking up into numerous competing entities. These interconnected conspicuous centres surrounded by circles of smaller replicas have been depicted in terms relating to the universe, as a *mandala* or 'galactic polity'.[45] The mainland polities in Southeast Asia, however, were connected not only to India, but also to the Chinese empire. At the same time, Chinese traders were a marked presence in the islands.

Moving from Europe to West and South Asia, the strong impact of religion on the ideals of rulership appears as a constant. A tension between religiously inspired ideals and the daily requirements of government was present in each of the regions considered. Once we move to East Asia, the burden on the shoulders of rulers is defined in different ways. Throughout the two millennia of Chinese imperial power, magistrates and scholars carefully glossed a number of texts mostly written in the centuries before the 'first emperor' Qin Shi Huang (221–210 BCE), notably including the works of Confucius (551–479 BCE). Confucius advocated rule through moral example and self-improvement. The *Analects* point to legendary exemplars of virtuous rule, notably the legendary emperors Yao and Shun: 'The Master said: "May not Shun be instanced as one who made no effort, yet the empire was well governed? For what effort did he make? Ordering himself in all seriousness, he did nothing but maintain the correct imperial attitude."'[46] What strikes the eye here is not the dignity that can be found in many ideals of princely behaviour, but the stress on stillness, repeated throughout the *Analects*: 'The Master said: "He who governs by his moral excellence may be compared to the pole-star, which abides in its place while all the stars bow towards it."'[47] The emperor was likened to the unmoving pole star, the still point of reference for active administrators who were expected to approach him from the south. Magistrates' buildings (*yamen*) and

---

[44] Ibid., 76–8.

[45] Stanley J. Tambiah, 'The galactic polity: the structure of traditional kingdoms in Southeast Asia', in Stanley A. Freed (ed.), *Anthropology and the Climate of Opinion* (New York, 1977), 69–97. On fusion and fission, see Andaya, 'Political development', 403; and Sunait Chutintaranond, 'Mandala, segmentary state and politics of centralization in medieval Ayudhya', *Journal of the Siam Society*, 78/1 (1990), 89–100.

[46] Confucius, *Analects*, trans. William Edward Soothill (Edinburgh, 1910; repr. London, 1995), Book XV, iv, 91–2.

[47] Ibid., Book II, i, 5.

imperial palaces consistently had their main entrance facing southwards: 'facing south' became a synonym for ruling.

Confucius' portrayal of impassive rule through exemplary morality provoked comments by 'legalist' writers proffering a more sceptical view of human nature, nurtured by the political turmoil in the 'warring states' period (403–221 BCE). The legalist school advocated a strict implementation of laws, stressing government through punishments and rewards rather than through moral example. At the other end of the spectrum stood a loose grouping of works and authors usually labelled as 'Daoist', including Laozi or the 'old master', possibly a contemporary of Confucius. His *Daodejing* or *Classic of the Way and of Virtue*, probably a compilation of works by several unnamed authors rather than the work of a single figure, fits neither the heavy social morality of Confucianism nor the legalists' pragmatic stance. The intentionally elusive poetic style of Daoism, never as sternly didactic as Confucius or as fixed on the ways of power as the legalists, confronts readers with the shortcomings of conventional wisdom without giving unequivocal solutions. It stresses withdrawal and reflection more than social engagement. However, aspects of Daoist thinking resonate in Confucius as well as in legalist texts, notably the idea of non-action or *wu wei*, the antithesis of active government interference.

A second round of discussion ensued in which Mencius (372–289 BCE) criticised the legalist approach and its 'rule through coercion' or 'rule of the hegemon', reverting to Confucius' 'rule through benevolence' or the 'kingly way'. Subsequently Han Feizi (280–233 BCE) provided a terse restatement of the legalist position as a pragmatic model of power. Han Feizi incorporated non-action into his work as a pragmatic princely strategy to confuse ambitious ministers, consorts, relatives, and servants: passivity concealed the ruler's intentions and made it very difficult to manipulate him.[48] Han Feizi also questioned the canonisation of early sage rulers, stressing the need to adapt policies to current situations.

Confucius and his numerous followers through the ages left room for laws, rewards, and punishments, but preferred ruling through moral example, characterised by simplicity and virtue more than by energetic activism. Their works became the dominant influence during the Han dynasty, and formed the core of an emerging orthodoxy under the Song dynasty. During the Ming and Qing dynasties the 'four books and five classics' of Confucianism formed the standard curriculum of the learned elite studying for the civil service examinations. Among the virtues of a

---

[48] See Han Fei Tzu, *Basic Writings*, trans. Burton Watson (New York, 1964); on the connection to Daoism, see 9–10.

good emperor, filial piety ranked high: he should respect his parents and ancestors, maintaining harmony in his family before he could effectively act as emperor. Filial piety and the correct performance of sacrifices and rituals were the essence of virtuous rulership. Involvement in the active ingredients of leadership, protecting the realm against outsiders and leading the daily routines of government, needed to remain within bounds. A large share should be left to leading ministers. These high state servants themselves exhorted the young princes under their tutelage to listen to wise counsel and refrain from impetuous actions disaffecting the people. The didactic use of ancient examples and classic texts persisted to the end in imperial China, supplemented by more recent additions from the historic record portraying the actions of good and bad emperors.[49]

This powerful didactic message was conveyed by a group that in some ways was more dominant than either *ulema* or priests. Confucian literati rising through examination success dominated government under the Song and the Ming; they maintained their position to a large extent under the Manchu Qing dynasty, sharing power with a conquest elite itself increasingly moulded by Confucian precepts.[50] These gentlemen-scholars never formed a caste of ritual specialists as did the Indic Brahmins; nor did they form a separate estate with marked worldly as well as spiritual powers as did the clergy in Europe; they depended more strongly on government office than did the ulema in West Asia. Yet the Chinese literati, too, educated princes and voluntarily offered moral guidance to the ruler, usually in highly deferential terminology. Occupying the same moral high ground as the ulema, priests, or Brahmins, they, too, acted as tutors, custodians, and critics. More strongly than these other religious and ritual elites, however, they dominated throughout the imperial bureaucracy.

The Chinese emperor or 'son of heaven' (*tianzi*) held the 'mandate of heaven' (*tianming*), yet celestial support for his rule could be jeopardised by his immoral behaviour or by wrongdoings perpetrated in his name. Harmony and order were vital to the Chinese conception of rulership. However, direct justice does not seem to have occupied the pivotal

---

[49] See a critical view of late Ming and Qing governance, reiterating the examples of Yao and Shun and deploring the decline in standards of rulership and state service: Huang Tsung-Hsi, *Waiting for the Dawn: A Plan for the Prince. Huang Tsung-Hsi's Ming-I Tai-Fang Lu*, trans. Wm. Theodore de Bary (New York, 1993). See Ebrey, 'Remonstrating against royal extravagance', on the didactic role of the tutor.

[50] On the civil service examinations, see Chapters 3 and 4 below, 211, 245–246; Benjamin A. Elman, *A Cultural History of Civil Examinations in Late Imperial China* (Berkeley, CA, 2000); and the same author's 'Political, social, and cultural reproduction via civil service examinations in late imperial China', *Journal of Asian Studies*, 50/1 (1991), 7–28.

position it did elsewhere, nor did the personal accessibility of the ruler for his peoples figure strongly in legitimising stories.[51] Complainants could make themselves heard by striking the 'petitioners' drum' or by sounding 'grievance bells' in the vicinity of the palace; the intrepid might consider 'stopping the royal cart' or voice complaints 'at the palace gate' hoping for a speedy and favourable response by the emperor. The only formally ruling empress in Chinese history, Wu Zetian (624–690–705), instituted 'petition boxes' allowing her to redress grievances as well as to punish her political rivals.[52] Censors had been instituted in the early empire to evaluate magistrates' careers. The Ming founder Zhu Yuanzhang (1328–1368–1398, also called Ming Taizu or the Hongwu emperor) gave them a more active role in investigating complaints.[53]

While taking care of the people was a key responsibility, appeals and complaints appear to have been seen with mixed feelings, as an inevitable requirement best kept within strict bounds rather than as an opportunity to generate popular support.[54] The Portuguese Jesuit Alvarez Semedo, staying at the Ming court in its final decades, enthusiastically reported the presence of several instruments for petitioners:

within the first gate of the Palace, there was always a Bell, a Drumme, and a Table overlaid with a white varnish, as it were, playstered over; upon this, he that would not speak to the King in person, wrote what his request was, which was presently carried to the King: But whosoever would speak with him, rang the Bell, or beat the Drumme, and presently they were brought in, and had audience.

While this old tradition continued, Semedo added, petitioners used it only rarely, and for good reasons:

for during twenty two years' time, I do not remember, that it was ever beaten above once: and he that did it, was presently paid his pension in ready Bastinadoes

---

[51] However, see John S. Major et al. (trans.), *The Huainanzi: A Guide to the Theory and Practice of Government in Early Han China* (New York, 2010), 309 and other places citing the need of 'soliciting opinions'.

[52] On Wu Zetian and her writings, see Denis Twitchett, '*Chen Gui* and other works attributed to Empress Wu Zetian', *Asia Major*, 16/1 (2003), 33–109.

[53] Chinese emperors held three different types of name. Zhu Yuanzhang is the family name with given name (in that order), Ming Taizu is the temple name, Hongwu is the reign name, formally written as 'the Hongwu emperor' rather than as 'Hongwu' or 'Emperor Hongwu'. In this book, most often the reign names will be used, sometimes in abbreviated form, as Kangxi rather than as the more correct 'the Kangxi emperor'.

[54] See Qiang Fang, 'Hot potatoes: Chinese complaint systems from early times to the late Qing (1898)', *Journal of Asian Studies*, 68/4 (2009), 1105–35; and earlier discussions by Edward A. Kracke, Jr, 'Early visions of justice for the humble in East and West', *Journal of the American Oriental Society*, 96/4 (1976), 492–8, and J.R. Perry, 'Justice for the underprivileged: the ombudsman tradition of Iran', *Journal of Near Eastern Studies*, 373 (1978), 203–15.

[beatings], for having disquieted the King, who was about halfe a league off. After this hard penance he was heard, and allowed, not to see or speak to the King, but according to the custome now in use, in a petition.[55]

Semedo's report makes clear that the ideals of rulership represented in 'complaint systems' in China and elsewhere were rarely embraced whole-heartedly in practice.

Confucian ethics remained dominant in imperial China, but they were always mixed with Buddhist and Daoist influences, in changing proportions during various dynasties. The 'three ways' overlapped, with Confucian scholars incorporating aspects of the Buddhist notion of the universal virtuous and benevolent 'wheel-turning king' and the Daoist concept of non-action. Empress Wu temporarily placed Laozi's *Daodejing* on the curriculum for the civil service examinations and lavishly sponsored Buddhism.[56] While the Song dynasty witnessed a powerful resurgence of Confucianism, a single emperor such as Huizong (1082–1100–1126) could develop a strong penchant for Daoism. Northern conquest dynasties infused the Han Chinese blend with a robust martial style, performing a similar role in East as well as in West and South Asia. In addition, their repeated incursions also changed religious priorities. Under the Mongol conquerors who ruled China as the Yuan dynasty (1271–1368) Buddhism again became a stronger presence. The Qing dynasty, ruling China proper primarily on the basis of its classic precepts, governed recently conquered peoples, most notably Mongols, Uyghurs, and Tibetans, according to different styles of rulership and different moral-religious positions, including shamanism and Tibetan Buddhism. Qing emperors were depicted as enlightened bodhisattvas and visited the Buddhist pilgrimage site at Mount Wutai.[57]

---

[55] Alvarez Semedo, *The History of that Great and Renowned Monarchy of China* (London, 1655), all quotations at 110.

[56] Twitchett, '*Chen Gui*'; T.H. Barrett, *The Woman Who Discovered Printing* (New Haven, CT, 2008).

[57] Bodhisattvas are 'beings who, having achieved nirvana or release from endless reincarnations, remain in this world to aid others towards release' – James L. Hevia, 'Rulership and Tibetan Buddhism in eighteenth-century China: Qing emperors, lamas and audience rituals', in Joëlle Rollo-Koster (ed.), *Medieval and Early Modern Ritual: Formalized Behavior in Europe, China, and Japan* (Leiden and Boston, MA, 2002), 279–302, at 280; David M. Farquhar, 'Emperor as bodhisattva in the governance of the Ch'ing empire', *Harvard Journal of Asiatic Studies*, 38/1 (1978), 5–34; Natalie Köhle, 'Why did the Kangxi emperor go to Wutai Shan? Patronage, pilgrimage and the place of Tibetan Buddhism at the early Qing court', *Late Imperial China*, 29/1 (2008), 73–119. See also Pamela Kyle Crossley, *A Translucent Mirror: History and Identity in Qing Imperial Ideology* (Berkeley, CA, 1999), 223–80, on Buddhism, bodhisattva-hood, the chakravartin, and Qing emperors.

Tributary polities around China, including Japan, more often Korea, Annam (Dai Viet or Vietnam) and a number of other entities such as Champa, Burma, and the Ryukyu islands, were all at some point influenced by the Confucian principle of rule based on virtuous example and learning. In each of these cases this shared imprint arose at a different moment and obtained a different character as it mixed with diverging political or social patterns and the equally strong Indic example. Soon after taking power, the Ming founder in truly Confucian style 'rectified the names' in his empire, extending this mission to include tributary polities:

the Emperor personally wrote sacrificial invocations and sent officials to the mountains, the towns, the seas and the rivers to change and to fix the names of the spirits and to announce the sacrifices ... others were sent to promulgate advice on the rectification of the spirits' names to Annam, Champa and Korea.

In 1372 the Hongwu emperor noted that not all tributaries were equally close:

Korea is very close to China and its people are familiar with the classics, histories and cultured things. Their music and ritual are much like those of China and it cannot be considered together with other foreign countries.[58]

Within a generation, the advent of the Ming dynasty was followed by a major dynastic change in this closest tributary state, from the Koryŏ to the Chosŏn lineage. After a millennium in which Buddhism had been the paramount influence, this changeover in 1392 brought with it a powerful reinforcement of neo-Confucianism, furthering an even greater accord with Ming China. The Manchu conquest (1644) was initially experienced as a setback by Chosŏn Korea, but disrupted neither the tributary relationship nor the staunch Confucianism of Korea. King Yŏngjo (1694–1724–1776), at times participating in three 'royal lectures' with his scholars, may have surpassed even his contemporary, the Qing Qianlong emperor (1711–1735–1796*), as a paragon of Confucian diligence.[59]

In Japan the first legendary emperor, Jimmu, who according to tradition started his reign in 660 BCE, traced descent to the sun goddess, Amaterasu Omikami. Divine descent and continuity into the twenty-first

---

[58] Geoff Wade (trans.), *Southeast Asia in the Ming Shi-lu: An Open Access Resource* (Singapore: Asia Research Institute and the Singapore E-Press, National University of Singapore), http://epress.nus.edu.sg/msl (accessed 22 October 2013), entries for 29 June 1370 and 16 November 1372.

[59] JaHyun Kim Haboush, *The Confucian Kingship in Korea: Yŏngjo and the Politics of Sagacity* (New York, 1988); on the royal lectures, see Yonung Kwon, 'The royal lecture and Confucian politics in early Yi Korea', *Korean Studies*, 6/1 (1982), 41–62.

century make this dynasty stand out in history.[60] The emergence of verifiable historic empresses and emperors – around 600 CE – coincides with the adoption of the Chinese calendar and other Chinese cultural influences; indigenous ritual Shinto practices became intertwined with Confucian phrases at the moment they were first recorded in writing. Chinese texts and examples were a formative influence, and the legendary Chinese sage kings of Yao and Shun can be found in Japanese Confucian texts, as well as the views of rulership connected to their example.[61] At the same time Buddhism became a powerful influence in Japan. In addition to some rituals familiar from imperial China, the imperial annual ritual observances (*nenju gyoji*) notably included Shinto and Buddhist practices. While adopting elements of Confucian thought, Japan cultivated its own style of rulership. Officials at the court of the Chinese Sui dynasty (561–618) quoted a Japanese envoy stating that 'The king of Wa [Japan] deems heaven to be his elder brother and the sun his younger. Before break of dawn he attends the court and, sitting cross-legged, listens to appeals. Just as soon as the sun rises, he ceases these duties, saying that he hands them over to his brother.'[62] The reference to the sun sets apart Japanese legitimacy from Chinese traditions. Interestingly, the requirement of listening to petitioners – familiar from European and West Asian tradition – is underlined here too. Notwithstanding its strong connections with China, Japan developed a specific style of rulership, with the emperors as increasingly symbolic figures leaving the practice of ruling to others. In early Japan the Fujiwara family, supplying imperial wives as well as regents, took power in its hands; while later, abdicated emperors ruled from Buddhist monasteries in the name of their sons. From the twelfth century onwards, the shogun emerged as the dominant military leader. Tokugawa Japan (1603–1868) consolidated a gradually evolving tradition where an emperor reigned and a shogun ruled, a separation of military and administrative power from ritual and cultural supremacy that was on occasion pictured as a combination of the two 'ways' of ruling: the way of the hegemon and the kingly way.[63] The practice of double

---

[60] In practice, several dynasties can be distinguished: continuity was as much a construction as divine descent, but both exerted a powerful influence.

[61] See several instances in Wm. Theodore de Bary et al. (eds.), *Sources of Japanese Tradition*, vol. I: *From Earliest Times to 1600* (New York, 2001), 420 in the context of petitioning, article 15 in the Kenmu code.

[62] Ben-Ami Shillony, *Enigma of the Emperors: Sacred Subservience in Japanese History* (Folkestone, 2005), 17.

[63] Mostly by critics among Tokugawa historians – see Wai-ming Ng, 'Redefining legitimacy in Tokugawa historiography', *Sino-Japanese Studies*, 18 (2011), 1–20, at 1. On the earlier traditions of separating the emperor's ritual authority from military and political power, see G. Cameron Hurst, 'Insei', in Donald H. Shively and William H. McCullough (eds.),

rulership, the marked presence of ruling empresses in early Japan, and the conspicuous role of a hereditary warrior elite indicate major differences between China and Japan beneath layers of cultural similarity. On closer observation, all lesser partners or tributaries of the Chinese empire mixed local tradition with Chinese and other influences. The Chinese model was never adopted wholesale and unchanged.[64]

Ideals of rulership established and reiterated in interconnecting literary traditions can be skimmed and summarised, a process limited here to the most obvious items in the catalogue of princely virtues. This task is more complicated for societies without long-standing written discourses on the prince, where oral traditions, myths of origins, and daily perceptions together convey far more diffuse and changing views. African, pre-Columbian American, and Polynesian views of rulership, however, can help to clarify aspects left aside in the literary ideals discussed here. I shall not attempt here to extrapolate more regional views of rulership from the scattered and unequal sources, but will look at ideas about kingship that extend and illuminate the preceding discussion and bring to light the problems these views engendered for incumbent kings.

Kings were often pictured as coming from elsewhere: as outsiders who through force, cunning, and celestial support defeated previous rulers and captured their wives or daughters. These 'stranger-kings' established their pre-eminence by transgressing common social norms: mythic royals could practise incest or use violence without risking social censure or punishment. Their successors could still be seen as possessing arcane knowledge and special skills, notably rainmaking. Royal incest, maintaining the bloodline through male and female lines, forms part of many myths of origin and indeed was sometimes put into practice, notwithstanding the powerful social prohibitions against it.[65] In the blurry changeover between myth and historical reality, conquest as the starting point

---

The Cambridge History of Japan, vol. II: Heian Japan (Cambridge, 1999), 576–643. On the emperors in general, see the long-term perspective in Shillony, Enigma of the Emperors.

[64] James A. Anderson, 'Distinguishing between China and Vietnam: three relational equilibriums in Sino-Vietnamese relations', Journal of East Asian Studies, 13/2 (2013), 259–80; Gregory Smits, 'Ambiguous boundaries: redefining royal authority in the kingdom of Ryukyu', Harvard Journal of Asiatic Studies, 60/1 (2000), 89–123.

[65] On Inka incest, see Yaya, Two Faces of Inca History, 77. On Hawaii, see Patrick Vinton Kirch, How Chiefs Became Kings: Divine Kingship and the Rise of Archaic States in Ancient Hawai'i (Berkeley, CA, 2010), 37, 205, 206. On Egypt, see Zahi Hawass, 'King Tut's family secrets', National Geographic, 218/3 (2010), 34–59; and Sheila L. Ager, 'The power of excess: royal incest and the Ptolemaic dynasty', Anthropologica, 48/2 (2006), 165–86. On incest generally, see Pierre L. van den Berghe and Gene M. Mesher, 'Royal incest and inclusive fitness', American Ethnologist, 7/2 (1980), 300–17; and more examples cited in David Dobbs, 'The risks and rewards of royal incest', National Geographic, 218/3 (2010), 60–1.

of dynasty is ubiquitous. Sons born into royal clans with many siblings, who had slight chances of succession and reasons to fear for their lives, had good grounds to move away. With their followers, they stood a better chance of obtaining power elsewhere. The dynamics of dynastic reproduction and succession, to be discussed in the next chapter, added to the proliferation of conquest dynasties arising in the periphery of existing African kingdoms.[66] Mobile pastoralists from the Nilotic area acting as conquerors, subjecting resident farming populations in the south and west, form a common pattern in Africa. This dynamic role of pastoralists is equally strongly attested for Central Asians moving in all directions.[67] Martial valour, for these conquering groups, was surely an essential ingredient of rulership. Actual conquests may have given rise to 'stranger-king' myths; such stories, however, were not always necessarily related to actual takeovers by outsiders.

Can stranger-kings ruling as outsiders over subjected peoples be presented as bringing harmony? In the kingdom of Ankole in Uganda, pastoral Bahima formed the dominant clan ruling over agricultural Bairu serfs. The order maintained by the Bahima king (*mugabe*) primarily advanced the interests of his own group. Above the ruling mugabe, however, stood the tribal fetish of all peoples of Ankole: the Bagyendanwa drum. This higher authority was impartial, 'as much interested in the Bairu as in the Bahima'. It protected all against infringement and injustice: a Bairu sentenced to death by the mugabe would be pardoned if he made it to the Bagyendanwa sanctuary and touched the drum.[68] The drum, standing above the power even of the mugabe, performs the same service here that we find elsewhere in the ideal of protection of the weak. This remarkable (but perhaps not very practicable) form of pardoning underlines the power of objects related to royal authority. Drums were connected to royalty and its rituals in many African kingdoms. Regalia were seen as embodying rulership, with their possessors serving merely as temporary bearers. Stools carried the power of ancestor-kings; royal power was activated only by 'enstoolment' (Plate 3a). Objects with magical powers sometimes brought commoners to royal status: charmed krises have reportedly acted as kingmakers in Southeast

---

[66] See Tardits (ed.), *Princes & Serviteurs*, 20, for the connection between dispossessed royal siblings and conquest. On conquest, see Vansina, 'Comparison of African kingdoms', 329; and Southall, 'Segmentary state', 61–3.

[67] On stranger-kings, see recently Sahlins, 'Stranger-king', discussing examples from many regions and myths. On nomadic pastoralists and sedentary farmers, see e.g. Edwin M. Loeb, 'Die Institution des sakralen Königtums', *Paideuma*, 10/2 (1964), 102–14.

[68] K. Oberg, 'The kingdom of Ankole in Uganda', in Fortes and Evans-Pritchard (eds.), *African Political Systems*, 121–62, at 150–7.

Asia.[69] Peoples throughout the world were awed by the powers of regalia, representing a higher force that could only temporarily be vested in a person.

As elsewhere, African kings and their peoples more often than not were seen as having strong mutual obligations: 'every one who holds political office has responsibilities for the public weal corresponding to his rights and privileges'.[70] The chief or king could raise taxes and demand tribute or labour service, but in return had the obligation to 'dispense justice to them, to ensure their protection from enemies and to safeguard their general welfare by ritual acts and observances'.[71] While this would hold true for conquest clans governing subjected peoples, there are numerous examples where representation and consent counterbalanced the powers of kingship. Where several kinship groups merged into one polity, kingship ideally served as an overarching function holding together these segments.[72] This responsibility, moreover, could be anchored in practice by alternating kingship among leading clans of the kingdom. Circulating forms of kingship, whether including a limited number of descent groups or a larger number of chiefly houses, not only entailed the possibility of future rule for each of these groups, but also made more likely a pattern of rule through negotiation and consent.

While the measure of power in the hands of kings throughout Africa varied, there was usually a strong presence of elders and councils.[73] The Asante, forming a federation of 'stools' or chiefs under the paramount king (*asantehene*), were portrayed by Robert Rattray as practising a form of democracy reminiscent of ancient Greece.[74] Interestingly, the awkward question how to deal with an incompetent or bad king could be solved here by the wholly accepted practice of 'destoolment'. Dissatisfaction among commoners set in motion a process that, by raising support and convincing elders, could lead to destoolment. Chiefs at all

---

[69] See Moertono, *State and Statecraft in Old Java*, 37, 65 on charmed objects (*pusakas*), 60–1 on signs of divine support and the ritual aspects of kingship; Jean-François Guermonprez, 'Rois divins et rois guerriers: images de la royauté à Bali', *L'Homme*, 25 (1985), 39–70, at 47, 50.

[70] Fortes and Evans-Pritchard (eds.), *African Political Systems*, 11–12.

[71] Ibid., 34, and see numerous other references to justice, including the obligation to protect the weak against evildoers at 69, reminiscent of *zulm* and *mazalim* in the Muslim context.

[72] Ibid., 22, and see also 293.

[73] Vansina, 'Comparison of African kingdoms', underlines this while also, at 332–4, suggesting a typology going from despotic via regal, incorporative, and aristocratic kingdoms to federations, linking the level of centralised power with exclusive or inclusive patterns of succession.

[74] Robert Sutherland Rattray, *Ashanti Law and Constitution* (Oxford, 1929), 401–6. See more recently Napoleon Bamfo, 'The hidden elements of democracy among Akyem chieftaincy: enstoolment, destoolment, and other limitations of power', *Journal of Black Studies*, 31/2 (2000), 149–73, stressing the checks and balances in various Akan polities.

levels, including the *asantehene* himself, could be destooled if they ignored the advice of elders, acted with undue cruelty, or forsook their ritual obligations.[75] Destooled chiefs were not allowed to take the property they had assembled during their incumbency, nor even the possessions they themselves had brought to the stool. This made it necessary to plan destoolments surreptitiously and execute them rapidly:

> The Chief might be enticed away from his 'palace' when he would be dragged out of his hammock, or he might have his Stool suddenly pulled from beneath him, so that his buttocks came in contact with the ground; he was also liable to be dragged on the ground; he was abused and slapped by the women and children.[76]

When a chief 'handed over the Stool voluntarily, his buttocks were not bumped on the ground'.[77] The sharp contrast between the usual highly reverential behaviour and this rather crude destoolment suggests the Asante people differentiated between the function and the person of chiefs: 'to the Ashanti, the stool was more important than the chief who, for the time being, sat upon it'.[78]

The role of kingship in bringing together the loosely integrated kinship segments can also be seen to some extent in the 'fourfold domain' of the Inka empire, where the royal descent group itself was divided into upper and lower (*hanan* and *hurin*) segments, each of which was again subdivided into left and right. The paramount ruler (*Sapa Inka*) needed to weld together the groups, but ritual as well as political responsibilities were divided among the sections.[79] Likewise the supreme king (*huey tlatoani*) of Tenochtitlan incorporated two other city-states under his rule, Texcoco and Tlacopan, headed by their kings (*tlatoque*). The supreme king 'carried his subjects in his cape': accepting responsibility for their welfare, he deserved their obedience.[80] As in many other places, justice and the protection of the weak were present in Aztec ideals of kingship.

---

[75] Rattray, *Ashanti Law and Constitution*, 406; William Tordoff, 'The Ashanti confederacy', *Journal of African History*, 3/3 (1962), 399–417, at 416.

[76] Rattray, *Ashanti Law and Constitution*, 146, and on destoolment, 85, 116, 133–4, 145–6, 196, 255, 406.

[77] Ibid., 196.   [78] Tordoff, 'Ashanti confederacy', 416.

[79] María Rostworowski and Craig Morris, 'The fourfold domain: Inka power and its social foundations', in Frank Salomon and Stuart B. Schwartz (eds.), *The Cambridge History of the Native Peoples of the Americas* (Cambridge, 1999), 769–863; Yaya, *Two Faces of Inca History*; Franklin Pease, 'The Inka and political power in the Andes', in Basham (ed.), *Kingship in Asia and Early America*, 243–56.

[80] Manuel Aguilar-Moreno, *Handbook to Life in the Aztec World* (Oxford, 2006), 75–6; J. Rounds, 'Dynastic succession and the centralization of power in Tenochtitlan', in George Allen Collier et al. (eds.), *The Inca and Aztec States, 1400–1800: Anthropology and History* (New York, 1982), 63–89, stressing the 'corporateness' of the ruling elites; see also Pedro Carrasco, 'Kingship in ancient Mexico', in Basham (ed.), *Kingship in Asia and Early America*, 233–42. Basham's 'Introduction', 5–12, in the same volume, suggests (9)

Father Bernardino de Sahagún noted in his *General History of the Things of New Spain* that 'The ruler watched especially over the trials; he heard all the accusations and complaints, the afflictions and the misery of the common folk, the orphans, the poor, and the vassals.'[81] Elsewhere, Sahagún refers to a stock of dried maize sufficient to feed the city for twenty years – an unlikely statement in general, but more specifically because he also reports a serious famine.[82]

The welfare of peoples, particularly in a context where different leaders competed for support, could be defined in terms of gift-giving and hospitality. For attracting followers and supporters, it was essential to amass wealth, produce, and often women – whose numbers were likely to be seen as a sign of power and who as a group were able to generate wealth. The Inka imperial venture was based on gift exchange: peripheral peoples accepting gifts lost autonomy. Expansion could be successfully consolidated only if the empire perpetually increased its stocks, amassing wealth to satisfy new tributaries.[83] In Melanesia and Polynesia, largesse and gift-giving formed the core of the households of 'big men' or chiefs, a practice that in the larger-scale institutionalised polities of Polynesia led to the building of storehouses to collect all sorts of goods: 'As the rat will not desert the pantry . . . where he thinks food is, so the people will not desert the king while they think there is food in his store-house.'[84] Conspicuous wealth and lavish entertaining, censured in moral-literary traditions, certainly rank among the most common characteristics of rulership. Without the writings of moral critics, it is not so easy to ascertain whether this show of luxury and hospitality was frowned upon by spiritual leaders.

The military, judicial, administrative, and redistributive roles of African kings were inextricably bound up with their ritual and magical functions. Numerous examples in African dynastic history show kings whose health was understood as closely connected to the health and wealth of their peoples, to rich harvests, good weather, and contented ancestors. In *The Golden Bough* James Frazer connected the deification of kings to the 'killing of the gods': once kings had lost their vigour, they

---

that the Inka held 'greater responsibility for the social security and economic welfare of his subjects' than the Aztec ruler.

[81] Bernardino de Sahagún, *Florentine Codex: General History of the Things of New Spain*, ed. Arthur J.O. Anderson and Charles E. Dribble (Santa Fe, NM, 1954), Book 8, 'Kings and Lords', 54, with other references to justice at 41–3, 59.

[82] Ibid., 44 and 41 respectively.   [83] Rostworowski and Morris, 'Fourfold domain', 778.

[84] David Malo, *Hawaiian Antiquities* (Honolulu, HI, 1903), 257–8, cited in Marshall Sahlins, 'Poor man, rich man, big-man, chief: political types in Melanesia and Polynesia', *Comparative Studies in Society and History*, 5/3 (1963), 285–303, at 296; see 298: 'Even the greatest Polynesian chiefs were conceived superior kinsmen to the masses, fathers of their people, and generosity was morally incumbent upon them.'

could actively imperil the realm and should be exterminated. The vigour and the spirits of the ancestors needed to be kept safe lest a sudden and unprepared death of the incumbent king prevent their well-ordered transmission to a successor. The king was only the temporary vessel of a quality bigger than man. Frazer's model, quite influential in the early twentieth century, was re-examined critically in the 1940s by E.E. Evans-Pritchard for the Shilluk of the Sudan; he confirmed the presence of the idea, but doubted whether the killing of a king had ever been put into practice.[85] However, the killing or suicide of kings is present in many stories, and appears to have been practised too. K. Oberg, rendering common views about the king of Ankole in Uganda, mentions the virtues of courage and largesse, before proceeding to more transcendent qualities:

He was called the 'drum', for like the drum he maintained the unity of the men under his power. He was called the 'moon', for through the moon he had power to drive away evil and bring fortune to the tribe. Power, then, both physical and spiritual, was the inherent quality of kingship. And when the physical powers of the king waned, through approaching age, these kingly powers were believed to wane with them. No king, therefore, was permitted to age or weaken. When sickness or age brought on debility, the Mugabe took poison, which was prepared for him by his magicians, and died, making way for a new, virile king who could maintain the unity of the kingdom and wage successful wars against external enemies.[86]

Whether or not kings were actually killed, it is clear that they were seen as possessing awesome powers that necessitated numerous ritual precautions restricting their own lives as well as their exchanges with other people. Among the Mamprusi of northern Ghana, *naam* was considered the essential quality shared by king and chiefs alike. Naam can be translated as 'office', but the term had strong connotations of the transcendent, of sacrifices and ancestors:

Naam is concentrated in the king's physical body in ways that make him powerful, but also vulnerable. He lives constrained by a host of prohibitions and it is not entirely clear if the prohibitions are to protect him, or to protect others. Thus, the king may not move quickly. He may not step barefoot on the ground, or endanger his body by holding any sharp instruments such as those used in farming or warfare. For him to shed blood on the earth would bring disaster. He may not see certain parts of his palace or certain ritual specialists who reside in his kingdom. He may not hear certain words. He may not cross either of the two streams

---

[85] E. E. Evans-Pritchard, 'The divine kingship of the Shilluk of the Nilotic Sudan: The Frazer Lecture, 1948', *HAU: Journal of Ethnographic Theory*, 1 (2011), 407–22.

[86] Oberg, 'Kingdom of Ankole', 137. On the suicide of the rain-queen, see Krige and Krige, *Realm of a Rain-Queen*, 167; W.D. Hammond-Tooke, *Boundaries and Belief: The Structure of a Sotho Worldview* (Johannesburg, 1981), 18, 21.

that traverse his village east and west of the palace. He sits only on the skins of animals that have been sacrificed by his ancestors, or those – such as the lion and leopard – which are embodiments of ancient kings.[87]

As a token of their elevated position, kings wore heavy regalia. In a 1929 study, Rattray portrayed the Asante king (*asantehene*) as so burdened with gold attire (Plate 3b) that he could move only with the assistance of his servants. In general, Blier concludes: 'Symbolically, rulers became the captives of the 'subjects' they served. Except for a yearly outing, many rulers could not leave the palace; most could never touch the ground. Nor generally could they eat, drink or speak in public except through (or accompanied by) an interpreter, linguist, or spokesperson.'[88] (See Plate 2.) This divine or sacral view of kingship, attributing awesome powers to kings while at the same time freezing them into immobility, does not seem to fit descriptions of European monarchs fighting and feasting, sultans on horseback pursuing the infidel, or Manchu emperors on campaign or hunting. It is also far from universal in Africa, where kings more often than not were expected to prove their prowess on the battle-field and flaunt their wealth through large-scale hospitality. The sacra-lised status of rulers, however, was present in each of these cases, though it often remained restricted to specific moments and constellations.

It is impossible to picture dynastic power anywhere without the ritual appurtenances that visibly demonstrated its status apart in society. Rituals are moments set apart from daily life, performed in a solemn or festive setting, usually including a set pattern of fixed actions, often involving special objects (regalia, religious insignia), and often accompanied by music and movement. Ritual calendars determined annually recurring feasts and sacrifices across the globe, a sequence sometimes specifically related to court activities, but often reflecting common social and religious practice. The fourth chapter of this book will deal with some of these occasions at greater length. Here it is relevant to mention them largely because they represent the incursion of the divine into dynastic routines.

The Chinese mandate of heaven, directly linking droughts, floods, and cosmic events to the performance of rulers, offers a powerful parallel for African ritual kingship. The Chinese record, moreover, suggests that

---

[87] S. Drucker-Brown, 'King house: the mobile polity in northern Ghana', in Quigley (ed.), *Character of Kingship*, 171–86, at 176–7 (Rattray is mentioned at 181). On *naam*, see also Meyer Fortes, 'The political system of the Tallensi of the northern territories of the Goldcoast', in Fortes and Evans-Pritchard (eds.), *African Political Systems*, 239–71, at 256–8. For a general and in many respects outdated discussion of 'untouchables', see Sigmund Freud, *Totem and Taboo* (London, 1950).

[88] Suzanne Preston Blier, *The Royal Arts of Africa: The Majesty of Form* (London, 1998), 29.

astute and clear-headed rulers were themselves taken aback by the powers of their office and its divine sanction. In 1832, a drought persisting even after a series of sacrifices, persuaded the Daoguang emperor (1782–1820–1850) to escalate the ritual ladder to its highest extreme, by performing the exceptional prayer for rain (*dayu*). The emperor himself took full responsibility: 'I tremble as I consider the causes of the drought: the fault must be mine.'[89] Among his predecessors, the Kangxi emperor, universally acclaimed as a highly accomplished and sensible figure, considered that 'From ancient times when there is error in human affairs the harmony of Heaven is affected. Perhaps there has been error in governance; I may have been found wanting in my personnel appointments.'[90] Elsewhere, Kangxi argued that for the ruler, 'Careless handling of one item might bring harm to the whole world, a moment's carelessness damage all future generations.'[91] To assuage the powers of heaven, emperors did not only examine their own behaviour; they could reduce expenditure, punish corruption, reform the magistracy, or seek to lighten the burdens of their peoples. During a prolonged drought in 1392, the formidable but hardly affable Hongwu emperor sent out judges and censors explicitly to examine the condition of prisoners all over the country: could their situation have caused heavenly displeasure?[92] Moreover, Hongwu was upset by the misdeeds of his sons:

People are the mandate of Heaven. He who has virtue Heaven will give it to him and people will follow. If he does not have [virtue], Heaven will withdraw [the mandate] and people will leave him. Now Zhou, Qi, Tan and Lu [Ming princes] have indiscriminately bullied and humiliated the soldiers and the people in their fiefs, will Heaven take away the mandate from them?[93]

In 1644, the final critical year of the Ming dynasty, the Chongzhen emperor (1611–1627–1644) issued an 'edict of self-blame' reflecting on the situation at some length:

I have inherited and abided by the imperial cause for seventeen years. Day and night, I have been cautious and vigilant and have not dared to be idle. At present, calamities are frequent: bandits become more active, people are tormented, and peaceful residences are nowhere to be found . . . I am personally at fault. Who else to blame? The people therefore suffer from spears and arrows; fires and floods follow in succession; the dead fill ravines; skeletons are heaped in mounds; these are all my transgressions. Causing the people to transport grains and fodder, to see

[89] Rawski, *Last Emperors*, 227.   [90] Ibid., 225.
[91] Jonathan D. Spence, *Emperor of China: Self-Portrait of K'ang-Hsi* (New York, 1974), 147.
[92] Fang, 'Hot potatoes', 1120.
[93] Hok-Lam Chan, 'Ming Taizu's problem with his sons: Prince Qin's criminality and early-Ming politics', *Asia Major*, 20/1 (2007), 45–103, at 87.

off the departing and supply food to the armies, the bitterness of imposing unregulated taxes and pre-collecting on debts, these are again my transgressions ... As for the lawlessness of the high officials I appointed, the dishonesty of the low officials I employed, the hesitancy and indecisiveness of the imperial censors, the arrogance, cowardice, and ineffectiveness of the military officials, are all because of my inadequate treatment and lack of compulsion. Even at midnight, whenever the situation comes to my mind, I feel extreme shame of myself. It is I who lack virtue and how could the people be held responsible?[94]

Chongzhen's self-blame did little to prevent the downfall of the dynasty.

Among China's tributaries, similar expressions can be found. Japanese emperors referred to their moral deficiencies when they explained their intention to resign or when the country was afflicted by natural adversities. In 705 Emperor Mommu (683–697–707) wrote: 'My virtue is insufficient to move Heaven and my humanity is inadequate to sway the people ... There is either too much rain or there is drought. Harvests have been meagre and the people suffer from hunger.'[95] The Dai Viet king, Le Thanh Ton (1442–1460–1497), pondered in 1467 after a long period without rains: 'I am a person without merit ... I am the father and mother of the people, sick at heart. If I do not dispense wide grace and generous forgiveness, then how can genuine blessings reach the people?'[96] Even minor incidents generated distress. In 1802 the Korean queen dowager-regent Chŏngsun was upset when lightning and thunder struck in winter, 'contrary to the regular rhythm and order'. After considering her own shortcomings and various possible faults in the government's treatment of the people, she admonished her ministers to mend their ways.[97]

Grave natural disasters, such as storms, floods, earthquakes, and volcanic eruptions, are still a test for government: tardy and ineffective responses can undermine legitimacy. In the premodern world, the tendency to attribute a certain responsibility for these occasions to the ruler, as intermediary with higher powers, further exacerbated the disruptive potential of natural phenomena. Extreme weather conditions and natural disasters threatened the well-being of the people and gave them a legitimate impulse to question the accomplishments of the individual ruler or the dynasty. Although most views of the polity underlined hierarchy and obedience, this was a moment

---

[94] Li Yuan, 'The Ming emperors' practice of self-examination and self-blame', *Chinese Studies in History*, 44/3 (2011), 6–30, at 16–17.

[95] Shillony, *Enigma of the Emperors*, 68–9, among several other examples.

[96] Andaya, 'Political development', 420, stressing several elements familiar from African kingship in Southeast Asia: the strong connection with kinship patterns, the special qualities attributed to kings, the special role of revered objects, and the general relevance of natural disasters, cosmic events, and deformities in man or beast.

[97] JaHyun Kim Haboush, *Epistolary Korea: Letters in the Communicative Space of the Chosŏn, 1392–1910* (New York, 2009), 38–9.

where rebellion could generate support and acquire legitimacy – successful usurpation of power, bringing an untarnished leader to the throne, could open a new era of harmony and well-being.[98]

All premodern variants of dynastic power cultivated a strong religious-moral underpinning as well as a connection to the celestial: they share at least some of these traits. The principal performances of imperial and royal legitimacy took place in or near places of religious observance and partially followed religious scenarios. Ottoman princes reached maturity with the ritual of circumcision, celebrated in prolonged festivals in which the city corporations of Istanbul took an important part. Friday prayer processions offered a less spectacular but more regular form of contact with the population. The dense ritual-ceremonial calendar was so pervasive for the Indic rajadharma that it constricted his role as an active ruler.[99] In Europe, Gottesgnadentum and *droit divin* were reflected in court practice. Addressing the young Louis XIV during a ceremony in the Parisian Parlement, one of its leading magistrates stated that 'Your Majesty's chair [*siège*] to us represents the living God, the orders of the kingdom pay their respects to you as to a visible divinity.'[100] French and English kings long performed the 'royal touch', healing their subjects suffering from the skin disease scrofula by serving as a vehicle for divine grace. When Louis XIV temporarily refrained from these activities early in his reign, he probably did so because his extramarital affairs prevented him from taking communion and hence left him unable to perform a rite based on divine grace. Louis XV, discontinuing the royal touch in most of his reign, explicitly used this soundly Catholic argument.[101] The populace did not forget the rite, however. Following the *sacre* (inauguration) of Louis XVI in 1775, more than 2,400 people presented themselves for the royal touch.[102] The royal touch was abolished by George I (1660–1714–1727) in 1714, but in France it persisted into the eighteenth century and briefly resurfaced in 1826.[103]

[98] Andaya, 'Political development', 420.

[99] Richards (ed.), *Kingship and Authority*, v; see also Heesterman, 'Conundrum of the king's authority', esp. 3–4, 8.

[100] Pascale Mormiche, *Devenir prince: l'école du pouvoir en France, XVIIe–XVIIIe siècles* (Paris, 2009), 212, citing Omer Talon, one of the advocates of limited monarchy in the Parlement.

[101] On Louis XV and his abandoning of the touch, see Jeroen Duindam, 'The dynastic court in an age of change', in *Friedrich300 – Colloquien: Friedrich der Große und der Hof*, in *Perspectivia* (2009), www.perspectivia.net/content/publikationen/friedrich300-collo-quien/friedrich-hof/Duindam_Court.

[102] Duindam, *Vienna and Versailles*, 139.

[103] Marc Bloch, *Les rois thaumaturges* (Paris, 1924), translated as *The Royal Touch: Sacred Monarchy and Scrofula in England and France*, trans. J.E. Anderson (Montreal and Kingston, 1973); Frank Barlow, 'The King's Evil', *English Historical Review*, 95/374 (1980), 3–27; C.J.Ch. Siret, *Précis historique du sacre de S.M. Charles X* (Reims, 1826), 95–6, 137.

Deep into the eighteenth century a dense sequence of religious processions and ceremonies connected Habsburg rulers to the urban environment of their palaces. Emperor Leopold I (1640–1658–1705) invoked heavenly support against two scourges arising during his reign: the Ottomans and the Plague. Heaven's direct warnings, punishments, and deliverances instigated new ritual practices. Upon recovering a wooden fragment of the holy cross miraculously untouched by the great fire in the imperial Hofburg, Eleonora II Gonzaga, the dowager empress, instituted the female Order of the Starry Cross. Her stepson Leopold I barely escaped when lightning struck his apartment in his hunting lodge at Laxenburg in 1691, and duly honoured this portentous miracle with an annual procession.[104] The age-old religious rite of the *pedilavium*, the washing of the feet of the poor in a re-enactment of the Last Supper, had come to represent full royal sovereignty in the early modern period. Briefly abolished in Joseph II's personal rule after the death of his mother Maria Theresa in 1780, it was soon reinstated. Francis Joseph (1830–1848–1916) practised the washing of the feet of the poor on Maundy Thursday into the twentieth century.[105]

Unattainable and inconsistent standards

This *tour d'horizon* shows the similarity of some key ideals of rulership: the universal stress on harmony, on the common good, and on the protection of the weak. While it is not surprising to find such lofty ideals in works intended to instil moral values into the minds of princes and rulers who in practice often behaved very differently, it is interesting to note that both the ideals outlined and the transgressions condemned overlap to a large extent.

Differences in tone and content of ideals and criticisms can be related to varying moral-religious backgrounds as well as to the diverging social positions of the groups voicing these views. In China and the regions influenced by its Confucian precepts, the priority of moral example coincided with a relatively passive and withdrawn ideal of rulership. The literati who educated and admonished Chinese princes and emperors were also the most important agents of government – there was no clash

---

[104] For the Stern-Creuz Orden, see Johann Christian Lünig, *Theatrum ceremoniale historico-politicum, oder historisch- und politischer Schau-Platz aller Ceremonien, welche so wohl an europäischen Höfen als auch sonsten bey vielen illustren Fällen beobachtet worden* (Leipzig, 1719–20), 1161–3. For Leopold's Laxenburg miracle, see Duindam, *Vienna and Versailles*, 140–1. On Habsburg piety, see literature cited in Duindam, *Vienna and Versailles*. For the parallel in the Spanish Netherlands, see Luc Duerloo, 'Pietas Albertina: dynastieke vroomheid en herbouw van het vorstelijk gezag', *Bijdragen en Mededelingen betreffende de Geschiedenis der Nederlanden*, 112 (1997), 1–18.

[105] Duindam, *Vienna and Versailles*.

here between the voices of clerical advisors and secular governors, although, of course, idealists and pragmatists quarrelled everywhere. On the other hand, the dominance of the literati in the written legacies of Chinese dynastic history may have deformed our view, by underplaying the presence of military elites and ignoring or criticising numerous examples of active and martial rulership.[106]

While European as well as most Asian views of rulership have a greater tolerance for an activist and outgoing style than the classic Chinese view, all ideals reviewed here stress the moral obligation of rulers, acting benevolently and justly towards their peoples while safeguarding cosmic order by appeasing divine powers through the painstaking performance of ritual.[107] Legitimacy was based on ritual propriety and religious sanction, translated into the need for the ruler to act in the shared interests of his peoples. European kings, in different measures, pointed to the divine sanction of their rule, but by doing so they accepted a responsibility for the welfare of their peoples. Persians cultivated the 'divine radiance' (*farr*) of kingship, a notion that permeated later Islamic forms of rulership, as can be seen through the adoption of Persian titles such as the 'shadow of god on earth' or the king of kings (*shahanshah*). Persian traditions and the newly acquired Islamic norms prompted the ruler to protect the flock against *zulm* (injustice). In China the mandate of heaven, obtained by successful claimants of the imperial dignity, engendered an overawing obligation to maintain the balance between heaven and earth through moral rectitude and ritual propriety. Popular disaffection, natural disasters, and cosmic events foreshadowed a violent end for any dynasty failing to redress the balance in time. The connection between the ruler's failings and divine wrath was equally strong in Southeast Asia and Africa.

This leads us to a second more important outcome: the duties of rulership as outlined in moral tracts were not only almost impossible to fulfil for most persons, they were also contradictory. Rulers were confronted by daunting responsibilities, too much for most talented persons and beyond the reach of the mediocrities that could be expected to sit on

---

[106] Robinson, *Martial Spectacles*.

[107] See Santucci, 'Vedic kingship', for the etymology and moral associations of the numerous Indo-European variants of *raj* and *rex*. Andaya, 'Political development', 408, 420, 421, indicates that views of rulership in mainland and island Southeast Asia fit well into this brief outline. However, note Spellman, *Monarchies*, who assumes four different types of monarchy (Asia, Africa and America, Byzantium and Islam, Europe) and underlines the differences between these styles. Wittfogel, *Oriental Despotism*, discusses some of the ideals traced in this chapter, but strongly underlines the instrumental character of the 'benevolence myth' (134–5); likewise, he sees the 'absolute loneliness' (154–6) of rulers largely as a consequence of the violence and terror he sees as inherent to the system he describes.

the throne where fixed rules of succession prevented selection. The expectation of moral and religious rectitude, a challenge for most individuals, awkwardly fitted the political challenges facing the ruler. Machiavelli's *Prince* was so influential and controversial precisely because it stated a truism that had often been denied. Pragmatic ruling often sullied the hands but it could be effective; conversely, rigidly sticking to ideals did not always advance the *bonum publicum* in the longer term. This posed a problem for the education of princes as well as an ongoing tension in the lives of rulers. Moral convictions and actual behaviour clash in the lives of most people, but here the tension was sharpened from two sides: lofty ideals of kingship seriously complicated the challenges of day-to-day government.

This permanent clash makes it understandable why reigning and ruling were often separated, creating differentiated roles for ritual figureheads and actual governors. Sometimes the separation between these roles was institutionalised. The paramount chief (*arii rahi*) of Tahiti escaped from the severe ritual constrictions placed upon him by abdicating upon the birth of a son, installing the child as chief while he himself ruled as regent – an adequate solution until the boy reached majority.[108] Japan offers a remarkable example of the separation between a largely sacerdotal supreme imperial power and a series of more active yet secondary rulers: regents from the dominant Fujiwara clan, abdicated emperors ruling 'from the cloister' (*insei*), and finally the 'military hegemon' (shogun). After the Heian period (794–1185) an almost continuous sequence of shogunal dynasties wielded power, whereas the imperial lineage held nominal sovereignty and ritual pre-eminence, ending only with the downfall of the Tokugawa shogunate and the restoration of the emperor in 1868.[109] While these explicit cases remain the exception, rulers across the world often found themselves limited to the ritual performance of omnipotence, while in practice they left government to key advisors. The Chinese tradition of governance, with its marked stress on a reticent emperor and active literati magistrates, left ample room for this solution. In the Ottoman empire, the grand vizier at times took over most of the sultan's active duties. In Europe, too, kings could maintain a high profile for distant audiences while in practice they were likely to follow the advice

---

[108] H.J.M. Claessen, 'Enige gegevens over taboes en voorschriften rond Tahitische vorsten', *Bijdragen tot de Taal-, Land- en Volkenkunde*, 118/4 (1962), 433–53.

[109] Hurst, 'Insei', 580, underlines the separation of ruling and reigning in Japanese dynastic history, with Fuijwara regents, abdicated emperors, and shoguns primarily dealing with the 'daily scramble for political and economic power' and the emperor serving as the 'repository of dynastic authority'. Shillony, *Enigma of the Emperors*, underlines the 'sacred subservience' as one of the possible explanations for the dynasty's longevity.

of their ministers. The guardians of kingship well knew the demoralising potential of the challenges facing a person elevated to extraordinary rank. They could use their moral suasion to keep the sovereign within the bounds dictated by tradition, but at times they effectively disempowered him while pursuing their own interests behind the smokescreen of royal omnipotence.

To these persistent tensions another complication needs to be added. The example of ancestors and their great deeds exerted a powerful influence that did not necessarily match the moral categories of the learned clerical or literary advisors of the king. In the dialogue on noble lineage and the virtues of the ideal courtier, Castiglione puts an interesting metaphor in the mouth of one of his discussants, Ludovico di Canossa:

for noble birth is like a bright lamp that manifests and makes visible good and evil deeds, and kindles and stimulates to virtue both by fear of shame and by hope of praise. And since this splendour of nobility does not illumine the deeds of the humbly born, they lack that stimulus and fear of shame, nor do they feel any obligation to advance beyond what their predecessors have done; while to the nobly born it seems a reproach not to reach at least the goal set them by their ancestors.[110]

The legacy of forebears could include examples of wisdom or justice – as in the case of Saint Louis under the oak or the legendary Yao and Shun emperors. However, great military campaigns, impressive monumental buildings, and hunting parties or lavish entertainments were likely to figure as examples for a ruler trying to establish himself in the footsteps of his predecessors – the very matters that in the eyes of Chinese literati were likely to overburden the people and estrange the heavens.

Which catalogue of virtues did kings need to embrace? Which group of relatives, advisors, and attendants should they listen to? They were taught to respect a set of ideals that was in itself contradictory and almost impossible to fulfil in its entirety. The inconsistent accumulation of moral demands, dynastic examples to follow, and daily challenges to cope with could never be moulded into a coherent and feasible model of rulership, because every single ruler displayed different strengths and weaknesses. No consistent and balanced set of precepts could be used effectively for the variety of characters on the throne. Moral pressure did not always suffice to keep in check particularly strong-minded or viciously tempered rulers; the examples of predecessors' great deeds could not always convince lethargic and insecure persons to adopt more active roles. Kingship itself, notwithstanding the overall support it aroused,

---

[110] Baldassar Castiglione, *The Book of the Courtier (1528)*, trans. Leonard Eckstein Opdyke (New York, 1903), 22.

was always associated with the awkward problem of the bad king. The ideals of kingship not only reflected the desire to prevent the rise of bad rulers, but also provided an instrument to contain them or at least limit the damage they could bring about. How did kings respond to the model imposed on them? What did it mean for these persons of flesh and blood to be fitted into this awkwardly elevated position? How did they cope with the burden on their shoulders during the various stages of their lives?

Life cycles

The day-to-day political actions of dynastic rulers cannot be traced here. It is certain that they never fitted the inconsistent ideals entirely and more often strayed far from them. Examining the performance of dynastic rulers amidst their advisors and servants, it is important to note that they sometimes rose to power as children and ended their lives on the throne as disabled elderly persons. In contemporary politics, heredity in office is the exception and only adults are elected or nominated to office. Elderly leaders usually retire into the margins of political life before the erosion of their faculties wreaks havoc. In one-party systems or in dictatorships where small elites predominate, leaders can monopolise office and retain it longer than in democracies. The gerontocracy ruling the Soviet Union in its pre-reform stages is an example of this tendency. Only very rarely, however, do we find people holding supreme office from their early youth to their death. In fixed systems of dynastic succession, or when only one successor was available, toddlers could be installed as kings, holding their elevated position while depending on parents, regents, and educators.[111] For these child-kings, reigning could last a lifetime: they experienced all the familiar stages from early youth to old age on the throne. The upheaval created by adolescents emancipating themselves from their environment could have considerable consequences for the realm in the case of dynastic rulers. The same holds true for the weakening of elderly kings – these phases of change could bring violence and contestation, as well as opportunities for ambitious figures operating in the proximity of the ruler.

Louis XIV of France (1638–1643–1715) and the Qing Kangxi emperor (1654–1661–1722) both started their rule as youngsters upon the early deaths of their fathers (see Plate 4). After reaching majority in 1651 and undergoing his ritual consecration and coronation in 1654, young Louis

---

[111] Competitive or open systems of succession changed this situation, creating a group of possible successors who were all preparing in practice for their bid for power upon – or sometimes before – the death of the ruler.

still remained in the background.[112] Only in 1661, after the death of his mentor and first minister, Mazarin, did Louis, aged twenty-two, choose to 'govern his peoples himself'. His Chinese contemporary the Kangxi emperor took less time. Fathering his first son in 1667 at age fourteen, he pushed aside the regency council in 1669 and personally assumed power with the support of his grandmother the empress dowager Xiaozhuang and other adherents. After these early years, the two rulers enjoyed three decades of relatively great personal power, the phase most commonly remembered. In the last two decades of their long reigns, however, these archetypally strong rulers experienced all sorts of setbacks, from the deaths of trusted advisors or relatives and the looming problems of succession to their own accumulating physical problems. They died saddened and with grave doubts about their own power.

While the reigns of Louis XIV and the Kangxi emperor were exceptional in length, numerous other rulers spent a fair share of their lives on the throne. They followed similar trajectories, starting out as boy-kings and ending as tormented old men. Safavid Shah Tahmasp (1514–1524–1576) ascended to power as a ten-year-old boy, gradually established himself as an astute ruler, but fell seriously ill and saw his authority evaporate a few years before this death. The Ming Wanli emperor (1563–1572–1620), a nine-year-old boy when his father died, spent his first decade on the throne under the tutelage of his grand secretary Zhang Juzheng and his mother empress dowager Li. Emancipating himself from these influences, he sought to take power in his own hands, but disillusionment with his officials made him gradually withdraw into the palace during the last three decades of his life.[113]

Mature women were called upon to bridge the gap in male succession by acting as regents, often for their own minor sons. Mothers throughout the globe were close to power when their young sons ascended to the throne. Where younger daughters or sisters ruled as sovereign queens or empresses in the absence of an acceptable male successor, they could hold power for many years. For these women rulers, the life cycle entailed a

---

[112] French kings reached majority at fourteen: see Pierre Dupuy, *Traité de la majorité de nos rois et des regences du royaume* (Paris, 1655).

[113] The gradual withdrawal of the Wanli emperor is the key theme in Ray Huang, *1587, A Year of No Significance: The Ming Dynasty in Decline* (Yale, CT, 1981); see also Ebrey, 'Remonstrating against royal extravagance'. On the religious patronage of Wanli as a form of competition with his mother, see Guoshuai Qin, 'In search of divine support: imperial inheritance, political power and Quanzhen Taoism at the court of the Wanli emperor, r. 1573–1620', a paper kindly given to me by the author. James B. Palais, *Confucian Statecraft and Korean Institutions: Yu Hyŏngwŏn and the Late Chosŏn Dynasty* (Seattle, WA, 1996), 603–4, cites a Korean mission to the Chinese court stressing the accessibility of the young emperor and the relatively close contacts between him and the officials – all contrasted positively with the withdrawal of the Korean kings.

special complication: childbirth. Maria Theresa (1717–1740–1780), succeeding to her father the 'last Habsburg' emperor Charles VI in 1740, was immediately subjected to grave military and political challenges. During these years she was either pregnant or recovering from childbirth: between 1737 and 1756 she gave birth to sixteen children.[114] Conversely, Elizabeth I of England (1533–1558–1603), shouldering an equally demanding burden, never married and hence never bore children, leaving her realm to James VI of Scotland. Mary of Hungary remained childless during her short tenure as queen (1521–7), nor did she remarry after the death of her husband on the battlefield in 1526. Her widowed state and childlessness made her particularly suitable to act as a viceroy for her brother, Emperor Charles V. The sixteenth-century patriarchal discourse asserting the inappropriateness of female sovereign power was belied in practice by the reigns of several successful queens. However, the question of marriage and childbirth made the exercise of power far more challenging for women than for men.[115]

In addition to the princes who spent almost a lifetime on the throne, numerous others started their reigns as children under the tutelage of their mothers and regents. These toddlers safeguarded dynastic continuity while learning the basic skills of life. Before Wanli, several Ming emperors had started reigning as minors.[116] Succeeding his father as emperor of the Manchu Qing dynasty in 1643, the Shunzhi emperor (1638–1643/4–1661) became the first Qing emperor of conquered China at age six in 1644.[117] Six years later, at age twelve, he started his personal rule following the death of the most important regent Dorgon in December 1650. After the accession of Shunzhi's minor son Kangxi, for more than a century only adults ascended the dragon throne. Several Qing ruling minors resurfaced in the second half of the nineteenth century, under the tutelage of the formidable dowager empress Cixi (1835–1908). The 'last emperor' Pu Yi (1906–1908–1912*) ascended to the throne as a two-year-old toddler; his reign soon ended in revolution.[118] The paragon of Mughal rulership, Akbar (1542–1556–1605) became

---

[114] See the relevant dates and children listed in e.g. Brigitte Hamann (ed.), *Die Habsburger: ein biographisches Lexikon* (Vienna, 1988), 341.

[115] Judith M. Richards, '"To promote a woman to beare rule": talking of queens in mid-Tudor England', *Sixteenth Century Journal*, 28/1 (1997), 101–21.

[116] The Zhengtong (seven), Zhengde (thirteen), Jiajing (thirteen) emperors, followed in the seventeenth century by the two somewhat older Tianqi (fifteen) and Chongzhen (sixteen) emperors.

[117] Though he had already succeeded his father Hong Taiji as Manchu Qing emperor in 1643.

[118] Bernardo Bertolucci's movie *The Last Emperor* (1987) evokes some of the bewildering experiences of many previous child-rulers.

shahanshah on the verge of adolescence. Several Ottoman sultans ascended to their supreme dignity before reaching maturity: Mehmed II (1432–1451–1481) ruled as a youngster when his Father Murad II stepped back from power between 1444 and 1446, before he assumed lasting control in 1451 (Plate 5). In the seventeenth century a series of young sultans started ruling under the guardianship of their mothers: Ahmed I (1590–1603–1617) and Osman II (1604–1618–1622) at thirteen, Murad IV (1612–1623–1640) at eleven, and Mehmed IV (1642–1648–1687) at six.[119] Notable European cases of youngsters on the throne include Edward VI (1537–1547–1553), James VI of Scotland (1566–1567–1625), and Charles II of Spain (1661–1665–1700). Edward reigned from his ninth to his fifteenth year under a regency, dying before reaching his majority. The 'cradle king' James, who ascended to the English throne in 1603 as James I, started his Scottish reign barely more than a year after his birth upon the forced abdication of his mother Mary Queen of Scots.[120] Charles II of Spain, the only son of Philip IV (1605–1621–1665), was only three years old when his father died. His physical and mental constitution was weak, and chances seemed slight that he would father any children. His death, awaited from the very beginning of his reign, caused a devastating succession war, ending Habsburg rule in Spain. Several French kings from the sixteenth to the eighteenth century ruled as minors – even if we accept as yardstick their formal majority at age fourteen: Charles IX (1550–1560–1574), Louis XIII (1601–1610–1643), Louis XIV, and Louis XV (1710–1715–1774).

This random selection shows that children on the throne were a regular occurrence. How were they trained for the tasks ahead? How did they relate to their teachers, who were subjects and masters at the same time? Did their parents play a marked role in educating them? Which responsibilities did they shoulder while young? In addition to child-kings put on the throne on account of the untimely deaths of their fathers, we find heirs-apparent awaiting succession and a wider group of princes eligible for the throne. For each of these groups, education could take a different shape. Proximity to succession created hierarchical differences among princes. Competitive patterns of succession, such as those practised by the Ottomans and the Mughals until respectively the early decades of the seventeenth and of the eighteenth century, made it likely to send out princes at an early age with

---

[119] Mehmed IV's rule ended by abdication rather than by his death, which occurred in 1693. On Ahmed I and Osman II, their mothers, and the concept of regency in the Ottoman context, see Baki Tezcan, 'The question of regency in Ottoman dynasty: the case of the early reign of Ahmed I', *Archivum Ottomanicum*, 25 (2008), 185–98, and the same author's 'The debut of Kösem Sultan's political career', *Turcica*, 40 (2008), 347–59.

[120] Alan Stewart, *The Cradle King: A Life of James VI & I* (London, 2003).

their mothers and tutors, allowing them to build up their households and acquire experience. Training heirs-apparent presented a dilemma: preparing them for high office and power could make them restive and scheming, whereas cultivating submission hardly prepared them for sovereign leadership.[121] The certainty or likelihood of future rule affected the attitudes of educators and the young princes themselves. Children imbued with their supreme dignity could prove to be notoriously intractable, whether as heirs-apparent or as minor rulers. In China, Confucian tradition underlined the deference of pupils vis-à-vis their teachers – Qianlong expected his sons, all in principle eligible for the throne, to adopt a subdued and respectful position, facing northwards towards the teacher who occupied the position of authority.[122] The officially appointed lecturers, always required to maintain a respectful attitude, could expect immunity against their powerful pupils' retaliations. Haughtily rebuking a youthful prince, however, would be asking for trouble – immediately or in the future.[123]

Some practices will have been similar for most child rulers, heirs-apparent, and princes qualifying for succession. The first phase of rearing was in the hands of women: sometimes notably including the mother herself supported by foster-mothers and wet-nurses, sometimes largely in the hands of these women.[124] In this phase, male physicians and tutors played a role, but women were in the forefront at least during the first four years of the lives of princes. Princesses were not generally eligible for the throne, but their education at court was seen as a vital matter.[125] It prepared them for multiple other tasks in the dynastic universe: educating their children, providing an example of cultural accomplishment and piety at court, leading their dynastic household, and functioning as a *trait d'union* between dynastic interests.[126] Princesses in Europe and elsewhere cemented dynastic alliances, either with other sovereign dynasties or with elite groupings. Hence the training of princesses in the separate female households present at most European courts was important for dynastic policies. The harem, in addition to its more familiar role in dynastic reproduction,

---

[121] See e.g. François Bluche, 'Dauphin', in François Bluche (ed.), *Dictionnaire du grand siècle* (Paris, 1990), 448.

[122] Harold L. Kahn, *Monarchy in the Emperor's Eyes: Image and Reality in the Ch'ien-Lung Reign* (Cambridge, MA, 1971).

[123] Huang, *Year of No Significance*, 44; Qin, 'In search of divine support', 4.

[124] Rawski, *Last Emperors*, 117, on Manchu.

[125] See above, note 5 in the Introduction, and the extended discussion of women and power in the first part of Chapter 2 below.

[126] On 'horizontal' affinal connections and women, see Michaela Hohkamp, 'Transdynasticism at the dawn of the modern era: kinship dynamics among ruling families', in Christopher H. Johnson et al. (eds.), *Transregional and Transnational Families in Europe and Beyond: Experiences since the Middle Ages*, (New York and Oxford, 2011), 93–106.

performed a similar function in educating female servants and potential consorts under the supervision of the incumbent ruler's mother.

In the Ottoman, Mughal, and Safavid empires, princes and princesses alike would spend their first years in the harem. For the princes, circumcision indicated the first step towards majority, yet it could be performed any time between the seventh day following birth and the fifteenth year.[127] Ottoman princes' circumcisions took place at very different ages: in 1675 Mehmed IV celebrated the circumcisions of his sons, the eleven-year-old Mustafa and the two-year-old toddler Ahmed. Circumcised Ottoman princes could expect to be sent out with their mother and their male tutor (*lala*) to governments in Anatolia – after the troubled interregnum in the early fifteenth century and subsequent rebellions by princes, they were no longer sent to Rumelia, the European border region.[128] While the mother was the most loyal supporter of her son, the *lala* as the ruling sultan's nominee represented a check on the ambitions of the young prince. There was no fixed age for the crucial moment of sending the princes with their mother to build up their own household as provincial governors. At one extreme we find the future Mehmed II who was sent as governor to Amasya in 1437 at five years and even before his circumcision; at the other extreme stands Mehmed III whose circumcision had been celebrated quite late in his fifteenth year, while he obtained his governorship of Manisa only towards the end of 1584 at the age of eighteen.[129] Mehmed III proved to be the last Ottoman prince to be sent out as a governor. Seventeenth-century Ottoman princes were kept in seclusion in a separate compound in the Topkapı harem, where their education necessarily became less attuned to the practices of warfare and government, reflecting and partially explaining a more withdrawn and passive role of ruling sultans.[130] Under the rule of Abbas I (1571–1588–1629; Plate 17), the Safavids, too, shifted from sending out their princes to educating them in seclusion and without formal responsibilities.[131]

Mughal princes (Plate 16) were most often circumcised at four or five years, an important event followed shortly by another great moment: the

[127] Murphey, *Ottoman Sovereignty*, 175.
[128] Metin Kunt, 'A prince goes forth (perchance to return)', in Karl Barbir and Baki Tezcan (eds.), *Identity and Identity Formation in the Ottoman World: A Volume of Essays in Honor of Norman Itzkowitz* (Madison, WI, 2007), 63–71.
[129] Gábor Ágoston and Bruce Alan Masters (eds.), *Encyclopedia of the Ottoman Empire* (New York, 2009), 364–5, 368.
[130] More on these changes in Chapter 2 below. On the princes in the harem, see N.M. Penzer, *The Harem: An Account of the Institution as it Existed in the Palace of the Turkish Sultans, with a History of the Grand Seraglio from its Foundation to the Present Time* (Philadelphia, PA, 1936), 24.
[131] Sussan Babaie et al., *Slaves of the Shah: New Elites of Safavid Iran* (London, 2004).

opening of their education.[132] Like Ottoman princes, they were accompanied by their mother and a male supervisor (*ataliq*). The circumcision and the start of education together made clear that the prince was now visible in political terms. Henceforth, princes could be expected to shoulder minor responsibilities. Once their education began, young princes gradually expanded their households, obtained formal rank, and governed increasingly important places, gradually distancing themselves from their early years at the court of their father or grandfather. As in the case of the Ottoman *lala*, the *ataliq* represented the Mughal emperor in the vicinity of the prince: he was likely to support the central court against the ambitions of his young master, whereas the mother usually was her son's devoted partisan. In addition to the mother, the *ataliq*, and the teachers, an interesting category of 'artificial kin' can be found around these princes. Princes shared their wet-nurses' milk with a group of boys their age (*kokas*). These foster-brothers often became their buddies, sharing their first military experiences and serving as confidants later in life. Even if no 'milk kinship' connected princes to other young boys, their youth companions were likely to form a loyal group of supporters later on. They formed the core of the households required for the princes' political-military careers.[133] Most Mughal rulers were not only literate but well-versed in learning and poetry. Akbar seems to have been an exception. He was circumcised at three and was educated from his fifth year onwards, yet to the dismay of his father Humayun the boy still could not read after five years of tutoring. Clearly, illiteracy did not prevent Akbar from being an effective ruler.[134]

When the Ming dynasty came to power, it could draw on a rich legacy of institutions and offices related to the education of the heir-apparent.[135] It is not quite clear which of these offices still functioned in practice: some of the resounding names may have turned into titles conferring rank without requiring tasks in the education of the prince. The early years of most emperors and princes remain shrouded. The Wanli emperor, during an audience in 1590, reminisced about his own upbringing, telling his grand secretaries that he could read at four. The high officials, who wanted Wanli to nominate an heir-apparent, reminded the emperor that he had been appointed heir in his eighth year, the starting point of his

---

[132] Murphey, *Ottoman Sovereignty*, 175; Ágoston and Masters (eds.), *Encyclopedia of the Ottoman Empire*, 370; Munis D. Faruqui, *The Princes of the Mughal Empire, 1504–1719* (Cambridge, 2012), 77.

[133] Faruqui, *Princes of the Mughal Empire*, 68–77.

[134] Vincent A. Smith, *Akbar the Great Mogul 1542–1605* (Oxford, 1917), 22–3.

[135] See Charles O. Hucker, *A Dictionary of Official Titles in Imperial China* (repr. Beijing, 2008), nos. 6239, 6244, 6249, 6251, 6256, 7102, 7538, and 7542 relating to the heir-apparent, and no. 7647 to the princes' school.

education. His eldest son was now approaching the same age and yet had not started any formal training: there should be no further delay. Wanli, who had been postponing this crucial decision because he favoured his third son, responded evasively that eunuchs were already teaching his eldest son to read.[136] Although six appears to have been the accepted age for the onset of formal schooling, practices were far more flexible and likely to vary according to political and personal priorities.[137] Wanli's statements underline the role of the eunuchs as domestic teachers of young princes. As soon as formal teaching began, their literati counterparts in the outer court would take charge of the curriculum. Wanli's tutor and chief advisor, Zhang Juzheng, appointed five lecturers, two calligraphers, and one 'academician attendant' for the education of the emperor during his ninth year. Every morning, the young emperor spent three separate periods learning Confucian classics, calligraphy, and history. In the interval between these classes, his eunuchs would bring memorials, an opportunity for Wanli to wield the vermilion brush signifying imperial assent. At noon the emperor was free, although he was expected to practise handwriting and memorise texts. Zhang Juzheng viewed young Wanli's passion for calligraphy with suspicion. Fearing calligraphy would turn into an empty distraction, he gradually purged it from his imperial pupil's curriculum.[138]

Wanli had undergone the rite of 'capping', doing the hair in a bun and wearing a cap signalling the end of boyhood, at the relatively young age of nine.[139] This practice made possible the entry of princes on the public stage, as did circumcision in the Islamic world. It usually took place later than the Muslim circumcision, after the twelfth or fifteenth year. Capping was followed by a second important step, with the prince 'leaving the pavilion to receive instruction' – the opening of a second formal stage of instruction.[140] Education would continue at least until marriage. For princes it would end with their enfeoffment and departure from the palace, which could be expected towards the end of their teens or in their early twenties. For the heir-apparent, education ideally continued indefinitely, even after his accession to the throne.

---

[136] Huang, *Year of no Significance*, Appendix A, 227–9.
[137] Ibid., 43; Rawski, *Last Emperors*, 117–18, on age of princes and the *Shangshufang* (palace school).
[138] Huang, *Year of no Significance*, 9–12.
[139] Ibid., 3. On capping and ages, see Kia-Li, *Livre des rites domestiques chinois*, ed. Charles de Harlez (Paris, 1889), 46, suggesting that the 'prise du bonnet viril' should take place between 15 and 20, an assessment that can also be found in Elman, *Cultural History of Civil Examinations*, 261 and note 60.
[140] Jérôme Kerlouégan helped me with the terminology, ages, and habits related to education, and provided the phrase given here.

Education was based first and foremost on the Confucian classics, with the lecturers pointing to historical examples of good and bad rulership. Wanli's tutor Zhang Juzheng himself compiled a book containing lessons from the past, warning his pupil in stern tones: 'The First Emperor exhausted the people's strength to build palaces and lavishly adorn them for his own pleasure. But the hearts of the people turned away from him and they rebelled, and [his palaces] were in the end reduced to ashes by [the rebel general] Xiang Yu. Take warning!'[141] The tone as well as the schedule of teaching seems to have continued unchanged until the emperor's marriage at sixteen in 1578, which offered partial escape from the tutelage of Zhang Juzheng and the dowager empress Li. His education continued in principle throughout his reign in the form of public study lectures, a ceremonialised practice which the emperor skipped in his last decades. The emperor's relationship with his high officials cannot be equated to the connection between princes and their teachers: the emperor enjoyed an unassailable pre-eminence. Yet high-minded or ambitious officials could submit memorials in which they voiced didactic remarks and criticisms in polite language. In any case they would make sure the Confucian legacy would be voiced time and time again. A particularly straightforward memorial, submitted to the Jiajing emperor (1507–1521–1567) following a violent crackdown on remonstrating officials, noted: 'I am especially eager that Your Majesty takes your ancestors as model, pays attention to learning, promotes the worthy and accepts criticism, distinguishes right and wrong, recognises loyalty and sycophancy, and thus nurtures the blessings of peace.'[142] The audacity of this particular official was rewarded: the emperor granted him the retirement he had asked for. The roles of ambitious sycophant and honest critical advisor had become literary clichés at most courts, yet acting as the proverbial good advisor often had dire consequences in practice.

Emperors' sons in the Qing dynasty on the whole must have followed roughly the same patterns. They usually lived with their birth mother until their sixth year, while wet-nurses, nurses, and personal servants organised daily life. The timing of the move to the world of male tutors and companions for formal schooling long remained somewhat hapha-zard. Kangxi received formal lessons from Confucian lecturers only from his sixteenth year; he initiated the education of his son and heir-apparent only at the boy's twelfth year. The Qianlong emperor learned the basics of

---

[141] Cited in Ebrey, 'Remonstrating against royal extravagance', 130.
[142] Carney T. Fisher, *The Chosen One: Succession and Adoption in the Court of Ming Shizong* (Sydney and London, 1990), 95.

reading at five while a more extended curriculum started at eight.[143] During the first years in the domestic setting, relatives played a key role. At several points in his long life, Kangxi recalled the all-important place of his grandmother the dowager empress Xiaozhuang: 'Since I was a toddler just learning to speak, I received my grandmother's kind discipline: in eating, walking, and in speaking she encouraged me to behave in the proper manner ... I credit her with the accomplishments of my entire career.'[144] Even before the early deaths of Kangxi's parents, his grandmother and her household servants occupied an important place in his life.[145] Kangxi took an active part in the education of his sons at a later stage, and his successor Yongzheng (1678–1722–1735), too, seems to have presided over the teaching of his sons with some frequency.

Some sources indicate the presence of a palace school in the inner court of the Forbidden City under the Kangxi emperor. The head of the heir-apparent's tutors, Tang Bin, pointed out the emperor's keen interest in the education of his sons:

At dawn, soon after the toll of the imperial clock, His Majesty arrived at the side chamber [of the Qianqing palace], where he called in his children one by one to recite the Classics they had just learned. He personally expounded on the Classics to his children before he went out to hold the morning audience with his ministers.[146]

A decade later, the French Jesuit Joachim Bouvet, visiting Beijing, likewise described how the princes, including the crown prince, could be seen daily attending the school for princes in a location close to the emperor, 'where they spend the entire day, partly to study and partly to engage in the exercises proper to their rank. His Majesty frequently visits them during their lessons.'[147] Bouvet was surprised to notice that the heir-apparent, although he was by now twenty-three years old, still attended these classes, and had not received his own palace and household. This, Bouvet suggested, was customary for princes at sixteen or seventeen.[148]

[143] Mark C. Elliott, *Qianlong: Son of Heaven, Man of the World* (New York and London, 2009), 4; Kahn, *Monarchy in the Emperor's Eyes*, 115–21, 150–2.

[144] Silas H.L. Wu, *Passage to Power: K'ang-Hsi and his Heir Apparent, 1661–1722* (Cambridge, 1979), 17, and see a similar quotation at 51; see also Joachim Bouvet, *Histoire de l'empereur de la Chine, présentée au roy* (The Hague, 1699), 133–4. Fresco Samsin brought to my attention Kangxi's letters to his grandmother, edited in Giovanni Stary, 'A preliminary note on some Manchu letters of the Kang-hsi emperor to his grandmother', in Giovanni Stary (ed.), *Proceedings of the 38th Permanent International Conference (PIAC)* (Wiesbaden, 1996), 365–76, in particular the letter expressing his longing and nostalgia at 369.

[145] Rawski, *Last Emperors*, 117–18.   [146] Wu, *Passage to Power*, 47.

[147] Bouvet, *Histoire de l'empereur de la Chine*, 142.

[148] Ibid., 141. The author could have connected this to the grand dauphin in France, who was no longer entitled to his own household, a practice developing after the two kings

Early in Yongzheng's reign the school for princes (*Shangshufang*) in the Qianqing palace was certainly in existence. At that point, the practice of openly appointing an heir-apparent had been discontinued, so all the emperor's sons were nominally in an equal position. Princes worked hard and long at their school, with classes from five in the morning to four in the afternoon. As Qing princes were no longer as a rule enfeoffed and sent out but stayed in the proximity of the Forbidden City, their education at court appears to have continued into their adult lives. The Qianlong emperor obtained his title as prince of Bao at twenty-two in 1733, and only in the last two years of his father's reign did he acquire some practical experience. However, he had represented the emperor in a variety of ritual and social roles in the preceding years, presiding over sacrifices and visiting trusted servants of the dynasty.[149] Qianlong later stipulated that even princes who were performing important ritual and political tasks should report to school directly after their missions had been accomplished. The French Jesuit Michel Benoit observed in 1774 that 'an advanced age and employment' did not exempt the emperor's sons and grandsons from attending school, noticing several men in their thirties among the pupils.[150] Benoit was surprised to see the ageing emperor's active involvement in the education of the princes, underlining that Qianlong was adamant about the princes maintaining a respectful attitude vis-à-vis their teachers. In addition to the Confucian classics, the Qing curriculum included Manchu and martial practice, notably archery.[151]

European practice as a rule entrusted royal children during their *infantia*, the phase up to their sixth or seventh year, primarily to women. Queens and princesses were not always actively mothering; in any case a high-placed noble female supervisor was present at most courts, assisted by wet-nurses and female servants. In France basic formal education for princes and princesses started at age four, most often in the hands of male teachers. Throughout Europe, princes passing from *infantia* to *pueritia* at

who started ruling as minors (and hence were served by a full court), Louis XIII and Louis XIV.

[149] Kahn, *Monarchy in the Emperor's Eyes*, 104–7; Elliott, *Qianlong*, 5–12. On ritual tasks of princes, see Nadia Maria El Cheikh, 'To be a prince in the fourth/tenth-century Abbasid court', in Duindam et al. (eds.), *Royal Courts in Dynastic States and Empires: A Global Perspective* (Leiden and Boston, MA, 2011), 199–216, at 214.

[150] Michel Benoit in Louis-Aimé Martin (ed.), *Lettres édifiantes et curieuses concernant l'Asie, l'Afrique et l'Amérique, avec quelques relations nouvelles des missions, et des notes géographiques et historiques*, 4 vols. (Paris, 1843), IV, 216.

[151] Kahn, *Monarchy in the Emperor's Eyes*, 115–21, 150–2; Rawski, *Last Emperors*, 118; see also Hyegyong, *The Memoirs of Lady Hyegyong: The Autobiographical Writings of a Crown Princess of Eighteenth-Century Korea*, ed. JaHyun Kim Haboush (New York, 1996), 251, on Prince Sado and the early stages of his life.

seven were ceremonially brought from the female into the male domain. They now moved to a protracted formal phase in their education, crossing from *pueritia* which ended at thirteen or fourteen into *adolescentia*. Teaching continued until their eighteenth or twentieth year, in practice ending only with their marriage or once they obtained an active political role.[152] On 1 May 1758, a French courtier reports the ceremonial transfer of the eldest grandson of Louis XV, the duke of Burgundy. The young prince was stripped naked to be examined by physicians before being presented by his *gouvernante* to the king, and by the king to his *gouverneur* the Duke of Vauguyon. The seven-year-old boy was then given an apartment and served a formal meal, with his newly appointed governor waiting upon him.[153] Between seven and thirteen years, princes were trained in a variety of disciplines and practices, by a series of specialised male tutors. In France a governor and a preceptor, each served by several substitutes, were responsible for the formation of princes. The governor, always a high nobleman and a soldier-courtier, permanently accompanied the prince from his seventh year to his maturity, representing the king and offering protection. Consequently, governors often held high court office when their pupil ascended the throne. They shared responsibility for the formation of the prince's character and attitude with the preceptor, usually a cleric, who took charge of the intellectual and moral formation of the prince.[154] This division of responsibilities between a high nobleman and a learned cleric or scholar, both served by substitutes and specialised teachers, was common in the education of princes throughout Europe.[155] The role of parents, however, varied immensely depending on the personalities and contingencies involved.

The French case suggests that, following the thirteenth year, more hours were spent studying. Moreover, from the seventeenth to the eighteenth century the number of hours princes studied rose from four or five to seven hours – a practice still not matching the ambitious Qing schedule. The curriculum notably included moral lessons. In addition to religious teachings, the dos and don'ts of monarchical governance were didactically demonstrated through the examples of historical rulers. Images, cards, and games were used to make knowledge more accessible; corporal punishment, not uncommon in the seventeenth century, gradually

---

[152] Mormiche, *Devenir prince.*
[153] Charles Philippe d'Albert, duc de Luynes, *Mémoires du duc de Luynes sur la cour de Louis XV (1735–1758)*, ed. L. Dussieux and E. Soulié, 17 vols. (Paris, 1860–5), XVI, 432 (1758).
[154] Mormiche, *Devenir prince*, 16; see the education of Charles V detailed in Anna Margarete Schlegelmilch, *Die Jugendjahre Karls V: Lebenswelt und Erziehung des burgundischen Prinzen* (Cologne, 2011).
[155] Schlegelmilch, *Die Jugendjahre Karls V.*

disappeared in the eighteenth century. Latin, rhetoric, modern languages, history, and heraldry were complemented by geography, mathematics, and techniques of fortification and warfare. Physical and martial training, including horsemanship, was necessary for princes. Their fathers and mentors gradually involved them in the practical business of council meetings and military campaigns.[156]

An important aspect of their education, moreover, was the inculcation of the bearing and manners befitting a good prince. The notes of physicians and tutors shed light on the obstacles young princes encountered in learning their roles. Even before the death of his father Henry IV, the heir-apparent (*dauphin*) Louis was expected to take part in the rituals of kingship. Upon being asked to perform the washing of the feet on Maundy Thursday in his father's stead, the six-year-old dauphin voiced, to his physician Jean Héroard, his aversion, telling him the poor had 'stinking feet'. In the end he could be persuaded to wash the feet only of girls, subverting the common gender arrangement of this ceremony, where the queen washed women's feet, the king men's feet. In 1619, after the regency of his mother and approaching full maturity at the age of nineteen, King Louis XIII expressed his doubts about performing an equally solemn and important rite, the royal touch. Could he be expected to touch his people during an outbreak of the plague? He was a person of flesh and blood, not a 'king of cardboard'.[157] Less dangerous experiences could still be challenging for youngsters. Young Louis XIV was a timid boy reluctant to engage in the social activities dictated by his function, from public dining to public ceremonies or speeches. In 1648, the nine-year-old king was expected to address the dignitaries in the Parlement of Paris; forgetting the text of his carefully prepared speech for the occasion, the boy burst out crying.[158]

Children were expected to perform their sovereign power in different contexts. Several prints depict Louis XV receiving ambassadors, one of them showing the rather tall Dutch diplomat Cornelis Hop towering over the boy king (Plate 6). The Ottoman ambassador Mehmed Efendi, whose visit in 1720-1 represented a major reorientation of Ottoman policies towards Europe, was charmed by the young king. During a first audience, however, the splendidly dressed eleven-year-old boy proved to be too timid to answer the ambassador's compliment. Later, when

---

[156] Mormiche, *Devenir prince*.

[157] Jean Héroard, *Journal de Jean Héroard sur l'enfance et la jeunesse de Louis XIII (1601–1628)*, ed. E. Soulié and E. de Barthélemy, 2 vols. (Paris, 1868), I, 255–7 (12 April 1607); II, 237 (17 October 1619).

[158] Orest A. Ranum, *The Fronde: A French Revolution, 1648–1652* (New York and London, 1993), 91.

the king's governor the duke of Villeroy invited Mehmed Efendi to a banquet, the ambassador had ample time to see the king in a less formal setting. Waiting for the meal to be served, Louis XV with his boy companions appreciatively examined the ambassador's exotic dress. Villeroy appeared eager to demonstrate the resourcefulness of his pupil, asking him to perform a sequence of stately and elegant movements. Mehmed Efendi, in the meantime, admired the king's appearance and attitude, patting his head while chatting with the governor.[159]

Several kings wrote long letters or tracts to prepare their sons for government. Louis XIV's memoirs, co-authored by several advisors, were explicitly intended for the education of the *dauphin* and were used for this purpose throughout the eighteenth century. German princes wrote lengthy 'political testaments' combining moral admonitions with practical instructions.[160] These texts were more practical than princely mirrors, yet most rulers presented moral standards they themselves had not been able to live up to – a common pattern in education. Louis XIV advised his son not to mix matters of the heart with those of the state while he himself was showering his mistress Madame de Montespan as well as her protégés with privileges.[161] Others, too, reiterated the admonitions of their tutors and confessors rather than their personal experiences. Charles V, in a highly personal instruction including numerous practical tips in an overall framework of devotion, advised his son Philip to study diligently, warning him against indulging in tournaments, hunting parties, and 'worse things' – a veiled reference to sex. Interestingly, he added that attendants around an inexperienced ruler could use such diversions to strengthen their own position – a warning that could easily have come from any Chinese minister.[162]

The three decades of maturity from twenty to fifty, labelled *iuventus* and *virilitas* in the European tradition, formed the period when kings and emperors stood the best chance of taking matters into their own hands. After the phase of education and initiation into their roles as future rulers, a critical moment arrived when young adults assumed personal power. This was the time to make their way, to show

---

[159] Yirmisekiz Çelebi Mehmed, *Le Paradis des infidels: relation de Yirmisekiz Çelebi Mehmed effendi, ambassadeur ottoman en France sous la Régence*, ed. Gilles Veinstein, trans. Julien Claude Galland (Paris, 1981), 98, 111–12.

[160] Duchhardt (ed.), *Politische Testamente*; Küntzel and Hass (eds.), *Politischen Testamente der Hohenzollern*.

[161] See Louis' sensible warnings in Louis XIV, *Mémoires de Louis XIV pour l'instruction du dauphin*, ed. Charles Dreyss, 2 vols. (Paris, 1860), II, 313–16.

[162] Charles V, *Das Vermächtnis Kaiser Karls V: die politischen Testamente*, ed. Armin Kohnle (Darmstadt, 2005), 48 (in the 1543 instruction). On Charles' education, see Schlegelmilch, *Die Jugendjahre Karls V*.

themselves to their peoples, to obtain glory on the battlefield, to develop their skills as supreme governors, and to demonstrate their ritual and cultural propriety – according to the dominant ideals of rulership. In Mughal as well as Ottoman history, enthronement was long the out-come of confrontation among the princes. Their violent clash most likely would bring to power a strong figure who had already assembled a circle of supporters. This did not necessarily mean that the new prince would take power into his own hands. More often than not, the eleva-tion to the throne of a new scion started a protracted reconfiguration of power relations: it remained to be seen whether the new prince would actually rule. The pace and outcome of this process depended on numerous factors, including the qualities and temperament of the ruler as well as the constellation of forces at court and the contingency of external challenges.

A portentous moment arrived with the death of a powerful mother or political mentor. Who would seize the reins of power: the ruler himself, or a favourite replacing the previous, trusted figure? Louis XIV remained compliant until Mazarin's death in 1661 but made his subsequent move to the heart of power conspicuously clear. His widely broadcast declara-tion of independence was underscored by legal proceedings against the most likely successor to Mazarin, the *surintendant des finances* Nicolas Fouquet.[163] Habsburg emperor Leopold I (1640–1658–1705), who unexpectedly came to the throne after the death of the emperor-elect Ferdinand IV (1633–54), had relied on the advice of his chief minister Johann Ferdinand Portia until the latter's death in 1665. Now, the emperor intended to follow the example of Louis XIV, planning to be his own first minister. This proved to be a difficult undertaking, he confided to his friend and ambassador in Spain. There was no disinter-ested person he could ask for advice or support: everybody was keen on finding out who would become the next favourite.[164] As soon as the emperor would seek to explain his predicament to a figure close to him, others would immediately interpret this as the onset of the new favourite's career. A similar changeover in Ming China, Zhang Juzheng's death in 1582, started a decade of increasing involvement of the Wanli emperor: 'the boy who had been a manipulated ruler had now awakened to vindi-cate himself'. The subsequent setbacks encountered by Wanli, 'too

---

[163] Marc Fumaroli, 'Nicolas Fouquet, the favourite manqué', in J.H. Elliott and L.W. B. Brockliss (eds.), *The World of the Favourite* (New Haven, CT, and London, 1999), 239–55.

[164] Leopold I, *Privatbriefe Kaiser Leopold I an den Grafen F.E. Pötting 1662–1673*, ed. A.F. Pribram and M. Landwehr von Pragenau, 2 vols. (Vienna, 1903–4), I, 104–7.

intelligent and sensitive to occupy the dragon seat', would lead to his frustration and withdrawal.[165]

Conversely, if death did not take away the figures presiding over the lives of adolescent princes, conflict became a distinct possibility. Louis XIII's reign started with his mother Marie de Médicis as regent, but their relationship soon turned sour. The king imposed an internal exile upon his mother in 1617, followed by a reconciliation in 1621 which proved to be temporary. Within a decade, the queen mother's renewed political activities triggered a second, now definitive, exile: Marie, staying in the southern Netherlands until 1638, finally died in Cologne in 1642 after a few more years of peregrination.[166] The young Kangxi, aided by his grandmother and other supporters, toppled the regents Oboi, Suksaha, Ebilun, and Sonin and took power into his own hands – only to find out, however, that he now needed to gradually break free from the Manchu grandees who had helped engineer his coup.[167]

Rulers could decide to rely on the services of favourites they themselves created, often youth companions or trusted attendants. Soon after his accession, Süleyman (1494–1520–1566) promoted his servant and companion Ibrahim Pasha to the rank of grand vizier, allowing his favourite to overstep the ranks of the *cursus honorum* and turning him into his *alter ego* with full powers. The grand vizier's career ended in downfall and execution without, apparently, damaging Süleyman's reputation.[168] His son and sole remaining successor, Selim II (1524–1566–1574; Plate 21),

[165] Huang, *Year of No Significance*, 67, 93. Huang concludes that Wanli's predicament was partly the necessary consequence of the ageing Ming apparatus, a conclusion contested in recent literature; see e.g. a stress on Wanli's, and more generally late Ming, efficacy in military policy in the work of Kenneth Swope.

[166] Toby Osborne, 'A queen mother in exile: Marie de Medicis in the Spanish Netherlands and England, 1631–41', in Philip Mansel and T. Riotte (eds.), *Monarchy and Exile: The Politics of Legitimacy from Marie de Medicis to Wilhelm II* (Basingstoke and New York, 2011), 17–43.

[167] Michael Chang, 'The recruitment of lower Yangzi (Jiangnan) literati to the Kangxi court, 1670s–1690s', paper presented at the conference 'Servants and administrators: from the court to the provinces', Leiden, 31 August – 2 September 2011.

[168] Zeynep Nevin Yelçe, 'The making of Sultan Süleyman: a study of process/es of image-making and reputation management', PhD thesis, Sabanci University (2009), on Ibrahim Pasha and Süleyman. There is a rich literature on the favourite in Europe: see Jean Bérenger, 'Pour une enquête européenne: le problème du ministériat au XVIIe siècle', *Annales ESC*, 29/1 (1974), 166–92; Elliott and Brockliss (eds.), *World of the Favourite*; Nicolas Le Roux, *La faveur du roi: mignons et courtisans au temps des derniers Valois (vers 1547 – vers 1589)* (Paris, 2000); Jan Hirschbiegel and Werner Paravicini (eds.), *Der Fall des Günstlings: Hofparteien in Europa vom 13. bis zum 17. Jahrhundert. 8. Symposium der Residenzenkommission der Akademie der Wissenschaften zu Göttingen* (Ostfildern, 2004); Michael Kaiser and Andreas Pečar (eds.), *Der zweite Mann im Staat: oberste Amtsträger und Favoriten im Umkreis der Reichsfürsten in der Frühen Neuzeit* (Berlin, 2003).

retained in office his father's last grand vizier, Sokollu Mehmed Pasha. More than a decade later under Murad III (1546–1574–1595), the all-powerful grand vizier would be pushed aside, with power reverting to the sultan and his circle of inner court favourites. Didactic history in East and West included notorious instances of attendants, eunuchs, or female favourites unsettling proper hierarchies and procedures at court. Rulers usually advised their potential successors to rule with a mixed group of advisors rather than depending on a single dominant figure. This was the best option for all groups at court. The dominance of a single person or faction raised doubts about the ruler's powers and inevitably triggered conflict at court, with the outsiders using every opportunity to overthrow the favourite or the faction in power.

The nominally all-powerful and morally supreme position of the ruler could not ensure the compliance and active support of key groups at court – relatives, spouses and concubines, personal attendants, state dignitaries, religious leaders, guards, and military commanders. Some exceptional rulers, such as first Ming emperor Zhu Yuanzhang or Napoleon, both rising to power after a phase of immense turmoil, could personally and forcefully reconstruct this constellation of powers. More often, as Louis XIV admitted, their prime task was the careful choice of talented and devoted ministers. In a mixed group of advisors, the 'jealousy of one would serve to check the ambitions of the others', the king perceptively noted in his memoirs. The appointment of several competing ministers would secure loyal service.[169] The ruler, however, still faced the question of how he could retain control of his leading agents' activities. The simplest answer to this question was: endless toil.

The tough schedule of education in Qing China prepared the princes for a daunting task ahead: dealing with an unending pile of paperwork. The three 'high Qing' emperors, all combining talent with diligence, appear to have worked very hard to adequately perform their office. Rising at five in the morning, the Qianlong emperor would be ready for a long morning's work with his councillors at seven, continuing with paperwork until the early afternoon, followed by audiences and inter-views with likely appointees.[170] Around three in the afternoon the emperor would dine before he could finally choose to devote the evening to one of his numerous artistic or scholarly pursuits, retiring at nine. His father, the Yongzheng emperor, was even keener to keep everything

---

[169] Louis XIV, *Mémoires*, ed. Dreyss, II, 267: 'La jalousie de l'un sert souvent de frein à l'ambition de l'autre', a remark referring to ministers but often misread to describe the power balances among courtiers enforced by the king.

[170] Elliott, *Qianlong*, 23–5.

under control, notably that core activity of all rulers, nomination to high office:

When I was still a prince, I did not have contact with ministers of the Outer Court, and thus I knew very few of them. When I succeeded to the Throne and there were vacancies in metropolitan and provincial posts, how could I not appoint people? I have had to search widely and appoint people whom I never knew. After I have appointed them and in due course observed them, then if I find them unworthy I have no choice but to change them. Therefore, every time there is an opening from governor-general ... down to local magistrate, if I do not find the right men, I pore through the monthly records of the Board of War and the Board of Civil Office repeatedly. Often I go without sleep all night. I must get the right man before I can relax. This is my predicament as a monarch, which words cannot describe.[171]

The emperor's commitment is confirmed by the comments he noted during hundreds of interviews with candidates for high positions.[172]

Yongzheng's father, the Kangxi emperor, though more easy-going than his perfectionist son, matched his capacity for work. The emperor allegedly once demoted a prefect who had boasted that he could handle seven or eight hundred administrative materials in one day, stating:

I've been ruling for forty years, and only during the Wu San-kuei rebellion did I handle five hundred items of business in one day. Nor did I myself hold the brush and write the documents, and even so I could not get to bed until midnight. You may fool other people, but you can't fool me.[173]

Looking back on his life at the end of his reign, Kangxi underlined that his toil could never be compared to that of a hard-working administrator: only the emperor carried the full burden of responsibility without a chance of respite: 'for decades I have exhausted all my strength, day after day. How can this just be summed up in a two-word phrase like "hard work"?'[174] The combined pressure of work and responsibility, he continued, made it understandable that earlier emperors had sometimes escaped into 'drink and sex'.

While the Mughal and Ottoman empires were certainly governed by paperwork as well as by horsemanship and archery, it is not clear how much time and effort individual rulers devoted to reading and commenting on administrative texts or to collegial decision-making and interviews. Akbar could not read but stood at the beginning of a major administrative reform and appears to have had a powerful memory. His

---

[171] Guy, *Qing Governors*, 121–2; Madeleine Zelin, 'The Yung-Cheng reign', in Willard J. Peterson (ed.), *The Cambridge History of China*, vol. IX: *The Ch'ing Empire to 1800* (Cambridge, 2002), 183–229, at 195. Both cite this passage.
[172] Guy, *Qing Governors*, 122.   [173] Spence, *Emperor of China*, 46.   [174] Ibid., 146.

successors must have been involved in the machinery of government by paper. Foreign agents were surprised by the endless letters and reports digested by high Mughal dignitaries.[175] Ottoman rulers could rely on the services of the grand vizier and his staff; they gradually withdrew from meetings with the council (*divan*) and communicated with the grand vizier through written reports (*telhis*) rather than in face-to-face consultation.[176] Apart from perfectionists disinclined to delegate their tasks, such as Philip II of Spain and Frederick II of Brandenburg-Prussia (1712–1740–1786), most European rulers seem lackadaisical in comparison with the three high Qing emperors. However, many among them experienced the same pressures. Their upbringing conveyed a sense of responsibility that made it difficult to evade the accumulation of administrative, ritual, and social tasks. Louis XIV straightforwardly addressed the issue in his memoirs: the prince can never adequately study all the documents in his ministers' portfolios. Therefore he should repeatedly and randomly make a detailed study of specific items to test his ministers' competence and loyalty. Performing this feat regularly and without a predictable pattern, he could retain control without losing himself in unending and detailed paperwork.[177] Still, the father stipulated to his son, an unremitting schedule of hard work was the *conditio sine qua non* of good kingship.

Emperor Leopold I excused himself to his confidant the Habsburg ambassador in Spain for his shortcomings as a correspondent: after five hours of concentrated paperwork, he found energy only to scribble a few hasty lines. Elsewhere he complained about the increasing workload: 'tasks accumulate day by day, but it is my obligation and profession, to which God has called me'.[178] The emperor looked forward to a stay at one of his hunting lodges, where opportunities for recreation would arise. Outdoor activity brought respite from social and administrative pressures. Leopold, who escaped from Vienna when the Ottoman army approached in 1683 and never performed any military feats, nevertheless was a passionate hunter. The Swedish diplomat Esaias Pufendorf saw him ferociously clubbing foxes in the Vienna Prater in the company of his

---

[175] See examples in Jos J.L. Gommans, *Mughal Warfare: Indian Frontiers and Highroads to Empire 1500–1700* (London and New York, 2003), 94. On Mughal scribal elites, see Kumkum Chatterjee, 'Scribal elites in sultanate and Mughal Bengal', *Indian Economic & Social History Review*, 47/4 (2010), 445–72.

[176] Murphey, *Ottoman Sovereignty*; Pal Fodor, 'Sultan, imperial council, grand vizier: changes in the Ottoman ruling elite and the formation of the grand vizieral telhis', *Acta Orientalia Academiae Scientiarum Hungaricae*, 47 (1994), 67–85.

[177] Louis XIV, *Mémoires*, ed. Cornette, 65.

[178] Leopold I, *Privatbriefe*, I, 118 (15 March 1665).

court dwarfs, a scene he found awkwardly remote from true imperial dignity.[179]

For Leopold and many of his fellow rulers, hunting represented a reprieve from the drudgery of government. Hunting is ubiquitous in the history of dynasty as a recreation and as a show of martial capabilities.[180] However, from a recreation in a small circle of intimates, the hunt could turn into a high-profile social activity with a circle of spectators watching the proceedings – another test to be passed. All social activities tended to acquire an element of representation and constraint. European kings with their relatively outgoing and interactive styles frequently tried to escape the bustle of courtiers and spectators and seek more secluded places, only to find that access to such select occasions was soon coveted as a special privilege. Some of them seized the opportunity this offered for the manipulation of ranks and reputations; others simply deplored the loss of leisurely and comfortable moments. Among the bustle of courtiers and petitioners, most rulers quickly adopted a reticent attitude, leaving the speaking to others and answering only briefly and in general terms. Louis XIV strongly advised his son to listen rather than talk, and never to respond directly to requests. Saint-Simon, the chronicler of the French court, reports the king's usual laconic answer: 'I shall see' (*je verrai*).[181] Louis XIII, hindered by persistent stammering, was dubbed 'the silent', an epithet he shared with many other rulers.[182] Habsburg emperors likewise were not noted for verbosity, usually answering in short and evasive statements.[183] Charles VI (1685–1711–1740), a talented linguist, was described by several unfriendly witnesses as being tongue-tied, speaking inaudibly if at all.[184] His daughter Maria Theresa, an easier personality in most respects at least until the death of her spouse in 1765, increased the social interaction of the Viennese court with the urban elites. No friend of gambling, she nevertheless advised her children to play cards and dice during the court's social gatherings because, she explained to them:

[179] Oswald Redlich, 'Das Tagebuch Esaias Pufendorfs, schwedischen Residenten am Kaiserhofe von 1671 bis 1674', *Mitteilungen des Instituts für Österreichische Geschichtsforschung*, 37 (1917), 541–97, at 568.

[180] Thomas Allsen, *The Royal Hunt in Eurasian History* (Philadelphia, PA, 2006).

[181] Louis XIV, *Mémoires*, ed. Dreyss, I, 195–7, II, 64–5; Louis de Rouvroy, duc de Saint-Simon, *Mémoires*, ed. A. de Boislisle, 43 vols. (Paris, 1876–1930), vol. XXVIII, 143–6.

[182] A. Lloyd Moote, *Louis XIII, the Just* (Berkeley, CA, 1989), 3, 139.

[183] Esaias Pufendorf, *Bericht über Kaiser Leopold, seinen Hof, und die Österreichische Politik 1671–1674*, ed. Carl Gustav Helbig (Leipzig, 1862), 59; Volker Press, 'Österreichische Großmachtbildung und Reichsverfassung: zur kaiserlichen Stellung nach 1648', *Mitteilungen des Instituts für Österreichische Geschichtsforschung*, 98 (1990), 131–54, at 146.

[184] Alphons Lhotsky, 'Kaiser Karl VI. und sein Hof im Jahre 1712–13', *Mitteilungen des Instituts für Österreichische Geschichtsforschung*, 66 (1958), 52–80, at 63–4.

'speaking amidst 100 persons keen to approach you is too difficult to sustain at length.'[185]

Withdrawing into the inner apartments of the court, surrounded only by trusted servants, could be an alluring alternative. The attendants in this comfortable environment, Louis XIV stated, who are 'the first to see the king's weaknesses, are also the first to take advantage of them'.[186] It made sense, therefore, to recruit companions from groups unlikely, because of some defect, to rise to high power: eunuchs, dwarfs, exiles, or low-ranking outsiders. Withdrawal among such groups, however, tended to annoy vested elites. French high court nobles were angered by Henry III's (1551–1574–1589) reliance on a small circle of favourites and by his attempts to create more distance between king and court. The retreat of Wanli and several of his fellow emperors into the inner court likewise was censured by high state dignitaries – even if they voiced their vexation in more respectful terms. French nobles and Chinese scholars shared a common anxiety: the rise to power of low-ranking inner court favourites. Princes, clearly, could not easily find a refuge free from the occupational hazards of their position without creating even more serious problems.

While the catalogue of moral virtues compelled rulers to attend to their responsibilities, negligence would not necessarily have dire consequences. As long as they were served by a mixed group of loyal advisors respecting the king's supremacy, nothing much would happen. In fact it is almost impossible for modern historians, as it was for contemporaries, to ascertain whether measures were taken on the initiative of the council or through the intervention of the ruler himself.[187] It is likely that even active figures were usually happy to follow the advice of their specialised servants. These would see little reason to complain or broadcast the passivity of the ruler: it ideally served their purposes. The team of advisors established at the outset of a personal reign, however, tended to break down within a few decades at most. As soon as open conflict arose among the advisors, or between a closed group of advisors and others who were trying to make themselves heard, it was essential for a king to step in and recreate order. This became more and more difficult with the passing of the years.

Moving from maturity to old age, rulers experienced a draining of their powers. The final two or three decades of life proved difficult even for formidable figures. From the 1690s onwards, Louis XIV gradually started

---

[185] Handwritten notes by Maria Theresa in Österreichische Nationalbibliothek, cod. ser. n. 1713, fol. 77^r.

[186] Louis XIV, *Mémoires*, ed. Dreyss, 288, 404; see a similar remark in Muḥammad Bāqir Najm-i Sānī, *Advice on the Art of Governance*, 60.

[187] Francis Bacon, 'Of Counsel', in *The Essays*, 120–4.

losing control (see Plate 7), a process caused by the deaths of his most talented and trusted ministers, the persistent political-military challenges facing France, increasing economic problems, and the changing physical condition of the king himself. His morganatic spouse, Madame de Maintenon, at the same time turned into a de facto first minister acknowledged by diplomats as a prime mover of court politics. In 1711 and 1712, a wave of deaths in the royal family soured the king's last years. After losing his only son, one of the numerous princes who never ascended to the throne, Louis also lost the duke of Burgundy, his cherished grandson and next in line for succession. The two young sons of the duke also fell ill, and the eldest died: now only a two-year-old boy, the future Louis XV, remained. The king decided to make his bastard sons eligible for succession, a step exacerbating factional strife at court. For these last years, numerous testimonies can be found on the king's anxious state of mind and declining health. A marginal comment in a text planning a banquet and ball included in the register for 1700 of the high noble servants in the king's chamber stipulates that 'only familiar faces should be placed around the king', suggesting that servants had long since been organising a comfort zone around their ageing monarch.[188]

The Kangxi emperor's long life likewise ended with fifteen years of increasing anxiety and ailments, caused to a large extent by his ongoing troubles with his sons and potential successors, most particularly his first (surviving) son Yinreng. In 1676 as an eighteen-month-old infant, this prince had been nominated heir-apparent by his proud father, but once he approached adolescence, tensions rose.[189] In 1708, after the death of a favoured younger son, the emperor's gradually mounting disgruntlement with the behaviour of his heir-apparent led to a distressing denouement in which Yinreng lost his position and was punished. Following the confrontation, the emperor feared that he had acted rashly and was beset by doubts. Reconsidering Yinreng's misdemeanours, he found indications that they had been caused by manipulations and possibly even by malicious spells. Kangxi's health was permanently affected by this crisis. By the end of 1708 he fell seriously ill and appeared to be dying. It took him until March 1709 to regain some strength, and he never fully recovered. Addressing his main officials when he felt death approaching, Kangxi himself stated that: 'After my serious illness in the forty-seventh year of my reign, my spirits had been too much wounded, and gradually I failed

---

[188] Duindam, *Vienna and Versailles*, 228: the *premiers gentilshommes'* register, cérémonies de toute espèce, 60–3, Bal masqué du 27 janvier 1700, note in the margin of 63. 'Nota: Eviter autant qu'il se peut de mettre des visages inconnus au roi sur l'échaffaud qui est vis à vis de lui.'

[189] Wu, *Passage to Power*, 31; Spence, *Emperor of China*, 123–39.

to regain my former state. Moreover, everyday there was my work, all requiring decisions; frequently I felt that my vitality was slipping away and my internal energy diminishing.'[190] Elsewhere in the same edict the emperor contrasts his position to that of the officials, who could at some point hope to enjoy retirement, asking himself: 'how can I attain the day when I will have no more burdens?'[191] In 1717 death seemed the only and desirable escape from a situation that seemed to become ever more wearying, saddening, and pointless. Typically, these powerful statements by the Kangxi emperor, who could not hold back his 'tears of bitterness' while sharing his thoughts with his officials (see Plate 8), were published in polished form after his death, without a trace of the emperor's despondency.[192] His grandson the Qianlong emperor (1711–1735–1796*) seems to have fared better. The French Jesuit Michel Benoit conversed at leisure with the emperor in 1774, during a session in which Qianlong posed for a Jesuit painter. At sixty-three, the emperor had gained some weight but still felt in good shape. The conversation suggests a keen and perceptive mind. Within a few years, however, Qianlong's grip on government diminished. From the late 1770s he allowed his favourite Heshen to accumulate offices, titles, and wealth, an example so conspicuous that it may well have contributed to corruption rampant among officials. Qianlong's powers waned, but he was able to maintain an unruffled outward image.

The Mughal emperor Aurangzeb (1618–1658–1707), grabbing the throne by defeating his brothers and imprisoning his ailing father Shah Jahan in 1658, enjoyed a particularly long life and ruled for almost fifty years. Shortly before his death in 1707 he wrote letters to several sons conveying fears of impending succession conflicts and a sense of the futility of his long activist reign: 'The instant which passed in power, hath left only sorrow behind it.' His sentiments appear close to those voiced by Kangxi, though in a less personal tone.[193] King Yŏngjo of Korea (1694–1724–1776), likewise ascending to the throne at a relatively advanced age, experienced the longest reign of his dynasty. When after a decade of ruling a son was born to him in 1735, the delighted Yŏngjo appointed him heir-apparent in his second year and groomed him for kingship. Gradually a gripping father–son tragedy unfolded around this 'prince of mournful thoughts' that in the end made Yŏngjo order his son to commit suicide in 1762. The king turned from 'a man of vision into a man of delusion', although he doggedly

[190] Spence, *Emperor of China*, 148.   [191] Ibid., 150.
[192] Ibid., 145, and 169–75 for the final published edict with an examination of the changes.
[193] See the letters printed in Eradut Khan, *A Translation of the Memoirs of Eradut Khan, a Nobleman of Hindostan ...*, trans. Jonathan Scott (London, 1786), 8–9.

pursued the ideal of the neo-Confucian scholar-prince to his death.[194] Three centuries earlier, the longest-reigning of all Ottoman sultans, Süleyman (1494–1520–1566), started his rule by successfully continuing his father's military triumphs.[195] At the very time the sultan's physical powers started declining, his brawny thirty-eight-year-old son Mustafa became increasingly popular among the janissary elite household infantry. In 1553 the Venetian *bailo* or ambassador wrote that 'it is impossible to describe how much he [Mustafa] is loved and desired by all as successor to the throne'.[196] The example of Bayezid II (1447–1481–1512), forced to abdicate by his activist son Selim I in 1512, may have been on Süleyman's mind: he took no risk and had Mustafa executed. Somewhat later, Habsburg ambassador Ogier Ghiselin de Busbecq noted that Süleyman, 'beginning to feel the weight of years', sought to improve his looks 'by painting his face with a coating of red powder'.[197] While Busbecq connected this habit to the sultan's wish to impress foreign ambassadors, it was clearly highly relevant for the Ottoman soldiery and leadership to see their sultan in good physical shape. During the 1566 Szigetvar campaign, the sultan, eager to demonstrate his personal leadership, proved unable to ride his horse without support. A book miniature pictures grand vizier Sokollu Mehmed Pasha supporting the sultan (Plate 9) – a scene commissioned by the grand vizier, who highlighted Süleyman's weakness as well as his own strength. The same series of miniatures shows how Süleyman had to dismount and ride in a carriage, which in the end became the hearse transporting his body. The aged sultan had tried to the end to perform a role that no longer fitted his physical capabilities.[198] Was riding into battle his version of the suicide practised by weakening Ankole kings?

In years of increasing vulnerability and anxiety, princes were no longer able to lead their soldiers into war and became less disposed to generate

---

[194] Haboush, *Confucian Kingship in Korea*, quotations at 230–2. See a portrayal of the rising tensions between King Yŏngjo and Prince Sado from the perspective of Sado's wife in Hyegyong, *Memoirs*, the memoir of 1805, 241–336.

[195] Yelce, 'Making of Sultan Süleyman'.

[196] On Mustafa and Süleyman, see Leslie P. Peirce, *The Imperial Harem: Women and Sovereignty in the Ottoman Empire* (Oxford, 1993), quotation at 56, more details at 81–3; as well as Ogier Ghislain de Busbecq, *The Turkish Letters of Ogier Ghiselin de Busbecq, Imperial Ambassador at Constantinople, 1554–1562: Translated from the Latin of the Elzevir Edition of 1663* (Oxford, 1927), 31–2.

[197] Busbecq, *Turkish Letters*, 65–6.

[198] Emine Fetvaci, *Picturing History at the Ottoman Court* (Bloomington, IN, 2013), 134–6, also printing another miniature with two servants supporting Süleyman; see also Nicolas Vatin and Gilles Veinstein, *Le sérail ébranlé: essai sur les morts, dépositions et avènements des sultans ottomans, XVIe–XIXe siècle* (Paris, 2003), 32.

support by touring their realm. Hours of paperwork and chairing meetings must have become increasingly burdensome. Dependence on a single trusted confidant became particularly tempting for these elderly rulers. Towards the end of his life, Habsburg emperor Rudolf II's (1552–1576–1612) low-ranking chamber servant monopolised access to the emperor, dominated the distribution of favours, and sold his influence to the highest bidder.[199] Rudolf had never been very outgoing, but more extrovert and forceful figures, too, tended to withdraw in a closed circle of companions. The problems of ageing kings were made worse by the restiveness of their now mature successors – who later in their lives could expect to replicate their fathers' anxieties. Leopold I, who ruled for almost fifty years, gradually became more comfortable in his role and continued in relatively good shape. However, his eldest son Joseph, emperor-elect since 1690, became impatient and attracted a 'young court' of people waiting for change.

Violent deposition occurred frequently in the Ottoman empire, with fifteen out of thirty-three sultans ruling between 1389 and 1918 forced out of their august office.[200] Interestingly, the abdications of Mehmed IV in 1687, Mustafa II in 1703, and Ahmed III in 1730 no longer automatically entailed the execution of the sultan – a pattern established earlier with the killing of Osman II in 1622 and Ibrahim in 1648. The elites pushing for abdication no longer even saw the retired sultans as a threat: they put another scion of the house of Osman on the throne who, hopefully, better fitted their expectations. Destoolment was an accepted and relatively peaceful pattern in several African kingdoms, but it served as a check on the behaviour of kings rather than as a solution to the problems of ageing rulers and impatient successors.

The Manchu grandee Songgotu sought to convince Kangxi of the desirability of abdicating in favour of his heir-apparent Yinreng in the late 1690s, but the emperor discarded the plan when his son's bad behaviour became more marked.[201] Kangxi's grandson, the Qianlong emperor, did in fact retire in 1796, leaving his illustrious grandfather Kangxi the honour of having enjoyed the longest reign in Chinese imperial history. In practice, however, Qianlong's son and successor the Jiaqing emperor (1760–1796–1820) could not rule without anticipating

[199] Friedrich Hurter, *Philipp Lang, Kammerdiener Kaiser Rudolphs II: eine Criminal-geschichte aus dem Anfang des siebenzehnten Jahrhunderts* (Schaffhausen, 1852).
[200] Murphey, *Ottoman Sovereignty*, 90; Anthony D. Alderson, *The Structure of the Ottoman Dynasty* (Oxford, 1956), 58.
[201] Wu, *Passage to Power*, 56–9, 69–70.

and respecting his father's wishes.[202] As 'supreme emperor' (*taishang huang*) Qianlong remained a notable presence from his abdication in 1796 to his death in 1799.[203] Abdications can be found in earlier Chinese history as well as in polities related to the Chinese Confucian model. In the period leading up to the Chinese Tang dynasty (618–907 CE), abdications were not infrequent. In Japan it almost became the norm: between the first abdication in 645 and the last in 1817, three quarters of all imperial reigns ended in abdication.[204] In addition, five of the fifteen Tokugawa shoguns voluntarily retired at least a year before they died.[205] In Korea and Vietnam, too, retired kings can be found. However, in each of these cases abdication did not primarily reflect a retreat to make room for a new generation but provided an instrument to deal with specific problems at court, securing a stabler succession pattern, circumventing powerful court factions, or simply dividing the heavy burden of rulership.

In Europe abdication remained rare; when it occurred, it was usually enforced by others or motivated by exceptional personal reasons. In 1567, after a series of confrontations, Mary Queen of Scots was forced to abdicate in favour of her one-year-old son James. In 1555–6, shortly before his death in 1558, a tired and disappointed Charles V retired after failing to contain the Reformation in his German territories, leaving his numerous lands and titles to his son Philip and his own brother Ferdinand. Queen Christina of Sweden abdicated in 1654 before departing to Rome and converting to Catholicism.[206] No regular pattern of abdication in favour of a younger ruler emerged, but arrangements for power-sharing between an elderly ruler and his successor can be found. The formal confirmation of a heir-apparent entailed a shift in responsibilities, increasing the difference in rank with others eligible to succeed to the throne. Where acclamation or election determined succession, kings

---

[202] The Japanese, Chinese, and Tahitian examples of emperors retiring for different reasons, often still actively ruling behind the scenes, are a different case. On the Chinese retired emperor from the fourth to the seventh century CE, see Andrew Eisenberg, *Kingship in Early Medieval China* (Leiden and Boston, MA, 2008).

[203] Kahn, *Monarchy in the Emperor's Eyes*; Elliott, *Qianlong*, 160.

[204] Shillony, *Enigma of the Emperors*, 49, underlining that most often emperors were forced to abdicate. At 109–10 Shillony mentions the shogun forcing the emperor's retirement in 1663 following signs of heavenly displeasure. See an overview of all abdicated emperors in Richard A.B. Ponsonby-Fane, *The Imperial House of Japan* (Kyoto, 1959), 287–9; the earlier phases are discussed in Hurst, 'Insei'. Hurst and Eisenberg present the practice of 'retiring' emperors as a strategy stabilising and reforming fluid succession practices (with shared sovereignty and female rulership) to male primogeniture, but this fails to account for the numerous retiring emperors in later periods.

[205] Personal communication from Anne Walthall.

[206] Also Philip V of Spain, John II Casimir Vasa of Poland, and several others.

often tried to have their sons elected during their lifetime (*vivente rege, vivente imperatore*) without themselves stepping back. Alternatively, sovereignty could be divided, by placing different responsibilities in different hands. Maria Theresa, ruling the Habsburg monarchy from 1740 to 1780, could not hold the male title of Holy Roman Emperor. Her husband Francis Stephen, regaining this title for the Habsburgs in 1745 after a short Wittelsbach tenure (1742–5), was made co-regent by his spouse. After the death of his father, Joseph II took over his position as co-regent as well as the imperial dignity, to which he had been elected *vivente imperatore* in 1764.[207] Mother–son co-rule, however, proved to be difficult for both parties, with restless Joseph adopting outspoken viewpoints that pained his level-headed mother. Nor did it prevent Maria Theresa from experiencing the troubles of ageing rulers. Shortly after the death of her beloved husband in 1765 Maria Theresa, now fifty, looked back on her early years, seeing that she had been inexperienced, timid, and insecure. She pointed to a handful of devoted servants, who were as important to her in 'old age and decrepitude' as they had been in her 'youthful impetuosity'. A few years later, a courtier reported that she was 'at extremes, considering even to part with her crown out of despair and disgust'. In 1773 Maria Theresa wrote to another of her associates that her situation was becoming intolerable and isolated, and could only be maintained thanks to the support of a few loyal friends and state servants.[208]

The burdens of rulership: agency and trust

Looking at numerous lives of sultans, kings, and emperors, a pattern can be established. Most kings could be effective only during a few decades: youth and old age on the throne entailed dependence and anxieties. Even during their years of strength and maturity, rulers faced

---

[207] Robert Oresko, G.C. Gibbs, and H.M. Scott (eds.), *Royal and Republican Sovereignty in Early Modern Europe: Essays in Memory of Ragnhild Hatton* (Cambridge and New York, 2006).

[208] *Correspondance secrète entre Marie-Thérèse et le Cte de Mercy-Argenteau. Avec les lettres de Marie-Thérèse et de Marie-Antoinette*, ed. Alfred von Arneth and Auguste Geffroy, 3 vols. (Paris, 1874–5), I, 146–7 (the empress reporting the death of Sylva-Tarouca to Mercy, 1 April 1771), quotation in note 1; Johann Josef Khevenhüller-Metsch, *Aus der Zeit Maria Theresias: Tagebuch des Fürsten Johann Josef Khevenhüller-Metsch, kaiserlichen Obersthofmeisters 1742–1776*, ed. H. Schlitter and R. Khevenhüller-Metsch, 7 vols. (Vienna, 1907–25), VII, 128–30 (20–5 May 1772), with an exchange of letters in endnotes 153 and 154, at 422–3. Compare Derek Beales, *Joseph II*, I, 288–9, 350–1; and Maria Theresa, *Briefe der Kaiserin Maria Theresia an ihre Kinder und Freunde*, ed. Alfred von Arneth, 4. vols. (Vienna, 1881), IV, 298–9.

daunting pressures. Paperwork, military action, ritual obligations, and social gatherings, mixed in different proportions for each place and period, formed a challenge for most incumbents. The moral responsibilities of kingship and the great examples of forebears did little to alleviate the burden. Shared patterns seem more important than any fundamental development over time or than any consistent regional divergence. Moreover, individual variation remains a strikingly important factor. Regional differences did determine conditions and expectations, leaving more room for a passively enacted moral example in the regions strongly influenced by Confucian thinking than elsewhere. Nevertheless, the alternation of outgoing and withdrawn rulers can be seen equally well in Europe or West Asia. Wanli, Murad III, Henry III, and Rudolf II, near-contemporaries, opted for an inward turn. A generation later, Murad IV and Henry IV developed more activist and outgoing styles, soon to be adopted by the new Qing emperors as well. Strong and weak figures chose different ways to deal with their kingship, but they were inevitably subject to the same pressures. Kangxi and Louis XIV, textbook examples of strong rulers, went through all the expected phases of the life cycle. Leopold I, often inaccurately pictured as a weak and indecisive ruler, experienced similar pressures and handled them no less sensibly than his more famous contemporaries. Murad III, most often seen as the typical bad sultan withdrawing into the harem, may have used his withdrawal to engineer the downfall of his overpowering grand vizier, in an attempt to regain the initiative. Lacking sources outlining the motives of the ruler and his proximates, we cannot be sure.

The political consequences of reigns have often determined judgements by contemporaries and historians. Military defeat, dynastic change, and political revolution all focus our attention on leaders' political errors or moral failures. Such dramatic endings, however, were not necessarily caused primarily by the incompetence of rulers, nor can successes always be explained by their wise deeds. Patricia Ebrey, carefully examining Song emperor Huizong (1082–1100–1126) on the basis of numerous sources, sees little reason to put the blame of the Jurchen triumph over Song China squarely on his shoulders.[209] She portrays a talented, well-intentioned young man ascending the throne unexpectedly. Common criticisms of Huizong, including the emperor's fancy for Daoism, his clashes with literati factions, and his spending on palaces and court life, hardly explain the Song fiasco. Ray Huang made an important remark about Wanli, another figure traditionally seen as weak. Wanli was

---

[209] Patricia B. Ebrey, *Emperor Huizong* (Cambridge, MA, 2014).

far from incompetent, but better grasped the constraints and contradic-
tions of his awkward position than many other emperors. His intelligence
and sensitivity made it more difficult for him to rule effectively.[210]
While Huang fits Wanli's trouble into a story of overall Ming decline,
the condition of princes more generally seems frustrating. They were,
on the one hand, nominally supreme in everything; yet, on the other hand,
they were bound by endless restrictions and guided by a staff offering
advice that could be disinterested or self-seeking.

Kings stood at the heart of the political machinery, yet they were not
always its prime movers. In his work on the 'theatre state' in Bali,
Clifford Geertz suggested the image of the icon-king or king of chess,
the passive centre of a dynamic and competitive world.[211] The metaphor is apt but presents one side only of kingship, or one specific type of
king. Who would call the Ming founder Hongwu or Kangxi icon-
emperors, Louis XIV or Süleyman kings of chess? These were active
figures, with great impact on society at large. Yet they, too, were subject
to the pressures that froze less formidable characters into passivity,
worrying about their mandate, their physical prowess, and their successors. More often than not, it remains unclear whether the decisions
attributed to individual rulers in contemporary discourse and later
national historiography were in fact the result of their personal agency.
The relevant point here is that we need to take into account the motives
and actions of a variety of groups around rulers. Scholars educated
youngsters, advised mature rulers, and wrote the history of their reigns.
Personal servants acted as daily companions and low-profile favourites.
Surrounded and served by all these groups, rulers nevertheless could
not confide in them without running risks. At the top of the hierarchy,
trouble-free trust was rare. Louis XIV seems to have recognised this
explicitly in an instruction preparing his grandson Philip for the
Spanish throne. In a series of thirty-three succinct phrases, moving
from moral admonition to pragmatic advice primarily stressing the
need to befriend the Spanish people, he laconically asks his grandson
'never to develop an attachment to anybody' – a dismal counsel based
on the potential misfortunes caused by friendship rather than on
conviction.[212] Who could be trusted without risk? Powerful ministers

---

[210] Huang, *Year of No Significance*, 67, 93.

[211] Clifford Geertz, *Negara: The Theatre-State in Nineteenth-Century Bali* (Princeton, NJ, 1980), 130.

[212] Louis XIV, *Mémoires*, ed. Cornette, 'instructions au duc d'Anjou (1700)', no. 5, 337. See the phrase cited at the outset of this chapter: 'Do not disclose the secret to anyone. Indeed, we have strolled the earth and found no confidant.' Wittfogel, *Oriental Despotism*, 154–6, underscores the prevalence of loneliness-at-the-top but presents a more sceptical reading.

or low-ranking inner court servants could abuse the ruler's confidence, or alternatively others could take offence at the privileged position of their rivals. Moreover, spouses and children, the category expected to be included in the innermost worlds of most persons, could become vicious rivals in dynastic settings. This fundamental tension at the heart of dynastic power took very different forms, depending on patterns of reproduction and succession. These patterns are the focus of the next chapter.

2 Dynasty: reproduction and succession

Prepare as you may against those who hate you, calamity will come to you from those you love.

Han Fei Tzu, 'Precautions within the palace', Basic Writings,
trans. Burton Watson (New York, 1964), 86.

He should guard against princes right from their birth. For princes devour their begetters.

'Guarding against Princes', The Kauṭilīya Arthaśāstra,
ed. R.P. Kangle, 3 vols. (Bombay, 1960–5), II, 44.

One obedient slave is better than three hundred sons; for the latter desire their father's death, the former his master's glory.

Anonymous poet quoted in Niẓam al-Mulk, The Book of Government or Rules
for Kings, ed. Hubert Darke (New York, 1960), chap. XXVII, 117.

Descent and rivalry

Texts outlining the duties of rulership include women only marginally, yet the practice of dynastic power shows women in a variety of commanding positions. These same texts convey ideals of harmony, justice, and protection of the weak, while at the heart of dynastic power violent competition was endemic. This chapter on reproduction and succession redresses the balance by shifting attention to women and conflicts among royals.

Rights or expectations of succession engendered tensions between fathers and sons, between ruling kings and their brothers, and more generally among all scions of the dynasty eligible for the throne. At the same time, relatives held high positions at court and in the country at large, served as regional chiefs or governors, commanded armies, and on occasion replaced the king in ritual performances. Members of the dynastic clan were eager to protect the institution of kingship as well as the birthright of their family: these were emphatically shared interests. Kings who founded their authority on descent and royal blood needed to accommodate their siblings; only rarely did they relegate them without further ado to the margins of society. Once in open conflict, kings could not shed royal blood with impunity, but they found alternative ways to silence their proximate rivals.[1] A potential for conflict was always present, particularly among the males at the heart of any dynasty. Dynastic power carried within itself a permanent invitation to violence.

Reproduction entails a series of choices and conventions. Any elite family aspiring to transfer its wealth and status to a next generation is faced by a dilemma. Its first imperative is to secure continuity by generating offspring. However, while numerous children may help to prevent extinction, they undermine a second goal: maintaining wealth and rank. Depending on the laws of inheritance, all children might expect a share of the family property: large families bring a risk of social demotion. Hereditary succession to high office exacerbates the problems that occur with inheritance of wealth and status.[2] Without relatives eligible for the throne, the dynasty is doomed; with numerous competitors for the throne, succession strife becomes likely. Division of sovereign rights could help to ensure a peaceful transition, but it causes fragmentation and entails a risk of conflict among the successor states. Male primogeniture, granting most rights and possessions to the first-born son, emerged in many European as well as in Han Chinese dynasties as the preferred solution. While it helped keep intact the territory held by the dynasty, it hardly removed conflict.

The physical reality of procreation and the cultural notion of dynasty do not neatly overlap. Dynasties are cultural constructs, based on a series of conventions regarding reproduction and eligibility for the throne. These constructs can differ fundamentally by stressing descent either in the male or in the female line, by opting for fixed rules such as male primogeniture, or by adhering to open and competitive patterns of succession. The following examination will show that dynasty cannot be equated with the practice of male primogeniture alone. Open and circulating forms of succession engendered violent changeovers, but left more room for merit and personal qualification. Many dynasties viewed their power in terms of a special quality or charisma that needed to be demonstrated and hence could not be fixed in advance. Moreover, no system of

[1] On conflict as well as on the prohibition against shedding royal blood, see Audrey I. Richards, 'African kings and their royal relatives', *Journal of the Royal Anthropological Institute of Great Britain and Ireland*, 91/2 (1961), 135–50; Ágoston and Masters (eds.), *Encyclopedia of the Ottoman Empire*, 274; Edna G. Bay, 'Servitude and worldly success in the palace of Dahomey', in Claire Robertson and Martin Klein (eds.), *Women and Slavery in Africa* (Madison, WI, 1983), 340–67, at 363 on king Tegbesu selling his unruly half-brothers as slaves. For variants of the 'gilded cage' metaphor, see the last section of this chapter below.

[2] See Jack Goody, 'Sideways or downwards? Lateral and vertical succession, inheritance and descent in Africa and Eurasia', *Man*, 5/4 (1970), 627–38, at 628 on the difference between succession and inheritance.

dynastic reproduction and succession ever steadily conformed to its own rules: dynastic history shows an endless series of ad hoc solutions to secure continuity in the absence of acceptable successors.[3] The survival of dynasties was often contingent on incorporating outsiders – adopting collaterals or even outsiders, temporarily empowering women, legitimising bastards. Immediately, however, such mishaps tended to be covered by genealogical fabrications. Dynastic succession always entailed a blend of demographic realities and ideological representations.

The role of women in dynastic power arrangements, almost wholly absent in the literary legacies of Asia and Europe, needs to be considered at length here. Women rarely acted only as passive vehicles of reproduction or as disinterested outsiders in succession conflicts. Even in dynasties based entirely on the notion of a male bloodline, women played marked roles. Mothers of potential successors exercised considerable influence in phases of transition; consorts created and consolidated ties with local or external elites. Outside of Christian Europe, polygyny was the rule in dynastic reproduction. The relatives of these multiple consorts became stakeholders in the dynastic venture. Yet at the same time, polygyny exacerbated succession conflict, with mothers defending their sons' claims. Everywhere, the exchange of sisters and daughters created networks of maternal affiliation that formed an alternative for the contentious relationships among males within the dynasty and could safeguard succession when no males were available. Matrilineal forms of descent, finally, entailed patterns of rule that contradict many characteristics commonly attributed to dynasty. This chapter approaches the pervasive conflicts over succession by examining the place of women in dynastic rule before turning to other variables determining the conditions of dynastic strife and solidarity among royals.

Women as rulers, royals, and affines

The literary traditions of rulership discussed in the first chapter sometimes include women who moved beyond their ascribed role as loyal, chaste, and devout spouses. The mother ruling temporarily as regent to bridge the gap between the reigns of two males was accepted with only minor misgivings, as long as she adopted a self-effacing attitude. The wife or concubine acting as the power behind the throne, abusing the weakness

---

[3] Robbins Burling, *The Passage of Power: Studies in Political Succession* (New York and London, 1974), includes case studies ranging from Africa and Asia to Europe and Latin America, covering early modern and contemporary examples. Burling stresses that succession rules tend to change and that in practice even these changing rules were often disregarded.

or infatuation of a male ruler, recurs as the cliché of the wicked woman transgressing time-honoured moral boundaries. Women, by definition present in a restricted sphere around the male ruler, were regarded with suspicion by outer court advisors who enjoyed only limited access. Consorts, these men feared, could bring a weak ruler under their control, undoing the advisors' counsel. Hence the histories these learned males compiled tend to convey wariness about inner court machinations, deploring female cunning and ambition. Finally, women could be hesitantly accepted as rulers in their own right, though usually only as a second choice, when no male successors were available. In any case, female power more often gave rise to caveats than to approval.

Incidental examples of ruling women can be given from many times and places, famously including Egypt, Nubia, and Hellenistic successor-states of Alexander the Great, as well as early modern England and Russia. However, the institutionalised succession of ruling women on the throne remains a rare exception.[4] In China only Empress Wu Zetian (624–690–705) ruled formally, although in a brief interlude after her death there seemed to be a chance of continued female rule. Wu Zetian's son, ruling as the Zhongzong emperor, was almost convinced by his empress Wei to appoint their daughter as heir-apparent – an act unprecedented in Chinese imperial history. However, within a few years

---

[4] Guida M. Jackson, *Women Rulers Throughout the Ages: An Illustrated Guide* (Santa Barbara, CA, 1999), lists numerous women, but doesn't differentiate between regencies of dowagers and women ruling as sovereigns in their own right. Her overview of regions and names shows few cases of regular succession from queen to queen. On traditions of ruling and fighting women, see Antonia Fraser, *The Warrior Queens: Boadicea's Chariot* (London, 2011); Marcus, 'Breaking the glass ceiling'; Beverly Mack, 'Royal wives in Kano', in Catherine Coles and Beverly Mack (eds.), *Hausa Women in the Twentieth Century* (Madison, WI, 1991), 109–29. On Ethiopian queens, powerful as regents more than as sovereign rulers, see Claire Bosc-Tiessé, '"How beautiful she is!" in her mirror: polysemic images and reflections of power of an eighteenth-century Ethiopia queen', *Journal of Early Modern History*, 8/3 (2004), 294–318, and in the same volume Hervé Pennec and Dimitri Toubkis, 'Reflections on the notions of "empire" and "kingdom" in seventeenth-century Ethiopia: royal power and local power', 229–58. See comments and interesting cases of queenship in an Islamic context in Farhad Daftary, 'Sayyida Hurra: the Ismāʿīlī Sulayhid queen of Yemen', in Gavin R.G. Hambly (ed.), *Women in the Medieval Islamic World: Power, Patronage, and Piety* (New York, 1998), 117–30; Stefan Amirell, 'The blessings and perils of female rule: new perspectives on the reigning queens of Patani, c. 1584–1718', *Journal of Southeast Asian Studies*, 42/2 (2011), 303–23; the introductory passages in McMahon, *Women Shall Not Rule*, 1–18. On the sole brief reign of a woman on the throne in the Delhi sultanate, Raziya Sultan (1236–1240), see the description in Farhat Jahan, 'Depiction of women in the sources of the Delhi sultanate (1206–1388)' PhD thesis, Aligarh Muslim University (2012), chap. 1. For an example of female rule in South India, see Lennart Bes, 'Toddlers, widows, and bastards enthroned: dynastic successions in early-modern South India as observed by the Dutch', *Leidschrift*, 27/1 (2012), 121–34. On Queen Suhita of Majapahit (1429–47), see J. Noorduyn, 'Majapahit in the fifteenth century', *Bijdragen Tot de Taal-, Land- En Volkenkunde*, 134/2 (1978), 207–74.

the situation had reverted to male imperial rule.[5] Wu Zetian would become a powerful negative cliché in didactic works produced by Confucian literati. More than a century after her rule, when eunuchs suggested to dowager empress Guo that she rule instead of her minor son, the dowager empress allegedly replied: 'Are you saying that I should become another Empress Wu? . . . Since ancient times, when has a woman ever ruled the world and established order like Yao and Shun?'[6] With few exceptions, powerful women in imperial China would henceforth cloak their ambition in explicit or implicit disavowal of Wu Zetian. Only in conquest dynasties and among nomadic peoples bordering China can female rule be found untainted by an air of impropriety and meddling.[7]

A somewhat longer phase of ruling women occurred in Silla Korea, with two queens in the seventh and another in the ninth century. The experiment remained without sequel and was condemned as an aberration by later Confucian scholars.[8] Another polity in close contact with Tang China, late Yamato and early Nara Japan, experienced a protracted phase with an exceptional presence of women on the throne. Empress Suiko (554–593–628) was the first sovereign of Japan to be styled *tenno* (emperor). Between 593 and 770 six empresses and eight emperors ruled Japan, two of these empresses reigning twice, returning to the throne after abdicating. Women ruled as many years as men in this period. The reign of Empress Jito (686–97) preceded the reign of Wu Zetian in China, and the Japanese example of female rule may have had an impact.[9] Chinese sources referred to Japan sometimes as *Nüwangguo*, kingdom of women rulers.[10] The women traditionally included among the legendary rulers of early Japan may actually have existed, paving the way for the first empresses whose reigns we can establish with certainty. However, the increasing impact of Confucianism pushed Japan towards a more limited patrilineal definition of rulership and succession, leaving no room for open female power. Only under the Tokugawa shogunate almost a

---

[5] McMahon, *Women Shall Not Rule*, 190–200, and his 'Women rulers in imperial China', *Nannü: Men, Women and Gender in Early and Imperial China*, 15/2 (2013), 179–218, kindly given to me by the author before publication. On contemporary empresses in Japan and queens in Silla Korea, see Jennifer W. Jay, 'Imagining matriarchy: "kingdoms of women" in Tang China', *Journal of the American Oriental Society*, 116/2 (1996), 220–9.

[6] Cited from two different texts in McMahon, 'Women rulers in imperial China'; see similar instances of women citing Empress Wu as a negative example in McMahon, *Women Shall Not Rule*, 226–8, 244–5.

[7] On female rule among the Khitan Liao, see Bruno De Nicola, 'Unveiling the Khatuns: some aspects of the role of women in the Mongol empire', PhD thesis, University of Cambridge (2011), 64–7, referring to Karl Wittfogel, and to F. Chia-Sheng, *History of Chinese Society: Liao (907–1225)* (Philadelphia, PA, 1949).

[8] Jay, 'Imagining matriarchy', 227.   [9] Shillony, *Enigma of the Emperors*, 23–56.

[10] Jay, 'Imagining matriarchy', 224.

millennium later do we again find two empresses. Their reigns, under the tutelage of the shogun, can be related to the revival of Shinto practices and attitudes.[11]

Two sultanates in Southeast Asia experienced a succession of female rulers: four *sultanas* ruled in Aceh (1641–99), seven in Patani (1584–1718). In both cases succession rules were relatively open; fights among male contenders eliminated candidates and opened the way to the women within the dynasty. A Chinese source describes the causes for the rise of the previous king's daughter Raja Ijau (?–1584–1616) to the throne of Patani: 'As he [the late king] was without a son, his relatives all fought for the throne, and there were killings all over the country until there was none of the relatives left. Thus, they enthroned a female chief as queen.'[12] In Aceh, Sultan Iskandar Muda (1583?–1607–1636) had his only son and successor murdered shortly before his own death in 1636. His son-in-law Sultan Iskandar Thani succeeded, but this hostage-prince from the conquered Malay sultanate of Pahang soon died. In 1641, his wife Sultana Taj al-Alam Safiyyat al-Din (?–1641–1675) ascended to the throne, starting the longest reign in seventeenth-century Aceh.[13] The strength and moderation of these first sultanas then convinced local elites that this experiment was to their advantage. However, chastity was seen as a necessary element in the queens' conduct: the absence of progeny complicated succession and may have hastened the return to male rule.[14]

Noteworthy examples of prolonged female rule can be found in Africa. The Ethiopian Solomonic dynasty, claiming descent from the mythical 'queen of Sheba', did not allow women on the throne. Nevertheless, after

---

[11] Shillony, *Enigma of the Emperors*, 23–56, 98–100. On the early phase, see Chizuko Allen, 'Empress Jingu: a shamaness ruler in early Japan', *Japan Forum*, 15/1 (2003), 81–98. On the preoccupation with succession, see Ross Bender, 'Auspicious omens in the reign of the last empress of Nara Japan, 749–70', *Japanese Journal of Religious Studies*, 40/1 (2013), 45–76.

[12] Amirell, 'Blessings and perils', 307.

[13] Leonard Y. Andaya, '"A very good-natured but awe-inspiring government": the reign of a successful queen in seventeenth-century Aceh', in Elsbeth Locher-Scholten and P.J. A.N. Rietbergen (eds.), *Hof en Handel: Aziatische vorsten en de VOC 1620–1720* (Leiden, 2004), 59–84, at 63–5; Sher Banu A.L. Khan, 'The sultanahs of Aceh 1641–1699', in Arndt Graf et al. (eds.), *Aceh: History, Politics and Culture* (Singapore, 2010), 3–25; Khan, 'Rule behind the silk curtain: the sultanahs of Aceh 1641–1699', PhD thesis, Queen Mary, University of London (2009), https://qmro.qmul.ac.uk/jspui/handle/123456789/1471 (accessed 1 February 2014).

[14] See also Andaya, *Flaming Womb*; Peter Carey and Vincent Houben, 'Spirited Srikandhis and sly Sumbadras: the social, political and economic role of women at the central Javanese courts in the 18th and early 19th centuries', in Elsbeth Locher-Scholten and Anke Niehof (eds.), *Indonesian Women in Focus* (Dordrecht and Providence, RI, 1987), 12–42; on competing consorts in Southeast Asia, see Michael Adas, '"Moral economy" or "contest state"? Elite demands and the origins of peasant protest in Southeast Asia', *Journal of Social History*, 13 (1980), 521–46.

the death of Emperor Bakaffa (?–1721–1730), dowager empress
Mentewwab ('how beautiful' in Amharic) took power in the name of
her son Iyasu II (1724–1730–1755), and continued ruling after the ascent
of her infant grandson Iyoas (?–1755–1769).[15] Mentewwab was powerful, but ruled in the name of her male offspring. In the kingdom of Kongo
women likewise were important as regents for male rulers, yet they also
served as heads of descent groups, as intermediaries between male factions, and as patrons of religion. In the second half of the seventeenth
century, a sequence of women openly wielded power, though not as fully
sovereign rulers. Moreover, a dependency of Kongo, the kingdom of
Ndongo-Matamba, was 'always ruled by women', a European observer
noted in the 1760s.[16] Queen Njinga (1583–1624–1663) started out as
regent for her deceased brother's son (Plate 10). Soon, she eliminated the
boy and ruled in her own right, a move that saddled her with a lifelong
burden of seeking legitimacy for her female usurpation, unwarranted by
tradition. Njinga tried a variety of expedients to cope 'with the barrier of
her female sex'.[17] First she copied male polygyny by adopting polyandry,
a habit apparently not uncommon among powerful women in Kongo.[18]
Later, she herself decided to 'become a man', turning her male followers
into concubines, requiring them to dress as women and to live among the
palace maids without touching them. She henceforth led her armies
personally in battle, showing remarkable dexterity. Njinga's efforts were
barely sufficient to bolster her authority, but they set a precedent. Now,
female power had apparently become acceptable: in the century following
her death, five queens ruled for eighty years, leaving only two decades
under male rule.[19] Perhaps the most enduring instance of institutionalised female succession can be found in South Africa, where the Lovedu
queen Modjadji's ability to produce rain for her people (or withhold it
from enemies) created the basis for a relatively stable pattern of female
primogeniture lasting from 1800 into the twenty-first century. The
Lovedu Modjadji was seen as masculine and received numerous women
as 'consorts' from her subjects. Her ritual and social pre-eminence did not
extend to military or narrowly political leadership. Among several

[15] On Mentewwab, see Remedius Prutky, *Prutky's Travels in Ethiopia and Other Countries*,
trans. and ed. J.H. Arrowsmith-Brown (London, 1991), 161–3, 170; Bosc-Tiessé, 'How
beautiful she is'. Mentewwab is pictured on the cover of this book, with her boy-son Iyasu
II in 1730.

[16] John K. Thornton, 'Elite women in the kingdom of Kongo: historical perspectives on
women's political power', *Journal of African History*, 47/3 (2006), 437–60, at 459;
Thornton, 'Legitimacy and political power: Queen Njinga, 1624–1663', *Journal of
African History*, 32/1 (1991), 25–40.

[17] Thornton, 'Queen Njinga', 39.   [18] Ibid., 39.   [19] Ibid., 38–40.

neighbouring tribes, queenship seems to have been adopted in response to the conspicuous success and popularity of the rain-queen.[20]

In France and in the Holy Roman Empire, the 'Salic Law' prevented women from ascending to the throne. This law, dating from the early Frankish kings and elaborated under the Merovingians and Carolingians, was rediscovered in the late fourteenth century and tailored to fit the arguments of authors defending France against English claims. In adapted form, it would later serve as a general argument against female rule.[21] These sentiments existed elsewhere, but they rarely hardened into fixed rules: numerous queens regnant can be found in Europe. Their reigns were not necessarily seen in negative terms, but female succession occurred only as a makeshift solution in the absence of males. The consecutive reigns of two queens in sixteenth-century England and the four empresses ruling in eighteenth-century Russia, interrupted by short reigns of ineffective tsars, reflected persistent dynastic crisis rather than the wholehearted acceptance of female power.

'Virgin queen' Elizabeth I of England (1533–1558–1603; Plate 11), Christina of Sweden (1626–1632–1654*), and Elizabeth of Russia (1709–1741–1762) remained unmarried and without issue, a condition matching that of many other 'chaste' ruling queens across the world. Some contemporary observers reasoned that by adopting typically male attitudes and responsibilities, female rulers forsook their fertility.[22] Moreover, it was feared that their male partners, by definition outside the royal bloodline and often found in distant countries, would dominate their wives and by extension their realms. Many Englishmen, particularly Protestants, had grave doubts about Mary Tudor's marriage to Philip II of Spain. Marriage was risky, but chastity did not offer a solution; female rule without progeny necessarily ended in succession crisis. Chastity did not become a general pattern for women on the throne. Tsaritsa Elizabeth's successor Catherine II (1729–1762–1796), who took over the reins of government after arranging a coup against her unlucky husband Peter III, engaged in a long series of amorous adventures preceding and following the birth of her son and successor Paul in 1754. Maria Theresa of Austria (1717–1740–1780) conspicuously cultivated family life with her husband Francis-Stephen and bore him sixteen children.

[20] On the rain-queen, see Krige and Krige, *Realm of a Rain-Queen*; Lebeuf, 'La rôle de la femme'; Luc de Heusch, 'Forms of sacralized power in Africa', in Quigley (ed.), *Character of Kingship*, 25–37 at 26–7.

[21] See recently C. Taylor, 'The Salic Law, French queenship, and the defense of women in the late Middle Ages', *French Historical Studies*, 29/4 (2006), 543–64; Sarah Hanley, 'The Salic Law', in Christine Fauré (ed.), *Political and Historical Encyclopedia of Women* (New York, 2013), 2–17.

[22] Richards, 'To promote a woman to beare rule'.

Overall, we can conclude that women held full sovereign power mostly when the dynasty could not provide males for the throne.[23] They rose to power on the basis of their pedigree, as an interim solution safeguarding dynastic continuity. Most often the throne reverted to male successors in one generation. However, once women were able to rise to power despite the dominant prejudice, we can find a recurring tendency towards continuation and imitation. This will have depended in part on the example and agency of the women on the throne, but a measure of acceptance and adjustment among the ruling elites must also have played a role: female rule appears to be clustered in time and place.

Far more often than ruling as the sole sovereign, women held separate responsibilities complementing or counterbalancing those of a male ruler. In Africa, where succession and inheritance tended to follow a pattern of 'homogeneous transmission' from males to males and females to females, leadership, too, could be defined in separate male and female compartments.[24] Next to male chiefs stood female leaders with their own ritual and political responsibilities, transmitted after their death to a succeeding generation of women. The queen mother (see Plate 12), a label commonly given to senior female office-holders but hiding a great variety of titles and statuses, was important in numerous African polities. The queen mother was not necessarily the ruler's actual birth mother: she represented motherhood both for the king and for his peoples, helping to establish harmony and concord – a key responsibility of kingship. An essential counterpart to the king leading the male conquest clan, the *kpojito* of West African Dahomey represented the women, the conquered, and the commoners. She was the king's ally or reign-mate, but not his mother; neither was she the king's sexual partner, nor did she give birth to successors. The *kpojito* often came from outlying or recently conquered regions of the kingdom, attaching them to the centre of power and replicating ritually the legendary first conquest in which the 'Leopard King' mated with a local woman. Moreover, the commoner or slave origin of the *kpojito* and her distant provenance made her a staunch ally of the king, as she had no other connections at court.[25] The court of the Leopard King was populated by thousands of women, many of them

---

[23] Noorduyn, 'Majapahit in the fifteenth century', 269, underlines that Queen Suhita (1429–47) rather than her younger brother succeeded; apparently here age preference overruled gender preference.

[24] Goody, 'Sideways or downwards', 627.

[25] Edna G. Bay, *Wives of the Leopard: Gender, Politics, and Culture in the Kingdom of Dahomey* (Charlottesville, VA, and London, 1998); Bay, 'Belief, legitimacy and the kpojito: an institutional history of the "queen mother" in precolonial Dahomey', *Journal of African History*, 36/1 (1995), 1–27. I wish to express my thanks to the author, who patiently answered my questions on these issues.

holding 'inner' offices that matched 'outer' offices held by men outside of the palace.[26]

Among the Asante, living somewhat further to the west, the king (*asantehene*) ruled jointly with the queen mother (*asantehemaa*). The asantehemaa had her own palace and staff, and held legal as well as ritual responsibilities. No *asantehene* could be nominated without the concurrence of the asantehemaa, and the same held true vice versa. The system of parallel male and female 'stools' (thrones) continued at regional and local levels in the Asante kingdom.[27] In addition to the queen mother, usually positioned a generation above the king, a queen sister of his own generation could play a role, as well as spouses or concubines of less exalted standing. Female dignitaries, present in many African kingdoms, were a potent force in succession. European traders and missionaries focusing on males in positions of authority sometimes failed to grasp the relevance of these women. In colonial times the female dimension of traditional power increasingly fell into abeyance; it was not perceived by colonial administrators or they may have feared it would unnecessarily encumber the elaborate double structure of colonial and 'native' government.[28] The principle of 'dual-sex' power structures, no exception in Africa, can also be found in other regions. Polynesian, Andean-Inca, and Egyptian polities share traits of dual forms of kinship and authority.[29] In these cases, the ideal of uncontaminated royal descent sometimes stipulated incestuous marriage practices within the dynastic clan, coinciding with a shared responsibility for government or separate prerogatives for dynastic men and women.[30]

[26] Bay, *Wives of the Leopard*, 11; Richard F. Burton, 'The present state of Dahome', *Transactions of the Ethnological Society of London*, 3 (1865), 400–8, at 405; see also Lynne Larsen, 'City of women: gendered space in the pre-colonial palace of Dahomey', *University of Toronto Art Journal*, 2 (2009), 1–11.

[27] Stoeltje, 'Asante queen mothers', and this entire volume 810 of *Annals of the New York Academy of Sciences*, 'Queens, queen mothers, priestesses and power: case studies in African gender'; Lebeuf, 'La rôle de la femme'.

[28] Stoeltje, 'Asante queen mothers', 44–5 and notes; Lebeuf, 'La rôle de la femme'.

[29] Yaya, *Two Faces of Inca History*; Valerio Valeri, 'Le fonctionnement du système des rangs à Hawaii', *L'Homme*, 12/1 (1972), 29–66; R. Alan Covey, 'Chronology, succession, and sovereignty: the politics of Inka historiography and its modern interpretation', *Comparative Studies in Society and History*, 48/1 (2006), 169–99.

[30] See general discussion in Berghe and Mesher, 'Royal incest and inclusive fitness'; Ray H. Bixler, 'Comment on the incidence and purpose of royal sibling incest', *American Ethnologist*, 9/3 (1982), 580–2; Bixler, 'Sibling incest in the royal families of Egypt, Peru, and Hawaii', *Journal of Sex Research*, 18/3 (1982), 264–81; Walter Scheidel, 'Brother-sister and parent–child marriage outside royal families in ancient Egypt and Iran: a challenge to the sociobiological view of incest avoidance?', *Ethology and Sociobiology*, 17/5 (1996), 319–40; more empirical assessments in Maria Rostworowski de Diez Canseco and John V. Murra, 'Succession, coöption to kingship, and royal incest among the Inca', *Southwestern Journal of Anthropology*, 16/4 (1960), 417–27; Yaya, *Two*

European and Asian consorts and dowagers could be key players in the absence of a mature male ruler, yet they rarely matched the established position of women in polities organised along dual lines. This can be related to the patrilineal practice dominant in Eurasian dynasties. It is easy to forget that an important minority of polities on a global scale was organised according to matrilineal principles of descent. The Akan peoples of Ghana, the Asante among them, traditionally viewed descent in matrilineal terms. A 'matrilineal belt' stretches from the Niger-Congo area in West Africa to Zambia in the southeast, reflecting the eastward migration of Bantu peoples.[31] Outside Africa, matrilineal influence was strongly present in the 'Malayo-Polynesian world' from Madagascar to Southeast Asia and West India.[32] Dynasties based on matrilineal descent accepted only the blood of women as transmitting royalty, although they more often than not preferred male over female rule. Audrey Richards describes the perspective of the Bemba people living in what is now northeastern Zimbabwe:

Among the Bemba it is believed that a child is made from the blood of a woman which she is able to transmit to her male and female children. A man can possess this blood in his veins, but cannot pass it on to his children, who belong to a different clan. Physiological paternity is recognized. Children are often described as being like their fathers, and are expected to give the latter affection and respect although they have no legal obligations to them under the matrilineal system. "We take our fathers' presents because they begot us", they say. But it is nevertheless the physical continuity of the mother's line of ancestors which is the basis of legal identification with her descent group. A Royal princess might even produce an heir by a slave father in the old days without lowering her child's prestige. The relationship between brother and sister, which is a very close one, legally and ritually, is based on the fact that the two were born from one womb, and in the case of the royal family it appears to be equally strong when the children are of different fathers. These theories of procreation account, not only for the matrilineal descent of the Bemba, on which succession to chieftainship is based, but also for the rank accorded to the royal princesses as mothers of chiefs, and the headmanships and other positions of authority given them.[33]

Faces of Inca History; Sheila L. Ager, 'Familiarity breeds: incest and the Ptolemaic dynasty', *Journal of Hellenic Studies*, 125 (2005), 1–34.

[31] See a discussion of matrilineal descent and Bantu migration in Malcolm Ruel, 'The structural articulation of generations in Africa', *Cahiers d'études africaines*, 165/1 (2002), 51–82. In general on matrilineal descent, see David Murray Schneider and Kathleen Gough, *Matrilineal Kinship* (Berkeley, CA, 1962), with a comparative analysis by David Aberle at 655–27 underlining the link between matrilineal kinship and horticulture, and its tendency to disappear with the emergence of plough agriculture.

[32] Paul Ottino, 'Ancient Malagasy dynastic succession: the Merina example', *History in Africa*, 10 (1983), 247–92, at 254; see also Yaya, *Two Faces of Inca History*, on matrilineal or double descent.

[33] Richards, 'The political system of the Bemba tribe – north-eastern Rhodesia', in Fortes and Evans-Pritchard (eds.), *African Political Systems*, 83–120, at 96–7; see also Stoeltje, 'Asante queen mothers', 53, on the view of female blood among the matrilineal West

Matrilineal descent breaks open the idea of dynasty in various ways. The closest male relationship within the matrilineal clan is not the connection between father and son, but between the sister's son and his maternal uncle. Succession more often proceeded first 'sideways' to uterine brothers, then 'downwards' to sister's sons. However, kings' sons were not always easily sidestepped, and their ambitions could complicate matters.[34] Matrilineal succession tends to be more diffuse and inclusive, attaching more groups to the dynastic enterprise through circulating or rotating forms of succession. While this pattern is also possible in patrilineal succession, 'downwards' succession to the next generation, to the king's sons, tends to be stronger there.[35] The matrilineal Asante recognised only the children of royal princesses as eligible for the position of *asantehene*. The king's sons were not eligible for succession, and hence less tension could be expected to arise between the king and his male offspring.[36] Sisters' children, often relatively carefree affiliates in patrilineal systems, now turned into competitors for high office. Most polities shaped by matrilineal descent were still strongly disposed to favour male authority; in combination with the common practice of exogamy, marrying outside of one's own group, this created an awkward puzzle. If the woman left her group to marry, her matrilineal clan would lose control over her children; if women stayed put and let the males move to other villages, brothers moved to places where they enjoyed no rights of inheritance or succession.[37] A variety of solutions emerged for this problem; most matrilineal societies tended to make room in one way or another for patrilineal descent – a statement equally true in the opposite direction.

Matrilineal descent had major consequences for dynastic reproduction. Polyandry could be practised, but it did not increase the number of births for any single female scion of the dynasty. How did high-ranking women representing the dynasty and responsible for its continuation select the

African Akan in general and the Asante in particular. On ideas about reproduction, see Clara Pinto Correia, *The Ovary of Eve: Egg and Sperm and Preformation* (Chicago, IL, 1998).

[34] Richards, 'African kings', 141.

[35] See tables in Goody, 'Sideways or downwards'. On matrilineality and its consequences in Congo, see Georges Balandier, *Le royaume de Kongo du XVIe au XVIIIe siècle* (Paris, 2009), 180–1.

[36] Meyer Fortes, 'Kinship and marriage among the Ashanti', in A.R. Radcliffe-Brown and D. Forde (eds.), *African Systems of Kinship and Marriage* (London, 1950), 252–84, at 269, stressing the alliance between fathers and their sons; Wilks, *Asante in the Nineteenth Century: The Structure and Evolution of a Political Order* (Cambridge, 1989), xxxix and 365, pointing to the offices held by the princes.

[37] See the classic passage on the puzzle in A.I. Richards, 'Some types of family structure amongst the Central Bantu' in Radcliffe-Brown and Forde (eds.), *African Systems of Kinship and Marriage*, 246–51.

fathers of their children? Their fertility was of the utmost importance, whereas the identity of the fathers mattered only in a negative way. Clearly identifiable high-ranking fathers were a liability because they might claim rights on the basis of their paternity. Interestingly, Bemba princesses, often themselves chiefs of villages, engaged in an active sex life, in sharp contrast to accepted social norms. Their promiscuity made it impossible for males to unequivocally claim paternity.[38] For the *asantehemaa*, divorce and remarriage were not uncommon, and 'Unlike every other woman, when a queen mother is married, she is not bound to her husband exclusively, and if she is not married, it is expected that she will have male friends.'[39] The Lovedu rain-queen, a woman holding masculine status, bore her successor, but she obscured the identity of her sex partners – conspicuous fatherhood was unwelcome in this patrilineal society governed by a queen.[40]

The position of princesses in patrilineal systems was characterised by a tension between their high birth rank and the common subservience expected of women in their relationships with men. Princesses of the Nilotic Shilluk could not marry: unions with their male relatives were considered incestuous, whereas common men were deemed inappropriate because of their low rank. In consequence a princess was allowed 'to select lovers as she chooses', while pregnancies were not accepted and had dire consequences for both partners.[41] In Dahomey, 'a princess was socially male', and the daughters of the Leopard King were known for their promiscuity. Men complained: 'Royalty is capable of anything … A princess will always betray you. Royalty has no morals, no ethics. They lie and cheat. All things are permitted to them.'[42] While the clash between birth and gender hierarchies complicated the lives of patrilineal princesses across the globe in various forms, they did not usually remain single. The marriage of princesses was complicated by their high rank: either they had only a very limited reservoir of marriage partners, or they faced 'hypogamy', marriage below their rank. This could be averted by refraining from marriage, for example by taking religious vows. Conversely, 'hypergamy', the 'upward marriage' of women, could be accepted more easily in patrilineal systems: male rank was maintained and the female alliance could bring material

---

[38] Richards, Political system of the Bemba tribe', 93.
[39] Stoeltje, 'Asante queen mothers', 59–60.
[40] Krige and Krige, *Realm of a Rain-Queen*, 173.
[41] C. G. Seligmann, 'Some aspects of the Hamitic problem in the Anglo-Egyptian Sudan', *Journal of the Royal Anthropological Institute of Great Britain and Ireland*, 43 (1913), 593–705, at 652, also mentioning the sexual licence of Baganda princesses.
[42] Bay, *Wives of the Leopard*, first quotation at 52, second at 245–7; Bay notes that this reputation reflected a change in marriage habits of princesses, shifting from dynastic alliances to local office-holders, and may also have been influenced by an increasing tendency to control (and complain about) female sexuality.

benefits and interesting connections. These gender labels were reversed in matrilineal systems. Any ruling house, whether it defined itself in matrilineal, patrilineal, or mixed terms, needed to conclude alliances with other groups to secure its continuity. The affiliations of dynasties were as important as their genealogy. Asante royal marriages show how matrilineal descent could go together with the formation of male royal houses. The sons of the ruling king, never eligible for the throne, frequently married women from the royal descent line. Sons born out of these unions could in principle ascend to the throne on the basis of their matrilineal descent. The *asantehene* maintained friendly relations with his sons, who were no competitors for the throne; at the same time he could hope for the enthronement of one of his grandsons. This practice led to the alternation of two male houses on the Asante throne.[43] Clearly an examination of marriage strategies is needed to find out social practice beyond genealogies. Whence did dynasties take their brides or concubines, and where did they find marriage partners for their princesses?[44]

European dynasties and nobilities formed a web of marriage and descent that can be pictured effectively only when affiliations and female connections are included. Michaela Hohkamp observes that 'if the gaze is shifted away from the male ego at the center of kinship events, then it becomes possible to detect horizontal kinship networks whose nodes are frequently formed by female relations, such as daughters, sisters, and aunts'.[45] While royalty and high noble families in Europe increasingly relied on male primogeniture, they adopted flexible policies when their house was at stake, relying on their daughters as well as on more distant female relatives to secure continuity of titles and wealth. In medieval Europe, noble families within a realm could hope to marry a daughter to a prince of their ruling house; marriages among the great sovereign houses had become the norm by the sixteenth century. Only Russian tsars still tended to marry among the upper layers of nobility until *c.* 1700.[46] A provisional hierarchy of sovereign houses was listed by Pope Julius II's master of ceremonies in 1504 to define the seating order in the papal chapel, serving as a starting point for endless adaptations and

---

[43] Wilks, *Asante in the Nineteenth Century*, 329, underlining marriages of *asantehene*'s sons or *ahenemma* with women of the royal line, opening the way to the throne for grandsons of kings; see also T.C. McCaskie, 'Office, land and subjects in the history of the Manwere Fekuo of Kumase: an essay in the political economy of the Asante state', *Journal of African History*, 21/2 (1980), 189–208, at 199.

[44] This holds true for princes as well, but as they usually enjoyed a right in succession too, their alliances will be discussed in the second part of this chapter.

[45] Hohkamp, 'Transdynasticism', 94.

[46] Russell Martin, *A Bride for the Tsar: Bride-Shows and Marriage Politics in Early Modern Russia* (DeKalb, IL, 2012).

contestations.[47] The list defined hierarchy primarily on the basis of pedi-gree and dignity, but it was subject to permanent fluctuations caused by shifts in the wealth and power of states. Rich social climbers such as the Medici of Florence found their way into royal and imperial dynasties; in the course of the seventeenth century the upstart Dutch Republic, on the basis of its wealth and military power, was granted full regal honours (*honores regii*), including the right to send ambassadors to Europe's main courts.

In this hierarchy, women often represented the connection with rival houses. Princesses travelled long distances to join the courts of their ruling husbands. Even in Vienna, where the junior Habsburg branch reigned, the arrival of a young Spanish Habsburg bride in 1666 could still cause upheaval in the city and at court, with people complaining about the 'Spanish habits' of the newly arrived empress with her house-hold and companions.[48] In the end, most major dynasties were comple-tely entangled: Louis XIV's sole legitimate son and *dauphin* of France, the product of two generations of intermarriage, was as much a Habsburg as a Bourbon.[49] Nevertheless, the dynastic union between Louis XVI and Marie-Antoinette, intended to seal the political alliance between these two traditional rivals, was never enthusiastically embraced by the French: for many the queen remained *l'autrichienne*, an object of mockery and vituperation.

Dynastic marriage was not restricted to Europe. The early Ottomans concluded marriages with Christian Byzantine princesses, Serbian royal princesses, and proximate Islamic Turkic principalities.[50] Military suc-cess drained this pool of candidates: the Ottomans gradually incorporated the territories and expelled or subjected the rulers. At the same time, a clear preference for slave concubinage developed that will be discussed below. The betrothals of the sultan's daughters (*sultanas*) followed a similar trajectory. Before the end of the fifteenth century they found marriage partners among the Anatolian princely houses gradually turning into vassals of the Ottomans. From the reign of Bayezid II onwards, sultanas increasingly wedded the upper ranks of the newly emerging *kul* (slave) office-holders. Numerous viziers and other high-ranking digni-taries of slave background now became the sultan's sons-in-law,

[47] Duindam, *Vienna and Versailles*, 185.

[48] John P. Spielman, *The City & the Crown: Vienna and the Imperial Court 1600–1740* (West Lafayette, IN, 1993), on quartering in Vienna and quarrels with the Spanish following of the new empress.

[49] H. Delacour et al., 'Louis XIV et Marie-Thérèse d'Autriche: un couple à travers le prisme de la génétique', *Immuno-analyse & biologie spécialisée*, 27/5 (2012), 272–5.

[50] Peirce, *Imperial Harem*, 29–31, 38–9.

a position that can be inferred from the term *damad* added to their names.[51] This union with the highest slave-servants of the state instituted a clear case of hypogamy for the princesses. While tying the administrative and military elites closer to the dynasty, this pattern of marital alliance had some awkward complications.[52] In the course of the seventeenth century, the marriages were typically arranged when princesses were still quite young, often under five years of age, yet their future spouses were usually greybeards already long in office. Ottoman chronicles tell stories about elderly viziers presenting child's clothing as a gift to their future spouses.[53] These men often died before the marriage could be consummated, particularly during phases of rapid turnover of high office, when disgrace, execution, and confiscation were commonplace. As a consequence of the age difference and the instability in office, princesses frequently remarried. Two daughters of Kösem Sultan (*c.* 1589–1651), favourite of Ahmed I and mother of Murad IV, married six and seven times respectively.[54] These practices came to a temporary halt in the later seventeenth century because Mehmed IV had no daughters, but they resumed in the eighteenth century. Paul Rycaut, secretary of the English embassy to the Ottoman court in the 1660s and later consul in Smyrna, lamented the fate of the *pashas* (provincial governors and viziers) marrying the sultanas. A pasha could not decline the honour to marry the sultan's kin, yet as a consequence, 'Instead of increasing power and glory, he becomes the miserablest Slave in the World to the Tyranny and Pride of an insulting Woman.'[55] The bridegroom, allowed four wives and an unrestricted number of concubines by Islamic law, now needed to do away with his other women: an Ottoman princess did not tolerate rivals or rivals' children. In addition, Rycaut noticed, princesses rarely became meek partners: 'in publick she keeps him at a distance, wears her Haniarre or Dagger by her side in token of her Superiority; and so frequently commands Gifts and Riches from him, until she hath exhausted him to the bottom of all his Wealth'.[56] Rycaut's concern for these husbands was not altogether out of place. We find examples of sultanas threatening their husbands with divorce and execution.[57] The progeny of these unions, Rycaut further argued, almost counted as outcasts: 'The children

---

[51] Ibid., 65–72.
[52] See Juliette Dumas, 'Les perles de nacre du sultanat: les princesses ottomanes (mi-XVe – mi-XVIIIe siècle', PhD thesis, École des hautes études en sciences sociales (2013), 125–94.
[53] Ibid., 143.   [54] Ibid., 142.
[55] Paul Rycaut, *The History of the Present State of the Ottoman Empire* ... (London, 1682), 132.
[56] Ibid., 134.
[57] Dumas, 'Les princesses ottomanes', examples at 111, 118, summary at 179.

of a Soltana married to a Pashaw are not capable of any office in the empire . . . They that are of this Race never dare vaunt their Pedigree, it is a contumaciousness and almost Treason to name it.'[58] The future of these children was not as bleak as Rycaut assumed: they formed an upper layer of office-holders within the state, retaining a connection with the dynasty without ever approaching the perilous honour of rights of succession. Nor were the marriages always a dismal failure. Sultan Murad IV's (1612–1623–1640) daughter Kaya Sultan married the high dignitary Melek Ahmed Pasha. The Ottoman writer Evliya Çelebi reports their happy union:

sometimes he [Melek] would have nice wrestling matches with his wife Kaya Sultan, for the propagation of the species. In the end he would overcome Kaya Sultan and bring her down. He engaged in this sort of 'greater jihad' forty-eight times a year—he did not indulge overmuch in sexual intercourse.[59]

Kaya Sultan died shortly after giving birth to her second child, leaving her husband inconsolable. Çelebi relates how the grand vizier Köprülü Mehmed Pasha responded to Melek's grief during the funeral: 'the pasha [Melek] had a falling fit over the sultana's grave and was covered with dirt. "My good man" said Köprülü, "aren't you ashamed to act like this for the sake of a woman? Don't fret over it. I'll give you another sultana. That's a promise."'[60] Melek's grief underlines that not all marriages were awkward business arrangements; the grand vizier's response, moreover, suggests that the alliance with a sultana could be attractive to high dignitaries.

In patrilineal Dahomey a remarkably similar development took place. Initially, princesses' marriages had cemented alliances with neighbouring kingdoms, but in the course of the nineteenth century Dahomean princesses married internally to high-ranking office-holders of the kingdom.[61] The king's two eldest daughters married the two highest officials; other women of the royal line were given in marriage to lesser officials. The parallel with the Ottoman situation continued at the level of the awkward position of spouses. Apparently, most Dahomean princesses actively cultivated the 'droit de cocufiage', their privilege of adultery. While their men, having been honoured by

---

[58] Rycaut, *Present State*, 131–2.

[59] Robert Dankoff, *An Ottoman Mentality: The World of Evliya Çelebi* (Leiden and Boston, MA, 2006), 121.

[60] Evliya Çelebi, *The Intimate Life of an Ottoman Statesman: Melek Ahmed Pasha (1588–1622) as Portrayed in Evliya Çelebi's Book of Travels*, ed. Robert Dankoff (Albany, NY, 1991), 234.

[61] Bay, *Wives of the Leopard*, 101, 247 (and preceding discussion, above).

receiving a royal daughter in marriage, were expected to go to great lengths to gratify their wives, they could at no point voice their exasperation to the king.[62] Children of Dahomean princesses, moreover, never joined their father's family but retained their mother's link to the royal Alladahonu clan.[63]

Safavid princesses were a force to be reckoned with in sixteenth-century Persia. They played leading roles during the temporary absence of male rulers, but also advised their governing male relatives.[64] In the sixteenth century princesses married either royal cousins or leading Qizilbash soldiers supporting the dynasty. Shah Abbas I, exasperated by the disturbances repeatedly created by the Qizilbash, redirected the alliances from the military leaders towards the religious elites. Henceforth, princesses would be given in marriage to religious notables, cementing the alliance between crown and turban.[65] The previously dominant Qizilbash were now partly replaced by slave-soldiers. Like the Ottomans, the Safavids turned primarily to elite slaves to staff the military and the administration; unlike the Ottomans, they did not accept marriages between their daughters and leaders of the new slave elite. The French jeweller and traveller Jean Chevalier de Chardin reported about the princesses: 'they are given in marriage to ecclesiastics of good family and pleasant looks; but never to a man of the sword or to a servant of the state, to prevent such men from forming plans undermining government'.[66] These ladies, Chardin stressed, were 'elevated in pride ... and of imperious humour'. He explained that the religious officials deemed suitable for marriage would get the shah's support for rapid promotion, as this reduced the uncomfortable dissonance with the princesses' prestige. Following the reign of Abbas I, the active political role of matriarchs from the patriline came to an end. The offspring of princesses, however, were in principle seen as eligible for succession. This honour, Chardin underlines, was a mixed blessing: all potential heirs to the throne

[62] Auguste le Hérissé, *L'ancien royaume du Dahomey: Moeurs, religion, histoire* (Paris, 1911), 34–5.

[63] Bay, *Wives of the Leopard*, 52.

[64] Maria Szuppe, 'La participation des femmes de la famille royale à l'exercice du pouvoir en Iran safavide au xvie siècle', *Studia Iranica*, 23/2 (1994), 211–58 (premiére partie), and 24/2 (1995), 61–122 (seconde partie); Shohreh Gholsorkhi, 'Pari Khan Khanum: a masterful Safavid princess', *Iranian Studies*, 28/3–4 (1995), 143–56; De Nicola, 'Unveiling the Khatuns', on the Mongol and Ilkhanid antecedents of women in Persia.

[65] Kathryn Babayan, *Mystics, Monarchs, and Messiahs: Cultural Landscapes of Early Modern Iran* (Cambridge, MA, 2002), 382; Babaie et al., *Slaves of the Shah*, 18, 42, citing the same development but including royal cousins and Tajik administrators among the marriage partners.

[66] Jean Chardin, *Voyages du Chevalier Chardin, en Perse, et autres lieux de l'Orient ...*, ed. L. Langlès, 10 vols. (Paris, 1811), V, 247.

risked being blinded in early youth. Blinding effectively eliminated them as rivals because no blind ruler could be accepted on the Persian throne.[67]

In the Mughal empire, marriage played an important role in bolstering alliances within the mixed imperial elite as well as with the recently conquered elites. Persian and Rajput connections were important: Akbar and Aurangzeb had Persian mothers, while Jahangir and Shah Jahan were born of Rajput princesses.[68] Mughal princesses were fitted into this scheme of creating cohesion through marriages. Following Abu'l-Fazl's stipulation that good offspring could be expected only from marriages with 'race on both sides', most alliances were concluded with 'exalted lineages', houses worthy of a lasting connection with the Mughal overlords. These included Uzbek and Safavid princes, as well as members of prestigious religious families. However, unwedded Mughal princesses were not uncommon, a situation that can partly be explained by the scarcity of candidates fitting their exalted pedigree. Activist young dynastic women emerging throughout Mughal history may have chosen this path deliberately to retain their freedom. Princesses from the patriline could not give birth to successors, as did their Safavid equals, but they did share in dynastic prestige.[69]

The three major West and South Asian Islamic empires show marked convergences: the predicament of high-ranking princesses from the patriline and their shifting alliances; and the sometimes awkward position of lesser-ranking males affiliated to the dynasty, particularly in the Ottoman but also in the Safavid context. Daughters could serve as their fathers' key advisors and supporters: notable examples are Shah Tahmasp's (1514–1524–1576) daughter Pari Khan Khanum (1548–78) and Shah Jahan's daughter Jahanara Begum Sahib (1614–81). Spouses could at times exert

---

[67] Ibid., V, 240–7, quotations at 247; Babaie et al., *Slaves of the Shah*, 18; and Stephen P. Blake, 'Returning the household to the patrimonial-bureaucratic empire: gender, succession, and ritual in the Mughal, Safavid, and Ottoman empires', in Peter F. Bang and C.A. Bayly (eds.), *Tributary Empires in Global History* (Basingstoke, 2011), 214–26, at 220, refers to the blinding of princesses, but in the Chardin pages cited here only the male children of princesses are described as subject to this procedure; in fact, Mohammad Khodabande (1532–1578–1587*) ruled although his eyesight was seriously restricted.

[68] Balabanlilar, 'Begims of the mystic feast', note 15 at 145.

[69] Abu'l-Fazl, *The Akbar Nama of Abu-l-Fazl (History of the Reign of Akbar Including an Account of His Predecessors)*, ed. Henry Beveridge, 3 vols. (New Delhi, 1973), III, 677–8. On the princesses' alliances, see Ruby Lal, *Domesticity and Power in the Early Mughal World* (Cambridge, 2005), 169–70. Blake, 'Returning the household', 224, states that 'for the Mughals the Indic obsession with hierarchy severely limited the marriage pool and, as a result, imperial daughters were often not married at all'. Balabanlilar, 'Lords of the auspicious conjunction: Turco-Mongol imperial identity on the subcontinent', *Journal of World History*, 18/1 (2007), 1–39, stresses the deliberate choice of politically active princesses to remain single, as well as the persisting relevance of descent in the maternal line. These perspectives cannot be brought in line easily.

power: Hürrem Sultan (*c.* 1500–58) and Nur Jahan (1577–1645) are commonly seen as major influences on, respectively, Süleyman I and Jahangir. Most lasting and general, however, was the role of senior women, elder female members of the patriline and most particularly mothers of rulers. A sequence of Ottoman valide sultans (queen mothers) wielded great power from the later sixteenth century (Plate 13) until the advent of Köprülü Mehmed Pasha as grand vizier in 1656.

China was staunchly patrilineal: women could not as a rule inherit property from their patriline and upon marriage moved to their husband's location and lineage.[70] Dynastic marriages with outside partners were usually seen as unacceptable: a steppe empress could hardly be accepted as the highest female authority, mother of the next emperor in line, and potentially as a regent of the realm during the minority of her son. Only under severe military pressure was such an arrangement accepted as a temporary and inevitable expedient. How, then, were suitable marriage partners for the emperor or heir-apparent selected in China? Mixed experiences during early dynasties gradually crystallised into a set of maxims regarding imperial marriage and the imperial clan.[71] Thus, the rise of powerful consort lineages from Han (206 BCE–220 CE) to Tang China (618–907 CE) had made later dynasties wary of selecting a main consort for the emperor from among the upper layers.[72] Song (960–1279) emperors gradually shifted marriage preferences from elite military families to scholars and officials, while restricting the careers of consorts' male relatives in office. The Ming founder (1328–1368–1398) initiated a more radical shift, selecting attractive and even-tempered girls from lower-ranking military families, mostly from the capital region. At the same time he tried to reduce the powers of the dowager empress. Manchu (1644–1911) emperors selected their concubines and consorts exclusively from the ranks of the mixed Manchu and Mongol conquest elite and its Han Chinese allies. The women selected, moreover, were 'socially and ritually severed from their natal families'.[73] Reflecting Mongol

[70] Rubie Watson and Patricia B. Ebrey (eds.), *Marriage and Inequality in Chinese Society* (Berkeley, CA, 1991), underline that lineages with only daughters used marriage and sometimes adoption to continue their existence, inverting the accepted pattern by fitting a man into their family.

[71] See the exemplary study by John W. Chaffee, outlining the specificity of all dynasties as well as the process of learning from previous experiences: *Branches of Heaven: A History of the Imperial Clan of Sung China* (Cambridge, MA, 1999).

[72] Jennifer Holmgren, 'Imperial marriage in the native Chinese and non-Han state, Han to Ming', in Watson and Ebrey (eds.), *Marriage and Inequality*, 58–97, notably at 73–5.

[73] Rawski, *Last Emperors*, 156; Jennifer Holmgren, 'A question of strength: military capability and princess-bestowal in imperial China's foreign relations (Han to Ch'ing)', *Monumenta Serica*, 39 (1990–1), 31–85; Holmgren, 'Imperial marriage', 73–5; Chaffee, *Branches of Heaven*, 10–11.

practice, the Manchus in general accepted a more active role for women, yet empresses and dowager empresses were not as a rule active players in Qing court politics; their families, moreover, remained firmly subjected to the hierarchy of the conquest clan. Only two Qing grand dowager empresses (ruling emperors' grandmothers), Kangxi's paternal grand-mother and Cixi in the later nineteenth century, became a major force in court politics.

In China, the discrepancy between the birth rank and the gender status of imperial princesses was at least as strong as in the Ottoman empire: the prestige of the imperial clan contrasted sharply with the female submis-siveness dictated by Confucianism.[74] However, marriages of imperial princesses offered an opportunity to create friends and followers, without the risk of elevating these families to uncomfortable power. The choice of marriage partners for dynastic siblings shows the same patterns as imper-ial marriage, alternating between military and scholar-official families and shifting preference from high-ranking to indifferent family background. Song princesses moved from marrying leading military men to alliances with prominent official and scholar families.[75] The Ming founder estab-lished strict norms for his progeny in many respects, but dictated no explicit rules about choosing marriage partners for either princes or princesses. An initial preference for military families changed in the early fifteenth century, when scholar-officials were usually selected as imperial in-laws. In the last century of Ming rule, lower local elites with a military background were favoured as spouses for princesses.[76] The Qing radically redirected matrimonial alliances. Imperial princes and princesses, like the emperor himself, sought partners in the mixed Manchu and Mongol conquest elite, with a smattering only of Han Chinese who had joined the conquest elite early on. The emperor and the princes exhibited a strong preference for Manchu women, with a minority of Mongol partners. The princesses, however, concluded more marriages with Mongol men. Princesses' marriages reflected alliance; princes' marriages proximity to succession.[77] Overall, the Qing imperial

---

[74] John W. Chaffee, 'The marriage of Sung imperial clanswomen' in Watson and Ebrey (eds.), *Marriage and Inequality*, 133–70, at 153, underlines the clash between imperial prerogatives and common considerations of gender and generation, and notes the gra-dual movement of the Song towards the general preferences.

[75] Chaffee, 'Sung imperial clanswomen', 148–9.

[76] Jérôme Kerlouégan provided information on Ming marriages on the basis of Chinese and Japanese literature as well as his own research. Rules for imperial kin can be found in Edward L. Farmer, *Zhu Yuanzhang and Early Ming Legislation: The Reordering of Chinese Society Following the Era of Mongol Rule* (Leiden, 1995), notably the 'August Ming Ancestral Instruction', nos. 69–71, at 141.

[77] Evelyn S. Rawski, 'Ch'ing imperial marriage and problems of rulership', in Watson and Ebrey (eds.), *Marriage and Inequality*, 170–204, tables at 177.

clan underlined its status apart through marriage, while seeking accommodation and contact with the Han Chinese in other forms.

In Japan, with an outspoken and lasting presence of noble families, women from the imperial family married emperors, crown princes, imperial princes within their own ranks, high-ranking nobles, or members of the warrior class. Emperors commonly married women from the Fujiwara clan, an alliance enduring for many centuries. The shoguns imitated this pattern, marrying imperial daughters and Fuijawara daughters to underpin their ascendancy in the state.[78]

Concubinage: why so many women?

Many authors have rightly observed that polygyny is the rule rather than the exception in world history from the advent of differentiated hierarchical societies to recent centuries.[79] Polygyny has been explained by combining Darwinian and sociopolitical perspectives. The natural inclination of men to reproduce was enhanced by power and wealth for some, thwarted by poverty for others. In other words, the emergence of 'greater resource inequality' led to 'differential reproduction'. In this view the rise of autocratic power in early empires necessarily entailed the maximisation of sexual and reproductive gratification for male rulers: the inclination was always there; the capabilities now ensured its fulfilment. Not only did autocratic sexual mass consumers accumulate women: they also emasculated poor men, creating flocks of eunuchs to serve and supervise their harems. Eunuchs occupied the extreme opposite of the grandees' advantaged position: they lacked the physical capability to procreate.[80] This

---

[78] Takie Sugiyama Lebra, *Above the Clouds: Status Culture of the Modern Japanese Nobility* (Berkeley, CA, 1995), table with percentages for all imperial and shogunal marriages on 186:

	Emperor	Shogun	Total
Imperial daughters	34 (22.5%)	7 (18.9%)	41 (21.8%)
Fujiwara daughters	97 (64.2%)	18 (48.6%)	115 (61.2%)
Other women	20 (13.2%)	12 (32.4%)	32 (17.0%)
Total consorts	151 (100%)	37 (100%)	188 (100.0%)

[79] See Patricia B. Ebrey on this question, 'Rethinking the imperial harem: why were there so many palace women?', in her *Women and the Family in Chinese History* (London, 2002), 177–93.

[80] Laura Betzig, 'Eusociality: from the first foragers to the first states', *Human Nature*, 25/1 (2014), 1–5; and numerous earlier contributions by the same author, e.g. 'Despotism and differential reproduction: a cross-cultural correlation of conflict asymmetry, hierarchy, and degree of polygyny', *Ethology and Sociobiology*, 3/4 (1982), 209–21. Compare several

perspective suggests that polygyny is self-evident, whereas it is the rise of monogamous marriage in the Christian tradition, anticipated by tendencies towards monogamy in Rome, that stands in need of explanation.[81] One of the Darwinist authors, Laura Betzig, states: 'In every one of the primary, or autochthonous, civilizations in Mesopotamia, Egypt, India, and China, and later on in Western civilizations from Greece to Rome, emperors collected as many as 100,000 women, who bore hundreds of children.' Repeating the statement briefly in her conclusion, she adds: 'up to 100,000 eunuchs filled sterile castes ... Then just 500 years ago, history reversed itself.'[82] These numbers are inflated, but literary sources frequently refer to large harems. The legendary Maurya Buddhist ruler Asoka (304–268–232 BCE) reportedly assembled a harem of 16,000 women: as an aspiring *chakravartin* he was expected to father 1,000 sons. A Dutch East India Company official believed that no fewer than 10,000 women dwelt at Amangkurat I's (?–1646–1677) Mataram court. In his idealised depiction of Akbar's court, Abu'l-Fazl noted that the emperor's well-ordered harem accommodated 5,000 women, each in a separate apartment. The palace of the Leopard King of precolonial Dahomey was populated by an exclusively female staff, numbering between 5,000 and 8,000 women.[83] European traders, diplomats, and missionaries in differing tonalities expressed their wonderment at the female cortèges accompanying rulers: in Europe kings were served almost exclusively by men, and female staff performed household tasks only for queens. European descriptions of the attire, charm, and number of women at distant courts tickled the imagination of a wide readership.

---

remarks in another work inspired by Darwinism, Azar Gat, *War in Human Civilization* (Oxford, 2008), 67–8, 415–17.

[81] See a clear assessment of the prominence of polygyny with a historical discussion of changes from Rome to Christianity in Walter Scheidel, 'Monogamy and polygyny in Greece, Rome, and world history', Social Science Research Network (Rochester, NY, 2008), http://papers.ssrn.com/abstract=1214729 (accessed 6 February 2014). On the imposition of monogamous marriage in France, see Georges Duby, *Le chevalier, la femme et le prêtre: le mariage dans la France féodale* (Paris, 1981), particularly 27–59 on the clashing views of priests and warriors, and 201–19 on the implications for the royal house.

[82] Betzig, 'Eusociality', (unpaginated) conclusion repeating earlier statements in the article; compare Ebrey's more careful assessments, 'Rethinking the imperial harem', 178, at 182 confirming the very high number of 10,000 women under Song emperor Renzong.

[83] On Asoka and Mataram, see Barbara Watson Andaya, 'Women and the performance of power in early modern Southeast Asia', in Walthall (ed.), *Servants of the Dynasty*, 22–44, at 23 and 28. On Akbar's harem, see Lal, *Domesticity and Power*, 166 (more numbers at 173); and Karuna Sharma, 'A visit to the Mughal harem: lives of royal women', *South Asia: Journal of South Asian Studies*, 32/2 (2009), 155–69, at 160. On the Leopard king, see Bay, *Wives of the Leopard*; and Bay, 'Servitude and worldly success'. See also Marilyn Booth (ed.), *Harem Histories: Envisioning Places and Living Spaces* (Durham, NC, 2010).

Later paintings of lascivious odalisques added a more explicitly erotic and perfumed fragrance to this clichéd depiction of the Orient.

Polygyny is indeed common in history and predominant in dynastic settings even where society as a whole adhered to monogamy. However, the association of the harem with unrestrained male sexual activity needs to be put into perspective. The huge numbers mentioned in literary sources usually represent wild overstatements, comparable to the combatants listed in records of battles. Reputations were at stake here; virility could be demonstrated through sexual prowess as well as on the battlefield. The presence of numerous women conveyed an image of royal strength, abundance, and fertility. Nevertheless, harems with hundreds of women were not uncommon, and examples numbering in the thousands can also be found. How can we best understand these establishments?

The term harem, an Ottoman variant of Arabic *harim*, refers in general to the part of a house to which access is restricted or forbidden, an inner sanctum not necessarily related to women.[84] The least accessible sections of palaces across the globe tended to include women's quarters. It would be wrong to imagine that all women in these restricted quarters served as the ruler's sexual reserve; in practice this honour was usually restricted to a fraction only. Can we assess the density of sexual encounters and the number of women concerned? Numbers of children and titled consorts provide an indication. In Chinese history, Song emperor Huizong holds the all-time record with sixty-five children, followed at some distance by Tang Xuanzong's fifty-nine and the Qing Kangxi emperor's fifty-six children. Huizong had twenty titled consorts, and we know his thirty-one sons were mothered by a dozen consorts. However, the emperor rewarded another 123 women with titles, possibly an indication of intimacy.[85] Thirty-nine consorts were listed for Kangxi in court genealogies, but fifty-four were buried in consort tombs. Kangxi's long-ruling

---

[84] See 'Ḥarīm', in P. Bearman et al. (eds.), *Encyclopaedia of Islam, Second Edition*, Brill Online Reference Works (Leiden, 1954–2005).

[85] Patricia B. Ebrey, 'Succession to high office: the Chinese case', in David Olson and Michael Cole (eds.), *Technology, Literacy, and the Evolution of Society: Implications of the Work of Jack Goody* (Mahwah, 2006), 49–71, at 60, mentioning '29 sons by about a dozen women'; Ebrey, *Huizong*, 301, 307, and table on 530 listing 31 sons; Ebrey, 'Rethinking the imperial harem', table with Northern Song emperors with consorts and children at 181, and a breakdown of women taken by the Jurchens, including 143 of Huizong's consorts, at 185–6. Richard L. Davis (Lingnan University, Hongkong) kindly sent me his 'Troubles in paradise: the shrinking royal family in the Southern Song', www.npm.gov.tw/hotnews/9910seminar/download/all/B01.pdf; this unpublished paper lists all Tang and Song emperors with their sons and daughters, reaching an average of 24.4 children for Tang and 13.2 for Song emperors. See Spence, *Emperor of China*, 119–22, with an overview of Kangxi's children.

favourite grandson, the Qianlong emperor, fathered seventeen sons and ten daughters, and had forty-one consorts.[86] High numbers of children and consorts can be found for early Japanese emperors, ranging around fifty and thirty respectively. Shogun Ienari holds the Japanese record, with sixteen consorts, forty-one concubines, and fifty-two children. A handful of imperial consorts with up to twenty concubines was the more common situation.[87] Among Ottoman sultans, Murad III is accepted as the keenest woman-lover; his reputation is usually underlined to exemplify the dated view of Ottoman degeneracy after Süleyman's golden age. Murad spent most of his time in Topkapı and in 1578–9 expanded the harem to include a sultanic residence;[88] by temperament and lifestyle he may indeed have been more given to sexual activities than most of his predecessors. One estimate suggests he must have taken to his bed forty harem women; by the time of his death forty-nine of his children were still alive and seven women were pregnant.[89] This exceeds the forty-seven Song dynasty children surviving their father Huizong. Taking these isolated and somewhat haphazard numbers as an indication, we can safely assume that the numbers of women present in polygynous dynastic households cannot be explained solely on the basis of either dynastic reproduction or imperial lust.

Many princes practised 'serial concubinage', moving from one favoured girl to another:

he [the sultan] chooses his consorts from slaves who are presented to him, and whenever it happens that one pleases him, he installs her in the palace . . . where he keeps her until he falls in love with another, then he repudiates the first and chooses the other, and this continues as long as he likes.[90]

Chinese polygynous lore held that concubines could never replace the main wife, that the empress should not be jealous, and that the emperor should not indulge in sexual excess or fall in love.[91] These restrictions, of course, were often disregarded in practice. The Wanli emperor's trouble with his main advisors and his mother were caused in part by his close relationship with his favourite concubine Zheng. Wanli promised her that

[86] Rawski, *Last Emperors*, 141–2; Elliott, *Qianlong*, 39.

[87] Shillony, *Enigma of the Emperors*, 58; Lebra, *Above the Clouds*, table of consorts at 201 and information on Ienari and others at 198.

[88] Gülru Necipoğlu, *Architecture, Ceremonial, and Power: The Topkapi Palace in the Fifteenth and Sixteenth Centuries* (Cambridge, MA, 1991), 165–7.

[89] A.H. de Groot, 'Murād III', in Bearman et al. (eds.), *Encyclopaedia of Islam, Second Edition*.

[90] Peirce, *Imperial Harem*, quotation at 43; one-son policy at 42–5; the hierarchy of the harem is discussed at 112–43, notably 125–34.

[91] Keith McMahon, 'The institution of polygamy in the Chinese imperial palace', *Journal of Asian Studies*, 72/4 (2013), 917–36; McMahon, *Women Shall Not Rule*, 9–18.

their son would become the heir to the throne – a promise which kept him from nominating the first-born son as heir and created endless political turmoil.[92] Neither Wanli's love nor the problems it caused were exceptional. Many princes, wearied by the challenges they faced and eager to share their concerns with a confidante, were devoted entirely to a special favourite. It is unlikely that Süleyman combined a profligate lifestyle with his infatuation for and marriage with Hürrem, celebrated in his love poems. The same can be said about Jahangir and his wife Nur Jahan (Plate 14), who landed in the Mughal harem after the death of her rebellious husband, while she had already given birth to a daughter. Nur Jahan may have shared Jahangir's favour with others, but her ascendancy cannot have left room for too many female competitors.[93] The rise of these powerful women had immediate consequences for power balances at court.

Akbar appears to have had no such special amorous connection, yet we find an intriguing statement by the Spanish Jesuit father Antonio Monserrate, serving as tutor to one of his sons: 'Zelaldinus [Akbar] has more than 300 wives, dwelling in separate suites of rooms in a very large palace. Yet when the priests were at the court he had only three sons and two daughters.'[94] Monserrate's 300 women contrast sharply with Abu'l-Fazl's 5,000.[95] Moreover, the Jesuit father suggests that only a small minority of this lower number of women ever had sex with Akbar, a view fitting Abu'l-Fazl's idealised presentation of Akbar as self-disciplined and moderate in eating as well as in sexual activities. Elsewhere this mouthpiece of Akbar's grandeur underlined that the emperor saw reproduction as the essence of sex.[96] Male hegemons themselves sometimes observed that undue revelling in sex and drinking undermined health and stature – a knowledge that did not prevent some of them from indulging in 'excessive drug and alcohol abuse'.[97] Dispositions of rulers towards the numbers of female companions and the types of relationships they maintained with them will have differed

[92] Qin, 'In search of divine support'.
[93] Lal, *Domesticity and Power*, 9–10, criticises the classic view of Nur Jahan, mostly because she is depicted as wholly unprecedented; at 224–5 she also appears to question Jahangir's devotion solely to Nur Jahan.
[94] Antonio Monserrate, *The Commentary of Father Monserrate, S.J. on his Journey to the Court of Akbar*, ed. S.N. Banerjee (Oxford, 1922), 202; see also Lal, *Domesticity and Power*, 153.
[95] See Lal's discussion, *Domesticity and Power*, 166.   [96] Ibid., 150–5.
[97] See Kangxi on sex and alcohol, in Spence, *Emperor of China*, 123, 146, 148; Akbar's ideas about sex, marriage, and fertility are mentioned in Rosalind O'Hanlon, 'Kingdom, household and body: history, gender and imperial service under Akbar', *Modern Asian Studies*, 41/5 (2007), 889–923, at 922; Lisa Balabanlilar, 'The Emperor Jahangir and the pursuit of pleasure', *Journal of the Royal Asiatic Society*, 3rd series, 19/2 (2009), 173–86, shows the other side of the coin.

immensely. The harem certainly performed a function in securing candidates for succession; this did not preclude the control and sometimes limitation of the ruler's sexual activities. Not only were these monitored carefully, they could also be restricted. Once an Ottoman favourite had given birth to a son, she was no longer expected to be sexually active: as a mother of a prince, she had 'post-sexual' status, a rule even the sultan needed to respect.[98] From the seventeenth century onwards, moreover, Ottoman princes were no longer allowed to father children 'until and unless they became sultan'.[99] Dynastic continuity and succession apparently were more important than the unrestricted indulgence of male princes.

Who were the other women in the harem, and what tasks did they perform? The Ottoman harem at the height of its existence in the seventeenth century numbered around 900 women.[100] A small segment of its population consisted of the sultan's relatives. From the reign of Murad III, the sultan resided in the Topkapı palace harem; from the start of the seventeenth century onwards, all relatives of the sultan stayed there during their youth and males were expected to move out only to ascend to the throne or to die. These relatives needed to be catered for, an explanation for rising numbers of harem staff.[101] The upper layer of the harem proper consisted of women who had achieved high rank through their role as the sultan's most favoured concubines. The favourite (*haseki* sultan) could rise to the pinnacle of female rank when her son ascended the throne: as *valide sultan* she towered above the others. Only once was this situation complicated by the emergence of two generations of mothers. Mehmed IV, enthroned in 1648, was torn between his mother Turhan Sultan and his grandmother Kösem Sultan.[102] Among the women placed below the valide and the haseki we find the wet-nurse, who through her services was seen as affiliated with the sultan, and the harem stewardess, who served as leading administrator. Under this upper category stood a group of women educating the newly arrived girls and managing the various services of this female household. The most numerous and lowest echelon consisted of the corps performing menial services. Newly arrived slave girls would start at this level; diligence, appearance, and intelligence determined a gradual ascent through the ranks; sultanic favour propelled girls upwards in the hierarchy more rapidly. The harem was as much a training institution and a boarding house for all women related to the

---

[98] Peirce, *Imperial Harem*, 39, 42, 58 (on Hürrem as an exception), and 108.
[99] Ibid., 21.   [100] Ibid., table at 122.   [101] Ibid., 132–3.
[102] Rycaut, *Present State*, 20–40, provides a vivid account.

dynasty as the sultan's reserve of sexual services. The slave girls in the harem match the slave boys in the palace school, separate from the harem but also located in the inner part of Topkapı palace.[103] These two slave-based training institutions were fundamental; the men and women emerging from them intermarried and formed the core of the Ottoman ruling establishment.

The same array of women and youngsters from the dynasty, teachers, managers, and young girls can be found in Safavid and Mughal harems. However, the prominence of Ottoman *hasekis* and *valide sultans* has no parallel in these establishments. Marriage, gradually abandoned in favour of concubinage by the Ottomans and somewhat later by the Safavids, remained important in Mughal India. Akbar's harem included eleven women given in marriage by Rajput princes to underpin their alliance.[104] While this exchange may have been seen as benefiting both sides, the reservoir of concubines could be replenished in less harmonious ways. Upon Akbar's 1569 conquest of Rambathore fort in Rajput Bundi, the first clause in the treaty decreed 'That the chiefs of Bundi should be exempted from that custom, degrading to a Rajput, of sending a dola (bride) to the royal harem.'[105] In 1581 a Mughal convoy crossed the Khyber Pass to subdue the rebellion of Mirza Muhammad Hakim. Jesuit Father Monserrate, part of the convoy, reports a remarkable group of elephant riders experiencing difficulty in the advance:

Amongst these riders were the queens, the princesses, the other noble ladies, and the chief queen of David, king of the Patanaei, by whom he had had several sons. Zelaldinus [Akbar] was taking her with him in honourable custody, both as a reminder and proof of his own victorious glory, and as a hostage in order to prevent any insurrection amongst the Patanaei, who were being kept in subjection by fear only. This queen had with her several of her daughters.[106]

[103] Peirce, *Imperial Harem*, 139–40.

[104] Frances H. Taft, 'Honor and alliance: reconsidering Mughal Rajput marriages', in Karine Schomer et al. (eds.), *The Idea of Rajasthan: Explorations in Regional Identity* (Manohar, 1994), 217–41, tables at 218–20, stressing the positive attitude of the Rajput princes towards the exchange.

[105] James Tod, *Annals and Antiquities of Rajasthan or the Central And Western Rajput States of India*, 3 vols. (Oxford, 1920), vol. III, 1482, also cited in Smith, *Akbar the Great Mogul*, 99.

[106] Monserrate, *Commentary*, 143, with a note pointing to Daud of Bengal. This must be the Afghan pretender Daud Khan Karrani, whose exploits are described at length in Abu'l-Fazl, *Akbar Nama*, III, 101, 140–3, 175–9, 253–5, with the submission of his mother and dependents mentioned at 376 and 420 (with thanks to Jos Gommans). On polygamy as a 'hostage institution', see Friedrich Katz, 'A comparison of some aspects of the evolution of Cuzco and Tenochtitlán', in Richard P. Schaedel et al. (eds.), *Urbanization in the Americas from its Beginning to the Present* (The Hague and Paris, 1978), 203–14, at 204.

These women, now on the march with the emperor's army, were no doubt accommodated in the female household once it took a more sedentary form.[107] The harem thus included ladies presented by vassals as well as others held in captivity to ensure the loyalty of their male relatives. In his typically exalted language, Abu'l-Fazl reports another occasion where the sister and a female companion of a Rajput prince, after miraculously escaping alive from the burning pile erected for them by their defeated relatives, 'obtained honour by being sent to kiss the threshold of the shahinshah': in other words they were incorporated in the harem.[108] By multiplying marriages beyond the conventional four, Akbar caused discomfort among his religious advisors.[109] Father Monserrate, decrying the practice of fourfold marriage and unlimited concubinage sanctioned by Islamic law, pointed to its primary purpose: 'Musalman kings employ this sanction and licence of the foulest immorality in order to ratify peace and to create friendly relationships with their vassal princes or neighbouring monarchs. For they marry the daughters and sisters of such rulers'.[110]

Chinese palace women were organised in a hierarchical pyramid from 'charwoman to empress dowager'. The emperor's grand empress dowager, his paternal grandmother, held highest rank. Only two such matrons are present in Qing history – Kangxi's grandmother Xiaozhuang, and Cixi ruling 'behind the curtain' in the last decades of the dynasty. More often the emperor's mother, the empress dowager, was the ranking woman at court. She could be either the preceding emperor's empress, or the birth mother of the incumbent emperor. Concubines' children were legally the children of the main wife – at court and in Chinese society. Eight ranks separated the empress from ordinary concubines, a hierarchy which could be escalated rapidly only through the emperor's favour. The imperial women, numbering somewhere between forty and a hundred, formed a minor proportion of the bulk of women in the palace, totalling around 2,000 or 3,000.[111] At the upper levels of the hierarchy we again encounter wet-nurses, forty of whom were annually selected for service at the Ming

[107] Lal, *Domesticity and Power*, outlines the gradual change from a moving world to a more secluded sedentary harem.
[108] Abu'l-Fazl, *Akbar Nama*, III, 331–2; see numerous other instances of women, mostly Rajput princesses, brought into the harem.
[109] Lal, *Domesticity and Power*, 171–5; O'Hanlon, 'Kingdom, household and body'.
[110] Monserrate, *Commentary*, 202.
[111] Numbers based on Bao Hua Hsieh, 'From charwoman to empress dowager: serving-women in the Ming palace', *Ming Studies*, 42/1 (2000), 26–80; Bao Hua Hsieh, *Concubinage and Servitude in Late Imperial China* (London, 2014), tables at 279–80; Rawski, *Last Emperors*, 127–59, tables at 141–2; also Jeanne Larsen, 'Women of the imperial household: views of the emperor's consorts and their female attendants', *Denver Museum of Natural History*, 3rd series, 15 (1998), 23–35; Shuo Wang, 'Qing imperial women: empresses, concubines, and aisin gioro daughters', in Walthall (ed.),

court. Other women in the upper echelons were midwives and physicians. The wet-nurse of a prince who became emperor was granted noble status. In Ming as well as in Qing China, two separate forms of recruitment or 'levies' were practised to select imperial consorts and young girls respectively for general service. There was no rigid separation: particularly alluring girls in the lower-ranking levy could be promoted to become concubines or even consorts. Under the Qing the girls at both levels were exclusively recruited from the military conquest elite, mixing Manchu, Mongol, and Han Chinese candidates, in a triennial draft of 'beautiful women' and an annual draft of palace maids. Of Ming imperial consorts, 64 per cent had started out as palace maids; under the Qing with their more restricted recruitment policies, this share reached 16 per cent.[112] Girls were brought into the palace at a relatively young age and underwent a long phase of training and education; most of them performed a variety of menial tasks.

The Tokugawa female establishment (Great Interior) likewise consisted of the females within the dynasty and their servants, consorts, and concubines, and other service personnel. These women, totalling *c.* 500 during the reign of Shogun Ienari, were recruited from many social layers. Their chances for promotion were twofold: becoming a concubine and bearing the shogun's child, or developing into an 'elder' who organised the Great Interior – no single woman, however, could combine these two positions.[113] The emperor's Kyoto court included a far smaller number of consorts and female personnel, reflecting its reduced position in the political structure.

Polygyny was common in Africa, certainly at the level of royal establishments. In the rare case of the Solomonic kings of Ethiopia, polygyny was combined with Christianity. In the kingdom of Kongo, interacting with the Portuguese and the papacy at an early stage, the introduction of monogamy induced by conversion was initially fiercely opposed by the king's female entourage, who feared losing their status; later these women turned into patrons of the new religion.[114] As elsewhere in Africa, the presence of Europeans with their military, commercial, and religious schemes offered opportunities to some locals, while it thwarted many others – the European challenge profoundly affected traditions and

Servants of the Dynasty, 137–58. On earlier and higher numbers under the Song, see Ebrey, 'Rethinking the imperial harem'.

[112] Hsieh, 'Charwoman to empress dowager', 47; Rawski, *Last Emperors*, 131.

[113] On Japan, see Hata Hisako, 'Servants of the inner quarters: the women of the shogun's Great Interior', in Walthall (ed.), *Servants of the Dynasty*, 172–90; see also Yi Jin, *Mémoires d'une dame de cour dans la cité interdite*, ed. Qiang Dong (Arles, 1996).

[114] Thornton, 'Elite Women', 441. On polygyny in general, see Murdock, *Africa*, who notes (25) a preponderance of 88 per cent in a sample of 154 societies.

power balances. Asante royalty maintained polygyny until the introduction of the British colonial regime. Serving the African Company of Merchants, Thomas Bowdich noted during his 1817 visit to the Asante capital of Kumase that 'The laws of Ashantee allow the King 3333 wives, which number is carefully kept up, to enable him to present women to those who distinguish themselves.' After listing the various places where these numerous women resided, including two streets in Kumase, Bowdich added that 'The King has seldom more than six wives resident with him in the palace. On the occasion of signing the treaty, as explained in the public letter, about 300 were assembled, and none but the King's chamberlain, and the deputies of the parts of the Government, were allowed to be present.'[115] These quotes make clear that a small group of women actually lived with the king in the palace, while greater numbers were summoned for solemn occasions. In addition, we learn that numerous women were brought together only to be redistributed again.[116] Upon his restoration under British colonial control, *asantehene* Agyeman Prempeh (1870–1888–1931) re-established the harem, not for his personal gratification but because he saw no other way to reconstruct the Asante tradition. Key families of the realm had 'provided the king with stool [throne] wives from generation to generation ... Asante administration is based on alliances serviced by marriage exchanges. To abolish the harem would have meant tearing down the Asante administrative structure, as Agyeman Prempeh knew it.'[117] The relevance of the harem as a connection with the realm becomes conspicuously clear in the case of the Dahomey Leopard King. His palace in the capital Abomey brought together an exclusively female staff of 5,000 to 8,000. These women formed a mixed group, executing very different tasks. The king's dependents (*ahosi*) consisted of three groups: the royal children (*ahovi*), the commoners (*anato*) presented by lineage heads, and the war captives (*kannumon* or *kanounnon*).[118] This 'city of women' was populated by all the lineages in the kingdom: 'marriage to the king was an idiom that in fact spoke of royal control over all lineages in Dahomey'.[119] Prominent men

---

[115] Thomas E. Bowdich, *Mission from Cape Coast Castle to Ashantee: With a Descriptive Account of that Kingdom* (London, 1873), 239–40.

[116] Confirmed in Bay, *Wives of the Leopard*, 126; see some details and complications in Robert Norris, *Memoirs of the Reign of Bossa Ahádee, King of Dahomy* ... (London, 1789), 88.

[117] Emmanuel Akyeampong, in Prempeh I, *The History of Ashanti Kings and the Whole Country Itself and Other Writings by Otumfuo, Nana Agyeman Prempeh I*, ed. Emmanuel Akyeampong et al. (Oxford, 2003), 51–2. See T. C. McCaskie, *State and Society in Pre-Colonial Asante* (Cambridge, 2003), 216–17, on the secluded and difficult lives of the palace women in the Asante harem or *hiaa*.

[118] See Bay, 'Servitude and worldly success', 341–3.

[119] Bay, *Wives of the Leopard*, 19.

from recently conquered regions could also technically 'marry' the king, a phrase indicating their loyalty and dependence rather than stipulating any specific service. Palace women and the exceptional men serving as *ahosi* were retainers, dependents most of whom would never engage in a close relationship with the king.[120] Maybe a thousand or so of the palace women were in principle sexually available to the king. The census compiled after the French conquest of Dahomey in 1894 lists 129 children surviving to maturity for Behanzin (1844–1889–1894*) and 77 for Glele (?–1858–1889), high figures when compared to the data from China and the Ottoman empire.[121]

Movement of the women outside of the palace was controlled carefully, as encounters with males were strictly forbidden. The English soldier and adventurer Richard Burton noticed that 'These being royal wives, cannot be touched without danger of death, they never leave their quarters unless preceded by a bell to drive men from the road.'[122] One of his compatriots in 1850 found his route barred several times by processions of the king's wives:

I was one morning near three quarters of an hour endeavouring to enter the Cumassee gate, from the constant succession of royal wives carrying food from one palace to the other. This morning, as we were leaving, we were desired not to go to the eastward, as 4000 of the king's wives ... were gone forth to bathe.[123]

Both English visitors, however, were struck especially by the conspicuous presence of women in the king's army. Burton positively commented on their sturdy physique and martial skills. He noted their 'marriage' to the king was most often, though not always, nominal: 'The fighting women are not de facto married to the king; but it may take place at his discretion. The first person that made the present ruler a father was one of his colonels.'[124] The amazons numbered 2,000–2,500, an important share of the king's dependents.[125]

---

[120] Ibid., 11, 19–20.
[121] Ibid., 251; Bay, 'Servitude and worldly success', 349–51. John Beattie, *Bunyoro: An African Kingdom* (New York, 1960), also notes more than a hundred children for a king.
[122] Burton, 'Present state of Dahome', 405–6.
[123] Frederick E. Forbes, *Dahomey and the Dahomans: Being The Journal of Two Missions to the King of Dahomey, and Residence at his Capital, in the Years 1849 and 1850* (London, 1851), 71, quoted in Bay, *Wives of the Leopard*, 209; Forbes in his annexes describes processions including numerous women who apparently played an important role in royal representation.
[124] Burton, 'Present state of Dahome', 405–6.
[125] On the female fighting force and its raison d'être, see Stanley B. Alpern, 'On the origins of the Amazons of Dahomey', *History in Africa*, 25 (1998), 9–25; Alpern, *Amazons of Black Sparta: The Women Warriors of Dahomey* (New York, 1998).

The Dahomey and Asante examples show how the harem connected numerous families to the kingship.[126] The same can be observed in the case of the Lovedu rain-queen. Ruling over a patrilineal people practising polygyny, she assembled a sizeable harem of women presented to her by subjects and allies. The wives could work for the queen and produce wealth; some of the women ruled areas or villages of their own. More often they were given in marriage to district heads and noblemen, who all became 'sons-in-law' to the queen. Any wife thus given was expected to return one of her daughters to the queen, creating a cycle of wife-giving that held together the loosely governed Lovedu realm.[127] In Central Javanese courts, wives (*ratu*) from high noble stock and concubines (*selir*) from village backgrounds linked the court with the country. Concubines' daughters, moreover, were given in marriage to village elites.[128] In general it can be said that the harem connected key families of a realm to the dynasty, willingly or grudgingly; it represented royal largesse, abundance, fertility, and virility. Its primary purpose was to secure dynastic succession by organising and regulating the ruler's sexual activity. Only a minority of the women was ever in touch with the ruler; most were active in a variety of tasks ranging from household service to productive labour and military activities. Training for these tasks, and for the eventuality of pleasing the ruler, was important in the harem.

Notwithstanding the numbers of women, the primary purpose of dynastic reproduction was not always accomplished. Polygyny did not preclude the threat of extinction. The Ottoman dynasty narrowly escaped extinction when in 1640 Sultan Ibrahim ascended to the throne as the only remaining brother of Murad IV – the future of the dynasty now hung on this diffident thirty-five-year-old sultan's untested ability to procreate. In Chinese history, too, several instances can be found where vertical succession from father to son failed. In the absence of sons, brothers or their sons were installed; in other instances adoption of more distant members from the plentiful imperial clan ensured the continuity of the main line.[129] The Japanese imperial and shogunal dynasties, too, practised adoption of scions from junior collateral branches to prevent extinction. This solution was particularly urgent for the Tokugawa shoguns,

---

[126] The same can be said for Buganda: see Nakanyike B. Musisi, 'Women, "elite polygyny", and Buganda state formation', *Signs: Journal of Women in Culture and Society*, 16/4 (1991), 757–86.

[127] Krige and Krige, *Realm of a Rain-Queen*, 174–85.

[128] Carey and Houben, 'Spirited Srikandas and sly Sumbadras', 25–9; elsewhere the article lists military and political roles held by women.

[129] See Günhan Börekci, 'Ibrahim', in Ágoston and Masters (eds.), *Encyclopedia of the Ottoman Empire*, 262–4; Fisher, *Chosen One*.

who consistently experienced difficulties in siring sons who survived childhood, notwithstanding polygynous reproduction.[130]

Patrilineal descent demanded the absolute chastity of the women groomed to please the ruler. Even where dynastic blood mattered less, the ruler's women required some form of control and protection. Two standard responses can be found in history: seclusion, and the employment of emasculated men as guardians and servants. No men were expected to enter the inner courts where the women resided (Plate 15); only eunuchs could serve them. Eunuchs are present across Asia and in large parts of Africa, especially in the regions influenced by Islam. They were not used in palace service in the Americas, where polygyny was practised, or in Europe, where it was not.[131] An estimated 200 black eunuchs staffed and guarded the harem in Topkapı palace; the pages in the palace school were supervised and trained by a smaller group of white eunuchs.[132] At the seventeenth-century Mughal and Safavid courts they performed similar roles. Greater numbers of eunuchs staffed the court of the Ming emperors, performing all household services as well as managing the harem. From 'a mere hundred' at the outset of the dynasty, they numbered around '10,000 in the 1520s', reaching 'the astonishing figure of 100,000 near the end of the dynasty'.[133] Many of these eunuchs were involved with government throughout the empire: the court employed a minor share of this number. In the 1620s, the Portuguese Jesuit Alvaro Semedo estimated, some 12,000 eunuchs worked in the palace.[134] At the

---

[130] Personal communication from Anne Walthall, who reports that Japanese scholarship explains the lack of surviving sons either by the fear of allowing too much power to consorts' families, or by the lead-based white paint that wet-nurses spread on their nipples to prevent the shogun's heir being confronted with a bare breast. On adoption and collateral houses, see Bob Tadashi Wakabayashi, 'In name only: imperial sovereignty in early modern Japan', *Journal of Japanese Studies*, 17/1 (1991), 25–57.

[131] Wittfogel, *Oriental Despotism*, 354, suggests without further proof that the absence of large domesticated animals, commonly subjected to castration in Europe and Asia, could account for the fact that no eunuchs were present in the Americas; the Japanese court, taking over many Chinese habits, apparently never employed eunuchs, although it did practise polygyny; the same seems to be true for Siam and parts of Southeast Asia less influenced by Islam.

[132] Numbers are contested: see Penzer, *Harem*, 132, citing 600–800 black eunuchs; Albertus Bobovius, *Topkapı: relation du serail du Grand Seigneur*, ed. Annie Berthier and Stéphane Yerasimo (Arles and Paris, 1999), 30, mentions 50 white eunuchs in the 1650s, whereas the Introduction, 15, mentions 350–400 pages supervised by 85 white eunuchs; Ignatius Mouradgea d'Ohsson, *Tableau général de l'empire othoman: l'état actuel de l'empire othoman*, 7 vols. (Paris, 1824), VII, 54–6, lists 200 black and 80 white eunuchs, a figure also given in Ezgi Dikici, 'The making of Ottoman court eunuchs: origins, recruitment paths, family ties, and "domestic production"', *Archivum Ottomanicum*, 30 (2013), 105–36, citing Ottavio Bon at 113.

[133] Tsai, *Eunuchs in the Ming Dynasty*, 26.

[134] Semedo, *History*, 114; the number is also cited in Hsieh, 'Charwoman to empress dowager', 26.

peak of the Qing dynasty, a century later, they barely exceeded 3,000.[135] Unfree bondservants (*booi*) attached to the Manchu conquest elite had supplanted them as household supervisors; the remaining eunuchs served in the female quarters and performed lesser household tasks.[136] Eunuchs and women populated the secluded area in many palace compounds. The impact of this relatively closed circle in which rulers spent much of their time is not easily verified but surely important. The next chapter will consider clashes between this secluded inner core and staffs working at a greater distance from the ruler.

In China, concubinage was combined with marriage: the empress at all times maintained precedence over concubines and she became the legal mother of their children. Consorts, who stood between the two ranks, held rights over their own children. The status of the empress in Japan was less clear: sometimes emperors had only consorts, and there are even instances where more than one empress can be found.[137] In the Ottoman harem, after the exceptional marriage of Süleyman and Hürrem sultan, there were no formal marriages: sultanic favour and reproductive success determined rank.[138] Safavid and Mughal practices included marriage as well as concubinage. In each of these cases, however, several women could nurture hopes for their own son's future career. Competition among women with a stake in dynastic succession was endemic. Consorts often chose to support their son's cause more eagerly than his father's, particularly in contexts where they competed with numerous other women for the ruler's sexual favours. Ageing concubines who noticed a diminution of their physical attraction feared the ascent of younger women successfully pushing their sons to power. In such circumstances the father's longevity tended to undermine the chances of older favourites' sons. The legalist thinker Han Feizi concluded that in polygynous circumstances 'it is likely his [the ruler's] consort, his concubines, or the son he has designated as heir to his throne will wish for his death'.[139] Han Feizi's caustic statement may be exaggerated, but it is undoubtedly true that multiple consorts, all pushing

---

[135] Rawski, *Last Emperors*, 164–5.

[136] On the gradual return of eunuchs to more influential roles, prefiguring their nineteenth-century position, see Kutcher, 'Unspoken collusions'. On late Qing eunuch experiences, see Dan Shi, *Mémoires d'un eunuque dans la Cité Interdite*, ed. Nadine Perront (Arles, 1995).

[137] Elliott, *Qianlong*, 39; Rawski, *Last Emperors*, 134–5, showing that most Qing emperors were sons of consorts rather than empresses; Larsen, 'Women of the imperial household', points to the rivalry between birth mothers elevated to the rank of empress dowager and the previous emperor's dowager. On the less unequivocal position of the Japanese empress, see Lebra, *Above the Clouds*, 199.

[138] However, note the exception of Ibrahim I's marriage: Ágoston and Masters (eds.), *Encyclopedia of the Ottoman Empire*, 263, label it 'an almost unprecedented step'.

[139] Han Fei Tzu, *Basic Writings*, 85.

their sons as candidates for the throne, stimulated violence and rivalry – a situation the Ottomans and the Mughals accepted and even encouraged until respectively the seventeenth and the eighteenth century. Open and violent or covert and subdued tensions among competing mothers and their factions occurred at all polygynous courts. The addition of an extra generation threatened to escalate such conflicts, as became clear in the brief co-regency of Mehmed IV's mother Hatice Turhan Sultan and his grandmother Kösem Sultan between 1648 and 1651: 'The two Queens were exasperated highly against each other; one to maintain the Authority of her Son, and the other her own.' The conflict worsened when Turhan started fearing for the life of her son. Alliances and counter-alliances were formed; finally leading officials forced the intimidated boy-sultan to sign his grandmother's death warrant. Consequently, while young Mehmed cried in the arms of his sword-bearer (*silahdar*) 'Pen and Ink being brought, the Mufti wrote the sentence, and the Grand Signior subscribed it, which was that the Old Queen should be strangled, but neither cut with sword, nor bruised with blows.' Kösem, 'being above 80 years old, and without Teeth', put up a fight, biting her attackers 'with her Gums only' before she finally was strangled.[140] This outburst of violence between mother and grand-mother was exceptional, but conflict between mothers and favourites, or among women of the same rank, was the rule at many courts. Did courts organised on the basis of monogamous marriage escape from this predicament? Apart from extinction, did monogamy entail other risks for dynastic continuity and harmony?

In the later Middle Ages, most European dynasties were organised primarily on the basis of male descent, with a more important secondary place for the female line than in the Chinese, Ottoman, and from the seventeenth century onwards also Mughal and Safavid cases. 'Exogamous' and 'isogamous' marriage, outside of a social group but at the same hierarchical level, became the norm. From the perspective of the European 'société des princes' this marriage practice was endogamous, connecting leading European dynasties in an increasingly dense network of interconnected families. Dynastic marriage was the outcome of a long process, related to the scale, rivalry, and proximity of European polities loosely united under the twin authority of pope and emperor. However, monogamous marriage had long since been the single religiously sanctioned form of reproduction, for dynasties as well as for anybody else.[141]

Royal adultery, not uncommon in most dynasties and an acclaimed practice in some, created two characters absent in harem-based reproduction: the mistress and the bastard. The Christian dictate of monogamy

[140] Rycaut, *Present State*, 24, 35, 38.   [141] See Duby, *Le chevalier, la femme et le prêtre*.

frequently went together with 'serial concubinage' outside of the hallowed bond of matrimony. Early sixteenth-century Valois and Tudor kings were notorious for their numerous affairs; Henry VIII (1491–1509–1547) was exceptional only because his liaisons turned into marriages. Bourbon kings, from Henry IV (1553–1589–1610), the *vert galant* (womaniser), to Louis XIV and Louis XV, frequently engaged in amorous adventures. The Sun King's contemporary Charles II of England (1630–1660–1685) demonstrated his procreative powers effectively with mistresses, while his marriage to Catherine of Braganza remained without issue. Among profligate princes, Augustus II 'the Strong' of Poland-Saxony (1670–1722, various reign dates) enjoyed a special reputation, which one of his detractors expressed using oriental terminology: 'The court of this prince was at that time the most brilliant of Germany ... The king maintained a sort of serail with the most beautiful women of his lands. Upon his death, it was calculated that he had sired three hundred and fifty four children with his mistresses.'[142] This description, written by a princess from the rival Hohenzollern house, was decidedly unfriendly, and its fanciful numbers (outclassing all other royals mentioned here) cannot be taken seriously. Still, Augustus had more than ten mistresses and fathered several bastards, among them Marshal Maurice of Saxony, an acclaimed general and military theorist in French service. Countless other profligate kings can be mentioned, including worldly as well as spiritual rulers in Europe.[143] Contemporary as well as modern audiences, eager to read saucy stories about royalty, have been served by numerous writers. A French pamphleteer opened his description of one of Louis XIV's extramarital affairs with a general apology for royal adultery:

If it is a crime to love, we have to admit that no crime is more willingly forgiven; the sweetness of this passion so easily implants itself into our souls that it disarms our moral senses ... of all men, the passions of kings deserve least censure ... what is a major offence for a subject, is but a slight imperfection for a sovereign ... whose marriage was arranged for reasons of state rather than to satisfy his person ... how can these sovereigns not be excused if they ... try to find a kindred soul to share delights.[144]

---

[142] Frédérique Sophie Wilhelmine of Bayreuth-Prussia, *Mémoires de Frédérique Sophie Wilhelmine, margrave de Bareith, soeur de Frédéric le Grand: depuis l'année 1706 jusqu'à 1742, écrits de sa main*, 2 vols. (Brunswick, 1845), I, 101.

[143] See examples and discussion in Andreas Tacke (ed.), *Wir wollen der Liebe Raum geben: Konkubinate geistlicher und weltlicher Fürsten um 1500* (Göttingen, 2006); Ludwig Schmugge and Béatrice Wiggenhauser (eds.), *Illegitimität im Spätmittelalter* (Munich, 1994); Simona Slanicka (ed.), *Bastarde*, WerkstattGeschichte 51 (Essen, 2009).

[144] [Gatien de Courtilz de Sandras,] *Le Passe-temps royal, ou Les Amours de Mademoiselle de Fontange* (s.l., 1680), avertissement, au lecteur (my translation); see Louis XIV on the subject of the mistress in his *Mémoires*, ed Dreyss, II, 313–16.

The rigidity of conventions dictating European succession, confirmed and enforced by the practice of intermarriage among sovereign dynasties, made it increasingly difficult to fit bastards into the royal line. In 1369 Henry (1333–1369–1379), one of the illegitimate sons of King Alfonso XI (1311–1312–1350) of Castile, took over the crown and established the house of Trastámara. Slightly later, the illegitimate son of Peter I (1320–1357–1367) ascended to the Portuguese throne as John I (1358–1385–1433), first ruler of the house of Aviz. No bastard lines would formally succeed in later centuries, although some came close. Henry IV's illegitimate son with Gabrielle d'Estrées became duke of Vendôme as a four-year-old boy in 1598. Vendôme gained increasing importance in the early decades of the seventeenth century. As late as 1714, after a series of deaths among his potential successors, Louis XIV granted his two favourite sons by Madame de Montespan, the duke of Maine and the count of Toulouse, the right to ascend to the throne. This extreme measure was applauded by Louis XIV's morganatic wife Madame de Maintenon, who had helped raise the boys. Typically, it was intensely disapproved by his sister-in-law the Palatine princess Elisabeth-Charlotte, whose son Philip was close to legitimate succession. Within two years after the death of the Sun King, during a formal session (*lit de justice*) of the Parisian Parlement, the regent Philip abolished the two bastards' right to the throne. In the years to follow, the quarrel between legitimate and illegitimate princes was markedly present in political contestation.

European dynastic customs invited friction between queens and mistresses as well as between legitimate lines and bastards. Queens were the sole vehicle of legitimate descent, yet they could be as vulnerable as Chinese empresses witnessing the rapid ascent of a new favourite concubine. In every century of early modern French history, at least one mistress proved able to ascend to a position of power rivalling that of a *premier ministre*. Not only did mistresses, contrary to the wishful statements in the Sun King's memoirs, hold power: they at times unabashedly confronted queens with their omnipotence. Madame de Montespan openly attended ceremonies and was awarded apartments in Versailles outshining those of Queen Marie-Thérèse.[145] The matron-mistress-minister Madame de Maintenon, whose position as queen was never openly acknowledged, made her de facto supremacy painfully clear to the Palatine princess Elisabeth-Charlotte, her senior according to court ranking. Feigning weak health, she usurped the right to sit or recline in the presence of the two highest-ranking ladies at court, the dauphine and the Palatine princess. In the gardens she maintained her strategic advantage by having herself transported in a *chaise*

---

[145] Pierre Clément, *Madame de Montespan et Louis XIV* (Paris, 1868), 45–6.

roulante or wheelchair. By the end of Louis' reign, Madame de Maintenon was perceived as a leading person by courtiers and diplomats alike.[146] Elsewhere in Europe, too, the meteoric careers of mistresses strike the eye. At most courts, conflict between women close to the ruler can be found, based either on the opposition between legitimate reproduction and illicit love, or on the generations within the royal family. Queen mothers were at times unfavourably disposed towards the queens who came to take away their sons as well as their crowns. Leopold I's stepmother Eleonora II Gonzaga hated to see her crown as queen of Hungary pass to her daughter-in-law in 1681.[147] While such discord brings to mind the conflicts at harem-based courts, it rarely gave way to open violence and did not fundamentally influence succession.

Queens who had not yet given birth to legitimate successors were under permanent pressure, facing a challenge that could turn into an ordeal.[148] Catherine of Braganza experienced several miscarriages without producing an heir for the English throne. Emperor Charles VI's (1685–1711–1740) spouse Elisabeth-Christine of Brunswick-Wolfenbüttel spent a lifetime trying to bear sons. While his wife toiled and fretted, Charles tried to convince the crowned heads of Europe to accept female succession to all Habsburg domains – a doomed effort. Elisabeth-Christine's predicament was not necessarily easier than that of a Chinese empress, who could have concubines bear children that would still legally be hers. At all courts, the position of women, whether they were empresses, queens, consorts, or concubines, was enhanced as soon as they gave birth to a son. Likewise the most lastingly powerful female position was reached by mothers whose sons ascended to the throne. While the mothers of rulers did not usually enjoy the power of a conspicuously successful mistress, the latter risked falling rapidly and steeply at the first signal of the ruler's interest fading.[149]

As the main households of European kings held few or no women, they could not serve as a hunting ground for mistresses. Very often, these were recruited among the girls serving in the queen's chamber. Prominent among Louis XV's favourites, Madame de Pompadour (1721–64) apparently was the first mistress to be recruited from outside rather than from among the

---

[146] Duindam, *Myths of Power*, 155; Augustin Cabanès, *Une Allemande à la cour de France* (Paris, 1916), 78–81, 158–61; Mark Bryant, 'Partner, matriarch and minister: the unofficial consort, Mme de Maintenon of France, 1669–1715', in C. Campbell-Orr (ed.), *European Queenship: The Role of The Consort 1660–1815* (Cambridge, 2004), 77–106.

[147] Duindam, *Vienna and Versailles*, 232.

[148] Marie-Thérèse's intense wish to get pregnant is depicted in Giovanni Battista Primi Visconti, *Mémoires de Primi Visconti sur la cour de Louis XIV, 1673–1681*, ed. Jean-François Solnon (Paris, 1988), 65.

[149] The Introduction and many other contributions in Walthall (ed.), *Servants of the Dynasty*, underline the role of mothers as the most stable female figures of power at court.

ladies serving in the female households of the court – hence she had to be formally presented at court before she could become the king's lover.[150] In the female households, young noble girls were educated in the ways of the world and prepared for marriage while serving the queen mother, the queen, dauphine, or princess. Not only did kings themselves sometimes cast a desirous glance on the girls: the noble relatives of these female novices could arrange for them to be seen by the king, hoping their beauty would strike him and induce a passion beneficial to family fortunes. Starting out as pawns in the competition between court factions, they sometimes became key players.

Comparisons have been made between European female establish-ments and harems.[151] Kings were often drawn to the young girls serving their female relatives. A French decision in 1674 to replace the young and unmarried *filles d'honneur* by more mature married ladies failed to resolve the issue.[152] Ladies-in-waiting were housed in the innermost sections of the palace, their interaction with male counterparts subject to strict limitations and continuously supervised by senior female office-holders.[153] Visiting the Burgundian court in 1477, the Habsburg heir Maximilian noted to his surprise that 'Women were not confined during day or night, and the whole house is full of young ladies ... who are allowed to walk around everywhere.'[154] Women at the German court apparently were more secluded than their equals in Burgundy, France, or Italy, but some protec-tion was practised everywhere. Like the harem, moreover, the female household was a training ground for young women being groomed to marry among the young nobles connected to the court. In addition, noble teenagers served as pages in the stables of households throughout Europe, receiving an education for careers in the army or in government. These parallel male and female training schools bring to mind the more numerous slave establishments at Topkapı palace. The boy teenagers and young women trained at court forged a connection with numerous noble families. On a more modest scale, this reflects two of the secondary

---

[150] From Mme de Pompadour onwards, we seem to find the indication 'maitresse en titre' used often but as far as I know without reference to sources. The presentation may have served as an 'official' introduction giving rise to this title, which I have not seen men-tioned before this phase, and never in official sources generated by the court. See an early example: Mathieu François Pidanzat de Mairobert, *Anecdotes sur M. la comtesse du Barri* (London, 1775), 58.

[151] See e.g. Peter Moraw, 'Der Harem des Kurfürsten Albrecht Achilles von Brandenburg-Ansbach', in Hirschbiegel and Paravicini (eds.), *Das Frauenzimmer*, 439–48.

[152] Duindam, *Vienna and Versailles*, 94.

[153] On the institutions, see Keller, *Hofdamen*; Duindam, *Vienna and Versailles*.

[154] Maximilian I, *Maximilians I vertraulicher Briefwechsel mit Sigmund Prüschenk Freiherr zu Stettenberg nebst einer Anzahl zeitgenössischer Briefe*, ed. Victor Felix von Kraus (Innsbruck, 1875), 28.

purposes of the polygynous harem: schooling youngsters and confirming elite alliances. Finally, the women serving queens and princesses can to some extent be pictured as an 'inner court': their influence on royalty could be substantial.[155] Leading ministers and advisors, never as distant from the king's apartment as the administrators in China or in the Ottoman empire, particularly resented the influence of mistresses they could not easily control.

Succession: eligibles

Who was eligible to succeed to the highest office in the realm? More often than not, succession retained an element of choice and flexibility, but at the same time candidates for the throne were usually to be found within a predetermined group. In its most open form this pool of eligibles could include all adults able to raise sufficient support for their candidacy: typically, martial leaders who allowed their followers a fair share in the booty stood a good chance. The most restricted variant limited succession to a single person: the eldest son of the preceding ruler. Only in the absence of this preferred candidate could other options be considered. Not only the practice of succession, but also the ideal of kingship was torn between these extremes: on the one hand it stipulated personal qualifications that were hard to find in any single individual; on the other hand it glorified pedigree. The superhuman qualities attributed to kings necessarily left open the door to divine designation through omens, exceptional battle luck, or remarkable personal characteristics.[156] Likely successors could be pushed aside by

---

[155] See examples in Akkerman and Houben (eds.), *Politics of Female Households.*

[156] Shelley Hsueh-lun Chang, *History and Legend: Ideas and Images in the Ming Historical Novels* (Ann Arbor, MI, 1990), 41–3, 170 (on birth myths), 193 (on charisma), and throughout (on the mandate of heaven as rewarding martial heroes who became founding emperors). In the Safavid context, *farr-i Izadi* (divine spark, divine effulgence) is often mentioned: see Babayan, *Mystics, Monarchs, and Messiahs*, xxx, xxxiii, 21, 26, 132, 211, and on a divine blessing or charisma (*barakat*) as being hereditary, see 214, 295; both terms can also be found in Colin P. Mitchell, 'Am I my brother's keeper? Negotiating corporate sovereignty and divine absolutism in 16th-century Turco-Iranian politics', in Colin P. Mitchell (ed.), *New Perspectives on Safavid Iran: Empire and Society* (Abingdon and New York, 2011), 33–58, at 45–7. Persian *farr* was taken up by the Mughals and connected to Akbar's special religious position by Abu'l-Fazl: see his *The Ain i Akbari*, ed. H. Blochmann, 3 vols. (Calcutta, 1873–94), I, 170–5. A Turco-Mongol variant can be found in Turkish *kut*, fortune or battle luck: see Murphey, *Ottoman Sovereignty*, 57; Mongol *qutlug* was included in the titles of many rulers. *Wahyu* (divine inspiration or consent) is mentioned in Moertono, *State and Statecraft in Old Java*, 60–1; *tuah* (fortune), in Andaya, 'A very good-natured but awe-inspiring government', 63; *wahyu* and *perwaba* are discussed in J.J. Ras, 'Geschiedschrijving en de legitimiteit van het koningschap op Java', *Bijdragen tot de Taal-, Land- en Volkenkunde*, 150/3 (1994), 518–38, at 536. These terms all appear to be related to the European concept of charisma, with its double meaning of divine election and personal magnetism.

candidates showing such signs of divine support. Even where primogeniture was the preferred rule, it could not always be maintained. The Solomonic dynasty ruling Ethiopia enjoyed great prestige; in addition social conventions in Ethiopia strongly supported the rights of the eldest son. Nevertheless, the dynasty could not translate this predilection into primogeniture: succession also required the flame of personal religious charisma and hence could never be entirely fixed. Of the thirty-nine kings who reigned between 1270 and 1755, only twenty came to the throne as sons of the preceding king, most of them eldest sons.[157] Pedigree was of vital importance for Southeast Asian royalty, yet outsiders announced by omens and equipped with magical objects could rise suddenly and be accepted as legitimate rulers, particularly in phases of turmoil.[158] In China the repetition of dynastic breakdown, roughly every two or three centuries, opened the door to outsiders fighting their way to the dragon throne. Every founding emperor started out as a general, though only the Ming founder Zhu Yuanzhang and the Han founder Liu Bang were upstarts.[159] The mandate of heaven confirmed rebels founding new dynasties, as well as helping dynastic princes to consolidate their rule once they succeeded.

The key problem of succession can be restated in a different form. Competition brought to power robust figures, but as a system it made inevitable repeated phases of bloodshed and disorder.[160] Fixed succession reduced internal contestation, but in the long run necessarily also empowered weaklings whose rule could turn out disastrously. The political contingencies faced by any particular community as well as the level of its administrative routines played a role here. Polities depending on activist military leadership were seriously hampered by a figurehead on the throne; polities where the king was largely a ritual figure or where princely rule was supported by extensive administrative routines could more easily endure straw men – here, weaklings could be welcomed by office-holders taking advantage of the situation. Hence it may not be a coincidence that fixed succession rules appeared in polities with an established administrative apparatus, whereas volatile martial dynasties left more room for divine inspiration, fortune, and 'war luck'. The legendary prowess of Timur and Chinggis put a high premium on descent from these ancestors, but fitted

---

[157] Eike Haberland, *Untersuchungen zum äthiopischen Königtum* (Wiesbaden, 1965), 63–71, numbers at 59; Prutky, *Travels in Ethiopia*, 170–6, presents election or acclamation by nobles as the common form of succession, and Mentewwab's astute manoeuvre to put her son on the throne as an usurpation. At 99 and 172 Prutky mentions that Isayu II wore a golden locket around his neck, with the genealogy of the Solomonids, including the queen of Sheba.

[158] Andaya, 'Political development', 419.   [159] Chang, *History and Legend*, 40.

[160] See numerous examples in Burling, *Passage of Power*, and his general conclusions, 254–70, mentioning the dilemma of fixed heredity and contested succession at 258 and 260.

uncomfortably the introduction of rigidly fixed succession rules among their descendants. In the long run, however, most successor dynasties moved from open and contested succession to less violent prearranged forms.

Primogeniture was only one among many rules determining succession practices. Porphyrogeniture designated as successor the first son born 'in purple', once his father had already ascended to the throne – the term is derived from Byzantium but the practice is also known elsewhere.[161] Not uncommon in Africa, ultimogeniture, the opposite of primogeniture, stipulated succession by the king's youngest son. Often rules did not designate a specific successor, but barred certain candidates from succession: prohibitions against eldest sons are frequent. Sometimes prohibitions excluded all sons of the reigning king, an arrangement that necessitated rotation of kingship among competing houses or lineages.[162] Succession frequently alternated between downwards succession to sons and sideways succession to brothers, the latter tending to be more inclusive.[163] The first *tlatoque* (kings) of Tenochtitlan came to the throne as sons of kings: the pure bloodline was deemed more important than personal attributes. In a critical phase of Aztec expansion, succession shifted from sons to brothers, stressing the 'corporateness of the ruling group' as well as the requirement of military prowess.[164] Even where father–son succession was seen as the best form and primogeniture was accepted in principle, it was frequently abandoned in practice. European visitors often rightly assumed an overall preference for primogeniture without verifying whether it determined succession in practice.[165] They were taken aback by habits they viewed as unworkable. In his *History of*

---

[161] Goody, *Succession to High Office*, 33, referring to the Nupe in Nigeria. In Byzantium, the term indicated either birth in the *porphyra*, a building covered with purple marble, or birth after the father had ascended to the throne: see Louis Bréhier, *Les institutions de l'empire byzantin* (Paris, 1949), 22, 33–7; as all children of emperors received the title *porphyrogenitus*, it did not have importance for succession. The name *porphyrogennetos* or *porphyrogenitus* was given to tenth-century emperor Constantine VII, to bolster his legitimacy: see Peter Schreiner, *Byzanz 565–1453* (Munich, 2011), 25, 76.

[162] Beattie, *Bunyoro*, 13, on ultimogeniture; Drucker-Brown, *Ritual Aspects of Mamprusi Kingship*, 135–46 on the general prohibition against the king's sons and other rules; Goody, *Succession to High Office*, 172–5, on circulating succession; Ottino, 'Ancient Malagasy dynastic succession', 254.

[163] In the eighteenth-century Oyo kingdom, not discussed in this chapter, succession changed from primogeniture to lateral succession with election by a small council: see Robin Law, 'Making sense of a traditional narrative: political disintegration in the kingdom of Oyo', *Cahiers d'études africaines*, 22/87 (1982), 387–401, at 389–90; Samuel Obadiah Johnson, *The History of the Yorubas: From the Earliest Times to the Beginning of the British Protectorate* (Lagos, 1921).

[164] Rounds, 'Dynastic succession', 67–73.

[165] This can be deduced from numerous discussions of succession in Africa or Southeast Asia in the literature: see e.g. Bay, *Wives of the Leopard*, 84–6; Kobkua Suwannathat-Pian, 'Thrones, claimants, rulers and rules: the problem of succession in the Malay

Java, Stamford Raffles, the English governor of Java in the Napoleonic age, recorded with exasperation the civil commotions among the 'Malay tribes', caused in part by 'the ill-defined succession to the throne, from the doctrine of primogeniture being imperfectly recognized'.[166] Colonial administrators were averse to the upheavals created by contested succession, preferring a fixed pattern of investiture or alternatively seeking to obtain the right to act as kingmakers themselves.[167] Their redefinition of power worldwide helped to generalise father-to-eldest-son succession, erasing other customs, including the parallel succession of male and female power-holders mentioned earlier.[168] Raffles' attitude, understandable for anybody eager to maintain public order, may reflect the attitudes of earlier leaders aiming for stability by narrowing the options in relatively open and contested succession systems. However, every dynastic crisis resurrected the problem: who could, in the absence of legitimate successors, guide the realm to calm and prosperity?

Polygynous reproduction generated numerous royals. The proliferation of Chinese imperial lineages based on polygynous reproduction made extinction inconceivable. At an early stage, Tang emperor Taizong wrote pointedly that 'a branch can get so heavy that it breaks the trunk; a tail can get too big to be wagged', arguing that a limited number of powerful relatives would be dangerous. Safety was to be found in numbers: 'the best way is to enfeoff many relatives to even up their power and to have them regulate one another and share one another's ups and downs'. Later he added in more general terms: 'neutralizing the power of subordinates so that none of them gets to be too strong or too weak is indeed the key to securing one's throne'.[169] Whether or not

sultanates', *Journal of the Malaysian Branch of the Royal Asiatic Society*, 66/2 (1993), 1–27, at 3–8: 'The rules of succession that never were'; David Henige, 'Akan stool succession under colonial rule – continuity or change?', *Journal of African History*, 16/2 (1975), 285–301, mentioning the anachronistic tendency to think in terms of a fixed 'constitution' (299).

166 Thomas Stamford Raffles, *The History of Java*, vol. I (London, 1830), 258, and see also 297 for another remark about primogeniture, showing a better understanding of the situation.

167 See Sophia Raffles, *Memoir of the Life and Public Services of Sir Thomas Stamford Raffles Particularly in the Government of Java, 1811–1816, Bencoolen and its Dependencies, 1817–1824: With Details of the Commerce and Resources of the Eastern Archipelago, and Selections from His Correspondence* (London, 1835), claiming this at 93.

168 See above, 95, 'homogeneous transmission'.

169 Section on 'Establishing one's kinsmen' in Tang Taizong's 'Plan for an emperor', in Twitchett, 'How to be an emperor', 58–63; note important differences in translation between Twitchett on one hand and Chiu-yueh Lai in Patricia B. Ebrey (ed.), *Chinese Civilization: A Sourcebook* (New York, 1993), 112–15. The final sentence quoted here suggests a *divide et impera* attitude, whereas Twitchett's translation leaves open mutual support in the clan – this is important because examples for both readings can be found in practice.

Taizong's advice was taken seriously, the Chinese imperial clans became enormous. Membership was carefully registered in genealogies based on 'mourning grades' up to eight generations, with eligibility to the throne being limited to the male line. Not only did the emperor practise poly-gyny, his sons and their sons did so too: hence imperial clans multiplied rapidly. The number of Ming princes before the Qing takeover in 1644 has been estimated variously between 80,000 and 200,000 or more; in the early twentieth century, the Qing imperial lineage counted 73,418 persons.[170] Maintaining the status of the princes represented a major investment. All princes and their wives received stipends, and this held true also for the princesses and their spouses – although they were not eligible for succession. In 1067 the Song imperial clan consumed almost twice as much as the entire central bureaucracy, the equivalent of nearly two thirds of the army based in the capital. Under the Ming these costs escalated further, at times threatening the solvency of the dynasty.[171] At the same time, the inflation of imperial clans did not prevent succession conflict among a more limited circle of uncles, brothers, sons, and grand-sons of ruling emperors.[172] The most successful Chinese dynasties endured between two and three centuries; however, the changeover to a succeeding ruling family was invariably long and violent.[173] With the rise of a new dynasty, the former imperial clan lost all rights. The costly reservoir of numerous potential successors did protect the dynasty against extinction, but it could neither prevent conflict among dynastic contest-ants for the throne, nor secure an exceptionally long life to Chinese dynasties.

In monogamous Europe, the pool of royalty within each country was far smaller, often limited to a handful of persons. The boundaries of this group were not necessarily better defined than the huge Chinese imperial clan. Illegitimate sons and their issue in the later Middle Ages could still

[170] Rawski, *Last Emperors*, on the Qing princes as a 'lean aristocracy' and their more numerous Ming predecessors, 91–5, also note 117 at 328–9. See Chaffee, *Branches of Heaven*, 271–5, for a comparison of the Song imperial clan with Ming and Qing practices, with somewhat diverging figures.

[171] Ray Huang, *Taxation and Governmental Finance in Sixteenth-Century Ming China* (Cambridge, 1974), tables at 178; Chaffee, *Branches of Heaven*, 66–8, with numbers on Song princes and their costs; on the Ming budgetary crisis of the 1570s and new regulation cutting princes' stipends I rely on a presentation by Jérôme Kerlouégan held at Leiden University on 10 April 2013, entitled 'Ming princes and the Ming polity' and given to me by the author.

[172] Fisher, *Chosen One*, discusses the choice of a brother or the adoption of a prince from the imperial clan upon the death of an emperor without successor.

[173] See a particularly impressive picture of one changeover in Lynn A. Struve, *Voices from the Ming–Qing Cataclysm: China in Tigers' Jaws* (New Haven, CT, 1993). My assessment of Chinese succession diverges somewhat from Ebrey, who underlines stability thanks to high numbers in 'Succession to high office'.

profit from dynastic crisis and end up on the throne. Succession through the female line, accepted in principle when the male line dried up, linked most European dynasties to each other in numerous ways. This made it difficult to establish an unchallenged priority of succession upon extinction of the main line. Could formal renunciations of succession rights by queens be accepted as valid, and, if so, were they undermined by the failure to pay dowries or comply with other agreements made during the marriage negotiations? Did the designation in the testament of a dying king overrule accepted conventions? In the early modern age, it became increasingly uncommon to look for alternative candidates among contending high-ranking noble families from within the realm. Monogamous alliances among sovereign royal dynasties and the increased reliance on primogeniture in late medieval and early modern Europe rendered internal conflict less likely and certainly more subdued. However, the conflict shifted rather than disappeared, moving from internal contestation to large-scale warfare among the dynasties of Europe connected through intermarriage. The death of the last Spanish Habsburg Charles II in 1700, causing a war of exceptional proportions, can be placed in a long series of military conflicts triggered by extinction: 'Succession wars were the standard type of interstate conflict in the ancien régime.'[174] These wars put into perspective the contrast between apparently peaceful patterns of succession in Europe and the violent contestations common among claimants in Islamic Asian empires or African kingdoms. The incidence of extinction and ensuing dynastic crisis in European history was high, and the cost in human lives caused by the ensuing succession wars was substantial. Moreover, genetic defects caused by repeated marriages between the same dynasties contributed to the low survival rates of legitimate children born from these unions. Repeated intermarriage increased the risk of extinction and created a tangle of succession claims that engendered numerous wars.[175]

In sharp contrast to the Chinese pattern of reproduction and succession, the Ottomans never allowed their dynasty to proliferate. Succession rules did not include a marked preference for the eldest son as they did in Europe and China. Sultans usually came to power after a violent contest among the sons. Mehmed II had his brothers killed upon his accession in 1451; this practice was far from new, but in 1479 Mehmed promulgated

---

[174] Johannes Kunisch, *Staatsverfassung und Mächtepolitik: zur Genese von Staatenkonflikten im Zeitalter des Absolutismus* (Berlin, 1979), 75, on succession wars as the 'Grundtyp zwischenstaatlicher Konflikte' in early modern Europe; see also Hermann Weber, 'Die Bedeutung der Dynastien für die europäische Geschichte in der Frühen Neuzeit', *Zeitschrift für bayerische Landesgeschichte*, 44 (1981), 5–32.

[175] Delacour et al., 'Louis XIV et Marie-Thérèse d'Autriche', 272–5.

regulations that declared fratricide acceptable 'when appropriate'.[176] Fratricide in battle or after obtaining victory remained the rule until the early seventeenth century. In this period, violent competition became inevitable as soon as more than one son survived the reigning sultan. Stepping out of the race apparently never was an option. When Bayezid II's son Korkud, under the mounting threat of fraternal onslaught, asked his father whether he could withdraw and pursue a career as a Muslim scholar, his request was refused adamantly. Royal blood and divine intervention were more important than individual preferences. Korkud briefly survived the rise to power of Selim I in 1512, but was executed within a year.[177] With numerous sons alive, the contest could be particularly ferocious, while at times succession went smoothly because only one son remained to take his father's place. The contest among the sultan's sons gradually developed into a set pattern. Sons were sent out with their mothers to govern provinces and gain experience as soldiers and leaders, building their households and followings in the process.[178] Upon the death of their father, they rushed to the capital or army camp to capture the throne. In Süleyman's reign, the competition started under the eye of the father, who himself was heavily involved, adding filicide to the accepted convention of fratricide and the incidental example of patricide.

Matters started changing with the accession of Süleyman's son Selim II and the latter's son Murad III. These sultans stayed in the palace more often than their mobile martial predecessors. Murad III's son Mehmed was sent out to govern the province of Manisa in 1582: however, he proved to be the last prince to gain experience as a governor. When Mehmed returned to ascend to the throne in 1595, he had his nineteen brothers as well as the pregnant harem women killed – a feat that apparently shocked the Mughals, who nevertheless also prided themselves on violent competition among brothers.[179] Mehmed III in 1603 ordered the execution of his eldest son Mahmud, leaving only two princes available for succession, thirteen-year-old Ahmed and his mentally unstable elder brother Mustafa. Ahmed, the first sultan to ascend the throne from within

[176] Murphey, *Ottoman Sovereignty*, 103, and Ágoston and Masters (eds.), *Encyclopedia of the Ottoman Empire*, 365–6, question whether Mehmed II turned fratricide into a 'law', but he had his brother executed. Conventionally this was done with a silk cord, as no blood of Ottoman princes was supposed to be shed – see Ágoston and Masters (eds.), 274.

[177] Peirce, *Imperial Harem*, 44; see a different perspective in Nabil Al-Tikriti, 'The Ḥajj as justifiable self-exile: Şehzade Korkud's Wasīlat al-aḥbāb (915–916/1509–1510)', *Al-Masaq*, 17 (2005), 125–46.

[178] On princes and governors, see Kunt, 'A prince goes forth'; and Kunt, 'Devolution from the centre to the periphery: an overview of Ottoman provincial administration', in Duindam and Dabringhaus (eds.), *Dynastic Centre*, 30–48.

[179] Balabanlilar, 'Lords of the auspicious conjunction', 19; Faruqui, *Princes of the Mughal Empire*.

the palace, did not touch his sickly elder brother Mustafa. When Ahmed fathered his first son and thus secured the bloodline, he still left alive his brother. After Ahmed's death in 1617, Mustafa spent a year as sultan before he was deposed. Osman II (1604–1618–1622), too, let Mustafa live: after his deposition he was interned in the *kafes* ('gilded cage') of the Topkapı harem, henceforth the residence of all male relatives of the house of Osman except the ruling sultan. Around the turn of the nineteenth century the Ottoman scions in the kafes were allowed more freedom, and Abdulhamid II (1842–1876–1909*) allowed princes to marry and have children.[180]

The benevolent policy towards Mustafa did not spell the end of fratricide. Leaving the capital for a military campaign in 1621, Osman took the precaution of having his younger brother Mehmed executed. He himself would be killed by the janissaries in a 1622 revolt – the first regicide by Ottoman elites. Mustafa was again briefly put on the throne, a measure adopted by palace elites to continue the dynasty. In 1635 and 1638 fratricide was practised by Murad IV who ordered the execution of his brothers Bayezid, Süleyman, and Kasım before departing on campaigns. These bloody precautions put the survival of the dynasty at risk. On his deathbed in 1640 Murad took a final step towards 'dynastic suicide' by ordering the execution of the single remaining scion of the house of Osman, his brother Ibrahim. Only a trick played upon the dying sultan by his mother Kösem Sultan saved Ibrahim's life and dynastic continuity.[181] Mehmed IV, too, initially planned to kill his brothers, but was persuaded to let them live. Gradually, and not without some exceptions, fratricide was abolished and succession proceeded through seniority. Before 1600, sons had commonly succeeded their fathers; after 1648 it became more common for brothers to ascend the throne. The Ottoman court practised polygynous concubinage, but as only the reigning sultan was allowed to reproduce, the number of eligibles remained relatively small. Continuity in the Ottoman empire was never wholly secure; several times the dynasty drew close to extinction due to reproductive failure as well as violence. The remarkable longevity of the Ottoman dynasty was supported at critical junctures by elites who apparently saw no better way to serve their interests than to help the dynasty survive.

The Mughal story shows a variant of the same pattern, starting with fierce competition among the sons of the incumbent ruler. From the 1580s onwards sons were integrated into the empire-wide distribution of a rank (*mansab*) combined with a share of the fiscal revenues of landholdings (*jagirs*), rather than receiving their own provinces as appanages.

---

[180] Alderson, *Structure of the Ottoman Dynasty*, 34–5.   [181] Ibid., 13–14.

Princes were expected to move from region to region, ascending the ladder of advancement, building their followings, and contributing to the expansion and consolidation of the empire. At the same time, collateral branches of the dynasty were no longer accepted as competitors for the throne: this prize was tied to the outcome of a fight among brothers. Each contest was to be definitive: princes grew up knowing that they would end 'on the throne or on the funeral bier'.[182] The succession of one of the brothers entailed the death of his competitors. There was no clearly privileged son in the contest – eldest sons enjoyed a head start, but tended to fall out with their fathers when these redirected their benevolence to other sons to balance the competition. The battle for the throne, if it was not repeated too often in a short time-span, could reinvigorate the Mughal hold on the empire, with the new emperor attracting the support of all contestants mobilised.[183] Around the turn of the eighteenth century, towards the end of Aurangzeb's long rule, a gradual change set in that empowered the nobles in the empire and made princes more dependent. As in the Ottoman case, the princes were no longer sent out as governors, learning how to rule and fight while assembling a following: they, too, were now kept in the imperial harem. The adoption of the confinement of princes in the Red Fort, the Mughal variant of the *kafes*, coincided with the collapse of the dynasty as the regional hegemonic force in the early decades of the eighteenth century.[184]

Under the Safavids the same tensions can be found, and a similar solution was adopted under Shah Abbas I. The dynasty was torn between an inclusive understanding of sovereignty with a share for all members of the ruling house and a more exclusive vertical father-to-son view. Competing princes could easily find support among the military tribal Qizilbash leaders, who were keen to use the alliance for their own purposes. The accession to power of Shah Tahmasp (1514–1524–1576), son of Shah Ismail I, did not go uncontested: between 1524 and 1536, Iran experienced a protracted civil war, eagerly watched by competitors across the border.[185] In the end, Shah Tahmasp was able to

---

[182] Faruqui, *Princes of the Mughal Empire*, 7, 8, 12, 18–19, 25, 30–1.

[183] This is the principal thesis of Faruqui, *ibid*.

[184] On the relatively loose nature of the princes' captivity, see Muzaffar Alam and Sanjay Subrahmanyam, 'Envisioning power: the political thought of a late eighteenth-century Mughal prince', *Indian Economic & Social History Review*, 43/2 (2006), 131–61. Apparently the fortress of Gwalior had served in earlier reigns to incarcerate unruly princes or high nobles: see Manucci, *Pepys of Mogul India*, 35: 'we arrived at the well-known fortress of Gualior (Gwaliyar), where it is usual for the Mogul to keep as prisoners princes and men of rank'.

[185] On Shah Tahmasp's redefinition of clientage and devotion, see Hani Khafipour, 'The foundation of the Safavid state: fealty, patronage, and ideals of authority (1501–1576)', PhD thesis, University of Chicago (2013).

restore his power, but after his death another round of succession-related warfare commenced, once more pitting Safavid princes with their Qizilbash supporters against one another. Rising to power in the middle of this turmoil, Shah Abbas I (1571–1588–1629) in 1590 started replacing Qizilbash governors with slaves, while at the same time he severely curtailed his own kin.[186] Transferring the capital from Qazvin to the new court city of Isfahan, he moved his male kinsmen into the seclusion of the harem, following the pattern that developed simultaneously at the Ottoman court. The gradual move from collective sovereignty to a restricted vertical view, based on the successions of sons only, was demonstrated with force. Abbas I blinded several of his sons, a treatment marking them as unacceptable for the throne. In 1632, shortly after his accession, Shah Abbas' grandson Safi (1611–1629–1642) blinded numerous children born from unions between Safavid princesses and grandees. At the same time Safi ordered some of the leading families around court executed, throwing their bodies onto Isfahan's great square. This was a forceful demonstration of royal power, levelling the field of potential successors, eliminating over-mighty subjects, and cautioning the Qizilbash elites that times had changed.[187]

The Ottoman, Mughal, and Safavid dynasties all had Turkic roots and traced their provenance to the steppe. The transition from open and combative succession practices to fixed routines has been related to the gradual changeover from nomadic steppe empires to sedentary empires.[188] Some of the changes were certainly initiated with force by rulers intending to consolidate their power, although it is unclear whether they pursued any longer-term goals. It is striking to see that in each of these empires the wider family, including collateral lines, was gradually pushed out of the competition for the throne. A second, even more remarkable pattern which these empires all adopted between c. 1590 and 1720 is the confinement of the princes. Steppe conventions in succession and governance can also be found in East Asia, among the Mongol and Manchu conquest dynasties repeatedly invading China.

---

[186] On the 1590–1632 changeover, see Babayan, 'Waning of the Qizilbash'; Babaie et al., *Slaves of the Shah*, 8–9, 14, 18–19, 20–5 (on the 1590–1632 changeover), 31–3, 37, 41, 102 (on the 1632 massacre).

[187] Babayan, 'Waning of the Qizilbash', and Babaie et al., *Slaves of the Shah*, present the massacre as signalling the changeover from Qizilbash to slaves, confirming the 1590 changes; Rudi Matthee, *Persia in Crisis: Safavid Decline and the Fall of Isfahan* (London and New York, 2012), 35–40, underlines the persistence of the Qizilbash and the balancing policies of the Safavid shahs.

[188] Peirce, *Imperial Harem*, 22, 91, 109.

The Manchus had adopted many Chinese conventions before the conquest; yet when they entered China proper, they still adhered to a collective view of dynastic power. The khan united tribes under his authority without necessarily restricting succession rights to his own sons only, leaving room for a measure of shared sovereignty, succession through acclamation, and hence competition. This pattern was evident in the regency councils installed under the first emperors starting their rule as minors, the Shunzhi and Kangxi emperors. When Kangxi came of age, he faced the challenge of breaking the Manchu grandees before he could turn to reining in the Chinese generals dominating the south.

Central Asia, the extended steppe area at the crossroads of the great empires in East, West, and South Asia, long remained in the shadow of its conspicuous neighbours. In recent decades, numerous scholars have focused on the impact of nomadic movements from the core area into contiguous dynastic empires. The Eurasian or Central Asian steppe has been presented as the source of a continent-wide model that stood at the heart of Turco-Mongol dynasties rising throughout Asia.[189] What was the influence of the steppe model on succession? Mongol women were closer to power than women in either the Arabic-Islamic or the Chinese-Confucian traditions. The Mongols did not view descent in narrow patrilineal terms. Mughal emperors claimed descent from Chinggis Khan through the female line, and the place of dynastic daughters and sisters in Mughal India and Safavid Iran, at least in their early phases, was more marked than in imperial China or among the Ottomans. Mongol succession did not follow matrilineal patterns, but it did entail a diffuse and inclusive definition of the dynasty that is typical for double forms of descent.

Did the Mongols at any point define clear succession rules, still operative under their successor peoples? Chinggis Khan (1162–1206–1227) himself had designated his third son Ögedei (1186–1229–1241) as successor, but a younger son temporarily took charge until his father's choice could be confirmed by the Mongol assembly (*kuriltai*). Chinggis Khan failed to dictate any clear rules for succession, and these do not seem to have emerged at later stages. Ögedei designated Köchü, the third son of his main wife Töregene, as successor. After Köchü's early death, Ögedei groomed his grandson Shiremün (Köchü's eldest son) for leadership and succession. These wishes were not respected by his widow and regent

[189] J. F. Fletcher, 'Turco-Mongolian monarchic tradition in the Ottoman empire', *Harvard Journal of Ukrainian Studies*, 3–4 (1979–80), 236–51; Fletcher, 'The Mongols: ecological and social perspectives', *Harvard Journal of Asiatic Studies*, 46/1 (1986), 11–50; Christopher I. Beckwith, *Empires of the Silk Road: A History of Central Eurasia from the Bronze Age to the Present* (Princeton, NJ, 2009).

Töregene (r. 1242–6): invoking the rule of primogeniture, she put on the throne her eldest son Güyük (1206–1246–1248).[190] Mongol succession was characterised by many conflicting rules: designation, primogeniture, acclamation by the kuriltai all seem equally important, while in practice the balance of power among claimants determined outcomes. This leaves a thin connection only with later Ottoman, Mughal, and Safavid practices. Their gradual disenfranchisement of more distant relatives was typical for sedentary dynasties rather than for the Mongols. Designation was not systematically practised by Ottomans, Mughals, or Safavids, although the preferences of the incumbent ruler and his consorts could play a marked role in the conflicts among sons. What remains is the violent nature of competition for the throne, but this was the rule rather than the exception across the globe.

Ongoing contestation among royals leading to an alternation of fission and fusion can be seen in many African and Southeast Asian domains as well as in the Central Asian steppe. The terminology found in the literature – '*mandala-states*', 'galactic states', 'segmentary states' – suggests a pattern of a centre with satellites, interacting with other such centres and undergoing kaleidoscopic change: satellites become centres, or shift adherence from one centre to another.[191] There is little reason to see these common practices as a specifically 'Mongol' model and even less ground for the conventional term applied to this model: 'bloody tanistry'. This term, referring to Gaelic practices of government, succession, and inheritance, seems to have entered the vocabulary of scholars via its pejorative use by sixteenth-century English administrators of Ireland. For them 'tanistry' indicated the downside of alternating and distributive patterns of succession: recurring competition.[192] Their limited understanding of tanistry matches Raffles' annoyance about the Malayans'

---

[190] De Nicola, 'Unveiling the Khatuns', 70.

[191] Southall, 'Segmentary state'; Tambiah, 'Galactic polity'. On fusion and fission, see Andaya, 'Political development', 403; Chutintaranond, 'Mandala'.

[192] The term tanist or *tanaise ríg* appears in Irish chronicles to mean the second-in-charge under the king; from the later Middle Ages onwards the term was increasingly used to indicate the successor designated by the incumbent king, mirroring the practice of early Scottish kingship. In the Republic of Ireland, the deputy prime minister is still called *tanaiste*. See references to tanistry or bloody tanistry in e.g. George Lane, *Genghis Khan and Mongol Rule* (Indianapolis, IN, 2009), 7, 197; Beckwith, *Empires of the Silk Road*, 322; David Morgan, *The Mongols* (Cambridge, MA, 1986), 38–9; Fletcher, 'Turco-Mongolian monarchic tradition', 240–1, is probably the source of this peculiar habit. See discussions of succession in Ireland and Scotland, showing that the terminology is at best awkward: Ian Whitaker, 'Regal succession among the Dálriata', *Ethnohistory*, 23/4 (1976), 343–63; Megan McGowan, 'Royal succession in earlier medieval Ireland: the fiction of tanistry', *Peritia*, 17–18/ (2003), 357–81. The succession of early Scottish kings of Dálriata (500–842) avoided sons and brothers of the king, and preferred the designation of a successor from a wider group descending from the ancestor-king Erc.

inability to understand primogeniture.[193] Outside administrators preferred orderly and well-defined procedures: rulers or grandees acting
under their authority were not expected to become popular leaders or
military heroes.

A violent scramble for the throne reduced the number of contestants.
In the Safavid case, further pruning of the dynastic tree was achieved by
the blinding of young princes. The fact that even the boy children of
princesses were blinded suggests that the shahs had not entirely embraced
the view of the dynasty as a father-to-son line only – or alternatively that
they expected rivals from the wider group to be able to generate sufficient
support to form a threat. Limiting eligibility to the direct descendants of
kings by taking away succession rights from collateral lines was not always
a violent process. Kings of Buganda (located in modern Uganda) found a
relatively peaceful way to do this:

Princes in the direct royal line are known as 'princes of the drum'. They are
divided into two categories, princes of the mujaguzo drum, the sons of the king,
and princes of the kanaba drum, the grandsons of the king. When a new Kabaka
[king] was chosen to ascend the throne, his brothers were told that their sons
would never succeed. Their descendants became 'peasant princes', bamabun-
dugu, or 'princes thrown away'. The division is made by ritual pronouncement.
The chief minister, who selects the heir, turns to the new Kabaka's rejected
brothers and says, 'You are peasants now. You can never succeed to the
throne' ... Actually, the royal brothers remained 'princes of the drum' until they
died and their sons 'princes of the kanaba drum'.[194]

In this way, there were always enough candidates for the throne, while
numbers – and hence competition and costs – remained limited.[195]
Elsewhere in Africa, families descending from cadet brothers were sometimes exiled; otherwise they themselves could take the initiative and try
their luck in contiguous regions, bringing distant provinces under their
authority or conquering border areas. Conversely, we find examples of
neighbouring peoples 'kidnapping' royal princes and turning them into

[193] See McGowan, 'Fiction of tanistry', 381; Henry Sidney, 'Sir Henry Sidney's memoir of
his government of Ireland. 1583', *Ulster Journal of Archaeology*, 3 (1855), 33–357, at 33,
52, 85–109, 336–57, and 5 (1857), 299–323.
[194] Richards, 'African kings', 148; see examples of 'subclans' losing the right of succession,
at 141.
[195] The opposite of this practice of permanent pruning of the royal tree is found where
'perpetual kinship' or 'positional succession' define the chiefdoms and offices given to
sons as hereditary and freeze the relationship between the descendants, creating tensions
with the new king, who cannot give these offices to his own sons. See Bay, *Wives of the
Leopard*, 38–9; Jan Vansina, *Kingdoms of the Savanna* (Madison, WI, 1966), 82–3 on
'perpetual kinship' or 'positional succession' among the Lunda and the Luba: 'Thus,
ancient kinship relations were re-enacted every generation and new links were created
only after all the "old positions" in the system had been filled.'

local kings, apparently because of their prestige and presumed magical qualities.[196]

The Japanese imperial dynasty excluded the lines descending from younger brothers from succession, creating the noble lineages of Minamoto and Taira, who would hold high office at court, counterbalancing the prominent Fujiwara family of regents and empresses. Other princely collateral lines (*shinno* houses) were established in due course: in the eighteenth century, four of these princely houses served as 'back-up lines' for imperial succession, and their numbers proliferated after the Meiji restoration:[197] 'The sun line could thus remain "unbroken" thanks to blood replenishment by the adoption of sons from the shinno houses. But blood flowed in a reverse direction as well: an emperor's blood son or grandson could be called upon to succeed the headship of a sonless shinnoke.'[198] The Tokugawa shoguns, too, used collateral lines, both to push other noble houses out of the highest echelon of court titles and to create a reservoir for succession – five of the Tokugawa shoguns were adopted into the main line from cadet branches.[199]

Going one critical step further, dynasties could be defined not in terms of downwards next-of-kin succession, but as a wider kin group barring father–son and brother–brother transmission.[200] A suspicion against the force of parent–child succession can be found in many places: communities established rules of avoidance preventing the lasting concentration of wealth and power in the hands of only a very limited segment. The prohibition of sons and brothers turned collateral lines into the preferred successors. In the absence of unequivocal rules for rotation or priority of these families, each of the potential candidates needed to solicit support, demonstrating princely qualities and distributing gifts among those expected to wield influence. As we have seen, alternating succession was practised in Europe in Gaelic regions; we can find examples across

---

[196] Temesgen G. Baye, 'The evolution and development of kingship and traditional governance in Ethiopia: a case of the Kefa kingdom', *Journal of Asian and African Studies*, 47/ 2 (2012), 190–203, mentioning exile at 194; Southall, 'Segmentary state', on 'hiving-off' and 'kidnapping' at 61–2; E. E. Evans-Pritchard, 'The Zande state', *Journal of the Royal Anthropological Institute of Great Britain and Ireland*, 93/1 (1963), 134–54, stresses the dynamics between princes and the king – and the fact that princes were primarily each other's rivals and hence as a rule couldn't threaten the king.

[197] Shillony, *Enigma of the Emperors*, 60–2.   [198] Lebra, *Above the Clouds*, 51.

[199] Wakabayashi, 'In name only', 39–40, 49; Conrad D. Totman, *Politics in the Tokugawa Bakufu, 1600–1843* (Cambridge, MA, 1967), 110–30, table at 112, discussion of place in succession at 119–20; Marius Jansen, *Warrior Rule in Japan* (Cambridge, 1995), 173–4; Totman and Jansen list the 'three houses' (*sanke*) Mito, Owari, and Kii, and the 'three lords' (*san kyo*) Hitotsubashi, Tayasu, and Shimizu.

[200] Drucker-Brown, *Ritual Aspects of Mamprusi Kingship*, 135–6, explains one example of this prohibition.

the world, with strong concentrations in Africa and Southeast Asia.[201] The Inka pattern of succession reflected not only an alternation between two segments, but also a permanent vacillation between pedigree and merit. A clearly stated preference for primogeniture was in practice often discarded when younger candidates appeared more promising.[202]

Defining eligibles for succession is one thing, while remembering them is another, particularly in cases where numerous descendants of previous rulers can compete for the throne. How did different polities organise dynastic memory? King-lists are available for many areas, but they were usually compiled after reigns. Genealogies can be found throughout the world, but these, too, tend to look towards the past even if they support claims in the present. Genealogies were carefully maintained by ruling houses and demonstrated in painting and sculpture; titles were reiterated in preambles to public statements and in inscriptions. The Chinese Imperial Clan Court kept track of all princely families and their marriages.[203] How well-informed were candidates and wider audiences about the details of kinship and descent? This is a difficult issue. On the one hand, we can accept a heightened awareness of such matters in environments where this information made a big difference.[204] On the other hand, it seems likely that the exact status of every single person in extended royal clans eluded the eligibles as well as the wider audiences. Genealogies allow manipulation, but they do facilitate the process of remembering. How did societies without script deal with this? A remarkable example of remembering and forgetting eligibles can be found in the Mamprusi kingdom. Drummers performed the king-lists there on major occasions, praising the names and deeds of former royals. The presence of royal eligibles was expected on these occasions:

any royal who hears his father's name performed must pay the drummer. Royals may choose not to attend public celebrations in order to avoid the expense. However, the fact that musicians must be paid suggests that the names of royals

---

[201] See Goody, *Succession to High Office*, overview at 172–5; Ottino, 'Ancient Malagasy dynastic succession', 254, mentions uterine succession, ultimogeniture, and rotation among several related lineages as widely attested in West Indonesia, the Malay Peninsula, and Sumatra; for numerous other examples, e.g. also in a matrilineal context, see Emmanuel Terray, 'Le royaume Abron du Gyaman', in Claude Tardits (ed.), *Princes & serviteurs du royaume* (Paris, 1987), 23–58; for rotation among four houses with the same father but different mothers, see Marjorie Helen Stewart, 'Kinship and succession to the throne of Bussa', *Ethnology*, 17/2 (1978), 169–82.

[202] Yaya, *Two Faces of Inca History*.

[203] Stevan Harrell et al., 'Lineage genealogy: the genealogical records of the Qing imperial lineage', *Late Imperial China*, 6/2 (1985), 37–47.

[204] Thus Horowski, *Die Belagerung des Thrones*, plausibly argues that even distant connections were readily perceived by the eighteenth-century French nobility.

with no descendants, or descendants who cannot afford to pay, will sooner or later be dropped from the lists.[205]

This flexible process of remembering and forgetting must be typical for many environments, with a mixture of current prestige and descent status determining chances for maintaining a high profile and pressing succession rights. Any cadet branch after three or four generations without high office could expect to gradually lose its royal allure, slowly merging with the population. Only in places where royals were maintained by stipends, as in imperial China, or in regions where they held leading regional office were they able as a rule to cling to their descent status. However, as we shall see, maintaining visible status was not always an advantage.

Kingmaking, kingmakers, and redundant royals

Who determined succession? Fixed patterns of succession, such as male primogeniture, do not require the intervention of others as long as there is a candidate. As soon as the vacancy cannot be filled according to the rules, or if these arrangements leave open various possibilities, active intervention becomes necessary. The first possible kingmaker is the king himself. Designating a successor allows rulers to reward proven capabilities and to punish misbehaviour. It also opens the door to endless complications. Father–son conflicts abound in the history of dynasty: succession rights generate tension. A distressing example occurred in eighteenth-century Chosŏn Korea between King Yŏngjo and his heir-apparent Sado. The father's high expectations aggravated the son's vacillation. Their long and painful conflict ended with Sado's slow suffocation in a rice chest, a ritual death imposed by the despondent father: no royal blood could be spilled. In England, the conflict between George II of Britain and his intractable son Frederick prince of Wales did not lead to violence, but the quarrel was publicly known and the prince of Wales became a focal point for opposition. In more muted form, the same structural tension can be seen at the French court, where the *dauphin* or heir-apparent was no longer granted his own household in the seventeenth century – a measure was implemented almost unthinkingly because these separate establishments had faded from memory after two dauphins, in 1610 and 1643, had inherited their father's court at a very young age.[206] Anywhere, the presence of an undisputed successor attracted ministers and elites sidelined by the father, who eagerly prepared their return to power under the son. Several father–son contests directly influenced succession policies,

---

[205] Drucker-Brown, 'King house', 177.
[206] Duindam, *Vienna and Versailles*, 58; Bluche (ed.), *Dictionnaire du grand siècle*, 448.

perhaps most notably the clashes between the Kangxi emperor and his heir-apparent, and between Tsar Peter I of Russia and his eldest son.[207]

Russian succession was a mixture of primogeniture, designation by the incumbent ruler, and acclamation by assembly – elements all present in Mongol succession practice. The Romanov dynasty was put on the throne through acclamation by the assembly in 1613; the practice continued with the eldest and only surviving son Aleksei I, who was still proclaimed tsar by the 'boyars and the people' in 1645. Peter the Great, the archetypal autocrat, was raised to power in preference over his feeble elder brother by an assembly in 1682: acclamation overruled primogeniture.[208] The troubled relationship between Peter and his eldest son Tsarevich Aleksei led to the flight of the latter to Vienna, where he started scheming against his father's unpopular policies. It is not clear whether Aleksei prepared a new policy for his future reign or actually intended to overthrow his father with the help of disgruntled Russian nobles and Swedish-Habsburg outside support. In any case, he planned for change and was put on trial in Russia. The affair ended in 1718 with the unexplained death of the tsarevich in prison.[209] Peter, aiming to break the power of the competing traditions of acclamation and primogeniture, in 1722 solemnly stated the tsar's exclusive sovereign right to designate a successor. However, by failing to proclaim a clear choice before his death, Peter left Russian succession a disjointed mixture of acclamation, heredity, and designation, marked by frequent coups and the intervention of court factions. At the end of her reign Catherine the Great unsuccessfully tried to transfer succession to her grandson Alexander rather than to her eldest son Paul. The resentful Paul made such practices impossible by instituting a new code for succession as well as for the imperial family in 1797. The code clearly opted for primogeniture, and thus aligned Russian succession with common European customs.[210] Typically, Paul himself

---

[207] On Yŏngjo and Sado, see Hyegyong, *Memoirs*, the memoir of 1805, 241–336.

[208] Richard Wortman, 'The representation of dynasty and '"fundamental laws" in the evolution of Russian monarchy', *Kritika*, 13/2 (2012), 265–300, at 270. See an example in Dahomey of a *vidaho* or heir being sent away by his father Tegbesu because he was too eager to succeed, in Bay, *Wives of the Leopard*, 160.

[209] Paul Bushkovitch, 'Power and the historian: the case of Tsarevich Aleksei 1716–1718 and N.G. Ustrialov 1845–1859, *Proceedings of the American Philosophical Society*, 141/2 (1997), 177–212; Bushkovitch, *Peter the Great: The Struggle for Power, 1671–1725* (Cambridge, 2001), 339–425.

[210] Wortman, 'Representation of dynasty'; see the relevant statement and defence in Antony Lentin, *Peter the Great: His Law on the Imperial Succession: The Official Commentary* (Oxford, 1996); on the court factions, see also Ernest A. Zitser, 'Post-Soviet Peter: new histories of the late Muscovite and early imperial Russian court', *Kritika*, 6/2 (2005), 375–92; on Paul and the nineteenth-century sequence, see Russell E. Martin, '"For the firm maintenance of the dignity and tranquility of the imperial

soon counteracted the code by designating his second son Konstantin as tsarevich and in 1801 even considered legitimising the children of one of his mistresses. In the nineteenth century Russian succession remained bumpy, with a rebellion following the enthronement of a brother in 1825. Heredity, moreover, was never 'deemed sufficient to justify the rulers' claims to the throne': power had to be manifested.[211]

A comparable sequence of events took place in Kangxi's reign. Qing succession had at first mixed Manchu and Han Chinese patterns, adding a notable presence of shared sovereignty and rule-by-council to Chinese centralised notions of power predicated on primogeniture. The first two Qing emperors started out as minors under regency councils. After taking power into his hands, Kangxi rapidly nominated his eighteen-month-old first son Yinreng heir-apparent in 1676. A series of altercations between father and son would lead to the heir-apparent being stripped of his rank in 1708. Following these experiences Kangxi made no further public announcement of the nomination of an heir-apparent. His successor, the Yongzheng emperor, who claimed to have been selected by the Kangxi emperor unbeknownst to others, turned secret succession into a principle and devised a procedure for it. The fact that a successor had been chosen was made public, but the name of the candidate remained secret – a secret confided to a small piece of paper in a damask-covered wooden casket that was placed some thirty feet above the throne in the audience hall at Qianqing palace. One or two confidants were told that the emperor himself also carried a note with the name of the successor, as a precaution.[212] In eighteenth-century Russia as well as in Qing China, emperors restated their personal right to designate their successors, whether or not they were first sons.

The wish of the dying ruler could be undone by the power of a regent or an assembly; each of these could override ingrained preferences for primogeniture or ultimogeniture. It is striking how easily numerous carefully stated principles could be pushed aside by unexpected contingencies demanding ad hoc solutions. Positive rules defining ideal candidates were easier to ignore than prohibitions, leaving open many choices while barring only some.[213]

In Europe heredity and primogeniture emerged late and hesitantly. Roman and Byzantine imperial dignity had included a strong element of

---

family": law and familial order in the Romanov dynasty', *Russian History*, 37/4 (2010), 389–411.

[211] Wortman, 'Representation of dynasty', 265–6, 281.

[212] Elliott, *Qianlong*, 2; Chia Ning, 'Qingchao Huangwei Jicheng Zhidu; The Institution of Qing Throne Succession (review)', *China Review International*, 14/1 (2007), 280–8.

[213] Suwannathat-Pian, 'Thrones, claimants, rulers and rules', 9.

personal achievement and acclamation, with numerous military leaders being 'raised on a shield' to signal their elevation.[214] The long list of Byzantine emperors reigning between 395 and 1453 includes only three dynasties able to maintain their hold on the throne for more than a century.[215] Most forms of kingship in Europe, whether or not they were vested in one particular family, had once combined elements of hereditary right, personal suitability, and some form of election by an assembly of peers.[216] By the end of the early modern age, in most realms only a ritual acclamation by peers embedded in the coronation ceremony still pointed to these earlier forms. However, the two nominally highest European dignities, that of pope and emperor, were still formally elected by cardinals and the limited body of worldly and spiritual electors respectively. In practice the Habsburgs secured a near-monopoly of the imperial title, partly by the designation and election of the successor during the lifetime of the emperor (*vivente imperatore*). Nevertheless, every new nomination necessitated a round of negotiations, a custom introduced by the Saxon elector, who withdrew in favour of Charles V after being elected in the first round of the 1519 election. Henceforth every election went together with a confirmation of the electors and other groups in the empire, embodied in a sequence of treaties gradually turning into an 'imperial constitution'. The short-lived incumbency of a Bavarian elector as emperor (1742–5) showed that the dignity could still be awarded to competing dynasties. Pope and emperor were only the highest-ranking examples of elective monarchical practice in Europe; it was common also in Central Europe and Scandinavia, although with the exception of Poland the tendency here was clearly towards hereditary succession.[217]

---

[214] Gilbert Dagron, *Emperor and Priest: The Imperial Office in Byzantium*, trans. Jean Birrell (Cambridge, 2003); Christopher Walter, 'Raising on a shield in Byzantine iconography', *Revue des études byzantines*, 33/1 (1975), 133–76.

[215] The Macedonian, Komnenian, and Palaiologan dynasties. See Bréhier, *Les institutions de l'empire byzantin*, 1–52, for an overview of the imperial institution, the family, and changing modes of succession; a brief discussion of the principle of dynasty in Byzantium can be found in Charles F. Pazdernik, 'Dynasty, idea of, Byzantine', in Bagnall et al. (eds.), *Encyclopedia of Ancient History*, 2243–4.

[216] Katharine Simms, 'Changing patterns of regnal succession in later medieval Ireland', in Frédérique Lachaud and Michael Penman (eds.), *Making and Breaking the Rules: Succession in Medieval Europe, c.1000–c.1600/Établir et abolir les normes: la succession dans l'Europe médiévale, vers 1000–vers 1600* (Turnhout, 2007), 161–72, at 162, with quotes from Irish sources including these three components, and references to the literature.

[217] See several chapters dealing with elective forms of monarchy in Lachaud and Penman (eds.), *Making and Breaking the Rules*; on election practices in early modern Transylvania, see Graeme Murdock, '"Freely elected in fear": princely elections and political power in early modern Transylvania', *Journal of Early Modern History*, 7/3 (2003), 213–44.

Heredity, primogeniture, and the indivisibility of sovereignty and territory were the consequence of a long and tangled process. As late as 1564, at the death of Ferdinand I, the Austrian Habsburg territories were divided among the sons of the deceased ruler: Styria and the Tyrol would be ruled by junior branches until 1619 and 1665 respectively. The Hungarian and Bohemian crowns united under Austrian Habsburg rule all proudly cultivated their own coronations and leading officers. In several major European monarchies, sovereign princes maintained their special rights into the eighteenth century. The Lorraine family cultivated connections in France and in the Empire, while it tried to maintain its own territories. The Liechtenstein family obtained sovereignty in the Empire by serving the Habsburgs and maintained its princely status after the demise of the former emperors.[218]

Machiavelli noted about the Mamluk sultan ('Soldan'): 'this state of the Soldan is different from that of all other princes, being similar to the Christian pontificate, for the sons of the dead prince are not his heirs, but he who is elected to that position by those who have authority.'[219] Mamluk succession, with alternating phases of hereditary father–son succession and election, was hardly as exceptional as Machiavelli assumed.[220] However, in one important respect, the Mamluk, papal, and imperial elections differ from elective forms of kingship elsewhere. The electors of the Holy Roman Empire, the cardinals united in the conclave, and the Mamluk emirs were themselves potential successors, whereas kingmakers across the globe were not usually eligible for the supreme honour they could confer on others. The right of determining the choice among a number of candidates was usually granted to relative outsiders. In the kingdom of Bunyoro, ultimogeniture was an established convention; the eldest son could not ascend to the throne but became the leader of the royal clan and could step in to decide succession. Such 'neutrals' can be found in many places: 'non-eligible royals, hereditary nobles, or commoners' who acted as regents, as guardians of regalia during an interregnum, as kingmakers, or as members of succession

---

[218] On the Lorraine, see Jonathan Spangler, *The Society of Princes: The Lorraine-Guise and the Conservation of Power and Wealth in Seventeenth-Century France* (Farnham, 2009). On the Liechtenstein, see Thomas Winkelbauer, *Fürst und Fürstendiener: Gundaker von Liechtenstein, ein österreichischer Aristokrat des konfessionellen Zeitalters* (Vienna and Munich, 1999); Volker Press and Dietmar Willoweit (eds.), *Liechtenstein – fürstliches Haus und staatliche Ordnung: Geschichtliche Grundlagen und moderne Perspektiven* (Vaduz, Vienna, and Munich, 1987).

[219] Niccolò Machiavelli, *The Prince*, trans. Luigi Ricci (London and Oxford, 1921), 81.

[220] On changing Mamluk succession practices, see Amalia Levanoni, 'The Mamluk conception of the sultanate', *International Journal of Middle East Studies*, 26/3 (1994), 373–92; and more recently Angus Stewart, 'Between Baybars and Qalāwūn: under-age rulers and succession in the early Mamlūk sultanate', *Al-Masaq*, 19/1 (2007), 47–54.

councils. Richards cites the device of a Bantu 'umpire prince', a royal son of high rank debarred from succession, who settled disputes among his brothers.[221] Among the matrilineal Bemba a similar pattern can be found, with a group of ineligibles coming to the fore during the changeover to a new king:

Who owns the historic charters of chiefship among the Bemba? Not the king, nor the royal dynasty but a class of hereditary priest-councillors (bakabilo) attached to the chief ... The bakabilo may be described as royal neutrals, that is to say men of royal descent but debarred by matrilineal succession from claiming the chiefship and hence never feared as rivals.[222]

The Aztec *cihuacoatl*, an office apparently barred from succession but vested hereditarily in the descendants of a high-ranking royal, was a key figure during interregna. In addition, the *cihuacoatl* acted as kingmaker with a 'council of four' and the kings of the two allied cities Texcoco and Tlacopan, although the new *tlatoani* still needed to be acclaimed by a broader elite grouping.[223] In general terms, groups excluded by the definition of descent in force could act as kingmakers and arbiters: maternal kin in patrilineal polities and vice versa.

In patrilineal Dahomey the royals, sent out from the palace in their youth, necessarily relied on the information and interventions of palace women in contested successions; the woman successfully supporting one of the contenders could then become his reign-mate or *kpojito*, representing the commoner and conquered element in the state.[224] The *asantehemaa* acted as the main kingmaker among the matrilineal Asante, with the *asantehene* taking the equivalent role in the succession of his female counterpart.[225] In China, women who could not themselves inherit and were expected to submissively fit into the male lineage acted as mediators among competing male heirs. At the level of imperial succession empress dowagers, who were unequivocally barred from formal imperial rule, fulfilled the same role in most Chinese dynasties. The empress dowager

[221] Numerous examples can be cited for Africa: Beattie, *Bunyoro*, 30; Richards, 'African kings', 140; Oberg, 'Kingdom of Ankole in Uganda', 138–9, on the Enganzi; Baye, 'Kefa kingdom', 194; Drucker-Brown, 'King house', 175–6; Haberland, *Untersuchungen zum äthiopischen Königtum*, on kingmakers as the 'Großen der Pfalz' or grandees of the palace at 137, also in general 58 and many other instances.

[222] Audrey I. Richards, 'Social mechanisms for the transfer of political rights in some African tribes', *Journal of the Royal Anthropological Institute of Great Britain and Ireland*, 90/2 (1960), 175–90, at 183–4; see also Rattray, *Ashanti Law and Constitution*, 86 and many other places, on the role of the Wirempefo in the interregnum.

[223] Rounds, 'Dynastic succession', 79–81, mentioning at 79 other examples of 'stand-ins' and kingmakers.

[224] Bay, *Wives of the Leopard*, 81–9 and many other places.

[225] Blier, *Royal Arts of Africa*, 137; Stoeltje, 'Asante queen mothers', 54.

was expected to choose among the various options when no son was available for succession. The throne could go to a younger brother, to a grandson, or via posthumous adoption to one of the princes from the imperial clan in the son's generation. In this special case, the empress dowager could overrule ministers. After the senior empress Xiang had announced the death of the Song Zhezong emperor (1076–1085–1100), a conversation ensued between the advisors and the dowager, reported by one of the participants:

> Zhang Dun (one of the four councillors) in a harsh voice said "According to the rites and statutes, Prince Jian should be installed, since as a brother with the same mother, he is the closest relative" . . . the empress dowager said "All of the brothers from Prince Shen on down are all Shenzong's sons. It is difficult to distinguish among them. Prince Shen has sick eyes. The next is Prince Duan (Huizong), so he should be established".

The empress dowager's choice of one of Zhezong's brothers was respected by the councillors. Soon afterwards, the new emperor Huizong himself summoned his advisors and stated that 'Just now I begged Mom to govern with me', an illustration of the two ways through which empress dowagers could wield very real power: kingmaking and regencies.[226] In the Ottoman empire between the death of Murad III in 1595 and the rise to power of the Köprülü viziers in 1656, the *valide sultan* was probably the key influence on succession, which she decided in accord with major inner and outer court officials such as the chief black eunuch of the harem and the *agha* of the janissaries.[227]

This brings us to another group of kingmakers: guards at the heart of the dynastic establishment, who at critical moments could sell their swords to the highest bidder or push forward candidates they expected to serve their interests. Accession donatives, or payments made to the troops upon succession to the throne, are conspicuously present in Roman and Ottoman history. Following a long-standing habit, Claudius in 41 CE raised the stakes by paying an unprecedented sum to the Praetorians to consolidate his position; this inflation would continue under his successors.[228] In the case of the Ottoman sultan, 'Until the

---

[226] Ebrey, 'Succession to high office', 56, 59.

[227] Peirce, *Imperial Harem*; Hathaway, *Beshir Agha*. On the rise of the chief black eunuch and his competition with the previously leading chief white eunuch, see Yıldız Karakoç, 'Palace politics and the rise of the chief black eunuch in the Ottoman empire', MA thesis, Boğaziçi University (2005).

[228] Richard Duncan-Jones, *Money and Government in the Roman Empire* (Cambridge, 1998), 86–7; on Claudius, see 'donative' in J.W. Roberts (ed.), *The Oxford Dictionary of the Classical World* (Oxford, 2007), with other references to 'donative' e.g. under 'Praetorians'.

distribution of the accession donatives his installation in office was considered incomplete and his authority circumscribed.'[229] Among the various key elements in the process of accession, the donative was probably the most important:

If one were called upon to choose between the girding of the sword, the swearing of oaths of allegiance and the payment of accession donatives as the defining act which conferred legitimacy and confirmation to a sultan's succession to rule, it was beyond a doubt the last that carried greatest weight and significance among followers, advisers, supporters and future subjects.[230]

The inflation of donatives in successive Ottoman reigns underlines the increasing presence of the janissaries in the Ottoman polity. Donatives were important mostly when legitimacy was in one way or another doubtful or when other candidates were present. In general largesse played an important role in accessions. The kingmakers in the Mamprusi kingdom expected to be feasted by the competitors for the throne. At greater remove from the actual choice, but still relevant for popular acclamation, audiences during the election and coronation of the early modern European emperors were indulged with wine-spouting fountains and the throwing of coins.

Once succession was decided, it was usually confirmed by accession rites that could vary from wild ordeals to serene confirmations, in intimate or public settings. The 'rites of passage' that transformed a royal eligible into a king were also a phase of fluidity and anxiety for society as a whole. Interregna were sometimes styled as counter-images of ordered society, as the world topsy-turvy. Violence and bloodshed in the palace, outsiders temporarily acting as mock-kings, and legitimate plunder can all be found.[231] In this anxious phase interference in succession by inner court powers, from women and eunuchs to elite guards, remained a distinct possibility. The pressure of outside administrators in China to fix an open situation by pushing for a public announcement of the choice of an heir

---

[229] Murphey, *Ottoman Sovereignty*, 86.

[230] Ibid., 129, with further elaboration at 120–3, 128–9.

[231] See in general Meyer Fortes, 'Of Installation Ceremonies', *Proceedings of the Royal Anthropological Institute of Great Britain and Ireland* (1967), 5–20. A rich literature exists describing specific rites or ceremonies for most of the regions discussed here. On the rites connected to papal interregnum or *sede vacante*, see Joëlle Rollo-Koster, *Raiding Saint Peter: Empty Sees, Violence, and the Initiation of the Great Western Schism (1378)* (Leiden and Boston, MA, 2008). For African examples of the interregnum, see Susan Drucker-Brown, 'The grandchildren's play at the Mamprusi king's funeral: ritual rebellion revisited in northern Ghana', *Journal of the Royal Anthropological Institute*, 5/2 (1999), 181–92; Bay, *Wives of the Leopard*, 16–17, 81; Norris, *Memoirs of the Reign of Bossa Ahádee*, 128–30; Rattray, *Ashanti Law and Constitution*, 142, 164, on looting after the death of a king or chief.

during the emperor's life was a manoeuvre to pre-empt such inner court machinations as well as to prevent a chaotic interregnum.

What to do with the royals, most of whom never ended up on the throne? And what to do with their descendants? Ottoman and Mughal restriction of eligibility to sons of the incumbent ruler and the violent struggle among these sons reduced numbers, as did Safavid blinding of princes.[232] The proliferation of Chinese imperial clans coincided with a strong preference for father–eldest son succession: a limited imperial family was combined with a huge imperial clan, raising the question how this extended group would be treated. The European distinction between *famille royale* and *sang royal*, or the vertical royal family and royal blood including collaterals, matches this distinction without approaching the numbers. Among the small number of royal collaterals, several caused problems for their ruling relatives by meddling in revolts or channelling discontent – as did the Orléans collateral line of the Bourbon house. The fundamental change seen in the Ottoman, Mughal, and Safavid cases makes clear the two dominant options for the treatment of royal eligibles by rulers across the globe. Princes were either sent out to govern, fight, and gain experience, or they were kept on a short leash at the centre of dynastic power. The changeover from frontier fighters to subdued occupants of the *kafes* in the harem – or the somewhat more open Red Fort of eighteenth-century Mughal princes – epitomises the two strategies commonly used to deal with princes. African practice suggests another related option: banishing princes to the periphery. Princes in several African kingdoms were sent out as 'banished heirs'. In Dahomey princes were sent out of the palace at age seven or eight, to be raised in other households, where they remained secluded from the court and ineligible for high office.[233] Ebrey considers how princes in imperial China could be kept out of harm's way: 'One way to do this was to send nonsucceeding sons out of the capital; another was just the opposite, to confine them to the capital to keep them under watch.'[234] Claude Tardits' examination of the relationship between princes and kings in Africa was summarised by Pierre Mounier in almost the same way: 'Either they are closely linked to the throne and we find them holding high office at court, or they are kept

[232] On mutilation, see also Tardits (ed.), *Princes & serviteurs*, 12, 15; Haberland, *Untersuchungen zum äthiopischen Königtum*, 185.

[233] Goody, *Succession to High Office*, 23, on the 'banished heir' among the Mossi and in other African kingdoms. On the Mossi, see Michel Izard, 'Le royaume Mossie du Yatenga', in Tardits (ed.), *Princes & serviteurs*, 61–106, underlining at 82 the fact that princes are not allowed to live close to the king, never even spending a night in the palace, a rule particularly strict for the successor. On Dahomey, see Hérissé, *L'ancien royaume du Dahomey*, 32–3; Bay, 'Servitude and worldly success', 350.

[234] Ebrey, 'Succession to high office', 68.

away from the court, sometimes violently.'[235] Ebrey stresses the need to keep princes away from power whether at the centre or in the provinces; Mounier sees the centre as powerful, the regions as more marginal. In the Ottoman, Mughal, and Safavid cases, the regional activity of the princes indicated their power and preparation for the succession battle, whereas during their confinement in the centre they passively awaited the choice of kingmakers. In Europe royals likewise could be found actively serving in the regions as viceroys, governors, and generals, or at the centre, serving in their relatives' establishments and living nearby in their own stately quarters. These roles, however, were often combined or alternated.

The Ming imperial clan, interestingly, shows yet another alternative: marginalisation in the regions. The Ming founder started out enfeoffing his sons with important military-strategic principalities, but during his reign started doubting the loyalty and moral stature of the princes. After the brief reign of his grandson, ousted from power by his forceful uncle who would rule as the Yongle emperor (1360–1402–1424), the enfeoffed princes were increasingly seen as a danger that needed to be reined in. Rules were decreed that limited the mobility of the princes as well as their functions and connections; this imperial clan was to be prestigious but basically unemployed. Only in the very last phase of Ming rule were clansmen finally entitled to enter the civil service examinations, the main road to office and preference – a limited reform that came too late to have any impact. It is clear that in the Ming case, regionalisation of the princes went together with an attempt at marginalisation or containment.[236] Regional marginalisation of collateral lines was also practised in Japan, with the houses of Minamoto and Taira.[237] Qing princes, conversely, were concentrated at the imperial capital. They were carefully educated and monitored by the regime; their performance influenced their ranking and their marriage opportunities.[238] Successful and loyal princes could rise to high office – they were after all the highest-ranking representatives of a conquest clan ruling over a vast Han Chinese

---

[235] Pierre Mounier, 'La dynamique des interrelations politiques: le cas du sultanat de Zinder (Niger)', *Cahiers d'études africaines*, 39/154 (1999), 367–86, summarising at 374 Tardits' Introduction to *Princes & serviteurs*.

[236] Hucker, *Dictionary of Official Titles*, 71: 'the nobility in general was an ornament on the Ming social scene, not a factor in government'. See revisions by Richard G. Wang, *The Ming Prince and Daoism: Institutional Patronage of an Elite* (Oxford, 2012); Jérôme Kerlouégan, 'Printing for prestige? Publishing and publications by Ming princes', *East Asian Publishing and Society*, 1 (2011), 39–73, and his paper given at Leiden University, 10 April 2013: 'Ming princes and the Ming polity'. See also the special issue of *Ming Studies*, 65 (2012), ed. David Robinson; and Craig Clunas, *Screen of Kings: Royal Art and Power in Ming China* (London, 2013).

[237] Thanks to Anne Walthall for this reference and countless other important suggestions.

[238] Rawski, *Last Emperors*, 96–126.

majority. In the nineteenth century, when the Qing imperial regime came under severe external as well as internal pressure, imperial clansmen and Manchu grandees adopted a more autonomous position, some of them becoming powerful players at court.

Endless variations can be plotted along the two axes of central–regional position and power–impotence or confinement. For one of these common tendencies, the restriction of movement or even literal incarceration of royals, remarkable examples can be found. Around 1300, a half-century after the Solomonids had replaced the preceding Zhagwe dynasty in Ethiopia, sources refer to the 'Mountain of Royals' (Amba Geshan). Here 'all sons of the reigning king who were eight years old or more, and all male descendants in the male line of former rulers of the reigning dynasty', possibly including the heir-apparent, were kept in custody. An unlikely story recounts that King (*Nagast*) Na'od (1494–1508), who himself had apparently stayed at Amba Geshan before coming to the throne, abolished the princely prison after witnessing the distress of a boy prince. Amba Geshan, which also served as a treasury, was razed by Muslim attackers in 1539. Another royal mountain was instituted at Wahni in 1647. Kings now sent their predecessor's children to the mountain 'since it was impossible for them to stay in the city (Gondar) in view of their rank as royal princes'. The princes at Wahni should have been treated as royals; however, governors often enriched themselves by reducing the budget intended to cater for the princes. Reports of Wahni and its princely prisoners suggest that it functioned until the end of the eighteenth century, 'as a reservoir of princes out of which the current power-holders could choose their puppets'.[239] The declining importance of the king's mountain coincided with the introduction of more violent procedures to keep royals from the throne: blinding or cutting off a hand or foot, operations that frequently led to the death of the victims. King John II ascended to the throne in 1769 through the intervention of a notorious kingmaker who had at an earlier stage cut off John's hand.[240] Kings had become the

---

[239] C.F. Beckingham, 'Amba Gesen and Asirgarh', *Journal of Semitic Studies*, 2/2 (1957), 182–8, at 182–3, 185; Haberland, *Untersuchungen zum äthiopischen Königtum*, 62, 82–9, quotation at 184–5.

[240] Haberland, *Untersuchungen zum äthiopischen Königtum*, 185; Crummey, 'Ethiopia in the early modern period', 195, on Amba Geshan and succession. In the same issue, see four other contributions to the history of Solomonic Ethipia, including Marie-Laure Derat, '"Do not search for another king, one whom god has not given you": questions on the elevation of Zär'ä Ya'eqob (1434–1468)', *Journal of Early Modern History*, 8/3 (2004), 210–28, discussing Amba Geshan at 211. Prutky, *Travels in Ethiopia*, 170–6, reports on Wahni ('Ohni') under Mentewwab.

instruments of the powers behind the throne, a situation that brings to mind the repeated successions of Mustafa (1617–18; 1622–3) and the summary executions of Osman II (1622) and Ibrahim I (1648) in the Ottoman empire.

Heredity and choice

The dominance of male primogeniture in recent European dynastic history predisposed not only English administrators in sixteenth-century Ireland or in Java around 1800 to see other succession practices as deviant. Dynastic history in predominantly patrilineal Europe and Asia has been seen largely in these terms. A global perspective makes clear that male primogeniture was far from universal. Matrilineal succession in a world usually preferring rule by men not only precluded father–son succession; it also led to a greater variety of candidates and created a margin of choice. 'Sideways' instead of 'downwards' patterns of succession, found in many patrilineal polities as well, created a strong potential for conflict, but at the same time offered a partial solution for the key problem of dynastic power: the fact that heredity does not guarantee military leadership, charisma, or strength of character. The involvement of outsiders and councils in the choice of a successor, designation by acclamation or by divine intervention, circulation of the paramount office among a number of groups, and the relevance of candidates' abilities to build support: these common practices suggest a permeable boundary between dynastic and non-dynastic forms of power. Not all dynasties operated on the basis of next-of-kin succession and increasing concentration of power in the hands of a diminutive royal lineage.

Stakeholders in the game of dynastic succession pulled in different directions, with fathers seeking to put their son on the throne opposing elders or office-holders keen to preserve their rights as kingmakers. Outcomes varied, but changes in either direction can be found: the European imperial dignity moved towards semi-heredity; the Mamluk sultanate confirmed designation by the group; numerous African polities protected the rights of elders and councils by prohibiting next-of-kin succession. Fathers cherished their right to designate a successor among their sons and sometimes long postponed this decision to prevent challenges to their power; leading administrators most of all wanted to establish clarity and continuity, preferring primogeniture or the early nomination of a successor. Sometimes, the rapid recurrence of violently contested successions allowed rulers or their advisors to push through a fixed pattern of succession promising stability. However, even where male

primogeniture had become the undisputed norm, the ravages of demography and the absence of obvious candidates caused frantic ad hoc
measures. Sometimes, when eldest sons were present but woefully incompetent or contested, others took their place through violence or manipulation. The instances where women, owing to the absence of males,
succeeded as sovereigns and started a sequence of female reigns, show
the strength of contingency and the pliability of rules. Changing power
constellations among elites and the performance of individual rulers –
exceptionally bad or unexpectedly competent – suspended or even altered
time-honoured rules. Dynastic power, left largely undefined in the
Introduction to this book, included a strong element of heredity and as
a rule restricted eligibility for the throne, but it was rarely determined
entirely by unchanging rules for succession. Succession adhered to certain rules and prohibitions connected to the ideals of rulership, but it left
room for the intervention of ruling elites, and notably for those present at
the heart of power at court.

A comparison of patrilineal and matrilineal patterns of descent illumi-
nates other aspects of dynastic rule. Tension between the high birth-rank
of princesses and their subservient status as women was marked in patrilineal systems. Dynastic daughters and sisters, nevertheless, were frequently used to cement alliances with the main elites of the realm. The
remarkable promiscuity of matrilineal princesses made invisible the
fathers of potential successors, and sheds a different light on the harem
of patrilineal rulers: the presence of numerous anonymous women
stressed the stature of patrilineal descent. Polygyny occurred in matrilineal as well as in patrilineal polities, although in the former it was of little
relevance for dynastic succession. The male ruler's sex drive was never the
sole explanation for polygyny. The remarkable occurrence of a polygynous establishment for the nominally 'male' rain-queen underlines the
role of the dynastic harems in integrating realms through the exchange of
women – voluntary or coerced. In patrilineal settings, concubines became
visible and powerful once their sons ascended to the throne. Perhaps
unsurprisingly, mothers appear in all forms of descent as the most powerful category of women.

Paternal and maternal descent were relevant in one way or another for
all dynastic polities – even staunchly patrilineal Chinese imperial advisors
carefully considered the impact of the ruler's maternal alliances. Patterns
of descent defined proximity to succession and hence determined rivalry
and alliance. Claude Tardits notes that the patrilineal kings of Bamoum
in Cameroon granted high office at the centre mostly to their maternal
kin, while they necessarily left authority in the regions to paternal princes.
Royal power was based on an ongoing balancing act between the princely

and the more dependent 'palatial' families.[241] Conversely, in West African Abron, matrilineal descent obtained: here the king's disenfranchised sons tended to act as confidants and allies, whereas maternal kin held important chiefdoms. In both cases, non-eligibles supported the king against the groups closest to succession.[242] Max Weber and Karl Wittfogel, among others, noticed a more general practice of counterbalancing hereditary power-holders by recruiting outsiders – including slaves, conquered peoples, exiles, and commoners. This practice can best be examined at the meeting point and clearing house of dynasty: the court.[243]

---

[241] Tardits (ed.), *Princes & serviteurs*, 114–17, and more generally in the Introduction, 17.

[242] Terray, 'Le royaume Abron du Gyaman', notably at 29–31; also the Introduction to Tardits (ed.), *Princes & serviteurs*, 15.

[243] Wittfogel, *Oriental Despotism*, 343–68; Weber, *Wirtschaft und Gesellschaft*, 130–70, specifically at 150–1, further elaborated by Nobert Elias in his *Court Society*, presenting noble–bourgeois (or 'sword and robe nobles') as the two forces competing under the king's eye.

3   At Court: spaces, groups, balances

Wearing a red hat the cockman accompanies the indications of dawn;
The wardrobe master now enters with the cloud-green furs.
The nine heavenly gates open to the palace court,
Ten thousand nations' robes and caps bow to the imperial cap and
    tassel.
The sun's rays at this moment reach the fairy hands;
Incense smoke floats around the dragon on the emperor's gown.
After the morning audience, you must cut open the five-colored imperial
    decrees,
And to the sound of jade pendants return to your office beside the
    Phoenix Pool.
Poem on the morning audience at the Tang Daming palace, by Wang
    Wei (699–759), in *Wang Wei*, trans. Marsha L. Wagner (Boston, MA,
    1981), 66–7.

Court: a universal term?

Many names have been devised for individuals wielding power: king and
emperor; *emir, sultan, shah, padishah* and *shahanshah, khan, khagan, raja,
wang, huangdi, tianzi, tenno, huey tlatoani, Sapa Inka,* and endless other
variants. Huge differences exist between the cultural associations of these
terms as well as between the levels of power of the incumbents. The single
term emperor in the European context, from Augustus via Charlemagne
and his Byzantine contemporaries to Napoleon and beyond, includes
powerful military leaders, ritual figureheads, and bureaucratically minded
managers. African names for paramount leaders, from the *nagast* (king-
emperor) of Ethiopia to the *mukama* of Bunyoro or the Asante *asantehene*,
each indicate different positions, and they change over time. Nevertheless,
the concept of a single dignitary, an anthropomorphic 'head' of the body
politic, is present in all these names. Likewise, the king's kin has been
labelled in many ways, often with distinct badges for sons, brothers, and
sons of brothers. Special titles could be given to the heir-apparent, the
queen mother, and other special positions. The group of royals was

determined by choices involving heredity and personal qualification, by distinct patterns of descent, and by policies vis-à-vis collaterals. While the results varied greatly, the idea of a clan deriving its authority in part from a mythical or historical ancestor can be found in many places.

Polities across the globe have been described in European terminology. The Dutch physician and writer Olfert Dapper (1636–89) compiled travellers' accounts without ever visiting the numerous territories he described. His 'Accurate description' of Africa sometimes explicitly contrasted distant examples with European models. The court of the king of Benin (Plate 19a), we learn, was as big as the Dutch city of Haarlem; it included numerous palaces and galleries, one of the latter on a par with the Amsterdam Exchange. Engelbert Kaempfer (1651–1716), an assiduous traveller-physician, accompanied a Swedish mission to Isfahan in the 1680s, before he served at the Dutch settlement on Dejima, and visited the court of the Japanese 'worldly emperor' or shogun in the 1690s. Kaempfer effortlessly provided common Latin and French translations for Persian court offices in Isfahan. In Edo's castle, he noticed the bustle of 'courtiers and soldiery' in the yard before the palace entry.[1] Dapper's and Kaempfer's habit of using common European terms to describe rulers and their spatial or social environments shows they recognised certain familiar characteristics. However, their practical choice may suggest equivalence where there is little or none. This problem is more vexing for 'court' than for 'palace'. It is possible to recognise the abode of a king notwithstanding huge variety in scale, permanence, luxury, and function.[2] The term 'court' raises confusions because it suggests far more than a house writ large. Germanic *Hof* as well as Romance *cour* have a

---

[1] Olfert Dapper, *Naukeurige beschrijvinge der Afrikaensche gewesten van Egypten, Barbaryen, Lybien, Biledulgerid, Negroslant, Guinea, Ethiopiën, Abyssinie. Vertoont in de benamingen ... steden, gewassen, dieren, zeeden, drachten, talen, rijkdommen, godsdiensten ...* (s.l., 1676), 122; Engelbert Kaempfer, *Amoenitatum exoticarum politico-physico-medicarum fasciculi V* (Lemgoviae, 1712), 78–88, with the *nasir* translated as grand master and the *mehter* as chamberlain. See also Kaempfer, *Engelbert Kaempfer am Hofe des persischen Grosskönigs 1684–1685*, ed. Walther Hinz (Leipzig, 1940), 79–87, using German titles; and Kaempfer, *De beschryving van Japan, behelsende een verhaal van den ouden en tegenwoordigen staat en regeering van dat ryk ... en van hunnen koophandel met de Nederlanders en de Chineesen. Benevens eene beschryving van het koningryk Siam* (Amsterdam, 1729), 371–85, courtiers at 379.

[2] See discussion of the term 'palace' in the pre-Columbian American context in Susan Toby Evans and Joanne Pillsbury (eds.), *Palaces of the Ancient New World: A Symposium at Dumbarton Oaks, 10th and 11th October 1998* (Washington, DC, 2004), Introduction and 2, 7–8, giving as the Nahuatl-Mexica term *'tecpan calli* or lord-place house' (7–8), and citing *hatun wasi* or 'big house' as the Inka term for palace (372); see also Susan Toby Evans, 'Aztec royal pleasure parks: conspicuous consumption and elite status rivalry', *Studies in the History of Gardens and Designed Landscape*, 20/3 (2000), 206–28, at 206, and *tecpanpouhque* or 'palace people' at 207.

variety of connotations based on their primary meaning, 'enclosed ground' or 'yard'. A court is the enclosed space as well as the social circle around the ruler: his abode as well as his retinue of kin, consort, guards, domestics, advisors, purveyors. The king and his followers wielded power: the court also stands for sovereignty and government – often affixed to the name of a specific location. Diplomats referred to Ottoman power as the 'Sublime Porte' and to the 'Court of St James' or to 'Versailles' for England and France respectively.[3] We still refer to the Vatican, the White House, or the Kremlin, using a location as *pars pro toto* for a government.

Princes and their retinues followed a ritual calendar that entailed solemn and festive occasions, some occurring only once in every reign, others repeated annually. European kings 'held court', assembling the grandees of their realms and attracting numerous spectators during religious and chivalric festivals. Their court was a string of special occasions as well as a location and a fixed group: it swelled at some points in the calendar and was reduced to a rump establishment at other times. Audiences and adjudication were common occasions at many courts. Rulers, we have seen, prided themselves on their role as supreme judges, listening to subjects' complaints, righting wrongs, and punishing wrongdoers. While this idealised picture rarely reflected actual practice, the court certainly developed a powerful association with justice – a connection persisting into our age in the naming of 'palaces' and 'courts' of justice.

The prince and his social as well as spatial environment formed the core of all contemporary European attempts to define the court. Can these two aspects be found elsewhere? European travellers often used *seraglio*, derived from the Persian *saray*, to refer to oriental courts. This term evoked the closed world of the harem. Yet its original meaning is far less specific, indicating a house, palace, inn, or even the world, depending on context and combinations with other terms. A related Persian term, *saraparda* or 'palace made of cloth', apparently refers to a cloth enclosure around the king, either within a camp or as a curtain in a palace defining royal presence.[4] In Arabic different sets of words were used to refer to

---

[3] See Tülay Artan, 'The making of the Sublime Porte near the Alay Köşkü and a tour of a grand vizierial palace at Süleymaniye', *Turcica*, 43 (2011), 145–206, on the misreadings of the term Sublime Porte and on early installation of the grand vizieral palace outside of Topkapı palace.

[4] David Durand-Guédy, 'Ruling from the outside: a new perspective on early Turkish kingship in Iran', in Lynette Mitchell and Charles Melville (eds.), *Every Inch a King: Comparative Studies on Kings and Kingship in the Ancient and Medieval Worlds* (Leiden and Boston, MA, 2012), 325–42, at 336; see explanations of other terms such as pavilion or *kushk* in this article.

either the physical abode of the ruler (*dar, qasr, qal'a*) or to his retinue (*bayt, hashiya, khassakiya*). The Mughal court was most often referred to as *darbar*: house or dwelling, but also the place for an audience and by extension the audience itself. Russian *dvor* can indicate both the palace and the retinue of a ruler – but like *saray* it can be used in a far more general sense. In China the court was most commonly referred to as *chao* or morning audience, although *ting* or courtyard was also used. Chao and ting could be used for the spatial as well as the social dimensions of the court, referring to a location, a group, or an occasion.[5] Asante households were structured around an oblong or square yard, called the *gyase*, 'a word which means literally beneath or below the hearth'; household slaves were called *gyasefo*, 'people round the hearth'.[6] The Asante federation as a whole functioned as a hierarchically organised pyramid of households culminating with the *asantehene*'s court. Here, the leader of all palace retainers was called the *gyasehene*.

Several issues complicate the equivalence suggested by overlapping terminology. First of all, while many courts were mobile, others seldom moved from their fixed abode. Do different levels of mobility and seasonal change of the courtly centre complicate comparison? Secondly, while all courts knew rules for access to the ruler, rights of entry diverged hugely. It is far from clear whether the notions of inner secluded spaces and their occupants at different courts were compatible. An examination of palace ground plans and patterns for access can clarify some of the discrepancies. Moving from the spatial to the social and functional divisions at court, a third question comes to mind. Do courts in different corners of the globe share specific staffs and offices catering for the daily lives of dynastic rulers? How were staffs recruited and fitted into court hierarchies? While the variety of offices defies attempts at typology and complicates the evaluation of numbers attending court, the court has often been seen in remarkably similar terms as an instrument in the hands of the ruler for controlling elites; the fourth section of this chapter assesses some key examples.

Cavalcade to palace?

In the 1690s Kaempfer was struck by the huge population of Edo out-growing the old imperial court city of Kyoto as well as by the massive

---

[5] Hans van Ess, 'The imperial court in Han China', in Antony Spawforth (ed.), *The Court and Court Society in Ancient Monarchies* (Cambridge, 2011), 233–66; on *neiting* and *waichao*, see Jianfei Zhu, *Chinese Spatial Strategies: Imperial Beijing, 1420–1911* (London, 2012), 99.

[6] Rattray, *Ashanti Law and Constitution*, 55–60 on the palace, 88–92 on the offices.

contours of the shogunal castle.[7] The dual powers of shogun and emperor seem to have been almost equally welded to their respective palaces and cities. Chinese imperial power, moving from one capital to another and often maintaining two capitals, had long exhibited a markedly urban and sedentary character. After the construction of the Forbidden City in Beijing by the Yongle emperor, this northern Capital soon overshadowed its southern counterpart at Nanjing. Ottoman sultans, first moving their capital from Bursa to Edirne, finally conquered the old imperial capital Constantinople. Appropriating Byzantine grandeur, they also constructed new palaces (Plate 19b) and mosques, creating an Ottoman imperial centre. Safavid Shah Abbas I's move from Qazvin to Isfahan (1590–1) and his subsequent major building activities turned the city into a showcase of royalty and permanence (Plate 22).[8] While Akbar's construction of a new palace at Fatehpur Sikri proved to be inauspicious and short-lived, the repeated renovations of imperial centres at Agra and Delhi by the Mughal emperors provided a strong urban basis for their dynastic power.[9] Cities stood at the heart of pre-Columbian American empires. Cuzco was the urban heart of Inka power at the junction of the empire's roads system; Tenochtitlan with its two fellow cities dominated a more densely populated and concentrated area.[10] Several African kingdoms, too, developed around urban cores. Dapper noted the 10-foot-high wall with gates enclosing Benin city and its royal court (Plate 19a), counting thirty major 120–foot-wide streets, matching the stateliest canals of Amsterdam. The walled city of Abomey, seat of the Leopard Kings of Dahomey, 'remained the core of a kingdom that was effectively centralized only within the roughly one thousand square miles of the Abomey plateau'.[11] The population of Kumasi, the capital of 'Greater Asante', was dominated by office-holders connected to the palace. A

---

[7] Kaempfer, *Beschryving van Japan*, 372.

[8] Kaempfer, *Amoenitatum exoticarum*, chaps. 11–14; and Kaempfer, *Am Hofe des persischen Grosskönigs*, 150–85. See Gülru Necipoğlu, 'Framing the gaze in Ottoman, Safavid, and Mughal palaces', *Ars Orientalis*, 23 (1993), 302–42; Sussan Babaie, *Isfahan and its Palaces: Statecraft, Shi'ism and the Architecture of Conviviality in Early Modern Iran* (Edinburgh, 2008).

[9] Stephen P. Blake, *Shahjahanabad: The Sovereign City in Mughal India 1639–1739* (Cambridge, 1991).

[10] Babaie, *Isfahan and its Palaces*; Michel M. Mazzaoui, 'From Tabriz to Qazvin to Isfahan: three phases of Safavid history', *Zeitschrift der Deutschen Morgenländischen Gesellschaft*, supplement 3 (1975), 514–22; Carla M. Sinopoli, 'Monumentality and mobility in Mughal capitals', *Asian Perspectives*, 33/2 (1994), 293–308, at 294–6; Katz, 'Evolution of Cuzco and Tenochtitlán'.

[11] Dapper, *Naukeurige beschrijvinge*, 121–2. On the city of Benin, see also Robert E. Bradbury, 'The kingdom of Benin', in his *Benin Studies*, ed. Peter Morton-Williams (London and New York, 1973), 44–75, at 51. Quotation on Abomey from Bay, *Wives of the Leopard*, 41.

string of villages populated by dependents catered for its needs. Kumasi was 'mentally mapped' as the hub of a wheel with spokes extending to the extremities of the Asante domain. Each of these outlying regions could be reached with a 'half-month' (twenty-one day) journey on foot, and the entire diameter of the circle could be crossed in forty-two days, a full month in Asante parlance.[12]

Europe's major cities, such as London or Paris, attracted courts with their diverse crafts, entertainments, financial power, and trade connections to distant luxuries. Conversely, the presence of the king's household brought cities to prominence. By the end of the sixteenth century, Giovanni Botero legitimately stated that 'it is of immeasurable assistance in making a city great and magnificent if the prince resides there'.[13] Ibn Khaldun, hardly a devotee of urban life, portrayed cities as a consequence primarily of dynastic power: 'Towns and cities are secondary products of royal authority ... dynasties and royal authority are absolutely necessary for the building of cities and the planning of towns'.[14] The centrality of capitals housing the royal court was reduced somewhat when European royals escaped into the countryside, constructing new and spacious outdoor palaces that outshone the cramped urban lodgings of their predecessors. Versailles, with its inexhaustible potential for hunting and other diversions, its amenities for councils and ministers, and its ability to accommodate up to 3,000 dignitaries and domestics in its auxiliary buildings, seemed to make movement superfluous. Other courts followed this example, sometimes creating new cities as accessories to magnificent palaces.

The urban focus of courts and the impressive palace complexes suggest permanence, yet palaces and capitals often coincided with a mobile court. The early Persian Achaemenid court (550–330 BCE) moved from city to

---

[12] Ivor Wilks, 'On mentally mapping Greater Asante: a study of time and motion', *Journal of African History*, 33/2 (1992), 175–90, esp.181–5; Wilks, *Asante in the Nineteenth Century*, 44–5; Gérard Pescheux, 'Centre, limite, frontière dans le royaume Asante précolonial', *Journal des africanistes*, 74 (2004), 180–201; Blier, *Royal Arts of Africa*, 130 and fig. 110.

[13] Giovanni Botero, *On the Causes of the Greatness and Magnificence of Cities, 1588*, ed. Geoffrey Symcox (Toronto and London, 2012), Book II, chap. 12, 'On the residence of the prince'. On courts and cities, see Werner Paravicini and Jörg Wettlaufer (eds.), *Der Hof und die Stadt: Konfrontation, Koexistenz und Integration im Verhältnis von Hof und Stadt in Spätmittelalter und Früher Neuzeit*, Residenzenforschung 20 (Ostfildern, 2006); Susanne Claudine Pils and Jan Paul Niederkorn (eds.), *Ein zweigeteilter Ort? Hof und Stadt in der Frühen Neuzeit* (Innsbruck, 2005); Malcolm Smuts and George Gorse (eds.), *The Politics of Space: Courts in Europe c. 1500–1750* (Rome, 2009). For a more general background, see Peter Clark and Bernard Lepetit (eds.), *Capital Cities and their Hinterlands in Early Modern Europe* (Aldershot, 1996); and the comparative volume, James McClain et al. (eds.), *Edo and Paris: Urban Life and the State in the Early Modern Era* (Ithaca, NY, and London, 1994).

[14] Ibn Khaldun, *Muqaddimah*, 263. See Blake, *Shahjahanabad*, 69 on the very real financial side to dynastic sponsoring of cities.

city, never settling definitively in one location – a pattern adopted by its Hellenistic successor courts.[15] Most courts retained a strong element of mobility, for a variety of reasons. Warfare necessitated movement wherever the ruler acted as commander or was supposed to be present as a mascot during campaigns. The court is 'where the prince resides', a German eighteenth-century writer stated succinctly: this could well turn out to be an army camp.[16] Courts and armies had a similar core of male retainers and household troops. Charlemagne started as a roving conqueror before he gradually developed a more settled pattern later in his life.[17] European royalty in the Middle Ages combined regular presence in one or more favoured cities with frequent movement. Elements of the military war band (*comitatus*, *Gefolgschaft*) can be found in the staffs and functions of European courts deep into the early modern age. Quartering and requisitioning, habits most often associated with armies, remained typical for court life into the seventeenth century. The stables, catering for movement, formed the biggest staff in most courts. Marshals and provosts organised quartering and discipline at court, matching similar functions in the army. Apparently, this apparatus was originally devised along military lines.[18] Deep into the period more often associated with powdered periwigs, the military household attached to the French court formed the elite core of the army, a pattern present at courts throughout Europe.

For the empires founded by the Seljuqs and the Mongols, mobility was the precondition of conquest. Their nomadic lifestyle persisted after the conquest of sedentary and urban peoples: it signalled the strength of the dynasty to its associates in battle. Nomadic and sedentary styles mingled. The Seljuq sultan camped outside of cities even when he at times listened to his subjects' complaints in the confined setting of urban palaces. Fixed elements were often included in the camps, most notably the *maidan* or open space for polo and other contests, but sometimes also gardens or pavilions.[19] Conversely, elements of the mobile camp can be recognised in palace complexes. Typically, the capitals arising in China after the Mongol conquest reflected two worlds: 'while the large palatial complexes of Qaraqorum, Shangdu and Dadu [Beijing] were typically Chinese in

[15] Lloyd Llewellyn-Jones, *King and Court in Ancient Persia 559 to 331 BCE* (Edinburgh, 2013), on the mobility of the Persian court and its various capitals; Rolf Strootman, 'Hellenistic court society: the Seleukid imperial court under Antiochos the Great, 223–187 BCE', in Duindam et al. (eds.), *Royal Courts*, 63–89.

[16] Johann Heinrich Zedler, *Grosses vollständiges Universal-Lexikon*, 64 vols. (Leipzig, 1732–50), XIII, 405–6.

[17] Rosamond McKitterick, 'A king on the move: the place of an itinerant court in Charlemagne's government', in Duindam et al. (eds.), *Royal Courts*, 145–69.

[18] Duindam, *Vienna and Versailles*, on staff organisation, numbers, and mobility.

[19] Durand-Guédy, 'Ruling from the outside', 335–6.

their design, they also included tents or buildings that evoked the shape of tents'.[20] Typically, Kaempfer reports that the great square in Safavid Isfahan still included two poles as targets for polo and horseraces.[21] The sovereign power of the Mughals was often referred to as the *rikab* or 'stirrup', reflecting their mobile and martial style of rulership.[22] Between 1556 and 1739, Mughal rulers spent nearly 40 per cent of their time in their peripatetic army camp, probably more than in any single city serving as their capital in this period.[23] Reports suggest that in the later seventeenth century the Mughal camp included 300,000 persons.[24] Until Süleyman's death during the 1566 Szigetvár campaign, Ottoman sultans, unambiguously based at their new capital Istanbul, were equally at home campaigning with their army. The imperial tents were prized luxury possessions and symbols of power; sections of the Topkapı palace with numerous relatively low pavilions resemble a tented camp.[25] Islamic raids and the threat of pastoral Galla peoples advancing from the south forced the Ethiopian Solomonids to keep on the move for two centuries before they started settling in their new capital Gondar in the 1630s. The white cotton imperial tents formed the heart of a frequently relocating caravan that shared the main characteristics of cities: numerous people living together in a small area predominantly pursuing non-agricultural activities. The structurally mobile court of the Solomonids included an inner court with women and their attendants.[26] We have seen that women accompanied the Mughal march across the Khyber Pass. Long-lasting dynastic mobility required the presence of women.

Climes and customs engendered distinct forms of seasonal alternation. Indic rulers led their troops to war in the cold winter season, retreated during the rainy season, and engaged in ritual interaction during the hot season.[27] Most climates prohibited war in certain seasons. Mongol incursions into India from the north were thwarted by the hot Indian summer.

---

[20] David Durand-Guédy, 'Introduction: location of rule in a context of Turko-Mongol domination', in Durand-Guédy (ed.), *Turko-Mongol Rulers, Cities and City Life* (Leiden and Boston, MA, 2013), 1–20, at 9. On the Mughal palace city of Fatehpur Sikri as a 'stone emcampment', see Alina Macneal, 'The stone encampment', *Environmental Design*, 11/1–2 (1991), 36–45.

[21] Kaempfer, *Am Hofe des persischen Grosskönigs*, 157.

[22] Personal communication from Jos Gommans; J. Deny, 'Rikab', in Houtsma et al. (eds.), *First Encyclopaedia of Islam*, VI, 1158: 'the sovereign himself or his presence, the foot of the throne'; apparently this habit was found throughout the Islamicate world.

[23] Sinopoli, 'Monumentality and mobility', 296; Blake, *Shahjahanabad*, 97–100.

[24] Sinopoli, 'Monumentality and mobility', 296.

[25] Necipoğlu, *Architecture, Ceremonial, and Power*; Nurhan Atasoy, *Otağ-I Hümayun: The Ottoman Imperial Tent Complex* (Istanbul, 2000).

[26] Ronald J. Horvath, 'The wandering capitals of Ethiopia', *Journal of African History*, 10 (1969), 205–19; Taddesse Tamrat, *Church and State in Ethiopia, 1270–1527* (Oxford, 1972), with a description and ground plan of the camp at 170.

[27] Richards (ed.), *Kingship and Authority*, iv–vii.

From late autumn to early spring, warfare in Europe was unusual and risky: horses could not feed off the land, provisions were difficult to obtain, and weather conditions fostered disease. Pastoralist ecology required more mobility, with nomadic peoples moving seasonally between summer and winter pastures. Variants of the Mongol *qishlaq* winter pastures and *yaylaq* summer pastures can be found among other pastoral peoples moving from winter valleys to higher summer pastures. Maintaining huge numbers of people and animals in one place for an extended period was a daunting challenge, overburdening the resources of any single area with the possible exception of metropolises with an organised hinterland as well as trade facilities. Like armies, courts often followed the dictates of provisioning and logistics. They lived off the land, sometimes ruining it like a swarm of locusts, or moved from city to city expecting to be fed and lodged. This form of resource extraction, depending on the mobility of the ruler's retinue, required little bureaucratic procedure.

Hunting, reflecting a mixture of provisioning, martial training, diversion, and representation, was practised eagerly by almost all dynasties: in the hunt all reasons for mobility merged.[28] Even when most of these practical grounds for hunting had become obsolete, the hunt still persistently lured royals out of their palaces, seeking entertainment in a form that underlined dynamism and strength. Ottoman sultans in the seventeenth century often staged hunting parties from the city of Edirne, which became the main sultanic residence under Mehmed IV and his successors.[29] Representations of the hunt can be found from the earliest dynasties up to the very recent past. The editions of the *Shahname* (Book of Kings) include glamorous hunting scenes. Distant echoes of this practice can be found in our own age as Vladimir Putin's widely broadcast hunting and fishing endeavours suggest.[30] Not only men hunted: dynastic history shows numerous examples of passionately hunting princesses. Louis XIV's sister-in-law, the Palatine princess, was a keen hunter, and she was no exception: eighteenth-century Russian tsaritsas hunted avidly,

---

[28] Allsen, *Royal Hunt*. For a film of hunting at the nineteenth-century German court, see www.youtube.com/watch?v=H619OMr8VqI.

[29] On Ottoman hunting, see Tülay Artan, 'Ahmed I's hunting parties: feasting in adversity, enhancing the ordinary', in Amy Singer (ed.), *Starting with Food: Culinary Approaches to Ottoman History* (Princeton, NJ, 2010), 93–138.

[30] Tom Parfitt, 'Vladimir Putin goes hunting to "beef-up action man" image', *Guardian*, 1 November 2010, and many other articles. See more recently the hunting débâcle of Juan Carlos, in Giles Tremlett, 'Spain's King Juan Carlos under fire over elephant hunting trip', *Guardian*, 15 April 2012. For a discussion of Horst Bredekamp's *Der schwimmende Souverän Karl der Große und die Bildpolitik des Körpers* (Berlin, 2014), and pictures, see Sebastian Hammelehle, 'Karl der Große: Horst Bredekamps *Der schwimmende Souverän*', *Spiegel Online*, 28 January 2014, www.spiegel.de/kultur/literatur/karl-der-grosse-horst-bredekamps-der-schwimmende-souveraen-a–945899.html.

and Kaempfer reported that several women in the Safavid harem were trained in archery, accompanying the shah on his hunting excursions.[31]

Ritual and political traditions contributed to dynastic peregrination. African royalty often resettled after succession, either by constructing a new habitat in the same palace area or, particularly in the case of rotating succession, by moving to a different region.[32] The Qing dynasty, taking over from their remarkably stationary late Ming predecessors, reintroduced movement for a variety of reasons. Qing emperors made a point of exercising the martial strength of the conquest clan (Plate 28b) by organising hunting expeditions at Mulan, beyond the great wall. In addition they devised a pattern of multiple capitals, with Beijing as prime location, Shengjing as Manchu capital, and the summer resort at Chengde, just beyond the wall, as a meeting point between the emperor and his non-Han tributaries.[33] Most kingdoms knew a hierarchy of religious and political centres related to the dynasty, comprising tombs of predecessors, key religious sanctuaries, and privileged urban centres. Pilgrimages to ancestors' tombs and holy places formed part of the ritual calendar. The occasional character of court life in Europe, at times assembling the retinues of numerous grandees, went together with a tradition of great open-air ceremonies, including acts of enfeoffment, banquets, and tournaments.[34]

From the later Middle Ages onwards, two developments contributed to a gradual and relative decrease in the mobility of European rulers and their retinues. Most royals adopted one urban centre as their main or winter residence. Their protracted annual stay there coincided with the Christmas and Easter cycles and formed the season for ceremonies and entertainments. At the same time, the increasing demands of financial accounting and judicial procedure made it expedient to allow specialised agencies to relocate from the court to the capital. These agencies now continued their

---

[31] Allsen, *Royal Hunt*, 129–30; J.T. Alexander, 'Favourites, favouritism and female rule in Russia, 1725–1796, in Roger P. Bartlett and Janet M. Hartley (eds.), *Russia in the Age of the Enlightenment: Essays for Isabel de Madariaga* (Basingstoke, 1990), 106–24, underlining at 108 that Anna, Elizabeth, and Catherine II were avid hunters; Kaempfer, *Am Hofe des persischen Grosskönigs*, 183. Princesses at many European courts shared the passion for hunting; Palatine princess Elisabeth Charlotte, Louis XIV's sister-in-law, reports hunting with the king frequently in her letters.

[32] Drucker-Brown, 'King house', 180; Blier, *Royal Arts of Africa*, 16, 38; Bay, *Wives of the Leopard*, 9; J. Cameron Monroe, 'Power by design: architecture and politics in precolonial Dahomey', *Journal of Social Archaeology*, 10/3 (2010), 367–97. Moving at the beginning of all reigns is stressed in Cato Lund, 'The royal capitals of the interlacustrine kingdoms: an urban legacy for Uganda', *Uganda Journal*, 45/1 (1999), 61–78, but she also underlines the urban character of the moving capitals.

[33] Rawski, *Last Emperors*, 19–23.

[34] Jeroen Duindam, 'The Habsburg court in Vienna: Kaiserhof or Reichshof?', in R.J. W. Evans and P.H. Wilson (eds.), *The Holy Roman Empire 1495–1806: A European Perspective* (Leiden and Boston, MA, 2012), 91–119.

administrative labours and record-keeping in the capital, undisturbed by the ruler's seasonal peregrinations: capitals became permanent whereas most royalty still moved. The consolidation of government services in the capital coincided with the rise of institutions and agents dealing with regional government. More often, local elites now needed to move to the centre to plead their cause or obtain office, with kings receiving them in their palaces rather than touring the country. Even the palace of Versailles, however, never became the sole location of the French court, which annually spent six autumn weeks in Fontainebleau and engaged in numerous shorter excursions. Courts-in-capitals such as Madrid, Vienna, or London escaped from the city frequently for protracted stays in other palaces from early spring to late autumn. These movements were dictated in part by the need to refurbish palaces, in part by the desire to visit different hunting grounds, and sometimes by specific motivations such as assemblies of estates, religious pilgrimages, or the threat of epidemics in the urban environment. Thus, from late spring to early autumn, court life was usually at a low ebb, with numerous courtiers away in the army, the prince with his retinue in hunting lodges, and a rump establishment taking care of matters in the capital.

In China, a settled capital administration had developed at a far earlier stage, in a context where the mobility of the ruler was generally frowned upon. Confucian literati cautioned their imperial pupils not to exploit the people and estrange heaven by military adventurism, senseless hunting parties, and voyages to outlying regions.[35] The 1449 Tumu incident, when Mongols captured the young Ming emperor Zhengtong at the head of an army, formed a particularly spectacular and recent example in the long repository of misadventures caused by imperial impetuosity or bad inner court advisors. Emperors could use Confucian arguments in support of movement by pointing out the need to show filial piety to ancestors or demonstrate compassion for the people, but the balance of opinion was against it.[36] Some emperors discounted the advice of their teachers. Soon after starting his reign in 1506, Zhengde literally escaped from the palace. An entry in the *shilu* (veritable records) notes his move to the 'Leopard Quarter' in Beijing: 'The emperor, having been duped by a pack of self-seekers, stayed there day and night and no longer entered the Forbidden City.'[37] In his new habitat, still within the Imperial City,

---

[35] Robinson, *Martial Spectacles*, underlines the growing distance between emperors with a taste for movement and martial exploits and their literati advisors in middle and later Ming.

[36] Michael G. Chang, *A Court on Horseback: Imperial Touring & the Construction of Qing Rule, 1680–1785* (Cambridge, MA, 2007), chaps. 1 and 2, shows the literati arguments in Qing contexts and how they were countered by the Qing emperors.

[37] James Geiss, 'The Leopard Quarter during the Cheng-Te reign', *Ming Studies*, 1 (1987), 1–38, at 2.

Zhengde engaged in martial pursuits and mixed with foreigners and out-siders not as a rule accepted at court. He died in 1521, soon to be transformed into a didactic example of yet another misguided emperor.

In the steppe world and among Arab desert peoples, the opposite argu-ment was dominant: that physical endurance and moral fibre would deteriorate once people moved into urban settings.[38] Ibn Khaldun's (1332–1406) cyclical scheme acted as a powerful warning against urban life. Desert leaders were drawn to the city once they established their rule. In the urban environment, they developed a taste for luxury which in the long run inevitably alienated their original supporters. Their urban dream declined and was doomed to end in takeover by fresh Bedouin migrants from the desert. Overspending, exploitation, and the loss of popular support loom large in Ibn Khaldun, as well as in Confucian remonstrations, yet these views clash in their explanations for decline: Ibn Khaldun pointed to urban effeminacy, the literati to the unnecessary dynamism. Few dynasties orga-nised their lives entirely along the lines of these positions; they cultivated lifestyles that fitted their personal preferences and political needs. The Manchus changed the sedentary Chinese style of rulership not only because of their 'nomadic tradition', but also as a consequence of their relationship with the peripheral peoples now under their authority and the need to show their special status as a conquest clan.[39] An emphatically nomadic style of rulership, as cultivated by the Seljuqs, Mongols, Timurids, and their suc-cessors, in practice entailed frequent stays in or near cities.

The most profoundly sedentary of dynastic powers still left room for some mobility, even in late Ming China and in Tokugawa Japan.[40] Typically mobility took shape as frequent movement within a relatively small circle around one or more residential cities, alternating with intermittent longer trips to more distant destinations. Differing levels of mobility had conse-quences for interactions with the realm, as will be examined in the next chapter. Most importantly, the prevalence of mobility in dynastic history shows that the image of the court as the heart of an immobile set of concentric circles has its limitations: the core itself moved. Moreover, dynastic power was often organised around several establishments rather

---

[38] Durand-Guédy, 'Location of rule', 1, citing the founder of the Aqqoyunly: 'Do not become sedentary, for sovereignty resides in those who practice the nomadic Türkmen way of life.'

[39] Durand-Guédy, ibid., 15 (and in other publications), makes the important point that 'these rulers were not nomadic out of atavism, but out of agency'; the same holds true for the Qing.

[40] Paradoxically, the term often used for the Tokugawa power, 'bakufu', literally meant 'tent-government', a style no longer practised by the Tokugawa shoguns; on terminology, see Wai-Ming Ng, 'Political terminology in the legitimation of the Tokugawa system: a study of "bakufu" and "shōgun"', *Journal of Asian History*, 34 (2000), 135–48.

than around a single figure. Queens, queen mothers, heirs, princes, and princesses were present, often with their own palaces and households. The persistent mobility and the multipolarity of many courts qualify the static view of a single centre radiating outwards.[41]

Many polities described here became less mobile while they consolidated rather than expanded their territories and worked out enduring administrative structures to solve the problem of governing an outstretched realm. In smaller African kingdoms, where the capital was located within a relatively short distance of the local chieftaincies, mobility of the court was not required to hold together the realm. In larger consolidated polities, such as imperial China or most European states after the 1650s, the burden of travel was transferred to intermediaries – groups dealt with at greater length in the next chapter.

Inner and outer

E.E. Evans-Pritchard described the heart of the Zande kingdom in South Sudan:

A king lived in the centre of his realm, like a queen bee in a hive. His court consisted of three parts: an outer court, an inner court, and the private quarters or harem. In the outer court cases were heard, wars were declared, and administration was conducted ... Between the outer court and the private quarters was a small inner court called 'the place of secrets', at the side of which the king's pages had their huts. Here food was served to nobles ... and to senior office-holders ... There also the king could discuss affairs privately with his more important retainers away from the general public. A path ran from this court to the royal harem which, as the king had many wives, might cover an extensive area.[42]

The layout of courts in an outer and inner section followed by residential spaces can be found in many places. The palace was called the 'king's village' in Bamoum (Cameroon); it included a multitude of gates and squares, showing the familiar sequence of spaces for 'open air government', residential quarters, and women's rooms (see Figure 2).[43] The sixteenth-century description of a Cuzco palace by Martín de Murúa highlights guarded gateways protecting access into a sequence of three

---

[41] On multipolarity and movement in the Habsburg case, see Jeroen Duindam, 'Palace, city, dominions: the spatial dimension of Habsburg rule', in Smuts and Gorse (eds.), *Politics of Space*, 59–90.

[42] Evans-Pritchard, 'Zande state', 149.

[43] Claude Tardits, *Le royaume Bamoum* (Paris, 1980), 601–2, and quotation at 694, 'gouvernement de plein air'; see explanations for exceptional spaces in the inner part of the palace, notably the 'cour de la guerre', at 597–8. See a reduced and clarified map of the palace in Blier, *Royal Arts of Africa*, 176.

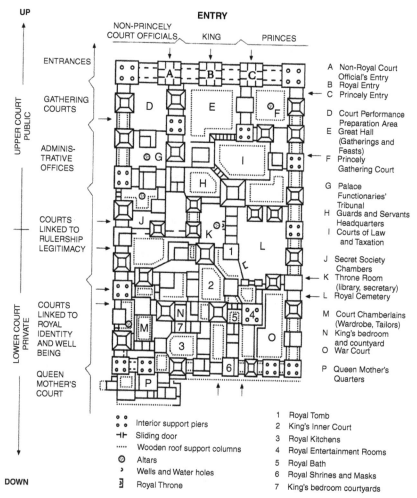

2 The Bamoum palace at Foumban (Cameroon). This structure from 1913 reflects earlier palace traditions: it shows an upper outer court and a lower inner court, with a right–left division between court officials (maternal kin) and princes (paternal kin). From Blier, *Royal Arts of Africa*, 176, and Tardits, *Le royaume Bamoum*, 601–2.

spacious courtyards, gradually moving towards the 'salons and rooms where the Inca lived'. Aztec palaces or *tecpan calli* were characterised by a great town plaza in front of a 'signature large entry courtyard', providing access to a 'dais room' in which the *tlatoani* received visitors. Beyond these administrative and ceremonial rooms followed the ruler's living quarters.[44]

Terms for inner and outer spheres at court abound in history. The Assyrians differentiated between the outer section of the palace (*babanu*) and the inner more secluded part (*bitanu*).[45] Safavids and Ottomans used Persian terminology, referring to the outer court as *birun* and to the inner court as *andarun* or *enderun*.[46] These spaces were typically related to the staffs pertaining to them, with eunuchs labelled as 'beardless men' serving in the Assyrian *bitanu*, as they did in the Ottoman and Safavid *enderun* (Plate 15). Much the same can be said for the Chinese terms *nei* for inner and *wai* for outer that can be found in various combinations with *chao* and *ting*.[47] The Tokugawa Chiyoda castle in Edo was divided into the Exterior (*omote*), the Middle Interior (*nakaoku*) housing the shogun, and the Great Interior (*ooku*) accommodating the palace women, replicating the Zande arrangement.[48]

The inner–outer pattern common to many ordinary households was replicated at an exceptional scale in palaces. Religious and cosmological models were important for the layout and orientation of palaces, sometimes conforming to and sometimes intersecting with inner–outer divides: upper–lower, left–right, north–south, east–west, safety–danger, pure–corrupt, divine–human, noble–commoner, stranger–local, male–female, warrior–scholar, administration–household, old–young, work–relaxation. Inner and outer were infused by a variety of normative and cosmological views and they cannot be equated with their most readily available modern variant: private and public.[49] The dynastic court did not

---

[44] Craig Morris, 'Enclosures of power: the multiple spaces of Inca administrative palaces', in Evans and Pillsbury (eds.), *Palaces of the Ancient New World*, 299–324, quotation at 300; Susan Toby Evans, 'Aztec palaces and other elite residential architecture', in the same volume, 7–58, at 7–8, with dais room at 19.

[45] Gojko Barjamovic, 'Pride, pomp and circumstance: palace, court and household in Assyria 879–612 BCE', in Duindam et al. (eds.), *Royal Courts*, 27–61, at 30–9. See Llewellyn-Jones, *King and Court in Ancient Persia*, 99, for several terms expressing the inner in the ancient world. In a personal communication Metin Kunt suggested that these semitic Assyrian terms relate to parallel Arabic and Turkish terms, for *bitanu*, respectively *bayt* and *beyt* (house), for *babanu*, *bâb* (gate).

[46] Babaie et al., *Slaves of the Shah*, 11; Murphey, *Ottoman Sovereignty*, 88.

[47] Zhu, *Chinese Spatial Strategies*, 133–4.

[48] Totman, *Politics in the Tokugawa Bakufu*, 95; Anne Walthall, 'Hiding the shoguns: secrecy and the nature of political authority in Tokugawa Japan', in Bernhard Scheid and Mark Teeuwen (eds.), *The Culture of Secrecy in Japanese Religion* (London, 2013), 332–56; Hisako, 'Servants of the inner quarters'; on similar inner–outer divides in Siam, see Tamara Loos, 'Sex in the inner city: the fidelity between sex and politics in Siam', *Journal of Asian Studies*, 64/4 (2005), 881–909.

[49] On some of these other divides, see Adam Kuper, 'The "house" and Zulu political structure in the nineteenth century', *Journal of African History*, 34/3 (1993), 469–87, esp. 474–9; Michelle Gilbert, 'The person of the king: ritual and power in a Ghanaian

represent 'family life' as distinct from political power or representation. Family life stood at the heart of the dynastic enterprise. Domestic service in the proximity of the ruler was understood as inherently political, if not in principle, then at least in practice. In Europe, important council meetings or individual consultation with advisors took place in the king's apartment or cabinet – hence the modern term for ministerial teams. The seclusion of women at court did not necessarily mean that they were limited to sexual, domestic, and 'private' roles.[50] Women at the heart of Topkapı palace shared in sovereign power and acted as cultural and political patrons. Grand viziers writing to the child-sultan Murad IV knew well that they in fact corresponded with his mother Kösem Sultan.[51] European princesses actively shared responsibility for the dynastic apparatus. Seclusion could underline sovereignty. The powerful shogun hid in the heart of Edo castle; his nominal superior the emperor, removed even further from the public gaze, was the epitome of continuity and sovereignty. The unseen inner, then, often represented the heart of power and 'public' responsibility. It cannot be rendered by the modern private; neither does outer necessarily fit our notion of public. It primarily reflected the level of visibility and access for wider audiences. Examining the parameters of access into the inner court is a requirement for the study of decision-making and power.

The idea of an enclosed space, present in *cour*, *Hof*, and their variants, found clear expression in European architecture. Most urban palaces and

state', in David Cannadine and Simon Price (eds.), *Rituals of Royalty: Power and Ceremonial in Traditional Societies* (Cambridge, 1992), 298–330, at 311–13; Larsen, 'City of women'; the ground plans in Lund, 'Royal capitals of the interlacustrine kingdoms', 66, 69, 71, 73, and explanation in the text. On Southeast Asia, see Behrend, 'Kraton and cosmos'. 'Facing south' as a synonym for ruling in the Chinese context has been referred to in Chapter 1; for a detailed discussion of various traditional types of city and the location of palaces, see Nancy Shatzman Steinhardt, 'Why were Chang'an and Beijing so different?', *Journal of the Society of Architectural Historians*, 45/4 (1986), 339–57; an analysis of Beijing and the Grand Sacrifices focusing on these issues can be found in Angela Zito, *Of Body and Brush: Grand Sacrifice as Text/Performance in Eighteenth-Century China* (Chicago, IL, 1997). On Mughal town and palace planning, see Blake, *Shahjahanabad*; on pre-Columbian America, see Evans and Pillsbury (eds.), *Palaces of the Ancient New World*. Numerous specialised works deal with the worldviews informing the orientation of building and palace complexes in various parts of the world.

[50] On women, see Peirce, *Imperial Harem*; and more recently, Elizabeth Thompson, 'Public and private in Middle Eastern women's history', *Journal of Women's History*, 15/1 (2003), 52–69, including the Sufi distinction between hidden and manifest, *batin* and *zahir*, also discussed in the conclusion of Blake, *Shahjahanabad*, 210.

[51] Halil İnalcık, *Devlet-i Aliyye: Osmanlı İmparatorluğu Üzerine Araştırmalar II. Tagayyür ve Fesad (1603–1656), Bozuluş ve Kargaşa Dönemi (The Sublime State: Studies on Ottoman Empire II. Transformation and Intrigue (1603–1656), the Age of Decline and Disorder)* (İstanbul, 2014), 371–429, cites *telhis* (petitions) from the grand vizier to Kösem Sultan, with the latter's responses. I thank Cumhur Bekar for the reference and translation.

castles included a sequence of courts, moving from an open square connecting city and court to more secluded inner courtyards on which the apartments of the sovereign and his family bordered. Court ordinances commonly tied access to these inner spaces to rank and function, stipulating who could enter in a carriage, on horseback, or on foot. This demarcation of the court into inner and outer spheres was never wholly rigid. Service personnel were active in all court spaces, often moving from outer into inner quarters and vice versa. Visitors and dignitaries entered the quarters close to the ruler as a function of their high rank or office. The apartments of princesses, served by marriageable noble girls, were more restricted. Even here, however, males could enter at certain times and interact with the ladies under the watchful eye of elder female chaperones. Overall, access at court was graded and limited, but boundaries shifted according to rank and occasion rather than being fixed spatially. In this respect, the absence of polygyny made a difference.

Within Europe there were major variations. Nobles at the French court prided themselves on their rights of access even into the king's personal quarters and protested vehemently when Henry III tried to create a more secluded living space for himself in the later sixteenth century. Repeated court ordinances (1574, 1578, 1585) convey Henry's discomfort with nobles leaning on his chair during meals, interrupting his walk back to his chambers with unending appeals, and bouncing into his rooms uninvited: the last Valois king wanted his obtrusive courtiers to stay at a distance, 'un peu loin'.[52] His regulations also highlight a politically tense situation in which regicide was wholly conceivable – as the deaths of Henry as well as his namesake and successor the first Bourbon king would show. The French court in its heyday during Louis XIV's reign was still relatively open and informal, with visitors of middling sort allowed to watch public dinners and even permitted into the royal bedroom after the king and his dignified guests had retired. While the court now redesigned Henry's ordinances into elaborate rules for subsequent entries into the king's bedroom, allowing the highest-ranking to come in first, to be followed later by a less exclusive crowd, it still maintained a policy of easy access. The differentiated entries into the king's bedroom organised at the *lever* and *coucher*, usually presented as the acme of ceremony, were a successful attempt to merge the French tradition of accessibility with the increasing demands of hierarchy imposed by diplomacy and a shared court culture.

Other courts, from Italy to England, had been more active in heightening standards. From the sixteenth century onwards European princes, engaged in competition and emulation, redefined forms of deference and

---

[52] Duindam, *Vienna and Versailles*, 162.

distance. Increasing the number of anterooms in the state apartment was one way to underline a ruler's supremacy vis-à-vis the agents of fellow monarchs as well as subjects. The Habsburg family venture with interacting establishments at Madrid, Brussels, and Vienna concocted a peculiar brew of Burgundian, Italian, Spanish, and German court traditions, seasoned with Counter-Reformation piety. The Habsburgs, dominant in the decades around 1600, only rarely allowed any visitors, whatever their rank, into their bedrooms. Incidentally, when the Austrian Habsburg emperor was plagued by gout of the big toe (*podagra*), he would accept an audience that could not easily be postponed at his bedside, but this practice never became common. Not only were the Habsburg courts in Spain and Austria more restricted in terms of spatial access than those of their European counterparts; their princes also spent far more time in a small company of relatives and servants. Before the eighteenth century, there was no daily salon-style sociable court life here. Outside of specially defined and announced occasions in the weekly calendar, the halls and corridors of the court were not intended as a meeting point for those with no specific assignment. Conversely, even during the protracted illness of Louis XIV in late 1686, Versailles retained its habitual style of numerous people coming, mingling, and going.[53]

The old urban palace-castles at the heart of major cities required frequent interaction with the urban populations. Any movement of the court passed through the streets and squares of the city (see Figure 3). Great squares and even palace halls could serve as public spaces for vendors, passers-by, and sightseers (Plate 32). Religious feasts and processions would typically be celebrated in the city rather than in the confined space of the court. A minor tourist industry developed around the major European palaces, offering guided tours and expert advice to elite young men on their Grand Tour. Visitors could admire the palace treasury or attend musical performances in the chapel. In the absence of the prince, they were allowed to visit the apartments.[54] The tourist business continued after the construction of outdoor hunting lodges, but the interaction with urban populations now became a choice rather than an inevitable circumstance: the court could move without passing through the city. The Versailles style of palace-building positioned the palace in the landscape, radiating outwards and inviting the admiring gaze of spectators (see Figure 4). The sequence of urban squares and inner courts around a vertical, inward-looking defensive structure was now projected

---

[53] Ibid., 165.
[54] Michaela Völkel, *Schloßbesichtigungen in der Frühen Neuzeit: ein Beitrag zur Frage nach der Öffentlichkeit höfischer Repräsentation* (Munich and Berlin, 2007).

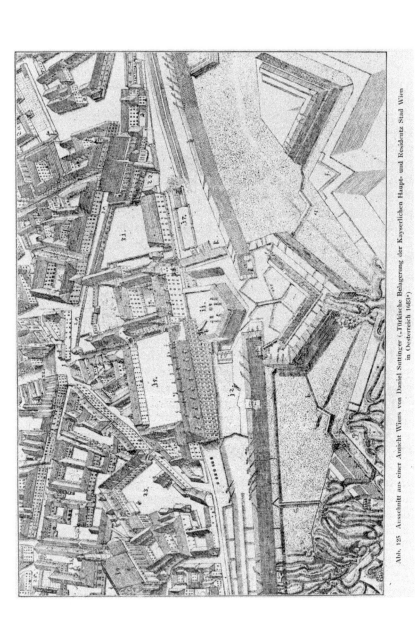

Abb. 125 Ausschnitt aus einer Ansicht Wiens von Daniel Suttinger („Türkische Belagerung der Kayserlichen Haupt- und Residentz Stad Wien in Oesterreich 1683")

3 The Vienna Hofburg gradually developed in constrained urban settings, set between the city and its fortifications. This was no luxury: Ottoman trenches can be seen in this 1683 picture. The main inner courtyard of the Hofburg was a relatively open space, and was used for court performances. From Suttinger, *Türckische Belagerung der Kayserlichen Haubt und Residentz Statt Wien in Oesterreich 1683*.

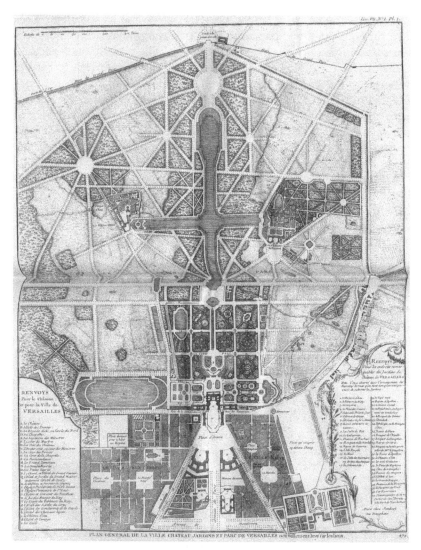

4 Plan of Versailles showing the lines radiating outwards from the chateau to the city and the gardens. Versailles was the most powerful example of a palace built outside the constraints inherent in older urban locations. Defensive structures were no longer relevant: open courts led from the city to the palace, from the place d'armes to the cour de marbre. From Blondel, 'Plan general de la Ville Jardins Chateau et Parc de Versailles', *Architecture française*, 4/1 (1752).

horizontally onto a wider landscape. The palace and its perimeter were fitted into a geometrical pattern of roads converging on a series of forecourts leading towards the heart of the palace. The pattern was replicated on the other side of the linear palace façade, inviting courtiers to behold the outward-looking perspective of the gardens. The geometrical lines radiating outwards from the great outdoor palaces resemble the lines of fire of 'trace italienne'-style fortifications; their elongated façades bring to mind the extended frontlines of linear armies. The distant outside perspective dominated, whereas the inner and outer spaces were now flattened into an enfilade of rooms in the state apartment.

Moscow's Red Square connected the city to the walled Kremlin citadel (Plate 25), a more imposing compound than most other European city residences. Courtiers or visitors allowed through the massive Spasski Gates passed a narrow street before reaching Cathedral Square, from whence high-ranking guests could proceed to one of the throne rooms via the 'Boyars' porch'.[55] Peter I's move to the new palaces in St Petersburg conformed Russian practice more closely to the patterns emerging at the same time elsewhere in Europe.[56] Palaces from Cuzco to Topkapı and the Forbidden City adhered to the format of an enclosed area including distinct courtyards, each with its own rules of access. The shogun's main residence, Chiyoda castle at Edo, was remarkable for the near-absence of great open spaces and its stress on defence rather than display. As in European urban castles, imposing gates connected outer and inner worlds in palace compounds throughout the world. Such gates represented sovereignty as well as the sovereign ruler in person. In Japan, 'the gates of the [imperial] palace, for which one Japanese word is "Mikado", were the outsider's usual token for the august personage inside'.[57] Ottomans used the majestic Imperial Gate (*Bab-ı Hümayun*) into the first courtyard of Topkapı palace as a synonym for sultanic power.

In the early eighteenth century, ambassadors visiting Topkapı palace made sure to have their mission commemorated in paint (see Figure 5). We see them entering (Plate 20) through the Middle Gate or Gate of Salutation (*Orta Kapı* or *Bab-us Selam*) into the second courtyard where janissaries awaited them, usually silently but sometimes loudly clamouring. The grand vizier then offered the ambassador hospitality in the council or

---

[55] Daniel Rowland, 'Two cultures, one throne room: secular courtiers and orthodox culture in the Golden Hall of the Moscow Kremlin', in Valerie A. Kivelson (ed.), *Orthodox Russia: Belief and Practice under the Tsars* (University Park, PA, 2003), 33–57, at 38–40.
[56] Keenan, *St Petersburg*.
[57] Herschel Webb, *The Japanese Imperial Institution in the Tokugawa Period* (New York, 1968), 68.

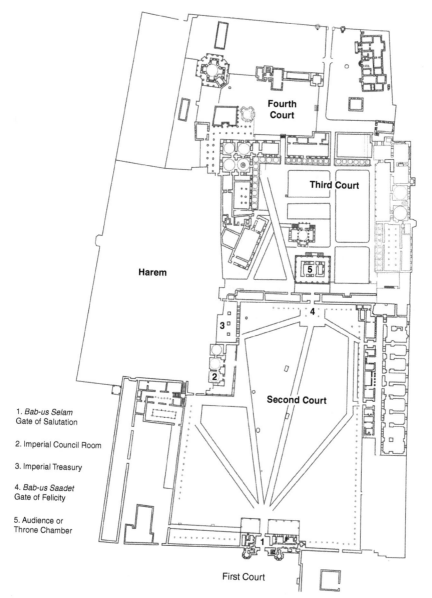

Fourth
Court

Third Court

Harem

5

4

3

2

1. *Bab-us Selam*
Gate of Salutation

2. Imperial Council Room

3. Imperial Treasury

4. *Bab-us Saadet*
Gate of Felicity

5. Audience or
Throne Chamber

Second Court

First Court

5 Topkapı palace ground plan, with the first open court left out. The second, outer court (*birun*), includes the Imperial Council Room and the Imperial Treasury on the upper left (northwest corner) and the court kitchens along the right (east). The third, inner court (*enderun*) has halls for the pages of the palace school along the sides of the court. Directly

divan room. This stately meal took place under a window covered by a metal grid; the absent sultan could in principle watch these proceedings from the harem (Plate 21), 'invisible but omniscient'.[58] Following the meal, the ambassador and his suite proceeded through the Gate of Felicity (*Bab-us Saadet*) to present their respects to the sultan in the throne or audience room, a construction shielding the secluded third court from prying looks. The latticed window in the council room, the Gate of Felicity, and the throne room all marked the outer–inner (*birun–enderun*) boundary. The third courtyard housed the page school supervised by the white eunuchs; the pages were also the servants of the sultan in his inner court chambers. No visitor was expected to cross into the inner court, but even for the inner court pages, the harem was forbidden territory.

Was seclusion typical for Islamicate courts? Neither the Mughal nor the Safavid rulers copied the isolation of the sultan in the *enderun* and the rigid inner–outer divide of the Ottoman court. The Safavid constellation of palaces and mosques around the great square of Isfahan was polycentric and flexible. The Âlî Qapu palace on the Isfahan Naqsh-e Jahan Square served as a viewing balcony, allowing the shah to watch the city while the people could watch him. However, there were clear limitations: visitors entering the gate soon found their way barred by a series of heavily guarded gates protecting the harem. On the other side of the palace, pleasure gardens likewise were not open to the public – although Kaempfer apparently was able to enter undisturbed. The lifestyle of Abbas I (Plate 17), builder of Isfahan in its Safavid shape, struck European visitors early in the seventeenth century as remarkably companionable. In 1609, a European friar wrote:

He [Abbas I] will go ... to the house of a private person and sit there two or three hours drinking with them, finding out what he wants to know ... He is also wont to go for a pastime to other places hardly respectable ... Sometimes passing through the city on foot he will come to the shops of the greengrocers, fruiterers, and those who sell preserves and sweetmeats: here he will take a mouthful, there another: in

---

Caption for 5 (cont.)

beyond the gate between the outer and inner courts stands the Audience or Throne Chamber. The fourth court with gardens and pavilions was added in the seventeenth century; the harem along the western side of the second and third courts is a sixteenth-century addition. Simplified plan based on Duindam et al. (eds.), *Royal Courts*, 294.

[58] Necipoğlu, 'Framing the gaze', 304.

one place taste a preserve, in another some fruit. He enters the house of a shoe-maker, takes the shoe that he fancies, puts it on at the threshold of the door, and then continues on his way.

The same visitor reports the shah's chat with a group of Augustinian friars: 'How does what I am doing appear to you, Fathers? I am a king after my own will, and to go about in this way is to be king: not like yours, who is always sitting indoors!' A year earlier another friar described similar encounters, with Shah Abbas now explaining his excursions in the city: 'He says that is how to be a king, and that the king of Spain and other Christians do not get pleasure out of ruling, because they are obliged to comport themselves with such pomp and majesty as they do.'[59] Kaempfer's impressions from the 1680s show the incumbent Shah Süleyman I (1647–1666–1694) moving around the city regularly but never in Shah Abbas I's easy-going mode. In the course of the seventeenth century, the Safavid shahs, following the earlier example of the Ottomans, increasingly restricted interaction with their advisors and with the outside world.[60]

Akbar's new palace city Fatehpur Sikri did include a separate palace for 'the queens', but on the whole this 'irregular agglomeration of courtyards' does not seem to have adhered to a rigid inner–outer divide.[61] The Red Fort of Delhi (Plate 23a), reconstructed by Shah Jahan between 1639 and 1648 and renamed Shahjahanabad, followed a north–south line moving from the Lahori Gate via three courtyards and gates to the inner sections (Figure 6). The first courtyard included a covered bazaar; the audience hall bordered on the second courtyard; the residential quarters of the emperor and palaces for women were located on the third courtyard, approaching

---

[59] Cited ibid., 307.

[60] Kaempfer, *Am Hofe des persischen Grosskönigs*, 31, 63, 186–8; Matthee, *Persia in Crisis*, 57–9. Ottoman chroniclers report the nightly wanderings of Sultan Murad IV through Istanbul, disciplining and punishing his peoples: 'The Late Sultan [Murad IV] used to stroll around the city all night long, and the people would hence be afraid to go even [to the mosque] for the prayer. At the time I had come to Istanbul, I was staying at the Hocapaşa quarter. At a certain night during those days, when the Sultan was walking in the neighbourhood, the son of the imam at the Hocapaşa Mosque came across him when the boy was returning home from the Mosque. The boy was shown no mercy and was killed, which I ran up and witnessed with my own eyes', reported in Ertugrul Oral in his 'Edition of Mehmed Halife, *Tarih-i Gılmani*', PhD thesis, Marmara University (2000). This reference, given to me by Cumhur Bekar, suggests a less withdrawn, though awe-inspiring sultan. Nicholas Rolamb, 'A relation of a journey to Constantinople', translated from the Swedish and printed in Awnsham Churchill and John Churchill (eds.), *A Collection of Voyages and Travels: Some Now First Printed from Original Manuscripts, Others Now First Published in English* ... 6 vols. (London, 1732), V, 669–716, cites Murad IV's violent wanderings (690) and mentions Mehmed IV as imitating his illustri-ous forebear (701).

[61] Lal, *Domesticity and Power*, 157–65, quoting Ebba Koch at 165.

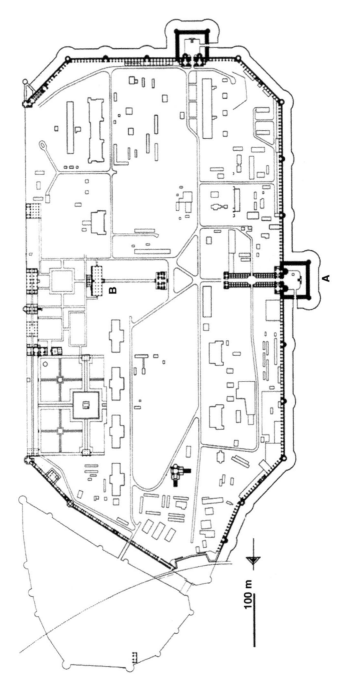

6 Ground plan of the Delhi Red Fort (north to the left) with (a) the main Lahori Gate connecting the city and the palace; (b) the Diwan-i Amm (Audience Hall).

100 m

the riverfront.[62] Akbar hardly fitted the model of the invisible and intro-verted monarch. Father Monserrate reported that he 'is so devoted to building that he sometimes quarries stone himself, along with the other workmen. Nor does he shrink from watching and even himself practising, for the sake of amusement, the craft of an ordinary artisan.'[63] Akbar, at other times, well knew how to impress his subjects through splendour and distance rather than camaraderie.

Neither the Ottomans nor the Mughals matched the 'festive informality' of the Safavid shahs, which declined after Shah Abbas I's reign.[64] The layout of the Mughal palace-fort in Delhi brings to mind the three courts of Topkapı palace, yet the commercial activities included in the Delhi and Isfahan compounds cannot be found in the Ottoman case. In addition, the ruler played a different role: the absence of the sultan was stylised in the Ottoman case, whereas the Mughal emperor in person stood at the heart of ceremonies. Notwithstanding the structurally different place of women and their attendants at Christian and Islamic courts, the diversity in Europe and in the western half of Asia undermines a straightforward typology contrast-ing Eastern seclusion and Western openness.

The Qing emperors adopted a more outgoing style than their late Ming predecessors, but they consolidated the secluded nature of the inner court (see Figure 7). The Kangxi emperor in 1669 moved his sleeping quarters from the outer court Hall of Preserving Harmony (*Baohedian*) into the inner court Palace of Heavenly Purity (*Qianqinggong*), confirming the inner–outer divide by this withdrawal.[65] From Yongzheng onwards, emperors in practice slept in the Palace of Mental Cultivation (*Yangxindian*), on the southern margins of the inner court, near its western gate.[66] Visits of diplomats to the Chinese court, rarely depicted by European painters, bring to mind Ottoman procedure: the company moved through several gates, gradually reaching more restricted court-yards before meeting the emperor in person.[67] Probably these missions entered through one of the secondary gates in the massive Meridian Gate

---

[62] Blake, *Shahjahanabad*, 36–44, groundplan at 37; see also Babaie, *Isfahan and its Palaces*, 252–3.

[63] Monserrate, *Commentary*, 199–200 on the palaces, quotation at 201.

[64] Necipoğlu, 'Framing the gaze', 313.

[65] Rawski, *Last Emperors*, 31; at the time of the move the Baohedian was called Qingning palace.

[66] Zhu, *Chinese Spatial Strategies*, 115, on formal versus actual residence, with a detailed ground plan at 124.

[67] Olfert Dapper, *Gedenkwaerdig bedryf der Nederlandsche Oost-Indische Maetschappye, op de kuste en in het keizerrijk van Taising of Sina* (Amsterdam, 1670), 349–69, describing the various meetings in the Imperial palace; see more briefly also Olfert Dapper, *Beschryving des keizerryks van Taising of Sina* (Amsterdam, 1670), 22–6. These descriptions do not allow a precise reconstruction of the embassy's trajectory.

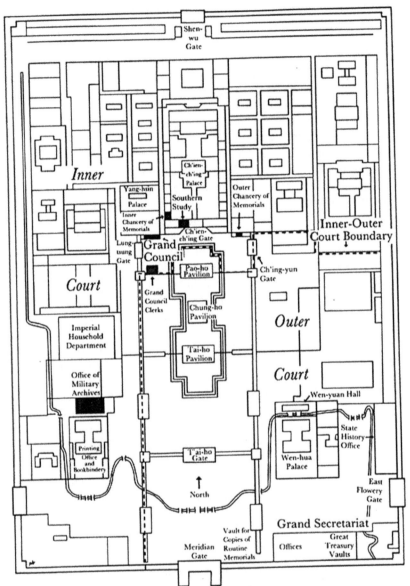

- - - - - Approximate Boundary of Inner-Outer Court

7 Inner and outer court of the Forbidden City at the Qing Chinese court. The three great halls for public ceremonies in the southern outer court are replicated in smaller form in the northern inner court, which houses the emperor and his close entourage. The key

(*Wumen*) – the main gate, opening only for the emperor in person – or through the Eastern Flowery Gate (*Donghuamen*) into the outer court of the Forbidden City. Only a privileged few could move beyond the Gate of Heavenly Purity into the inner court, reserved for the emperor and his close entourage. Most ceremonial transactions between inner and outer court staffs took place at the Gate of Good Fortune (*Jingyunmen*).[68] The report of a United States commissioner visiting Qing China on the verge of its collapse reflected this pattern:

> In going to and returning from solemn audiences the representatives of the powers shall be borne in their chairs to the outside of the Ching-yun gate [*Jingyunmen*]. At the Ching-yun gate they shall alight from the chairs in which they have come and will be borne in small chairs (*i chiao*) to the foot of the steps of the Chien-ching gate. On arriving at the Ch'ien-ching gate the Representatives of the Powers shall get out of their chairs, and shall proceed on foot into the presence of His Majesty in the Ch'ien-ching Kung hall.[69]

The dominance of the empress dowager Cixi and her 'government behind the curtain' during the last half-century of Qing rule should not obscure the fact that Qing emperors were never wholly secluded. They moved out on many occasions and interacted easily with high visitors – without ever matching Shah Abbas I's fraternising attitude.

Kaempfer reported at length the repeated visits of the Dutch mission at Dejima to the shogun's castle. The perceptive physician noticed many

---

Caption for 7 (cont.)

Qing body of decision-making, the Grand Council, stands at the eastern connecting point between inner and outer. The core of the previous Ming dynasty government, the Grand Secretariat, was still located in the southwestern corner of the palace complex. The western gate connecting inner and outer, (*Jingyunmen*) was most commonly used for ceremonial interactions. Plan based on Bartlett, *Monarchs and Ministers*, 14.

---

[68] Zhu, *Chinese Spatial Strategies*, mentions the *Qianqingmen* or Gate of Heavenly Purity as boundary; Rawski, *Last Emperors*, 30–2, gives the two southward side gates *Longzonmen* and *Jingyunmen* as entries into the inner court redefined after 1669; Beatrice S. Bartlett, *Monarchs and Ministers: The Grand Council in Mid-Ch'ing China, 1723–1820* (Berkeley, CA, 1991), 15, draws a line that leaves Longzon Gate in the inner court, while stressing the relevance of *Jingyunmen* and *Qianqingmen*; Preston M. Torbert, *The Ch'ing Imperial Household Department: A Study of its Organization and Principal Functions, 1662–1796* (Cambridge, MA, 1977), 31, prints yet another variant of inner and outer; see also Zito, *Of Body and Brush*, 134–52.

[69] William Woodville Rockhill, *Report of William W. Rockhill, Late Commissioner to China, with Accompanying Documents* (Washington, DC, 1901), 281, 338.

8 Kaempfer's sketch of Edo, with Chiyoda castle in the centre. No major thoroughfare or even small alley approached the castle entrances in a straight line. From Kaempfer, *De beschryving van Japan*, 372–3.

things. No ground plans or drawings of Chiyoda castle had been made
available to him, and he was prohibited to draw maps himself – a command
he disobeyed (Figure 8). Edo, Kaempfer writes, was built 'irregularly',
showing signs of haphazard expansion as well as careful planning.[70] No
road approached Edo castle directly, and the many turns and twists in its
interior challenged his memory: 'It has so many intersections, different
moats, and ramparts that I was [un]able to work out its ground plan.'[71]
The castle was a huge moated terrain including several enceintes. The main
enceinte of the castle consisted of 'a rambling set of interconnected wooden,
single-story buildings covering nine acres of land' – small wonder Kaempfer
lost track. Once in the audience room of the Exterior (Plate 23b), Kaempfer
noted other strategies of concealment. The shogun and his relatives were
made invisible by blinds. Kaempfer glimpsed the face of the shogunal
consort and heard the shogun's voice, yet all communication was handled
indirectly, through court servants. The visitors were asked all sorts of
questions and invited to perform songs and dances to amuse the court
ladies. The ladies apparently enjoyed the performances; Kaempfer reports
their use of small pieces of paper wedging open the blinds to allow better
vision.[72] Foreign visitors were granted only limited access and were not
allowed to see the shogun. In general at the shogunal court, access was
based on a mixture of family ranking, service to the shogun, and 'rank and
office bestowed by the monarch in Kyoto at the behest of the shogun'.[73]
Visitors holding the appropriate rank and pedigree could proceed from the
formal audience room (*ohiroma*) deeper into the castle to a section with a
room for more restricted audiences (*shiroshoin*). Rank and access were made
visible by assigning different places to the visitors in each of these audience
rooms. Beyond lay the Middle Interior, with spaces for the shogun's officials
as well as his living quarters; the audience room here (*kuroshoin*) was used
sometimes for less formal meetings with the leading regional power-holders
(*daimyo*). Two 'bell corridors' connected this Middle Interior to the female
Great Interior, 'officially off-limits to all men except the shogun' (see
Figure 9).[74] Edo castle lacked the open grounds that attracted the attention

[70] Kaempfer, *Beschryving van Japan*, 372; Kaempfer, *Kaempfer's Japan: Tokugawa Culture Observed*, ed. and trans. Beatrice M. Bodart-Bailey (Honolulu, HI, 1999), 351.
[71] Kaempfer, *Kaempfer's Japan*, 353.
[72] Kaempfer, *Beschryving van Japan*, 381; Kaempfer, *Kaempfer's Japan*, 362–3.
[73] Walthall, 'Hiding the shoguns', 336.
[74] Ibid., 334–5, quotation at 335; Totman, *Politics in the Tokugawa Bakufu*, 97–9, with somewhat differing focus and terminology; Hisako, 'Servants of the inner quarters', 173–5, on the seclusion of the Great Interior; Anna Beerens, 'Interview with two ladies of the ōoku: a translation from Kyūji Shimonroku', *Monumenta Nipponica*, 63/2 (2008), 265–324, at 284, with notes on the two 'bell passageways' connecting the Great Interior to the Middle Interior (50–1).

9 Map of Chiyoda castle, Edo, showing the shogun's main Honmaru palace, with its sequence of outer (*omote*), Middle Interior (*nakaoku*) housing the shogun, and the great Interior (*ooku*) with women. The sequence is replicated in palaces for heirs and retired shoguns. See the marks indicating officials' and daimyo entry routes. Drawing based on Totman, *Politics in the Tokugawa bakufu, 1600–1843*, 94.

of visitors to majestic structures elsewhere. No great square or avenue led up to its gates; in the interior, the big open spaces of Topkapı or the Forbidden City are conspicuously absent.[75] More than the shogun's castle at Edo, the imperial palace at Kyoto fitted the model of the Forbidden City, with a great southern gate to be used only by the emperor, and a gradual movement from ceremonial spaces in the south to residential quarters and the empress's palace in the north, with open spaces both in and around the major palace compound (*Kindairi-Gosho*). The emperor and his court, however, represented religion, rank, refinement, and continuity rather than military and political power. Ensconced in his palace city, the emperor remained a distant presence for almost all Japanese.[76]

Interaction with sovereigns was limited in many ways. Blinds hid the shogun during audiences; a latticed window suggested the presence of the Ottoman sultan in the *divan* room. Screens and curtains can be found elsewhere. The fourteenth-century Muslim king of Kanem in Africa, likewise, was not as a rule visible: 'Hidden by a screen, he is only seen on the days of the two fetes when he appears at the morning and evening prayer. For the rest of the year he addresses no one, not even an Amir, except from behind a screen.'[77] Beaded crowns concealed the faces of Yoruba kings in West Africa; the king of Kefa in Ethiopia donned a veiled crown and was seated behind a curtain.[78] In Europe, royals were more visible to the public, but many among them attended religious celebrations in a canopied booth open only towards the altar, or in a special compartment in the court chapel.[79] During public audiences at the court of Dahomey, a line of palm-branches made clear to male officials and visitors alike where their access and gaze should end.[80] Kings' names or characters were sometimes banned from common speech or writing, another form of deferential avoidance or concealment.[81] Neither the shogun nor the sultan communicated directly with outsiders: a

---

[75] Beatrice M. Bodart-Bailey, 'Urbanisation and the nature of the Tokugawa hegemony', in Nicolas Fieve and Paul Waley (eds.), *Japanese Capitals in Historical Perspective: Place, Power and Memory in Kyoto, Edo and Tokyo* (Abingdon and New York, 2013), 100–28, at 103–4.

[76] See the short description in Webb, *Japanese Imperial Institution*, 65–71; and see a re-evaluation of the imperial court in Lee A. Butler, *Emperor and Aristocracy in Japan, 1467–1680: Resilience and Renewal* (Cambridge, MA, 2002).

[77] H.R. Palmer, 'The kingdom of Gaògha of Leo Africanus. Part II', *Journal of the Royal African Society*, 29/116 (1930), 350–69.

[78] Blier, *Royal Arts of Africa*, 10; Baye, 'Kefa kingdom', 195.

[79] Duindam, *Vienna and Versailles*, 142.

[80] Bay, 'Servitude and worldly success', 358; Larsen, 'City of women'.

[81] See examples cited in Luke Fleming, 'Name taboos and rigid performativity', *Anthropological Quarterly*, 84/1 (2011), 141–64, referring to Tahiti, Hawaii, and the Zulu kingdom; Hongxu Huang and Tian Guisen, 'A sociolinguistic view of linguistic taboo in Chinese', *International Journal of the Sociology of Language*, 81 (1990), 63–85;

conversation was engaged through intermediaries. Qing emperors could be viewed and approached by ambassadors, and often communicated with them directly, as was the case in Europe. At the Qing court, as in most other East Asian examples, the handing over of letters or other objects would normally pass through intermediaries. Bodily contact, even if only through the handing over of objects, was not usually accepted. The French ambassador Chevalier de Chaumont, visiting the Siamese court in 1685 (Plate 30a), was allowed to present his sovereign's letter to King Narai only indirectly, putting it in a gold cup for the king, who was positioned higher on a balcony.[82] This was a world with many layers protecting the main occupants and demonstrating their special status. A legion of servants was necessary to organise the details of the hide-and-seek of court life.

Staffs, recruitment, ranks

Most courts were mobile; this required a staff able to organise the movement of large numbers of people and their belongings. All courts in one way or another limited access into the king's chambers, a task that in major palaces could be enforced only with the help of numerous guards, doorkeepers, or chamberlains. Many of those present at court, servants and visitors alike, expected to be nourished. Therefore, the staffs that could be found at most courts were structured around sleeping, hospitality, and transport. These three activities and the staffs responsible for them conform to the inner–outer layout of palaces, with the services for sleeping located at the heart of the palace, for eating and hospitality in the intermediate spaces, and for movement on the outer margins. A string of supplementary services could be attached to the basic services for the chamber, the table, and the stables: devotion, ceremony, wardrobe, outfitting, medicine, education, security, washing, cleaning, armoury, hunting, treasury and accounting, gardens, cellars, entertainment, music, crafts production, engineering and construction. The tasks performed show substantial similarity, but each court organised the services in very different ways. Some court offices – chamberlains, doorkeepers,

H.G. Quaritch Wales, *Siamese State Ceremonies: Their History and Function* (London, 1931), 32–41, cites various taboos related to Siamese royals; on the 'iconography of absence' in Japan, see Timon Screech, *Shogun's Painted Culture: Fear and Creativity in the Japanese States, 1760–1829* (London, 2000), 112–18, cited in Walthall, 'Hiding the shoguns', 331.

[82] Alexandre de Chaumont, *Relation de l'ambassade de Mr. le Chevalier de Chaumont a la cour du roy de Siam, avec ce qui s'est passé de plus remarquable durant son voyage* (Amsterdam, 1686), 46–54; on Kangxi and the Russian ambassador Ismailov in 1721, see John Bell, *A Journey from St. Petersburg to Pekin, 1719–22*, ed. J.L. Stevenson (Edinburgh, 1966).

cupbearers, guard captains, and falconers among them – can be found in many places. However, no easy concordance can be established in the organisation and offices of the court.

In Benin, the royal court was organised through three 'palace associations', the first responsible for the *oba*'s (king's) throne, 'his ceremonial wardrobe and accoutrements', the second for his household and personal service – including a number of pages and sword-bearers as well as doctors – and the third supervising his wives and children, including the provisioning of this substantial group.[83] All palace societies were connected to Benin guilds; in the government of Benin, their leaders stood next to the hereditary nobles (*uzama*) and the appointed town chiefs (*eghaevbo n'ore*). No clear connections can be found with the Asante palace organisation. Under the *gyasehene*, the leader of all palace retainers at the *asantehene*'s court, we find cooks, stool-carriers, fan-bearers, sword-bearers, eunuchs, heralds, and many others. The Asante compound notably included a mausoleum with its own leading officer and courtyard with adjacent rooms containing the 'blackened stools' of previous rulers.[84] Lists of offices can be gleaned from many works on African kingship, but the variety of names defies typology on a continental, let alone on a global, scale.[85] Information on the functioning of these staffs is usually meagre – a situation that holds true for pre-Columbian America as well. No modern study is available that brings together all relevant information on the Mughal or Safavid courts. The shogunal establishment has been dealt with in several works, but the Japanese imperial court in Tokugawa times has been treated less generously.[86] More works deal

---

[83] Bradbury, *Benin Studies*, 60–2; Victor Osaro Edo, 'Hierarchy and organization of the Benin kingdom and palace', 91–101, and Daniel Inneh, 'The guilds working for the palace', 102–17, both in Barbara Plankensteiner (ed.), *Benin Kings and Rituals: Court Arts from Nigeria* (Vienna, 2007): see a diagram of the various palace-related elites (92), and of the guilds related to the palace societies (104).

[84] Rattray, *Ashanti Law and Constitution*, 55–60 on the palace, 88–92 on the offices.

[85] Oberg, 'Kingdom of Ankole in Uganda', 136–45, on the personnel of the royal kraal, including concubines and eunuchs; Mounier, 'Le cas du sultanat', 369–71, provides a list of offices; Johnson, *History of the Yorubas*, 57–68, provides a full description of court staffs, including eunuchs and court ladies; Holly Hanson, 'Mapping conflict: heterarchy and accountability in the ancient capital of Buganda', *Journal of African History*, 50/2 (2009), 179–202, at 190–3, analyses Buganda palace and city plans with some indication of buildings and staffs; on palaces, see also Blier, *Royal Arts of Africa*, 176, on the Foumban palace in the late nineteenth century, with less detailed plans of Dahomey (103), Bamileke, Batufam (179), and Kuba (242).

[86] On the Mughal court, see Muhammad Azhar Ansari, *Social Life of the Mughal Emperors 1526–1707* (Allahabad and New Delhi, 1974). More academic discussions dealing with aspects of the court include Blake, *Shahjahanabad*, 122–60, and the comparative conclusion at 182–211; Lal, *Domesticity and Power*, 155–66, on Fatehpur Sikri; S.A.A. Rizvi, *The Wonder that was India*, vol. II: *A Survey of the History and Culture of the Indian Sub-Continent from the Coming of the Muslims to the British Conquest 1200–1700* (London,

with the Ming and Qing, the Ottoman, and several European courts, but even here many questions remain unanswered.

The Ming court was managed by eunuchs organised in twelve directorates, four departments, and eight bureaus, almost all located in the imperial palace, with an additional group of eunuchs leading accessory services throughout the empire.[87] These numerous agencies covered all activities mentioned above, including a remarkable bureau for the production of luxury toilet paper and a nursing home for retired palace personnel. The Qing dynasty replaced the eunuch-controlled household with a more mixed 'imperial household department' (neiwufu), divided into seven different bureaus led by Manchu princes and bondservants. The highly stratified eunuch workforce included an upper level of around 300 office-holders. At the top stood a chief eunuch with his own staff of forty-four highly trained eunuch scribes. His status was equalled in practice by lesser-ranking eunuchs serving the emperor in person.[88] The tasks of the imperial household department went far beyond the management of household activities: it held the monopoly of jade and ginseng trades, collected precious objects, and hoarded wealth in its vaults. To some extent, the Household Department's services mirrored the outer court government organisation with its 'six ministries' for nominations (personnel), finance (revenue), rites (ceremony), war, punishments (justice), and works (construction), responsible for the imperial government.[89]

Inner and outer referred to different tasks as well as different groups. Hucker's Dictionary of Titles lists as occupants of the inner court (neichao) 'imperial family, palace women, eunuchs ... and a few eminent persons or institutions having close relations with the Emperor as administrators of the imperial household, intimate counsellors'. He continues to point out that the neichao was habitually contrasted with the waichao (outer court), referring to 'the established hierarchy of administrative, military,

---

1987), esp. 167–75; Kaempfer, *Am Hofe des persischen Grosskönigs*, 79–87 on court offices, and 134–49 on court customs; court offices can also be taken from Vladimir Minorsky (ed.), *Tadhkirat Al-Muluk: A Manual of Safavid Administration* (London, 1943), and Mirza Naqi Nasiri, *Titles & Emoluments in Safavid Iran: A Third Manual of Safavid Administration*, trans. Willem Floor (Washington, DC, 2008). On the Japanese courts in the Tokugawa period, Butler, *Emperor and Aristocracy*, and Webb, *Japanese Imperial Institution*, provide information on the imperial court; Totman, *Politics in the Tokugawa Bakufu*, gives detailed information on the shogunal organisation; but these studies give no full institutional view of the household – in the imperial case, the continuity with the Nara and Heian periods may have been considerable.

[87] Tsai, *Eunuchs in the Ming Dynasty*, Appendix 1, 231–3. Eunuchs took over most of the court ladies' tasks from the last years of the Yongle emperor onwards.

[88] Rawski, *Last Emperors*, 162–6, 178–81; Torbert, *Ch'ing Imperial Household Department*, 27–51.

[89] Torbert, *Ch'ing Imperial Household Department*, 33.

censorial [censors checked the activities of magistrates], and other agencies that managed the empire for the ruler'.[90] Qing emperors adopted a long-standing divide of inner and outer staffs, but modified it by infusing the inner court with conquest clan personnel. Manchu bondservants were added to the eunuchs as supervisors of the household administration; Manchu notables were present as trusted councillors and intermediaries at the highest levels, a role no longer primarily confided to eunuchs. The Forbidden City was embedded in the Imperial City (Plate 24), where outer court ministries were based. The Imperial City, in turn, formed the heart of a Manchu city: Ming Beijing was repopulated by the hereditary conquest elite. Manchu soldiers, with their Mongol and Chinese allies, were organised in eight semi-tribal hereditary 'banners', located in garrisons in various Chinese cities, but massively present in the Beijing area. The banners resided in the Manchu city, a third tier around the Forbidden and Imperial cities. The expelled Han Chinese constructed a new settlement on the southern margins of the city.[91]

At the Topkapı palace the inner court (*enderun*) included separate male and female hierarchies in the palace school and the harem, supervised by white and black eunuchs respectively. The youths in the palace school could 'graduate' to inner or outer court offices. Once they had left the confines of the inner court to serve in the Ottoman military or bureaucracy, however, they could no longer enter the world of their youth and education: the *enderun* was barred to all outer court (*birun*) staff, up to and including the grand vizier. At the highest level of the inner court, pages served the sultan in the four 'chambers', the privy chamber, the treasury, the larder, and the campaign chamber. Leading offices included the chief of the privy chamber (*hass oda başı*) sword-bearer (*silahdar*), stirrup-holder (*rikabdar*), the keeper of the garment (*çuhadar*), and the keeper of the linen (*dülbend oğlani*). A library, privy kitchens, the sultan's physicians, and the imperial tutor were also located in the inner court.

The Ottoman outer court staff included the departments necessary for organising the contact between the palace and the outside world: stables, gatekeepers, palace kitchens, gardens, palace workshops (including wardrobe, outfitting, book production), tent pitchers and standard bearers, and finally the keepers of the sultan's birds of prey.[92] In addition to the guards included in the inner court and in the outer court gatekeeper

---

[90] Hucker, *Dictionary of Official Titles*, 342–3, no. 4142; see also 352, no. 4267 *neiting*; 559, no. 7576 *waichao*; 561, no. 7606 *waiting*.

[91] On the banners, see Mark C. Elliott, *The Manchu Way: The Eight Banners and Ethnic Identity in Late Imperial China* (Stanford, CA, 2001).

[92] Murphey, *Ottoman Sovereignty*, 168–74; Halil İnalcık, *The Ottoman Empire: The Classical Age, 1300–1600* (London, 1973), 76–88.

service, janissary infantry and six cavalry (*sipahi*) divisions were related closely to the court establishment. The services for the government of the realm were initially concentrated in the second court, but tended to move outwards to the residence of the grand vizier. The imperial council (*divan*) brought together a mixed group, including the grand vizier and a growing number of lesser viziers, treasurers (*defterdars*), and a Keeper of the Seal (*nişancı*). Muslim legal scholars (*ulema*) were represented by the chief jurisconsult (*şeyhülislam*) and by two military judges (*kadıasker*). The leader (*agha*) of the janissaries, the grand admiral, and the governor (*beylerbey*) of Rumelia completed this highest council of the Ottoman empire. A group of scribes took care of the paperwork related to its decisions.[93]

The Ottoman, Safavid, and Mughal courts included workshops; in the New World, dynastic establishments likewise appear to have functioned as centres for the production as well as the consumption of luxury items.[94] Courts in Africa, Asia, and pre-Columbian America included numerous women producing precious textiles; polygyny created as well as demonstrated conspicuous wealth.[95] Large-scale production was present at the Chinese court, but cannot be found within the perimeter of European courts – although luxury production of tapestries, silk, and porcelain was initiated by the court as well as kept alive by its demands.[96]

Notwithstanding great variety in organisation, European courts were all based on the three staffs for the chamber, the table, and the stable. In the early modern age, the leaders of these staffs were the most important dignitaries at court, taking their oaths in the hands of the sovereign and usually accepting the oaths of numerous dependents. The chamberlain, the steward, and the master of the horse were served by lower-ranking staffs who did the actual work; the same pattern was replicated in a varying set of accessory services (wardrobe, treasury, silverware, kitchen)

---

[93] Gabor Agoston, 'Administration, central', in Ágoston and Masters (eds.), *Encyclopedia of the Ottoman Empire*, 10–13; Murphey, *Ottoman Sovereignty*, 253–68, on scribes.

[94] The presence of workshops is stressed in Blake, *Shahjahanabad*, in many places, including the Conclusion where it is generalised to include Ottoman, Safavid, Chinese, and Japanese examples. On the relatively great importance of workshops or *karkhanas* in the Mughal context, see Rizvi, *Wonder that was India*, 169–70; Faruqui, *Princes of the Mughal Empire*, 107–8; Kaempfer, *Am Hofe des persischen Grosskönigs*, 117–25.

[95] Susan Toby Evans, 'Concubines and cloth: women and weaving in Aztec palaces and colonial Mexico', in Walthall (ed.), *Servants of the Dynasty*, 215–31; Heidi J. Nast, 'Women, royalty and indigo dyeing in northern Nigeria, circa 1500–1807, in the same volume, 232–60; in general on women as wealth, see Evans-Pritchard, 'Zande state', 147.

[96] Rawski, *Last Emperors*, 175–8, at 176 citing an estimate of 10,000 palace artisans, with others employed at other locations and on a temporary basis. In Europe most luxury production was outside of the court, for instance the court-related porcelain production at Meißen or Sèvres. Ceramics were mostly produced at a distance from the court, as witnessed by the position of Ottoman Iznik, and Chinese Jingdezhen.

and independent additional services, notably the chapel, hunt, and guards.[97] The great court dignitaries long combined their domestic service with related responsibilities in government, with chamberlains serving as treasurers, stewards as leading advisors, and marshals or masters of the horse as military commanders. The rise of specialised services and leading secretaries or ministers from the later Middle Ages to the seventeenth century reduced many of these responsibilities to empty formulae, but court dignitaries ranked among the top echelons of most European monarchies until the end of the *ancien régime*.

Impressive numbers of people attending court can be found throughout the literature. Even relatively small African polities maintained big courts. By the late nineteenth century an estimated 8,000 persons, most of them females, served the Leopard King of Dahomey in his various establishments.[98] King Njoya (1860–1886–1933) of Bamoum in the Cameroon grasslands had around 1,000 wives and 2,000 servants.[99] Estimates of court numbers in a more distant past usually remain fragile and tentative. They can reach reasonable precision only if they are based on a breakdown of staffs and services.[100] Assessments vary widely, not only because of limited information in the sources, but also because it is never entirely clear who should be included. For many courts, several points in the seasonal calendar would lead to different outcomes: numbers may reflect a reduced travelling court or a court inflated during festive occasions. Do we count only household services, or should some administrative or military units be included? Are princes or grandees with their staffs taken into account? Do we accept artisans or labourers commissioned for certain projects as part of the court?

Louis XIV's royal household in the late 1690s included somewhat more than 2,000 persons; adding the households of other royals we reach 5,000; with the military elite units attached to the court 15,000 becomes a more likely figure. Numbers inflate if we count the crowds of visitors with their dependents in the environment of the chateau, or commissioned labourers.[101] Drawing the line between the domestic core of the household and its numerous fringes is not always easy. The Ottoman court at its greatest expanse in the early seventeenth century included almost 11,000 persons in its outer services and another estimated 2,000 in the inner services, not counting the janissary and *sipahi*

---

[97] Duindam, 'Royal courts'.   [98] Bay, *Wives of the Leopard*, 8.
[99] Tardits, *Le royaume Bamoum*, 573.
[100] Blake, *Shahjahanabad*, 190, 196, 201, 206, mentions figures that may be correct, but cannot be verified because no categories (or sources) are indicated.
[101] See my overview on European courts, 'Royal courts'.

household troops.[102] Numbers were higher at the late Ming court. The Portuguese Jesuit Semedo calculated that 13,000 eunuchs and 3,000 women populated the inner court of the Ming Forbidden City: 'Besides there are colledges for the Eunuches, for the Litterati, Priests, singing men, comedians &c. and almost infinite habitations for . . . people that are employed there, who are at the least 17000 persons.'[103] Semedo's 17,000 can be accepted as a minimum. Under the Qing the eunuchs were reduced sharply to 3,000 or fewer; the reorganisation of the imperial household department introduced Manchu overseers and staff, rising to more than 1,500 in the eighteenth century. The number of women in the inner court probably remained more constant, close to the 3,000 level. In addition, 10,000 palace artisans and 1,000 actors were active at court. Male and female labourers in diverse capacities added anything from 5,000 to 35,000 persons at different times.[104] A conservative estimate based on only the core groups would still suggest at least 8,000 persons for the early Qing court; including wider categories of personnel the figure easily rises to 20,000 or more, particularly during the Qianlong reign. While the Chinese court tended to grow during the reigns of the three 'high Qing' emperors, the Ottoman court reached its peak shortly after 1600. European courts expanded from the fifteenth into the seventeenth century, stabilised after the 1660s, and were reduced from the 1770s onwards. In absolute numbers, the Chinese court surpassed the other courts, while the Ottoman court still easily exceeded all European courts. As a proportion of the population, African courts appear as the most impressive establishments.

In Europe as well as in Asia two simultaneous tendencies can be found: the inward movement of rulers and the outward movement of government services. In Europe, specialised agencies for law and finance moved 'out of court', whereas monarchs tended to withdraw deeper into the sequence of rooms inside their palaces. Some European monarchs refrained from frequent council meetings, preferring to write their comments in the margins of advisors' reports; most continued meeting their key advisors on an almost daily basis. This was not the case in the Ottoman empire. After Mehmed

---

[102] On the outer court, see detailed information in Murphey, *Ottoman Sovereignty*, tables at 167, 171–4. On harem women, see Peirce, *Imperial Harem*, 122. On eunuchs and pages there is less clarity – see various assessments: Penzer, *Harem*, 132, citing 600–800 black eunuchs; Ohsson, *Tableau général*, 54–6, lists 200 black and 80 white eunuchs, figures also given in Dikici, 'Making of Ottoman court eunuchs', 113; Bobovius, *Topkapı*, 30, mentions 50 white eunuchs in the 1650s, and his Introduction, 15, lists 350–400 pages in the fifteenth century; Ohsson, *Tableau général*, 48–9, mentions 400 pages at Topkapı.

[103] Semedo, *History*, 112.

[104] Rawski, *Last Emperors*, 165–79; Spence, *Emperor of China*, 45, shows Kangxi stating that he employed only 400 eunuchs.

II's conquest of Constantinople, sultans reduced their presence among household troops and no longer attended *divan* (council) meetings. Following Murad III's reconstruction and expansion in the 1570s, sultans withdrew into the harem. Daily government was increasingly left to grand viziers, who held divan meetings in their own residences. From the later sixteenth century, communication between the grand vizier and the sultan usually proceeded in writing.[105] The more accessible Safavid shahs gradually became more reclusive in the seventeenth century. Kaempfer reports that Süleyman I most often communicated with his grand vizier 'through the intervention of eunuchs, rarely eye to eye'.[106]

The Qing Kangxi emperor moved his residential quarters into the inner court and changed the pattern of communication with outer court dignitaries. Under the Ming, the Grand Secretariat (*neige*) had co-ordinated the transfer of paperwork and decisions between inner and outer court services. In Qing times, the Grand Secretariat, located on the southeastern tip of the Forbidden City, still channelled formal memorials from the ministries to the palace. However, Kangxi initiated a second line of communication, asking his confidants for frank advice sent to him secretly and written in Manchu. Starting out as a circumvention of due administrative procedure, these 'palace memorials' gradually evolved into a full-blown confidential channel of communication in Manchu, bypassing the six ministries and the Grand Secretariat. The Yongzheng emperor devised an intermediate body to deal with decision-making. This 'Grand Council' (*junjichu*), initially dealing largely with military matters, had a stronger Manchu presence than the ministries and retained an air of informality. Its meetings took place in the 'strategic, transitional area between the inner and outer courts of the Palace City', close to the Palace of Mental Cultivation where the emperor resided de facto.[107]

The increasing distance between the domestic and administrative spheres exacerbated a tension universal in court life, between the agents of formal decision-making and the groups daily attending the ruler in person. Global history shows endless examples of servants in the immediate environment of the ruler outwitting outer court advisors.[108] This

[105] Fodor, 'Sultan, imperial council, grand vizier'.

[106] Kaempfer, *Am Hofe des persischen Grosskönigs*, 31, repeated at 63, though with the addition that the vizier and the shah rode out together in the evening, suggesting direct contact; Matthee, *Persia in Crisis*, 57–9.

[107] Zhu, *Chinese Spatial Strategies*, quotation at 102, map on 116; Rawski, *Last Emperors*, 32.

[108] Hereditary princes can be substituted for high-ranking outer court dignitaries: Mounier, 'Le cas du sultanat', construes the opposition between *gado* and *amana*, or 'héritage' and 'proximité', 376, 378, 379, and its consequences for social mobility and political dynamics, with slave-soldiers 'qui se curialisent progressivement' whereas princes, apart from a minority consolidating elite status, tended to submerge in the general

tension, however, took very different shapes, depending on the recruitment and status of court servants. A sharp divide pitted outer court magistrates against inner court eunuchs in imperial China. Magistrates recruited through civil service examinations saw themselves as the epitome of learning and culture. Court eunuchs, conversely, were recruited from lowly levels of society, qualifying for their menial tasks by enduring a demeaning operation that damaged their bodies in a way abhorrent to Confucian ideals.[109] Nobody denied that eunuchs could reach positions of great power, but few applauded this situation. Eunuchs were commonly presented as trifling figures reaching power only through subterfuge, on a par with concubines and consorts manipulating a weak emperor – the 'pack of self-seekers' referred to in the *Veritable Records* cited above.[110] By putting eunuchs under the leadership of bondservants from the conquest clan, Qing emperors changed the balance: the inner court now represented not only the despised influence of eunuchs and women, but also the clout of the ruling Manchus.

At the Ottoman court, the sharp status barrier between Chinese literati magistrates and inner court eunuchs was not replicated. Recruitment of staffs for the *enderun* and *birun* uniformly relied on slavery: from the later fifteenth century onwards Ottoman leading elites styled themselves as 'the sultan's slaves'. Eunuchs and concubines in the harem were recruited in slave markets. Palace pages were hand-picked from among the young boys gathered as slaves in the margins of the empire in the increasingly systemic 'selection' (*devshirme*) process. All groups were replenished by slaves captured as war booty. While black eunuchs usually underwent castration in North Africa, a share of the white eunuchs appears to have been castrated locally, on the basis of voluntary enrolment among the pages.[111] In the course of the seventeenth century, the devshirme levies declined; increasing numbers of local elite boys now voluntarily entered the palace school.[112] This important change does not seem to have

---

population. See a similar analysis projected onto the map of the palace and the city in Hanson, 'Mapping conflict', 179–202. On the 'domesticité dorée' of the princes in Dahomey, see Hérissé, *L'ancien royaume du Dahomey*, 32–3.

[109] On Chinese eunuchs, see Tsai, *Eunuchs in the Ming Dynasty*; Kutcher, 'Unspoken collusions'; Dan Shi, *Mémoires d'un eunuque*; Jennifer W. Jay, 'Another side of Chinese eunuch history: castration, marriage, adoption, and burial', *Canadian Journal of History*, 28/3 (1993), 459–78.

[110] Geiss, 'Leopard Quarter', 2. See above, 166.

[111] Dikici, 'Making of Ottoman court eunuchs', makes clear that white eunuchs could be recruited among devshirme boys, with the pages and their eunuch supervisors coming from the same background. They were sometimes castrated in the palace, whereas the harem's black eunuchs were more often castrated in their region of origin.

[112] Metin Kunt, *The Sultan's Servants: The Transformation of Ottoman Provincial Government, 1550–1650* (New York, 1983).

reduced the sharp inner–outer boundaries. However, neither the inner nor the outer court staff could claim the moral high ground unequivocally held by the literati in late imperial China. A parallel for them can be found in the *ulema*. The Muslim legal scholars were not tied to the inner or to the outer court service groups and could seek alliances with either. No counterpart existed in China for the Ottoman page school: eunuchs performed domestic tasks in the proximity of the ruler, and the inner court school groomed only the emperor's relatives for imperial service – although talented scholars were present in several learned institutions in the margins of the inner court, acting as tutors and advisors.[113]

The basic congruence in inner–outer court layout of the Chinese and Ottoman courts cannot be found in Japan. The shoguns practised poly-gyny but did not employ eunuchs at their court. Women guarded access into the female quarters. Numerous *bozu*, shaved women and men adopt-ing religious garb and renouncing their sexual activity, served at the sho-gun's court and communicated between its various layers. While women serving in lower ranks in the Great Interior could be recruited among commoners, almost all staff at the shogun's court were recruited from the military class. This elite, representing 6 per cent of the population, could be entered at its lower levels by commoners, with parents paying for the adoption of their children.[114] At the top, leading *daimyo* occupied the upper 'sixty or so' positions in the Tokugawa establishment; other 'mili-tary, administrative, ceremonial, and attendant' offices were filled by *c.* 17,000 liege vassals. This group performed service both in household and government: these domains were thus staffed by different layers of the same group, matching the Ottoman rather than the Chinese pattern.[115]

In Japan, inner–outer antagonism could take shape as conflict between hierarchically separated layers within the warrior group. Lesser-ranking pages starting out their careers attending the shogun's son and accom-panying his gradual ascendancy to power were likely to obtain positions as confidants. The favour they received could bring political influence as well as rapid promotion and hence antagonised distinguished families.

---

[113] Schools for imperial bondservants and for non-Chinese minorities were established in the *neiwufu* in the eighteenth century: see Torbert, *Ch'ing Imperial Household Department*, 38; Robert B. Crawford, 'Eunuch power in the Ming dynasty', *T'oung Pao*, 49/1 (1962), 115–48, at 134, refers to the training of young eunuchs in the palace by Hanlin academicians; titles of Hanlin academicians and the role of the 'southern study' or *nanshufang* under the Qing represent the literati element in the inner court, or on the margins between inner and outer.

[114] Personal communication from Anne Walthall; Totman, *Politics in the Tokugawa Bakufu*, Appendix B, 270–7.

[115] Totman, *Politics in the Tokugawa Bakufu*, 131–3, quotation at 131. On groups in Edo castle, on the collateral houses, and on the pages sometimes rising to prominence as 'grand chamberlains', see 91–109, 110–30, 214–21.

Shoguns gradually strengthened the position of their close attendants, establishing the function of chamberlain for them. In 1681, a year after succeeding his elder brother Ietsuna, Shogun Tsunayoshi (1646–1680–1709) created the office of grand chamberlain for his 'guardian or foster-father'. This man, Makino Narisada, was promoted to *daimyo* rank and became the dominant power at court. Even an outsider like Kaempfer was able to point out the grand chamberlain as the shogun's 'most intimate councillor and the only one whom the shogun trusts'.[116] After Narisada's retirement, Yanagisawa Yoshiyasu, who had served the shogun in his youth, purportedly also by offering sexual comforts, ascended to power and controlled access to his master.[117] Apart from the discord caused by the incidental rise of favourites, it is likely that rivalry was strongest among compeers in each of the hierarchical layers of the warrior class.

The predominance of the warrior class at the shogun's court needs to be put into the perspective of the imperial court at Kyoto. In the early decades of the seventeenth century, a new balance took shape between the emperor and the shogun that was based on the clear separation of the warrior class (*buke*) from the small group of Kyoto court nobles (*kuge*) and their elevated sovereign. In 1606, Shogun Ieyasu made the granting of ranks and titles to warriors by the imperial court contingent upon his explicit authorisation. Henceforth all nominations and promotions of warriors needed the shogun's sanction, a rule which gradually turned the imperial ranking system into an extension of shogunal power.[118] Ieyasu's 1615 code for the court nobles (*kuge shohatto*) never explicitly took away political power from the emperor, but did make painstakingly clear that any imperial effort to seek support among the *daimyo* by distributing titles was out of bounds. The supreme legitimacy of the imperial court, its strong residual cultural power, and its ranking system were harnessed to support Tokugawa power. Lee Butler points out that the redaction of the kuge shohatto suggests that, whereas Ieyasu's first priority was disconnecting the daimyo from direct imperial patronage, his second priority was to uphold the order and dignity of the imperial court. Thus, his regulations aimed to reduce the rivalry of leading families at court, often divided between the princes of the imperial house (*shinno*)

---

[116] Totman, *Politics in the Tokugawa Bakufu*, 99–103, 214–17; Kaempfer, *Kaempfer's Japan*, 357.

[117] Anne Walthall, 'Histories official, unofficial and popular: shogunal favourites in the Genroku era', in James C. Baxter and Joshua A. Fogel (eds.), *Writing Histories in Japan: Texts and their Transformations from Ancient Times through the Meiji Era* (Kyoto, 2007), 175–99; Beatrice M. Bodart-Bailey, *The Dog Shogun: The Personality and Policies of Tokugawa Tsunayoshi* (Honolulu, HI, 2006), 103–27.

[118] See more detail on rankings and rewards in Chapter 4.

and the members of regental families (*jugo*) serving in ministerial office. These two groups both aspired to supreme rank as well as to the emperor's confidence and hence had a long tradition of rivalry. Ieyasu's efforts to reduce this tension suggest that he saw the maintenance of the imperial court's prestige as his own best interest.[119]

The secluded position of women at the shogun's court resembled patterns observed in Beijing and Istanbul, though without the presence of eunuchs. Monogamous marriage and the mixing of high-ranking princesses and their suites with the male court mitigated the female–male divide in Europe. However, the dynamics of rank and proximity in Tokugawa Japan were closer to those in Europe than to either the Ottoman or the Chinese examples. Throughout *ancien régime* Europe, nobles held the highest ranks and performed honorary domestic service in the direct proximity of the king, matching the situation found in Japan. Noble rank, primarily defined by lineage and valour, was required for leading offices in the domestic sphere as well as in the upper levels of government. Structurally, the high ranks and ambitions of great nobles invited kings to seek support among talented lesser servants – clerics whose celibacy complicated patrimonial ambitions, or daily companions in every conceivable capacity, could be catapulted to high rank and political prominence. Mistresses, as we have seen, could also step in as confidantes and managers. While the rise of these favourites can be found throughout history, the gradual ascent of administrators trained in law and finance from the later Middle Ages to the eighteenth century created a growing and more structural tension, pitting vested noble dynasties against new men rising through office and preferment. While signs of this rivalry can be found in many European polities, it does not fit the inner–outer divide of imperial China or the Ottoman empire. The challenge of the specialised advisors emerged primarily in the council and its subordinate administrative agencies. In these upper layers of decision-making, ministers and secretaries, initially doing the paperwork for their noble superiors, gradually reached ascendancy. However, they never formed as prestigious a group as the upper layers of the Chinese magistracy: their highest ambition usually was to merge with the greater noble families. From the fifteenth century onwards a limited number of ministerial

---

[119] Lee A. Butler, 'Tokugawa Ieyasu's regulations for the court: a reappraisal', *Harvard Journal of Asiatic Studies*, 54/2 (1994), 509–51, and more generally on the relevance of the imperial court, his *Emperor and Aristocracy*; see also Eva-Maria Meyer, *Japans Kaiserhof in der Edo-Zeit: unter besonderer Berücksichtigung der Jahre 1846 bis 1867* (Münster, 1999).

dynasties were able to integrate through marriage and political alliance into the noble houses dominating court office. In France, a phase of ministerial mobility to higher rank ended in the later seventeenth century after the rise of the Le Tellier and Colbert families. Elsewhere short phases of exceptional mobility can be found, but nobles retained or regained their social prominence. As in Tokugawa Japan, it is likely that apart from general noble outcries against the inordinate rise of low-ranking favourites or ministers, nobles most often saw their near-equals as their main rivals while regarding social climbers as dispensable temporary allies or useful clients.

What to conclude from these dispersed and inconsistent data? Staffs were responsible for common household activities that can to some extent be fitted into the inner–outer framework. The presence of women and eunuchs or other lower domestics defined the innermost part of many courts. Conversely ministers, soldiers, and a second set of domestics usually served on the outer fringes of the court. The quarters of the king stood between the two domains. The positions of royals, successors, and nobles varied greatly, going from one extreme to another, or combining various locations as did the *daimyo* and many European grandees. Groups were recruited in very different ways, and hierarchies show some congruity only on a limited regional basis: within Europe, or among the Islamicate West Asian empires, or in China and some of its tributaries. Similarities of the inner–outer format cannot be extended to the level of social groups, hierarchies, and recruitment. At all courts, however, different hierarchies clashed. Generally accepted ranking systems introduced or adapted by the dynasty never wholly fitted hierarchies of office-holding, let alone the volatile 'shadow hierarchy' based on access to the ruler and favour. Hereditary grandees often found themselves distant from an active role at the heart of power and from the ruler's confidence. Likewise, rulers could turn a cold shoulder to their supreme political dignitaries, sometimes reducing their office to an empty show of power. Conversely, low-ranking servants without extended social connections were attractive candidates for favour and promotion. A recurring element in the staffs around the ruler seems to be the consistent dissonance created by conflicting hierarchies of descent, office, and access. The ruler's grace was a powerful instrument of social mobility, and the court itself has been pictured as an instrument for elite control, manipulating rivals by generating new elites, and controlling all by a fine-tuned machinery of checks and balances. Courts have rightly been pictured as places of contention and bargaining; at the same time they were the main stage for the solemn enactment of dynastic power. How did these reputations fit together and who pulled the strings?

Temple, cage, arena

Three images persist in historiography: the court as a temple of glory where all elites enacted obedience; the court as a gilded cage confining formerly recalcitrant elites; and finally, the court as an arena of competition controlled by the arbiter-king. Detailed historical examples can be given for each of these images; they have been understood largely as corroborating the agency of rulers and enforcing the compliance of their office-holders. Undoubtedly the initiative sometimes lay in the hands of a powerful king supported by loyal advisors. However, the constellation of personalities and contingencies at other moments shows rulers manipulated by a handful of their servants, or courts where all took part in a shameless scramble for spoils. In all but the most extreme situations these practices would be carefully veiled by deference to the incumbent prince as well as to higher moral notions. Can we see the difference at a distance? Sources may be available outlining nominations and events, but few texts remain in which rulers or their key advisors carefully and credibly describe their motives. While it is only rarely possible to ascertain the intentions of rulers, it is even more difficult to establish with precision the motives and actions of the multiple servants at court. Surely these foot-soldiers of dynastic power were not expected to openly voice their personal ambitions, let alone confide them to paper.[120]

The royal court naturally brings to mind the temple. Many sources stress the immutable order and dignity of court life, the unchanging rhythms of the prince, the benevolent and just nature of his rule, the ingrained subservience of all. The metaphor of the sun can be found in temples as well as in palaces, indicating not only the sun's radiance, but also its steadfast appearance, and sometimes the accessory roles of orbiting bodies.[121] Across the globe, from the Americas and Africa to Europe and Asia, court-related rituals could take very different shapes, changing from violent, moving, and transformative to more stately and sedate events. Everywhere, however, they shared certain characteristics. Solemn ceremonies followed detailed rules kept alive by ritual specialists – in memory, writing, songs, and pictures. Artefacts played a key role in ceremonies: courts included repositories of such objects and workshops to create more. The spaces of the court were designed for the enactment of rituals and were furnished for the occasion with the paraphernalia tradition called for. Ritual performances were repeated in set patterns based on seasonal rhythms (liturgical

---

[120] See Rawski, *Last Emperors*, on the master–servant tension and on the agency of subservient staff (160–1), and on the dominant security agenda of the court and on transgression by court personnel (182–94).
[121] Necipoğlu, 'Framing the gaze', 313–14.

and agricultural calendars), on the cycle of rulership (death–accession–maturity–marriage–birth–death), and on specific occasions (assemblies, warfare, hunt, drought, illness). At fixed moments, set apart from ongoing everyday routines, rituals were consciously performed, often for a wider audience – if only the extended group of participants.

Ideally the great rites of court life were insulated against any disturbance or contestation. They represented the natural order of hierarchies terrestrial and celestial. Painstaking performance of ritual was essential for rulers in many places: by their unwavering adherence to ritual propriety they ensured celestial benevolence. The court establishment as a whole put a high premium on the undisturbed performance of ritual and seriously punished offenders undermining this splendid collective show of hierarchy and order. No *daimyo* was expected to disrupt the order described for audiences in the shogunal castle; no Chinese eunuch or magistrate should misbehave during any of the Grand Sacrifices. Ceremonial order was to be eternal. Stone place markers indicated the positions of participants in audiences in the Forbidden City.[122] Detailed written protocols outlined the time-honoured proceedings. Great ceremonies only partially conformed to the ideal of the immaculate performance; people made mistakes and sometimes did so intentionally to improve their position in the show. Meddling with the rituals, however, cannot have been trouble-free for any of the participants, including the ruler who often performed – or underwent – the most visible part. Kings were the hub of court ritual but not necessarily its prime movers. Demanding that their courtiers conform to age-old imperatives, they could not discard these rules offhandedly themselves.[123] Changing rituals undoubtedly was possible for some rulers; inevitably all rulers to some extent adapted their personal roles in the performances. But did ritual offer a good opportunity to settle scores?

Perhaps the most famous examples of manipulation through ceremony are the bedside conventions at the French court under Louis XIV, with the king singling out courtiers for the privilege of handing him his nightshirt (*chemise*) or candle-holder (*bougeoir*). It is beyond doubt that Louis was keenly aware of the value attached to minor honours and distinctions, yet his prime activity in devising new honours was not connected to ceremony.[124] Moreover, the morning and evening conventions were not

---

[122] Dapper, *Beschryving des keizerryks van Taising of Sina*, 25.

[123] Elias, *Court Society*, on the whole overrates the power of the king, but Elias did include an important passage on the 'Verkettung' of the king, 'chained' by the rules he dictated to others.

[124] See a famous quotation from Louis XIV, *Oeuvres de Louis XIV*, ed. Philippe Henri de Grimoard and P.A. Grouvelle, 6 vols. (Paris, 1806), I, 143, in the context of orders of chivalry and similar honorary distinctions: 'nulle ne touche plus les cœurs bien faits que ces distinctions de rang, qui sont presque le premier motif de toutes les actions

usually seen as ceremonies by contemporaries; only with the presence of diplomats did these daily meetings obtain ceremonial status, documented in official records, and organised by the relevant ceremonial specialists. More importantly, the privilege of the *chemise* was strictly tied to rank: the unexpected entry of a higher-ranking prince would mean that the king needed to suspend activity until the newly arrived grandee handed him his shirt – there was little room for manipulation here. Only the presentation of the *bougeoir* was left to the king's discretion, but this was a minor exception in the set-up of court life, usually predicated wholly on the rank of those present. Likewise, the right to present the king's napkin during the dinner was given to the highest-ranking person present. Contestations over daily service were not as a rule instigated by the king, nor did he appreciate them. When in March 1688 the first gentle-man of the bedchamber and the grand master of the wardrobe disputed the right to hand the *surtout* (coat) to the king, we hear that the king refrained from deciding and simply waited glumly.[125] Such conflicts were awkward without necessarily offering chances for manipulation and could not constitute the basis for a system of ceremonial divide-and-rule.

In France a strong tendency towards heredity and venality of court office threatened to make servants in all ranks unmanageable. Office was seen as a family heirloom, to be protected at all cost against incursions by rivals. The unclear division of labour between offices and staffs formed the occasion for numerous battles. Thus, the 'wine runner' (*courreur de vin*) and the 'conductor of the ambler' (*conducteur de la haquenée*) were engaged in a protracted fight over the locations where they were allowed to serve refreshments to the king. A quarrelsome master of ceremonies under Louis XIV picked fights with his superior, the grand master, and even with ambassadors – dignitaries representing their sovereign in per-son. His aversion to sharing information about due procedure with his colleagues, because he hoped their mishaps would improve his career chances, was not uncommon.[126] At the highest levels court dignitaries contested the perquisites of their offices and the spoils of the ceremonies

humaines, mais sur-tout des plus nobles et des plus grandes; c'est d'ailleurs un des plus visibles effets de notre puissance, que de donner, quand il nous plaît, un prix infini à ce qui de soi-même n'est rien'.

[125] Philippe de Courcillon Dangeau, *Journal du Marquis de Dangeau*, ed. Eud. Soulié and L. Dussieux, 19 vols. (Paris, 1854–60), II, 123, 25 March 1688: 'Il y eut une contesta-tion à Saint-Cyr (Salut) entre M. de la Rochefoucault, grand maître de la garderobe, et le marquis de gesvres, premier gentilhomme de la chambre, à qui donneroit le surtout au roi. Quand le roi est hors de sa chambre, c'est au premier gentilhomme de la chambre à lui donner son manteau ou sa casaque; M. de la Rochefoucault prétend qu'un surtout c'est un justaucorps.'

[126] Duindam, *Vienna and Versailles*, 206–9.

to which they were entitled. If the well-ordered courtly universe in Europe at times resembled a perennial whirlwind of competition, what does this tell us about other courts? The parameters of office-holding, the power of cultural example, and the threat of punishment will have been proportioned differently, but it seems unlikely that court servants elsewhere failed to pursue personal goals, even if these at times mixed uncomfortably with their responsibilities. A submissive demeanour was indispensable in court service as well as in the polite turns of courtly epistolary culture, but individual and family interests surface whenever we have detailed information on attitudes and motives.

It would be wrong to assume that court life consisted of an unbroken chain of ritual occasions. Most examples of rivalry at the French court did not occur during the great ceremonial highlights of the dynasty, where they would not have been tolerated, but during daily patterns of court life in the wide margins between ceremonial publicity and dynastic seclusion. Depending on the traditions of the court, kings could spend an important part of their lives behind the gates and barriers of the inner court. We know little about their lives there, but what we can find out suggests familiarity and relaxation rather than undiminished ritual severity.

Kings and their advisors were keenly aware of the demonstrative value of grand ceremonial performances. Solemn rituals defined and visualised ranks; if the order they presented was contested, disagreements could arise. This was certainly the case in diplomatic interaction, which gradually embraced increasingly distant territories in the early modern age. Conflict surfaced invariably where no single institution wielded supreme authority or could dictate hierarchies. In European diplomacy, ceremonial contestation served to publicly demonstrate the advantages secured on the battlefield and at the conference table. In the years following the 1659 Peace of the Pyrenees, the changing balance of power between Spain and France was at stake in several ceremonial conflicts. Ambassadors in their impressive coaches, typically pulled by six horses as a sign of the occupants' high dignity, were often unwilling to grant priority to their rivals. In London in 1661 this recurrent ceremonial contest for *préséance* turned into a miniature battle between the footmen of the French and Spanish ambassadors. The episode ended with the Spanish ambassador's public apology at the French court, celebrated by a painting in the Versailles Hall of Mirrors: 'French pre-eminence recognised by Spain'.[127] A minor incident at court in Vienna shortly after the Peace of Rijswijk (1697) led to protracted sabre-rattling by the French,

[127] Lucien Bély and Gérard Poumarède (eds.), *L'incident diplomatique (XVIe–XVIIIe siècle)* (Paris, 2010).

again demanding and obtaining a full apology.[128] Ceremonial strife helped define rankings in the grey area between war and peace.

Diplomatic encounters between China and the lesser powers in its proximity were framed by the Chinese as the bringing of tribute, even when the tributaries themselves were often eager to be treated in a more equal way.[129] European missions to China were fitted into this pattern of tribute-bringing, until the rising military strength of Europe gradually tilted the balance after 1800. Russian–Chinese relations were an exception: the 1689 treaty of Nerchinsk put the two powers roughly at the same level. The account of Peter the Great's ambassador Ismailov to Beijing in 1721 shows the old Kangxi emperor in good shape. Ismailov had alienated the Qing ceremonial specialists in preliminary discussions by demanding special rights. The emperor, apparently unmoved, allowed Ismailov to advance with his sovereign's letter in his hands into the main audience hall:

Count Ismailof then entered, and immediately prostrated himself before the table, holding up the Czar's letter with both hands. The Emperor, who had at first behaved graciously to Ismailof, now thought proper to mortify him, by making him remain some time in this particular posture. The proud Russian was indignant at this treatment, and gave unequivocal signs of resentment by certain motions of his mouth, and by turning his head aside, which under such circumstances was very unseemly. Hereupon his Majesty prudently requested that the ambassador himself should take up the letter to him, and when Count Ismailof did so, kneeling down at his feet, he received it with his own hands, thus giving him another mark of regard, and granting what he had previously refused.[130]

Kangxi's alternation of affront and preference suggests a conscious action to put the ambassador in his place without compromising his mission. Examples of exchanges between European ambassadors and the Ottomans show similar cases of wrestling through ceremonial forms; perhaps the most notorious incident involved the visit of Süleyman Ağa to Louis XIV's court in 1669. The king's unwillingness to receive the sultan's letter standing and the diplomat's unceremonious withdrawal formed the occasion for the composition of the 'cérémonie turque' in the *Bourgeois*

---

[128] Duindam, *Vienna and Versailles*, 17.

[129] Sylvie Pasquet, 'Quand l'empereur de Chine écrivait à son jeune frère, empereur de Birmanie ... Analyse d'une correspondance diplomatique sur "feuilles d'or" (XVIIIe siècle)', *Journal asiatique*, 300/1 (2012), 265–313.

[130] Bell, *Journey from St. Petersburg to Pekin*, 133, and Appendix 219 from the memoirs of Father Ripa. Bell's account does not include this particularly vivid scene. The Kangxi emperor did entertain his guests in a friendly and approachable way during several hunting parties.

Gentilhomme by Molière and Lully.[131] Outsiders and opponents could be ridiculed with impunity. In 1582, the Safavid ambassador witnessing the major festival for the circumcision of Murad III's son Mehmed in Istanbul was expelled when his countrymen violated the truce. Miniatures depicting the occasion show buffoons playing with Safavid turbans.[132] This slight was replicated in 1619 when during one of Shah Abbas I's popular excursions, 'The unpopular Ottoman ambassador was humiliated by a group of courtiers who pushed him so hard that he fell on the ground and his turban came off to roars of laughter. The astonished ambassador swore at this unseemly behavior which was so foreign to the "serious gravity of his nation".'[133] Among the reasons behind the failure of the Ottoman mission to Louis XIV, the lack of clarity of Süleyman Ağa's rank had played a role: full ambassadors were received with higher honours. Only after crucial changes in the balance of power between 1683 and 1718 did the Ottoman sultan send full ambassadors to Europe. China, similarly, fitted into the European patterns of exchange of diplomats only after the rupture of the Opium Wars (1839–42, 1856–60) and the Taiping Rebellion (1850–64).

The diffuse and contested ranking of diplomacy, always related to the changing military-political balances, differed from practice at court.[134] Hierarchies were more clear-cut within the confines of a single court, and malpractice during ceremonies was more likely to provoke sharp punishment by unchallenged authorities. A court marked by disorder and conflict reflected badly on the character of the ruler who apparently could not establish order even in his own household. Conflict manifestly undermined the principle of monarchy and dishonoured the ruler in person. Therefore, it is difficult to accept ceremonial conflict as a widely practised stratagem of government. On the whole, rulers defended rank and order, punishing those who disturbed these ideals by misbehaving. Kings could choose to engage in a sophisticated balancing act through ceremony; most often, however, this was not in their best interest. They had far more direct and efficient means to punish arrogant figures.

Officiating as the high priest in the temple of glory, the prince was limited in his freedom to manoeuvre. Surely, it was easier to bring together at court, under close supervision, his most important potential rivals. We have seen several examples of caged successors: Ottoman, Safavid, and Mughal

---

[131] See a relatively neutral description of the audience in Laurent d'Arvieux, *Mémoires du chevalier d'Arvieux, envoyé extraordinaire du Roy à la Porte ...*, ed. R.P. Jean-Baptiste Labat, 6 vols. (Paris, 1735), IV, 157–65.

[132] Derin Terzioglu, 'The imperial circumcision festival of 1582: an interpretation', *Muqarnas*, 12 (1995), 84–100, at 86.

[133] Necipoğlu, 'Framing the gaze', 311.

[134] Christian Windler, 'Diplomatic history as a field for cultural analysis: Muslim–Christian relations in Tunis, 1700–1840', *Historical Journal*, 44/1 (2001), 79–106.

princes were confined in palace compounds, and Qing princes were kept close to the centre on a short leash. 'Hostage systems' guaranteeing the loyalty of subjected elites stipulated the presence of daughters and sons at court, in the harem or as pages. At the Ottoman court a list of 'captive dignitaries' produced in the 1540s included 'sons and descendants of subordinated dynasties, such as the Crimean Tatars and the Mamluk sultans of Egypt'.[135] At the court of Aceh, scions of subjected Malay principalities were held as hostages – one of them even ascended to the throne in 1636.[136] Leading dignitaries from the core provinces of the Mataram sultanate were expected to reside at court, leaving regional government in the hands of their representatives. The sultans accepted in marriage princesses from subjected polities, and pages were educated in the households of leading officials.[137] The Mughal harem recruited women from subjected princes, and sons of vassals were educated at court. In Cuzco, elite polygyny brought together women from across the Inka domains; at the same time nobles' sons were attracted to the capital as pages, whereas lesser-ranking groups were forced to work there temporarily.[138] In Bunyoro, the great chiefs were supposed to maintain residences at the king's capital Hoima and to 'attend there constantly'.[139]

Among these numerous examples a few stand out. The Tokugawa shoguns in Japan stipulated the frequent presence of the *daimyo* lords at their court. Following the common Japanese practice of using hostages as a means of ensuring the loyalty of vassals, Shogun Iemitsu in 1635 revised the 'Laws for the Military Houses' (*buke shohatto*), outlining a system of 'alternate attendance' (*sankin kotai*). He decreed the regular attendance at the shogunal castle in Edo of the *tozama* or 'outside' daimyo (Plate 29b), former equals of the Tokugawa who had not supported the founder Ieyasu in the decisive Battle of Sekigahara (1600). Iemitsu's 1642 revision of the *buke shohatto* also required the presence of the loyal hereditary (*fudai*) daimyo, who had been vassals from before Sekigahara.[140] The

---

[135] Murphey, *Ottoman Sovereignty*, 157–8.

[136] Andaya, 'A very good-natured but awe-inspiring government', 64.

[137] Moertono, *State and Statecraft in Old Java*, 94–5, and at 108 recapitulating strategies, including alliances between sultanas and key officials.

[138] Katz, 'Evolution of Cuzco and Tenochtitlán', 204–5; R. Alan Covey, 'Intermediate elites in the Inka heartland, A.D. 1000–1500, in Christina M. Elson and R. Alan Covey (eds.), *Intermediate Elites in Pre-Columbian States and Empires* (Tucson, AZ, 2006), 112–35, at 124–7 on polygyny and its consequences.

[139] Beattie, *Bunyoro*, 36; on chiefs in capitals, see also Lund, 'Royal capitals of the inter-lacustrine kingdoms', 64–7.

[140] Toshio G. Tsukahira, *Feudal Control in Tokugawa Japan: The Sankin Kōtai System* (Cambridge, MA, 1966), 43–6, on the gradual accumulation of rules in the buke shohatto from 1615 onwards; the buke shohatto of subsequent shoguns can be found translated in John Carey Hall, 'Japanese feudal laws, III: the Tokugawa legislation',

'related' daimyo (*shimpan*), collateral houses of the Tokugawa who could be adopted into the main line to safeguard succession, were also included in the system of alternate attendance. This law required all daimyo lords to stay in Edo during twelve-month periods according to a fixed schedule including different arrangements for different ranks. After this prolonged stay in Edo, the daimyo could retire to his castle to manage his fief, while his wife, sons, daughters, and a number of his vassals remained in Edo. As a consequence, 'The shogun remained fixed, stationary in his castle palace, while his retainers, the daimyo, were in orbit around him.'[141] This system enforced the obedience of the daimyo, repeatedly and clearly demonstrated in court audiences, but at the same time left them relatively great autonomy in governing their own fiefs. The daimyo lords, leaders of the warrior class, numbered 195 houses in 1602, ruling over numerous vassals; in 1866 these high-ranking houses had risen to a total of 265.[142] At court the daimyo were expected to come to audiences three times a month, in a carefully graded pattern of access and honour. High rank was respected and made visible, but key positions of power at the centre were rarely confided to the highest-ranking: 'Here, as elsewhere in the bakufu, however, high status went hand in hand with separation from power.'[143] Alternate attendance represented a major investment for the daimyo, who not only had to organise movement between their domains and Edo, but also had to maintain a stately mansion and lifestyle at the capital. The enforced frequent stays at the capital never deprived the daimyo of political power in their domains.[144] The permanent movements, moreover, turned out to have a major significance for the culture and economy of Japan.

The metaphor of the cage has been used for Versailles, often presented as a splendid prison for the French nobility.[145] Some similarities with the

---

Transactions of the Asian Society of Japan, 38/4 (1911), 269–331. On the *kuge shohatto* or rules for the imperial nobility, see Lee A. Butler, 'Tokugawa Ieyasu's regulations for the court'; and Constantine N. Vaporis, *Tour of Duty: Samurai, Military Service in Edo, and the Culture of Early Modern Japan* (Honolulu, HI, 2008), on the experiences of daimyo and samurai, and the wider impact of alternate attendance. At 2, Vaporis criticises superficial comparisons between Louis XIV's Versailles and Tokugawa policies vis-à-vis daimyo lords.

[141] Vaporis, *Tour of Duty*, 7.

[142] Tsukahira, *Feudal Control*, 22–7, citing for 1602 119 tozama, 72 fudai, and 4 shimpan daimyo, and for 1866 97 tozama, 145 fudai, and 23 shimpan houses.

[143] Totman, *Politics in the Tokugawa Bakufu*, 116.

[144] A point underlined by S.N. Eisenstadt, *Japanese Civilization: A Comparative View* (Chicago, IL, 1996), 184–9, who presents an outdated view of French nobles.

[145] Norbert Elias, *Die höfische Gesellschaft: Untersuchungen zur Soziologie des Königtums und der höfischen Aristokratie, mit einer Einleitung: Soziologie und Geschichtswissenschaft* (Neuwied, 1969), 367, uses the terminology; the French case is cited in many works dealing with Tokugawa Japan, e.g. Tsukahira, *Feudal Control*, 27.

Tokugawa experience can be found. In the memoirs for his son, Louis XIV explicitly voiced a policy that has been inferred from Tokugawa actions by several historians.[146] As a young king establishing his reputation, Louis stated, it had not been in his interest to employ noble grandees as ministers: the public would expect these prestigious figures to rule behind the king's back, whereas they themselves were liable to develop 'higher hopes than it pleased the king to fulfil'.[147] Grandees would not serve as key advisors in Louis' privy council or act as prime ministers. This separation of 'grandeur and power' did not imply a negative attitude to nobles in general: it reflected a strong determination to prevent the challenges to royal power that had characterised the turbulent preceding decades.[148]

Did the king force nobles to attend court? No written regulations in the style of the *buke shohatto* were ever proclaimed. In fact, the Sun King accomplished a remarkable feat that controverts the notion of enforced presence of numerous nobles. In a reform only rarely matched by his European fellow monarchs, Louis XIV sharply reduced the numbers of the French court, which had undergone uncontrolled expansion during the political crisis following 1648. The king re-established a stable balance, disturbed in preceding decades, by sending away many supernumerary noble office-holders and stipulating fixed numbers for most offices. At the same time, he confirmed the rights and privileges of those still employed at court, making court office more exclusive and attractive for noble grandees, some of whom had earlier joined the rebellion. When supplementary staff were necessary for construction, entertainment, or maintenance, Louis had them hired on the basis of commission and without special rights – a measure resembling the modern practice of 'outsourcing'. Nobles at Versailles held the highest offices as honorary domestics in the immediate presence of the king. They organised the king's daily schedule in the chamber, at the table, and during the hunt – settings most often used to illustrate the king's alleged ceremonial balancing act. The leading office-holder at the French court, the steward or head of the household, was a prince of royal blood distant from but entitled to succession. He combined his leading (and lucrative) court office with the governorship of several provinces, a pattern replicated by

---

[146] Totman, *Politics in the Tokugawa Bakufu*, 30, cites the same passage from Louis' memoirs, relating it to Ieyasu's use of lesser-ranking men from the military class; Bodart-Bailey, *Dog Shogun*, 103, opens her chapter on the 'shogun's new men' with a reference to Saint-Simon.

[147] Louis XIV, *Mémoires*, ed. Cornette, 71.

[148] On *pouvoir* and *grandeur*, see the early and lucid work by Henri Brocher, *Rang et l'étiquette sous l'ancien régime* (Paris, 1934).

others in the upper echelons of court office. The families confirmed in office by Louis not only successfully maintained their presence at court from the 1660s onwards, they also acquired a lasting grip on high office throughout France in government, army, diplomacy, and the Church.[149] Domestic service at court did not usually mix easily with a leading role in the king's councils, but it provided privileged access to the king as well as to the offices he distributed. Royals at the French court, by definition at the upper levels of the ranking system, were not necessarily close to power. The political roles of Louis' heir-apparent and his brother were carefully circumscribed – their proximity to succession did not allow any tomfoolery. Supreme rank restricted access to political power but brought a regal share of wealth and honour. Holding court office and residing at Versailles were coveted rights within the exclusive reach of high nobles. The French court was a gilded cage only in the sense that it restricted membership – and hence the chance of access to power – to a limited circle. The overwhelming majority of French nobles saw themselves locked out rather than locked in.

The metaphor of the cage fits the Ottoman *kafes* and the Ethiopian 'royal mountains' at Amba Geshan or Wahni, with their permanent confinement of all potential successors. Neither in Versailles nor in Edo were successors the prime target of measures to ensure court attendance. Only a minuscule share of the nobles present at these courts could in theory ascend to the throne. However, attracting nobles was surely relevant for the shoguns as well as for Louis XIV. Their measures were intended to forestall the rise of noble challengers and establish beyond doubt the hierarchical supremacy of the ruler. They demanded subservience at court while confirming in different ways the dominant position of the upper layers of nobles. Frequent presence was enforced in Japan, whereas it was largely determined by the benefits available for courtiers in France.

In Japan and in France, hereditary grandees did not habitually enjoy access to political decision-making at the highest levels: lesser-ranking groups were preferred as advisors and political managers. Did rulers act as social engineers by promoting confidants and bypassing high-ranking candidates for leading political office? Did the court resemble an arena rather than a cage, with kings dividing their opponents to maintain power?[150] This is the most complicated but potentially the most instructive image. It needs to be examined at various levels, from social engineering to the distribution of honours, from groups to individual grandees.

---

[149] Horowksi, *Die Belagerung des Thrones*.

[150] This classic formula was rephrased with great power by Elias, *Court Society*, as the 'Königsmechanismus' or the king's balancing between robe and sword nobles.

Finally, as in so many other questions related to dynastic power, we need to relate it to the variable individual capabilities and dispositions of rulers.

Overseeing the arena of court politics and the social setting of court life, several rulers successfully confronted social elites by empowering alternative groups as leading servants. The Ottoman *devshirme* system perhaps represents the most articulate and far-reaching variant of recruitment and training of slaves for high office at court, in the army, and in government. Between the late fourteenth and the early sixteenth century, devshirme recruits replaced leading families in all sectors except the *ulema* establishment. The early introduction of civil service examinations in China likewise fundamentally changed the recruitment and nature of elites. Training and selection through examination, developed to a remarkable extent in post-Tang imperial China, proved to be a lasting alternative to hereditary office-holding. After the end of the Tang dynasty and the advent of the Song dynasty in the tenth century, noble grandees were no longer a major political force: the examinations had profoundly changed elite recruitment. The requirement of examination success made next-of-kin succession in office very unlikely; at the same time it demonstrated the possibility of social ascent through hard work to wider audiences. Stories about country boys rising from rags to riches opened the vista of social ascent for many. However, while heredity in office was no longer possible on an individual basis, the examinations maintained the grip of lineages on office and privilege. Training for the examinations required so much time and money that, although mobility was a real possibility, it remained exceptional. On the whole, the examinations ensured the lasting dominance of the gentry class. Nevertheless, they underpinned the moral legitimacy of the empire in general and the literati magistrates in particular.[151]

A mystical connection through shared beliefs could become a truly dominant element in Islamicate rulership. Safavid Shah Ismail (1487–1501–1524), claiming descent from the mystic Shaykh Safi al-din (d. 1334), commanded the loyalty of his 'Turkmen armed disciples, who venerated him as the incarnation of God on earth'.[152] The confidence of these 'redhead' Qizilbash in their leader went so far that some apparently entered the battlefield unarmed. A Venetian traveller reported in 1518: 'This sophy [Shah Ismail] is loved and reverenced by his people as a God and especially by his soldiers, many of whom enter into battle without armour, expecting their master Ismael to watch over them in

[151] Elman, *Cultural History of Civil Examinations*; and Elman 'Political, social, and cultural reproduction'.
[152] Babayan, *Mystics, Monarchs, and Messiahs*, 296.

fight ... The name of God is forgotten throughout Persia and only that of Ismael remembered.'[153] Under Ismail I's successors, the mystical-religious tie was gradually supplemented by patronage networks based on the distribution of benefits.[154] In the same period, the Mughal padishahs entertained close connections with several competing Sufi orders.[155] Akbar's personalised and eclectic form of devotion, however, included Hindus as well as Muslims of different creeds among its followers. In 1579, the objections of more orthodox *ulema* to their leader's various heterodox initiatives were pre-empted by a decree assigning to Akbar the final word in any religious controversy:

we declare that the King of Islam, Amir of the Faithful, Shadow of God in the world, Abul Fath Jalal-ud-din Muhammad Akbar Padshah Ghazi (whose kingdom God perpetuate), is a most just, most wise, and a most God-fearing king. Should, therefore, in the future, a religious question come up, regarding which the opinions of the mujtahids are at variance, and His Majesty, in his penetrating understanding and clear wisdom, be inclined to adopt, for the benefit of the nation, and as a political expedient, any of the conflicting opinions, which exist on that point, and issue a decree to that effect, we do hereby agree that such a decree shall be binding on us and on the whole nation.[156]

The prince as spiritual guide (*pir*) was mystically present among his followers (*murids*), even when they were fighting for him in distant corners. As a form of recruitment of supporters, spiritual leadership could be as effective as examinations or *devshirme*. However, it relied on the personal charisma of the leader as well as on the lasting devotion of his followers, and these qualities were not necessarily reproduced in a second or third generation.

---

[153] Henry Edward John Stanley (ed.), *Travels to Tana and Persia by Josafa Barbaro and Ambrogio Contarini* (New York, 1873), 206, a sixteenth-century translation by William Thomas. On the Qizilbash and earlier Sufi traditions, see Riza Yildirim, 'Inventing a Sufi tradition: the use of the Futuwwa ritual gathering as a model for the Qizilbash Djem', in John Curry and Erik Ohlander (eds.), *Sufism and Society: Arrangements of the Mystical in the Muslim World, 1200–1800* (Abingdon and New York, 2012), 165–82.

[154] In addition to Babayan, *Mystics, Monarchs, and Messiahs*, see Khafipour, 'Foundation of the Safavid state'.

[155] Muzaffar Alam, 'The Mughals, the Sufi shaikhs and the formation of the Akbari dispensation', *Modern Asian Studies*, 43/1 (2009), 135–74.

[156] 'Abd al-Qādir ibn Mulūk Shāh (Badā'ūnī), *Muntakhabu-T-Tawārikh*, trans. W.H. Lowe et al. 3 vols. (Patna, 1973), II, 279–80 (reprint of older Calcutta edition). Badā'ūnī was highly critical of Akbar's unorthodoxy and Abu'l-Fazl's attitudes: see Catherine B. Asher, 'A ray from the sun: Mughal ideology and the visual construction of the divine', in Matthew T. Kapstein (ed.), *The Presence of Light: Divine Radiance and Religious Experience* (Chicago, IL, and London, 2004), 161–94, at 172, 176. The article as a whole outlines Akbar connections with the Sufi Chistiyya order and Abu'l-Fazl's creation of a Mughal ideology of illumination.

The elites recruited in these alternative ways rapidly became essential components of the dynastic state, but they rarely flaunted claims to hereditary power as brazenly as did European, Japanese, and some African noble elites. The Ottoman slave elite developed into a semi-hereditary upper layer of the empire, strengthening its rights particularly during contested accessions. In the long term these *osmanlı*, leading servants of the house of Osman, became the main beneficiaries of the regime, at times intervening in the fortunes of the dynasty to consolidate their positions. In the course of the sixteenth century, Qizilbash religious fervour was diluted by the rewards of military and political power. The religious disciples soon adopted patterns familiar for any vested elite, competing for power and mingling in succession disputes. Abbas I reduced the dominance of the Qizilbash in the Safavid venture and harnessed the power of religion.[157] The civil service examinations in imperial China, highly conducive to the consolidation of the imperial state, entrenched in power a magistracy that took seriously the elevated principles of Confucianism without necessarily forgetting lineage inter-ests. Sultans, shahs, and emperors instituted several mechanisms con-trolling and limiting the powers of their leading elites, as will be elaborated in the next chapter.

Recruitment and training of outsiders for high office at court and in the realm was effective at least temporarily in diminishing the intransigence of elites. These more dependent groups could be used as counterweights. The ruling elite of Benin included non-hereditary town chiefs and leaders of palace organisations as well as prestigious hereditary *uzama* chiefs.[158] The *oba* seems to have played a sophisticated game offsetting the uzama chiefs, kingmakers who allegedly preceded the dynasty, by the town chiefs and the palace leaders, whose offices were in his gift:

His main political weapon lay in his ability to manipulate the system of Palace and Town offices. By making appointments to vacant titles, creating new ones, trans-ferring individuals from one order to another, introducing new men of wealth and influence into positions of power, and redistributing administrative competences, the kings tried to maintain a balance between competing groups and individuals ... His interests lay in fostering competition for his favours, both within and between chiefly orders and palace associations.[159]

Hereditary elites in many places were circumscribed in their power by the rise of competing groups, initially relying on the support of the ruler.

---

[157] See Babayan, 'Safavid synthesis'; Matthee, *Persia in Crisis*, 32, underlines the persistence of hereditary power in Persia under Abbas I, 'in practice if not in theory'.

[158] Bradbury, *Benin Studies*, 55; Edo, 'Hierarchy and organization of the Benin kingdom and palace', 92–4.

[159] Bradbury, *Benin Studies*, 62, 70, 71.

Eunuchs occupied a special position for several reasons. They tended to be disconnected from dominant elite networks because of their ambiguous status that also made impossible their reproduction: hence they could be granted special powers with a reduced risk of elite collusion and transmission of power to succeeding generations.[160] As harem guards they were present in the most secluded part of the palace, where they could expect to find the ruler at his ease. Finally, eunuchs served as intermediaries with outer court officials, particularly where the status of the ruler was so exalted – or where inner–outer boundaries were so strict – that he no longer communicated directly with his chief advisors. These conditions make it easy to understand the remarkable power of eunuchs in court history. Japanese imperial and shogunal dynasties as well as the Aztec and Inka practised polygyny without employing eunuchs; the Byzantine empire adhered to monogamous marriage while employing eunuchs.[161] More often in dynastic history, polygyny and eunuchs appear in tandem. The origins of this age-old practice are difficult to pinpoint, hence it is not possible to assign to any particular ruler the idea of using eunuchs as a counterweight against outer court dignitaries. Nevertheless, if any ruler at any point had felt undermined by the ambitions or attitudes of ministers or grandees, he could easily have sought support among these inner court companions.

At the Safavid court, where the shahs in the course of the seventeenth century gradually withdrew into the palace, eunuchs exerted a growing influence. The French traveller Jean-Baptiste Tavernier reported: 'When the King is young, the Prime Minister has a hard game to play, for then the Favourite Eunuchs and the Sultanesses annul and cancel in the night whatever orders he makes in the day time.'[162] Writing several decades later, Kaempfer stressed that communication between leading officers and the shah took place mostly through the intervention of eunuchs. He also pointed out that after the convening of the court council, a protracted meeting enlivened by theatrical performances, an inner court council met with the shah, leading eunuchs, and the queen mother to consider outcomes: 'Occasionally it even happens that decisions taken in the court

---

[160] This brings to mind the marked role of clerics as administrators, and prelates as leading advisors and governors, in Europe: see Hélène Millet and Peter Moraw, 'Clerics in the state,' in Wolfgang Reinhard (ed.), *Power Elites and State Building* (Oxford, 1996), 173–88; Cédric Michon, *La crosse et le sceptre: les prélats d'état sous François Ier et Henri VIII* (Paris, 2008). Michon shows that French prelates were closely connected to noble families at court, whereas English prelates were new men in power, connected by their shared university training rather than by family networks.

[161] On the Byzantine case, see Ringrose, *Perfect Servant*.

[162] Jean-Baptiste Tavernier, *The Six Voyages of John Baptista Tavernier through Turkey into Persia and the East-Indies, Finished in the Year 1670: Together with a New Relation of the Present Grand Seignor's Seraglio, by the Same Author* (London, 1678), 221.

council are withdrawn under the pressure of the eunuchs and the queen-mother ... two black eunuchs ... who served under three shahs ... are commonly consulted on all important matters by the ruler.'[163] Under Shah Süleyman this informal inner court privy council became the dominant power, leaving the outer court officials in grave uncertainty.[164] Several European travellers tell another revealing story, confirmed in Persian sources, about the succession after the death of Shah Abbas II in 1666. Not only did eunuchs convey the information about the shah's death and start the process of electing a new shah: they also reversed the proposal reached by the assembled notables. After the convened dignitaries had decided in favour of a young boy, discarding Safi, the twenty-year-old first son of the deceased shah, the eunuch-tutor of the younger prince voiced a powerful complaint against the assembly. Acting against his own immediate personal interests, he supported the candidature of the elder son Safi (who would later rule as Süleyman I). The assembled dignitaries, the tutor argued credibly, were intent on securing their own advantage by preferring a pliable minor over a grown prince: 'The true motive for your decision, as you know as well as I do, is the desire to govern Persia according to your wishes for a long time; therefore you chose an infant, during whose minority everything will be possible for you, allowing you to wield absolute power.'[165] Particularly in China, outer court leaders, dominating the literary legacies of the dynastic past, traditionally depicted eunuchs as immoral insiders taking advantage of the prince's weakness. In this incidental well-documented Persian case, a eunuch defended a moral position against the pragmatic self-interest of the leading outer court dignitaries. There is no reason to see the example as unique.

The confidence and companionship that must sometimes have existed between eunuchs and the ruler could lead to manipulation, with inner court confidants played against outer court ministers. In the Chinese case, eunuchs have consistently been seen as the emperors' counter-weights against outer court dignitaries.[166] After describing the powerful impact of leading Ming eunuchs on upper-level magistrates, particularly

---

[163] Kaempfer, *Am Hofe des persischen Grosskönigs*, 185, with references to indirect communication at 31, 63; see also Matthee, *Persia in Crisis*, 59–62.

[164] Matthee, *Persia in Crisis*, 62.

[165] Ibid., 56–8; see a short version of the story in Kaempfer, *Am Hofe des persischen Grosskönigs*, 37–8, and a detailed version with speeches and letters in Chardin, *Voyages*, IX, 397–573, with the key speech of the eunuch-tutor at 435–7, quotation at 436.

[166] See Zhu, *Chinese Spatial Strategies*, on the minister–emperor or jun–chen tension and the traditional role of the inner court; see a review of this dimension of the inner–outer discussion in Sabine Dabringhaus, 'The monarch and inner–outer court dualism in late imperial China', in Duindam et al. (eds.), *Royal Courts*, 265–87.

in the Grand Secretariat, Henry Tsai presents the censorate and the eunuchs as the two opposed forces that kept the Ming dynasty afloat:

In the final analysis, however, the Ming autocrat was the sole beneficiary, as these two irreconcilable forces [eunuchs and the censorate] fought to check one another. The survival of the Ming dynasty for over two and a half centuries involves too many factors for one encompassing generalization, but the dynasty's "check and balance" system should nevertheless be considered one of the most important reasons.[167]

Individual eunuchs, Tsai continues, were commonly executed or degraded after several years in power, undergoing 'the predestined eunuch tragedy'.[168] This position, showing some of the overstatement of Wittfogel's typology of 'oriental despotism', presents the emperors as engaged in crude balancing acts. Inevitably, however, many among them were puppets rather than masters of the game: their escaping into the inner court could have very different grounds and consequences. In her careful study of the Qing court, Evelyn Rawski shows how the Qing emperors refined the Ming balancing system, reducing not only eunuch power by adding a layer of Manchu managers to the imperial household department, but also restraining the empress dowager and circumscribing the role of the imperial clan. The Qing as outsiders necessarily charted a middle course between several traditions. The challenge of maintaining minority control over a huge population helped create cohesion among the conquest elite. Finally, the first Qing emperors were remarkable in their diligence and insight. Even their measures, however, cannot all have reflected foresight and planning, nor did they prevent the emergence of several familiar problems of dynastic power by the later eighteenth century.

Sometimes the clash between inner and outer court defined a reign. When in 1574 the Ottoman sultan Murad III assumed power, he accepted as his second-in-command his predecessor's grand vizier Sokollu Mehmed Pasha. Starting his tenure as grand vizier in the last year of Süleyman's reign, Sokollu had outlasted the whole reign of Selim II. During his decade in office before the ascent of Murad, Sokollu had become the leader of the Ottoman enterprise, a position that was to be eroded within five years. Murad brought to court opponents of his venerable grand vizier and dismissed from office loyal supporters of the Sokollu clan. He instituted a pattern of rule through court favourites, strengthening the inner court vis-à-vis outer court office-holders, whose tenure in office now more and more often tended to be short and insecure. With the

---

[167] Tsai, *Eunuchs in the Ming Dynasty*, 228.   [168] Ibid., 229.

expansion of the harem, the chief black eunuch gradually became more important than the chief white eunuch of the palace page school, who had previously dominated (Plate 18).[169] A flexible pattern of alliances emerged in which the power of the grand vizier was balanced by numerous other players: leading eunuchs, the sultan's mother and favourites, the imperial tutor, the *agha* of the janissaries and the leader of the mounted *sipahi*, the chief jurisconsult in the *divan*, and others such as the grand admiral and foremost provincial governors.[170]

In this phase of shifting power balances, with the new sultan seeking support among his inner court staff and using nominations to counterbalance the commanding presence of Sokollu, others were involved actively. Emine Fetvaci recently demonstrated how several high-ranking figures from the inner as well as the outer court redefined the Ottoman sultan and the identity of the court as a whole through their patronage of illustrated history books. Telling shifts of focus and representation in lavishly illustrated historical works sponsored by Sokollu himself, by the chief black eunuch Mehmed Agha, by the chief white eunuch Ganzafer Agha, and by several high-ranking figures from the outer court military show how these leading figures all sought to frame history for a wider audience of Ottoman dignitaries at court. Patronage of books was part of a political discourse: Mehmed Agha used it to promote his outer court ally Ferhad Pasha and to cast some doubt on the accomplishments of his rival, the current grand vizier Sinan Pasha.[171] Although inner and outer courts in their various manifestations loom large in the discussions of political intrigue at court, we can assume that in practice rivals within the inner as well as the outer court at times sought allies in the opposite camp. The rise of the chief black eunuch to power in Murad III's reign provoked the chief white eunuch.[172] Fetvaci's analysis shows how inner and outer court dignitaries could be connected. At the same time, she stresses that the military establishment as a whole was concerned about the rise of the inner court. During the 1603 revolt of the *sipahi*, the two leading court eunuchs were murdered. More often leaders of the janissaries and the sipahis were each other's rivals. It is likely that the same can be said about the white and black eunuchs and about women in the palace – the exceptional clash between sultan-grandmother Kösem Sultan and

[169] Karakoç, 'Palace politics'.

[170] Günhan Börekci and Şefik Peksevgen, 'Court and favorites', 151–4, Şefik Peksevgen, 'Murad III', 401–3, and Şefik Peksevgen 'Sokollu family', 534–6, all in Ágoston and Masters (eds.), *Encyclopedia of the Ottoman Empire*. On patronage at court in this period, see Fetvaci, *Picturing History*.

[171] Fetvaci, *Picturing History*, 185–8.   [172] Karakoç, 'Palace politics', 40–6.

sultan-mother Turhan Sultan has been mentioned earlier.[173] Inner court agents would look to outer court agents to best their proximate rivals, rather than always seeking alliances within their own sphere. Factions or ad hoc alliances of groups at court therefore usually crossed the apparently impenetrable inner–outer boundaries. Only in cases where collective interests were at stake did rivals in each of these domains close ranks.

Murad's moves against Sokollu, and the *oba* of Benin's balancing act against the hereditary chiefs, relied on the same instrument: control of nominations. Most practical guides to governing written by rulers expand on the subject of nominations, underlining first and foremost that the ruler should carefully guard this right. Han Feizi presents the emperor as a tiger, punishments and rewards as his claws and teeth; leaving these to his ministers, he will be controlled by them.[174] The distribution of favours makes it easy to acquire a following: 'Take warning when there are many men gathered at the gates of the high ministers!' Han Feizi added ominously.[175] Personally supervising patronage allowed rulers to retain control over intermediary elites, who needed access to the royal bounty to satisfy their own dependents.[176] Nominations were a key instrument for any ruler, but they demanded hard work. Qing rulers, in their painstaking commitment to government, carefully checked the files of nominees, taking personal notes to prepare interviews and evaluations.[177] Louis XIV underlined the importance of the distribution of honours and offices time and time again in his memoirs.[178] All rulers of some calibre knew that they risked disaster when they allowed nominations to slip from their hands. Leaving control to a single favourite generally meant that a sizeable group of candidates would be bypassed and aggravated. Louis XIV's decision to rule without the intervention of a minister-favourite, usually understood as a sign of the king's desire to be the absolute master, was also an attempt to create more stability in office-holding and a better-

---

[173] Prutky, *Travels in Ethiopia*, 174 and note 9, mentions the rivalry between Mentewwab and her son Iyasu's wife, with Mentewwab banishing her along with her two sons to the king's mountain at Wahni; see the more detailed later descriptions of Mentewwab's actions in James Bruce, *Travels to Discover the Source of the Nile, in the Years 1768, 1769, 1770, 1771, 1772, and 1773*, vol. II (London, 1790), 608–706, at 658–9 on the rivalry between mother and spouse.

[174] Han Fei Tzu, *Basic Writings*, 30–4.   [175] Ibid., 39.

[176] A vast literature is available on patronage, in its original sense of control over nominations, in art historical literature on princes commissioning works of art, and in anthropological studies on patron–client relationships; see a compact discussion in Duindam, 'Royal courts'. More on rewards, rankings, and intermediary elites follows in Chapter 4.

[177] Guy, *Qing Governors*, 121–2; Madeleine Zelin, 'Yung-Cheng reign', 195; Pierre-Étienne Will, 'Views of the realm in crisis: testimonies on imperial audiences in the nineteenth century', *Late Imperial China*, 29/1 (2008), 125–59.

[178] Louis XIV, *Mémoires*, ed. Dreyss, II, 20–1, 42–3, 238–9, 341–2.

balanced distribution of offices. The changeover of the two preceding favourite ministers, Richelieu and Mazarin, entailed a sharp swing in nominations which fuelled discontent in the later 1640s.

Discussing Ming decline, the Kangxi emperor argued that eunuchs had been blamed falsely. Clearly, he argued, 'there were indeed evil eunuchs', yet it would be 'completely incorrect to say it was the eunuchs' power that caused the dynasty's fall. It was, rather, a problem of factionalism, in which the Ming officials were fighting for power at court, competing with each other, and ignoring the needs of the country.'[179] Kangxi did not expand on the nature of 'factionalism'; otherwise he could hardly have ignored the widespread opposition to the court eunuch Wei Zhongxian who dominated the Tianqi emperor (1605–1620–1627). Serving the future emperor's mother and befriending his wet-nurse, Wei had acquired the boy's full confidence even before he became emperor. Wei's rise to power during his pupil's reign triggered a collective response organised by the literati 'Donglin faction'. Other equally staunch Confucians were more hesitant, arguing that not even Wei Zhongxian's crude abuse of power justified the formation of political associations that threatened to undermine harmony, unity, and subservience to the emperor.[180] During the final decades of the eighteenth century, when the Qianlong emperor heaped favours on his notoriously corrupt former Manchu imperial guard Heshen, concerted literati criticism can again be found. Qianlong's successor the Jiaqing emperor purged Heshen but again relied on the agency of a favourite grand councillor: Nayancheng. Only after Nayancheng's failure did he opt for a different style of rule, employing several leading advisors.[181]

In China as elsewhere, the emergence of favourites monopolising the ruler's distribution of honours created discomfort and conflict. Did factions operate at the Chinese court outside of incidental clashes over favourites? Political trafficking and alliances were invariably seen in a negative light. Only the most urgent moral grounds legitimised the collective action of magistrates vis-à-vis the emperor. Ming officials staged five dramatic mass demonstrations between 1449 and 1524, but

---

[179] Spence, *Emperor of China*, 87, also relates several conversations with his eunuchs that gave a different picture, hence showing indirectly his relationship to eunuchs. Kangxi (45–6) does underline that he never involved eunuchs in government; on Yongzheng's and Qianlong's similar critical attitudes to faction, see Benjamin A. Elman, 'Imperial politics and Confucian societies in late imperial China: the Hanlin and Donglin academies', *Modern China*, 15/4 (1989), 379–418, at 395, 402–3.

[180] Elman, 'Imperial politics', 395.

[181] On Heshen and the question of the 'favourite' under the Jiaqing emperor, see Yingcong Dai, 'Broken passage to the summit: Nayancheng's botched mission in the White Lotus War', in Duindam and Dabringhaus (eds.), *Dynastic Centre*, 49–73, at 53–4.

no self-respecting magistrate would openly confess to belonging to any grouping aiming for mundane political goals.[182] Ideally only 'petty men' were interested in the machinery of power and promotions; serious scholars refrained from partisanship: 'Confucius had said, "I have heard that the gentleman does not show partiality." Siding with a faction went against the public interests represented ideally by the ruler.'[183] The high moral profile of the Chinese magistrates and their dominance in the creation of history make it difficult to find out more about the political transactions in their ranks. Patronage, recommendation, and rival networks of friends undoubtedly played a role among Chinese magistrates, but they appear to have left few traces in the records.[184] In the equally Confucian context of Chosŏn Korea, dynastic factionalism was omnipresent. Recruitment through examinations here went together with the persistence of a relatively small hereditary class of office-holders. Moreover, the inner court agency of eunuchs was less important. No lasting inner court power bloc emerged around the king's women and servants. It was almost impossible for officials to establish furtive personal connections to the king: strict rules forbade the king's secret consultations with individual officials. Conflict at court was characterised by a sharp rift between two groupings in the bureaucracy, starting as a conflict between 'easterners' and 'westerners' (terms relating to the location of their residences). These factions clashed over nominations, the principles of dynastic succession, the interpretation of Confucianism, and the political responses of Korea to its powerful neighbours. In the seventeenth and eighteenth centuries, further subdivisions arose and the factions obtained a hereditary character – atypical in a comparative perspective. Conflict between the factions was sometimes accepted and used by kings, whereas others desperately tried to prevent it. Yŏngjo (1694–1724–1776) followed a policy of 'grand harmony achieved through a rule of impartiality', conforming to the ideal of order created through dynastic example. His lofty intentions did not reduce the conflict.[185]

---

[182] Elman, 'Imperial politics'. On the mass demonstrations, see John W. Dardess, 'Protesting to the death: the *Fuque* in Ming political history', *Ming Studies*, 47 (2003), 86–125; Li Jia, 'Conflicts between monarch and ministers: a political and cultural interpretation of the Ming-Dynasty officials' collective "petitions to the palace"', *Chinese Studies in History*, 44/3 (2011), 72–89.

[183] Elman, 'Imperial politics', 395.

[184] R. Kent Guy, 'Routine promotions: Li Hu and the dusty byways of empire', in Duindam and Dabringhaus (eds.), *Dynastic Centre*, 74–93, with remarks on patrons and recommendations at 82–5.

[185] James B. Palais, 'Confucianism and the aristocratic/bureaucratic balance in Korea', *Harvard Journal of Asiatic Studies*, 44/2 (1984), 427–68; Haboush, *Confucian Kingship in Korea*, 16–20, 31, 117–22; Keith Pratt, and Richard Rutt, *Korea: A Historical and Cultural Dictionary* (Richmond, 1999), 'Factions', 115–19.

The Korean example, occurring in a profoundly different setting, cannot be taken as an indication of the presence of faction in China. Still, it is difficult to accept at face value the principled attitudes of Chinese magistrates. In Europe as in China few courtiers would admit to 'membership' in a faction; the term was almost always used pejoratively, accusing others of belonging to a faction. Here, too, policy-making was seen not as a playground for all but as the prerogative of the ruler and his advisors. Decisions with potentially major repercussions, for instance on war and peace, or matters of great ideological importance were as a rule limited to a small circle of influential key figures. It seems likely that in most polities a highly variable mix of figures active in the administrative agencies and in the proximity of the ruler belonged to this circle. The ideal was secrecy and restriction of influence, and in practice the number of people actively involved remained limited. In the case of nominations, where the interests of numerous groups were involved directly while the importance of individual cases, apart from a few key nominations, was relatively minor, the number of players was much larger. There was a keen awareness among social elites that power and wealth were redistributed at court. Lobbyists have besieged political centres in past and present. In order to advance the interests of their patrons, they needed a foothold at court – anybody in the ruler's proximity or in government. In Europe, all groups at court, whether domestics, nobles, or advisors, could expect to be approached by outsiders. Office-holders in any capacity who spent part of their time in the proximity of the ruler could hope to intercede for friends and relatives, unobtrusively dropping their names as candidates for employment or rewards. Chamber ordinances typically forbade servants to pass on supplications, an indication that this must have been common practice. The archives of great noblemen holding court office or ministers in power contain numerous supplications. Networks of friends and followers, based on regional family connections, on military command, on high office at court or in central government, were a key element in nominations. Such behaviour was the practice not only of 'petty men': the ministry of Jean-Baptiste Colbert has been labelled a 'family business'. The talented minister of finance and organiser of the French navy used his extended ministerial portfolio to place his relatives and clients in lucrative and powerful positions. He constructed his own dynasty while loyally serving the interests of his master.[186] The same held true for other leading ministerial dynasties. The most lasting contest at the French court under Louis XIV was that between the rival

---

[186] Jean-Louis Journet and Daniel Dessert, 'Le lobby Colbert: un royaume ou une affaire de famille?', *Annales: économies, sociétés, civilisations*, 30/6 (1975), 1303–36.

ministerial clans of Colbert and Louvois, both promoting their clients to positions in their purview.

The 'micropolitics' of the redistribution of wealth and honour was probably more important on a daily basis than the major political choices – although the latter could have more radical outcomes. Only a detailed examination of individual instances of inner–outer competition and decision-making can substantiate these thoughts. This is a notoriously difficult task: usually archives contain the decisions reached, sometimes with a good overview of the various options considered at the council table. Only with a rare accumulation of different types of sources – memoirs, diplomats' reports, correspondences of participants – can we find out more about the influences and groupings behind the decisions.

The king was the prime focus of court competition: numerous competitors strove to approach him, attract his attention, and solicit his favours. Kaempfer's description of the Safavid court under Süleyman I underlines this, while making painfully clear that the figure at the heart of this competition was sometimes reduced to impotence. Escaping from the pressures of formal representation and decision-making in the outer court into the confines of the inner court, the king was awaited by another set of servants pushing him to satisfy their demands. Court dignitaries, Kaempfer stated, were preoccupied mostly with their own limited perspectives and interests.[187] As soon as they managed to secure the shah's favour, they all had the same purpose: 'Their first priority now is to keep away from the Shah all knowledge of public matters, to freeze him in a distracted state, allowing them to pursue their own interests unobstructed. All courtiers, even the most inveterate enemies, follow the same plan.'[188] During extended council meetings Süleyman I was served refreshments and entertained by live performances. The grand vizier expertly manipulated the agenda, alternating entertainment with complicated and boring dossiers, at critical junctures inserting apparently easy matters on which he wanted a rapid decision. If necessary the shah's state was further eased by opium or other sedatives. In the end, Kaempfer concludes, the distribution of graces was in the hands of avaricious grandees, limited only by the jealousy of their peers and the fear that the latter could speak ill of them in front of the shah. Considering whether this was typically Persian or a more general phenomenon, Kaempfer added cautiously that at European courts similar situations could be found.[189]

---

[187] Kaempfer, *Am Hofe des persischen Grosskönigs*, 30.   [188] Ibid.

[189] Ibid., 30–3, mentioning opium explicitly at 28 and 82, and the accumulation of offices among friends and relatives of the grand vizier at 65–6.

In contrast to Kaempfer's example, relevant wherever a ruler incapacitated by youth, old age, or any other weakness found himself in the midst of ambitious advisors and servants, we can point to the moments when powerful figures on the throne confronted their opponents head-on, or where subtle characters were able to subdue them through careful manipulation. Louis XIV underlined hard work, a careful choice of advisors, and the absolute requirement never to rely on a single advisor or confidant. Kangxi, outdoing Louis in discipline and intelligence, in addition counselled moderation in sex and the consumption of alcohol. Numerous rulers who expressed their views on government emphasised the need to hold on to the prerogative of nomination. Following these sensible admonishments, dynastic scions of average intellect and character could with some luck manage the challenges of rulership at least for a time. We cannot, however, assume that the hierarchical pre-eminence of the ruler and his nominal control over the distributions of graces automatically turned him into the arbiter in the arena of court competition.

It is evident that several rulers and their advisors consciously countered the power of groups at court by elevating others. The process tended to be repeated *ad libitum* because newly created elites in turn became less dependent and pliable. In shorter-term oscillations at court, nominations were an all-important instrument not only to secure good government, but also to prevent damaging concentrations of power in the hands of any single subject. In these respects *divide et impera* was a commonplace of dynastic power, creating long-term ways of dealing with overmighty groups as well as of bypassing overbearing candidates for promotions. Not all individual kings could make this solution work. Under weaker rulers the promotion of inner court favourites took shape as a consequence of the ruler's blind dependence and anxiety rather than as a carefully premeditated stratagem, and it could have disastrous consequences for royal power and overall stability. The distribution of offices, moreover, was typically the result of numerous reports and recommendations, providing infinite opportunities for manipulation of the paperwork by the agents responsible for it – ending only with the hushed suggestions of the ruler's personal entourage.

Finally, no servant or office-holder at court would forget that dismissal, confiscation, and execution were distinct possibilities and legitimate sanctions against any form of disobedience. Why would kings use subtle ruses when coercion offered an accepted and rapid alternative? At the Ottoman court and under some of the more pugnacious Chinese emperors, retribution was swift and could involve numerous office-holders. Examples are sparser in European history, but here, too, leading statesmen and soldiers could be prosecuted and executed when they were perceived as failing in the tasks assigned to them. In 1619, during the first decades of the Dutch Republic, a commonwealth of provinces with a semi-dynastic, non-hereditary prince-stadholder, the leading statesman Johan van Oldenbarnevelt was executed following a conflict with the prince. After lengthy moral reflections, Emperor Ferdinand II in 1634 decided to have his overmighty general Wallenstein executed. Thomas Wentworth, earl of Strafford, was executed in 1641, followed in 1645 by Archbishop Laud. The incidental cases of Charles I in 1649 and Louis XVI in 1793 show that even kings were not inviolable. Rebellion and treason, here as elsewhere, were liable to be punished by death, and these major offences would be defined by those in power. Violence, moreover, was not always legally sanctioned: other kings and high statesmen were murdered, while doubts remained about the motives and sponsors of the assassins. In 1672 another key leader of the Dutch Republic, Grand Pensionary Johan de Witt, was violently murdered by a mob. In 1579 Sokollu, at seventy-three and during his fifteenth year in office, was stabbed, creating the occasion for endless speculations.

Court, government, realm

Several of the dynasties discussed in this chapter evolved from a highly mobile to a more sedentary pattern – without ever entirely giving up movement. More generally a pattern can be seen where specialised agencies of government not only moved out of the domestic environment of the prince but also expanded and differentiated. In the process, the distance between domestic and administrative domains of rulership tended to widen, and the connection between the two underwent frequent redefinition. In none of the dynastic polities discussed here, however, was power ever entirely dissociated from the personal environment of the ruler. All dynastic polities to some extent remained 'palace polities', although the level of power wielded personally by the ruler could vary immensely.

The relative importance attached to dynastic courts can be inferred to some extent from numbers. The household serving Louis XIV's brother, approximately half the size of the king's own household, was bigger than the combined staffs of the six ministries running the French state at the central level.[190] The inner and outer services of the Ottoman court outnumbered by far the leading offices of the *divan* and the scribes supporting them. For most European countries and for the Ottomans it is difficult

---

[190] Jeroen Duindam, 'Vienna and Versailles: materials for further comparison and some conclusions', *Zeitenblicke*, 4/3 (2005), www.zeitenblicke.de/2005/3/Duindam.

to draw a sharp line between the agents of central power in the provinces and their local auxiliaries operating outside the bounds of strict state service. Universally, the army was the biggest and most expensive state-run operation. In late Ming times, the budget spent on the imperial clan came perilously close. Ming princes by the end of the dynasty far outnumbered the entire Chinese magistracy in the capital and in the provinces. In Qing times, with a reduced court and a strengthened administrative structure, the proportions of the court, the magistracy, and the population at large still give pause for thought. Around 1800 a thinly spread magistracy of *c.* 35,000 governed a population of 300 million, organised around a conspicuous centre that in the most conservative assessment formed one third of the magistracy as a whole.[191]

Discussion of state formation on a global scale has tended to concentrate on the efficiency of 'resource extraction', reaching new heights in early modern Europe. The military competition among Europe's major states, wholly entangled with expansion and empire-building on a global scale, exerted immense pressures. Most European monarchies first experienced a phase of expanding direct taxation and a strengthening of government agencies, followed by a phase of 'fiscalism' where governments tried desperately to raise funds by selling future tax income to private contractors, by selling offices, or by privatising state ventures. In the course of the seventeenth and eighteenth centuries, focus shifted from taxation to public debt and other credit instruments relying on the wealth of private buyers. The credit of a state as represented in the interest rates it needed to pay became an indicator of political strength – as the French monarchy would notice when attempts at a fundamental overhaul of the fiscal-political set-up failed miserably in the 1780s. The Western European logic of competition, military expansion, and the gradually increasing reliance on private wealth to finance the state without recourse to open coercion has provided the standard scenario of political modernisation. It leads to a state with greater income and greater

---

[191] On numbers of magistrates, see Benjamin A. Elman, 'The social roles of literati in early to mid-Ch'ing', in Peterson (ed.), *Cambridge History of China*, vol. IX, 360–427, at 384, citing 20,400 positions for licentiates in 1500, expanding to 24,680 in 1625; G.W. Skinner, 'Introduction: urban development in imperial China', in G.W. Skinner (ed.), *The City in Late Imperial China* (Stanford, 1977), 21, underlined the gradual decrease of magistrates as a proportion of the population since Han times; Guy, *Qing Governors*, stresses the strengthening of the structures of administration under the Qing (35, 43) but also points to the Qing emperors' effort to weed out redundant positions (52, 56). To the officials recruited through the civil service examinations and integrated in the nine-rank system (see Chapter 4) lesser servants ('clerks and runners') can be added, according to one estimate, four times the regular officials, i.e. *c.* 100,000 in mid-Ming: see Charles O. Hucker, 'Governmental organization of the Ming dynasty', *Harvard Journal of Asiatic Studies*, 21 (1958), 1–66, at 18.

responsibilities, connected through a variety of links to the populations at large. Modern states have become far more influential in the lives of their inhabitants, but they grant them a higher level of involvement in setting priorities.

These fundamentally changing notions of legitimacy have determined our views of history. The modern view of dynastic power has rightly underlined the haphazard and sometimes appalling violence surfacing in premodern history. It has on the whole failed to accept the other side of the logic of state formation, the remarkable fact that whole societies were organised around a dynastic centre supported by an exceedingly thin administrative machinery. While military force could be used for conquest and violent repression of rebellions, it was of limited use in regular government and the maintenance of order. The question to ask here is not why Europe broke through the ceiling of resource extraction used primarily for the organisation of military power, but how the conspicuous dynastic centre, alien to modern sensibilities, could invoke the acquiescence or loyalty of large populations. How did the court fit into the larger whole? How did it cultivate its connections to the realm?

4 Realm: connections and interactions

By his grace they drank and ate. He gave them contentment and he gave them gifts; he bestowed upon them whatsoever they needed.

Sahagún, Florentine Codex: General History of the Things of New Spain, Book 8, 'Kings and Lords', 54.

When the *sur* was concluded on the fifteenth day
The masses were summoned to join in the fray
No matter how countless the inhabitants o' the land
Among merchants, the poor and the empty of hand
They hastened one and all to the place of the feasting
To add their high hopes for their sovereign's prospering
So bounteous the food on that day of contentment
That sufficient remained for both fishes and fishermen
When all had completed their measure of duty
The doors of bestowal were opened completely
None remained untouched by the sovereign's bounty
And not the least person's pocket stayed empty of booty
The whole world rejoiced together in the sultan's beneficence
And all, great and small, took their share in his boundless munificence

Ottoman poet Yusuf Nabi (1642–1712) on the 1675 circumcision festival, in Murphey, Ottoman Sovereignty, 203.

Heaven is high and the Emperor far away.
Chinese proverb, in Ebrey (ed.), *Chinese Civilization*, 281.

Virtue, honour, fear

How did the court fit into the larger whole of the kingdom or empire? What made people willing to comply? In *The Spirit of the Laws*, Montesquieu replaced Aristotle's classic typology of governments ruled by 'one, several, and many' with another tripartite scheme: republic, monarchy, and despotism. He assumed that republics, including democracies and aristocracies, were driven by virtue and concern for the common good, whereas monarchies thrived on the principle of honour. Despotic power, finally, was based on fear more than on anything else, with subjects fearing harsh punishments and despots awaiting violent rebellion. Republics gradually moved from democracy to aristocracy and finally to monarchy when their virtue was eroded; monarchies risked tilting towards despotism once their rulers no longer respected either the laws or the honour of their elites.

Aristotle had presented good and degenerate variants for each of the three governments: monarchy/tyranny, aristocracy/oligarchy, polity/democracy.[1] Montesquieu's three forms, however, represent a single line of declining moral fibre. He appears to have viewed the democratic republic as a historic ideal rather than as a practicable form of government, an attitude strengthened by his travel in Italy and in the Dutch Republic. Negative experiences convinced Montesquieu that the patricians governing the Dutch Republic had no real virtue and hence needed the semi-monarchical stadholder to establish an equilibrium between virtue and honour, republic and monarchy. Throughout Montesquieu's work, the intermediate categories of aristocracy and monarchy appear as the most sensible and pragmatic polities, sensible compromises between human rectitude and frailty. France in the days of Louis XIV, he argued tacitly, had been moving away from the principle of honour, at times skirting the boundary between monarchy and despotism. Despotism, to be found primarily in the Orient, was the unmitigated rule of whim and fear, reflecting the utter degeneration of monarchy. Montesquieu had no patience with his Jesuit fellow countrymen presenting Chinese government as a balanced mixture of his three principles. China with its polygyny, harsh punishments, and luxury, Montesquieu stressed, was the classic instance of despotism. The Chinese people, he claimed, 'act only through fear of being bastinadoed', a statement bringing to mind his equally bold pronouncement that 'you must flay a Muscovite alive to make him feel'. Voltaire, always ready to criticise his rival, adopted a far more positive view of China, and questioned the stark contrast between European and Asian forms of monarchical power – a question raised again in current research.[2]

---

[1] On dynasty in Aristotle's typology and its connotations of oligarchy and tyranny, see Bearzot, 'Dynasteia'.

[2] Charles de Secondat, baron de Montesquieu, *The Spirit of the Laws*, trans. Thomas Nugent (London, 1752), quotations at 143 (Book VIII, chap. 21) and 248 (Book XIV, chap. 2); Voltaire, 'Commentaire sur l'esprit des lois', in *Oeuvres complètes de Voltaire: avec des notes et une notice historique sur la vie de Voltaire*, vol. V (Paris, 1835), 444–75, at 456; see also Myrtille Méricam-Bourdet, 'Voltaire contre Montesquieu?', *Revue Française d'Histoire des Idées Politiques*, 35/1 (2012), 25–36. For debates on governance in China and Russia, see on Russia e.g. Charles J. Halperin, 'Muscovy as a hypertrophic state: a critique', *Kritika*, 3/3 (2002), 501–7, with contributions by Marshall Poe and Valerie Kivelson to the same issue; and in the same line, the moderate and positive appraisal in Nancy Shields Kollmann, *Crime and Punishment in Early Modern Russia*

Montesquieu's three principles turn into a caricature when each is seen as distinctive for only one particular form of government. However, the combination of ideals, interests, and force – mixed in different proportions – is a necessary foundation for all governments.[3] In the last resort the sanction of violence stands behind any ordered polity. Laws, as Montesquieu well knew, operate only when infractions can be punished. Nevertheless, regimes cannot endure through the permanent threat of violence alone: to last longer, they need to pacify, gratify, and integrate elites. Montesquieu's view of 'honour' hinted not only at the ethos of the noble upper layers, but also at the material advantages enjoyed by the elites: titles, offices, exemptions. Governments attract and reward elites; alternatively, as we have seen, they create new elites, dependents who initially accept the preservation of the dynasty as their own best interest. In turn these elites rely on local associates to ensure their intermediary position. Finally, all forms of government cultivate a mixture of religion, time-honoured tradition, ideals of equity and representation, with views of their racial-ethnic or ideological superiority, sharing these ideals with a portion of their subjects or citizens. While such views do not universally dictate policies, they set priorities and define limitations – implicitly or explicitly, government actions can be measured against these fluid and often contradictory standards.

Premodern capacities for organised violence were less impressive than those of the modern state, but they could be wielded with fickleness and ferocity, at times wholly unrestrained by compassion or justice. The threat of violent retribution was always present, but it did not suffice to create stability and social cohesion. This chapter focuses on the interests and ideals connecting rulers, elites, and the populace. How could the dynastic centre, an extended household consuming an inordinate proportion of resources, function as the pivot of outstretched and relatively loosely governed polities? Which groups were connected to this conspicuous centre and what attitudes, institutions, and occasions shaped their interactions? How, if at all, did common people relate to the dynasties

(Cambridge, 2012), on Russian legal practices, showing how attendance at a public execution in 1697 in Amsterdam played a role in Peter's introduction of more violent and public forms of retribution (408–10). While appraisals of Qing governance, after the massacres of the Ming-Qing changeover, tend to be relatively positive, James L. Watson, 'Waking the dragon: visions of the Chinese imperial state in local myth', in Stefan Feuchtwang and Hugh Baker (eds.), *An Old State in New Settings: Studies in the Social Anthropology of China in Memory of Maurice Freedman* (Oxford, 1991), 162–77, shows that villagers in the southeast had a negative view of the Chinese emperor – and the modern state – as bringing terror and massacre rather than support.

[3] Tilly, *Trust and Rule*, tables at 31, 105, presents a formula of governments based on coercion, capital, and commitment in differing proportions that can be read as a variant of this scheme.

holding power in the centre? What was the relevance of the court and its activities for the coherence of the polity? The key question of political power was phrased gracefully by David Cannadine: 'how are people persuaded to acquiesce in a polity where the distribution of power is manifestly unequal and unjust, as it invariably is'?[4] Select groups served in the dynastic household; others spent a formative phase of their lives there, adopting some of its forms and norms. Elites without such direct experiences were tied to the centre through hierarchies of titles and offices defined there. Higher echelons of agents serving the dynasty were expected to intermittently visit the court for evaluation and relocation. Others looked to the court for justice or material betterment. Subjects of diverse ranks could participate in or watch the great events connected to dynastic power, particularly if they lived close to the capital. These rituals of royalty could take very different shapes, but they always relate to the traditions and ideals of rulership outlined in the first chapter. The groups most distant in social and spatial terms probably saw dynasty only reflected in the presence of local agents of central power, in religious-ritual observances, on coins, or in folk stories.[5]

Hospitality and service

Households catering for royals and their retinues gave numerous others a chance to share in the spoils. 'Big men' throughout the world underlined their status by conspicuously redistributing the foods and riches they had accumulated. 'Even the greatest Polynesian chiefs were conceived superior kinsmen to the masses, fathers of their people, and generosity was morally incumbent upon them.'[6] The African king of Mamprusi was obliged to allow beggars, children, lepers, and blind or insane persons access to his court. For others, kindness to these groups was considered

---

[4] David Cannadine, 'Introduction', in Cannadine and Price (eds.), *Rituals of Royalty*, 1–19, at 19.

[5] Neither Chinese nor Japanese coins carried representations of rulers; Chinese coins were bundled in strings through a hole in the coin; on Chinese coins and monetary policies, see Richard Von Glahn, *Fountain of Fortune: Money and Monetary Policy in China, 1000–1700* (Berkeley, CA, 1996). Coins in most Islamicate countries carry inscriptions referring to the ruler rather than images, but the Mughals did produce remarkable coins with rulers' images.

[6] Sahlins, 'Poor man, rich man', 298, followed by the statement that many paramounts seemed inclined to 'eat the power of the government too much'. On hospitality, gift-giving, and 'big men', see e.g. Luc de Heusch, 'Autorité et prestige dans la société tetela', *Zaïre*, 10 (1954), 1001–27; Eugene Cooper, 'The potlatch in ancient China: parallels in the sociopolitical structure of the ancient Chinese and the American Indians of the northwest coast', *History of Religions*, 22/2 (1982), 103–28; Mattison Mines and Vijayalakshmi Gourishankar, 'Leadership and individuality in South Asia: the case of the South Indian big-man', *Journal of Asian Studies*, 49/4 (1990), 761–86.

virtuous; for the king it was a requirement.[7] In the palace of the Bamoum kingdom in the Cameroon grasslands, a sizeable open space was aptly called 'the court where the realm unites and eats'. Lineage elders could enter to enjoy the king's bounty, eating his food and drinking his wine. A dozen or so palace granaries filled with corn and dried meat were kept in reserve to feed the crowds attending court, and to succour the populace in times of famine.[8]

Groups serving African royals reflected a wider society of lineages, crafts, and regions. At court in Bamoum, 'secret societies' representing elite groupings had their own quarters, with paternal princely lineages of regional chiefs situated in the right half of the palace compound, maternal relatives active at the centre in its left half. In Bunyoro, all crafts were represented in the palace, while court offices were vested hereditarily in particular clans: 'In these ways, the huge royal establishment served to integrate the Nyoro people around their center and so to sustain the political system itself.'[9] The three Benin palace associations (*otu*) were closely connected to urban guilds. The *oba* distributed numerous titles related to palace service through the society at large:

Every freeborn man in the Benin kingdom considered himself a member of one of the palace otu. In nearly every village there were a few men who had actually 'entered the palace', that is had been initiated into an association, but the majority had only a nominal affiliation inherited from their fathers. Nominal membership gave no access to the otu's apartments, no voice in its affairs or share in its revenue ... What [it] did was to afford each individual a sense of personal identification with the central institutions of the state; and thus they helped to maintain popular support for a highly exploitative political system.[10]

For villagers and townspeople alike, the palace represented chances for social mobility and success: 'Many young men from all over the kingdom were initiated as ... 'children' or 'servants' of the apartments. The candidate spent an initial period of seven days in the apartments of his *otu* during which he paid fees to its chiefs, swore oaths of loyalty and secrecy, and received instructions in his duties.'[11] Having entered the palace service, a ladder of advancement emerged; while service demanded a serious investment in fees and training, it opened the possibility of lucrative and prestigious office. The palace connection, once it existed, was rarely given up in favour of alternative career paths.

---

[7] Drucker-Brown, *Ritual Aspects of the Mamprusi Kingship*, 162–3.

[8] Tardits, *Le royaume Bamoum*, 580, 601, 592.   [9] Beattie, *Bunyoro*, 32.

[10] Bradbury, *Benin Studies*, 44–75, quotation at 62–3, on the palace association (56), on the relevance of titles (60–7), as part of a balancing act (71); on the guilds, see also Inneh, 'Guilds working for the palace'.

[11] Ibid., 62–7, quotation at 63; Tardits, *Le royaume Bamoum*, 73–602.

The numerous royal women discussed in Chapter 2 turned the court into the pivot of wife-taking and wife-giving. Women at court in Dahomey could obtain positions of great influence and authority: the move to the court was not necessarily a loss for the woman or for her family. The 'male' Lovedu rain-queen in Sotho accumulated countless women, distributing them to create a continuing pattern of wife-exchange holding together society. In the early 1930s, trying to reconstruct the Asante kingdom after deep crisis, Agyeman Prempeh II reintroduced the harem and wife-exchange as indispensable for the integration of elites.[12]

Courts in bigger polities cannot have been connected as directly to their populations, yet the same notions can be found. In his advice for kings, the Seljuq vizier Nizam al-Mulk stressed that 'Kings have always paid attention to having well-supplied tables in the mornings, so that those who come to the royal presence may find something to eat there.' In response to reports about a ruler's lack of hospitality, he reiterated that 'it is necessary that his [the king's] housekeeping, his magnanimity and generosity, his table and largesse should accord with his state and be greater and better than that of other kings'.[13] The public was not supposed to share the emperor's food in the Forbidden City, but the imperial responsibility for the sustenance of the people was taken seriously. In Qing China well-stocked granaries were used to control prices; the needy were fed by soup kitchens in times of crisis. While these facilities were largely urban, tax remits were used to alleviate the predicament of provinces hit by crop failures, diseases, or natural disasters.[14] In Europe, urban governments tried to secure grain supplies to prevent scarcity, escalating prices, and bread riots, but they could not as a rule cope with major crop failures.[15] Courts did even less for hungry urban crowds, but most provided token support for the needy in less extreme situations. The practice of eating in several hierarchically ordered tables or shifts commonly ended with the leftovers being served to outsiders or left to beggars in the main hall or in an adjacent public square. In the course of several

---

[12] Prempeh I, *History of Ashanti Kings*, 51–2; see a less optimistic view of the palace women in McCaskie, *State and Society in Pre-Colonial Asante*, 216–17.

[13] Nizam al-Mulk, *Book of Government*, 126–7.

[14] Pierre-Étienne Will and R. Bin Wong, *Nourish the People: The State Civilian Granary System in China, 1650–1850* (Ann Arbor, MI, 1991); see early examples mentioned in Victoria Tin-bor Hui, *War and State Formation in Ancient China and Early Modern Europe* (Cambridge, 2005), 83; Lillian M. Li and Alison Dray-Novey, 'Guarding Beijing's food security in the Qing dynasty: state, market, and police', *Journal of Asian Studies*, 58/4 (1999), 992–1032.

[15] On provisioning, government, order, and popular rebellion in Paris, see Steven L. Kaplan, *Provisioning Paris: Merchants and Millers in the Grain and Flour Trade during the Eighteenth Century* (Ithaca, NY, 1984).

centuries, most courts exchanged board for wages, reducing the number of tables at court.[16] Support for the needy continued in different ways, as the various categories of alimony and pensions in court budgets show.[17]

Connections to social corpora were present at court in a variety of forms. Certain prestigious honorific court offices were held by grandee families, who rarely performed actual service but cherished the status conferred by the office.[18] Different sets of such hereditary offices existed particularly for regions recently acquired by the crown. In the Habsburg monarchy, several regionally based 'courts' of high office-holders slumbered in anticipation of princely visits. Sixteenth-century scholars stipulated that high officers at the French court served as patrons for the Parisian crafts (métiers) closest to their tasks – the pantler for baker's shops, the butler for taverns and inns, and so on.[19]

A share of the populations in the urban winter residences in Europe would figure on the payroll of the court. Numerous guardsmen, purveyors, artisans, and labourers combined meagre court wages with a privileged status and the hope of advancement. These court servants, living in lodgings in the city procured by the court's quartering system, were exempt from urban taxes and justice. This special status allowed them to commit minor misdeeds with impunity. Guardsmen opened illicit taverns, underselling and angering local publicans. The effrontery of court pages, noble boys educated in the stables, became proverbial, with several expressions referring to it in contemporary French dictionaries.[20] City authorities were squeezed between locals complaining about disorder or unfair competition and the supreme authority of their sovereign, master of his household as well as ruler of the realm. When in the eighteenth century the legal and fiscal exemptions of the court were gradually eroded, the label of court purveyor obtained new relevance, particularly for luxury shops, suggesting quality and elegance to rich urban customers. Even nowadays a royal clientele can help to attract other buyers.

---

[16] Duindam, *Vienna and Versailles*; on the English reforms in the early 1660s, see Andrew Barclay, 'Charles II's failed restoration: administrative reform below stairs 1660–64', in Eveline Cruickshanks (ed.), *The Stuart Courts* (Stroud, 2012), 158–70.

[17] Duindam, 'Vienna and Versailles'.

[18] Duindam, 'Habsburg court'; more on election and coronation below.

[19] Charles Loyseau, *Les oeuvres de maistre Charles Loyseau* ... (Paris, 1678), 224; Jean Du Tillet, *Les mémoires et recherches de Jean Du Tillet, greffier de la cour de Parlement à Paris, contenans plusieurs choses memorables pour l'intelligence de l'estat des affaires de France* (Paris, 1578), 238–46.

[20] See *Dictionnaires d'autrefois*, http://artfl-project.uchicago.edu/content/dictionnaires-dautrefois, under 'page': 'On appelle, Un tour de Page, Une malice où il y a quelque espieglerie; On dit proverbialement, d'Un homme hardi jusqu'à l'impudence, qu'Il est effronté comme un Page de Cour.'

Like bureaucracies, courts expanded easily, providing a living for many people who henceforth staunchly defended their source of income. Inflation of court numbers did not always occur at the prince's behest. Henry III's leading courtiers attracted their own followers into the French court, granting them office, sustenance, and payment without even consulting the king.[21] Instances of rapid court inflation in Europe occurred in phases of political turmoil rather than at times when rulers were in steady control. Much of the administrative energy of European court 'controllers' (financial managers) was directed against scroungers eating at the king's table and emptying his coffers without good reason. Kings expressed regret at the expansion of their courts, but more often than not accepted it as inevitable. While they sometimes were simply lackadaisical, they were hesitant to reduce numbers because this meant alienating their followers.

Numerous individuals held privileged status as members of the ruler's *familia* without actually staying at court on a regular basis. This custom involved all social layers, but was most developed for nobles. Nobles were associated with the court through their nominal status as servants in the chamber, table, and stable staffs. In addition to these chamberlains, cupbearers, carvers, and equerries, administrative staffs could also include absent titular servants: long lists of councillors only marginally connected to actual deliberation can be found throughout Europe. The service of these supernumerary titled office-holders could be arranged through an elaborate system of job rotation with alternating quarter or semester shifts of service, as was pioneered in Burgundy and France. Alternatively the dignitaries were simply expected to turn up intermittently during ceremonial and festive occasions, without receiving regular pay for their nominal service. More often, candidates for titles implying membership of the court were expected to pay for their honours, a common practice developed in its most extended form in France.

Part-time honorific connections to the court occurred in many forms; in addition to the supernumerary office-holders, two variants were common at all European courts: the training of youngsters and the rewarding of distinguished servants. Adolescent boys and girls spent a few years at court as pages or court ladies to absorb courtly mores and learn skills, an apprenticeship ideally ending with office for the boys, with marriage for the girls. Orders of chivalry, proliferating from the late Middle Ages onwards, formed the upper echelon of this noble extension of the court. The number of royal orders expanded and membership in many orders increased. Most dynasties retained one supreme and exclusive order for

---

[21] Duindam, *Vienna and Versailles*, 145.

royalty and grandees – the Burgundian-Habsburg Order of the Golden Fleece, the French Order of the Holy Spirit, the English Order of the Garter, and so on. In addition dynasties founded several less prestigious orders rewarding outstanding service in war, government, arts, and sciences.

The multiple honorary connections helped to turn the European court into a meeting point for elites from different regions. These diffuse elites attached to the court through titular office or irregular services formed the basis of a wider 'court society'. This society of courtiers occupied an intermediate position between full-time membership of the court and outsider status. They were entitled to serve at court, but combined this right with occupations elsewhere. A 'season' developed around court cities, drawing in those in occasional attendance, while simultaneously attracting other elites as well as servants, artisans, and purveyors catering to their various needs. Purchasing luxury articles, pursuing family matters, arranging marriages, or engaging in legal and business transactions, these visitors reinforced the appeal of the capital. Never as coerced, systemic, and well-ordered as the Tokugawa practice of enforced 'alternate attendance', European elites in many countries nevertheless developed their own, voluntary 'tour of duty' to the dynastic heart of their realms.[22]

'Courtier' is the accepted expression for these part-time honorific servants as well as for the upper layers of office-holders permanently staying at court. However, this term has been used also as a convenient label for anybody at court. In his *Book of the Courtier*, Baldassare Castiglione created an even broader cultural category, using his discussion of the courtier to redefine the ideal of gentlemanly behaviour. Castiglione depicted a fluid elite, ennobled by blood or talent, competing in the multipolar world of Italian courts: princes sought the presence of the best and the brightest, courtiers vied for the rewards of princely grace. Flocking to the court, these courtiers undoubtedly had in mind some of Castiglione's hints about unaffected elegance as the best way to attract the ruler's benevolence. Rulers could offer actual court offices, titular court offices conferring the right of presence at court, or stipends. Alternatively they could commission works of art or scholarship. *The Book of the Courtier* became a literary model for court life and an example for European elites. It explicitly discussed the place of women at court and the ideal of the female courtier: wholly male households increasingly saw their interaction with the women in princesses' establishments as a

---

[22] See Vaporis, *Tour of Duty*, on the social, cultural, and economic impact of alternate attendance.

necessary aspect of civility. In most respects, Castiglione's views were far removed from daily practice at court, where a majority of low-ranking staff catered for the ruler with his kin and followers. These lesser servants daily mixed with an upper layer of nobles, perhaps sometimes in affable companionship, but never as social equals. The gap between stable boys and the master of the horse was at least as wide as that between a managing director and the blue-collar workers in his factory. Labelling both groups as courtiers blurs distinctions vital for contemporaries, who applied the term only to the higher echelons.

More importantly, using 'courtier' for occupants of courts worldwide suggests a deceptive equivalence.[23] The inner–outer divide in Topkapı or in the Forbidden City makes it difficult to find one single term for higher service at court.[24] Furthermore, it is far from clear that court elites could easily move outwards and return to the inner services, a feature characteristic for European courtiers. In the Persianate-Islamicate world we find *musahibs* ('boon companions') joining the ruler in his diversions. Their role seems to be closer to the favourite than to the courtier; they enjoyed a far more personal connection with their prince than most European courtiers could expect to have. It seems unlikely, moreover, that such confidants could easily move between inner and outer spheres.[25] The outer court literati and the inner court eunuchs in the Forbidden City cannot be combined in one category as courtiers without overstretching the term. No generic word for all upper layers serving at court can be found in Chinese, while numerous terms refer to officials serving the emperor. There is a word for imperial favourites which holds strong negative overtones.[26] Chinese eunuchs who were sent out on confidential

---

[23] Llewellyn-Jones, *King and Court in Ancient Persia*, 4, proposes this, rightly stressing the need to look at the whole court rather than only at its upper layers; however, this can be done without using the term courtier for all present at court.

[24] Fetvaci, *Picturing History*, 20–3, 139, 239, 243–4, 258–64, 268, refers to her main elite protagonists in the inner and outer court as courtiers.

[25] Ottoman eunuchs, particularly white eunuchs, apparently were able to move outside of the palace: see Mustafa bin Ahmet Ali, *The Ottoman Gentleman of the Sixteenth Century: Mustafa Ali's Mevaidun-Nefais Fi Kavaidil-Mecalis 'Tables of Delicacies Concerning the Rules of Social Gatherings'*, trans. Douglas S. Brookes (Cambridge, MA, 2003), 20–1: 'Nowadays even the lowest eunuch guard has obtained a house outside the palace'. On Ottoman favourites, e.g. Artan, 'Ahmed I's hunting parties', 107, mentions *nedims* and *musahibs* in the sultan's company; Murphey, *Ottoman Sovereignty*. On the boon companion (*nadim*) in Arabic tradition, see Samer Ali, 'Boon companion', in Fleet et al. (eds.), *Encyclopaedia of Islam, Three* (accessed January 2015).

[26] Hucker, *Dictionary of Official Titles*, uses 'courtier' in the explanation of several of his entries referring to honorary nominations; a longer entry on *chŭng-sàn* (192, no. 1589) suggests this is the translation of a foreign term. Patricia Ebrey (personal communication) sees no direct parallel for courtier in Chinese; Jérôme Kerlouégan suggested a number of related terms, while confirming the absence of a term with the associations common in Europe; his suggestions include *shicong* (suite), *shichen* (officials serving [the emperor]),

missions still had a chance of returning to the emperor's proximity. While they could aspire to integrate into the elite through religious patronage or philanthropy, they would rarely reach social pre-eminence. The *daimyo* lords frequently moving to the shogun's court and the prestigious *kuge* families around the emperor in Kyoto come closer to the European courtier elite, although their numbers were more restricted, matching the uppermost layers of the European court elites.

In the European context the dispersed 'court society' was an essential accessory to the permanent staffs serving the ruler at court.[27] The education and temporary presence at court of elites helped to define and broadcast court rankings and court culture, particularly in the patchwork-polities common in *ancien régime* Europe. The Habsburg court in Vienna served as focal point for a variety of domains, each cherishing its own traditions. Local nobles, connected to the centre through their court office and recurring stays in the capital, flaunted their court titles and fashions in their region of provenance. The combination of access at court, a court rank, and a style polished by court attendance trumped local rivals lacking these advantages. This situation benefited the court as well as its inadvertent spokesmen. European chivalric culture was imbued not only with honour and personal fidelity; it could resemble a religious brotherhood and create a strong religious bond. Vows to fight the infidel together were made during banquets and festivities; religious celebrations formed an important part of the regular meetings of orders of chivalry. In the Islamicate context, the role of princes as spiritual leaders ideally created a group of proximates who could be distant from the court, but close to the ruler.[28] Other instruments were necessary to secure the loyalty even of such devotees over a longer period.

Rankings and rewards

From Benin to Versailles, presence at court created a layer of men and sometimes women absorbing and spreading courtly social mores. Other groups were connected to the court without regularly staying there. The European pattern of part-time courtiers connecting centre and periphery

jinshi chen, jinshi guan, jinshi li (officials serving [the emperor] closely) all including the term *shi*, to serve or to attend, as well as *chaochen*, (court official), *chaoshi* (court scholar), and finally a more specific and pejorative term *ningxing* (favourite) for anybody who wins the emperor's trust but whose influence is judged bad according to the orthodox Confucian canon. Lindsey Hughes, *Russia in the Age of Peter the Great* (New Haven, CT, 2000), 5–6, 180, cites *tsaredvortsy* among other terms connected to the Duma as the Russian term for courtiers, used for non-Boyar nobles.

[27] Spawforth (ed.), *Court and Court Society*, considers this in various contexts.
[28] See above, Chapter 3, 211–212.

cannot be found at all courts. However, almost universally courts did play a marked role in defining ranks and hierarchies. The social status of elites depended on numerous factors, some of which could be influenced by dynastic policy. Rulers nominated and rewarded office-holders who were subject to evaluation on the basis of their performance. Soldiers and administrators in the highest positions were requested to report back to the capital, receiving new assignments and sometimes meeting the ruler in person. Hierarchies of offices, payments, and ranks were determined at court. Particularly loyal and talented servants could be granted special tokens of distinction or honorific titles. All courts evaluated, rewarded, and punished intermediaries, but major differences can be found in the nature of the intermediary elites and in the distribution of honours.

Mughal, Ottoman, and Safavid rulers paid their commanders and governors through the allocation of the fiscal usufruct of lands.[29] Ideally, these land grants, following earlier examples such as the Seljuq *iqta* or Mongol *soyurghal*, never entailed either ownership or overall administrative control of the lands.

The Mughal system of *mansab* (office) ranks connected to *jagir* land grants was elaborated under Akbar, who expropriated land and redistributed it under restricted conditions. *Mansabdar* office-holders were listed with numbers of *zat* indicating their pay and rank, followed by *sawar*, the numbers of horsemen they were expected to maintain. Zat ranks went from starting rank 10 to the upper rank 5,000, later rising to 7,000 and 10,000. From 500 zat upwards, mansabdars were seen as nobles, although their title and assigned revenues never became hereditary. Mansabdar rankings were placed on top of a pre-existing pattern of local hereditary elites (*zamindars*). In 1595 Akbar's administrators counted 1,283 men serving him as mansabdars, together maintaining 141,053 followers.[30] This mansabdar elite comprised Arabs, Persians, Uzbeks, Chaghatai Turks, Indian Rajputs, and others; adherents of various shades of Islam were represented as well as Hindus. The jagir land assignments were not connected to land ownership or full governmental responsibility: they were limited to the fiscal revenues. Ranks, assigned lands, and pay could change every two or three years, a process intensely preoccupying the mansabdars.

Ottoman *sipahi* cavalrymen were paid by a modest land grant (*timar*). Higher levels of the Ottoman bureaucracy, usually recruited through

---

[29] Halil İnalcık, 'Autonomous enclaves in Islamic states: Temlîks, Soyurghals, Yurdluḳ-Ocalḳlıḳs, Mâlikâne-Muḳâta'as and Awqâf', in Judith Pfeiffer and Sholeh A. Quinn (eds.), *History and Historiography of Post-Mongol Central Asia and the Middle East: Studies in Honor of John E. Woods* (Wiesbaden, 2006), 112–35.

[30] Richards, *Mughal Empire*, 58–78, at 63.

devshirme and trained in the palace school, enjoyed more substantial *hass* grants. Both types of assigned income were subsumed under the generic term *dirlik*: 'The whole system can be defined as consisting of the sultan and all the independent officeholders with assigned revenue sources as livings, dirlik in Ottoman usage: the sultan, a few dozen vezirs and pashas, several hundred provincial officers, and tens of thousands of cavalrymen around the realm made up this Ottoman class.'[31] All office-holders could expect to be dismissed frequently and often waited several months before being awarded another appointment with assigned income. The highest echelons, the main provincial governors (*beylerbeys*) and the viziers in the *divan*, held the title of *pasha*. Promotion was expected to proceed along the lines of seniority and performance, but inevitably it was often influenced by alterations at the top of the hierarchy. With every new sultan or grand vizier, the balance among office-holders would change and the dismissal of a patron at any level would entail the removal of his clients: 'The higher the rank gained by an appointee, the greater the number of associates who fell with him on his dismissal from office.'[32] Sultanic favour could override common procedures based on seniority and performance by rapid promotions of confidants, whose rise disappointed the expectations of others.

In the Safavid domains, the Qizilbash elite held land assignments called *teyul* (or *tuyul*, *tiyul*). These continued to function as payment for military command and regional high office throughout the Safavid dynasty and lasted into the nineteenth century under the Qajar dynasty.[33] *Jagir*, *dirlik*, and teyul all fitted the same purpose: rewarding office-holders without alienating lands. Alongside payment through land grants, cash wages were present in these three empires. The Mughals, rich in bullion and ruling over a populous empire, paid wages to soldiers and labourers recruited on the labour market, and provided a cash complement to the land-based income of the *mansabdar* elite. The Ottomans and the Safavids paid wages primarily to slave elites. Shah Abbas I's reforms, reducing the predominant role of the Qizilbash in the Safavid venture, were made possible by the payment of salaries to the slaves (*ghulam*) in the service of the dynasty. In the Ottoman empire, the expansion of the

---

[31] On assigned sources of income (*timar*, *dirlik*, *hass*), see Metin Kunt, 'Ottomans and Safavids: states, statecraft, and societies, 1500–1800', in Youssef M. Choueiri (ed.), *A Companion to the History of the Middle East* (Chichester, 2008), 191–205; see a detailed discussion in the same author's *Sultan's Servants*.

[32] Murphey, *Ottoman Sovereignty*, 131–7, on dismissal and reappointment, or *mazuliyet* and *mülazemet*, quotation at 132.

[33] Nasiri, *Titles & Emoluments*, lists the teyuldars (*teyul*-holders) for the early eighteenth-century phase of transition.

central musket-bearing janissary infantry, paid by cash salaries, reduced the relevance of the cavalry, holding *timar* land grants.

Office-holders obtained their office, rank, and revenue assignment at court, and frequently returned to court to await new placements and rewards. Rankings among office-holders can be inferred from the relative standing of their revenue allocations. During major occasions of the year, including dynastic anniversaries, solar and lunar New Year, and the breaking of the fast of Ramadan (*Id al-Fitr*), dignitaries flocked to the court to pay their compliments to the ruler, hoping their tributes in the form of gifts *(piskes, pishkesh, pishkash)* would be rewarded with promotions.[34] The Mughal emperor Jahangir repeatedly reports their visits in his memoirs, providing detail about the awarding of *mansabs* and the gift-giving during these meetings: 'About this time many of the Amirs and Uzbeg soldiers . . . came to Court and waited on me. They were all honoured with robes of honour, horses, cash, mansabs, and jagirs.'[35] Visits occasioned by the distribution of honours immersed the disparate Mughal elites in a shared court culture. The exchange of gifts with attendant nominations was a common occurrence at the Safavid, Ottoman, and Mughal courts, sharing several of the observances included in the Islamic calendar.

The elites maintained by revenue assignments were expected to form their own households, imitating that of the ruler on a smaller scale. They assembled followers and advisors, and more often than not took these with them upon their reassignment to other places. The dynastic states of the Ottomans, Safavids, and Mughals can be represented as pyramids of households related to their leading figures more than to specific territories – with the royal princes fitting into the upper layers of this hierarchy until their change of status brought confinement in the palace. These high dignitaries could behave like miniature rulers, as John Richards' description of Mughal grandee households underlines:

---

[34] Stewart Gordon, 'Robes of honour: a "transactional" kingly ceremony', *Indian Economic & Social History Review*, 33/3 (1996), 225–42; Murphey, *Ottoman Sovereignty*, mentions the exchange of gifts and robes of honour in many places, noting (194) the very substantial amounts given by the office-holders during festivities; on Mughal *piskes*, see Annemarie Schimmel, *The Empire of the Great Mughals: History, Art and Culture* (London, 2004), 71; on the Safavid context, see Nasiri, *Titles & Emoluments*, 78, noting the office of Recorder of Presents or *pishkesh-nevis-e divan- a'la l*; on *pishkash*, Rudolph Matthee, 'Gifts and gift-giving in the Safavid period', in *Encyclopaedia Iranica* (2012), www.iranicaonline.org/articles/gift-giving-iv, stresses that gift-giving was 'tribute in return for patronage', a system of exchange converging on the royal household; Anne K.S. Lambton, 'Pīshkash', in Bearman et al. (eds.), *Encyclopaedia of Islam, Second Edition*, defines pishkash as an intermediate form of tribute and gift-giving.

[35] Jahangir, *Tuzuk-I-Jahangiri*, 202.

Wherever they were posted, whether at court or in the provinces, the patrimonial households of the nobles were a focal point for aristocratic life and culture. To the extent his resources permitted, each nobleman emulated the style, etiquette, and opulence of the emperor. Each held near-daily audiences or *durbars,* essentially public events, seated on his elevated cushion in the royal style, in which all manner of business was conducted.[36]

While the leading agents of dynastic power were expected to build a magnificent household, their success risked antagonising their rivals in office, sometimes including the ruler himself.

Several factors determined the efficacy of the revenue allocation system. The ruler's ability to evaluate and reassign or cashier office-holders was critical. Akbar, who defined and improved the Mughal *mansab* system, was closely involved in the distribution of honours: 'The emperor personally reviewed all changes in rank, titles, and official postings for all save the lowest ranked officers. Changes in rank could come at any time – without reference to procedure or rules. The sole criterion remained the emperor's favor.'[37] Rulers tried to maintain a strong grip on key nominations, but as we have seen, they were always subject to pressures of groups and figures in their daily environment. As soon as it became clear that nominations were no longer in the hands of the ruler, conflict among key leaders and their allies in the inner court became likely: the rankings and rewards became a bone of contention rather than an instrument connecting groups to the dynastic centre.

Expansion and consolidation of dynastic polities influenced the capacity of rulers to satisfy their soldiers and administrators with grants of land and honour. Elites of newly conquered territories were pacified by integrating them into the system of revenue allocation, but their numbers did not necessarily match the lands becoming available through conquest. The ruler's powers of reallocation were undermined by the powerful tendency towards hereditary devolution, the spectre of all forms of government combining delegation of power with land grants. In all three empires, examples can be found of officials turning into hereditary local lords, contending with the dynasty rather than supporting it. The French traveller Chardin reports that the holders of *teyul* land grants in the Safavid lands profited from the growth of the population and the economy, reaping far more benefits than stipulated for their teyuls. In addition, Chardin adds, 'The lands assigned for the payment of wages are not under close inspection of the king's men: they are almost like the property of the grant holders.'[38] The concentration of revenue grants in the hands

---

[36] Richards, *Mughal Empire*, 61.   [37] Ibid., 64.
[38] Chardin, *Voyages*, V, 412–18, quotation at 418.

of noble family networks undermined the flexibility of the Mughal allocation system in the last decades of Aurangzeb and under his successors.[39]
Distant provinces under Ottoman authority gradually moved away from
central control, with long-lasting governors acting independently.[40] The
'classic' phase of Ottoman power, based on the recruitment of elites
through *devshirme* and the sharp divide between ruling elite (*askeri*) and
commoners (*reaya*), was dissolving. In the decades around 1600, warfare
required increasing numbers of janissaries who needed to be paid in ready
cash, forcing the Ottoman government to put up for sale rights of taxation. Tax contracts were largely sold to government-employed elites, but
these dignitaries often leased them to lesser agents at the local level.[41] Tax
leases issued at various moments of fiscal-military crisis gave locals the
opportunity to rise from the 'flock' (reaya) layer and turn into a new local
elite; these *ayan* (notables) were also active as military entrepreneurs,
organising troops at the regional level. At the same time, service in the
great households of Ottoman dignitaries, who scouted talents at the local
level, provided another channel of advancement.[42] The personal connection (*intisab*) of household staff with their patron made possible appointment in the higher offices of the Ottoman polity. These tendencies
increased the relevance of household-based elite networks and restricted
the powers of the sultan.

[39] Gommans, *Mughal Warfare*, 84–6; Satish Chandra, *Parties and Politics at the Mughal Court, 1707–1740* (Oxford, 2002; repr. of the 1959 publication with an extended new preface), 40–9, on the concentration of *zat* and *sawar* in the hands of two groups. The new preface reconsiders aspects of the 'jagirdar crisis' under Aurangzeb.

[40] Bruce Masters, 'Semi-autonomous forces in the Arab provinces', in Suraiya N. Faroqhi (ed.), *The Cambridge History of Turkey*, vol. III: *The Later Ottoman Empire, 1603–1836* (Cambridge, 2006), 186–206, on tenure at 194–5; see also in this volume, Fikret Adanir, 'Semi-autonomous provincial forces in the Balkans and Anatolia', 157–85; Dina Rizk Khoury, 'The Ottoman centre versus provincial power-holders: an analysis of the histor-iography', 133–56; and see Kunt, 'Devolution'.

[41] From the fifteenth century onwards *Iltizam* grants and from 1695 onwards lifelong *malikane* leases: see the terms in Gustav Bayerle, *Pashas, Begs, and Effendis: A Historical Dictionary of Titles and Terms in the Ottoman Empire* (Istanbul, 1997), 85, 103, 11; and further explanantion in F. Müge Göçek, 'Mültezim', in Bearman et al. (eds.), *Encyclopaedia of Islam, Second Edition*; on the *ayan* local elites and tax farming, see Robert W. Zens, 'Provincial powers: the rise of Ottoman local notables (ayan)', *History Studies*, 3 (2011), 433–47.

[42] See Kunt, *Sultan's Servants*, with visualisations of rise to high office around 1550 (34) and around 1650 (68), the first adapting the channels of advancement given in İnalcık, *Ottoman Empire*, 82, the second showing the opening of other channels in the course of the seventeenth century as well as the diminution of devshirme levies. This brief discus-sion leaves out the rights of appointment and transferral of *ulema* in the three empires, who on the whole were less frequently uprooted than leading soldiers and administrators; see Madeline C. Zilfi, 'The Ottoman ulema', in Faroqhi (ed.), *Cambridge History of Turkey*, III, 207–25, notably at 221–3.

The European practice of creating supernumerary court titles was not entirely unknown in these regions. Hellenistic courts included a category of the king's friends or *philoi*. At the peripatetic Seleukid court under Antiochus the Great (241–223–187 BCE), philoi adopted a shared Greek culture on top of their local identities and languages, shaping a lasting connection between the court and the cities in the realm.[43] The Cairo Bahri Mamluks (1250–1382) tried to bring Arab Bedouins at least nominally under their authority by conferring on them the title of *amir* – related to military command rather than to service at court.[44] Jochid Mongols of the Golden Horde had rewarded loyal local elites with the dignity of *tarkhan*, confirming properties and privileges while granting them access to court without stipulating any active government service.[45] While Abu'l-Fazl mentions that Akbar incidentally bestowed the title tarkhan as a supreme honour, agents sent outwards to govern the empire were almost universally fitted into the *mansab* ranking.[46]

In the Ottoman empire several titles can be found that connected the court to regional groups. As a consequence of the sultanic passion for hunting, remarkable numbers of falconers (*doğanci*) were employed in the Ottoman provinces, mostly among the commoners (*reaya*): 2,171 *doğanci* were listed for Anatolia and 1,520 for Rumeli (the European provinces) in 1564.[47] This huge provincial corps of falconers faded in the seventeenth century. At that time, however, the rising numbers of local elites seem to have coveted the title of palace doorkeeper (*kapucubaşı*).[48] Other groups at the Ottoman court may reflect an honorary connection. The status of Süleyman Aga, visiting the French court in 1669, was a puzzle for Louis XIV's officials. Trying to ascertain his formal ranking, they were taken aback by the title 'gardener' (*bostancı*), before they discovered the honorific title *müteferrika*. Rightly or wrongly, French dignitaries equated this term with the 'ordinary gentlemen' of the French

---

[43] Strootman, 'Hellenistic court society', 70.

[44] Kurt Franz, 'The castle and the country: spatial orientations of Qipchaq Mamlūk rule', in Durand-Guédy (ed.), *Turko-Mongol Rulers*, 347–84, at 368–76; in Durand-Guédy's Introduction to the volume, 11, this is labelled as 'politics of notables'.

[45] Marie Favereau-Doumenjou kindly showed to me her forthcoming article, 'Tarkhan: the free citizens of the khan. A case study of the Golden Horde at the end of the fourteenth century'.

[46] Abu'l-Fazl, *Akbar Nama*, I, 450; for further explanation of the title and its rights, see Abu'l-Fazl, *Ain i Akbari*, I, 393–4. On earlier use of the title, see P.B. Golden, 'Ṭarkhān', in Bearman et al. (eds.), *Encyclopaedia of Islam, Second Edition*; apparently the title, by extension, was also used for a particularly martial people in the Punjab. On elite groups in the centre, see Gommans, *Mughal Warfare*, 61, 83; in their household Mughal rulers cultivated the personal loyalty of *chelas*, or slaves redefined into disciples, and a sizeable group of *ahadi* bodyguards, but these were not sent to the provinces.

[47] Halil İnalcık, 'Doghandjī', in Bearman et al. (eds.), *Encyclopaedia of Islam, Second Edition*.

[48] Kunt, 'Devolution', 46; Zens, 'Provincial powers'.

court, a body typically comprising mixed elites rarely present at court – at one point including Voltaire.[49] Numbers of *müteferrika* or 'distinguished persons' at the Ottoman court expanded from 40 in the late fifteenth century to more than 400 in the early seventeenth century. Initially they mostly comprised sons of distant allies or clients as well as viziers' and *pashas*' sons, honouring the connections with these grandees as well as securing their loyalty.[50] In the eighteenth century they were largely recruited from the *bostancı* corps at court. In their earlier shape the *müteferrika* can be compared to pages at European courts, while the later form reflected a career at the centre rather than a loose honorary connection with relative outsiders.

Leaders in the margins of empires could be integrated in different ways, retaining traditional titles as did tributaries in the European and African fringes of the Ottoman empire. However, for the core lands and key provinces of the early modern Islamicate empires in West and South Asia, the revenue allocation ranks were the most important administrative-honorific connection between ruler and elites.[51]

Chinese hierarchies of office-holders followed an age-old grid of nine ranks, moving upwards from the lowest level, nine, to the highest level, one. Each rank was split into two grades and in addition the lower six ranks were divided into upper and lower levels. The outlines of this finely graded hierarchy in thirty positions predated the Tang dynasty and were maintained to the end of the Qing dynasty. The first three ranks reflected high office, ranks four to seven middling office, and the last two ranks junior appointments. Recruitment was limited mostly to licentiates of the civil service examinations. The examinations were based on the classics and did not test specific administrative or technical skills; they stood at the heart of the imperial regime and had a powerful impact on Chinese culture.[52] Those successfully passing the second level of the examinations (*juren*) could enter the magistracy, usually at lower ranks. The 'presented scholars' (*jinshi*) passing the final third level of the examinations could hope for more rapid advancement. Ranks came with stipends in silver and

---

[49] Arvieux, *Mémoires*, IV, 124–5; see Bayerle, *Pashas, Begs, and Effendis*, 23, 117.
[50] Murphey, *Ottoman Sovereignty*, 157–8; Bayerle, *Pashas, Begs, and Effendis*, 116–17.
[51] See Moertono, *State and Statecraft in Old Java*, 99–108, 116, for an examination of similar practices at the Mataram sultanate, where *lungguh* lands were granted to leading officials, who nevertheless resided in the capital. A share of the usufruct of these lands was expected as gift or tribute to the sultan, resembling the *pishkesh* described above. The grandees were expected to attend the rituals of Islamicate festivities and probably were expected to present their gifts on these occasions. For reasons of space, I leave aside here the ruler's rights of nomination over leading functions in law and religion, a significant aspect of patronage and control both in Europe and West and South Asia.
[52] Elman, *Cultural History of Civil Examinations*.

rice, specific privileges, and a dress code. Under the Ming, six military ranks followed similar principles, and there were special military examinations. However, these never matched the pervasive influence of the civil examinations, and military leadership advanced more often through recommendation and performance.[53] Ranks were represented visually by emblems, or 'mandarin squares', on the breast of garments worn by office-holders, with birds for civil officials and mammals for military ranks.[54]

Frequent relocation prevented collusion between magistrates and locals, while 'laws of avoidance' prohibited situations where members of the same family worked together or where magistrates governed their own region of provenance.[55] The performance of officials was evaluated continuously, a process comprising the writing of self-evaluations for higher ranks and triennial merit ratings by superiors for all ranks. A separate 'great reckoning' of all provincial officials was performed every three years, and independent censors continually assessed the performance of their fellow literati in office. In general, the accumulation of three merit ratings provided grounds for deciding promotion, demotion, or punishment. Matteo Ricci's report on the 1607 'great reckoning' conveys the awe it could inspire:

Every third year the ranking officials of all provinces, districts, and cities ... must convene in Pekin to express their solemn fealty to the King. At that time a rigorous investigation is made concerning the magistrates of every province in the entire kingdom, including those present and those not called. The purpose of this inspection is to determine who shall be retained in public office, how many are to be removed, and the number to be promoted or demoted and punished, if need be. There is no respect for persons in this searching inquisition. I myself have observed that not even the King would dare to change a decision settled upon by the judges of this public investigation. Those who are punished are by no means few or of lower grade ... a list of the names of those concerned is published in a single volume and circulated throughout the land.[56]

As early as the Tang, the common tribulations of a career in government service provided inspiration for a board game including a thousand

---

[53] Charles O. Hucker, 'Ming government', in Denis C. Twitchett and Frederick W. Mote (eds.), *The Cambridge History of China*, vol. VIII: *The Ming Dynasty* (Cambridge, 1998), 9–105, at 41–61 on civil and military hierarchies. See an updated but short explanation of recruitment and ranking in Endymion Porter Wilkinson, *Chinese History: A New Manual* (Cambridge, MA, 2013), 265–8.

[54] Valery M. Garrett, *Mandarin Squares: Mandarins and their Insignia* (Oxford and Hong Kong, 1990); Yuan Zujie, 'Dressing for power: rite, costume, and state authority in Ming dynasty china', *Frontiers of History in China*, 2/2 (2007), 181–212.

[55] Hucker, *Dictionary of Official Titles*, 263, no. 2887; 397, no. 4862.

[56] Hucker, 'Ming government', 44.

positions and numerous obstructions called 'struggling to advance in officialdom'. Various combinations of two dices determined advancement: thus, a pair of sixes brought 'recognition for talent', a pair of ones 'revealed corruption', and so on. In each dynasty, the game was adapted to fit changes in the system.[57] The infusion of Manchus into the upper layers of officialdom and the separate channels of confidential communication developing between the emperor and his trusted servants under the Qing cannot have made matters easier for Han Chinese officials.

The results obtained in the civil service examinations and the ensuing placement and advance in the nine ranks of officialdom formed the core of a far more elaborate system of ranking. Following positive evaluation, officials at all ranks could be granted 'prestige titles' befitting their rank. These forty-two titles included lofty indications such as the 'grand master for splendid happiness' and the 'grand master for proper consultation'. Outstanding achievements were rewarded by 'merit titles' reserved to the upper ranks five to one, including the (left or right) 'pillars of the state' for the two highest ranks. Titles conferred the right to wear visible status markers, mostly special accoutrements such as headgear. On special request of the chosen ones, titles could be extended to include fathers and grandfathers; extra honours were sometimes conferred posthumously. The Jesuit Ferdinand Verbiest (1623–88), gaining the recognition and friendship of the Kangxi emperor by his improvement of the calendar, was promoted to director of the astronomical bureau and rank two; the merit title attached to this promotion was extended to include his parents and grandparents.[58] This intricate machinery, ill-fitting to modern sensibilities and easily ridiculed, stood at the heart of power relations at court and helped define status in the provinces. Ming scholars eagerly discussed the niceties of rank in their notebooks (*biji*).[59]

Military ranks followed the same pattern, but they were somewhat less extended and, on the whole, lower in prestige.[60] Outside the ranks of officialdom stood other forms of distinction often granted to military commanders. 'Meritorious subjects' could be rewarded with titles of nobility: duke (*gong*), marquis (*hou*) and count (*bo*).[61] These titles could

[57] Wilkinson, *Chinese History*, 268.
[58] Charles Louis Carton, *Notice biographique sur le père Ferdinand Verbiest, missionaire à la Chine* (Bruges, 1839), 31–7, prints translations of the various grants; see Jean-Baptiste Du Halde, *Description géographique, historique, chronologique, politique, et physique de l'empire de la Chine et de la Tartarie chinoise*, 4 vols. (The Hague, 1739), II, 69–75 on nobility, mentioning Verbiest's success.
[59] Personal communication from Jérôme Kerlouégan, whose advice for this paragraph as well as other parts of this book was invaluable.
[60] See tables for these special privileges in Hucker, 'Ming government', 50–1, 59–60.
[61] Ibid., 28, listing 'earl' for 'count'.

be granted for life, with full or with limited heredity – for several generations, or declining one step every generation. Some cases of nobility stood
out in a hierarchy that was based on the rankings of service and officialdom. The Kong lineage, descendants of Confucius, held ducal rank.
Imperial in-laws were often granted nobility in the Ming. As we have
seen, every dynasty formed its own imperial clan, consisting of a separate
hierarchy of princely ranks. Ming princes were ordered in eight ranks; the
first two levels of full princes and commandery princes (*qinwang* and
junwang) followed by six less exalted ranks with numerous princes.
Incidentally, survivors of earlier dynasties were granted noble rank: a
favour granted by the Yongzheng emperor in 1724 to a Ming
descendant.[62]

Qing emperors gradually developed a hierarchy for princes in the
imperial clan (*aisin gioro*), counting eighteen ranks after 1748.[63] The
Qing takeover, made possible by the support of Manchu and Mongol
grandees, made nobility into a mainstay of the state. Manchus and
Mongols dominated the banner military forces and were notably present
in the inner court. While Manchus entered the civil service examinations
and the dynasty on the whole conformed to accepted Han Chinese
practice, the conquerors' superior status transformed the system. The
conquest elite and its noble allies governed the outer provinces and held a
privileged position in the upper ranks of central and provincial
government.[64] In the outer provinces as well as in the inner court, nobility
and descent had now become dominant, whereas examination success
and promotion through the nine ranks still formed the backbone of
China's core provinces.

How can we picture the emperor at the junction of these differentiated
hierarchies and rewards? Ideally, seniority and performance determined
all status changes, and escalations up the ladder of advancement proceeded gradually: promotion was restricted to two degrees, demotion to
three degrees in rank. The emperor was not tied to these rules, yet
appointments to higher ranks were not made entirely at his pleasure.
In Ming times, 'emperors disposed only when ministers proposed, the
emperor was generally bound to consider for appointment only men
nominated by the officialdom'.[65] The sheer numbers of files to be looked
at and appointments to be decided on must have left considerable

---

[62] Rawski, *Last Emperors*, 72.   [63] Ibid., 76–7, 304.

[64] See Guy, *Qing Governors*, 146–7, on the privileged position of bannermen in high office
and more specifically on the Qianlong emperor's effort to strengthen the Manchu grip on
governorships; Guy mentions (15) that fewer than half of the governors held the *jinshi*
degree.

[65] Hucker, 'Ming government', 47.

leeway to the leading officials around the emperor, preparing advice and recommendation. In Qing times, the remarkable diligence of emperors and the fact that they used the confidential channel of the palace memorials as well as the formal channels of bureaucratic communication may have made a gradual difference. The hard work of the three 'high Qing' emperors and their keen interest in appointments have been mentioned earlier. Their nineteenth-century successors, not usually presented in the same light, likewise appear to have been quite active in studying personnel files and conducting interviews.[66] While the emperors' personal grip on nominations must have been restricted largely to leading offices and some room must have been granted to networks of office-holders preparing appraisals and recommendations, the overall strength of central evaluation and reallocation cannot be doubted. Corruption was endemic and sometimes blatant; officials may have been baffled by the numbers of people they had to oversee and higher authorities rarely monitored their day-to-day operations. Nevertheless, the pull of the central overseers would make itself felt regularly and powerfully.

The *yamen* (headquarters) of local officials was no close parallel of the households of Mughal or Ottoman office-holders. Clearly, however, the office-holders were the local representatives of imperial power in more than just an administrative capacity. They performed the Confucian rites at set times and made imperial power visible to their communities. The dynastic prestige of the emperor, too, sometimes had a local face. Numerous Ming princes in their fiefs lived in smaller replicas of the imperial palace.[67] Semedo, describing the situation of the high-ranking Qin prince of Xi'an, wondered about the strange mixture of prestige and impotence: 'all the Officers of the Province were obliged to pay him respect suitable to his Title; whence every first and fifteenth day of the Moone they went to do him reverence in like manner, as is done at Court to the King'. At the same time, 'Authority and Jurisdiction . . . he had nothing at all; neither over the people, nor in the government; the King reserving all that to himself; neither hath he libertie to go out of the City and Territorie, where he hath his residence.'[68] Under the Qing, the princes lived mostly in or around Beijing and their presence elsewhere was limited to specific missions. They operated as leading agents in the emperor's name, but as a rule remained in the vicinity of the Forbidden City.

[66] Will, 'Views of the realm'.   [67] Wang, *The Ming Prince and Daoism.*
[68] Semedo, *History*, 122.

The two courts in Tokugawa Japan functioned as interrelating hierarchies, one based on political power, the other on time-honoured prestige. The leading *daimyo* lords showed their deference in attending the shogun's court, but were not usually involved in decision-making; lower daimyo lords as well as other groups from the warrior class held office in the shogunal government. Yet these hierarchies of birth and service were topped by the supreme ranking of imperial court office still nominally distributed by the emperor. Kaempfer commented at length on the reduced powers of the 'spiritual emperor', stressing the dominance of the 'worldly emperor': the shogun. The 'giving and conferring of honorific titles to grandees and their children or friends', he continued, was still in the hands of the emperor, who 'enriched his treasury' through it.[69] An ancient law on court service decreed in 702 linked offices to a hierarchy of thirty imperial court ranks. This ranking persisted throughout Japanese history while gradually changing function. Positions that had reflected actual offices in the eighth or ninth century now retained importance as honorary titles. A historian of early Japan reports: 'Thus, for instance, as late as the end of the Tokugawa period, Bakufu officials bore such titles as Controller of the Bureau of Weaving (Oribe no sho), although this particular office had been abolished nearly 1,000 years before, the title only surviving as a mark of honour.'[70] In this hierarchy the shoguns themselves were nominated as Minister of the Left (*sadaijin*) or First Minister (*dajodaijin*), offices conferring the first court rank. Imperial court offices and their concomitant ranks were distributed to *kuge* (the emperor's courtiers), as well as to daimyo and the uppermost layers of the direct vassals of the shogun (*hatamoto*). For daimyo, promotions to offices such as provincial governors matching the fifth court rank were possible and sought after.[71] Such grants could be awarded only with the full sanction of the shogun and on his initiative: no daimyo was allowed to petition the emperor directly. Kaempfer described the Tokugawa policy vis-à-vis the daimyo in no uncertain terms:

They do not suppress them, neither keep them subjected with force of arms, nor do they overburden them with heavy tributes: but they try to win their friendship and affection by polite and friendly behaviour, and by showing them imperial

---

[69] Kaempfer, *Beschryving van Japan*, 108.

[70] George B. Sansom, 'Early Japanese law and administration', *Transactions of the Asiatic Society of Japan*, 9 (1932), 67–109, at 72; see also Robert K. Reischauer, *Early Japanese History, c. 40 B.C. – A.D. 1167* (Princeton, NJ, 1937), 87–105.

[71] Daimyo could rise to the fourth court rank. See a vehement critique of the disarray of ranks and offices in Bob Tadashi Wakabayashi, *Japanese Loyalism Reconstrued: Yamagata Daini's Ryūshi Shinron of 1759* (Honolulu, HI, 1995), esp. 129–33, 'Making name and actuality conform'. My thanks go to my Leiden colleague Wim Boot for explaining the ranking system and providing references.

benevolence . . . those wrapped by them in friendship and high titles . . . are kept in obedience and subordination.[72]

An imperial court office obtained for daimyo, who were at the same time engaged in their habitual train back and forth to Edo, was yet another security for the shogun: it delighted the lords and invited them to demonstrate their newly acquired prestige through conspicuous spending.

After his military triumph at Sekigahara (1600), Shogun Ieyasu engaged in a major operation of confiscation and reassigning of daimyo lands, adding up to 'the greatest transfer of landholding in Japanese history'.[73] Confiscations (*kaieki*) and transfers (*tenpu*) continued even after the gradual pacification of Japan and the repression of a major peasant rebellion in 1637–8, but their punitive character gradually subsided. While shoguns became more reticent, no longer transferring daimyo lords like 'potted plants', they retained the ability to do so.[74]

The process of recommendation for court rank and endorsement by the emperor and the shogun has been studied only in incidental cases. At least once the shogun and the emperor clashed in a 'title incident'. This atypical case followed a succession anomaly common in Japan and to a lesser extent in China. Emperor Go-Momozono (1758–1770–1779) died leaving only a daughter, with succession going to a minor relative from a cadet branch who would rule as Emperor Kokaku (1771–1779–1817★). The new emperor, torn between filial duties to his deceased imperial father and his biological father, decided to promote his father from prince to former emperor by conferring the title *Dajo-tenno*.[75] This initiative was steadfastly blocked by Shogun Ienari's (1773–1787–1837★) senior councillor Sadanobu. In a long-drawn-out political ballet with his counterpart at the imperial court, the leading advisor Sukehira, the matter was stalled

---

[72] Kaempfer, *Beschryving van Japan*, 489–90, a long and outspoken digression continuing with: 'Without even mentioning the endless other tricks and subterfuges the Emperors (shoguns) use, to prevent their (daimyos) mutual alliances and sympathies, penetrating their most secret conversations, pushing them to friendships, suspicion or enmity, depending on their own interests.'

[73] John Whitney Hall, 'The Bakuhan system', in John Whitney Hall (ed.), *The Cambridge History of Japan*, vol. IV: *Early Modern Japan* (Cambridge, 1991), 128–82, at 144; at 150–2 Hall presents an overview of later confiscations; in the same volume Harold Bolitho, 'The Han', 183–234, shows that the shoguns acted with increasing reticence (208–11).

[74] Philip C. Brown, 'The political and institutional history of early modern Japan', *Early Modern Japan: An Interdisciplinary Journal*, 11 (2003), 3–30, at 28, refers to 'potted plants' and questions the 'absolutist' perspective, pointing to his *Central Authority and Local Autonomy in the Formation of Early Modern Japan: The Case of Kaga Domain* (Stanford, CA, 1993), and Mark Ravina, *Land and Lordship in Early Modern Japan* (Stanford, CA, 1998).

[75] Herman Ooms, *Charismatic Bureaucrat: A Political Biography of Matsudaira Sadanobu, 1758–1829* (Chicago, IL, 1975), 105–21; see very similar circumstances in China studied in Fisher, *Chosen One*.

in the expectation it would be dropped: precedents were to be studied while no action was taken. However, the emperor persisted, putting pressure on the shogun by postponing his ritual performance in the Harvest Festival. In the end, several imperial courtiers were punished and dismissed, whereas the emperor's father was placated by a raise of his stipend.[76] To settle the affair, Sadanobu at one point even suggested that the shogun should visit the emperor, a feat last effected in 1634. This incident, underlining the political relevance of titles at the highest levels, may also have been a sign of changing times, announcing the gradual shift between shogunal and imperial favour.

The marked presence of *daimyo* lords processing back and forth between their fiefs and Edo, combined with the powerful presence of these lords in their own fiefs, suggested the supremacy of the invisible shogun to wider audiences. On his way back to Nagasaki, Kaempfer encountered the procession of a daimyo of high rank, numbering more than a thousand persons preceded by a long baggage train and guards.[77] The daimyo were as conspicuously visible as the leading Mughal *mansabdar* households moving from region to region, and certainly more so than Chinese magistrates with their more modest followings. At the same time, the mixture of substantial power in the regions, high honour, and public subservience towards the shogun, capped by the possibility of transferral and confiscation, made rebellion unattractive in all respects.

In each of these examples, honour and rank were related to coercive potential. The bestowing of office and rank was most effective in situations where honours could be withdrawn and transferred. Typically in Europe short-term commissions based on cash wages, evaluations, and reassignments were added to the common practice of hereditary and long-term office-holding. These innovations, familiar from the previous paragraphs, cannot be seen as either European or early modern inventions. Throughout the early modern period, birth rank remained central, but it was confronted by changes on two fronts: education and the system of ranks.

Training in law and finance played an increasing role in the recruiting of administrators. Rulers tended to open government to social climbers, or alternatively expect nobles to obtain the relevant knowledge. University training became a requirement for specialised administrators

---

[76] Ooms, *Charismatic Bureaucrat*, 182, note 20, reports one other public punishment of courtiers in 1629; the situation in the 1780s was complicated by the fact that Shogun Ienari, too, had succeeded as a collateral adopted into the main line, and maybe even considered promoting his own father to the title of abdicated shogun (*ogosho*); see ibid., 115.

[77] Kaempfer, *Beschryving van Japan*, 385–6.

at middling levels. Social mobility was possible in the army, with distinguished service traditionally leading to ennoblement. However, military
commanders, particularly those responsible for siege warfare, now
needed far more schooling, a fact reflected in the curriculum of pages at
court. The key importance of fortification and artillery explains the rapid
rise of engineers such as Sebastien le Prestre de Vauban (1633–1707) to
noble rank and the marshalcy. In the course of the eighteenth century
military schools were founded for officers across Europe, sometimes with
separate establishments for the various components of the army.
Promotion from the ranks on the basis of seniority and outstanding
service became more common, although nobles dominated the upper
ranks.[78] Specialised schools for administrators developed only in the
nineteenth century. Entry tests for university-trained legal scholars seeking office in state service were decreed in early eighteenth-century
Brandenburg-Prussia. In the 1770s, examinations became somewhat
more important in Prussia, but they remained the exception elsewhere.[79]
Systemic nationwide competitive examinations for state service were
proposed in 1791 during the French Revolution and became more common only very gradually after Napoleon's consolidation and reform of
education.

European rulers created a new upper layer of titled nobles connected to
the court. While they could not gainsay impressive genealogies of local
lords, they were quite able to elevate their favourites and most competent
servants to higher nobility. Across Europe, the nobility, never a single
cohesive group, was torn apart. It split into an upper group approaching
the court and benefiting from its perks and a lower group that saw its
economic power eroded while being barred from access to the advantages

---

[78] On seniority based on the 'ordre du tableau' and other ingredients of promotion in the
French army under Louis XIV, see Bertrand Fonck, 'Le commandement des armées et
ses enjeux sous Louis XIV', *Revue historique des armées*, 263 (2011), 17–27; Guy
Rowlands, *The Dynastic State and the Army under Louis XIV: Royal Service and Private
Interest, 1661–1701* (Cambridge, 2002); Rowlands, 'Louis XIV, aristocratic power and
the elite units of the French army', *French History*, 13/3 (1999), 303–31.

[79] On the Berlin Generaldirektorium and its examination committee
(Oberexaminationskommission zu Berlin) established in 1770, see Hans Martin Sieg,
*Staatsdienst, Staatsdenken und Dienstgesinnung in Brandenburg-Preussen im 18. Jahrhundert
(1713–1806): Studien zum Verständnis des Absolutismus* (Berlin, 2003), 138–55; see also
Axel Rüdiger, *Staatslehre und Staatsbildung: die Staatswissenschaft an der Universität Halle
im 18. Jahrhundert* (Tübingen, 2005), 272; Wilhelm Bleek, *Von der Kameralausbildung
zum Juristenprivileg: Studium, Prüfung und Ausbildung der höheren Beamten des allgemeinen
Verwaltungsdienstes in Deutschland im 18. und 19. Jahrhundert* (Berlin, 1972), 38–44,
56–60, 73–82; for French examinations, see Talleyrand's 1791 report to the assembly:
Charles-Maurice de Talleyrand-Périgord, *Rapport sur l'instruction publique, fait au nom du
Comité de constitution de l'Assemblée nationale, les 10, 11, et 19 septembre 1791* (Paris, 1791).
Other examples can be found from the nineteenth century onwards.

of the court. At the upper levels, the peers of the realm were redefined and replenished, now comprising a mixed group of grandees, royal favourites, and ministers who had risen through state service. French kings inserted their candidates into the reformed corps of dukes and peers; Habsburg emperors enticed their key supporters with the near-sovereign status of prince of the empire. Conferring these supreme ranks was effective only with limited numbers: inflation ruined the prestigious character of the titles and provoked those already in place. Moreover, promotions needed to conform to certain criteria which were not necessarily wholly at the discretion of the ruler. Nevertheless, this was a powerful instrument to attract supporters. The beneficiaries accumulating supreme rank, orders of chivalry, and leading offices, gradually coalesced into a new upper layer.

The construction of a new, mixed upper layer did not entail the demise of noble power. It created a leading court-connected group based on service and hereditary rank that persisted into the twentieth century. These families mimicked the strategies of ruling dynasties, adopting male primogeniture and protecting their landed wealth against the whims of single family members through trusts and family settlements.[80] They profited from new opportunities such as banking and the exploitation of overseas wealth or mineral resources in their extended domains. Russia, increasingly connected to mainstream European developments, underwent a parallel change in its upper layers between the 1650s and 1800. Peter's radical intervention in succession, leaving matters undecided upon his death, was matched by his ambitious but open-ended redefinition of nobility. In the later seventeenth century Moscow's leading noble *boyars*, often connected by marriage to the ruling house, dominated high office and had free access to the tsar.[81] The balance between heredity and service, however, was gradually changing. The 'code of precedence' or *mestnichestvo*, basing the hierarchy of command on a combination of family prestige, family service record, and personal seniority within the family, was abolished in 1682, leaving more freedom to the ruler's appointments.[82] In his 1722 Table of Ranks Peter introduced a concordance of ranks and offices at court, in the military, and in the administration. Copying several titles and offices from Scandinavian

[80] On these transformations, see the forthcoming book by Hamish M. Scott, *Forming Aristocracy: The Reconfiguration of Europe's Nobilities, c. 1300–1750*, which the author kindly allowed me to read in unpublished form.

[81] On Russian dynastic marriages, see Martin, *Bride for the Tsar*.

[82] Hughes, *Russia in the Age of Peter the Great*, 5–6, 172–9; on *mestnichestvo*, see Nancy Shields Kollmann, *By Honor Bound: State and Society in Early Modern Russia* (Ithaca, NY, 1999); on the abolition, see also Bushkovitch, *Peter the Great*, 120–3.

and German examples, Peter with this document defined service as the basis of all ranks. Nobles were expected to serve in higher ranks, whereas others rising through loyal service would acquire noble rank. The obligation of lifelong service for nobles was soon dropped, but state service remained an accepted stage in the lives of male nobles to the end of the Russian empire. Catherine II's Noble Charter of 1785 strengthened the hereditary position of nobles, but did not touch the logic of state service.[83] The ties between state service and noble rank were not as formalised elsewhere in Europe, yet concordances of civil, military, and court status became commonplace, and the logic that long-standing as well as outstanding service should be rewarded by noble status was generally accepted.

The control of hierarchy, service, and income in the hands of the rulers, whether or not they personally supervised distribution, was of prime importance in holding together the realm. African village chiefs sharing in royal largesse, Islamicate military dignitaries moving around with their households, Chinese magistrates governing their counties, daimyo moving between their domains and Edo, nobles alternating court attendance with stays in their local mansions: they all in one way or another represented the powers of the paramount prince at local levels. Ensuring the loyalty of these intermediaries to the dynastic centre was a precondition for the allegiance, or grudging submission, of the population at large. A pyramid of patronage built on the expectation of reciprocal services connected the court to the intermediary elites, and these elites to local middlemen. The intermediaries acted as brokers, using their access to the distribution of honours at court to satisfy their followers at local levels. Although nobody expected reciprocity to be fully symmetrical, patrons disappointed the expectations of many clients: there were always more dependents than rewards. In this lottery, the success of some kept alive the hopes of others.[84] Leading patrons were in the same position vis-à-vis the prince. Factional strife among grandees at court reflected the

---

[83] Dominic Lieven, 'The elites', in Dominic Lieven (ed.), *The Cambridge History of Russia*, vol. II: *Imperial Russia, 1689–1917* (Cambridge, 2006), 227–83, at 229.

[84] I cite only a few titles from the rich historical and anthropological literature on clientage and patron–client relations: Ernest Gellner and J. Waterbury (eds.), *Patrons and Clients in Mediterranean Societies* (London, 1977); S.N. Eisenstadt and Louis Roniger, 'Patron–client relations as a model of structuring social exchange', *Comparative Studies in Society and History*, 22/1 (1980), 42–77; S.N. Eisenstadt and René Lemarchand (eds.), *Political Clientelism, Patronage and Development* (London, 1977); Yves Durand (ed.), *Hommage à Roland Mousnier: clientèles et fidélités en Europe à l'époque moderne* (Paris, 1981); Antoni Maczak (ed.), *Klientelsysteme im Europa der Frühen Neuzeit* (Munich, 1988); Sharon Kettering, *Patrons, Brokers and Clients in Seventeenth-Century France* (Oxford, 1986). Many other titles could be mentioned, including more recent work on trust in political systems: see e.g. Tilly, *Trust and Rule*, examining several types of connection

competition for scarce benefits more often than major policy choices. In smaller polities, the pyramid of patronage reached only from the central establishment to its clients in surrounding chiefdoms or provinces. In bigger polities, brokerage connected multiple layers. A highly developed administrative machinery made personal connections less imperative, but recommendations and friendships remained significant.

The capacity to befriend and enthrall supporters depended on the distribution of honours and rewards as well as on shared ideas and experiences. Elites could plausibly hope for rewards, yet local subjects were not expected to share directly in the dynastic feast. At best, dynastic intervention alleviated the consequences of local droughts, famines, or pestilences; at its worst it brought increased taxation and violent retribution. The compliance of wider groups hinged on the attitudes of the intermediaries. Was it also shaped by their perception of the dynastic centre and its activities?

Power and pageantry

Dynastic households invariably included experts in the ritual choreography of power. Across the globe dynastic rituals could take very different shapes. Everywhere, however, they shared certain characteristics.[85] First of all, solemn ceremonies followed detailed rules kept alive by ritual specialists, in learned written discourse, in songs and stories, and in objects and spaces. While these rules were pictured as age-old and unchanging, they were usually pliable and varied over time. Secondly, more often than not special artefacts played a key role in ceremonies: drums, parasols, stools or thrones, canopies, daises and carpets or animal skins, crowns, swords, relics. Courts included repositories of such objects and workshops to create more. Thirdly, spaces in the palace and in its vicinity were designed for the enactment of rituals and were furnished for the occasion with the paraphernalia called for by tradition. Moving courts were expert at recreating the desired ambiance for their rituals in other

between rulers and 'trust networks' (31–2), typical top-down strategies (105), and bottom-up responses (33, 104). In practice, Tilly's categories (e.g. particularistic ties, brokered autonomy, patronage systems) overlap. While he plausibly defines rulers and governments as the most conspicuous predators in history (86–7), he leaves little room for the weakness of rulers (inseparable from 'governments under a ruler' in his book) and for the shared ideals and hopes of all involved. Geoffrey Hosking, 'Trust and distrust: a suitable theme for historians?', *Transactions of the Royal Historical Society*, 6th series, 16 (2006), 95–115, makes clear that trust invites more historical research but sticks to the familiar catalogue of European breakthroughs as examples of trust-building moments.

[85] I use ritual and ceremony as synonyms. Etymology and early modern usage place the terms in the same category, and modern definitions differ in various disciplines.

locations. Fourthly, ritual performances were repeated in set patterns based on cosmological and seasonal rhythms (recurring liturgical and agricultural calendars), on the cycle of rulership (death–accession–maturity–marriage–birth–illness–death), and on ad hoc or recurring specific occasions (assemblies, warfare, hunt, drought). Finally, rituals were consciously enacted by rulers and their retinues at moments set apart from routine concerns. Devotion, audiences, banquets, and entertainments formed part of daily routines as well as of special occasions, but the great ritual events related to the calendar and to dynastic demography stood out for the participants.

These generic remarks leave open the question whether a common denominator can be found for the profound diversity of ritual practices related to dynastic rule across the globe. Moreover, they fail to clarify how we should understand these solemn and scripted practices. Did court ritual fit into religious categories, or was it first and foremost a political statement? Did the ritualised meeting points of the dynastic past form a collective demonstration of a shared worldview binding together different social groups? Or, conversely, was this a predetermined strategy of power, consciously organised by a ruling elite impressing subjected populations with a show of splendour and hierarchy? This survey of select rituals related to dynastic power shows that such outspoken positions are misleading rather than helpful.

Court ritual followed liturgical-cosmological calendars, but it included markedly political events such as enthronements, consultations with grandees, and the obeisance of subjected peoples. Celestial and terrestrial hierarchies merged in the liturgies of power elevating the dynasty; the humble prostration of the ruler before higher powers underlined his role as intermediary. The most important ceremonies at court combined placating the supernatural with political rituals defining earthly relationships. After performing his Grand Sacrifice at the Altar of Heaven in the southern outskirts of Beijing during the winter solstice, the emperor returned to the Forbidden City, where he met his greatest dignitaries in a Grand Audience in the main hall (*Taihedian*).[86] French kings after their coronation and oath in Rheims cathedral employed their newly acquired divine grace to perform the royal touch, healing crowds affected by the skin disease scrofula. Their *sacre* was a restatement of connections with heaven, with the grandees, and with the populace of the realm – and it was

---

[86] Zhu, *Chinese Spatial Strategies*, 197–221, esp. 204; for a different approach and discussion of interpretations, see Zito, *Of Body and Brush*, 125–8, 142–3; for an insightful analysis of the local dimensions of Qing ritual and their considerable overlap with magic and folklore, see Jeffrey Snyder-Reinke, *Dry Spells: State Rainmaking and Local Governance in Late Imperial China* (Cambridge, MA, 2009), discussing the Grand Sacrifices at 50–9.

followed by numerous worldly celebrations. Much the same can be said about the election and coronation of the nominally highest secular ruler of Europe. After being elected, the Holy Roman Emperor went to the church to be inaugurated and clothed in Charlemagne's vestments. Following this event, he was escorted by his imperial elites to the town square of Frankfurt to enjoy a festive banquet in the town hall, cheered along the road by thousands of spectators. The Ottoman, Mughal, and Safavid rulers celebrated the breaking of the fast (*Id al-Fitr*), gradually moving through the solar year because its timing followed the Islamic lunar calendar, by attracting their agents and tributaries from across the realm.[87] These great celebrations all underline that religious and worldly ceremonies overlapped: separating rigidly the two aspects denies the vital connection that existed for the participants.[88]

The accessibility and visibility of ceremonies varied considerably; the absence of audiences affected the impact of ceremony. Which groups performed ceremonies and which groups witnessed them? Chinese emperors performed the Grand Sacrifices during winter and summer solstice and spring and autumn equinoxes in relative isolation. After lengthy preparations in the palace for the prayer and sacrifices at the Altar of Heaven, the emperor

with his entire entourage, in a strict formation ... slowly moved out of the Palace City, amidst the ringing of the bell and the beating of the drum at the Meridian Gate. The procession followed the sacred way on the axis of the whole city from the Meridian Gate of the Palace City to the southwestern gate of the Altar of Heaven. All street intersections on the two sides of this avenue were blocked by timber fences and covered by large curtains. Shops on the two sides were also closed. Guards and soldiers knelt on the two sides all the way through.[89]

Arriving at the Altar of Heaven, prayer and libations were performed by the emperor with his most exalted servants; dynastic women were barred from attending these rites and no outside spectators were present. Other Grand Sacrifices followed the same pattern. The major ceremonies

---

[87] On calendars and ceremony in the Islamicate empires, see Stephen P. Blake, *Time in Early Modern Islam: Calendar, Ceremony, and Chronology in the Safavid, Mughal, and Ottoman Empires* (Cambridge, 2013).

[88] The terms ritual and ceremony are sometimes understood to refer to the religious and the secular respectively; alternatively they are used to indicate different social groups (popular ritual, court ceremony) or regions of the earth (African royal rituals, European royal ceremonies). I leave aside these shaky distinctions and use the words ceremony and ritual as interchangeable. The same holds true for *rituale* or *ceremoniale*, books recording ceremonial practices, as does the *Rituale Romanum* for the Catholic Church. On secular ritual, see Sally Falk Moore and Barbara G. Myerhoff (eds.), *Secular Ritual* (Assen and Amsterdam, 1977), with contributions by, among others, Jack Goody and Victor Turner.

[89] Zhu, *Chinese Spatial Strategies*, 216.

related to imperial rule, the ascension to the throne, audiences, and the 'declaration of imperial decrees' likewise were performed among the restricted company of the emperor with magistrates and servants, now in the halls of the Forbidden City rather than at the main altars of greater Beijing.

In Song times, the rehearsal of processions with drums and elephants created a stir among the populace of Kaifeng.[90] Such events apparently remained exceptional in Ming and Qing China. Only incidentally did the emperor show himself in festive processions: two such occasions are reported in the eighteenth century, the first on the occasion of the Kangxi emperor's sixtieth birthday in 1713 (Plate 28a), the second for Qianlong's eightieth birthday in 1790.[91] Depictions of these events suggest some interplay between the imperial procession and the population. Imperial processions, hidden from view or overt, must have formed a regular aspect of life in Qing Beijing. The Kangxi emperor undertook 128 tours between 1688 and 1722, more than two outings every year. His excursions included more than fifty northern tours beyond the wall (mostly hunting expeditions), six southern tours to the heart of the literati culture and commercial wealth in Jiangnan, six western tours to the Shanxi and Shaanxi provinces, and three eastern tours to the secondary Manchu capital of Shengjing.[92] After a lull in the reign of the Yongzheng emperor, Qianlong revived his grandfather's remarkable mobility, matching his average of two to three tours every year and staying in Beijing not more than two thirds of most years.[93] This frequent movement must have been noticed in the capital and in the provinces the emperors visited. The interaction with the people they encountered may have been toned down in the official sources generated at court, which invariably stressed the stately and distanced character of the imperial progress.[94] An indirect reflection of imperial grandeur, the frequent Korean and incidental

---

[90] Patricia B. Ebrey, 'Taking out the grand carriage: imperial spectacle and the visual culture of Northern Song Kaifeng', *Asia Major*, 12/1 (1999), 33–65.

[91] Susan Naquin, *Peking: Temples and City Life, 1400–1900* (Berkeley, CA, 2000), 249–50; see the 1713 entry depicted in the painting commemorating the Kangxi emperor's entry into Beijing on his sixtieth birthday in 1713 (Plate 28a); in a series of prints by Isidore Stanislas Helman we find a similar scene depicting Qianlong's 'marche ordinaire' in 1786 rather than in 1790 (see British Museum, 1877,0714.1522.1–3: Marche ordinaire de l'Empereur de la Chine lorsqu'il passe dans la ville de Péking / Suite des seize estampes représentant les Conquêtes de l'Empereur de la Chine). Illustrations in this series include the ploughing of the first furrow by emperor and dignitaries (Plate 26). On the Siamese variant of the ploughing ceremony, see Quaritch Wales, *Siamese State Ceremonies*, 256–64, showing the Brahmanic character of this ceremony. On the warlike connotations of the Inka ploughing ritual (Plate 27a), see Brian S. Bauer, 'Legitimization of the state in Inka myth and ritual', *American Anthropologist*, 98/2 (1996), 327–37.

[92] Chang, *Court on Horseback*, 73.   [93] Ibid., 74; see also the overviews at 116–18.

[94] See an analysis of central and local sources in Chang, 'Historical narratives'.

European missions to the palace must have attracted some attention. The ten richly caparisoned elephants accompanying the exceptional Burmese mission to the Forbidden City in 1750–1 – eight to be given to Qianlong, two to his mother – can hardly have gone unnoticed.[95]

Eighteenth-century European observers were particularly impressed by the Chinese emperor's habit of opening the tilling season by 'ploughing the first furrow' with his dignitaries at the Altar of Agriculture on the first auspicious day of the second month of spring (Plate 26). Montesquieu understood this 'excellent custom' as an example for common peasants: 'The historical relations of China mention a ceremony of opening the ground which the emperor performs every year. The design of this public and solemn act is to excite the people to tillage.'[96] Montesquieu's appreciative description of the sacrifice as a public act is confusing: this was a solemn act of state visible to only a relatively small group of participants. However, his source, the Jesuit Du Halde, adds an important element that held true for most state rituals. The 'mandarins of each town', Du Halde stated, 'perform the same ceremony'.[97] The Grand Sacrifices, performed by the emperor in seclusion, were enacted at the same time throughout China by his magistrates. The same holds true for other rituals performed at the central level by the emperor, notably the sacrifices prompted by droughts and other forms of celestial displeasure. Local representatives of power freely added popular and magical practices to their ritual activities, distancing themselves from the highly scripted and sedate imperial ritual code. The emperor's rituals may have remained hidden to the eye, but their more lively and less codified local variants were markedly present in the social fabric of imperial China.[98]

The emperor in Tokugawa Japan did not budge from his Kyoto palace complex. Leaving the palace would endanger the purity of the emperor, who was not supposed to pollute his elevated stature through hunting or other mundane activities embraced by his fellow dynasts around the world. In the palace compound he engaged in a round of ceremonies performed with his servants and the *kuge* court nobles. Highlights of the

---

[95] On the Burmese mission, see Pasquet, 'Quand l'empereur de Chine écrivait à son jeune frère'.

[96] Montesquieu, *Spirit of the Laws*, Book XIV, chap. 8.

[97] Du Halde, *Description*, II, 82.

[98] Snyder-Reinke, *Dry Spells*; see David Faure, 'The emperor in the village: representing the state in South China', in Joseph P. McDermott (ed.), *State and Court Ritual in China* (Cambridge, 1999), 267–98, on the role of Daoists and literati integrating imperial power in their roles at the village level. I leave aside here the Manchu shamanic and Buddhist rituals practised in the inner court: see Nicola Di Cosmo, 'Manchu shamanic ceremonies at the Qing court', in McDermott (ed.), *State and Court Ritual*, 352–98; and Rawski, *Last Emperors*, 231–63.

Shinto ritual calendar, including the *niinamesai* harvest festival, were celebrated at court. A special variant of the festival, the *daijosai*, took place when a new emperor shared newly harvested rice with his legendary divine ancestress. These rites remained invisible, but the population celebrated the same festivities and must have known about court traditions. Some emperors cultivated ties with elite and artist segments of the urban population of Kyoto, but their interaction remained restricted.[99] Only in the formative phase of the relationship between shoguns and emperors do we find exceptional processions outside of the palace. In 1620 Emperor Go-Mizunoo (1596–1611–1629*) was pressured to marry Tokugawa Masako (1607–78), the daughter of Shogun Hidetada (1579–1605–1623*). This highly exceptional instance of an emperor accepting a spouse from a warrior clan was celebrated by a splendid procession as well as by the building of a new palace.[100] Shortly afterwards, in 1626, the emperor and empress were summoned to proceed in state to the Tokugawa castle of Nijo in Kyoto.[101] After the abdication of Emperor Go-Mizunoo, the imperial dignity was again held by a woman: Hidetada's granddaughter ruled as Empress Meisho (1623–1630–1643*). In 1634 Shogun Iemitsu himself led a substantial military force to Kyoto to visit the court, a meeting that would not be replicated by his successors. No further direct contact between the shogun and the imperial court would take place until 1863: all communication was handled by intermediaries.

The shoguns, never as locked into their palaces as the emperors, showed themselves to the populace only in closed palanquins. Hunting was an appropriate activity for the martial shogun and it inspired frequent movement.[102] Shogun Ienobu in particular was a keen visitor of the hunting pavilion he constructed at Edo Bay. Among the few longer excursions of the shoguns we find the procession to the Nikko shrine, honouring Tokugawa founder Ieyasu. This particularly important dynastic pilgrimage was carefully cultivated by Ieyasu's first three successors. After 1700 it was

---

[99] Elizabeth Lillehoj, *Art and Palace Politics in Early Modern Japan, 1580s–1680s* (Leiden and Boston, MA, 2011), 192–4, on connections with the Kyoto population, including commoners. Towards the end of the Tokugawa, connections between commoners and the emperor became more frequent: see a remarkable example of a peasant woman visiting the emperor in 1862 in Anne Walthall, *The Weak Body of a Useless Woman: Matsuo Taseko and the Meiji Restoration* (Chicago, IL, 1998), 144–53.

[100] Lillehoj, *Art and Palace Politics*, 121–53, including prints of the painted folding screens representing the procession.

[101] Ibid., 155–65.

[102] See references to the shogun's and the princes' hunting in the calendar in Isaak Titsingh, *Illustrations of Japan; Consisting of Private Memoirs and Anecdotes of the Reigning Dynasty of the Djogouns, Or Sovereigns of Japan ...* (London, 1822), 115–44; Titsingh also lists the audiences of daimyo, or 'levee days', in his calendar.

performed only three times by shoguns in person: until 1867 an emissary was sent annually to represent the shogun in Nikko.[103] In Tokugawa Japan, we can conclude, ceremonies took place mostly in the palaces, far away from public observation. The exceptional processions of shoguns and their relatives in closed palanquins represented royalty to the people who could not penetrate the thick walls of Edo castle or enter the palace compound in Kyoto. The processions of Korean and Dutch emissaries (Plate 29a) indicated the power of the shogun, but surely the persistent, numerous, and impressive convoys of *daimyo* throughout the country were far more present in the public eye (Plate 29b).

Indirect representation and concealment were common elements of courts in Europe as well as in West and South Asia. In Europe, however, the great moments of the calendar more often than not were witnessed by the population. Following the calendar of seasonal and religious festivities familiar to the public at large, court celebrations often involved wider participation. The Christmas and Easter cycles in Europe entailed religious observances and processions shared by city and court at least in Catholic countries. In Vienna on several occasions, particularly during Holy Week, court and emperor paraded through the city with the religious orders, guilds, and other city corporations. Baroque piety welded together different segments of the population in a shared experience during great public processions and in more secluded settings. Catholic rulers adopted the practice of washing the feet of the poor during their annual re-enactment of the Last Supper; this *pedilavium*, copied from religious practice, became one of the prime indicators of sovereign status. Similar rites can be observed in Muscovite Russia (Plate 30b). Samuel Collins, an English physician serving Tsar Aleksei Mikhailovich in the 1660s, reported the tsar's Palm Sunday progress on foot with his *boyars* to church. In preparation, 'an hundred Scavingers' were sent out 'to clear the way', then the emperor,

accompanied with all his Nobility and Gentry, richly clad in cloth of Gold . . . goes to a Church, called Jerusalem . . . from whence after an hour he returns with the end of the Patriarchs Bridle upon his right Arm, whose Reins are four yards long, supported by three Noblemen behind his Majesty: The Patriarch fits sidelong upon an Horse covered all over with fine white Linnen, in his hand he holds a rich Cross, and blesses the people.[104]

---

[103] Personal communication from Anne Walthall (citing 1728, 1776, and 1843 as the isolated years of personal pilgrimages by shoguns).

[104] Samuel Collins, *The Present State of Russia* (London, 1671), 16, available online in an edition by Marshall T. Poe at http://ir.uiowa.edu/cgi/viewcontent.cgi?article=1000 &context=history_pubs; on the Palm Sunday ceremony, see also John Bancks, *The History of the Life and Reign of the Czar Peter the Great, Emperor of All Russia and Father of His Country* (London, 1740), 56–7.

In this re-enactment of Christ's entry into Jerusalem, the tsar served as equerry by leading the Patriarch's horse by the bridle. During a ceremonial procession on Epiphany, the Patriarch sprinkled the standing, bareheaded tsar and his boyars with water taken from a hole in the frozen river, before the people of Moscow took some of the water and put the sick in it to be healed. These characteristic rites stressed the supreme status of the Church as well as the tsar's position as first among equals, and included a marked element of popular participation. During the seventeenth century the choreography gradually changed, with the tsar occupying a more dominant position vis-à-vis the Patriarch and the nobles. In the 1690s Peter discontinued these ceremonies, but they were restored under his successors and in muted form continued until 1905.[105]

Popular participation could take many shapes. The coronation and election of the emperor, most often in Frankfurt during the early modern age, tripled the population of the city. Delegations from all over the empire converged in Frankfurt, with their presence attracting numerous others offering services of many kinds. Crowds witnessed the processions through the streets and received their share of the spoils. As soon as the emperor had passed, they were allowed to tear the rich cloth from the wooden plankings covering the streets. During the festive banquet, the electors or their substitutes performed a remarkable table service on horseback, ritually serving oats, meat, and drink to the emperor, while another elector threw coins to the public. These practices had been decreed in the Golden Bull of 1356, a key document defining the relationship between the emperor and the electors, but they persisted to the end of the Empire. Following the electors' acrobatics on horseback, the populace was allowed to rush in, enjoy the wine-spouting fountain, and tear down the kitchen with the emperor's festive roast. This *Preisgabe* of gifts to the crowd usually caused several fatalities, yet their involuntary sacrifice was accepted as a necessary ingredient of the proceedings.[106] In 1681, an envoy visiting the coronation of a new Hungarian queen

[105] Michael S. Flier, 'The iconography of royal procession: Ivan the Terrible and the Muscovite Palm Sunday ritual', in Heinz Duchhardt et al. (eds.), *European Monarchy: Its Evolution and Practice from Roman Antiquity to Modern Times* (Stuttgart, 1992), 109–25; Flier, 'Seeing is believing: the semiotics of dynasty and destiny in Muscovite Rus', in Nicholas Howe (ed.), *Ceremonial Culture in Pre-Modern Europe* (Notre Dame, IN, 2007), 63–88; Paul Bushkovitch, 'The Epiphany ceremony of the Russian court in the sixteenth and seventeenth centuries', *Russian Review*, 49/1 (1990), 1–17; Robert O. Crummey, 'Court spectacles in seventeenth century Russia: illusion and reality', in Daniel Waugh (ed.), *Essays in Honor of A. A. Zimin* (Columbus, OH, 1985), 130–58; Collins, *Present State of Russia*; on the Russian court at St Petersburg and its connections with the city, see Keenan, *St. Petersburg*.

[106] Duindam, 'Habsburg court'.

underlined the dominance of the imperial model by stating his surprise that 'no money was thrown, no wine sprang ... no ox was roasted'.[107]

Religion formed a point of contact in Russia as well as in Catholic Europe. Lutheran, Anglican, and Calvinist forms of piety seem less attuned to interaction between dynasty and populace, yet Protestant courts actively practised time-honoured rituals. When in 1660 Charles II returned to England as king, he immediately started touching his subjects for the 'King's Evil'. During his first six months on the throne he 'healed' over seven thousand sufferers of scrofula; in his entire reign around a hundred thousand were touched by the king, 2 per cent of the entire population.[108] William III discontinued the practice, but Queen Anne revived it, touching up to two hundred sufferers at a time, twice a week during the court season. Apparently her assiduity still left many eager applicants waiting. In 1703 the archbishop of York explained to one of these: 'There are now in London several thousands of people, some of them ready to perish, come out of the country waiting for Her Healing.'[109] In 1714 the royal touch was finally abolished with the advent of George I.[110]

Following his 1660 restoration, Charles II also took up avidly the Royal Maundy washing of the feet, a practice he continued even in plague years. From the late seventeenth century onwards, royals no longer washed the feet of the poor, but the ceremony continued in a reduced form as a symbolic act of royal charity. Interestingly, the single occasion where a Scandinavian king performed the *pedilavium* seems to have occurred in Stockholm in 1594, when the fervent Catholic Sigismund III Vasa (1566–1592–1599*) with his queen Anne of Austria washed the feet of twelve beggars.[111] In the Lutheran and Calvinist principalities and kingdoms of the Holy Roman Empire and Scandinavia, the ceremonies most directly

---

[107] Justus Eberhard Passer, 'Berichte des Hessen-Darmstädtischen Gesandten Justus Eberhard Passer an die Landgräfin Elisabeth Dorothea über die Vorgänge am kaiserlichen Hofe und in Wien von 1680–1683', ed. L. Baur, *Archiv für Österreichische Geschichte*, 37 (1867), 273–409, at 321; on echos of the imperial election and coronation in the Swedish coronation, see Fabian Persson, '"So that we Swedes are not more swine or goats than they are": space and ceremony at the Swedish court within an international context', in Birgitte Bøggild Johannsen (ed.), *Beyond Scylla and Charybdis: European Courts and Court Residences outside Habsburg and Valois/Bourbon Territories, 1500–1700* (Copenhagen, 2015), 123–36.

[108] Anna Keay, *The Magnificent Monarch: Charles II and the Ceremonies of Power* (London and New York, 2008), with numbers of people touched in the appendix.

[109] R.O. Bucholz, '"Nothing but ceremony": Queen Anne and the limitations of royal ritual', *Journal of British Studies*, 30/3 (1991), 288–323, at 298.

[110] Bloch, *Royal Touch*; Barlow, 'King's Evil'.

[111] Sigismund was deposed in 1599; he ruled Poland-Lithuania until his death in 1632. Fabian Persson kindly pointed out this reference to the washing of the feet of the poor, cited in Erik Gustaf Geijer, *Svenska folkets historia* (Stockholm, 1852), 321.

related to sacral status and biblical example do not seem to have flour-
ished, whereas coronations, weddings, funerals, and entries continued to
be performed.

The waning of conspicuous collective piety in eighteenth-century
Europe led to a reduction of religious meeting points, but this shift
entailed a transformation rather than a decline of contacts. Affluent
citizens drew closer to the court and its expanding sequence of social
entertainments, while other points of contact and forms of largesse were
made available to the wider population. During his personal reign,
Emperor Joseph II, the most radical of later eighteenth-century reforming
monarchs, discontinued some of the major rites connecting the dynasty
with popular pious ritual. At the same time, however, he took care to
broadcast his own outspoken variant of accessible rulership, conversing
with low-ranking Viennese townspeople in the service area of the
Hofburg, or interacting with peasants during his incognito travels. One
of Joseph's much-celebrated actions during his travels was the ploughing
of a furrow (Plate 27b) – an action resembling the Chinese emperor's
solemn and secluded ritual and fitting Joseph's ideal of strong-willed but
benevolent rule.[112] As in the case of Peter the Great, religious rituals were
resumed under Joseph's successors and would last until the end of
Habsburg monarchy.

The enthronements, birthdays, religious festivities, and seasonal festivals of the Mughal, Safavid, and Ottoman court attracted not only the
great dignitaries, who presented their tribute while hoping for nominations and honours. Lavish entertainments lasting several weeks accompanied the circumcision festivals (*sur-i-hümayun*) of Ottoman princes in
1457, 1530, 1539, 1582, 1675, and 1720, several of them depicted in
lavishly illustrated books. Other circumcisions were celebrated with less
pomp, but must have followed some of the habitual patterns. The sultan
witnessed processions of guilds and distributed largesse in a variety of
forms. Coins were thrown to the public, and banquets were organised for
several groups, including remarkable 'food scrambles' with crowds rush-
ing in to procure food. Also, the sultan paid for numerous circumcisions
coinciding with those of his own son or sons.[113] The festival aimed to
incorporate all social groups in one way or another, an ideal reflected in
the poem cited at the start of this chapter.

---

[112] On Joseph II ploughing in 1769, see Beales, *Joseph II*, I, 338, mentioning a 'repeat
performance' in Reichenberg in 1779.

[113] Murphey, *Ottoman Sovereignty*, 175–205; on food distribution during *garebeg* processions, see Karel Steenbrink, 'Groggy bij Garebeg: Nederlanders bij de Javaans-
islamitische feesten in Yogyakarta', *Indische Letteren*, 21/1 (2006), 57–69; Winter,
Beknopte beschrijving', 61–6.

The Safavid ceremonial style brings to mind European examples of religious humility: 'In popular imagination, the shah's public display of humility, such as his preferred titles as the dog or slave of the threshold of Ali, was fused with his personal deeds of humility, as at the sacred thresholds of the shrines in Najaf and Mashhad.'[114] Like many European rituals, it stressed spectacle and visibility rather than withdrawal. The Âli Qapu palace on the Maydan square, as we have seen, was a viewing platform allowing the shah to watch performances while enabling the public to see the ruler.[115] The Maydan (Plate 22) with its commercial and other urban functions served as a stage for splendid shows:

Military parades, mock battles with towers and fortifications built like a stage set for an opera – including, presumably, one instance of a naval combat for which a vast portion of the Maydan was filled with water and ships were floated – and equestrian sports and shows (a game of polo being supreme among them), elaborate fireworks, and displays of sudden and simultaneous lighting of thousands of torches and lamps number among the staged spectacles.[116]

Visiting grandees offering their *piskes* (gift-tribute) were integrated into the proceedings. As elsewhere, this was particularly relevant in the case of foreign missions, whose processions and gifts were often noteworthy.[117] Persian New Year (*Nauruz*), on 21 March, was the start of a festive period of several days, including celebrations in the palace as well as outdoor spectacles and equestrian sports. An 1818 description of Nauruz in Qajar Teheran highlights the presence of dense crowds outside the palace, the perfect dignity of the proceedings in the palace, and the lively attendance at the horseraces a few miles outside the city.[118]

Following a similar ritual calendar, the Mughals celebrated many of the festivals familiar from Ottoman and Safavid examples. Several ceremonies, however, show a special Mughal touch. The emperors practised a daily series of stylised public appearances on their viewing balcony, distant and aloof but visible. Abu'l-Fazl notes that after his morning devotions, Akbar would show himself to 'people of all ranks'.[119] Shahjahan's chronicler Lahori added later that Akbar consciously planned the viewing (*jharoka-i darshan*) in the early morning hours 'to enable his Majesty's subjects to witness the simultaneous appearance of the sky-adorning sun and the world-conquering emperor'.[120] Mughal emperors and princes celebrated their birthdays with a ceremony that fascinated European

[114] Babaie, *Isfahan and its Palaces*, 133.   [115] Ibid., 131–2.   [116] Ibid., 237.
[117] Ibid., 238.
[118] See a lengthy description of the 1818 *Nauruz* ('nowroose') festivities in Teheran rather than in Safavid Isfahan by Robert Ker Porter, *Travels in Georgia, Persia, Armenia, Ancient Babylonia ... during the Years 1817, 1818, 1819, and 1820* (London, 1821), 316–36.
[119] Abu'l-Fazl, *Ain i Akbari*, I, 165.   [120] Cited in Necipoğlu, 'Framing the gaze', 314.

observers. Twice every year, following the lunar Islamic and the solar calendars, they were weighed. Precious articles were put in the scales, ranging from jewels and gold to iron, silks, and edibles. Abu'l-Fazl listed Akbar's two birthdays (15 October and 5 Rajab) and outlined the various articles used for weighing him. On these occasions, he continued, 'animals are set free as usual' and 'donations, or grants of pardon, are bestowed upon people of all ranks'.[121] Seventeenth-century travellers reported the ceremony with keen interest, focusing on the rich furnishings of the pavilions erected for the weighing and the precious jewellery put in the scales. They describe the arrival of numerous grandees bringing their tributes, who admired the riches in the scales and rejoiced loudly when the emperor had gained weight. The festival lasted five days and included outdoor performances such as firework displays and battles of elephants. The role of the city inhabitants is less clear, although one traveller noted that 'For five days everybody rejoices in the city as well as in the palace.'[122] Mughal paintings depicting the weighing and viewing ceremonies do not tell us much about the presence of outside audiences: the focus is on the elites, arranged harmoniously and hierarchically at the feet of the emperor. It is unclear whether the 'people of all ranks' underlined in Abu'l-Fazl's idealised view were present; we cannot ascertain confidently either that the populace remained involved or that it became more distanced in the course of the seventeenth century.

Justice played a part in most ceremonial calendars: amnesties were pronounced on ceremonial occasions; conspicuous acts of mercy – in the Mughal case apparently including beast as well as man – were performed.[123] Mehmed IV announced a general amnesty for prisoners during the 1675 circumcision festival, a practice common at the beginning of a reign.[124] During their hunting expeditions, sultans sometimes championed the rights of their people, showing mercy and reducing taxation.[125] In China, amnesties were announced on the occasion of anniversaries and enthronements. In Europe wrongdoers were pardoned during royal entries. Common people witnessed these practices and used them to their best advantage. A peasant woman from Troyes moved to Dijon to attend Henry II's 1548 entry and be pardoned for her crime. Two years later, on the occasion of Henry II's 1550

[121] Abu'l-Fazl, *Ain i Akbari*, I, 276–7.

[122] Jean de Thévenot, *Voyages de Mr de Thévenot contenant la relation de l'Indostan, des nouveaux Mogols et des autres peuples & pays des Indes* (Paris, 1684), 138–40, quotation at 140; François Bernier, *Voyages de François Bernier, docteur en medecine de la Faculté de Montpellier: contenant la description des états du grand Mogul, de l'Hindoustan, du royaume de Kachemire*, vol. II (Amsterdam, 1711), 51–65, with combat of elephants at 63–6; Tavernier, *Six Voyages*, 122–3.

[123] Abu'l-Fazl, *Ain i Akbari*, I, 276–7.   [124] Murphey, *Ottoman Sovereignty*, 192, 241.

[125] Ibid., 246.

entry in Fécamp, an apprentice dyer from Lyon travelled more than 600 kilometres to profit from the king's redeeming powers.[126] A steady stream of petitioners followed the trajectories of royalty to obtain grace. Others moved to the capitals to beseech the ruler's support in lawsuits and conflicts. The ceremonialised forms of mercy and justice were continued by institutions at centres of dynastic power on a day-to-day basis, a protracted and often frustrating process for the petitioners, who could rarely approach royalty directly there.[127]

Crowds witnessing ceremonies from a certain distance behind rows of guards were common in Europe and West Asia. Many ceremonies relied on the presence of cheering crowds attracted by the spoils as well as by the show, but active popular involvement in the ceremonies remained limited. Europeans present at the ritual high points at African courts were sometimes shocked by the violent and saturnalian character of celebrations. The Asante Yam festival (Plate 31) brought together all chiefs and tributaries of the Asante king – a pattern fitting the great ceremonies in Europe and Islamicate Asia. The English traveller Thomas Edward Bowdich reported that it opened a phase of lawlessness and licence for the population of the capital Kumasi: 'neither theft, intrigue, nor assault are punishable during the continuance, but the grossest liberty prevails, and each sex abandons itself to its passions'. During this phase of abandon, royal power was staged in a ferocious way:

All the heads of the Kings and caboceers [headmen] whose kingdoms had been conquered, from Sai Tootoo [Osei Tutu 1660–1701–1717] to the present reign, with those of the chiefs who had been executed for subsequent revolts, were displayed by two parties of executioners, each upwards of a hundred, who passed in an impassioned dance, some with the most irresistible grimace, some with the most frightful gesture: they clashed their knives on the skulls, in which sprigs of thyme were inserted, to keep the spirits from troubling the King. I never felt so grateful for being born in a civilized country.[128]

---

[126] Murphy, 'Royal grace', 293; on the Troyes woman and the Lyon apprentice, see also Natalie Zemon Davis, *Fiction in the Archives: Pardon Tales and their Tellers in Sixteenth-Century France* (Stanford, CA, 1987), 161, note 46; on pardoning and early European kingship, see Geoffrey Koziol, *Begging Pardon and Favor: Ritual and Political Order in Early Medieval France* (Ithaca, NY, and London, 1992).

[127] There is a rich literature on petitioning and litigation in Europe and on capital appeals in China. On the legal superstructure of the Holy Roman Empire, see (in English) Ralf-Peter Fuchs, 'The Supreme Court of the Holy Roman Empire: the state of research and the outlook', *Sixteenth Century Journal*, 34/1 (2003), 9–27; Karl Härter, 'The early modern Holy Roman Empire of the German nation (1495–1806): a multi-layered legal system', in Duindam et al. (eds.), *Law and Empire*, 111–31. On Qing China, see Jonathan K. Ocko, 'I'll take it all the way to Beijing: capital appeals in the Qing', *Journal of Asian Studies*, 47/2 (1988), 291–315; and Fang, 'Hot potatoes', 1105–35.

[128] Bowdich, *Mission from Cape Coast Castle to Ashantee*; the customs are described at 226–53, quotation at 226–7.

Bowdich expressed his horror at the sacrificing of slaves and convicts upon the arrival of new groups in Kumasi. He painted vivid scenes of drunkenness and immorality, caused by the king's free distribution of huge quantities of rum. In Dahomey the kings annually honoured their ancestors in a festival ('customs') that obtained special significance when a new king had taken power. He would organise 'grand customs' to demonstrate his rise to power, often after a difficult interregnum and a contested succession. We recognise again the convergence of tributaries, the gift-giving, and the distribution of spoils. As in the Asante case, defeated enemies, convicts, or slaves were sacrificed, and the population was invited to indulge in enjoyments of all kinds.[129]

African ceremonies manifest the transformative powers of ceremony, a trait not always taken into account in the description of European or Asian cases. Kingship can be hereditary or rotate among several houses; kings may well be elected by elders or other representatives; the candidate, however, becomes king only through the performance of ritual. The protracted ritual practised to turn the king-elect of the kingdom of Akuapem in Ghana into a king is likened in a proverb to the process of making oil from palm nuts. During the ritual following the election of a candidate for the throne, kingship – represented by the stools of ancestors – takes possession of the king. The ritual forces all participants out of their ordinary routines; it forces the king-elect to submit to challenges gradually conferring sacredness on him, bringing him back to ordinary life as a true king. Sacrifices were a necessary element of this undertaking on the margins of living and dead, connecting higher powers and ordinary humans. Among the Akuapem, animal sacrifice had replaced human sacrifice, but the participants still 'gasp in fear' when the blood of a castrated ram flows, understanding it as the sacrifice of a man.[130] In the increasingly worldly ambiance of eighteenth-century European scholarship, the German erudite Johann Jakob Moser denied that the intricate ceremonies in Frankfurt, with two sets of court dignitaries first stripping the emperor-elect and then dressing him in Charlemagne's costume, were necessary to transform the candidate into emperor – the question,

---

[129] Hérissé, *L'ancien royaume du Dahomey*, 178–94; Bay, *Wives of the Leopard*, 66–7, 125–8, 164–5, and, on changes in the ceremonial cycle, 213–22.

[130] Gilbert, 'Person of the king', on sacrifice (302) and transformation (316–20); I leave out of the text the extended discussion on ritual and liminality and on rites of passage: see e.g. Victor Turner, 'Variations on the theme of liminality', 36–52, and Terence Turner, 'Transformation, hierarchy and transcendence: a reformulation of Van Gennep's model of the structure of *rites de passage*', 53–70, both in Moore and Meyerhoff (eds.), *Secular Ritual*.

however, apparently was still judged relevant.[131] Wine-spouting fountains, the popular rejoicing following the *Preisgabe*, and the inevitable
ensuing casualties show that at least some European ceremonies retained
characteristics of the carnivalesque and of violence, so abhorrent to
Bowdich and others watching African spectacles.[132]

Sacrifices straddled the border between living and dead, infusing ritual
with transformative powers and providing supernatural guidance for royalty. The dignified Chinese Grand Sacrifices, distant in atmosphere and
style from African rituals, included libations and animal offerings: they,
too, were meant to assuage heavenly powers. The redeeming and transformative powers of the sacrifice of Christ stand at the heart of Christian
beliefs. Miraculous stories of Catholic martyrs and the often gruesome
torments they suffered before death underline the equivalence of painful
sacrifice and holiness. In Europe the most sacral of royal ceremonies were
founded on the redeeming powers of Christ, passed on by the king's
touch. The strong presence of bloody self-sacrifice in Christianity did
not inure the Spanish conquistadores to Aztec human sacrifice. Spanish
warriors in the Americas perpetrated violent deeds and were hardly
tenderhearted. Moreover, they had a cynical reason to overstate the
barbarity of Aztec human sacrifice, as this would form a keystone in
their argument in favour of enslavement and subjection of the natives.
Nevertheless, the awe of one of Cortes' companions, Bernal Diaz del
Castillo, rings true:

there was sounded the dismal drum of Huichilobos and many other shells and
horns ... and the sound of them all was terrifying ... we all looked towards the
lofty pyramid where they were being sounded and saw that our comrades ... were
being carried by force up the steps ... they forced them to dance before
Huichilobos and after they had danced they immediately placed them on their
backs on some rather narrow stones which had been prepared as places for

---

[131] Johann Jacob Moser, *Teutsches Staats-Recht: darinnen von des Römischen Kaysers Foro,
Absterben, Abdanckung und Absetzung, von der Römischen Kayserin, von des Römischen
Königs Wahl, Crönung, Regierungs-Antritt* ... (Leipzig, 1742), 15–16, 95; Moser, *Neues
teutsches Staatsrecht: von dem Römischen Kayser, Römischen König und denen Reichs-
Vicarien* (Frankfurt, 1767), 313, asking whether the coronation was indispensable.

[132] There are reports about executions of convicts integrated in festive entries, but pardoning surely was far more common: see Murphy, 'Royal grace'; Neil Murphy, 'Ceremonial
entries and the confirmation of urban privileges in France, c. 1350–1550, in Duindam
and Dabringhaus (eds.), *Dynastic Centre*, 160–84; and the story about a convict being
executed while performing Holofernes' part in a play on Judith and Holofernes on the
occasion of Prince Philip's entry into Tournai in 1549, reported in Frédéric Jules Faber,
*Histoire du théâtre français en Belgique depuis son origine jusqu'a nos jours: d'apres des
documents inédits reposant aux archives générales du royaume*, 5 vols. (Brussels and Paris,
1878), I, 14–15, questioned in Margaret E. Owens, *Stages of Dismemberment: The
Fragmented Body in Late Medieval and Early Modern Drama* (Newark, NJ, 2005), 24–6,
but confirmed in Paul Rolland, *Histoire de Tournai* (Tournai and Paris, 1956), 194.

sacrifice, and with some knives they sawed open their chests and drew out their palpitating hearts and offered them to the idols that were there, and they kicked their bodies down the steps, and the Indian butchers who were waiting below cut off their arms and feet and flayed the skin of their faces . . . and the flesh they ate in chilmole.[133]

Blood and sacrifice permeated Aztec culture, with ritual voluntary sacrifice playing a role in addition to coerced sacrifice. Conquest and the sacrificing of prisoners captured in raids or victims demanded as tribute were founded on the mythic aggression of Huitzilopochtli, who upon his birth killed the mother goddess and annihilated his four hundred divine siblings. Aztec sacrifice seems to have escalated in the decades preceding the Spanish conquest, with diminishing economic returns of conquest triggering domination and retribution through sacrifice. The small band of Spanish warriors, relying on the support of numerous discontented subjected peoples, demanded an even greater display of ferocity.[134]

The bloody show at the Temple Mayor in Tenochtitlan drew a razor-sharp line between insiders and outsiders, lords and slaves. Most dynastic rituals, from serene to violent and from secluded to public, defined and showed hierarchies. The choreography of distance and visibility differentiated the ruler from elites, ranks among the elites, and boundaries between insiders and outsiders, participants and spectators. Instrumental uses of ritual, overawing subjected populations, can be inferred from some of the descriptions offered here. Akbar, we have seen, carefully timed his public appearance to coincide with sunrise, impressing the spectators by combining the radiance of the sun with his own 'divine effulgence'. An awareness of the impact of staging and appearance of rulership was present across the world. The conscious withdrawal from public view, with royalty living in massive walled palaces and moving in closed palanquins, can be understood as a strategy of representation through concealment. Kings and advisors thought carefully about these matters. Louis XIV noted his subjects' apparent inability to grasp the complexities of government and their innate disposition to base

[133] David Carrasco, 'Myth, cosmic terror, and the Templo Mayor', in J. Broda et al. (eds.), *The Great Temple of Tenochtitlan: Center and Periphery in the Aztec World* (Berkeley, CA, 1987), 124–69, at 124–5; see a full translation in Bernal Diaz Del Castillo, *The History of the Conquest of New Spain by Bernal Diaz Del Castillo*, ed. David Carrasco (Albuquerque, NM, 2008); John M. Ingham, 'Human sacrifice at Tenochtitlan', *Comparative Studies in Society and History*, 26/3 (1984), 379–400.

[134] Ingham, 'Human sacrifice'; Carrasco, 'Myth, cosmic terror, and the Templo Mayor', 134–6, 153–6. The role of Moctezuma in the proceedings is not made explicit in these texts so it may be questionable to rank the sacrifices as a 'dynastic' ceremony.

judgement on 'what meets the eye': spectacle and splendour.[135] His variant of 'bread and circuses' included a keen eye for the ranks and appurtenances in public processions. A French ceremonial specialist somewhat earlier carefully pondered how fire, smoke, colours, 'lugubrious' sounds, rows of guards, canopies, and the positioning of key protagonists in processions would affect spectators.[136] Protestant German scholars of ceremony, who rejected the sacraments of the Catholic Church as unauthentic and unnecessary, by the later seventeenth century reluctantly accepted the Sun King's conclusion that the common people (the *Pöbel* or rabble as they would say) could be convinced only by outward show.[137]

Undoubtedly, those in power well knew that a fine show could make a difference. However, this did not mean they themselves were not spellbound by ritual; neither did it necessarily undermine their respect for the time-honoured scripts outlining their performance. Ritual mixed instrumental and mundane concerns with deeply held convictions: it stood at the heart of power and surely was more than a trick captivating spectators.[138] Democratic leaders, too, can wholeheartedly believe in their mandate and constituencies, while at times instrumentally using the inbuilt options of the electoral process to manipulate results. Are spin doctors undemocratic? Can politicians retract promises made during campaigns? A fully principled and consistent attitude will be maintained by some, whereas most will combine acceptance of the basic rules of the game with a willingness to use them to their best advantage. The same manoeuvring between ideals and pragmatic politics must have determined attitudes in premodern history.

Leaders, elites, and the populace at large accepted hierarchy and dynastic rule as an order sanctioned by celestial powers. Individual rulers and even dynasties that violated the moral rules dictated by tradition could be ousted, but others would take their place to continue the unchallenged order. Rituals confirmed the harmonies between terrestrial and celestial hierarchies, past and present, the mighty and the powerless. The shared experience of ritual could join groups and help to overcome strife and social tensions. Most ritual calendars included phases where ordinary rules and statuses were suspended during interregna or

---

[135] Louis XIV, *Mémoires*, ed. Dreyss, II, 15, 368.

[136] Duindam, *Vienna and Versailles*, 183.

[137] See Miloš Vec, *Zeremonialwissenschaft im Fürstenstaat: Studien zur juristischen und politischen Theorie absolutistischer Herrschaftsrepräsentation* (Cologne and Weimar, 1998).

[138] Geertz, *Negara*, 130: 'Power served pomp, not pomp power'; see a lucid discussion of the late imperial Chinese context in James Laidlaw, 'On theatre and theory: reflections on ritual in imperial Chinese politics', in McDermott (ed.), *State and Court Ritual in China*, 399–416.

carnival-like festivals, confirming hierarchy by temporarily allowing disorder. Rebellion created its own rituals subverting the language of power. The janissaries, slaves partaking of the sultan's 'bread and salt', overturned their soup cauldrons to signal their periodic defiance of sultanic power.[139] The language of ritual could be used by all, though rarely with impunity. Entries into European cities entailed a battle of symbols between rulers aiming to show their dominance and urban elites clinging to their privileges. Results depended on shifting balances of power.[140] With big audiences witnessing the proceedings, the stakes could be high for all participants.

For all examples discussed here, cosmologies, calendars, and normative orientations formed a foundation for repositories of ritual. These legacies were continually reinvented and applied to changing circumstances by designers and performers usually keen to preserve or restore tradition. Traditions varied immensely: scripted, serene, and learned rituals fitting in the Chinese imperial Confucian canon seem distant from violent and transformative rituals in African contexts – yet they share animal sacrifice and a grave concern with the harmonies of heaven and earth, the living and their ancestors. The responsibility of rulers for rainmaking indicates this shared background. Many rituals, we have seen, attracted grandees and tributaries, forming an occasion for receiving gifts and distributing rewards. Ceremonies and festivals, hence, were fundamentally intertwined with the rankings and rewards at the heart of the political set-up. Even in China, with its intricate rules for evaluation and relocation of magistrates, solemn events such as enthronements, dynastic births, or anniversaries were the occasion for bestowing honorific titles and special rewards.

Rulers, as the main protagonists of dynastic ritual, acted out a script based on their cultural and dynastic legacies. However, their performance was inevitably influenced by political contingencies as well as by their disposition and character. Extroverted characters loved to mingle with their subjects and widened the margins of access and interactions. Others painstakingly followed rules without questioning them, deeply convinced that ritual propriety formed the core of true royalty. Introverted and insecure figures hated the bustle of grandees and cheering crowds and escaped into the haven of the inner court. Traditions could be reshaped by personal idiosyncrasies, sometimes absorbed into the ceremonial record as age-old and unchanging rules. A sequence of several rulers with different approaches to their ceremonial roles can easily be mistaken

---

[139] Murphey, *Ottoman Sovereignty*, 30.
[140] Murphy, 'Royal grace'; Murphy, 'Ceremonial entries'; Margit Thøfner, '"Willingly we follow a gentle leader . . . ": joyous entries into Antwerp', in Duindam and Dabringhaus (eds.), *Dynastic Centre*, 185–202.

for a long-term development caused by the wider social, cultural, and political changes more often central to historians' work. While it is imperative to move away from dynastic history based on anecdotes and personalities, no attempt at a comparative or long-term history of dynasties can safely ignore either political contingencies or the impact of the personalities involved.

From court culture to popular culture

From the preceding paragraphs the role of intermediaries has become clear at several stages. These agents, moving between centre and periphery, were not the only carriers of the dynastic message. The imposing architecture and splendid show of the court exerted their influence beyond the outskirts of the capital. Court culture comprised palaces and ceremonial practices, specialised workshops, artists and designers, scholars and writers. The images created by the court, multiplied in numerous media, could spread over large territories. Images, objects, and stories generated could maintain the charm of the courtly centre for ages – at times persisting long after the collapse of the political entities.

Courts could be seen as the epitome of culture, savoir faire, and luxury. A connection between the court and polished social mores can be found in many places. African peoples prided themselves on the high culture of their court, contrasting its sophistication with the uncouth customs of outsiders.[141] The subsequent position of Italy and France as paradigms of European elite culture was at least in part based on the conspicuous courts of these regions, numerous and competing in the Italian case. Persianate court traditions, harking back to a pre-Islamic past, formed a powerful example in the western half of Asia – even in polities hostile to Safavid Iran, such as the Ottoman empire.[142] The politically marginalised Japanese imperial court still served as a ritual and cultural centre. Burgundy disappeared as a separate political entity in the late fifteenth century, but the reputation of its courtly splendour, dignity, and refinement was effectively appropriated by the Habsburgs, with the Order of

---

[141] Richards, 'Political system of the Bemba tribe', 111: 'The ordinary people do not attend the ceremonies except in the case of some inhabitants of the capital, but they value their secret nature and speak contemptuously of the Bisa and neighbouring tribes with less complex rites'; see similar statements on greeting and language in Drucker-Brown, *Ritual Aspects of the Mamprusi Kingship*; and see Southall, 'Segmentary state', 62, on peoples 'kidnapping' a king's sons to obtain their royal services, or asking the king for the favour of sending a royal.

[142] The Ottomans saw themselves as heirs of Alexander the Great and Persian kings – Achaemenids and Sasanids; they looked upon the Safavids as uncouth Turks (personal communication from Metin Kunt).

the Golden Fleece acting as the concrete centrepiece of this elusive but powerful legacy.[143]

The panache of court culture was often frowned upon. Moral censure of luxury and ambition at court can be found in all religious traditions as well as among Confucian literati in China. The idealised reputation of the court was perilously tied to its antithesis: a locus of greed, lust, ambition, and vanity. Popular proverbs in several European languages echo the German statement *bei Hof, bei Höll*, 'near the court, near hell'.[144] The eastwards march of court culture in Europe, visible in styles of palace architecture and court fashions, was perceived by some as the spread of moral corruption.[145] In China, it is doubtful whether the court can be seen as the model for polished social mores. The court in late imperial China, operating within the constraints and ideals of Confucian tradition, stood at the apex of the body politic without necessarily guiding elite behaviour. The literati elite depended on the court for careers and ranks, but its lifestyle was not built on the example of the court. Conversely, literati in or out of office associated the inner court with the pejorative downside of court reputations worldwide: excess, ambition, intrigue, and immorality. Parallels to the rich urban heartland of literati culture in Jiangnan province can be found in other regions where urban culture with its traditions based on commerce, learning, and religion formed a counterpoint to court culture.

The potential of the court to disseminate its image through a variety of media could be considerable. Illuminated manuscripts with texts, such as Ferdowsi's *Shahnama*, celebrated court traditions throughout the western half of Asia; great court events were likewise celebrated in illustrated manuscripts or, particularly at the Mughal court, in paintings. The patronage of mosques, markets, hostels, and schools, carrying the signature of their founders, underlined the benevolence of rulers. Coins distributed their titles and sometimes their profiles throughout the realm. Coins made expressly to be thrown at audiences during ceremonial occasions can be found in Europe (*jetons*) as well as in Islamicate Asia (*nithar*). Commoners in China were not allowed to possess images of their

---

[143] Duindam, 'Burgundian-Spanish legacy'.
[144] Helmuth Kiesel, *'Bei Hof, bei Höll': Untersuchungen zur literarischen Hofkritik von Sebastian Brant bis Friedrich Schiller* (Tübingen, 1979).
[145] Visconti, *Mémoires*, 13, uses 'Italian vice' for sodomy; the Palatine princess frequently used 'Franzoßen' as shorthand for sodomy as well as for venereal diseases: Elisabeth-Charlotte von Orléans, *Briefe*, ed. Wilhelm Ludwig Holland, 6 vols. (Stuttgart, 1867–81), on sodomy as 'franzoßen krankheit' or 'franzoßen' (VI, 94), and on 'franzoßen' for venereal disease (I, 172, 197). On 'mal de Naples' and 'morbus gallicus' in general, see Joan Lane, *A Social History of Medicine: Health, Healing and Disease in England, 1750–1950* (London and New York, 2012), 151.

emperor, nor did coins carry rulers' profiles – the same holds true for the Japanese emperor and the shogun. Rather than distributing their images, Chinese emperors acted as moral teachers, exhorting their subjects to behave in good Confucian manner, by erecting steles (stone slabs or pillars) with inscriptions. At various stages, the Ming founder also issued instructions in print to local officials, who were expected to regularly expound these imperial lessons to the masses. Qing emperors picked up the tradition and added their own exhortations.[146]

Print magnified the potential for the dissemination of royalty. The Chinese civil service examinations stimulated the production of numerous books for eager students seeking to enhance their chances of examination success. While these works cannot be read as 'imperial propaganda', they were necessarily imbued with the presence of the emperor at the apex of the edifice. From the late fifteenth century onwards, printing was present in the Ottoman empire, yet the first state-sponsored press founded in 1727 disappeared within a few decades. Printing was to be actively used as an instrument of Ottoman propaganda only in the nineteenth century.[147] Conversely, on the European stage the emergence of print was soon exploited by princes. Emperor Maximilian I experimented with illustrated prints to broadcast his reputation as a heroic knight and remarkable king. His interest in print did not prevent him from pursuing representation in many other forms, from armour, artillery, building, and painting to ephemeral shows.[148]

Prints, portraits, and statues created a world of royal representation that was no longer primarily connected to direct interaction and attendance at events. Books conveyed the proud splendour of processions and the thrill of illuminations, fireworks, and tournaments to outsiders; opera libretti showed the refinement of court culture to distant enthusiasts. An increasingly dense network of pamphlets, journals, and news books reported on court events. The splash of ephemeral court culture could not be captured wholly in these works, but they reached audiences far beyond the groups able to attend. Consequently, the battle of prestige

---

[146] Farmer, *Zhu Yuanzhang*; Farmer, 'The great Ming commandment (ta Ming ling): an inquiry into early-Ming social legislation', *Asia Major*, 6 (1993), 181–99; Sarah Schneewind, 'Visions and revisions: village policies of the Ming founder in seven phases', *T'oung Pao*, 87/4 (2001), 317–59; Victor H. Mair, 'Language and ideology in the written popularizations of the "sacred edict"', in Nathan Johnson and Evelyn S. Rawski (eds.), *Popular Culture in Late Imperial China* (Berkeley, CA, 1985), 325–59.

[147] John-Paul Ghobrial, 'Printing', in Ágoston and Masters (eds.), *Encyclopedia of the Ottoman Empire*, 471–4.

[148] Larry Silver, *Marketing Maximilian: The Visual Ideology of a Holy Roman Emperor* (Princeton, NJ, 2008); see the richness and variety of Maximilian's patronage in Eva Michel and Maria Luise Sternath (eds.), *Kaiser Maximilian I. und die Kunst der Dürerzeit* (Munich and Vienna, 2012).

among European courts was now extended into the domain of print. The festival books produced as programmes for the occasion or the descriptions published after the event did not necessarily faithfully reproduce the celebrations: they celebrated the success of the performance, making rival performances look pale and conventional.[149] Louis XIV's ministers organised a campaign to 'fabricate' the kingship of their prince systematically by creating or expanding royal academies. These institutions harnessed the powers of scholars and artists by granting them honorary memberships and pensions – a variant of the policies relating to rankings and rewards discussed above. Illustrated prints and numerous paintings described palaces and court festivities, while equestrian statues were placed in major urban centres throughout the country.[150]

The show of monarchical splendour in transportable and lasting media did change the parameters of courtly representation. It is far easier, however, to outline the top-down fabrication than to weigh the responses and attitudes of the wider population. Popular culture cherished its own views of royalty, in popular stories, songs, and verses, including good as well as bad kings. Top-down representation may have had a limited impact on these popular attitudes.[151] In the Holy Roman Empire, where the Habsburgs propagated their image far less actively than did the French kings in their realm, others stepped in. Jesuits were keen supporters of the dynasty, organising numerous events and publishing laudatory works. In addition, entrepreneurs throughout the empire, including Protestants, printed works friendly to imperial reputation, from pamphlets and broadsheets to medals and learned books. They were not in the service of the dynasty, but hoped to earn money. These indirect multipliers of the royal image defined views that imperfectly fitted dynastic representation. Emperor Leopold I was seen mostly as a clumsy but reasonable and mild figure, the antithesis of a war hero, who nevertheless stood between the Empire and its two main outside threats, the

---

[149] Helen Watanabe-O'Kelly, '"True and historical descriptions"? European festivals and the printed record', in Duindam and Dabringhaus (eds.), *Dynastic Centre*, 150–9; J.R. Mulryne et al. (eds.), *Europa Triumphans: Court and Civic Festivals in Early Modern Europe*, 2 vols. (London, 2004).

[150] Peter Burke, *The Fabrication of Louis XIV* (New Haven, CT, 1994); on the limitations of the statue campaign, see Roger Mettam, 'Power, status and precedence: rivalries among the provincial elites of Louis XIV's France', *Transactions of the Royal Historical Society*, 38 (1988), 43–62.

[151] Jens Ivo Engels, *Königsbilder: Sprechen, Singen und Schreiben über den französischen König in der ersten Hälfte des achtzehnten Jahrhunderts* (Bonn, 2000); Dorothy R. Thelander, 'Mother Goose and her goslings: the France of Louis XIV as seen through the fairy tale', *Journal of Modern History*, 54/3 (1982), 467–96; František Graus, 'Die Herrschersagen des Mittelalters als Geschichtsquelle', *Archiv für Kulturgeschichte*, 51/1 (1969), 65–93.

Turks and the French.[152] This reputation deviated from the heroic imagery of court spectacle, but was probably nearer to the mark. The Sun King's more active propaganda was countered by an equally active response: numerous libels and caricatures decried Louis XIV's military exploits and poked fun at his illicit sexual liaisons. In multipolar Europe, the printing press could never be monopolised.

In his *Characters*, Jean de la Bruyère, preceptor of one of the French princes of the blood, stated that 'The common people are so blindly prepossessed in favour of the great, and so enthusiastic about their bearing, looks, tone of voice, and manners, that if the latter would take it into their heads to be good, this prepossession would become idolatry.'[153] La Bruyère was critical and his statement implicitly judges the behaviour of the grandees. Roughly at the same time, the Dutch writer Pieter de la Court, sternly warning his compatriots against the perils of monarchical government, deplored the inevitable fondness of the common people for 'idle and foolish royal and princely pomp'.[154] Was the populace always in favour of royalty?

Numerous rebellions show that populations everywhere at times lost all confidence in their dynastic overlords or their advisors. Urban discontent, food riots, and peasant rebellions recur in European history from the thirteenth to the eighteenth century. This holds true for West and East Asia as well, although Chinese dynasties, the Qing in particular, developed sophisticated ways to alleviate urban food shortages. Rebellions often mixed with religious movements; moreover, they challenged a particularly bad ruler or advisor rather than the principle of dynastic power. Anti-Manchu sentiments, Ming loyalism, and an intriguing mixture of religious influences characterised rebellions in late Qing history.[155]

---

[152] Jutta Schumann, *Die andere Sonne: Kaiserbild und Medienstrategien im Zeitalter Leopolds I.* (Berlin, 2003).

[153] Jean de la Bruyère, *The Characters of Jean de La Bruyère*, trans. Henri van Laun (London, 1885), 221.

[154] Pieter de la Court, *Aanwysing der heilsame politike gronden en maximen van de Republike van Holland en West-Vriesland* (Leiden and Rotterdam, 1669), 9, citing the famous passage from Juvenal's *Satires* (Book X) on 'bread and circuses'.

[155] On rebellion in the Ottoman context, see Karen Barkey, *Bandits and Bureaucrats: The Ottoman Route to State Centralization* (Cambridge, 1994). On Qing China, see Ho-fung Hung, 'Cultural strategies and the political economy of protest in mid-Qing China, 1740–1839', *Social Science History*, 33/1 (2009), 75–115; Ho-fung Hung, *Protest with Chinese Characteristics: Demonstrations, Riots, and Petitions in the Mid-Qing Dynasty* (New York, 2013); Will and Bin Wong, *Nourish the People*; Li and Dray-Novey, 'Guarding Beijing's food security'. On riots and rebellions in Europe, see e.g. Julius R. Ruff, *Violence in Early Modern Europe 1500–1800* (Cambridge, 2001); Andy Wood, *Riot, Rebellion and Popular Politics in Early Modern England* (Basingstoke, 2002); Kaplan, *Provisioning Paris*.

Popular culture echoed the semi-magical potential of royals, but did not necessarily see them in a positive light. Where we have information on popular attitudes, they mirror the Janus-faced reputation of royalty, including just and virtuous princes as well as cruel tyrants. Sleeping kings or emperors awaiting their turn to succour their unhappy peoples can be found in several European folk stories.[156] Likewise prophecies announced the return of the Javanese messianic *ratu adil* (just king), who was invoked during many rebellions. Prince Diponegoro (1785–1855), the leader of the Java Rebellion (1825–30), viewed himself as the living embodiment of the *ratu adil*. His followers prized him as a 'human *jimat* (amulet) rather than as a battlefield commander'.[157] A belief in tsars or their offspring miraculously surviving violent usurpations persisted in Russian history. Here and elsewhere 'false pretenders' acting as survivors were hailed as saviours in popular movements, providing legitimacy and the chance of celestial support. Reflecting a similar state of mind, other legends relate how princes, expelled from court at an early age and raised elsewhere, were finally recognised as royals because of marks on their body or special objects in their possession. After proving their status by performing great deeds, they would recapture their rightful heritage.[158]

Kings and emperors were sometimes portrayed in popular stories as affable and folksy figures. In the *Thousand and One Nights*, Harun al-Rashid and his grand vizier wander through Baghdad at night, enjoy chance encounters with ordinary people, and right their wrongs. In one such story, Harun expressed his desire to 'go down into the city and question the common folk concerning the conduct of those charged with its governance; and those of whom they complain we will depose from office and those whom they commend we will promote'.[159] Numerous legends about Emperor Charles V revolve around the theme of his incognito meeting with simple peasants or artisans, enjoying their

---

[156] See an overview of 'sleeping hero legends' at the webpage of D.L. Ashliman, www.pitt. edu/~dash/sleep.html#Barbarossa, and a great variety of other categories at www.pitt. edu/~dash/folktexts.html#k (accessed 11 June 2014).

[157] Peter Carey, *The Power of Prophecy: Prince Dipanagara and the End of an Old Order in Java, 1785–1855* (Leiden, 2008), 124.

[158] Maureen Perrie, '"Royal marks": reading the bodies of Russian pretenders, 17th–19th centuries', *Kritika*, 11/3 (2010), 535–61, on other European stories at 561; Perrie, *Pretenders and Popular Monarchism in Early Modern Russia: The False Tsars of the Time of Troubles* (Cambridge, 1995); other examples in Thelander, 'Mother Goose', 472–5.

[159] Richard F. Burton (trans.), *The Book of the Thousand Nights and a Night* (s.l., 1885), 186; see other stories where the caliph and his Barmecid vizier Ja'afar move around Baghdad, discussed in Ulrich Marzolph and Richard van Leeuwen, *The Arabian Nights Encyclopedia*, 2 vols. (Santa Barbara, CA, 2004), I, 201–6, II, 487–9, 585–7; Robert Irwin, *The Arabian Nights: A Companion* (London, 1994), 122–5, 128, 198–9; and a general discussion of these 'urban legends' in H.T. Norris, 'Fables and legends', in Julia Ashtiany et al. (eds.), *Abbasid Belles Lettres* (Cambridge, 1990), 136–45, at 144.

pastimes and sharing their saucy humour. Upon discovering the true identity of their guest, the shocked peasants show obeisance while the emperor heartily laughs and pursues his way. Popular stories along these lines can be found mostly for rulers who represent a 'golden age', preceding a phase of strife and decline. This holds true for Harun as well as for Charles. The latter's image may have become so outspokenly companionable to increase the contrast with his son Philip, who in the course of the Dutch revolt was pictured in increasingly dark tones. One 'urban legend', probably originating in the late sixteenth or early seventeenth century, pictures a remarkable scene from Philip's 1549 Tournai entry, during a play staged for the young prince. A young convict playing the role of Holofernes was decapitated by a youngster playing Judith, in front of Philip who reportedly stayed unperturbed while coldly remarking 'bien frappé' (well struck).[160]

Popular Chinese stories represent emperors in various guises. Magical proportions were attributed to founding emperors: wondrous events accompanied their births and special marks were seen on their bodies. Their remarkable prowess and resilience indicated divine favour. Conversely, the last emperors of dynasties were cast as muddleheaded weaklings or debauched pleasure seekers. In popular historical fiction, the stereotype of the sage king was 'overshadowed by the common images of *baojun* (tyrannical ruler) or *hunjun* (muddleheaded ruler)'.[161] In addition hero-emperors can be found 'checking the misdeeds of officials and ... helping the oppressed'. A nineteenth-century story depicts the Qianlong emperor as a 'formidable fist-fighter' defending the weak.[162] In stark contrast to these images of heroic saviours, villagers in China represented the distant emperor as a dangerous dragon best left slumbering. A particularly negative view of power-holders in general was found in the far

---

[160] On the numerous stories about Charles, see Martina Fuchs, *Karl V., eine populäre Figur? Zur Rezeption des Kaisers in deutschsprachiger Belletristik* (Münster, 2002); Harlinde Lox, *Van stropdragers en de pot van Olen: verhalen over Keizer Karel* (Leuven, 1999); Joan de Grieck, *De heerelycke ende vrolycke daeden van keyser Carel den V.* (Brussels, 1674). The Tournai entry in 1549 is reported in Rolland, *Histoire de Tournai*, 194, and Faber, *Histoire du théâtre français en Belgique*, I, 4, 14–15; the story cannot be found in the long description of Philip's voyage by Juan Cristóbal Calvete de Estrella, *El felicissimo viaie d'el muy alto y muy poderoso Príncipe Don Phelippe ...* (Antwerp, 1552), 146–61 on Tournai; see discussion in Jody Enders, *Death by Drama and Other Medieval Urban Legends* (Chicago, IL, 2005).

[161] Chang, *History and Legend*, quotation at 132, with *pao chün* and *hun chün* changed to pinyin transliteration; on founding emperors and birth myths, 40–3, 170, 193; on evil last emperors, 150–3. Also see Sarah Schneewind, *A Tale of Two Melons: Emperor and Subject in Ming China* (Cambridge, MA, 2006), on Ming Taizu's responses to the story of two melons miraculously growing on a single stem.

[162] Wilt L. Idema, *Chinese Vernacular Fiction: The Formative Period* (Leiden, 1974), xix, with other and less flattering images at 26, 28–9, 124–5.

southeast corner of the Chinese empire. Villagers in Guangdong and Fujian remembered the arrival of central power on the local scene largely in terms of 'rivers of blood'. Invoking the emperor, village lore stressed, could have dire consequences.[163] These views may reflect an actual case of harsh retribution by the first Ming emperor against a local strongman, mixed with the extreme violence of the Ming–Qing changeover, and possibly boosted by experiences with contemporary communist leadership. The origin of the negative image cannot be established beyond doubt; neither is it clear how strong this view may have been elsewhere in the empire, or whether peasants were generally more distrustful of imperial power than literati elites.

Peasants in the southeast corner of the Chinese empire lived some 3,000 kilometres away from the Chinese imperial capital. Most of these villagers rarely encountered the county magistrate, but might see his underlings once in a while. Notwithstanding the huge distance and the marginal presence of agents from the centre, imperial power was ubiquitous in folklore and daily practice. Emperors were present not only as fearful avengers. Stories related how a Song boy-emperor fleeing the Mongol onslaught aboard a ship was found dead on the coast; his memory was honoured in a shrine maintained by lineages with the Song imperial surname Zhao. Other lineages claimed special status on the basis of their alleged descent from a Song princess. Literati lineages constructed their ancestral halls and celebrated their genealogies, always fitting their filial piety in an overall scheme of loyalty to the emperor. Magistrates performing the sacrifices of the state religion at the local level made clear that hierarchies on earth and in heaven were connected. A stele dedicated to a city god in the late imperial period stated that 'While it is the magistrates who rule in the world of light, it is the gods who govern in the world of shadows. There is close cooperation between the two authorities.'[164] Yet the imperial dignity had more powerful proxies. The Jade Emperor, a Daoist divinity, figured prominently among the gods in local religion: 'Petitions sent to heavenly deities, audience rituals adapted from what the priests believe to be court ceremony ... are symbolic of the villager's representation of imperial authority.'[165] Daoist priests guiding the village rituals 'intercede between local deities and the heavenly pantheon in much the same way as the imperial magistrate might have interceded

---

[163] Watson, 'Waking the dragon', with the opening quote: 'The Emperor is like a sleeping dragon. You wake him at your own peril.'

[164] Lloyd E. Eastman, *Family, Fields, and Ancestors: Constancy and Change in China's Social and Economic History, 1550–1949* (Oxford, 1988), 58; see also Chang, *History and Legend*, 166–7, 188.

[165] Faure, 'Emperor in the village', 273.

between local politics and the state'.[166] The intermittent activity of imperial agents in the region mixed with numerous other practices and customs, fitting villagers under the ritual-cultural umbrella of the Chinese imperial state.

Differing experiences of royalty among the population at large led to a continuum of views from idealised to menacing figures. In popular fiction, clichés of the charismatic but sometimes violent first emperor and the weak last emperor form the familiar extremities of a world that includes sage-kings as well as lascivious characters. They all fit into a worldview predicated on the inevitable presence of an emperor.[167] Images of kings and emperors were strongly present among populations in China and elsewhere. Folk perceptions of dynastic power made room for villains on the throne, but never called into question the principle of kingship.[168] Chardin reports that Persian expressions indicated a deep distrust of royalty. The phrase 'act the king' could be rendered as 'repress somebody and violate justice': variants of the saying all suggest the profound unreliability of kings. Nevertheless, obedience and loyalty were taken for granted, as was the supernatural aura of kings.[169]

Persistence and change

Looking at the connections between royalty and populations, continuity and congruity of form strike the eye. The household was the starting point for networks based on presence and representation. The ideals of hospitality and largesse were demonstrated on a grand scale in most dynastic centres. Elites were attracted by a variety of honours and perks; they brokered access to these benefits for others. Vital for dynastic rule, the intermediaries often shared some of its characteristics: a household and a show of power. United under a single dominant court, the miniature courts of the grandees functioned like the components of 'galactic polities': their cohesion was maintained by the potential of the exemplary centre to attract, punish, dismiss, reward, and promote. Rituals were a formative experience as well as an occasion for effecting reallocation.

---

[166] Ibid., 274.

[167] Harold L. Kahn, 'Some mid-Ch'ing views of the monarchy', *Journal of Asian Studies*, 24/2 (1965), 229–43, on 'unofficial histories' at 236–40; Robert Rhulman, 'Traditional heroes in Chinese popular fiction', in Arthur F. Wright (ed.), *The Confucian Persuasion* (Stanford, CA, 1960), 141–76, on the prince at 155–61; Chang, *History and Legend*, 129–56, stresses (147) that disapproval of individual bad rulers never developed into a critique of the imperial institution.

[168] D.L. Ashliman, *Folk and Fairy Tales: A Handbook* (Westport, CT, 2004), 16.

[169] Chardin, *Voyages*, V, 214–24, explains critical attitudes vis-à-vis the shah, and presents a series of alleged 'deathbed sayings' conveying the normative ideals of kingship (90–7).

While the connections between rulers and elites can be traced with some precision, the attitudes of the wider population can only be surmised from limited and uncertain sources. Folk stories described incompetent or malicious individual rulers, but developed no alternatives to dynastic power. The overall legitimacy of dynastic power remained unscathed until the revolutionary wave of the later eighteenth century.

The apparent congruity and continuity of these forms is correct only in a limited sense. All dynastic forms of power frequently experienced phases of crisis and renewal caused either by external conquest or by gradual inner disintegration. The permanent requirement to pacify intermediary elites through the distribution of honours drained the centre and pushed towards devolution. Ongoing conquest, replenishing the potential for distribution, could bring temporary relief. In the longer run, however, it engendered overextension and financial crisis. Polities subject to severe fiscal-military crisis frequently opted for solutions bringing cash without delay: the sale of offices or titles, the auctioning of rights of taxation, and other practices now subsumed under the label of privatisation. Such short-term solutions eroded the powers of the centre and frequently led to rebellions. Sometimes dynasties could avert breakdown by inaugurating sweeping reform. Often reform was implemented as a consequence of breakdown and violent dynastic change, with a strong new first emperor or post-rebellion strongman restoring order.

These fluctuations bring to mind Ibn Khaldun's cyclical model: rulers rose to power through the support of their armed retainers, but consolidated their dynasty and established a luxurious sedentary lifestyle with the help of administrative elites. In the process they forsook the *asabiyya* (group feeling) of their original supporters: continuous rewards were now required to maintain loyalty among their new followers. This constant demand on the state coffers led to the exploitation of the common people and opened the way to conquest by fresh desert tribes.[170] While luxury and exploitation of the people are given as the causes of decline both in Ibn Khaldun's model and in the classic representations of the Chinese dynastic cycle, the changing relationship between rulers and their military-administrative elites can be seen as the main force at work, in addition to outside pressures. European countries experienced the same 'dynastic cycle' in miniature, with the successes of Spain and France in the sixteenth and seventeenth centuries respectively leading to phases of overextension and financial crisis. Urgent financial needs were

---

[170] See many passages in Ibn Khaldun, *Muqaddimah*, 97–100, 188–90, 231–56, and remarks about population at 255–6 that can be connected to Jack Goldstone, *Revolution and Rebellion in the Early Modern World* (Berkeley, CA, 1991), who presents demography as the main agent in this process.

solved by short-term solutions that brought in ready cash, but in the long run empowered vested elites and undermined the state's capacity for reform. The lasting success of several European states from the eighteenth century onwards is a powerful exception. However, it cannot be dissociated from the global military hegemony that developed in the same period, and it is intertwined with the major economic and political breakthroughs that ended the early modern period. Distribution of graces, a key instrument of all premodern polities, could easily lead to erosion of central powers. The ties created though patronage were increasingly fitted into administrative rules and procedures, but these innovations never entirely replaced personal contacts and networks of loyalty.

Continuity took shape as the sequence of rise and fall and the repeated reinvention of age-old maxims of dynastic power in a range of different polities. Nevertheless, the sequence of disruptions and restorations could go together with a gradual strengthening of the political centre. Techniques of resource extraction, military power, and administrative control waxed in Asia as well as Europe in the centuries discussed here.[171] This process, following different formats in various regions, did not stop in 1789 or 1815. Napoleon put together a variety of images and stratagems of dynastic power, mixing them with sound administrative logic. He combined expanded state institutions with a redesigned monarchical apparatus, a pattern imitated by most Restoration kings. The dignities of the Legion of Honour and the spoils of conquest throughout Europe were used to form a new elite assimilating former revolutionaries and ci-devant nobles on the basis of their loyalty to Napoleon, a policy matching that of numerous earlier successful conqueror-kings. The presence of Napoleon in French folk culture, moreover, shows how a short-lived, powerful ruler could obtain a formidable place in the minds of people. Former soldiers telling miraculous stories to peasants, peddlers selling cheap printed images and tales about the emperor, local museums stockpiling memorabilia, together created a legend that permeated all social layers. Typically the legend assimilated views ranging from the invincible general and the righteous lawgiver to the ogre condemning endless numbers of youths to an early death on the battlefield.[172]

Congruity, too, needs to be qualified: scale and development did make a difference. The big royal households of small African kingdoms could

---

[171] This is one of the conclusions in Lieberman, Strange Parallels.
[172] See Honoré de Balzac, Histoire de l'empereur (Paris, 1842), on soldiers telling their stories to a peasant audience; numerous soldiers on half-pay propagating Napoleonic legend populate the novels of Balzac's Comédie humaine, outlining a process that seems plausible for this as well as for some earlier periods. On the legend, see Sudhir Hazareesingh, The Legend of Napoleon (London, 2005).

literally bring together the realm, at times welcoming the heads of all important lineages and including people from every village in their staffs. This was not feasible for the bigger empires in Asia or for most European polities. The machinery of government varied immensely from immediate and personal 'open-air government' in Bamoum to lengthy formalised paperwork in China. The direct exchange of goods through tribute and largesse in small-scale polities could not be practised in major kingdoms and empires, where fiscal extraction and central redistribution were organised through numerous intermediary bodies and would be expressed in bullion or currency rather than in goods. Nevertheless, in the small kingdom of Mamprusi, chiefs represented the power of the king in villages, as did the great *mansabdars* throughout the extended realm of Mughal India. 'Paramount' kings were almost by definition chiefs-of-chiefs, but the intermediary layers separating king and population could vary from single to multiple and from nearby to distant.[173] The polities at the greatest remove in terms of scale and development also differed in styles of ritual and behaviour. Nevertheless, the key responsibilities of the Chinese emperor overlapped with those of most African kings, treading the thin line between ancestors and the living, heaven and earth. Many characteristics of complex and extended polities can be understood as extensions and differentiations of patterns found in the less developed areas. The growth of specialised institutions somewhat reduced the role of the incumbent king in government and war, yet an ineffective ruler unwilling to listen to his advisors could still wreak havoc. Conversely, less differentiated polities found ways to solve the problem of weak rulers. In Africa and elsewhere, most kings reached the throne through competition, and could be forced to resign when they no longer fulfilled their tasks according to the expectations of their elites.

Reputation determines the strength of any person or institution. This truism, often stated by Louis XIV, is equally relevant for our age. Companies rely on advertising, and they know that share prices on the stock exchange can respond dramatically to bad news. States predicate their international actions on credibility and prestige as much as on other criteria. At the personal level, the demands and possibilities of representation have been escalated by the Internet. These examples of contemporary attitudes should make it easy for us to understand how polities based on the relationship between rulers and elites as well as on the perceptions of wider audiences could persist ad infinitum.

---

[173] Claessen, 'Kings, chiefs and officials', 204, defines the two-level structure as a chiefdom, the three-level structure with intermediaries between the king and local chiefs as typical for an 'early state'.

Intermediaries were attracted by rewards, intimidated by the risk of retribution, and charmed by the show of power in which they themselves occupied an important place. Wider populations commonly viewed dynastic power only from a distance, as a *Wayang* or shadow play projected onto the horizon. Their distant view, however, included all elements necessary for basic compliance: images of moral rectitude and celestial endorsement mixed with bloody action and fierce retribution. These powerful contrasting images were enough to secure compliance as long as the king or emperor remained distant and his local agents were not unduly demanding. Natural disasters, wars, and the misbehaviour of local power-holders could stir populations to ask the paramount for help or to rise in rebellion against his unjust rule. In the end, whether or not the ruler was ousted or a new dynasty ascended to power, the situation was restored – with a new set of memories entering folklore.

Only during the protracted redefinition of political authority and global power balances between 1750 and 1918 did this process change radically and irreversibly. Which elements of the dynasty and household-based form of government persist into our own age? How can this book serve to reconsider the role of dynastic power in global history?

Conclusion

I see a good king, I die happy.

> Woman embracing the knees of Louis XVI on 21 June 1786
> during his visit to Cherbourg.[1]

We have a great resource in the paternal feelings of the king and I cannot tell you how much love and respect he inspires in us.

> Jean-François Campmas, deputy to the Estates General in a letter to his
> brother, 30 May 1789, cited in Timothy Tackett, *Becoming a
> Revolutionary* (Princeton, NJ, 1996), 151.

One cannot reign innocently. The folly of doing so is evident. Every king is a rebel and a usurper. Did kings themselves treat differently the usurpators of their authority?[2]

> Saint-Just, 'Discours concernant le jugement de Louis XVI',
> 13 November 1792.[3]

Outcomes

How can this bird's-eye view of themes in global dynastic power contribute to our understanding of the human experience? After recapitulating some outcomes of the previous chapters, I will consider regional typologies and change over time, and finally explore the legacies of dynastic power in our own age.

Kings and emperors were universally expected to safeguard harmony, justice, and the common good. Rulers held responsibility for the well-

---

[1] Évelyne Lever, *Les dernières noces de la monarchie: Louis XVI* (Paris, 2005), 294: 'Je vois un bon roi, je meurs contente.' Lever does not provide a source for these words, but several versions of the meeting can be found in contemporary sources; see Louis Pierre Couret de Villeneuve, *Recueil amusant de Voyages, en vers et en prose; faits par différents auteurs, auquel on a joint un choix des epîtres, contes & fables morales qui ont rapport aux voyages* (Paris, 1787), 5–6.

[2] 'On ne peut point régner innocemment: la folie en est trop évidente. Tout roi est un rebelle et un usurpateur. Les rois mêmes traitaient-ils autrement les prétendus usurpateurs de leur autorité?'

[3] Louis Antoine Léon de Saint-Just, *Oeuvres complètes de Saint-Just*, ed. Charles Vellay, 2 vols. (Paris, 1908), I, 369.

being of their peoples and for the harmonious connections between heaven and earth. These ideals were taken seriously by princes and by their subjects, yet they took different shapes across the globe. In the Confucian canon, exemplary moral behaviour and ritual propriety were valued above political acumen or military activism. The ideal of the ruler as virtuous world-renouncer was strongly present in Indic kingship, yet it competed with the equally compelling model of the active world-conqueror. In the nomadic polities of Central Asia, prowess and martial leadership were indispensable assets for any ruler. West Asian sultans and European kings, too, were expected to lead their armies on the field of battle, to outmanoeuvre rivals, and to befriend elites. In Africa, outspoken martial and active ideals of kingship can be found alongside views stressing the ritual, magic, and moral supremacy that severely restricted the activities of incumbents. The status of Confucian literati, Brahmins, Buddhist or Daoist monks, *ulema*, African witch doctors, and Christian priests, as well as the measure to which the ruler himself could aspire to a supreme sacral role, moulded dynastic traditions. The moral role of the king was perhaps most pronounced when no separate religious hierarchy existed and the ruler in person held supreme responsibility for the balance between heaven and earth, the living and their ancestors. Rulers could engage more easily in potentially polluting political activities where others held prime responsibility for propitiating higher powers.[4]

How did youngsters learn to become kings and what did it mean for them to hold this inflated and exposed position, sometimes for their entire lives? Everywhere princes shouldered a moral burden they could rarely fulfil; everywhere there was a clash between moral responsibility and the demands of ruling. Even the more attainable virtues of rulership demanded moderation and insight: largesse risked turning into profligacy, yet self-restraint could easily become stinginess – painfully inappropriate for any king. Educators of royalty needed to instil in their pupils the capability to balance contradictory ideals and irreconcilable demands. This task was complicated by the contrasts among personalities groomed for the throne. How could tutors devise a single formula for dealing with stupid or bright, assertive or reticent princes? The burdensome responsibilities of kingship could intimidate princes into inactivity and withdrawal; alternatively they could trigger aggression and fickleness. Princes taking government in their own hands could be a calamity as well as a blessing. Little could be done against intractable and violent rulers, the spectre of dynastic power worldwide. Advisors tried to reduce the damage by invoking the moral catalogue and they bided their time. Bad kings were

[4] Webb, *Japanese Imperial Institution*, 18–19; Spellman, *Monarchies*.

added to the repository of examples used to teach princes; their misdeeds also permeated popular stories.

All kings experienced phases of weakness and frustration, unavoidably in adolescence and old age but frequently present in the prime of life as well. A show of royal omnipotence more often than not veiled ongoing competition among power-holders pursuing their own interests – with a dignified but unmoving chess-king in the centre watching the fray. This recurring situation could arouse resentment and suspicion in perceptive and well-intentioned individuals, whereas less talented incumbents might unperturbedly play the dignified role dictated to them by others. The elevated status not only circumscribed the activity of kings: it also made it difficult for them to establish satisfying human relationships. Once rulers cultivated close friendships, these friends could use the king's trust to attain their own goals. Even if they proved to be loyal servants, jealous rivals would decry their role as favourites. Trouble-free and peaceful family life was an exception in dynasties: succession strife frequently made spouses and children a source of anxiety and rivalry.

A vertical view of dynasty has become dominant, with downwards father-to-eldest-son succession emerging as the leading principle in Europe, East Asia, and many other regions. Male primogeniture was transported to – and sometimes wrongly perceived in – other realms by European colonial administrators, who hoped to establish uncontested continuity of local princelings under their overarching rule. However, dynastic power world-wide was never entirely dominated by primogeniture, neither was it always transmitted through the male line, nor was heredity the only ingredient. In a majority of polities, men ruled and pedigree was defined primarily in male terms. In this patrilineal context, succession of eldest sons was sometimes prohibited, while horizontal ('sideways') succession to brothers or to cadet branches was common. Moreover, women frequently stepped in to secure continuity, temporarily acting as regents or ruling with full powers. Where succession was not conclusively fixed on the eldest son, heredity was sup-plemented by an element of choice. This entailed contestation but at the same time left room for rewarding individual qualities and for the participa-tion of outsiders in the process of king-making. Bloody interregna could be accepted as the inevitable cost of a process that led to stronger rulers and helped to reinforce connections with the realm. Powerful figures emerging successfully from the contest were seen as supported by divine favour. Charisma, in its double meaning of divine election and personal magnetism, was often more important than heredity.

Sideways succession allowed kingship to circulate among different seg-ments of the dynasty or even among different royal houses. In matrilineal systems of descent, men on the throne by definition could not pass on their dignity directly to their sons, since royalty could be transferred only by women. The ruler's sisters' sons or his uterine brothers succeeded: horizontal diffusion of succession rights and competition or election were common. Depending on the goodwill of electors, or on support among the powerful, rival candidates actively campaigned to obtain their position. Circulating and elective forms of rulership underline that heredity was only one of the building blocks of dynastic power. A combination of circulating kingship, the powerful influence of elders as kingmakers, and the practice of destoolment can be found among many African peoples. On closer inspection, numerous examples of succession through circulation and election emerge in medieval Europe, Southeast Asia, and elsewhere. A mixture of hereditary status, competition among candidates, and a measure of influence for relative outsiders remained typical for dynastic succession in many places. Forms of elective and circulating rulership suggest that dynastic power mixed characteristics usually seen as typical of either monarchy or aristocracy in contemporary European political discourse.[5] Fixed rules defining the eldest son or the eldest male royal as successor became common in polities where established military and administrative hierarchies made the personal qualities of the king as general or leader somewhat less essential: in these domains repeated violent succession disputes entailed greater risks than a weakling on the throne. Nevertheless, this tendency never became a general rule, nor can we establish with certainty the motivation behind changes in succession patterns.

Succession rights universally generated conflict: incumbent kings were often at loggerheads with males eligible for succession, seeking alliances instead with families distant from such rights. A comparison of patrilineal and matrilineal succession shows that contrary definitions of descent can reverse alliances: paternal relatives, rivals in patrilineal settings, become harmless allies in matrilineal polities – and vice versa. Dynasties are cultural constructions usually emphasising either male or female descent; dynastic power networks, however, can be traced effectively only by including both male and female lines. Matrilineal succession among the Asante in practice coincided with the alternating kingship of two male houses: a king's sons, ineligible for the throne, married female royals, making it possible for a king's grandsons to ascend to the throne.[6] Alliances contracted through marriages of royal women were equally important in patrilineal societies. Many examples can be given of emperors, kings, or sultans giving their sisters and daughters in marriage to their key supporters. European dynasties formed a dense network of marriage

---

[5] See examples in Beattie, 'Checks on the abuse of political power'.
[6] Wilks, *Asante in the Nineteenth Century*, 327–73.

alliances, an inextricable knot of male and female connections. Everywhere, women could hold leading positions as mothers and sisters of the male prince. They were key intermediaries transferring power from generation to generation, linking the dynasty to its supporters, or tying together a patchwork of dynasties. However, an ongoing line of female paramount rulers remains the exception. Women ascended to the throne most often as an ad hoc solution for the absence of suitable male candidates. Powerful and effective queens sometimes started a series of female successions, but in almost all cases male rule again predominated after a few generations.

Rulers treated male royals eligible for succession in remarkably similar ways. Two patterns can be found around the world: princes were either sent out to govern frontier areas, or they were kept close to the court under some form of supervision. The Islamicate empires of West and South Asia shifted from the first to the second option, a change coinciding with the abandonment of violent contestation for the throne. Elsewhere, too, the two variants can be found alternating in different periods. The tension between the ruler and his potential successors was one of the constituent elements of infighting at court. Supreme birth rank and eligibility for succession created a potential for conflict with the incumbent ruler and made leading positions in central government questionable.

Dynastic rule took shape in the extended family of kings. This household of spouses, kin, servants, administrators, and soldiers varied from highly mobile to sedentary: it combined characteristics of a warband and a cloister. Courts of nomadic rulers camped near cities and cultivated urban life; most sedentary courts located in great capitals still moved regularly. The differentiation of government routines demanded a fixed residence for specialised services and their record-keeping. Administrators tended to move outwards from the domestic core of the court. A growing separation between relatively static administrative services and more mobile domestic staffs can be found in many places. The physical separation between domestic and administrative services was deepened by the divide between male and female domains. Polygyny was almost universal in the world of dynastic rule: it was prohibited only in Christian Europe. The secluded female inner quarters of polygynous courts were barred to all men except the prince and his emasculated harem servants. Numerous rulers fixed their abode in the harem and limited their strenuous contact with the outer world to a series of well-defined interactions: intermediaries and intermediate zones became necessary for the consultation between administrators and rulers. This recurring situation turned inner court confidants into key political operators. At most Asian and many African courts, a relatively sharp boundary separated innermost female quarters adjoining the ruler's apartment from outer sections of the court devoted to administrative purposes, hospitality, and interaction with a wider public. A restriction of access into the domestic heart of the court can be found in Europe, but the separation between domestic and administrative or male and female domains was far less rigid here.

The inner–outer divide was reflected in palace layout and court organisation. Staffs were responsible for different activities, moving outwards from the inner core around the ruler: sleeping, hospitality, movement, government. The inner staffs could influence the ruler once he withdrew and relaxed; outside magistrates held leading political offices and offered advice. High birth rank did not necessarily confer access to either of these domains. Rank, access to institutions of decision-making, and access to the ruler created overlapping, but never entirely coinciding hierarchies. High-ranking princes or nobles could find themselves excluded from leading political office. Few leading administrators or high-ranking grandees were able to fully control the daily and nocturnal environment of the prince. Therefore inner–court female, eunuch, or male confidants were often able to outsmart their outer court rivals by manipulating the sovereign. The hierarchies based on rank, access to the institutions of decision-making, and access to the prince, created different power groups; yet within each of these segments there was strife. Inner and outer interests could at times be opposed *en bloc*, but more often grandees, outside ministers, and inside domestics and concubines sought support in the opposite domain against rivals in their own direct environment. In each of these spheres, patrons commanded the loyalty of supporters at court and elsewhere. Socially and functionally diverse alignments based on personal loyalties formed the most persistent and lasting power groups at court.

Servants at court, catering for the daily needs of the ruler and organising the representation of dynastic power, have rarely been studied as agents pursuing their own interests. The sources available, however, strongly suggest that they actively intervened in the distribution of honours at court. Major policy choices were out of reach for most of them: only leading advisors and key inner court confidants could expect a prominent role here. However, all personnel serving in person the ruler, his spouse, or one of their leading office-holders could hope to share in the spoils – nominations, rewards, honours. Petitioners frequently tried to obtain a foothold at court by asking these servants to act as go-betweens.

Uncovering the agendas and actions of subservient staff is one of the most relevant, but also most difficult questions of court 'politics'. It was not in the interest of these groups to openly manifest their ambitions: they operated best under the veil of deference and respect for royal supremacy.

This helps to explain why later observers have seen the court primarily as an instrument in the hands of the ruler: a temple celebrating his glory, a gilded cage confining grandees, and an arena allowing him to play groups and individuals off against their rivals. Each of these plausible metaphors can be supported by numerous examples and by verbatim quotes from sources. However, at the same time, multiple occasions can be found where the ceremonial show turned the ruler into a prisoner in magnificent confinement. Likewise, the astute prince ruling by fomenting competition among his elites can be contrasted with figureheads on the throne manipulated by dignitaries and servants. A varying set of examples – notably including Louis XIV's Versailles, Tokugawa 'alternate attendance', the cage (*kafes*) at the Ottoman court, and the 'Mountain of Royals' (Amba Geshan) at the Solomonic court in Ethiopia – has been understood as evidence of a general pattern of kings taming their elites.[7] This persuasive formula is imprecise and cannot be accepted as generally valid. These examples targeted different groups: royals eligible for the throne versus high nobles. Potential successors were more often controlled and confined than other elites. More importantly, the formula fails to leave room for the numerous cases where elite stakeholders of dynastic power monopolised the spoils and controlled the king. The instances where royal policies effectively outmanoeuvred powerful elites, reducing their power or replacing them with lesser-ranking and more pliable servants, rarely endured. After one or two generations, countervailing movements took shape, with the newly instituted elites reducing the power of the ruler – sometimes to a mere semblance. The persistent alternation of these processes is as obvious as the long-term tendency towards the strengthening of central power that can be seen in recent centuries, perhaps most particularly in Europe.[8]

How relevant was the show of power for society at large? How could the court hold together the extended empires and fragmented kingdoms of the premodern age? It was the hub of networks of hospitality, officeholding, marriage alliance, and patronage. Extended households with huge numbers of concubines and servants brought together people from many groups and regions, sharing in the ruler's largesse and hospitality

---

[7] Textbooks briefly refer to these parallels without examining or explaining them, e.g. Steven Wallech et al., *World History: A Concise Thematic Analysis* (Malden, MA, and Oxford, 2012), 350, on the Solomonids and Louis XIV's Versailles; Milton W. Meyer, *Japan: A Concise History* (Plymouth, 2009), 105, on Versailles and alternate attendance (also see this parallel mentioned in many scholarly works cited above); on the gilded cage and the classic view of Versailles as model for *ancien régime* rulership more generally, see e.g. K.J. Holsti, *Taming the Sovereigns: Institutional Change in International Politics* (Cambridge, 2004), 33–4.

[8] Lieberman, *Strange Parallels*, I, 533–41.

while hoping to better the future of their kin. Families sent their daughters to court and sought their spouses there; young boys stayed at court for a few years as pages or trainees before entering service or returning to their regions. Supernumerary servants in all staffs constituted a lasting connection with the outside world. Relatively numerous households in African polities included representatives of villages, lineages, and urban guilds from the entire country. European honorary supernumeraries, serving in rotation or only occasionally, broadcast court style to outlying areas. The inflated numbers of households connected many to the dynastic enterprise. Even in polities with extended hierarchies of administrators responsible for regional government, the household remained vital. At court, rewards, promotions, and punishments were meted out: dignitaries periodically progressed from the province to the centre, awaiting evaluation, carrying presents, and hoping for promotion. These intermediaries were more than vehicles of royal power: they acted as brokers of patronage, holding out the promise of advancement to their regional adherents while using their connections at the centre to generate rewards. Everywhere intermediary elites formed the backbone of dynastic power in the provinces. Attaching the *corps intermédiaires* to the court through a balanced distribution of honours secured at least a modicum of coherence in the realm. The emergence of powerful hereditary elites could undermine central dynastic power. Sophisticated systems of competitive training, evaluation, and relocation emerging in imperial China and elsewhere reduced the traditional role of such elites and prevented heredity in office at the individual level. The introduction of slave elites or other low-ranking outsiders in the ruler's household, too, checked the power of vested groups, although slaves as well as outsiders soon proved able to consolidate their positions. The same holds true for the disciples initially blindly following the lead of their charismatic spiritual leaders, the Safavid shah or the Mughal emperor. The administrative and coercive machinery of premodern government was never strong enough to control all layers of society directly: it retained its dependence on intermediaries and hence on the dynastic court. Conversely, the loose structures of dynastic government also help to explain the acquiescence of the populace: rulers and their agents most often remained behind the horizon.

Advantages and honours were not the only reason to move to the centre: in all realms a calendar of solemn ceremonies and festivities attracted participants and spectators. Chinese imperial rites were visible only for performers joined by a small group of male dignitaries; in Japan neither shogun nor emperor showed himself to the populace in outdoor ceremonies. The stately processions of *daimyo* lords and the magistrates performing rites locally in China underlined the dignity of a distant and mostly invisible ruler. Across the globe rites varied immensely in levels of popular participation, visibility, and styles – ranging from ferocious collective rejoicing to dignified proceedings performed in isolation. Rites could be used instrumentally by rulers to impress populations, yet these same rulers were most often deeply convinced of their own place between heaven and earth, mediating between the living and the dead. Taking people out of their ordinary daily habits, rituals could promote change, create cohesion, and transform the status of groups or individuals: the dignity of kingship was acquired during accession ceremonies. While rituals were most often viewed as eternal and unchanging, leaving little room for the designs of individual princes, any incumbent would slightly adjust conventions. Changes in ceremonial practice – withdrawal from the public, change of ceremonial styles – should be considered in the light of ad hoc adaptations and personal idiosyncrasies before they can be accepted as long-term developments. Rituals were defined by religious beliefs and fitted into liturgical calendars. Hence, changes in the forms of piety and religion did have an enduring impact on ceremony. In Europe, from the Reformation onwards and particularly in the eighteenth century, a questioning attitude towards sacraments and ostentatious collective piety undercut the festive and collective side of dynastic-religious rites, weakening an important component of traditional rulership.

Why did ordinary people accept the dominion of dynasty and court? The most important answer undoubtedly is that it fitted their view of a harmonious social order, sanctioned by heaven and celebrated in collective ritual. More than the consequence of top-down propaganda or coercion, support for dynastic power was ingrained in a widely shared mentality present in all social settings. The demonstrative show of royal power must have had some impact, even where the key players remained invisible behind screens, walls, and moats. The populace, however, was not necessarily swayed by the images emanating from the court. They appraised dynastic power in their own categories, including fearful images of ruthless tyrants as well as friendly paragons of virtue. Both the heroes and the villains supported the edifice of dynastic power: the Janus-faced view allowed the populace to explain deviations from ideals they approved of or in any case accepted as inevitable. A mixture of ideals, rewards, and threats, proportioned differently for various social groups, kept together dynastic realms. The populace might hope for support in times of hunger and for the righting of wrongs, yet their expectations were often disappointed. Ideally entitled to the paternal care of the ruler, they were not usually eligible for the honours and perks that tied the intermediary layers to the centre. The direct impact of dynastic rule – sometimes bloody, incidentally merciful – remained limited. In terms of popular culture and mentality, dynasty was everywhere: for most people, a world without rulers was simply inconceivable.

The preceding chapters considered examples of dynastic power over five centuries, across the globe, and in polities of very different character and scale. Changes were part and parcel of dynastic power: dynasties rose to power, consolidated their domains, and underwent phases of rebellion and reform. Several dynasties were able to survive remarkably long. The Japanese imperial dynasty secured demographic survival by common strategies such as adoption of successors from collateral lines and incidental female succession. Perhaps more strikingly, the conflicting roles of kingship were entrusted to different office-holders in Japan: the distant and untarnished emperor could survive more easily than the active hegemon. The Habsburgs in Europe show that a dynasty could endure while its domains and titles changed frequently: in every century the Habsburg dynastic enterprise obtained a markedly different character – and its long-term survival, too, depended on junior branches and female succession. Narrowly escaping extinction at several points notwithstanding the practice of polygyny, the Ottomans match Habsburg longevity. The Ottoman record, more explicitly than other cases, indicates that survival cannot be explained only by the dynasty's reproductive success or by the political acumen of its leaders. Many times Ottoman elites decided the fate of the dynasty, killing one sultan and enthroning another.[9] Why would these elites opt for a new dynasty, likely a figure from their own ranks, if they could reshuffle power arrangements and at the same time preserve the prestige of the house of Osman? Dynastic continuity was a collective effort here, with long phases during which sultans reigned under the tutelage of their mothers or powerful grand viziers. The accumulation of dynastic prestige was an important factor for the Ottoman elites as well as for the shogun, who accepted the emperor as his nominal sovereign. Habsburg prestige and the devotion of administrative and military services to the emperor defined the Dual Monarchy in the later nineteenth century. Imperial prestige was a key factor in China, but it could more easily be appropriated by a new rivalling house – the Chinese imperial tradition was never affixed to any single house: on the contrary, change of dynasties formed an accepted

---

[9] Murphey, *Ottoman Sovereignty*, 90: 'the reigns of 15 of the 33 sultans (45 per cent) who ascended the throne between 1389 and 1918 came to a premature end through deposition'; see the table in Alderson, *Structure of the Ottoman Dynasty*, 58. Compare the figures on Roman emperors between 44 BCE and 392 CE: 39 killed or dethroned, 5 killed in battle, and 19 dying peacefully; and Byzantine emperors between 395 and 1453: 65 deposed by force, 8 killed in battle and 39 concluding their reigns in peace, given in Bréhier, *Les institutions de l'empire byzantin*, 17. Note that neither in Rome nor in Byzantium was heredity ever as strong as in the Ottoman empire.

part of an ongoing tradition.[10] Everywhere, prestige was founded on legacies that predated the rise of a particular dynasty mixed with distinctive new claims. The Ottoman and Chinese cases indicate that the proportioning of specific dynastic achievements, most notably battlefield success, and long-term cultural legacies varied considerably.

Several of the realms studied here experienced a sequence of expansion and consolidation, coinciding with the changeover from open to more fixed patterns of succession and with the establishment of a capital city. These tendencies can be observed in West Asian Islamicate empires, but they have also been suggested for African kingdoms in the eighteenth and nineteenth centuries.[11] East Asian and European examples, too, appear to show a steady consolidation of central power. However, a long-term global view suggests that changes in dynastic power tend to be cyclical rather than linear: a repeated alternation of rise and fall coincided with the fusion and fission of dynastic domains. Charismatic new leaders replace their ineffective and weary predecessors, restore power, and strengthen the grip of the centre on the peripheries. Under their successors the once eager supporters of the dynasty gradually lose their dependence and loyalty: the restored empire starts falling apart. In his wide-ranging study on the sources of social power, Michael Mann toyed with the idea of a 'dialectic between two types of development', an oscillation between centralising 'empires of domination' and decentralised 'multi-power-actor civilizations': a view approaching that of Ibn Khaldun.[12] The cyclical view of dynasty, dominant throughout human history, does not easily fit recent history with its long-term tendency towards the strengthening of power centres. How can this global examination of dynastic power be aligned with the fundamental breakthroughs of state power occurring in recent centuries?

Global change and East–West typologies

This book examines comparative questions rather than linear historical change, yet its time frame coincides with a period of profound long-term

[10] This point is made with great clarity in Yuri Pines, *The Everlasting Empire: The Political Culture of Ancient China and its Imperial Legacy* (Princeton, NJ, 2012); it is equally valid for Byzantium and Rome, where short-lived dynasties fitted into the more durable concept of imperial rule: see Bréhier, *Les institutions de l'empire byzantin*, 17–26. Long-lasting examples and legacies can be construed for all dynasties; the Ottomans, for example, connected to the Persian tradition, to Islamic examples and the caliphate, to the legacy of the Romans, and to steppe traditions.

[11] Bay, *Wives of the Leopard*, 259–73; Ivor Wilks, 'Aspects of bureaucratization in Ashanti in the nineteenth century', *Journal of African History*, 7 (1966), 215–32; Wilks, *Asante in the Nineteenth Century*, xiv and chaps. 12–15.

[12] Michael Mann, *The Sources of Social Power*, vol I: *A History of Power from the Beginning to AD 1760* (Cambridge, 1986), 533–41.

transformation concentrated in Europe: the strengthening of global connections and trade networks, the collapse of religious uniformity in
Christendom, and an unrelenting competition that triggered the rise of
fiscal-military states. A late arrival on the global stage, Europe within
three centuries became the undisputed hub of the world economy. In
the same period, fiercely competing European states became dominant
forces worldwide.

Change was not limited to Europe. The growth of populations, the
expansion of economies, military innovations, and the differentiation of
government institutions can be found elsewhere during this period.[13]
The Ottomans were intimately involved in the first stages of the military
revolution, experimenting with musket-bearing infantry, artillery, and
logistics. The Mughals, developing their military capacity in a profoundly different context, likewise proved able to adopt and develop
many of these innovations. Renaissances, reading revolutions, and a
consumer culture have been construed plausibly for China between the
Tang–Song changeover and late Ming. The rule of the 'high Qing'
emperors coincided with an immense economic and demographic
spurt.[14] Chinese government, at least since the Song and in some
respects long before, was far more differentiated and organised than
anything Europe could muster before the later seventeenth century. In
terms of population, production, and bullion imports, India and China
retained their traditional roles as global giants. European urban centres
approached the population of major cities in Asia only towards the end of
the eighteenth century. By this time the economic and political contours
of Europe were undergoing unprecedented change. Between 1750 and
1850, the balance shifted dramatically in favour of Europe. In the
decades following 1850, none of the major Asian polities of the premodern world escaped from Europe's overbearing tutelage, although some
retained independence and Japan would soon create its own formula of
modernisation. In the nineteenth century Europe became synonymous
with global hegemony and modernity; by the early twentieth century
dynastic rule was rapidly becoming the exception rather than the rule
in Europe and elsewhere.

Once the timing and explanation of long-term change occupy centre
stage, global comparison alters in scope and character. In the first place, it

[13] Lieberman, *Strange Parallels*; Goldstone, *Revolution and Rebellion*; Goldstone, 'The rise of
the West – or not? A revision to socio-economic history', *Sociological Theory*, 18/2 (2000),
175–94.
[14] Clunas, *Screen of Kings*; Jeroen Duindam, 'Early modern Europe: beyond the strictures of
modernization and national historiography', *European History Quarterly*, 40/4 (2010),
606–23; Goldstone, 'Problem of the "early modern" world'.

tends to deal only with the main players: Europe and Asia.[15] The Americas, Africa, Southeast Asia, and Oceania retain relevance mostly as subsidiaries fitted into the emerging network of trade, slavery, and war centred on Europe. Within the Eurasian continent the focus is usually further restricted to the leading economic powers: China and northwestern Europe. In the second place, explanations for the success of northwestern Europe easily blend with the traditional story of political modernisation. The incentives for economic innovation have been connected to the institutional conditions structured by the political set-up: the security of property, the interest of leadership in commerce and industry, the levels and forms of resource extraction. The Dutch Republic and the mixed monarchy emerging in England, united in their war effort against Ludovician France, defined themselves in opposition to 'absolute' monarchy. Their economic successes were more remarkable and lasting than those of their continental rivals. Spain rose and declined; France took over Spain's leading position but could not withstand the pressure of the English. England succeeded because of its participatory political structure and its state apparatus based on public credit.

Apparently, state power balanced with private interests offered the best prospect for growth; European 'absolute' monarchies failed to establish this balance and lost the competition. It is difficult to disentangle the factual basis of these views from their ideological underpinning. Different power structures may well have added force to the booming economies of the Dutch Republic and England, yet political contingency and geography contributed their share. Continental monarchies, never as despotic as the Dutch and English propaganda would have it, experienced long phases of remarkable growth. Conversely, coercion and military power were part and parcel of Dutch and later English successes. Once these political-economic views are extended to explain the outcomes of global competition, they approximate age-old clichés of stagnant Asian empires doomed to lose the battle with dynamic European mixed monarchies and republics.

The academic debate on the 'rise of the West' suggests important differences that can be confirmed in historical practice; at the same time it evokes age-old East–West clichés and tends to reflect modern political ideology. This study, concentrating on the period preceding the breakthroughs of the eighteenth and nineteenth centuries without trying to determine their causes, suggests a far greater equivalence in the social

---

[15] See a powerful summary of this research in Jean-Laurent Rosenthal and Roy Bin Wong, *Before and Beyond Divergence: The Politics of Economic Change in China and Europe* (Cambridge, MA, and London, 2011).

and political environments of rulers than these typologies concede.[16] Nevertheless, some of the fundamental differences encountered in dynastic power arrangements approach the commonplaces of East–West comparison. They need to be considered at some length here.

Kingship has often been seen as a conservative force thwarting rather than stimulating progress. Hippocrates hazarded a general contradiction between royal power and individual initiative, cited on the first page of this book:

where there are kings, there must be the greatest cowards. For [here] men's souls are enslaved, and refuse to run risks readily and recklessly to increase the power of somebody else. But independent people, taking risks on their own behalf and not on behalf of others, are willing and eager to go into danger, for they themselves enjoy the prize of victory.[17]

Several influential Greek authors writing in the wake of the Persian Wars contrasted the spiritedness of Europeans with the meekness of Asians. Aristotle's *Politics* suggests the Greeks were the ideal mixture:

The nations inhabiting the cold places and those of Europe are full of spirit but somewhat deficient in intelligence and skill, so that they continue comparatively free, but lacking in political organization and capacity to rule their neighbours. The peoples of Asia on the other hand are intelligent and skilful in temperament, but lack spirit, so that they are in continuous subjection and slavery. But the Greek race participates in both characters, just as it occupies the middle position geographically, for it is both spirited and intelligent; hence it continues to be free and to have very good political institutions, and to be capable of ruling all mankind if it attains constitutional unity.[18]

This Greek view of the Orient was restricted largely to West Asia, but remarkably similar notions would later be extended to East Asia. A fourteenth-century compilation of earlier European travel reports published under the name of John Mandeville, mixing depictions of social conventions such as footbinding with grotesque fantasies, adds a peculiar touch in a comment on the life of a rich Chinese gentleman:

For he hath, every day, fifty fair damosels, all maidens, that serve him evermore at his meat, and for to lie by him o'night, and for to do with them that is to his pleasance ... they cut his meat, and put it in his mouth; ... And when that he eateth no more of his first course, then other ... fair damsels bring him his second

---

[16] Peer H.H. Vries, 'Governing growth: a comparative analysis of the role of the state in the rise of the West', *Journal of World History*, 13 (2002), 67–138; Lieberman, *Strange Parallels*, stresses convergence and equivalence rather than the European *Sonderweg*.

[17] Hippocrates, *Airs, Waters, Places*, 133.

[18] Aristotle, *Politics*, trans. H. Rackham, Loeb Classical Library 264 (Cambridge, MA, 1932), Book VII, 566–7; see a discussion of these views in Andrew L. March, *The Idea of China: Myth and Theory in Geographic Thought* (New York, 1974), 23–43, 61–7.

course, always singing as they did before. And so they do continually every day to the end of his meat. And in this manner he leadeth his life. And so did they before him, that were his ancestors. And so shall they that come after him, without doing of any deeds of arms, but live evermore thus in ease, as a swine that is fed in sty for to be made fat.[19]

The combination of polygyny and comfortable wealth made the Chinese impervious to the lure of martial exploits or other outstanding deeds. The East was rich, sophisticated, and therefore inert.[20] These images were in place long before the West could boast global leadership. The bounty of nature afforded by the climate, a relative uniformity among the people, and a submissive attitude towards despotic rule recur in texts about China by Montesquieu and his contemporaries. By now, however, the ideal mixture of clime and mentality was located in northwestern Europe rather than in Greece. Montesquieu and his fellow *philosophes* in addition stressed the pernicious consequences of polygyny: 'It is with lust as with avarice, whose thirst increases by the acquisition of treasure.'[21] The pleasure-seeking oriental ruler, who withdrew from his advisors and neglected state matters, surely existed in historical fact, but was this type dominant in Asia and exceptional in Europe?

Different models of dynastic power arose in the macro-regions of the Eurasian continent, in Africa, in the Americas, and in the maritime worlds bordering these continents. Distinct characteristics have been described by numerous scholars for Sinic, Indic, Persian-Islamicate, and European-Christian civilisations with their overlapping borderlands. Two important discrepancies mentioned in the preceding paragraphs are mutually rein-forcing and match common typologies. An aloof style of rulership based on serene moral example was stronger in East and South Asia than else-where. The Confucian sage-kings were closer to the Indic rajadharma than to the more active Inner Asian, Persian-Islamicate, or European-Christian rulers.[22] In Japan the roles were divided between the emperor and the shogun. These differences in views on rulership, always subject to

---

[19] John Mandeville, *The Travels of Sir John Mandeville* (London, 1900), 204–5; see the source of this description in Odoric of Pordenone's travels, in Manuel Komroff (ed.), *Contemporaries of Marco Polo, Consisting of the Travel Records to the Eastern Parts of the World of William of Rubruck (1253–1255), the Journey of John of Pian de Carpini (1245–1247), the Journal of Friar Odoric (1318–1330) & the Oriental Travels of Rabbi Benjamin of Tudela (1160–1173)* (New York, 1928), 245–6.

[20] See also the far more sophisticated notion of a 'high-level equilibrium trap' as developed in Mark Elvin, *The Pattern of the Chinese Past: A Social and Economic Interpretation* (Stanford, CA, 1972).

[21] Montesquieu, *Spirit of the Laws*, Book XVI, chap. 6.

[22] On the immobile ruler in Southeast Asia, see Geertz, *Negara*; Soemarsaid Moertono, 'The concept of power in Javanese tradition', *Indonesia Circle: School of Oriental & African Studies: Newsletter*, 2 (1974), 16–17.

personal and regional variations, were deepened by the far sharper divide between polygyny and monogamy. Monogamous dynastic marriage was common only in Christian Europe. Dynasties almost universally relied on concubinage for reproduction and succession. Mistresses and bastards were part and parcel of the dynastic venture in Europe and princesses with their women servants lived in relatively secluded apartments. Nevertheless the closed compounds inhabited by women and eunuchs were characteristic only for polygynous settings. The aloof style of rulership and the presence of polygyny created an environment for rulers in Asia that differed from the ambiance of their fellow princes in Europe. Viewed at some distance, the movement eastwards from Europe to Asia coincided with a gradual shift from accessibility and activity to withdrawal and passive moral example.

The previous chapters, however, offer numerous examples crosscutting this tendency. At the individual level, active and involved rulers can be found repeatedly in all Asian polities, some fitting the cliché of the ferocious despot, others with benevolent and outgoing styles. European history, conversely, provides many examples of withdrawn rulers dominated by favourites: while some cases, such as the Habsburg emperor Rudolf II or the Bourbon king Philip V of Spain, have been attributed to mental deficiencies, less extreme examples underline the continuing alternation of extrovert and introvert personalities on the throne. Individual variability is not the only complication of the typology; within the various regions, different styles coexisted. In Europe, rules for access into the inner apartments and the sociability of court life varied greatly, with France epitomising accessibility and the Spanish Habsburgs representing a more closed style. A comparable variety of styles can be seen in the Ottoman, Safavid, and Mughal empires. Life cycles, moreover, had the same impact everywhere, with ageing rulers withdrawing into a smaller circle.

Change over time, too, complicates East–West typologies. Many dynastic polities discussed in this book, in Asia as well as in Europe, have been depicted in terms of a gradually declining interaction with the wider public. Consolidation and strengthening of power at the centre have rightly or wrongly been related to withdrawal. European princes are presented as withdrawing from the dense medieval interaction with the urban world, moving to country hunting lodges and increasingly eschewing ritual connections to the populace.[23] Roughly in the same period, Ottoman consolidation from Mehmed the Conqueror onwards

---

[23] See discussion of change and continuity in ritual connections in Duindam, 'Royal courts'; Duindam, *Vienna and Versailles*.

has been connected to withdrawal into the third court and under Murad III into the harem of Topkapı palace. In the early seventeenth century, Safavid Shah Abbas I poked fun at his reclusive European fellow monarchs, but his successors, too, gradually withdrew into the inner court. A similar development may have occurred at the Mughal court from Akbar to Aurangzeb, but this is uncertain. Late Ming China and Tokugawa Japan serve as the standard examples of distant and invisible rule, associated with ineptitude and decline under Wanli and his successors, with consolidation and effective government under the Tokugawa shoguns. The Qing Kangxi emperor moved his sleeping quarters into the inner court and concentrated decision-making there; yet both he and his grandson Qianlong cultivated a markedly outgoing style of rulership. Was withdrawal a common process that connected dynasties from across the globe at the same moment? In the late sixteenth century Henry III of France, the Ottoman Sultan Murad III, and the Ming Wanli emperor all proved to be far less given to movement and interaction than their predecessors – yet in a few decades, with the advent of Henry IV, Murad III, and the Qing emperors, the tendency was reversed.

Traditions of rulership and the spatial-social-gender structures of the palace made withdrawal more likely as well as more acceptable in the East Asian context. Nevertheless, the difference can be turned neither into a typology neatly following the East–West axis, nor into a consistent development from the fifteenth to the eighteenth century. Physical withdrawal, moreover, did not always go together with inactivity, let alone ineptness. Murad III hardly budged from his quarters but used inner court favourites to reduce the power of outer court dignitaries. Withdrawal into the palace and away from the needs of the populace does fit the critical cyclical views of dynastic power ubiquitous in history. New dynasties necessarily started on the basis of active leadership, obtaining the highest dignity through force and charisma. Ming founder Zhu Yuanzhang worried that his successors, born in the palace, would lose the force and stamina that had brought him to the throne.[24] His observations fitted into common concerns about dynastic decadence and the loss of the mandate of heaven. Around 1600, Ottoman elites observing the changes in leadership style and succession, feared a downturn in the powers of the dynasty along the lines of Ibn Khaldun's model.[25]

The cliché of oriental seclusion contains more than a grain of truth, but it leaves insufficient room for variation in personalities, regions, and

---

[24] Chan, 'Ming Taizu's problem', focusing on the wrongdoings of the sons.
[25] Cornell H. Fleischer, 'Royal authority, dynastic cyclism, and "Ibn Khaldunism" in sixteenth-century Ottoman letters', *Journal of Asian and African Studies*, 18 (1983), 198–220.

periods. Also it fails to acknowledge the universal pressures on individuals at the centre of dynastic polities. Notwithstanding major differences between regions and periods, the inner court favourite, male or female, emerges as a universal phenomenon in the global history of dynastic power. Finally the cliché obscures the fact that all dynastic rulers, in one way or another, were concerned with their presence in a wider society, even if they withdrew into the palace, prohibited the dissemination of their image, and forbade the use of symbols, words, or characters related to their name.

Intimately linked to withdrawal and passive voluptuousness is the view of the prince as a fickle despot. Picking up classic themes, in *The Prince* Machiavelli contrasted despotic rulers and servile elites in Asia with European princes dealing with hereditary elites:

all principalities known to history are governed in one of two ways, either by a prince to whom everyone is subservient and whose ministers, with his favour and permission, help govern, or by a prince and by nobles whose rank is established not by favour of the prince but by their ancient lineage. Such nobles have states and subjects of their own, and these acknowledge them as their lords and bear a natural affection towards them.[26]

The preceding comparative examination of numerous individuals at the heart of power underlines the universal contrast between their overstated positions and their variable personal characteristics. Rulers wielding uninfringeable authority in theory were dependent and insecure in practice. Strong kings and emperors, we have seen, underwent bouts of depression and hesitation; even in their most successful years, moreover, they necessarily relied on the support of numerous groups and individuals in their direct environment. The cliché of the oriental despot leaves room for honey-tongued advisors and court intrigue, for the malicious tyrant and the lascivious weakling – yet there is no place for the sensible king trying to solve key issues in accordance with the advice of his councillors. I see little reason to assume that such sensible characters were more common in Europe than elsewhere. The written legacies of rulers in Europe and Asia underline common predicaments rather than any structural difference in character.

Lord Acton, in a famous passage on European kings and popes, stated that 'Power tends to corrupt, and absolute power corrupts absolutely. Great men are almost always bad men.'[27] The ideals of rulership

[26] Niccolò Machiavelli, *The Prince*, trans. George Bull (London, 1961), 14–16.

[27] John E.E. Dalberg Acton, *Essays on Freedom and Power*, ed. Gertrude Himmelfarb (London, 1956), 335–6, 'Acton–Creighton Correspondence', letter of 5 April 1887; see a recent variant in Wolfgang Reinhard, 'Staat machen als organisiertes Verbrechen?

everywhere condemn the classic type of the oriental despot, but bad rulers can be found in many places, in the past as well as in the present. We need to turn to the nature of elites and institutions to find out whether the checks on power were more consistent and effective in Europe than in Asia. The manifest importance of 'ancient lineage' in Europe contrasts with the muted role of heredity in most Asian polities. Slave-elites were common in the Arabic-Islamicate past; the Ottomans as well as the Safavids used slave administrators and slave-soldiers to offset hereditary elites. The elaborate Mughal *mansabdar* rankings remained in the hands of the ruler and were superimposed on local hereditary power-holders. In late imperial China the predominant role of civil service examinations and the elaborate evaluations marginalised noble families. In each of these examples, personal qualifications and the ruler's discretion were more important than the birth rank of the candidates. The rise of the Qing dynasty, however, empowered a small minority of Manchu and Mongol nobles in the dynastic core and in the outlying provinces of China, leaving in place the governance of China proper. On the margins of the Eurasian continent, Europe and Japan both had powerful hereditary landholding noble elites, whose status had increasingly become contingent on their loyalty to the dynastic ruler. Hereditary wealth and birth status were recognised as important in Europe and Japan, whereas in China and in the Ottoman empire service to the ruler counted as the key status marker. Safavid Iran and Mughal India appear to have held an intermediate position.

Heredity plays a subdued role in the grand narrative of European exceptionalism, probably because it does not fit the ideals of modernity. Full heredity in office, or election and co-optation from a small group of candidates defined by heredity, was common in almost all European polities, from Venice and the Dutch Republic to France and the Holy Roman Empire or England: this presents a striking difference with most Asian dynastic polities. Here, too, family wealth and power could persist through the ages, but personal heredity in high office was less common and it was rarely as proudly proclaimed as in Europe.[28]

Did hereditary status make European elites less susceptible to rapacious or violent rulers? Leading individuals and sometimes entire noble families were executed for rebellion or treason, and religious dissent provided another cause for large-scale violence as well as individual

---

Die Kriminalität der Mächtigen aus der Perspektive der Geschichte der Staatsgewalt', in C. Prittwitz (ed.), *Kriminalität der Mächtigen* (Baden-Baden, 2008), 174–84.

[28] Jeroen Duindam, 'Dynasty and elites: from early modern Europe to late imperial China', in Liesbeth Geevers and Mirella Marini (eds.), *Dynastic Identity in Early Modern Europe: Rulers, Aristocrats and the Formation of Identities* (forthcoming).

punishment in the sixteenth and seventeenth centuries. However, executions of high nobles declined in the seventeenth century and became truly exceptional in the eighteenth. Individual nobles would be bypassed for promotion and in rare cases they could be severely punished, but the group as a whole was so intertwined with the dynastic state that it could not be challenged. Can the same be said for Ottoman *pashas*, viziers, and janissaries, for leading office-holders in Mughal India and Safavid Iran, for Tokugawa *daimyo* lords or for Chinese literati office-holders? Unfree status cannot be read as powerlessness; janissaries repeatedly acted as kingmakers at the Ottoman court. When they were finally wiped out and disbanded at the behest of Mahmud II after a revolt in 1826, they could look back on a long history of close involvement in the Ottoman dynastic polity. Dismissals of leading viziers and pashas and confiscations of their properties were common in the Ottoman empire. Harsh reprisals against office-holders, particularly those affiliated with the dynasty, occurred in 1632 and at several other points in Safavid history. The insurrections of Mughal princes were followed by executions of their noble followers and confiscations of properties.[29] After the turbulent first decades of Tokugawa rule from the Battle of Sekigahara (1600) to the Shimabara rebellion (1637–8), the daimyo lords enjoyed relative security – later instances of *seppuku* (forced suicide) among them were exceptional. The Ming founder purged the office-holding elite following his abolition of the chancellorship in 1380, with an estimated 100,000 officials losing their lives in the following two decades. Clashes between emperors and leading office-holders recurred later, but never approached the exceptional scale of the Hongwu emperor's purges. After the violent Ming–Qing dynastic changeover, a cataclysm of terrifying proportions,[30] the Qing *cursus honorum* reflected a sensible pattern of evaluation and relocation, with confiscation, demotion, and sometimes executions occupying an important place.[31]

Many European travellers claimed that rapid upward as well as downward mobility and severe punishment were more common in Asian

[29] Jorge Flores, 'Two Portuguese visions of Jahangir's India: Jerónimo Xavier and Manuel Godinho de Erédia', in Jorge Flores and Nuno Vassallo e Silva (eds.), *Goa and the Great Mughal* (Lisbon, 2004), 44–66, at 54–5 on Khusrau's 1605 rebellion and on executions and confiscation in general.

[30] See e.g. a short discussion in Ebrey, *Cambridge Illustrated History of China*, 192; Fisher, *Chosen One*; Dardess, 'Protesting to the death'. See common comparisons of Mao and the Ming founders, e.g. Anita Andrew and John Rapp, *Autocracy and China's Rebel Founding Emperors: Comparing Chairman Mao and Ming Taizu* (Lanham, MD, 2000); on the Ming–Qing changeover, see Struve, *Voices from the Ming–Qing Cataclysm*.

[31] Guy, *Qing Governors*; Torbert, *Ch'ing Imperial Household Department*, 117–20; Norman A. Kutcher, 'The death of the Xiaoxian empress: bureaucratic betrayals and the crises of eighteenth-century Chinese rule', *Journal of Asian Studies*, 56/3 (1997), 708–25.

polities than in Europe. Some of the travellers, most notably Busbecq visiting the Ottomans under Süleyman and the numerous Jesuits reporting about China, were pleased to note that the emperor rewarded talent rather than descent. Travellers frequently reported violent and capricious despots in the East as a circumspect form of criticising tendencies in Europe: Louis XIV was pictured as an oriental despot by his opponents and the ministry of Jean-Baptiste Colbert was later labelled as a 'demi-vizierate'.[32] In these cases, the East served as a mirror for the West and observations may have been twisted to serve this purpose.

Wealth and inheritance did not always easily go together with dynastic overlordship. All assets could in principle be seen as belonging to the ruler, underpinning the dynastic right to confiscate and redistribute at will. Legal definitions of private property diminished the impact of dynastic transgressions. Urban corporations and religious institutions throughout Europe were able to define their own spheres of action and were never wholly absorbed by the dynasty or the state before the French Revolution.[33] The patchwork of rights and exemptions in European early modern cities caused endless negotiations and unclear outcomes, a world far removed from the radical measures Mehmed II adopted to repopulate and restructure Istanbul or the overhaul of Beijing and other major cities in the aftermath of the Qing conquest. Everywhere elites looked to the rewards in the hands of the dynastic ruler, yet the same groups keenly sought ways to protect their own wealth and status against the appetite of a rapacious dynasty. In the Islamicate world, pious foundations (Arabic *waqf*; Ottoman *vakif*) served high moral purposes but at the same time safeguarded family property and funds against the infringements of rulers. Once vested in foundations, supporting mosques, schools, markets, or hospitals, family wealth generated high office and social respect without risking dynastic interference. In China, wealthy gentry lineages could secure long-term access to examination success for talented males in their networks. In East and West, acute need for ready

---

[32] On Bernier's travels as a comment on Louis XIV, see Sylvia Murr, 'Le politique "au Mogol" selon Bernier: appareil conceptuel, rhétorique stratégique, philosophie morale', in J. Pouchepadass and H. Stern (eds.), *De la royauté à l' état: anthropologie et histoire du politique dans le monde indien* (Paris, 1991), 239–311. On Colbert as vizier, see Charles-Irénée Castel de Saint-Pierre, *Discours sur la polysynodie: où l'on démontre que la polysynodie ou pluralité des conseils, est la forme de ministère la plus avantageuse pour un roi, et pour son royaume* (Amsterdam, 1719), 21. On the deformation inherent in travel accounts, see Sven Trakulhun, 'The view from the outside: Nicolas Gervaise, Simon de la Loubère and the perception of seventeenth century Siamese government and society', *Journal of the Siam Society*, 85/1–2 (1997), 75–84.

[33] On diverging patterns of law, see Teemu Ruskola, 'The East Asian legal tradition', in Mauro Bussani and Ugo Mattei (eds.), *The Cambridge Companion to Comparative Law* (Cambridge, 2012), 257–77; Duindam et al. (eds.), *Law and Empire*.

cash, often during military crises, disposed leaders to lease rights of taxation or sell offices, measures reinforcing existing elites or creating new stakeholders.

Official descriptions of court life invariably suggest undisturbed hierarchy and order. In Europe, numerous letters, journals, and memoirs allow us to redraw the picture. These sources disclose the endemic contestation among near-equals in the highest ranks, against the express wish of the sovereign. Neither in Europe nor in Asia can we take at face value the commissioned descriptions of dynastic grandeur and elite servility, even where they offer great detail. Such sources, however, predominate in the legacies of Asian dynasties. The contrasts between elites in East and West may therefore in part reflect the difference in source materials. Only with equivalent sources will it be possible to more effectively reassess the images.

In the end the clear dichotomy posited by Machiavelli breaks down into a continuum where the interplay between the ruler's favour and elite families' resources defines outcomes. Moreover, in Europe as well as in Asia, the distribution of favours at the centre was controlled in part by persons related to these elites. Studies of local elites throughout the world show how these groups 'dominated local arenas and interacted with elites in other arenas'.[34] Local elites were 'neither simply representing state interests nor opposing them but rather manipulating the system to serve their own interest'.[35] This was rarely a contest between two parties, with a unified leadership at the centre overpowering distant elites. The 'state' never was a monolith based on the will of the ruler: it reflected competition among several groups and individuals. Regional elites were naturally dispersed and easily divided, but they keenly cultivated their brokers at the centre.

Several 'elite theorists' in the early twentieth century described the inevitable drift of democratic organisations to the leadership of a small political class. The 'iron law of oligarchy', put forward by one of these theorists, can be applied to dynastic power structures as well.[36] None of the polities examined here ever neatly conformed to the cliché of absolute or despotic power held effectively by a sequence of rulers. In all cases,

[34] Joseph Esherick and Mary Backus Rankin, *Chinese Local Elites and Patterns of Dominance* (Berkeley, CA, 1990), 305.

[35] Szonyi, *Practicing Kinship*, 205–6. In general see Tilly, *Trust and Rule*, 34, 92, 104, on 'bottom-up' strategies of intermediary and local elites.

[36] Robert Michels, *Zur Soziologie des Parteiwesens in der modernen Demokratie: Untersuchungen über die oligarchischen Tendenzen des Gruppenlebens* (Leipzig, 1911), 'Die Demokratie und das eherne Gesetz der Oligarchie' (362). See also Gaetano Mosca, *The Ruling Class* (New York, 1939); and a lucid discussion by Robert D. Putnam, *The Comparative Study of Political Elites* (Englewood Cliffs, NJ, 1976).

mixed groups of office-holders and confidants developed into a political class, limiting access to the ruler, controlling his patronage, and manipulating him. Violence against elites and agents of dynastic power can be found in all regions during phases of rebellion or dynastic change, but hereditary power groups were stronger in Europe than in most Asian polities. Massive violence against leading groups was exceptional in Europe. Certainly, it is difficult to find parallels for the Ming Hongwu emperor's violent purges here – but the same can be said about Asia. The attempt to make sense of these differences far exceeds the themes and ambitions of this book. A more elaborate assessment of clichés and actual conditions needs further comparative study.

Europe, the region presented by Machiavelli and Montesquieu as leaving most leeway to private property and birth, also pioneered systemic fiscal extraction at levels unseen elsewhere.[37] In 1711–12 the Kangxi emperor, eager to exhibit his stature as a sage ruler, froze the tax lists – a measure with serious consequences for his successors.[38] Each subsequent round in European warfare from the late fifteenth to the late eighteenth century proved a financial nightmare for the combatants. The protracted and costly conflict between 1739 and 1763 made inevitable a series of fundamental reforms; these top-down measures and the angry popular responses they triggered were a major factor in the outbreak of the American as well as the French Revolution. The ensuing political turmoil and the long-term process of economic modernisation fundamentally changed the parameters of power. How did dynasty and court fit these developments?

The modern state and the end of dynasty

East–West clichés do not comfortably fit the paradigm of European modernisation. Machiavelli underlined the powerful role of 'ancient lineages' in Europe, contrasting it with servile elites and strong rulers in the East. The traditional story of state formation in Europe, however, depicted kings as winning the contest with their nobles and creating service elites, now wholly dependent on royal favour. Seventeenth-century 'absolute' monarchs, supported by increasingly effective bureaucracies, concentrated the reins of power in their hands. The consolidation of the state apparatus reduced the function of the king's entourage and in

---

[37] There is a tension between the key arguments of the old view of European exceptionalism based on birth rank and the modern view based on effective fiscal extraction, with the relative safety of property serving as common ground.

[38] Spence, 'The K'ang-hsi reign', in Peterson (ed.), *Cambridge History of China*, vol. IX, 120–82, at 124, 178.

the end made his crown superfluous. Societies were now able to take control of the state and push aside their kings – gradually through the rise of Parliament in England, radically through the Revolution in France. Europe was subjected to absolute monarchical authority only briefly and as part of its trajectory into the modern world.

Recent interpretations show that noble elites maintained power through their integration into the monarchical edifice. They underline that the state itself was a compromise between various groups and interests, the outcome of protracted bargaining rather than the king's instrument or a self-willed abstraction setting its own targets.[39] These revisions do not question the strengthening of government institutions in the centre and their increasing presence in the periphery. Moreover, the entourage did change character: executive office in government, once a responsibility held by people who also served the ruler in person, became a specialised occupation. Staffs and departments in the household as well as in the new ministries expanded and differentiated, while there was an increasing separation of these domestic and administrative spheres. Ministers gradually matched the status of high noblemen and frequently surpassed them in actual power. Did the fixed routines of the modern state render irrelevant the patterns of dynastic rule sketched in this book? Was the household at some point reduced to a mere catering institution, where service no longer entailed access to power? A modern author writing on state formation plausibly suggests that in the course of the eighteenth century 'The household was swallowed by its own offspring, so to speak, it became simply one of a great many administrative departments whose responsibility happened to be looking after the monarch's person, his residences, his property, and the like.'[40] The statement rings true: in most European polities, specialised departments had taken over responsibilities earlier held by household dignitaries. The French royal household had become one among several responsibilities in the portfolio of a single secretary of state. However, at this point the household in France as well as in most European states was still bigger than the combined staffs of central ministries.[41] It consistently performed the typical roles outlined earlier: conspicuous hospitality and royal representation. The comparative horizon is helpful here: a rigid separation of household and government, we have seen, was characteristic for several Asian courts. This did not mean, however, that inner court staffs could

---

[39] Ronald G. Asch, *Nobilities in Transition, 1550–1700: Courtiers and Rebels in Britain and Europe* (London, 2003); Hillay Zmora, *Monarchy, Aristocracy, and the State in Europe* (London, 2001); Scott, *Forming Aristocracy*.

[40] Martin van Creveld, *The Rise and Decline of the State* (Cambridge, 1999), 130.

[41] Duindam, 'Vienna and Versailles'.

not wield power or that the court had lost its exemplary status in the body politic. The imperial household department of the Chinese court fitted into an impressive array of ministries and departments, and most high state officials remained outside the domestic inner court perimeter, but this did not diminish the lasting importance of the court. The growth of state institutions in the European setting, hardly as unique as often supposed, only very gradually reduced the relevance of the domestic apparatus around the ruler. Until the first decades of the eighteenth century the consolidation and differentiation of the state machinery coincided with a prolonged movement towards increasing court magnificence.

A formal division of domestic and administrative responsibilities was solidly in place in most eighteenth-century kingdoms, yet 'inner court' male and female favourites with extensive powers were markedly present until the end of the *ancien régime*. What conditions could alter the setting and impact of the dynastic court more profoundly? As long as the king remained a key figure in decision-making, his daily companions and confidants were expected to be influential – an anticipation that defined them as political actors even in cases where their actual influence was limited.[42] Anybody seeking to influence decisions or nominations made sure to cultivate connections both with courtiers in the proximity of the ruler and with ministers in the council. Once political power was taken from the hands of the ruler, matters changed: perceptive petitioners would now redirect their energies from the princely entourage to other places. Even the loss of power did not necessarily render the ruler and his court insignificant. The Japanese emperor no longer held a share in political decisions; his acclaimed nominations were in practice dictated by the shogun. In this reduced role, however, the emperor still enjoyed great cultural and religious prestige.

Only a weakening of kingship's religious-ritual foundation combined with the reduction of the ruler's political power profoundly eroded the *raison d'être* of court and dynasty. Partial moves in this direction can be seen in England, where Protestant monarchs were limited in power by a parliament that voted on the court's finances, or in France where Louis XV forfeited some of the rituals defining his sacral status. More radical moves by Habsburg emperor Joseph II, a self-styled bureaucrat who expanded the government while reducing the court and trimming its ceremonies, went together with a new and personal style of monarchical rule, in some ways echoing the 'benevolent despotism' of his Chinese fellow emperors. To his dismay, Joseph noticed that the officials in the expanding bureaucracy copied the practices of the old court, with its

---

[42] On types of power, see Putnam, *Comparative Study of Political Elites*, 5–8.

proclivity for protocol and *Vielschreiberey* – endless writing.[43] Indeed, the expanding state apparatus, with its rankings and procedures, honorary supernumeraries, inflating numbers, and its scrounging on the ruler's coffers, continued many of the court's proclivities. In differing proportions, later eighteenth-century dynastic polities in Europe adapted to changing intellectual horizons and political needs – yet nowhere did this process eliminate the familiar components of dynastic power. Throughout Europe, changes in the legitimation of rulership and in the patterns of decision-making were absorbed into the flexible framework of dynastic power. It needed a revolution to fundamentally uproot the tradition and create states and populations that either managed their polity wholly without crowned heads or relegated them to very minor positions. In the turbulent decades of revolution and warfare, the traditional, self-evident form of monarchy was effaced everywhere. In most places monarchs regained power, but nowhere did they continue unaffected. Even where dynastic continuity remained unbroken, rulership was undergoing a process of redefinition.

The reinvention of monarchical traditions in the nineteenth century was hardly unprecedented. Following rebellions and wars, upstart dynasties had always engaged in bricolage to establish their place among rival houses, appropriating old forms and ideas while adapting them to current needs. However, the changeover of 1789–1815 was different for several reasons: it profoundly shook elites and populations in their beliefs, convincing some to pursue new ideals, others to revere order in its ancient form. The instruments the state wielded to control its populations, growing incrementally over the previous centuries, now expanded rapidly. Numbers of administrators and policemen inflated, and improvements in infrastructure and communication eased their tasks. *Ancien régime* monarchy, with the court serving as a conspicuous centre of dynastic grandeur, a point of orientation bringing together regional elites often cherishing different identities and holding distinctive rights, was gone. The relatively loose power of earlier rulers, inconsistent in their application of rules and at times blatantly violent as well as unjust, was now replaced by a more consistent rule of law and application of force that penetrated far deeper into all levels of society. In the ensuing century, the question of who could determine the agenda of this more powerful state became a central issue, resolved in Western Europe first by constitutions

---

[43] Peter G.M. Dickson, 'Monarchy and bureaucracy in late eighteenth-century Austria', *English Historical Review*, 110/436 (1995), 323–67, mentioning Joseph's complaints at 324. See also Joseph's 'Hirtenbrief', point 8, in Harm Klueting, *Der Josephinismus: ausgewählte Quellen zur Geschichte der theresianisch-josephinischen Reformen* (Darmstadt, 1995), 334. On numbers, see Duindam, 'Vienna and Versailles'.

reducing the political role of dynastic rulers, and subsequently by the extension of the franchise. In the process, state institutions swelled, the impact of the state on society waxed, and some of the interests of the expanded electorate were incorporated into the state agenda. These processes reduced the position of royals where they were still on the throne. Courts became civil lists, honorary memberships rather than full-time households with numerous servants representing different groups and regions as well as performing very real tasks. Representative assemblies, ministries, and the emerging political parties now became the hubs attracting petitioners.

Rewards and rankings related to royalty did not disappear: if anything, orders of chivalry and royal distinctions of service seem to have become more popular and widespread. Surprisingly, the festive and ceremonial show of European monarchs, too, proved remarkably successful, particularly in the later nineteenth century. As symbols of national unity and pride, monarchs were much esteemed – conversely, where national unity and pride were under severe pressure, monarchs could be held responsible. Western dominance presented the Ottoman and the Qing dynasties with an awkward dilemma: how could they modernise and adapt without imitating the very model that was undermining their prestige? The common pattern of dynastic rule from an exemplary centre, incorporating different provinces loosely and on different conditions, now came under pressure. This formula seemed ineffective and undesirable to reformers who hoped to establish a powerful cohesive state on the basis of a single leading nationality. Minority rule of 'Manchu invaders' over Han Chinese did not easily fit the national model; it was further undermined by the repeated humiliations of Qing leadership by local rebels and bullying outsiders.[44] The cosmopolitan Ottoman sultans, who had long been served by elites recruited elsewhere and whose mothers came from distant places, underwent an ongoing process of change, including the adoption of Western-style reforms as well as the active use of the title of caliph leader of Sunni Islam, a dignity slumbering since the Ottoman conquest of Cairo in 1517.[45] In addition the Ottomans redefined their

---

[44] Joseph Esherick, 'How the Qing became China', in Joseph Esherick et al. (eds.), *Empire to Nation: Historical Perspectives on the Making of the Modern World* (Lanham, MD, 2006), 229–59; Pamela Crossley, 'Nationality and difference in China: the post-imperial dilemma', in Joshua Fogel (ed.), *The Teleology of the Modern Nation-State: Japan and China* (Philadelphia, PA, 2005), 138–58.

[45] Carter Vaughn Findley, 'The Ottoman lands to the post-First World War settlement', in Francis Robinson (ed.), *The New Cambridge History of Islam*, vol. V: *The Islamic World in the Age of Western Dominance* (Cambridge, 2010), 29–78; Selim Deringil, 'The invention of tradition as public image in the late Ottoman empire, 1808 to 1908', *Comparative Studies in Society and History*, 35/1 (1993), 3–29.

connection to the various groups in their shrinking empire, relying increasingly on the Turkish population – a portent of more radical changes to follow in the twentieth century. Similar adaptations in representation surfaced in the Habsburg lands, where, between the end of the Holy Roman Empire (1806) and the crisis that ignited the First World War, the dynasty adapted its formula of rule various times with mixed success. Was it essentially German or did it cultivate multinational cosmopolitanism? Did it embody the Catholic faith, or could it accommodate all religious groups? Did it rule through consent, or with high-handed authority?[46]

Military defeat looms large in the demise of dynasty: the First World War ended most dynastic houses still ruling over empires and composite monarchies. Previously, losing a war in many cases inaugurated dynastic change and renewal, but now the changeover heralded a different political system. In East and West, dynasties persisted with greater facility where wars were won and where national identity was less riven by diversity. With some notable exceptions, in victorious polities kings henceforth reigned without ruling: others were responsible for the political machinery and could be held accountable for failures. In Africa royalty subsisted under the overarching structure of colonial and modern independent states. In the Arabic world, with the retreat of the Ottomans, several dynasties rose to power, some succumbing to revolutions during the twentieth century, others successfully defending their thrones. In Southeast Asia, too, dynasties retained a marked position. In some of these places, modernity coincides with royalty in an undiminished leadership role.[47]

The *Entzauberung der Welt*, or disenchantment of the world, ranks among the causes of dynastic decline.[48] A willingness to accept and believe in the wondrous powers of rulers long stood at the heart of dynastic power; without this aura the show of power staged in a dynastic centre lost much of its significance for audiences nearby and distant. Once regional elites and agents of power no longer flocked to the court for rewards and relocation, the overblown domestic apparatus at the heart of the dynastic set-up, too, became embarrassing rather than appealing.

---

[46] R.J.W. Evans, 'Communicating empire: the Habsburgs and their critics, 1700–1919', *Transactions of the Royal Historical Society*, 19 (2009), 117–38; Gary B. Cohen, 'Neither absolutism nor anarchy: new narratives on society and government in late imperial Austria', *Austrian History Yearbook*, 29 (1998), 37–61.

[47] Roger Kershaw, *Monarchy in South-East Asia: The Faces of Tradition in Transition* (London and New York, 2001); Michael Herb, *All in the Family: Absolutism, Revolution, and Democracy in Middle Eastern Monarchies* (New York, 1999).

[48] Max Weber, 'Wissenschaft als Beruf', in *Gesammelte Aufsätze zur Wissenschaftslehre*, vol. I (Tübingen, 1922), 536.

How can modern kings, queens, princes, and princesses, in the absence of the religious underpinning and the spoils system so critical for dynastic power, retain their remarkable appeal for wider audiences? Does this low-key version of the fairy tale of high birth and special status indicate the persistence of old popular attitudes, or is it more akin to the modern adoration of celebrities in sports and entertainment?

Legacies

After more than two centuries of political change and experimentation moving from hierarchy, birthright, and unchallengeable authority to the ideals of social mobility, accepted political contestation, and the popular vote, what remains of the stubborn patterns around persons in power?

Tensions between the norms and the practices of political power are a common fact of political life: idealists survive politically only if they are able to circumvent the moral foundation of their position. Election brings leaders to power in a less haphazard way than heredity or selection from a group of royals. The qualities allowing leaders to win elections, however, do not invariably predispose them to successfully tackle major problems. Nor is the requirement to cultivate popular support always conducive to wise government. Finding the right balance between instrumental and idealist motives appears to be a continuing dilemma of political leadership. Modern chosen leaders are not immobilised by the awkwardly exalted position of royals; neither do they to the same extent experience personal vulnerability. The democratic mandate, depending on public scrutiny and personal responsibility, is less intimidating than the all-seeing eye of heaven. Democratically chosen leaders, moreover, no longer spend a lifetime in office, and hence avoid the moments of soul-searching befalling frail and anxious veterans on the throne. Succession in democracies is contested more often with words than with weapons. Long-lasting leaders, of any ideological colour, do obtain some of the traits of the dynastic ruler. The metaphor of the crown prince is frequently used when long-serving leaders contemplate retirement; anticipating the new situation, factions form around potential successors.

These similarities become far stronger where individuals spend their lives in power. Modern-day autocrats rising to power through force resemble founding emperors; the powers of their governments, however, are far more intimidating than those of premodern rulers. Dictators often tend towards next-of-kin succession, disguising the designation of their offspring by rigged elections or legitimating it by broadcasting the stunning talents of the future leader to wide audiences. Successors need to demonstrate their power and determination. Kim Jong-un's execution of his paternal aunt's husband Jang Song-thaek in 2013 brings to mind a pattern common in dynastic power: the marriage of dynastic sisters or daughters to key supporters, the role of these in-laws as leading powers behind the throne, and their elimination by a next generation of royalty ascending to power. With semi-dynastic succession or co-optation among a small group of leaders, competition among eligibles emerges, and alliances forming around candidates characterise political conflict under ageing rulers. In anticipation, potential candidates can be purged: after Lenin's death Stalin gradually consolidated power by eliminating rivals from the first generation of revolutionary heroes. The genealogies are different, the processes similar. Both Stalin and Mao savagely purged the elites who assisted their rise to power in the country, reflecting earlier dynastic retribution against agents who were becoming too powerful. Problems of limited access and the power of confidants serving in capacities technically irrelevant to the political set-up, too, will inevitably arise around dictators. By the end of their lives, leaders hiding in their inner quarters can become so suspicious that their attitude verges on paranoia.[49] In fact, Karl Wittfogel's entirely understandable aversion to contemporary totalitarian dictators impelled him to write his epoch-making study of oriental despotism – an inspiration that unfortunately persuaded him to look only for examples confirming his comprehensive condemnation. His acute observations show one side only of a pattern that was not consistently present either in the East or in the West.

The dynastic court was a hub of redistribution. Modern democratic states by definition also redistribute wealth and status. They tap more wealth from the population than earlier regimes could dream of, yet this wealth is redistributed ideally to achieve shared social and political ideals. Modern forms of regional-numerical representation will secure a more equitable reallocation than the hierarchically organised networks of power in premodern polities. It is clear, however, that the process of redistribution turns the major capitals of decision-making, from Washington, DC, to Brussels and from Beijing to Moscow, into centres of lobbying. State institutions compete for funding, industries try to improve their market and profit conditions, myriad other groups voice their goals and invest heavily to accomplish them by influencing decision-making processes. Parties, the leading vehicles of political power, not only represent certain ideals and aims but also generate financial support to facilitate their ascendancy to power and their members' access to high

---

[49] This has been depicted by numerous novelists and journalists: see e.g. Ryszard Kapuscinski, *The Emperor* (London, 2006); on the dynastic aspects of modern dictators, see Montefiore, *Stalin*; Martin, *Under the Loving Care of the Fatherly Leader*.

office. Where are the borders between legitimate lobbying and collusion or corruption?[50] Surely no political system can function entirely without the grey area between formal decision-making, political representation, and the involvement of private and sector interests.[51] The gift-giving of grandees moving to the centre and their competition for the ruler's graces, so conspicuously present in many dynastic centres, have their parallels in the modern world. Upon the election of a new president of the USA, not only the White House staff changes: numerous supporters of the previous administration throughout the state apparatus make way for followers and patrons of the new president. Campaign sponsors obtain high diplomatic office, working together with highly professional staffs. In many ways, representative institutions reflect the functions traditionally held by the court: bringing together different regional and social segments at the centre, organising the distribution of favours, and collectively performing the unity of the realm.

We rightly associate dynasties with an elaborate choreography of power: Akbar showing his profile against the radiance of the rising sun, rulers parading under canopies or being transported in elevated palanquins. The calendar of court life included many occasions where elites performed together in rites demonstrating the ruler's power as well as their own pre-eminence. The visual performance of power was an essential ingredient of dynastic rule, but it did not end with Louis XVI's decapitation. In the French Revolution royal ceremonial was redefined into large-scale outdoor festivals, initially with the king listlessly playing his role, soon without him. Republican festivities were grander than royal ceremonies. Napoleon designed his own show of power and grandeur, bringing together many earlier examples. Rallies and parades have been present in most regimes. Thanks to modern media, the popular presentation of power-holders has reached unprecedented heights. Engineered spontaneity and carefully prepared televised performances can determine shifts in power. In our age, the link between politics and performance seems closer than ever. Nineteenth-century scholars, looking for political

---

[50] Mounira M. Charrad and Julia Adams, 'Introduction: patrimonialism, past and present', *Annals of the American Academy of Political and Social Science*, 636/1 (2011), 6–15, and the contributions to this issue discussing patrimonialism in modern contexts, not limited to dictatorships or the 'global South'.

[51] Carl J. Friedrich, *The Pathology of Politics: Violence, Betrayal, Corruption, Secrecy, and Propaganda* (New York, 1972); James C. Scott, *Comparative Political Corruption* (Englewood Cliffs, NJ, 1972). See also Wolfgang Reinhard, 'Die Nase der Kleopatra: Geschichte im Lichte mikropolitischer Forschung. Ein Versuch', *Historische Zeitschrift*, 293/3 (2011), 633–66; and the recent important synthesis by Jens Ivo Engels, *Die Geschichte der Korruption* (Frankfurt, 2014), which differentiates sharply between the changing discourse on corruption and persistent 'micropolitical' practices.

decision-making, trawled through endless description of rankings and ceremonies. In their works and source editions, they omitted these details, separating politics from its domestic and dynastic context. Much of contemporary politics would fall within the rubrics of trimmings these scholars deemed unworthy of their attention. A cursory glance at dynastic and modern political settings suggests powerfully that performance is an inevitable part of politics, in past and present.

Populations accepted dynastic power as preordained and natural; it reflected a shared moral order and offered some hope of support and betterment. At the same time they well knew that kings could have a ruinous impact on their lives. Their image of the distant court and ruler involved admiration, expectation, censure, and fear. Compliance easily mixed with complaining. The reputation of the court in the past approached that of the Washington Beltway or Brussels: people hope to obtain benefits but on the whole are sceptical and tend to have a critical view of the groups active at the centre.

Kinship and kingship were connected in many ways, but kinship retains a marked position in modern society. The Bush and Kennedy families show that dynasties persist in the domain of democratically elected heads of state and leading politicians.[52] Private companies, too, have often taken the shape of family businesses. A recent study describes the marked success of families in banking and the automobile industry, and argues that their companies are more than a passing stage in the development of the modern economy.[53] The study of contemporary political and industrial dynasties shows that choices pertaining to succession – male primogeniture, succession of women, designation by the incumbent, adoption of talented outsiders affiliated through marriage – are still entirely relevant. Remarkably, even the dynastic cycle recurs, in the literary imagining of families as well as in the practice of businesses – self-made men founding their company, first generations of successors consolidating it, and spendthrift youngsters raised in opulence squandering their predecessors' achievements in the third or fourth generation. Thomas Mann's *Buddenbrooks* provides one among many powerful literary examples of a similar model. Do these family cycles correspond to the Chinese dynastic cycle and Ibn Khaldun's model of generations?

World history after 1750 has followed a linear rather than a cyclical trajectory in most respects. Notwithstanding long-term developments in the political domain, notably those relating to the enfranchisement of

---

[52] Ralph G. Martin, *Seeds of Destruction: Joe Kennedy and His Sons* (New York, 1995); Baker, *Family of Secrets*.

[53] See examples from the business world in Pina-Cabral and Lima (eds.), *Elites*; and Landes, *Dynasties*.

previously excluded social groups and the strengthening of their rights, a residue of the cyclical fluctuations can be found. An alternation of centralising and regionalising forces has been suggested for Chinese history from the Song to modern post-Mao China.[54] Incisive events, mostly wars, can create a mentality of rebuilding and solidarity. Such phases of intense ideological commitment and strong social coherence have been followed by the breakdown of overarching identities and loyalties in many places. Critics connect the loosening of social and moral ties with a booming economy and the predominance of self-interest, echoing some of the older normative cyclical views. Current concerns about the increased distance between political parties and the electorate, the distrust of many groups vis-à-vis political leadership, and the overwhelming importance of material interests bring to mind the notion of declining group feeling (*asabiyya*).

Past and present parallels between rule in East and West are worth pursuing. Profound ideological cleavages separate premodern and modern political cultures, yet they should not prevent comparative examination of everyday political practices. The same holds true for all shades of state from liberal democracies to totalitarian regimes. This comparative study of dynasty suggests that forms of government situated at opposite poles can share basic characteristics. It raises uncomfortable questions about continuities of power and leadership in past and present, East, West, and worldwide. Most importantly it pioneers a form of worldwide comparison centred on concrete settings and specific questions rather than on predetermined typologies of scale, development, or contiguity.[55] Any comparison will find similarities and differences, but satisfying results can be expected only when we define and understand the fundamental differences in the similarities and the equivalences hiding behind differences.

---

[54] Bol, 'Localist turn'.

[55] Other candidates for global comparison, such as armies or cities, may be tied to scale and development more stringently than dynasty: dynastic power can be seen as a relatively constant factor in a changing world.

Glossary

adharma (Sanskrit). 'That which is not in accord with the law'; antonym of *dharma*.

adolescentia (Latin). Age from fourteen to twenty.

agha. 'Chief, master, lord': title for a civilian or military officer in the Ottoman empire.

ahosi. Dependents or wives of the Dahomey king.

ahovi. Children or descendants of Dahomey kings.

aisin gioro. Chinese imperial clan of the Qing dynasty.

Âlî Qapu palace. 'Lofty Gate', a Safavid royal palace located on the western side of the Naqsh-e Jahan Square in Isfahan.

Amba Geshan. 'Mountain of Royals', a mountain in northern Ethiopia and prison for the male heirs to the emperor of Ethiopia.

anato. Free commoners in the Dahomey kingdom.

arii rahi. Paramount chief of Tahiti.

asabiyya. Sense of community or group feeling; an important concept in Ibn Khaldun's *Muqaddimah*.

asantehemaa. Queen mother of the Asante federation.

asantehene. Paramount king of the Asante federation.

askeri. 'Military', ruling class of imperial administrators in the Ottoman empire (as opposed to *reaya*, taxpaying commoners).

Asta-brata. 'The eight life-rules': Javanese rendering of part of the Indic epic *Ramayana*.

ataliq or **atalïk.** Guardians or tutors of khan's children or princes in the Mughal empire.

ayan. 'Notables', local or provincial elites in the Ottoman empire.

babanu. Outer court of the palace in Assyria, as opposed to *bitanu*, the inner court.

Bab-ı Hümayun. The Imperial Gate, leading into the open first court of the Ottoman Topkapı palace.

Bab-us Saadet. Gate of Felicity, leading into the third courtyard in the Ottoman Topkapı palace.

Bab-us Selam (also Orta Kapı). Gate of Salutation, leading into the second courtyard in the Ottoman Topkapı palace.

bailo or **baylo**. Venetian ambassador and resident consul in Istanbul.

Baohedian. Hall of Preserving Harmony in the outer section of the Forbidden City.

baojun (Chinese). Tyrannical ruler.

bayt (Arabic). Retinue of the ruler; see also *hashiya, khassakiya*.

beylerbey or **beylerbeyi**. 'Bey of the beys', a provincial governor of the Ottoman empire.

biji. 'Notebook', a genre in classical Chinese literature.

birun. 'Outside', the outer departments of the Ottoman imperial household, as opposed to *enderun*.

bitanu. Inner court of the palace in Assyria, as opposed to *babanu*, the outer court.

bo. Count (Chinese title).

bonum publicum (Latin). Common good.

booi. Manchu phrase, meaning 'of the household', referring to unfree bondservants.

bostancı. Ottoman title, literally 'gardener'; also, the *bostancı* corps of troops at the Ottoman court.

boyar. High-ranking Russian noble.

bozu (Japanese). 'Shaved head', referring to male and female monks who acted as servants and intermediaries at the shogun's court.

buke shohatto. 'Laws for the Military Houses', a collection of laws promulgated by Japan's Tokugawa shogunate governing the responsibilities and activities of *daimyo*.

buke. Japanese warrior class.

chakravartin or **cakkavatti**. Ancient Indian concept of the world ruler, or 'wheel-turning monarch'.

chao (Chinese). Court, morning audience.

Chiyoda castle. See Edo castle.

cihuacoatl. Aztec title, 'Woman Snake', kingmaker and advisor to the king.

comitatus (Latin). Germanic warband; see *Gefolgschaft*.

conducteur de la haquenée. Conductor of the ambler, a staff position at the French court.

courreur de vin. Wine runner, a staff position at the French court.

çuhadar. Keeper of the garment, an Ottoman office at the Topkapı palace.

daijosai. Great Thanksgiving festival, a Japanese Shinto inauguration ritual.

daimyo. Territorial lord in Japan; upper layer of the warrior class.

daire-i 'adliye (Arabic). 'Circle of justice', view of society whereby all social groups have set responsibilities.

dajodaijin. Prime minister, highest office of Japan's early imperial government, persisting in systems of ranking in later times; see *sadaijin*.

Dajo-tenno. Honorific title for a Japanese emperor who abdicated in favour of a successor.

damad. A Persian word meaning son-in-law, used as a title for officials married to princesses of the Ottoman dynasty.

dar or **darbar** (Persian). Door, gate, or dwelling, also used to refer to the ruler's court or a government bureau.

dauphin. Title given to the heir-apparent to the throne of France.

dayu (Chinese). Special ritual for rain.

defterdar. 'Keeper of the Registers', an Ottoman term for the chief financial officer.

devshirme. Ottoman term for the periodical levy of Christian children employed at court and in military-administrative functions.

dharma (Sanskrit), **dhamma** (Pali). Cosmic law and order.

dirlik (Turkish). Living or livelihood, in the Ottoman empire referring to an income provided by the state for the support of persons in its service.

divan, Divan-ı Hümayun. Imperial council of the Ottoman empire.

doğanci. Falconers serving the Ottoman sultan.

Donghuamen. Eastern Flowery Gate, the east gate of the Forbidden City.

droit divin (French). Divine right of kings, a doctrine in defence of monarchical absolutism.

dülbend oğlani. Keeper of the linen, Ottoman office at the Topkapı palace.

dvor (Russian). Palace or retinue of a ruler.

Edo castle. Fifteenth-century castle built in Edo (Tokyo) used as residence and seat of government by the Tokugawa shoguns.

eghaevbo n'ore. Appointed town chiefs in Benin.

enderun (Turkish), **andarun** (Persian). 'Inside' service, the inner court of the imperial household of the Ottoman sultan, as opposed to *birun* or 'outside' service.

farr or **farr-i Izadi** (Persian). Essential quality of rulers, divine radiance, divine effulgence.

Fatehpur Sikri. Palace city in North India near Agra, founded by the Mughal emperor Akbar and shortly thereafter serving as capital of the Mughal empire.

Forbidden City. The Chinese imperial palace complex in Beijing. It served as residence to the emperors and was the centre of government during the Ming and Qing dynasties.

fudai daimyo. Hereditary lords who pledged loyalty to the Tokugawa dynasty before the Battle of Sekigahara.

Gefolgschaft. Following, Germanic warband, see *comitatus.*

ghulam (Arabic). Boy, servant, slave, commonly used for slave-soldiers.

gong. Duke (Chinese title).

gyase. Akan word meaning beneath or below the hearth, referring to an oblong or square yard, the courtyard of an Asante household.

gyasefo. People around the hearth: servants and household slaves of an Asante household.

gyasehene. In the Asante federation, the leader of all palace retainers at the *asantehene*'s court.

hanan. Inka/Quechua term for upper; upper moiety or kinship group; see *hurin.*

haseki. Title for an Ottoman sultan's favourite consort who had given birth to a child.

hashiya (Arabic). Entourage of a ruler; see *bayt, khassakiya.*

hass. A land grant in the Ottoman empire worth more than 100,000 akçe.

hass oda başı. Chief of the privy chamber in the Ottoman Topkapı palace.

hatamoto. 'Under the banner', a term used by the Tokugawa for direct vassals of the shogun.

hiaa. Harem of the Asante king.

Hofburg palace. Habsburg palace and main residence located in the centre of Vienna.

hou. Marquis (Chinese title).

huey tlatoani. Supreme king of Tenochtitlan.

hunjun (Chinese). Muddleheaded ruler.

hurin. Inka/Quechua term for lower; lower moiety or kinship group; see *hanan.*

Id al-Fitr. Feast of Breaking the Fast, an Islamic festival marking the end of Ramadan.

infantia (Latin). Age up to six or seven.

insei. Japanese, 'cloistered government', rule by emperors who retired to a Buddhist cloister.

intisab. Personal connections, patron–client relationships in the Ottoman empire.

iuventus (Latin). Age between adolescence and full maturity, usually seen as ending with marriage.

jagir. 'Holding land', the usufruct of landholdings in the Mughal empire.

jetons (French). Coins or tokens distributed during ceremonial occasions in Europe.

jharoka-i darshan. Regular public appearance or 'viewing' by the Mughal emperor.

jimat (Javanese). Amulet.

Jingyunmen. Gate of Good Fortune, main connection between inner and outer court during ceremonial occasions in the Forbidden City.

jinshi. 'Presented scholar' who had passed the third and highest level of Chinese civil service examinations.

jugo. Members of regental families serving in the ministerial office of the Tokugawa shogunate.

junjichu. Grand Council of the Qing dynasty.

junwang. Commandery, second princely rank during the Ming and Qing dynasties.

juren. 'Recommended man' who had passed the second level of Chinese civil service examinations.

kadıasker. A chief judge in the Ottoman empire, originally restricted to military affairs.

kafes. 'Cage', Ottoman term for the restricted area in the Topkapı harem where princes lived from the seventeenth century onwards.

kaieki (Japanese). Confiscation of fiefs and status.

kannumon or **kanounnon.** Fon word for slave, used for prisoners of war and raids in the Dahomey kingdom.

kapucubaşı. Palace doorkeeper, Ottoman office at the Topkapı palace and honorary rank.

khassakiya. Arabic term for retinue; see also *bayt, hashiya.*

Kindairi-Gosho. Major Kyoto palace compound.

kokas. Foster-brothers of princes in the Mughal empire.

kpojito. 'She who helped the leopard', female reign-mate to the king of Dahomey.

kraton or **keraton** (Javanese). Royal palace.

Kremlin. A fortified complex in Moscow which served as residence to various Russian rulers from the fourteenth century onwards before their move to St Petersburg.

kuge. Kyoto court nobles.

kuge shohatto. Code for court nobles, issued by Tokugawa Ieyasu.

kul. Ottoman term for palace slaves and more generally for all servants of the sultan and his military retainers (*kapikulu*).

kuriltai or **kurultai** (and various other spellings). Assembly of Mongol chieftains gathered to decide on military matters or choose the successor to the khan.

kuroshoin. Audience room in the shogun's quarters in Chiyoda castle.

lala. Preceptor or male tutor to Ottoman princes.

lit de justice. Session of the Parisian Parlement in the presence of the king.

maidan. In the camps of the Seljuq dynasty, an open space for polo, other contests, and troop exercises; urban square (Istanbul, Isfahan).

mandala (Sanskrit). Circle; often used to describe the diffuse distribution of political power in Southeast Asia.

mansab. Office, dignity, rank in the Mughal empire.

mansabdar. An official of the Mughal empire, holder of a *mansab*.

mazalim (Arabic). Grievances. Rulers listened to their subjects' grievances in mazalim courts; see *zulm*.

mestnichestvo. 'Code of precedence', a hierarchical system in early modern Russia.

mugabe. Title of the king of Ankole.

mukama. Title of the king of Bunyoro.

murid. 'He who seeks', a novice or seeker of enlightenment on the Sufi path.

musahib. 'Boon companion' of the sultan.

müteferrika. 'Distinguished person' entering into Ottoman court service, later a corps of guards, used for important public or political missions.

naam. Among the Mamprusi people of northern Ghana and Togo, *naam* refers to the essential quality of kings, the chiefly or kingly power.

nagast. Title of king-emperor of the Ethiopian empire.

nakaoku. Middle Interior of Chiyoda castle in Edo.

Nauruz or **Nowruz.** Persian New Year.

nei (Chinese). Inner.

neichao (Chinese). Inner court.

neige. Grand Secretariat, leading advisory body during the Ming dynasty.

neiwufu. 'Imperial household department' of the Qing dynasty.

nenju gyoji. 'Annual events', Japanese imperial annual ritual observances.

nggogol (Javanese). Collective processions.

niinamesai. Japanese harvest festival.

nişancı. 'Keeper of the Seal', the chancellor in the Ottoman empire.

nithar. Noun of *nathara*, 'to scatter, spread abroad', referring to the showering of valuables and coins during ceremonial occasions in the premodern Middle East; it can also refer to the coins themselves (see *jetons*).

oba. Benin king. Word for king in the Nigerian Yoruba language.

ohiroma. Great Hall and audience room of the Tokugawa Chiyoda castle in Edo.

omote (Japanese). Front or exterior; also used to refer to the exterior of Chiyoda castle.

ooku. Great Interior, referring to the female quarters of Chiyoda castle.

osmanlı. Leading servants of the house of Osman.

otu. The three palace associations of Benin.

pasha. Highest official title in the Ottoman empire, given to provincial governors and viziers.

pedilavium (Latin). Christian rite of washing the feet of the poor on Maundy Thursday, performed by secular rulers.

pepe. Javanese imploring the king's help by sitting unprotected from the sun in full in view of the palace.

philoi (ancient Greek). 'Friend', a title for royal friends and advisors of the king.

pir. Spiritual guide or director among the Sufis.

piskes, pishkesh, pishkash (Persian). Gifts, or tribute in the form of gifts.

podagra. Gout of the big toe.

pueritia (Latin). Age from seven to thirteen or fourteen.

qadi court. Court of justice in accordance with Islamic religious law.

qal'a (Arabic). Physical abode of the prince; see *dar, qasr*.

qasr. Islamic castle, fortress, large house, or palace.

Qianqinggong. Palace of Heavenly Purity, in the inner section of the Forbidden City in Beijing.

qinwang. Full prince, first-rank prince during the Ming and Qing dynasties.

qishlaq. Turkic term for winter pastures, as opposed to *yaylaq*, summer pastures.

ratu. Javanese princess, royal wife.

ratu adil. 'Just king', a messianic figure in Indonesian folklore.

reaya. 'Flock', taxpaying commoners in the Ottoman empire, differentiated from leading group of *askeri*.

Red Fort. Mughal fort in Old Delhi (Shahjahanabad) that served as the residence and seat of government of multiple Mughal emperors.

rikab (Persian). Stirrup; also used as a term for Mughal power.

rikabdar. Stirrup-holder, an Ottoman court office.

sadaijin. 'Minister of the Left', a senior office of Japan's early imperial government, persisting as a supreme rank in later times; see *dajodaijin*.

sangha. Buddhist monks.

sankin kotai. 'Alternate attendance', referring to the regulated residence of *daimyo* in Tokugawa Edo.

Sapa Inka. Paramount ruler of the Inka.

saraparda (Persian). 'Palace made of cloth', cloth enclosure, curtain, palace.

saray (Persian). House, palace, inn.

sawar (Persian). Horseman; used in the Mughal empire to refer to the number of horsemen a *mansabdar* was required to maintain.

selir. Javanese royal concubine.

seraglio (Italian). Oriental courts or the living quarters of the harem.

şeyhülislam. Chief jurisconsult in the Ottoman empire.

shahanshah. 'King of kings' (Persian title).

Shangshufang. Chinese palace school for princes.

shari'a (Arabic). Holy law.

shimpan daimyo. Collateral lines of the Tokugawa shoguns.

shinno. Japanese imperial prince; collateral houses of the imperial dynasty.

shiroshoin. Audience room in Chiyoda castle.

shogun. Military commander or general; title of leading governors of Japan since 1192, most notably the Tokugawa dynasty.

silahdar. 'Sword-bearer', a court title in the Islamic world.

sipahi (Persian). Horseman; Ottoman household cavalry corps.

speculum principis (Latin). 'Princely mirror', advice literature for princes.

sultana. Sultan's daughter.

sur-i-hümayun. Ottoman circumcision festival.

Taihedian. Hall of Supreme Harmony, the largest hall of the Forbidden City, in its outer section.

taishang huang. 'Supreme emperor', retired emperor and father of ruling Chinese emperor.

tarkhan. Central Asian title, used by the Jochids.

tecpan calli. Aztec word for palace.

telhis. Written reports summarising important matters for the Ottoman sultan, a form of written communication between grand vizier and sultan.

tenno. 'Heavenly sovereign', title for the emperor of Japan.

tenpu (Japanese). Transfers of territory.

teyul, or **tuyul, tiyul.** A grant of land as revenue for soldiers and officials in Persia.

tianming. Mandate of heaven, an ancient Chinese belief that heaven bestowed upon the emperor the right to rule, which demanded painstaking ritual and moral propriety.

tianzi. Son of heaven, the Chinese imperial title.

timar. 'Care, attention', a land grant meant to sustain an Ottoman cavalry army (see *dirlik, hass*).

ting (Chinese). Courtyard.

tlatoani. Aztec king. See *huey tlatoani*.

tlatoque. Plural of *tlatoani*.

Topkapı palace. Name of the palace complex in Istanbul that served as residence of the Ottoman sultans from the fifteenth to the nineteenth century.

tozama daimyo. 'Outside daimyo', former peers of the Tokugawa who had not supported the founder Ieyasu in the decisive battle of Sekigahara.

ulema. Muslim legal scholars.

umma. Community of Muslims.

uzama. Hereditary nobles in Benin, founders of the first dynasty.

vakif. See *waqf*.

valide sultan. 'Mother sultan', the queen mother of a ruling sultan in the Ottoman empire.

Versailles, Palace of. French royal residence and centre of government from 1682 to 1789.

virilitas (Latin). Age from twenty to forty or fifty.

vivente rege or **vivente imperatore.** 'With the king still living', the designation or election of a successor during the lifetime of the ruler.

wai (Chinese). Outer.

waichao (Chinese). Outer court.

waqf (Arabic) or **vakif** (Ottoman). Islamic term for pious foundations.

wazīr (Arabic). Vizier or chief minister.

wu wei. Daoist principle of non-action.

Wumen. Meridian Gate, the southern gate of the Forbidden City.

yamen. The office or residence of a Chinese magistrate.

Yangxindian. Palace of Mental Cultivation, actual residence of the Chinese emperors in the eighteenth century.

yaylaq. Turkic term for summer pastures, as opposed to *qishlaq*, winter pastures.

zamindar. Local hereditary elite in the Mughal empire.

zat. In the Mughal system of office ranks, *zat* constituted the personal rank of an official, indicating pay and rank. It was subject to change by the prince.

zulm (Arabic). Unjust acts, wrongdoings, oppression, tyranny. See *mazalim*.

Bibliography

Source editions

Abu'l-Fazl, *The Ain i Akbari*, ed. H. Blochmann, 3 vols. (Calcutta, 1873–94). *The Akbar Nama of Abu-l-Fazl (History of the Reign of Akbar Including an Account of his Predecessors)*, ed. Henry Beveridge, 3 vols. (New Delhi, 1973).

Acton, John E.E. Dalberg, *Essays on Freedom and Power*, ed. Gertrude Himmelfarb (London, 1956).

Aristotle, *Politics*, trans. H. Rackham, Loeb Classical Library 264 (Cambridge, MA, 1932).

Arvieux, Laurent d', *Mémoires du chevalier d'Arvieux, envoyé extraordinaire du Roy à la Porte . . .*, ed. R.P. Jean-Baptiste Labat, 6 vols. (Paris, 1735).

Babur, *The Baburnama: Memoirs of Babur, Prince and Emperor*, trans. Wheeler M. Thackston (New York and Oxford, 1996).

Bacon, Francis, *The Essays*, ed. John Pitcher (London, 1985).

Badā'ūnī, 'Abd al-Qādir ibn Mulūk Shāh, *Muntakhabu-T-Tawārikh*, trans. W.H. Lowe et al., 3 vols. (Patna, 1973).

Balzac, Honoré de, *Histoire de l'empereur* (Paris, 1842).

Bancks, John, *The History of the Life and Reign of the Czar Peter the Great, Emperor of All Russia and Father of his Country* (London, 1740).

Bary, Wm. Theodore de, Donald Keene, George Tanabe, and Paul Varley (eds.), *Sources of Japanese Tradition*, vol. I: *From Earliest Times to 1600* (New York, 2001).

Bell, John, *A Journey from St. Petersburg to Pekin, 1719–22*, ed. J.L. Stevenson (Edinburgh, 1966).

Bernier, François, *Voyages de François Bernier, docteur en medecine de la Faculté de Montpellier: contenant la description des états du grand Mogul, de l'Hindoustan, du royaume de Kachemire*, vol. II (Amsterdam, 1711).

Blondel, Nicolas-François, 'Plan general de la Ville Jardins Chateau et Parc de Versailles', *Architecture françoise*, 4/1 (1752).

Bobovius, Albertus, *Topkapı: relation du serail du Grand Seigneur*, ed. Annie Berthier and Stéphane Yerasimo (Arles and Paris, 1999).

Bossuet, Jacques-Bénigne, *Politique tirée des propres paroles de l'Écriture sainte* (Paris, 1709).

Botero, Giovanni, *On the Causes of the Greatness and Magnificence of Cities, 1588*, ed. Geoffrey Symcox (Toronto and London, 2012).

Bouvet, Joachim, *Histoire de l'empereur de la Chine, presentée au roy* (The Hague, 1699).

Bowdich, Thomas Edward, *Mission from Cape Coast Castle to Ashantee: With a Descriptive Account of that Kingdom* (London, 1873).

Bruce, James, *Travels to Discover the Source of the Nile, in the Years 1768, 1769, 1770, 1771, 1772, and 1773*, vol. II (London, 1790).

Bruyère, Jean de la, *The Characters of Jean de La Bruyere*, trans. Henri van Laun (London, 1885).

Burton, Richard F. (trans.), *The Book of the Thousand Nights and a Night* (s.l., 1885).

Busbecq, Ogier Ghislain de, *The Turkish Letters of Ogier Ghiselin de Busbecq, Imperial Ambassador at Constantinople, 1554–1562: Translated from the Latin of the Elzevir Edition of 1663* (Oxford, 1927).

Calvete de Estrella, Juan Cristóbal, *El felicissimo viaie d'el muy alto y muy poderoso Príncipe Don Phelippe . . .* (Antwerp, 1552).

Carton, Charles Louis, *Notice biographique sur le père Ferdinand Verbiest, missionaire à la Chine* (Bruges, 1839).

Castiglione, Baldassar, *The Book of the Courtier (1528)*, trans. Leonard Eckstein Opdyke (New York, 1903).

Çelebi, Evliya, *The Intimate Life of an Ottoman Statesman: Melek Ahmed Pasha (1588–1622) as Portrayed in Evliya Çelebi's Book of Travels*, ed. Robert Dankoff (Albany, NY, 1991).

Chardin, Jean, *Voyages du chevalier Chardin en Perse, et autres lieux de l'Orient . . .*, ed. Louis Langlès, 10 vols. (Paris, 1811).

Charles V, *Das Vermächtnis Kaiser Karls V: die politischen Testamente*, ed. Armin Kohnle (Darmstadt, 2005).

Chaumont, Alexandre de, *Relation de l'ambassade de Mr. le Chevalier de Chaumont a la cour du roy de Siam, avec ce qui s'est passé de plus remarquable durant son voyage* (Amsterdam, 1686).

Churchill, Awnsham and John Churchill (eds.), *A Collection of Voyages and Travels: Some Now First Printed from Original Manuscripts, Others Now First Published in English . . .* 6 vols. (London, 1732).

Clément, Pierre, *Madame de Montespan et Louis XIV* (Paris, 1868).

Collins, Samuel, *The Present State of Russia* (London, 1671), and online edn, ed. Marshall T. Poe, http://myweb.uiowa.edu/mapoe/Publications/Collins.pdf.

Confucius, *Analects*, trans. William Edward Soothill (Edinburgh, 1910; repr. London, 1995).

Couret de Villeneuve, Louis Pierre, *Recueil amusant de Voyages, en vers et en prose; faits par différents auteurs, auquel on a joint un choix des epîtres, contes & fables morales qui ont rapport aux voyages* (Paris, 1787).

Court, Pieter de la, *Aanwysing der heilsame politike gronden en maximen van de Republike van Holland en West-Vriesland* (Leiden and Rotterdam, 1669).

[Courtilz de Sandras, Gatien de], *Le Passe-temps royal, ou Les Amours de Mademoiselle de Fontange* (s.l., 1680).

Dan Shi, *Mémoires d'un eunuque dans la Cité Interdite* (Arles, 1991).

Dangeau, Philippe de Courcillon, *Journal du Marquis de Dangeau*, ed. Eud. Soulié and L. Dussieux 19 vols. (Paris, 1854–60).

Dapper, Olfert, *Beschryving des keizerryks van Taising of Sina* (Amsterdam, 1670).
Gedenkwaerdig bedryf der Nederlandsche Oost-Indische Maetschappye, op de kuste en in het Keizerrijk van Taising of Sina (Amsterdam, 1670).
Naukeurige beschrijvinge der Afrikaensche gewesten van Egypten, Barbaryen, Lybien, Biledulgerid, Negroslant, Guinea, Ethiopiën, Abyssinie. Vertoont in de benamingen ... steden, gewassen, dieren, zeeden, drachten, talen, rijkdommen, godsdiensten ... (s.l., 1676).

Diaz del Castillo, Bernal, *The History of the Conquest of New Spain by Bernal Diaz del Castillo*, ed. Davíd Carrasco (Albuquerque, NM, 2008).

Duchhardt, Heinz (ed.), *Politische Testamente und andere Quellen zum Fürstenethos der Frühen Neuzeit* (Darmstadt, 1987).

Dupuy, Pierre, *Traité de la majorité de nos rois et des regences du royaume* (Paris, 1655).

Eradut Khan, *A Translation of the Memoirs of Eradut Khan, a Nobleman of Hindostan ...*, trans. Jonathan Scott (London, 1786).

Faber, Frederic Jules, *Histoire du théâtre français en Belgique depuis son origine jusqù'a nos jours: d'apres des documents inédits reposant aux archives générales du royaume*, 5 vols. (Brussels and Paris, 1878).

Forbes, Frederick Edwyn, *Dahomey and the Dahomans: Being the Journals of Two Missions to the King of Dahomey, and Residence at his Capital, in the Years 1849 and 1850* (London, 1851).

Frederick II of Prussia, *Anti-Machiavel, ou essai de critique sur Le Prince de Machiavel* (Brussels, 1740).

Ghazali, *Ghazali's Book of Counsel for Kings (Naṣīḥat al-mulūk)*, ed. Frank R.C. Bagley (New York, 1964).

Grieck, Joan de, *De heerelycke ende vrolycke daeden van keyser Carel den V.* (Brussels, 1674).

Halde, Jean-Baptiste Du, *Description géographique, historique, chronologique, politique, et physique de l'empire de la Chine et de la Tartarie chinoise* (The Hague, 1739).

Han Fei Tzu, *Han Fei Tzu: Basic Writings*, trans. Burton Watson (New York, 1964).

Hérissé, Auguste le, *L'ancien royaume du Dahomey, moeurs, religion, histoire* (Paris, 1911).

Héroard, Jean, *Journal de Jean Héroard sur l'enfance et la jeunesse de Louis XIII (1601–1628)*, ed. E. Soulié and E. de Barthélemy, 2 vols. (Paris, 1868).

Hippocrates, *Airs, Waters, Places*, in *Hippocrates*, vol. I, trans. W.H.S. Jones, Loeb Classical Library (Cambridge, MA, 1923).

Huang Tsung-Hsi, *Waiting for the Dawn: A Plan for the Prince. Huang Tsung-Hsi's Ming-I-Tai-Fang Lu*, trans. Wm. Theodore de Bary (New York, 1993).

Hyegyong, *The Memoirs of Lady Hyegyong: The Autobiographical Writings of a Crown Princess of Eighteenth-Century Korea*, ed. JaHyun Kim Haboush (New York, 1996).

Ibn Khaldun, *The Muqaddimah: An Introduction to History*, ed. Franz Rosenthal (Princeton, NJ, and Oxford, 1967).

Ivan IV, *The Correspondence between Prince A.M. Kurbsky and Tsar Ivan IV of Russia*, ed. J.L.I. Fennel (Cambridge, 1963).

Jahangir, Nur-ud-din Muhammad, *The Tuzuk-i-Jahangiri; or, Memoirs of Jahangir*, ed. Henry Beveridge and Alexander Rogers (London, 1909).

Jin, Yi, *Mémoires d'une dame de cour dans la Cité Interdite*, ed. Qiang Dong (Arles, 1996).

Johnson, Samuel Obadiah, *The History of the Yorubas: From the Earliest Times to the Beginning of the British Protectorate* (Lagos, 1921).

Joinville, Jean de and Geffroy de Villehardouin, *Chronicles of the Crusades*, ed. Caroline Smith (London and New York, 2009).

Kaempfer, Engelbert, *Amoenitatum exoticarum politico-physico-medicarum fasciculi V* (Lemgoviae, 1712).

De beschryving van Japan, behelsende een verhaal van den ouden en tegenwoordigen staat en regeering van dat ryk ... en van hunnen koophandel met de Nederlanders en de Chineesen. Benevens eene beschryving van het koningryk Siam (Amsterdam, 1729).

Engelbert Kaempfer am Hofe des persischen Grosskönigs 1684–1685, ed. Walther Hinz (Leipzig, 1940).

Kaempfer's Japan: Tokugawa Culture Observed, ed. Beatrice M. Bodart-Bailey (Honolulu, HI, 1999).

Kautiliya, *The Kauṭilīya Arthaśāstra*, ed. R.P Kangle, 3 vols. (Bombay, 1960–5).

Khevenhüller-Metsch, Johann Josef, *Aus der Zeit Maria Theresias: Tagebuch des Fürsten Johann Josef Khevenhüller-Metsch, kaiserlichen Obersthofmeisters 1742–1776*, ed. R. Khevenmüller-Metsch and H. Schlitter, 7 vols. (Vienna, 1907–25).

Kia-Li, *Livre des rites domestiques chinois*, ed. Charles de Harlez (Paris, 1889).

Komroff, Manuel (ed.), *Contemporaries of Marco Polo: Consisting of the Travel Records to the Eastern Parts of the World of William of Rubruck (1253–1255), the Journey of John of Pian de Carpini (1245–1247), the Journal of Friar Odoric (1318–1330) & the Oriental Travels of Rabbi Benjamin of Tudela (1160–1173)* (New York, 1928).

Küntzel, Georg and Martin Hass (eds.), *Die politischen Testamente der Hohenzollern nebst ergänzenden Aktenstücken* (Stuttgart, 1911).

Leopold I, *Privatbriefe Kaiser Leopold I an den Grafen F.E. Pötting 1662–1673*, ed. A.F. Pribram and M. Landwehr von Pragenau, 2 vols. (Vienna, 1903–4).

Louis IX, Saint Louis, *The Teachings of Saint Louis: A Critical Text*, ed. David O'Connell (Chapel Hill, NC, 1972).

Louis XIV, *Mémoires de Louis XIV pour l'instruction du dauphin*, ed. Charles Dreyss, 2 vols. (Paris, 1860).

Mémoires, suivis de Manière de montrer les jardins de Versailles, ed. Joël Cornette (Paris, 2007).

Oeuvres de Louis XIV, ed. Philippe Henri de Grimoard and P.A. Grouvelle, 6 vols. (Paris, 1806).

Louis XVI, *Mémoire du Roi, adressé à tous les François, à sa sortie de Paris* (Paris, 1791).

Loyseau, Charles, *Les oeuvres de maistre Charles Loyseau ...* (Paris, 1678).

Lünig, Johann Christian, *Theatrum ceremoniale historico-politicum, oder historisch- und politischer Schau-Platz aller Ceremonien, welche so wohl an europäischen Höfen als auch sonsten bey vielen illustren Fällen beobachtet worden* (Leipzig, 1719–20).

Luynes, Charles Philippe d'Albert, duc de, *Mémoires du duc de Luynes sur la cour de Louis XV (1735–1758)*, ed. L. Dussieux and E. Soulié, 17 vols. (Paris, 1860–5).

Machiavelli, Niccolò, *The Prince*, trans. George Bull (London, 1961).

The Prince, trans. Luigi Ricci (London, 1921).

Mairobert, Mathieu François Pidanzat de, *Anecdotes sur M. la comtesse du Barri* (London, 1775).

Major, John S. et al. (trans.), *The Huainanzi: A Guide to the Theory and Practice of Government in Early Han China* (New York, 2010).

Mandeville, John, *The Travels of Sir John Mandeville* (London, 1900).

Manucci, Niccolao, *A Pepys of Mogul India, 1653–1708: Being an Abridged Edition of the "Storia do Mogor" of Niccolao Manucci*, ed. William Irvine and Margaret L. Irvine (New York, 1913).

Maria Theresa, *Briefe der Kaiserin Maria Theresia an ihre Kinder und Freunde*, ed. Alfred von Arneth, 4 vols. (Vienna, 1881).

Correspondance secrète entre Marie-Thérèse et le cte de Mercy-Argenteau. Avec les lettres de Marie-Thérèse et de Marie-Antoinette, ed. Alfred von Arneth and Auguste Geffroy, 3 vols. (Paris, 1874–5).

Handwritten notes in Österreichische Nationalbibliothek, cod. ser. n. 1713, fol. 77^r.

Martin, Louis-Aimé (ed.), *Lettres édifiantes et curieuses concernant l'Asie, l'Afrique et l'Amérique, avec quelques relations nouvelles des missions, et des notes géographiques et historiques*, 4 vols. (Paris, 1843).

Maximilian I, *Maximilians I vertraulicher Briefwechsel mit Sigmund Prüschenk Freiherr zu Stettenberg nebst einer Anzahl zeitgenössischer Briefe*, ed. Victor Felix von Kraus (Innsbruck, 1875).

Minorsky, Vladimir (ed.), *Tadhkirat Al-Muluk: A Manual of Safavid Administration* (London, 1943).

Monserrate, Antonio, *The Commentary of Father Monserrate, S.J. on his Journey to the Court of Akbar*, ed. S.N. Banerjee (Oxford, 1922).

Montesquieu, Charles de Secondat, baron de, *The Spirit of the Laws*, trans. Thomas Nugent (London, 1752).

Moser, Johann Jacob, *Neues teutsches Staatsrecht: von dem Römischen Kayser, Römischen König und denen Reichs-Vicarien* (Frankfurt, 1767).

Teutsches Staats-Recht: darinnen von des Römischen Kaysers Foro, Absterben, Abdanckung und Absetzung, von der Römischen Kayserin, von des Römischen Königs Wahl, Crönung, Regierungs-Antritt . . . (Leipzig, 1742).

Muḥammad Bāqir Najm-i Sānī, *Advice on the Art of Governance (Mau'izah-I Jahangiri) of Muhammad Baqir Najm-I Sani: An Indo-Islamic Mirror for Princes*, ed. Sajida Sultana Alvi (New York, 1989).

Mustafa bin Ahmet Ali, *The Ottoman Gentleman of the Sixteenth Century: Mustafa Ali's Mevaidun-Nefais Fi Kavaidil-Mecalis 'Tables of Delicacies Concerning the Rules of Social Gatherings'*, trans. Douglas S. Brookes (Cambridge, MA, 2003).

Nasiri, Mirza Naqi, *Titles & emoluments in Safavid Iran: A Third Manual of Safavid Administration*, trans. Willem Floor (Washington, DC, 2008).

Niẓām al-Mulk, *The Book of Government or Rules for Kings: The Siyar Al-Muluk or Siyasat-nama of Nizam Al-Mulk*, ed. Hubert Darke (New York, 1960).

Norris, Robert, *Memoirs of the Reign of Bossa Ahádee, King of Dahomy, an Inland Country of Guiney: to which are added, the Author's Journey to Abomey, the Capital; and A Short Account of the African Slave Trade* (London, 1789).

Ohsson, Ignatius Mouradgea d', *Tableau général de l'empire othoman: l'état actuel de l'empire othoman*, 7 vols. (Paris, 1824).

Orléans, Elisabeth-Charlotte von, *Briefe*, ed. Wilhelm Ludwig Holland, 6 vols. (Stuttgart, 1867–81).

Passer, Justus Eberhard, 'Berichte des Hessen-Darmstädtischen Gesandten Justus Eberhard Passer an die Landgräfin Elisabeth Dorothea über die Vorgänge am kaiserlichen Hofe und in Wien von 1680–1683', ed. Ludwig Baur, *Archiv für Österreichische Geschichte*, 37 (1867), 271–409.

Pigeaud, Theodore Gauthier Th., *Java in the 14th Century: A Study in Cultural History. The Nagara-Kertagama by Rakawi Prapanca of Majapahit, 1365 A.D. III translations*, Koninklijk Instituut voor Taal-, Land-, en Volkenkunde 4/3 (The Hague 1960).

Polybius, *The Histories*, ed. F.W. Walbank, Chr. Habicht, and W.R. Paton (Cambridge, MA, 2011).

Porter, Robert Ker, *Travels in Georgia, Persia, Armenia, ancient Babylonia ... during the years 1817, 1818, 1819, and 1820* (London, 1821).

Prempeh I, *The History of Ashanti Kings and the Whole Country Itself and Other Writings by Otumfuo, Nana Agyeman Prempeh I*, ed. Emmanuel Akyeampong et al. (Oxford, 2003).

Prutky, Remedius, *Prutky's Travels in Ethiopia and Other Countries*, trans. and ed. J.H. Arrowsmith-Brown (London, 1991).

Pufendorf, Esaias, *Bericht über Kaiser Leopold, seinen Hof und die Österreichische Politik 1671 – 1674*, ed. Carl Gustav Helbig (Leipzig, 1862).

Raffles, Sophia, *Memoir of the Life and Public Services of Sir Thomas Stamford Raffles Particularly in the Government of Java, 1811–1816, Bencoolen and its Dependencies, 1817–1824: With Details of the Commerce and Resources of the Eastern Archipelago, and Selections from his Correspondence* (London, 1835).

Raffles, Thomas Stamford, *The History of Java*, vol. I (London, 1830).

Rockhill, William Woodville, *Report of William W. Rockhill, Late Commissioner to China, with Accompanying Documents* (Washington, DC, 1901).

Rycaut, Paul, *The History of the Present State of the Ottoman Empire ...* (London, 1682).

Sahagún, Bernardino de, *Florentine Codex: General History of the Things of New Spain*, ed. Arthur J.O. Anderson and Charles E. Dribble (Santa Fe, NM, 1954).

Saint-Just, Louis Antoine Léon ˙de, *Oeuvres complètes de Saint-Just*, ed. Charles Vellay, 2 vols. (Paris, 1908).

Saint-Pierre, Charles Irenée Castel de, *Discours sur la polysynodie: où l'on démontre que la polysynodie, ou pluralité des conseils, est la forme de ministère la plus avantageuse pour un roi, et pour son royaume* (Amsterdam, 1719).

Saint-Simon, Louis de Rouvroy, duc de, *Mémoires*, ed. A. de Boislisle, 43 vols. (Paris, 1879–1930).

Semedo, Alvarez, *The History of that Great and Renowned Monarchy of China* (London, 1655).

Sima Guang, *Comprehensive Mirror in Aid of Governance*, 10 vols. (Beijing, 1956).

Skertchly, J.A., *Dahomey As It Is : Being a Narrative of Eight Months' Residence in that Country* ... (London, 1874).

Speke, John Hannig, *Journal of the Discovery of the Source of the Nile* (Edinburgh, 1864).

Stanley, Henry Edward John (ed.), *Travels to Tana and Persia by Josafa Barbaro and Ambrogio Contarini* (New York, 1873).

Stary, Giovanni, 'A preliminary note on some Manchu letters of the Kang-hsiemperor to his grandmother', in Giovanni Stary (ed.), *Proceedings of the 38th Permanent International Conference (PIAC)* (Wiesbaden, 1996), 365–76.

Stella, Joannes Christophorus Calvetus, *El felicissimo viaie d'el muy alto y muy poderoso Príncipe Don Phelippe, hijo d'el Emperador Don Carlos Quinto Maximo, desde España à sus tierras dela baxa Alemaña : con la descripcion de todos los Estados de Brabante y Flandes* (Antwerp, 1552).

Talleyrand-Périgord, Charles-Maurice de, *Rapport sur l'instruction publique, fait au nom du Comité de constitution de l'Assemblée nationale, les 10, 11, et 19 septembre 1791* (Paris, 1791).

Tavernier, Jean-Baptiste, *The Six Voyages of John Baptista Tavernier through Turkey into Persia and the East-Indies, Finished in the Year 1670: Together with a New Relation of the Present Grand Seignor's Seraglio, by the Same Author* (London, 1678).

Thévenot, Jean de, *Voyages de Mr de Thévenot contenant la relation de l'Indostan, des nouveaux Mogols et des autres peuples & pays des Indes* (Paris, 1684).

Tillet, Jean Du, *Les mémoires et recherches de Jean Du Tillet, greffier de la cour de Parlement à Paris, contenans plusieurs choses memorables pour l'intelligence de l'estat des affaires de France* (Paris, 1578).

Titsingh, Isaak, *Illustrations of Japan; Consisting of Private Memoirs and Anecdotes of the Reigning Dynasty of the Djogouns, Or Sovereigns of Japan* ... (London, 1822).

Visconti, Giovanni Battista Primi, *Mémoires de Primi Visconti sur la cour de Louis XIV, 1673–1681*, ed. Jean-François Solnon (Paris, 1988).

Voltaire, 'Commentaire sur l'esprit des lois', in *Oeuvres complètes de Voltaire: avec des notes et une notice historique sur la vie de Voltaire*, vol. V (Paris, 1835), 444–75.

Wade, Geoff (trans.), *Southeast Asia in the Ming Shi-lu: An Open Access Resource* (Singapore: Asia Research Institute and the Singapore E-Press, National University of Singapore), http://epress.nus.edu.sg/msl.

Wei, Wang, *Wang Wei*, trans. Marsha L. Wagner (Boston, MA, 1981).

Wilhelmine, Frédérique Sophie, of Bayreuth-Prussia, *Mémoires de Frédérique Sophie Wilhelmine, margrave de Bareith, soeur de Frédéric le Grand: depuis l'année 1706 jusqu'à 1742, écrits de sa main*, 2 vols. (Brunswick, 1845).

Winter, J.W., 'Beknopte beschrijving van het Hof Soerakarta in 1824', ed. G.P. Rouffaer, *Bijdragen tot de Taal-, Land- en Volkenkunde van Nederlandsch-Indië*, 54 (1902), 15–172.

Yirmisekiz, Çelebi Mehmed, *Le paradis des infidèles: relation de Yirmisekiz Çelebi Mehmed efendi, ambassadeur ottoman en France sous la Régence*, ed. Gilles Veinstein, trans. Julien Claude Galland (Paris, 1981).

Zedler, Johann Heinrich, *Grosses vollständiges Universal-Lexikon*, 64 vols. (Leipzig, 1732–50).

Secondary literature

Adanir, Fikret, 'Semi-autonomous provincial forces in the Balkans and Anatolia', in Faroqhi (ed.), *Cambridge History of Turkey*, III, 157–85.

Adas, Michael, '"Moral economy" or "contest state"? Elite demands and the origins of peasant protest in Southeast Asia', *Journal of Social History*, 13 (1980), 521–46.

Ager, Sheila L., 'Familiarity breeds: incest and the Ptolemaic dynasty', *Journal of Hellenic Studies*, 125 (2005), 1–34.

'The power of excess: royal incest and the Ptolemaic dynasty', *Anthropologica*, 48/2 (2006), 165–86.

Ágoston, Gábor, 'Administration, central', in Ágoston and Masters (eds.), *Encyclopedia of the Ottoman Empire*, 10–13.

Ágoston, Gábor, and Bruce Alan Masters (eds.), *Encyclopedia of the Ottoman Empire* (New York, 2009).

Aguilar-Moreno, Manuel, *Handbook to Life in the Aztec World* (Oxford, 2006).

Akarli, Engin, 'The ruler and law making in the Ottoman empire', in Duindam et al. (eds.), *Law and Empire*, 87–109.

Akkerman, Nadine, and Birgit Houben (eds.), *The Politics of Female Households: Ladies-in-Waiting across Early Modern Europe* (Leiden and Boston, MA, 2013).

Alam, Muzaffar, 'The Mughals, the Sufi shaikhs and the formation of the Akbari dispensation', *Modern Asian Studies*, 43/1 (2009), 135–74.

Alam, Muzaffar, and Sanjay Subrahmanyam, 'Envisioning power: the political thought of a late eighteenth-century Mughal prince', *Indian Economic & Social History Review*, 43/2 (2006), 131–61.

Alderson, Anthony D., *The Structure of the Ottoman Dynasty* (Oxford, 1956).

Alexander, J.T., 'Favourites, favouritism and female rule in Russia, 1725–1796', in Roger P. Bartlett and Janet M. Hartley (eds.), *Russia in the Age of the Enlightenment: Essays for Isabel de Madariaga* (Basingstoke, 1990), 106–24.

Alexander, S., 'The Serengeti: the glory of life', *National Geographic*, 169 (1986), 584–601.

Ali, Samer, 'Boon companion', in Fleet et al. (eds.), *Encyclopaedia of Islam, Three*.

Allen, Chizuko, 'Empress Jingu: a shamaness ruler in early Japan', *Japan Forum*, 15/1 (2003), 81–98.

Allsen, Thomas, *The Royal Hunt in Eurasian History* (Philadelphia, PA, 2006).

Alpern, Stanley B., *Amazons of Black Sparta: The Women Warriors of Dahomey* (New York, 1998).

'On the origins of the Amazons of Dahomey', *History in Africa*, 25 (1998), 9–25.

Al-Tikriti, Nabil, 'The Ḥajj as justifiable self-exile: Şehzade Korkud's Wasīlat al-aḥbāb (915–916/1509–1510)', *Al-Masaq*, 17/1 (2005), 125–46.

Ames, Roger T., *The Art of Rulership: A Study in Ancient Chinese Political Thought* (Albany, NY, 1994).

Amirell, Stefan, 'The blessings and perils of female rule: new perspectives on the reigning queens of Patani, c. 1584–1718', *Journal of Southeast Asian Studies*, 42/2 (2011), 303–23.

Andaya, Barbara Watson, *The Flaming Womb : Repositioning Women in Early Modern Southeast Asia* (Honolulu, HI, 2006).

'Political development between the sixteenth and eighteenth centuries', in Nicholas Tarling (ed.), *The Cambridge History of Southeast Asia*. vol. I: *From Early Times to c. 1800* (Cambridge, 1992), 402–59.

'Women and the performance of power in early modern Southeast Asia', in Walthall (ed.), *Servants of the Dynasty*, 22–44.

Andaya, Leonard Y., '"A very good-natured but awe-inspiring government": the reign of a successful queen in seventeenth-century Aceh', in Locher-Scholten and Rietbergen (eds.), *Hof en Handel*, 59–84.

Anderson, Frank Maloy (trans.), *The Constitutions and Other Select Documents Illustrative of the History of France, 1789–1907* (Minneapolis, MI, 1908).

Anderson, James A., 'Distinguishing between China and Vietnam: three relational equilibriums in Sino-Vietnamese relations', *Journal of East Asian Studies*, 13/2 (2013), 259–80.

Andrew, Anita and John Rapp, *Autocracy and China's Rebel Founding Emperors: Comparing Chairman Mao and Ming Taizu* (Lanham, MD, 2000).

Ansari, Mohammad Azhar, *Social Life of the Mughal Emperors, 1526–1707* (Allahabad and New Delhi, 1974).

Arjomand, Saïd Amir, 'The salience of political ethic in the spread of Persianate Islam', *Journal of Persianate Studies*, 1/1 (2008), 5–29.

The Shadow of God and the Hidden Imam: Religion, Political Order, and Societal Change in Shi'ite Iran from the Beginning to 1890 (Chicago, IL, 1984).

Artan, Tülay, 'Ahmed I's hunting parties: feasting in adversity, enhancing the ordinary', in Amy Singer (ed.), *Starting with Food: Culinary Approaches to Ottoman History* (Princeton, NJ, 2010), 93–138.

'The making of the Sublime Porte near the Alay Köşkü and a tour of a grand vizierial palace at Süleymaniye', *Turcica*, 43 (2011), 145–206.

Asch, Ronald G., *Nobilities in Transition, 1550–1700: Courtiers and Rebels in Britain and Europe* (London, 2003).

Asher, Catherine B., 'A ray from the sun: Mughal ideology and the visual construction of the divine', in Matthew T. Kapstein (ed.), *The Presence of Light: Divine Radiance and Religious Experience* (Chicago, IL, and London, 2004), 161–94.

Ashliman, D.L., *Folk and Fairy Tales: A Handbook* (Westport, CT, 2004).

Atasoy, Nurhan, *Otağ-i Hümayun: The Ottoman Imperial Tent Complex* (Istanbul, 2000).

Babaie, Sussan, *Isfahan and its Palaces: Statecraft, Shi'ism and the Architecture of Conviviality in Early Modern Iran* (Edinburgh, 2008).

Babaie, Sussan, Kathryn Babayan, Ina Baghdiantz-McCabe, and Massumeh Farhad, *Slaves of the Shah: New Elites of Safavid Iran* (London, 2004).

Babayan, Kathryn, *Mystics, Monarchs, and Messiahs: Cultural Landscapes of Early Modern Iran* (Cambridge, MA, 2002).

'The Safavid synthesis: from Qizilbash Islam to imamite Shi'ism', *Iranian Studies*, 27 (1994), 135–61.

'The waning of the Qizilbash: the spiritual and the temporal in seventeenth century Iran', PhD thesis, Princeton University (1993).

Babb, Lawrence A., *Absent Lord: Ascetics and Kings in a Jain Ritual Culture* (Berkeley, CA, 1996).

Bailey, Anne Caroline, *African Voices of the Atlantic Slave Trade: Beyond the Silence and the Shame* (Boston, MA, 2005).

Baker, Russ, *Family of Secrets: The Bush Dynasty, America's Invisible Government, and the Hidden History of the Last Fifty Years* (New York, 2009).

Balabanlilar, Lisa, 'The Begims of the mystic feast: Turco-Mongol tradition in the Mughal harem', *Journal of Asian Studies*, 69/1 (2010), 123–47.

'The Emperor Jahangir and the pursuit of pleasure', *Journal of the Royal Asiatic Society*, 3rd series, 19/2 (2009), 173–86.

'Lords of the auspicious conjunction: Turco-Mongol imperial identity on the subcontinent', *Journal of World History*, 18/1 (2007), 1–39.

Balandier, Georges, *Le royaume de Kongo du XVIe au XVIIIe siècle* (Paris, 2009).

Bamfo, Napoleon, 'The hidden elements of democracy among Akyem chieftaincy: enstoolment, destoolment, and other limitations of power', *Journal of Black Studies*, 31/2 (2000), 149–73.

Barclay, Andrew, 'Charles II's failed restoration: administrative reform below stairs 1660–64', in Eveline Cruickshanks (ed.), *The Stuart Courts* (Stroud, 2012), 158–70.

Barjamovic, Gojko, 'Pride, pomp and circumstance: palace, court and household in Assyria 879–612 BCE', in Duindam et al. (eds.), *Royal Courts*, 27–61.

Barkey, Karen, *Bandits and Bureaucrats: The Ottoman Route to State Centralization* (Cambridge, 1994).

Barlow, Frank, 'The King's Evil', *English Historical Review*, 95/374 (1980), 3–27.

Barrett, T.H., *The Woman Who Discovered Printing* (New Haven, CT, 2008).

Bartlett, Beatrice S., *Monarchs and Ministers: The Grand Council in Mid-Ch'ing China, 1723–1820* (Berkeley, CA, 1991).

Basham, A.L. (ed.), *Kingship in Asia and Early America* (Mexico City, 1981).

Bauer, Brian S., 'Legitimization of the state in Inca myth and ritual', *American Anthropologist*, 98/2 (1996), 327–37.

Bay, Edna G., 'Belief, legitimacy and the kpojito: an institutional history of the "queen mother" in precolonial Dahomey', *Journal of African History*, 36/1 (1995), 1–27.

'Servitude and worldly success in the palace of Dahomey', in Claire Robertson and Martin Klein (eds.), *Women and Slavery in Africa* (Madison, WI, 1983), 340–67.

Wives of the Leopard: Gender, Politics, and Culture in the Kingdom of Dahomey (Charlottesville, VA, and London, 1998).

Baye, Temesgen G., 'The evolution and development of kingship and traditional governance in Ethiopia: a case of the Kefa kingdom', *Journal of Asian and African Studies*, 47/2 (2012), 190–203.

Bayerle, Gustav, *Pashas, Begs, and Effendis: A Historical Dictionary of Titles and Terms in the Ottoman Empire* (Istanbul, 1997).

Beales, Derek, *Joseph II*, 2 vols. (Cambridge, 1987–2009).

Bearman, P., et al. (eds.), *Encyclopaedia of Islam, Second Edition*, Brill Online Reference Works (Leiden, 1954–2005).

Bearzot, Cinzia, 'Dynasteia, idea of, Greece', in Roger S. Bagnall et al. (eds.), *The Encyclopedia of Ancient History* (Oxford, 2012), 2240–1.

Beattie, John, *Bunyoro: An African Kingdom* (New York, 1960).

'Checks on the abuse of political power in some African states: a preliminary framework for analysis', in Ronald Cohen and John Middleton (eds.), *Comparative Political Systems: Studies in the Politics of Pre-Industrial Societies*, (New York, 1967), 355–73.

Beck, Brenda, 'The authority of the king: prerogatives and dilemmas of kingship as portrayed in a contemporary oral epic from south India', in Richards (ed.), *Kingship and Authority*, 168–91.

Beckingham, C.F., 'Amba Gesen and Asirgarh', *Journal of Semitic Studies*, 2/2 (1957), 182–8.

Beckwith, Christopher I., *Empires of the Silk Road: A History of Central Eurasia from the Bronze Age to the Present* (Princeton, NJ, 2009).

Beerens, Anna, 'Interview with two ladies of the ōoku: a translation from Kyūji Shimonroku', *Monumenta Nipponica*, 63/2 (2008), 265–324.

Béguin, Katia, 'Louis XIV et l'aristocratie: coup de majesté ou retour à la tradition?', *Histoire, économie et société*, 19/4 (2000), 497–512.

Les princes de Condé: rebelles, courtisans et mécènes dans la France du grand siècle (Paris, 1999).

Behrend, Timothy, 'Kraton and cosmos in traditional Java', *Archipel*, 37 (1989), 173–87.

Beik, Paul (ed.), *The French Revolution* (London, 1970).

Bély, Lucien, and G. Poumarède (eds.), *L'incident diplomatique (XVIe–XVIIIe siècle)* (Paris, 2010).

Bender, Ross, 'Auspicious omens in the reign of the last empress of Nara Japan, 749–770', *Japanese Journal of Religious Studies*, 40/1 (2013), 45–76.

Bérenger, Jean, 'The demise of the minister-favourite, or a political model at dusk: the Austrian case', in Elliott and Brockliss (eds.), *World of the Favourite* (New Haven, CT, and London, 1999), 256–68.

'Pour une enquête européenne : le problème du ministériat au XVIIe siècle', *Annales ESC*, 29/1 (1974), 166–92.

Berghe, Pierre L. van den, and Gene M. Mesher, 'Royal incest and inclusive fitness', *American Ethnologist*, 7/2 (1980), 300–17.

Bes, Lennart, 'Toddlers, widows, and bastards enthroned: dynastic successions in early-modern south India as observed by the Dutch', *Leidschrift*, 27/1 (2012), 121–34.

Betzig, Laura, 'Despotism and differential reproduction: a cross-cultural correlation of conflict asymmetry, hierarchy, and degree of polygyny', *Ethology and Sociobiology*, 3/4 (1982), 209–21.

'Eusociality: from the first foragers to the first states', *Human Nature*, 25/1 (2014), 1–5.

Bhattacharya, Bhaswati, Gita Dharampal-Frick, and Jos Gommans, 'Spatial and temporal continuities of merchant networks in South Asia and the Indian Ocean (1500–2000)', *Journal of the Economic and Social History of the Orient*, 50/2–3 (2007), 91–105.

Bixler, Ray H., 'Comment on the incidence and purpose of royal sibling incest', *American Ethnologist*, 9/3 (1982), 580–2.

'Sibling incest in the royal families of Egypt, Peru, and Hawaii', *Journal of Sex Research*, 18/3 (1982), 264–81.

Black, Antony, *The History of Islamic Political Thought: From the Prophet to the Present* (Edinburgh, 2001).

Political Thought in Europe, 1250–1450 (Cambridge and New York, 1992).

Blake, Stephen P., 'The patrimonial-bureaucratic empire of the Mughals', *Journal of Asian Studies*, 39/1 (1979), 77–94.

'Returning the household to the patrimonial-bureaucratic empire: gender, succession, and ritual in the Mughal, Safavid, and Ottoman empires', in Peter F. Bang and C. A. Bayly (eds.), *Tributary Empires in Global History* (Basingstoke, 2011), 214–26.

Shahjahanabad: The Sovereign City in Mughal India 1639–1739 (Cambridge, 1991).

Time in Early Modern Islam: Calendar, Ceremony, and Chronology in the Safavid, Mughal, and Ottoman Empires (Cambridge, 2013).

Bleek, Wilhelm, *Von der Kameralausbildung zum Juristenprivileg: Studium, Prüfung und Ausbildung der höheren Beamten des allgemeinen Verwaltungsdienstes in Deutschland im 18. und 19. Jahrhundert* (Berlin, 1972).

Blier, Suzanne Preston, *The Royal Arts of Africa: The Majesty of Form* (London, 1998).

Bloch, Marc, *Les rois thaumaturges* (Paris, 1924).

The Royal Touch: Sacred Monarchy and Scrofula in England and France, trans. J.E. Anderson (Montreal and Kingston, 1973).

Blockmans, Wim, 'Beau, fort et fertile: l'idéal du corps princier', *Micrologus*, 22 (2014), *Le Corps du Prince*, 767–81.

Bluche, François (ed.), *Dictionnaire du grand siècle* (Paris, 1990).

Bodart-Bailey, Beatrice M., *The Dog Shogun: The Personality And Policies of Tokugawa Tsunayoshi* (Honolulu, HI, 2006).

'Urbanisation and the nature of the Tokugawa hegemony', in Nicolas Fieve and Paul Waley (eds.), *Japanese Capitals in Historical Perspective: Place, Power and Memory in Kyoto, Edo and Tokyo* (Abingdon and New York, 2013), 100–28.

Boesche, Roger, 'Han Feizi's legalism versus Kautilya's *Arthashastra*', *Asian Philosophy*, 15/2 (2005), 157–72.

Bol, Peter Kees, 'The "localist turn" and "local identity" in later imperial China', *Late Imperial China*, 24/2 (2003), 1–50.

Bolitho, Harold, 'The Han', in John Whitney Hall (ed.), *The Cambridge History of Japan*, vol. IV: *Early Modern Japan* (Cambridge, 1991), 183–234.

Booth, Marilyn (ed.), *Harem Histories: Envisioning Places and Living Spaces* (Durham, NC, 2010).

Börekci, Günhan, 'Ibrahim', in Ágoston and Masters (eds.), *Encyclopedia of the Ottoman Empire*, 262–4.

Börekci, Günhan and Şefik Peksevgen, 'Court and favorites', in Ágoston and Masters (eds.), *Encyclopedia of the Ottoman Empire*, 151–4.

Bosc-Tiessé, Claire, '"How beautiful she is!" in her mirror: polysemic images and reflections of power of an eighteenth-century Ethiopia queen', *Journal of Early Modern History*, 8/3 (2004), 294–318.

Bradbury, Robert E., *Benin Studies*, ed. Peter Morton-Williams (London and New York, 1973).

Bréhier, Louis, *Les institutions de l'empire byzantin* (Paris, 1949).

Brocher, Henri, *Rang et l'étiquette sous l'ancien régime* (Paris, 1934).

Brown, Philip C., *Central Authority and Local Autonomy in the Formation of Early Modern Japan: The Case of Kaga Domain* (Stanford, CA, 1993).

'The political and institutional history of early modern Japan', *Early Modern Japan: An Interdisciplinary Journal*, 11 (2003), 3–30.

Bryant, Mark, 'Partner, matriarch and minister: the unofficial consort, Mme de Maintenon of France, 1669–1715', in C. Campbell-Orr (ed.), *European Queenship: The Role of The Consort 1660–1815* (Cambridge, 2004), 77–106.

Bucholz, R.O., '"Nothing but ceremony": Queen Anne and the limitations of royal ritual', *Journal of British Studies*, 30/3 (1991), 288–323.

Burke, Peter, *The Fabrication of Louis XIV* (New Haven, CT, 1994).

Burling, Robbins, *The Passage of Power: Studies in Political Succession* (New York and London, 1974).

Burton, Richard F., 'The present state of Dahome', *Transactions of the Ethnological Society of London*, 3 (1865), 400–8.

Bushkovitch, Paul, 'The Epiphany ceremony of the Russian court in the sixteenth and seventeenth centuries', *Russian Review*, 49/1 (1990), 1–17.

Peter the Great: The Struggle for Power, 1671–1725 (Cambridge, 2001).

'Power and the historian: the case of Tsarevich Aleksei 1716–1718 and N.G. Ustrialov 1845–1859', *Proceedings of the American Philosophical Society*, 141/2 (1997), 177–212.

Butler, Lee A., *Emperor and Aristocracy in Japan, 1467–1680: Resilience and Renewal* (Cambridge, MA, 2002).

'Tokugawa Ieyasu's regulations for the court: a reappraisal', *Harvard Journal of Asiatic Studies*, 54/2 (1994), 509–51.

Cabanès, Augustin, *Une Allemande à la cour de France* (Paris, 1916).

Cannadine, David, 'Introduction', in David Cannadine, Simon Price (eds.), *Rituals of Royalty: Power and Ceremonial in Traditional Societies* (Cambridge, 1987), 1–19.

Canseco, María Rostworowski de Diez and John V. Murra, 'Succession, coöption to kingship, and royal incest among the Inca', *Southwestern Journal of Anthropology*, 16/4 (1960), 417–27.

Carey, Peter, *'The Power of Prophecy: Prince Dipanagara and the End of an Old Order in Java, 1785–1855* (Leiden, 2008).

Carey, Peter, and Vincent Houben, 'Spirited Srikandhis and sly Sumbadras: the social, political and economic role of women at the central Javanese courts in the 18th and early 19th centuries', in Locher-Scholten and Niehof (eds.), *Indonesian Women in Focus*, 12–42.

Carrasco, Davíd, 'Myth, cosmic terror, and the Templo Mayor', in J. Broda and et al. (eds.), *The Great Temple of Tenochtitlan: Center and Periphery in the Aztec World* (Berkeley, CA, 1987), 124–69.

Carrasco, Pedro, 'Kingship in ancient Mexico', in Basham (ed.), *Kingship in Asia and Early America*, 233–42.

Chaffee, John W., *Branches of Heaven: A History of the Imperial Clan of Sung China* (Cambridge, MA, 1999).

'The marriage of Sung imperial clanswomen', in Watson and Ebrey (eds.), *Marriage and Inequality*, 133–70.

Chan, Hok-Lam, 'Ming Taizu's problem with his sons: Prince Qin's criminality and early-Ming politics', *Asia Major*, 20/1 (2007), 45–103.

Chandra, Satish, *Parties and Politics at the Mughal Court 1707–1740* (Oxford, 2002).

Chang, Michael G., *A Court on Horseback: Imperial Touring & the Construction of Qing Rule, 1680–1785* (Cambridge, MA, 2007).

'Historical narratives of the Kangxi emperor's inaugural visit to Suzhou, 1684', in Duindam and Dabringhaus (eds.), *Dynastic Centre*, 203–24.

'The recruitment of lower Yangzi (Jiangnan) literati to the Kangxi court, 1670s–1690s', paper presented at the conference 'Servants and administrators: from the court to the provinces', Leiden, 31 August – 2 September 2011.

Chang, Shelley Hsueh-lun, *History and Legend: Ideas and Images in the Ming Historical Novels* (Ann Arbor, MI, 1990).

Charrad, Mounira M., and Julia Adams, 'Introduction: patrimonialism, past and present', *Annals of the American Academy of Political and Social Science*, 636/1 (2011), 6–15

Chatterjee, K., 'Scribal elites in sultanate and Mughal Bengal', *Indian Economic & Social History Review*, 47/4 (2010), 445–72.

Chutintaranond, Sunait, 'Mandala, segmentary state and politics of centralization in medieval Ayudhya', *Journal of the Siam Society*, 78/1 (1990), 89–100.

Claessen, H.J.M., 'Enige gegevens over taboes en voorschriften rond Tahitische vorsten', *Bijdragen tot de taal-, land- en volkenkunde*, 118/4 (1962), 433–53.

'Kings, chiefs and officials: the political organization of Dahomey and Buganda compared', *Journal of Legal Pluralism and Unofficial Law*, 19/25–6 (1987), 203–41.

Van Vorsten en volken: een beschrijvende en functioneel-vergelijkende studie van de staatsorganisatie in vijf schriftloze vorstendommen (Amsterdam, 1970).

Claessen, H.J.M., and Peter Skalnik (eds.), *The Early State* (The Hague, 1978).

Clark, Peter, and Bernard Lepetit (eds.), *Capital Cities and their Hinterlands in Early Modern Europe* (Aldershot, 1996).

Clunas, Craig, *Screen of Kings: Royal Art and Power in Ming China* (London, 2013).

Cohen, Gary B., 'Neither absolutism nor anarchy: new narratives on society and government in late imperial Austria', *Austrian History Yearbook*, 29 (1998), 37–61.

Cooper, Eugene, 'The potlatch in ancient China: parallels in the sociopolitical structure of the ancient Chinese and the American Indians of the northwest coast', *History of Religions*, 22/2 (1982), 103–28.

Cosmo, Nicola Di, 'Manchu shamanic ceremonies at the Qing court', in McDermott (ed.), *State and Court Ritual*, 231–63.

Covey, R. Alan, 'Chronology, succession, and sovereignty: the politics of Inka historiography and its modern interpretation', *Comparative Studies in Society and History*, 48/1 (2006), 169–99.

'Intermediate elites in the Inka heartland, A.D. 1000–1500', in Christina M. Elson and R. Alan Covey (eds.), *Intermediate Elites in Pre-Columbian States and Empires* (Tucson, AZ, 2006), 112–35.

Crawford, Robert B., 'Eunuch power in the Ming dynasty', *T'oung Pao*, 49,/1 (1962), 115–48.

Creveld, Martin van, *The Rise and Decline of the State* (Cambridge, 1999).

Crone, Patricia, *God's Rule – Government and Islam: Six Centuries of Medieval Islamic Political Thought* (New York, 2004).

Crossley, Pamela, 'Nationality and difference in China: the post-imperial dilemma', in Joshua Fogel (ed.), *The Teleology of the Modern Nation-State: Japan and China* (Philadelphia, PA, 2005), 138–58.

A Translucent Mirror: History and Identity in Qing Imperial Ideology (Berkeley, CA, 1999).

Crummey, Donald E., 'Ethiopia in the early modern period: Solomonic monarchy and Christianity', *Journal of Early Modern History*, 8/3 (2004), 191–209.

Crummey, Robert O., 'Court spectacles in seventeenth century Russia: illusion and reality', in Daniel Waugh (ed.), *Essays in Honor of A. A. Zimin* (Columbus, OH, 1985), 130–58.

Curry, John, and Erik Ohlander (eds.), *Sufism and Society: Arrangements of the Mystical in the Muslim World, 1200–1800* (Abingdon and New York, 2012).

Dabringhaus, Sabine, 'The monarch and inner–outer court dualism in late imperial China', in Duindam et al. (eds.), *Royal Courts*, 265–87.

Daftary, Farhad, 'Sayyida Hurra: the Ismāʿīlī Sulayhid queen of Yemen', in Gavin R.G. Hambly (ed.), *Women in the Medieval Islamic World: Power, Patronage, and Piety* (New York, 1998), 117–30.

Dagron, Gilbert, *Emperor and Priest: The Imperial Office in Byzantium*, trans. Jean Birrell (Cambridge, 2003).

Dai, Yingcong, 'Broken passage to the summit: Nayancheng's botched mission in the White Lotus War', in Duindam and Dabringhaus (eds.), *Dynastic Centre*, 49–73.

Dakhlia, Jocelyne, 'Les miroirs des princes islamiques : une modernité sourde?', *Annales: histoire, sciences sociales*, 57/5 (2002), 1191–206.

Dankoff, Robert, *An Ottoman Mentality: The World of Evliya Çelebi* (Leiden and Boston, MA, 2006).

Dardess, John W., 'Protesting to the death: the Fuque in Ming political history', *Ming Studies*, 47 (2003), 86–125.

Darling, Linda T., 'Circle of justice', in Fleet et al. (eds.), *Encyclopaedia of Islam, Three*.

A History of Social Justice and Political Power in the Middle East: The Circle of Justice from Mesopotamia to Globalization (New York, 2013).

Davis, Natalie Zemon, *Fiction in the Archives: Pardon Tales and their Tellers in Sixteenth-Century France* (Stanford, CA, 1987).

Davis, Richard L., 'Troubles in paradise: the shrinking royal family in the Southern Song', unpublished paper, www.npm.gov.tw/hotnews/9910seminar/download/all/B01.pdf.

Delacour, H., F. Ceppa, and P. Burnat, 'Louis XIV et Marie-Thérèse d'Autriche: un couple à travers le prisme de la génétique', *Immuno-analyse & biologie spécialisée*, 27/5 (2012), 272–5.

Deny, J., 'Rikab', in M.Th. Houtsma et al. (eds.), *First Encyclopaedia of Islam: 1913–1936*, (Leiden, 1993).

Derat, Marie-Laure, '"Do not search for another king, one whom god has not given you": questions on the elevation of Zär'ä Ya'eqob (1434–1468)', *Journal of Early Modern History*, 8/3 (2004), 210–28.

Deringil, Selim, 'The invention of tradition as public image in the late Ottoman empire, 1808 to 1908', *Comparative Studies in Society and History*, 35/1 (1993), 3–29.

Dickson, Peter G.M., 'Monarchy and bureaucracy in late eighteenth-century Austria', *English Historical Review*, 110/436 (1995), 323–67.

Dikici, Ezgi, 'The making of Ottoman court eunuchs: origins, recruitment paths, family ties, and "domestic production"', *Archivum Ottomanicum*, 30 (2013), 105–36.

Diskul, M.C. Subhadradis, 'Ancient kingship in mainland Southeast Asia', in Basham (ed.), *Kingship in Asia and Early America*, 133–59.

Dobbs, David, 'The risks and rewards of royal incest', *National Geographic*, 218/3 (2010), 60–1.

Drucker-Brown, Susan, 'The grandchildren's play at the Mamprusi king's funeral: ritual rebellion revisited in northern Ghana', *Journal of the Royal Anthropological Institute*, 5/2 (1999), 181–92.

'King house: the mobile polity in northern Ghana', in Quigley (ed.), *Character of Kingship*, 171–86.

Ritual Aspects of the Mamprusi Kingship (Leiden and Cambridge, 1975).

Duby, Georges, *Le chevalier, la femme, et le prêtre: le mariage dans la France féodale* (Paris, 1981).

Duchhardt, Heinz, *Politische Testamente und andere Quellen zum Fürstenethos der Frühen Neuzeit* (Darmstadt, 1987).

Duerloo, Luc, 'Pietas Albertina: dynastieke vroomheid en herbouw van het vorstelijk gezag', *Bijdragen en Mededelingen betreffende de Geschiedenis der Nederlanden*, 112 (1997), 1–18.

Duindam, Jeroen, 'The Burgundian-Spanish legacy in European court life: a brief reassessment and the example of the Austrian Habsburgs', *Publications du Centre européen d'etudes bourguignonnes*, 46 (2006), 203–20.

'The dynastic court in an age of change', in *Friedrich300 – Colloquien: Friedrich der Große und der Hof*, in *Perspectivia* (2009), www.perspectivia.net/content/publikationen/friedrich300colloquien/friedrichhof/Duindam_Court.

'Dynasty and elites: from early modern Europe to late imperial China', in Liesbeth Geevers and Mirella Marini (eds.), *Dynastic Identity in Early Modern Europe: Rulers, Aristocrats and the Formation of Identities* (forthcoming).

'Early modern europe: beyond the strictures of modernization and national historiography', *European History Quarterly*, 40/4 (2010), 606–23.

'The Habsburg court in Vienna: Kaiserhof or Reichshof?', in R.J.W. Evans and P.H. Wilson (eds.), *The Holy Roman Empire 1495–1806: A European Perspective* (Leiden and Boston, MA, 2012), 91–119.

Myths of Power: Norbert Elias and the Early Modern European Court (Amsterdam, 1995).

'Palace, city, dominions: the spatial dimension of Habsburg rule', in Smuts and Gorse (eds.), *Politics of Space*, 59–90.

'Royal courts', in Hamish Scott (ed.), *The Oxford Handbook of Early Modern European History, 1350–1750*, vol. II: *Cultures and Power*, (forthcoming, 2015).

'Vienna and Versailles: materials for further comparison and some conclusions', *Zeitenblicke*, 4/3 (2005), http://www.zeitenblicke.de/2005/3/Duindam.

Vienna and Versailles: The Courts of Europe's Dynastic Rivals, 1550–1780 (Cambridge, 2003).

Duindam, Jeroen, Jill Harries, Caroline Humfress, and Nimrod Hurvitz (eds.), *Law and Empire: Ideas, Practices, Actors* (Leiden and Boston, MA, 2013).

Duindam, Jeroen, and Sabine Dabringhaus (eds.), *The Dynastic Centre and the Provinces: Agents and Interactions* (Leiden and Boston, MA, 2014).

Duindam, Jeroen, Tülay Artan, and Metin Kunt (eds.), *Royal Courts in Dynastic States and Empires: A Global Perspective* (Leiden and Boston, MA, 2011).

Dumas, Juliette, 'Les perles de nacre du sultanat. Les princesses ottomanes (mi-XVe – mi-XVIIIe siècle', PhD thesis, École des hautes études en sciences sociales (2013).

Dumézil, George, *L'idéologie tripartite des Indo-Européens* (Brussels, 1958).

Duncan-Jones, Richard, *Money and Government in the Roman Empire* (Cambridge, 1998).

Durand, Yves (ed.), *Hommage à Roland Mousnier: clientèles et fidélités en Europe à l'époque moderne* (Paris, 1981).

Durand-Guédy, David, 'Introduction: location of rule in a context of Turko-Mongol domination', in David Durand-Guédy (ed.), *Turko-Mongol Rulers, Cities and City Life* (Leiden and Boston, MA, 2013), 1–20.

'Ruling from the outside. a new perspective on early Turkish kingship in Iran', in Lynette Mitchell and Charles Melville (eds.), *Every Inch a King: Comparative Studies on Kings and Kingship in the Ancient and Medieval Worlds* (Leiden and Boston, MA, 2012), 325–42.

Eastman, Lloyd E., *Family, Fields, and Ancestors: Constancy and Change in China's Social and Economic History, 1550–1949* (Oxford, 1988).

Ebrey, Patricia B., *The Cambridge Illustrated History of China* (Cambridge, 1996).

Emperor Huizong (Cambridge, MA, 2014).

'Remonstrating against royal extravagance in imperial China', in Duindam and Dabringhaus (eds.), *Dynastic Centre*, 127–49.

'Rethinking the imperial harem: why were there so many palace women?', in *Women and the Family in Chinese History* (London, 2002), 177–93.

'Succession to high office: the Chinese case', in David R. Olson and Michael Cole (eds.), *Technology, Literacy, and the Evolution of Society: Implications of the Work of Jack Goody* (Mahwah, 2006), 49–71.

'Taking out the grand carriage: imperial spectacle and the visual culture of Northern Song Kaifeng', *Asia Major*, 12/1 (1999), 33–65.

(ed.), *Chinese Civilization: A Sourcebook* (New York, 1993).

Edo, Victor Osaro, 'Hierarchy and organization of the Benin kingdom and palace', in Barbara Plankensteiner (ed.), *Benin Kings and Rituals: Court Arts from Nigeria* (Vienna, 2007), 91–101.

Eisenberg, Andrew, *Kingship in Early Medieval China* (Leiden and Boston, MA, 2008).

Eisenhofer, Stefan, 'The Benin kinglist/s: some questions of chronology', *History in Africa*, 24 (1997), 139–56.

Eisenstadt, S.N., *Japanese Civilization: A Comparative View* (Chicago, IL, 1996).

Eisenstadt, S.N., and Louis Roniger, 'Patron–client relations as a model of structuring social exchange', *Comparative Studies in Society and History*, 22/1 (1980), 42–77.

Eisenstadt, S.N., and René Lemarchand (eds.), *Political Clientelism, Patronage and Development* (London, 1977).

El Cheikh, Nadia Maria, 'To be a prince in the fourth/tenth-century Abbasid court', in Duindam et al. (eds.), *Royal Courts*, 199–216.

Elias, Norbert, *The Court Society* (Oxford, 1983).
  Die höfische Gesellschaft: Untersuchungen zur Soziologie des Königtums und der höfischen Aristokratie, mit einer Einleitung: Soziologie und Geschichtswissenschaft (Neuwied, 1969).

Elliott, J.H., and L.W.B. Brockliss (eds.), *The World of the Favourite* (New Haven, CT, and London, 1999).

Elliott, Mark C., *Emperor Qianlong: Son of Heaven, Man of the World* (New York and London, 2009).
  The Manchu Way: The Eight Banners and Ethnic Identity in Late Imperial China (Stanford, CA, 2001).

Elman, Benjamin A., *A Cultural History of Civil Examinations in Late Imperial China* (Berkeley, CA, 2000).
  'Imperial politics and Confucian societies in late imperial China: the Hanlin and Donglin academies', *Modern China*, 15/4 (1989), 379–418.
  'Political, social, and cultural reproduction via civil service examinations in late imperial China', *Journal of Asian Studies*, 50/1 (1991), 7–28.
  'The social roles of literati in early to mid-Ch'ing', in Peterson (ed.), *Cambridge History of China*, IX, 360–427.

Elvin, Mark, *The Pattern of the Chinese Past: A Social and Economic Interpretation* (Stanford, CA, 1972).

Enders, Jody, *Death by Drama and Other Medieval Urban Legends* (Chicago, IL, 2005).

Engels, Jens Ivo, *Die Geschichte der Korruption* (Frankfurt, 2014).
  Königsbilder: Sprechen, Singen und Schreiben über den französischen König in der ersten Hälfte des achtzehnten Jahrhunderts (Bonn, 2000).

Esherick, Joseph, 'How the Qing became China', in Joseph Esherick, Hasan Kayali, and Eric Van Young (eds.), *Empire to Nation: Historical Perspectives on the Making of the Modern World* (Lanham, MD, 2006), 229–59.

Esherick, Joseph, and Mary Backus Rankin, *Chinese Local Elites and Patterns of Dominance* (Berkeley, CA, 1990).

Ess, Hans van, 'The imperial court in Han China', in Spawforth (ed.), *Court and Court Society*, 233–66.

Evans, R.J.W., 'Communicating empire: the Habsburgs and their critics, 1700–1919', *Transactions of the Royal Historical Society*, 19 (2009), 117–38.

Evans, Susan Toby, 'Aztec palaces and other elite residential architecture', in Evans and Pillsbury (eds.), *Palaces of the Ancient New World*, 7–58.

'Aztec royal pleasure parks: conspicuous consumption and elite status rivalry', *Studies in the History of Gardens and Designed Landscapes*, 20/3 (2000), 206–28.

'Concubines and cloth: women and weaving in Aztec palaces and colonial Mexico', in Walthall (ed.), *Servants of the Dynasty*, 215–31.

Evans, Susan Toby, and Joanne Pillsbury (eds.), *Palaces of the Ancient New World: A Symposium at Dumbarton Oaks, 10th and 11th October 1998* (Washington, DC, 2004).

Evans-Pritchard, E.E., 'The divine kingship of the Shilluk of the Nilotic Sudan: the Frazer Lecture, 1948', *HAU: Journal of Ethnographic Theory*, 1 (2011), 407–22.

'The Zande state', *Journal of the Royal Anthropological Institute of Great Britain and Ireland*, 93/1 (1963), 134–54.

Fang, Qiang, 'Hot potatoes: Chinese complaint systems from early times to the late Qing (1898)', *Journal of Asian Studies*, 68/4 (2009), 1105–35.

Farmer, Edward L., 'The great Ming commandment (ta Ming ling): an inquiry into early-Ming social legislation', *Asia Major*, 6 (1993), 181–99.

Zhu Yuanzhang and Early Ming Legislation: The Reordering of Chinese Society Following the Era of Mongol Rule (Leiden, 1995).

Faroqhi, Suraiya, *Another Mirror for Princes: The Public Image of the Ottoman Sultans and its Reception* (London, 2008).

(ed.), *The Cambridge History of Turkey*, vol. III: *The Later Ottoman Empire, 1603–1836* (Cambridge, 2006).

Farquhar, David M., 'Emperor as bodhisattva in the governance of the Ch'ing empire', *Harvard Journal of Asiatic Studies*, 38/1 (1978), 5–34.

Farrar, Tarikhu, 'The queenmother, matriarchy, and the question of female political authority in precolonial West African monarchy', *Journal of Black Studies*, 27/5 (1997), 579–97.

Faruqui, Munis D., *The Princes of the Mughal Empire, 1504–1719* (Cambridge, 2012).

Faure, David, 'The emperor in the village: representing the state in south China', in McDermott (ed.), *State and Court Ritual*, 267–98.

Fernandes, Léonor, 'On conducting the affairs of the state: a guideline of the fourteenth century', *Annales islamologiques*, 24 (1988), 81–91.

Fetvacı, Emine, *Picturing History at the Ottoman Court* (Bloomington, IN, 2013).

'The production of the Şehnâme-i Selīm Ḫān', *Muqarnas*, 26 (2009), 263–315.

Ficquet, Eloi, 'L'intervention des Oromo-Wällo dans la dynastie éthiopienne salomonide sous les règnes de Bäkaffa, Iyasu et Iyo'as, 1721 à 1769', *Annales d'Éthiopie*, 16 (2000), 135–46.

Findley, Carter Vaughn, 'The Ottoman lands to the post-First World War settlement', in Francis Robinson (ed.), *The New Cambridge History of Islam*, vol. V: *The Islamic World in the Age of Western Dominance* (Cambridge, 2010), 29–78.

Finer, S.E., *The History of Government from the Earliest Times* (Oxford and New York, 1997–9).

Fisher, Carney T., *The Chosen One: Succession and Adoption in the Court of Ming Shizong* (Sydney and London, 1990).

Fleet, Kate, et al. (eds.), *Encyclopaedia of Islam, Three*, Brill Online Reference Works (Leiden, 2007–).

Fleischer, Cornell H., *Bureaucrat and Intellectual in the Ottoman Empire: The Historian Mustafa Ali (1541–1600)* (Princeton, NJ, 1986).

'Royal authority, dynastic cyclism, and "Ibn Khaldunism" in sixteenth-century Ottoman letters', *Journal of Asian and African Studies*, 18 (1983), 198–220.

Fleming, Luke, 'Name taboos and rigid performativity', *Anthropological Quarterly*, 84/1 (2011), 141–64.

Fletcher, J.F., 'The Mongols: ecological and social perspectives', *Harvard Journal of Asiatic Studies*, 46/1 (1986), 11–50.

'Turco-Mongolian monarchic tradition in the Ottoman empire', *Harvard Journal of Ukrainian Studies*, 3–4 (1979), 236–51.

Flier, Michael S., 'The iconography of royal procession: Ivan the Terrible and the Muscovite Palm Sunday ritual', in Heinz Duchhardt et al. (eds.), *European Monarchy: Its Evolution and Practice from Roman Antiquity to Modern Times* (Stuttgart, 1992), 109–25.

'Seeing is believing: the semiotics of dynasty and destiny in Muscovite Rus', in Nicholas Howe (ed.), *Ceremonial Culture in Pre-Modern Europe* (Notre Dame, IN, 2007), 63–88.

Flores, Jorge, 'Two Portuguese visions of Jahangir's India : Jerónimo Xavier and Manuel Godinho de Erédia', in Jorge Flores and Nuno Vassallo e Silva (eds.), *Goa and the Great Mughal* (Lisbon, 2004), 44–66.

Fodor, Pal, 'Sultan, imperial council, grand vizier: changes in the Ottoman ruling elite and the formation of the grand vizieral Telhis', *Acta Orientalia Academiae Scientiarum Hungaricae*, 47 (1994), 67–85.

Fonck, Bertrand, 'Le commandement des armées et ses enjeux sous Louis XIV', *Revue historique des armées*, 263 (2011), 17–27.

Fortes, Meyer, 'Kinship and marriage among the Ashanti', in Radcliffe-Brown and Forde (eds.), *African Systems of Kinship and Marriage*, 252–84.

'Of installation ceremonies', *Proceedings of the Royal Anthropological Institute of Great Britain and Ireland* (1967), 5–20.

'The political system of the Tallensi of the northern territories of the Goldcoast', in Fortes and Evans-Pritchard (eds.), *African Political Systems*, 239–71.

Fortes, M., and E.E. Evans-Pritchard (eds.), *African Political Systems* (London, 1940).

Franz, Kurt, 'The castle and the country: spatial orientations of Qipchaq Mamlūk rule', in David Durand-Guédy (ed.), *Turko-Mongol Rulers, Cities and City Life* (Leiden and Boston, MA, 2013), 347–84.

Fraser, Antonia, *The Warrior Queens: Boadicea's Chariot* (London, 2011).

Frazer, J.G., *The Golden Bough: A Study in Magic and Religion* (London, 1987 [1922]).

Freud, Sigmund, *Totem and Taboo* (London, 1950).

Friedrich, Carl J., *The Pathology of Politics: Violence, Betrayal, Corruption, Secrecy, and Propaganda* (New York, 1972).

Fuchs, Ralf-Peter, 'The Supreme Court of the Holy Roman Empire: the state of research and the outlook', *Sixteenth Century Journal*, 34/1 (2003), 9–27.

Fuchs, Martina, *Karl V., eine populäre Figur? Zur Rezeption des Kaisers in deutschsprachiger Belletristik* (Münster, 2002).

Fuess, Albrecht, 'Zulm by mazalim? The political implications of the use of mazalim jurisdiction by the Mamluk sultans', *Mamluk Studies Review*, 13/1 (2009), 121–47.

Fumaroli, Marc, 'Nicolas Fouquet, the favourite manqué', in Elliott and Brockliss (eds.), *World of the Favourite*, 239–55.

Garrett, Valery M., *Mandarin Squares: Mandarins and their Insignia* (Oxford and Hong Kong, 1990).

Gat, Azar, *War in Human Civilization* (Oxford, 2008).

Geertz, Clifford, *Negara: The Theatre State in Nineteenth-Century Bali* (Princeton, NJ, 1980).

Geiss, James, 'The Leopard Quarter during the Cheng-Te reign', *Ming Studies*, 1 (1987), 1–38.

Gellner, Ernest, and J. Waterbury (eds.), *Patrons and Clients in Mediterranean Societies* (London, 1977).

Ghobrial, John-Paul, 'Printing', in Ágoston and Masters (eds.), *Encyclopedia of the Ottoman Empire*, 471–4.

Gholsorkhi, Shohreh, 'Pari Khan Khanum: a masterful Safavid princess', *Iranian Studies*, 28/3–4 (1995), 143–56.

Gilbert, Michelle, 'The person of the king: ritual and power in a Ghanaian state', in David Cannadine and Simon Price (eds.), *Rituals of Royalty: Power and Ceremonial in Traditional Societies* (Cambridge, 1992), 298–330.

Gillespie, Susan D., *The Aztec Kings: The Construction of Rulership in Mexica History* (Tucson, AZ, 1989).

Glahn, Richard Von, *Fountain of Fortune: Money and Monetary Policy in China, 1000–1700* (Berkeley, CA, 1996).

Göçek, F. Müge, 'Mültezim', in Bearman et al. (eds.), *Encyclopaedia of Islam, Second Edition*.

Golden, P.B., 'Ṭarḵẖān', in Bearman et al. (eds.), *Encyclopaedia of Islam, Second Edition*.

Goldstone, Jack A., 'New patterns in global history: a review essay on *Strange Parallels* by Victor Lieberman', *Cliodynamics*, 1/1 (2010), 92–102.

'The problem of the "early modern" world', *Journal of the Economic and Social History of the Orient*, 41/3 (1998), 249–84.

Revolution and Rebellion in the Early Modern World (Berkeley, CA, 1991).

'The rise of the West – or not? A revision to socio-economic history', *Sociological Theory*, 18/2 (2000), 175–94.

Gommans, Jos J.L., *Mughal Warfare: Indian Frontiers and Highroads to Empire 1500–1700* (London and New York, 2003).

Goody, Jack, 'The mother's brother and the sister's son in West Africa', *Journal of the Royal Anthropological Institute of Great Britain and Ireland*, 89/1 (1959), 61–88.

'Sideways or downwards? Lateral and vertical succession, inheritance and descent in Africa and Eurasia', *Man*, 5/4 (1970), 627–38.

'Strategies of heirship', *Comparative Studies in Society and History*, 15/1 (1973), 3–20.

(ed.), *Succession to High Office* (Cambridge, 1966).

Gordon, Stewart, 'Robes of honour: a "transactional" kingly ceremony', *Indian Economic & Social History Review*, 33/3 (1996), 225–42.

Graus, František, 'Die Herrschersagen des Mittelalters als Geschichtsquelle', *Archiv für Kulturgeschichte*, 51/1 (1969), 65–93.

Groot, A.H. de, 'Murād III', in Bearman et al. (eds.), *Encyclopaedia of Islam, Second Edition*.

Guermonprez, Jean-François, 'Rois divins et rois guerriers: images de la royauté à Bali', *L'Homme*, 25 (1985), 39–70.

Guy, R. Kent, *Qing Governors and their Provinces: The Evolution of Territorial Administration in China, 1644–1796* (Seattle, WA, 2010).
   'Routine promotions: Li Hu and the dusty byways of empire', in Duindam and Dabringhaus (eds.), *Dynastic Centre*, 74–93.

Haberland, Eike, *Untersuchungen zum äthiopischen Königtum* (Wiesbaden, 1965).

Haboush, JaHyun Kim, *The Confucian Kingship in Korea: Yongjo and the Politics of Sagacity* (New York, 1988).
   Epistolary Korea: Letters in the Communicative Space of the Chosŏn, 1392–1910 (New York, 2009).

Halkias, Georgios T., 'The enlightened sovereign: Buddhism and kingship in India and Tibet', in Steven M. Emmanuel (ed.), *A Companion to Buddhist Philosophy* (Malden, MA, and Oxford, 2013), 491–510.

Hall, John Carey, 'Japanese feudal laws, III: the Tokugawa legislation', *Transactions of the Asian Society of Japan*, 38/4 (1911), 269–331.

Hall, John Whitney, 'The Bakuhan system', in John Whitney Hall (ed.), *The Cambridge History of Japan*, vol. IV: *Early Modern Japan* (Cambridge, 1991), 128–82.

Halperin, Charles J., 'Muscovy as a hypertrophic state: a critique', *Kritika*, 3/3 (2002), 501–7.

Hamann, Brigitte (ed.), *Die Habsburger: ein biographisches Lexikon* (Vienna, 1988).

Hammelehle, Sebastian, 'Karl der Große: Horst Bredekamps *Der schwimmende Souverän*', *Spiegel Online*, 28 January 2014, www.spiegel.de/kultur/literatur/karl-der-grosse-horst-bredekamps-der-schwimmende-souveraen-a–945899.html.

Hammond-Tooke, W.D., *Boundaries and Belief: The Structure of a Sotho Worldview* (Johannesburg, 1981).

Hanley, Sarah, 'The Salic Law', in Christine Fauré (ed.), *Political and Historical Encyclopedia of Women* (New York, 2013), 2–17.

Hanson, Holly, 'Mapping conflict: heterarchy and accountability in the ancient capital of Buganda', *Journal of African History*, 50/2 (2009), 179–202.
   'Ḥarīm', in Bearman et al. (eds.), *Encyclopaedia of Islam, Second Edition*.

Harrell, Stevan, Susan Naquin, and Ju Deyuan, 'Lineage genealogy: the genealogical records of the Qing imperial lineage', *Late Imperial China*, 6/2 (1985), 37–47.

Härter, Karl, 'The early modern Holy Roman Empire of the German nation (1495–1806): a multi-layered legal system', in Duindam et al. (eds.), *Law and Empire*, 111–31.

Hathaway, Jane, *Beshir Agha: Chief Eunuch of the Ottoman Imperial Harem* (London, 2005).

Hawass, Zahi, 'King Tut's family secrets', *National Geographic*, 218/ 3 (2010), 34–59.

Hazareesingh, Sudhir, *The Legend of Napoleon* (London, 2005).

Heesterman, J.C., 'The conundrum of the king's authority', in Richards (ed.), *Kingship and Authority*, 1–27.

Henige, David, 'Akan stool succession under colonial rule – continuity or change?', *Journal of African History*, 16/2 (1975), 285–301.

Herb, Michael, *All in the Family: Absolutism, Revolution, and Democracy in Middle Eastern Monarchies* (New York, 1999).

Heusch, Luc de, 'Autorité et prestige dans la société tetela', *Zaïre*, 10 (1954), 1001–27.

'Forms of sacralized power in Africa', in Quigley (ed.), *Character of Kingship*, 25–37.

Hevia, James L., 'Rulership and Tibetan Buddhism in eighteenth-century China: Qing emperors, lamas and audience rituals', in Joëlle Rollo-Koster (ed.), *Medieval and Early Modern Ritual: Formalized Behavior in Europe, China, and Japan* (Leiden and Boston, MA, 2002), 279–302.

Hirschbiegel, Jan, and Werner Paravicini (eds.), *Der Fall des Günstlings: Hofparteien in Europa vom 13. bis zum 17. Jahrhundert. 8. Symposium der Residenzenkommission der Akademie der Wissenschaften zu Göttingen* (Ostfildern, 2004).

(eds.), *Das Frauenzimmer: die Frau bei Hofe in Spätmittelalter und Früher Neuzeit* (Stuttgart, 2000).

Hisako, Hata, 'Servants of the inner quarters: the women of the shogun's Great Interior', in Walthall (ed.), *Servants of the Dynasty*, 172–90.

Hocart, Arthur M., *Kings and Councillors: An Essay in the Comparative Anatomy of Human Society*. Classics in Anthropology (Chicago, IL, 1970 [1936]).

Kingship (London, 1927).

Hodgson, Marshall G.S., *The Venture of Islam: Conscience and History in a World Civilization* (Chicago, IL, 1974).

Hohkamp, Michaela, 'Transdynasticism at the dawn of the modern era: kinship dynamics among ruling families', in Christopher H. Johnson et al. (eds.), *Transregional and Transnational Families in Europe and Beyond: Experiences since the Middle Ages* (New York and Oxford, 2011), 93–106.

Holmgren, Jennifer, 'Imperial marriage in the native Chinese and non-Han state, Han to Ming', in Watson and Ebrey (eds.), *Marriage and Inequality*, 58–97.

'A question of strength: military capability and princess-bestowal in imperial China's foreign relations (Han to Ch'ing)', *Monumenta Serica*, 39 (1990–1), 31–85.

Holsti, K.J., *Taming the Sovereigns: Institutional Change in International Politics* (Cambridge, 2004).

Horowski, Leonhard, *Die Belagerung des Thrones: Machtstrukturen und Karrieremechanismen am Hof von Frankreich 1661–1789* (Stuttgart, 2012).

Horvath, Ronald J., 'The wandering capitals of Ethiopia', *Journal of African History*, 10/2 (1969), 205–19.

Hosking, Geoffrey, 'Trust and distrust: a suitable theme for historians?', *Transactions of the Royal Historical Society*, 6th series, 16 (2006), 95–115.

Hsieh, Bao Hua, *Concubinage and Servitude in Late Imperial China* (London, 2014).

'From charwoman to empress dowager: serving-women in the Ming palace', *Ming Studies*, 42/1 (2000), 26–80.

Huang, Hongxu, and Tian Guisen, 'A sociolinguistic view of linguistic taboo in Chinese', *International Journal of the Sociology of Language*, 81 (1990), 63–85.

Huang, Ray, *1587, A Year of No Significance: The Ming Dynasty in Decline* (1981).

Taxation and Governmental Finance in Sixteenth-Century Ming China (Cambridge, 1974).

Hucker, Charles O., *A Dictionary of Official Titles in Imperial China* (repr. Beijing, 2008).

'Governmental organization of the Ming dynasty', *Harvard Journal of Asiatic Studies*, 21 (1958), 1–66.

'Ming government', in Denis C. Twitchett and Frederick W. Mote (eds.), *The Cambridge History of China*, vol. VIII: *The Ming Dynasty* (Cambridge, 1998), 9–105.

Hughes, Lindsey, *Russia in the Age of Peter the Great* (New Haven, CT, 2000).

Hung, Ho-fung, 'Cultural strategies and the political economy of protest in mid-Qing China, 1740–1839', *Social Science History*, 33/1 (2009), 75–115.

Protest with Chinese Characteristics: Demonstrations, Riots, and Petitions in the Mid-Qing Dynasty (New York, 2013).

Hurst, G. Cameron, 'Insei', in Donald H. Shively and William H. McCullough (eds.), *The Cambridge History of Japan*, vol. II: *Heian Japan* (Cambridge, 1999), 576–643.

Hurter, Friedrich, *Philipp Lang, Kammerdiener Kaiser Rudolphs II: eine Criminal-Geschichte aus dem Anfang des siebenzehnten Jahrhunderts* (Schaffhausen, 1852).

Hurvitz, Nimrod, 'The contribution of early Islamic rulers to adjudication and legislation: the case of the *mazalim* tribunals', in Duindam et al. (eds.), *Law and Empire*, 135–56.

Idema, Wilt L., *Chinese Vernacular Fiction: The Formative Period* (Leiden, 1974).

İnalcık, Halil, 'Autonomous enclaves in Islamic states: Temlîks, Soyurghals, Yurdluḳ-Ocalḳlıḳs, Mâlikâne-Muḳâta'as and Awqâf', in Judith Pfeiffer and Sholeh A. Quinn (eds.), *History and Historiography of Post-Mongol Central Asia and the Middle East: Studies in Honor of John E. Woods* (Wiesbaden, 2006), 112–35.

Devlet-i Aliyye: Osmanlı İmparatorluğu Üzerine Araştırmalar II. Tagayyür ve Fesad (1603–1656), Bozuluş ve Kargaşa Dönemi, (The Sublime State, Studies on Ottoman Empire II. Transformation and intrigue: (1603–1656) the age of decline and disorder) (Istanbul, 2014).

'Doghandji', in Bearman et al. (eds.), *Encyclopaedia of Islam, Second Edition*.

The Ottoman Empire: The Classical Age 1300–1600 (London, 1973).

Ingham, John M., 'Human sacrifice at Tenochtitlan', *Comparative Studies in Society and History*, 26/3 (1984), 379–400.

Inneh, Daniel, 'The guilds working for the palace', in Barbara Plankensteiner (ed.), *Benin Kings and Rituals: Court Arts from Nigeria* (Vienna, 2007), 102–17.

Irwin, Robert, *The Arabian Nights: A Companion* (London, 1994).

'Toynbee and Ibn Khaldun', *Middle Eastern Studies*, 33/3 (1997), 461–79.

Izard, Michel, 'Le royaume Mossie du Yatenga', in Tardits (ed.), *Princes & serviteurs du royaume*, 61–106.

Jackson, Guida M., *Women Rulers Throughout the Ages: An Illustrated Guide* (Santa Barbara, CA, 1999).

Jahan, Farhat, 'Depiction of women in the sources of the Delhi sultanate (1206–1388)', PhD thesis, Aligarh Muslim University (2012).

Jansen, Marius, *Warrior Rule in Japan* (Cambridge, 1995).

Jay, Jennifer W., 'Another side of Chinese eunuch history: castration, marriage, adoption, and burial', *Canadian Journal of History*, 28/3 (1993), 459–78.

'Imagining matriarchy: "kingdoms of women" in Tang China', *Journal of the American Oriental Society*, 116/2 (1996), 220–9.

Jia, Li, 'Conflicts between monarch and ministers: a political and cultural interpretation of the Ming-dynasty officials' collective "petitions to the palace"', *Chinese Studies in History*, 44/3 (2011), 72–89.

Journet, Jean-Louis, and Daniel Dessert, 'Le lobby Colbert : un royaume ou une affaire de famille?', *Annales: économies, sociétés, civilisations*, 30/6 (1975), 1303–36.

Kahn, Harold L., *Monarchy in the Emperor's Eyes: Image and Reality in the Ch'ien-Lung Reign* (Cambridge, MA, 1971).

'Some mid-Ch'ing views of the monarchy', *Journal of Asian Studies*, 24/2 (1965), 229–43.

Kaiser, Michael, and Andreas Pečar (ed.), *Der zweite Mann im Staat: oberste Amtsträger und Favoriten im Umkreis der Reichsfürsten in der Frühen Neuzeit* (Berlin, 2003).

Kaiser, Thomas, 'The evil empire? The debate on Turkish despotism in eighteenth-century French political culture', *Journal of Modern History*, 72/1 (2000), 6–34.

Kaplan, Steven L., *Provisioning Paris: Merchants and Millers in the Grain and Flour Trade during the Eighteenth Century* (Ithaca, NY, 1984).

Kapuscinski, Ryszard, *The Emperor* (London, 2006).

Karakoç, Yıldız, 'Palace politics and the rise of the chief black eunuch in the Ottoman empire', MA thesis, Boğaziçi University (2005).

Kathirithamby-Wells, Jeyamalar, '"Strangers" and "stranger-kings": the Sayyid in eighteenth-century maritime Southeast Asia', *Journal of Southeast Asian Studies*, 40, Special Issue 3 (2009), 567–91.

Katz, Friedrich, 'A comparison of some aspects of the evolution of Cuzco and Tenochtitlán', in Richard P. Schaedel, Jorge E. Hardoy, and Nora Scott-Kinzer (eds.), *Urbanization in the Americas from its Beginning to the Present* (The Hague and Paris, 1978), 203–14.

Keay, Anna, *The Magnificent Monarch: Charles II and the Ceremonies of Power* (London and New York, 2008).

Keenan, Paul, *St Petersburg and the Russian Court, 1703–1761* (Basingstoke, 2013).

Keller, Katrin, *Hofdamen: Amtsträgerinnen im Wiener Hofstaat des 17. Jahrhunderts* (Vienna, 2005).

Kerlouégan, Jérôme, 'Printing for prestige? Publishing and publications by Ming princes', *East Asian Publishing and Society*, 1 (2011), 39–73.

Kershaw, Roger, *Monarchy in South-East Asia: The Faces of Tradition in Transition* (London and New York, 2001).

Kettering, Sharon, *Patrons, Brokers and Clients in Seventeenth-Century France* (Oxford, 1986).

Khafipour, Hani, 'The foundation of the Safavid state: fealty, patronage, and ideals of authority (1501–1576)', PhD thesis, University of Chicago (2013).

Khan, Sher Banu A.L., 'Rule behind the silk curtain: the sultanahs of Aceh 1641–1699', PhD thesis, Queen Mary, University of London (2009), http://qmro. qmul.ac.uk/jspui/handle/123456789/1471 (accessed 1 February 2014).

'The sultanahs of Aceh, 1641–99', in Arndt Graf, Susanne Schroter, and Edwin Wieringa (eds.), *Aceh: History, Politics and Culture* (Singapore, 2010), 3–25.

Khoury, Dina Rizk, 'The Ottoman centre versus provincial power-holders: an analysis of the historiography', in Faroqhi (ed.), *Cambridge History of Turkey*, III, 133–56.

Kiesel, Helmuth, *'Bei Hof, bei Höll': Untersuchungen zur literarischen Hofkritik von Sebastian Brant bis Friedrich Schiller* (Tübingen, 1979).

Kirch, Patrick Vinton, *How Chiefs Became Kings: Divine Kingship and the Rise of Archaic States in Ancient Hawai'i* (Berkeley, CA, 2010).

Klueting, Harm, *Der Josephinismus: ausgewählte Quellen zur Geschichte der theresianisch-josephinischen Reformen* (Darmstadt, 1995).

Köhle, Natalie, 'Why did the Kangxi emperor go to Wutai Shan? Patronage, pilgrimage, and the place of Tibetan Buddhism at the early Qing court', *Late Imperial China*, 29/1 (2008), 73–119.

Kollmann, Nancy Shields, *By Honor Bound: State and Society in Early Modern Russia* (Ithaca, NY, 1999).

Crime and Punishment in Early Modern Russia (Cambridge, 2012).

Koziol, Geoffrey, *Begging Pardon and Favor: Ritual and Political Order in Early Medieval France* (Ithaca, NY, and London, 1992).

Kracke, Jr, Edward A., 'Early visions of justice for the humble in East and West', *Journal of the American Oriental Society*, 96/4 (1976), 492–8.

Krige, E. Jensen, and J.D. Krige, *The Realm of a Rain-Queen: A Study of the Pattern of Lovedu Society* (Oxford, 1943).

Kunisch, Johannes, *Staatsverfassung und Mächtepolitik: zur Genese von Staatenkonflikten im Zeitalter des Absolutismus* (Berlin, 1979).

Kunt, Metin, 'Devolution from the centre to the periphery: an overview of Ottoman provincial administration', in Duindam and Dabringhaus (eds.), *Dynastic Centre*, 30–48.

'Ottomans and Safavids: states, statecraft, and societies, 1500–1800', in Youssef M. Choueiri (ed.), *A Companion to the History of the Middle East* (Chichester, 2008), 191–205.

'A prince goes forth (perchance to return)', in Karl Barbir and Baki Tezcan (eds.), *Identity and Identity Formation in the Ottoman World: A Volume of Essays in Honor of Norman Itzkowitz* (Madison, WI, 2007), 63–71.

The Sultan's Servants: The Transformation of Ottoman Provincial Government, 1550–1650 (New York, 1983).

Kuper, Adam, 'The "house" and Zulu political structure in the nineteenth century', *Journal of African History*, 34/3 (1993), 469–87.

Kutcher, Norman A., 'The death of the Xiaoxian empress: bureaucratic betrayals and the crises of eighteenth-century Chinese rule', *Journal of Asian Studies*, 56/3 (1997), 708–25.

'Unspoken collusions: the empowerment of Yuanming Yuan eunuchs in the Qianlong period', *Harvard Journal of Asiatic Studies*, 70/2 (2010), 449–95.

Kwon, Yonung, 'The royal lecture and Confucian politics in early Yi Korea', *Korean Studies*, 6/1 (1982), 41–62.

Lachaud, Frédérique, and Michael Penman (eds.), *Making and Breaking the Rules: Succession in Medieval Europe, c.1000–c.1600/Établir et abolir les normes: la succession dans l'Europe médiévale, vers 1000–vers 1600* (Turnhout, 2007)

Laidlaw, James, 'On theatre and theory: reflections on ritual in imperial Chinese politics', in McDermott (ed.), *State and Court Ritual*, 399–416.

Lal, Ruby, *Domesticity and Power in the Early Mughal World* (Cambridge, 2005).

Lambton, Anne K.S., 'Pīshkash', in Bearman et al. (eds.), *Encyclopaedia of Islam, Second Edition*.

State and Government in Medieval Islam: An Introduction to the Study of Islamic Political Theory: The Jurists (Oxford, 1981).

Landes, David S., *Dynasties: Fortunes and Misfortunes of the World's Great Family Businesses* (New York, 2006).

Lane, George, *Genghis Khan and Mongol Rule* (Indianapolis, IN, 2009).

Lane, Joan, *A Social History of Medicine: Health, Healing and Disease in England, 1750–1950* (London and New York, 2012).

Lange, Dierk, 'The kingdoms and peoples of Chad', in D.T. Niane (ed.), *General History of Africa*, vol. IV: *Africa from the Twelfth to the Sixteenth Century* (Berkeley, CA, 1984).

Larsen, Jeanne, 'Women of the imperial household: views of the emperor's consorts and their female attendants', *Denver Museum of Natural History*, 3rd series, 15 (1998), 23–35.

Larsen, Lynne, 'City of women: gendered space in the pre-colonial palace of Dahomey', *University of Toronto Art Journal*, 2 (2009), 1–11.

Law, Robin, 'Dahomey and the slave trade: reflections on the historiography of the rise of Dahomey', *Journal of African History*, 27 (1986), 237–67.

'Making sense of a traditional narrative: political disintegration in the kingdom of Oyo', *Cahiers d'études africaines*, 22/87 (1982), 387–401.

Lebeuf, Annie M.D, 'Le rôle de la femme dans l'organisation politique des sociétés africaines', in Denise Paulme (ed.), *Femmes d'Afrique noire* (Paris, 1960), 93–120.

Lebra, Takie Sugiyama, *Above the Clouds: Status Culture of the Modern Japanese Nobility* (Berkeley, CA, 1995).

Le Goff, Jacques, *Saint Louis* (Paris, 1996).

Lentin, Antony, *Peter the Great: His Law on the Imperial Succession: The Official Commentary* (Oxford, 1996).

Levanoni, Amalia, 'The Mamluk conception of the sultanate', *International Journal of Middle East Studies*, 26/3 (1994), 373–92.

Lever, Évelyne, *Les dernières noces de la monarchie: Louis XVI* (Paris, 2005).

Lewicka, Paulina, 'What a king should care about. two memoranda of the Mamluk sultan on running the state's affairs', *Studia Arabistyczne i Islamistyczne*, 6 (1998), 5–45.

Lewis, Bernard, *The Political Language of Islam* (Chicago, IL, and London, 1988).

Lhotsky, Alphons, 'Kaiser Karl VI. und sein Hof im Jahre 1712–13', *Mitteilungen des Instituts für Österreichische Geschichtsforschung*, 66 (1958), 52–80.

Li, Lillian M., and Alison Dray-Novey, 'Guarding Beijing's food security in the Qing dynasty: state, market, and police', *Journal of Asian Studies*, 58/4 (1999), 992–1032.

Lieberman, Victor, *Strange Parallels: Southeast Asia in Global Context, c. 800–1830*, 2 vols. (Cambridge, 2003).

Lieven, Dominic, 'The elites', in Dominic Lieven (ed.), *The Cambridge History of Russia*, vol. II: *Imperial Russia, 1689–1917* (Cambridge, 2006), 227–83.

Lillehoj, Elizabeth, *Art and Palace Politics in Early Modern Japan, 1580s–1680s* (Leiden and Boston, MA, 2011).

Llewellyn-Jones, Lloyd, *King and Court in Ancient Persia 559 to 331 BCE* (Edinburgh, 2013).

Lloyd, Peter C., 'The political structure of African kingdoms. an explanatory model', in Michael Banton (ed.), *Political Systems and the Distribution of Power* (London, 1965), 63–112.

Locher-Scholten, Elsbeth, and Anke Niehof (eds.), *Indonesian Women in Focus* (Dordrecht and Providence, RI, 1987)

Locher-Scholten, Elsbeth, and P.J. A. N. Rietbergen (eds.), *Hof en Handel: Aziatische vorsten en de VOC 1620–1720* (Leiden, 2004).

Loeb, Edwin M., 'Die Institution des sakralen Königtums', *Paideuma*, 10/2 (1964), 102–14.

Loos, Tamara, 'Sex in the inner city: the fidelity between sex and politics in Siam', *Journal of Asian Studies*, 64/4 (2005), 881–909.

Lox, Harlinde, *Van stropdragers en de pot van Olen: verhalen over Keizer Karel* (Leuven, 1999).

Lund, Cato, 'The royal capitals of the interlacustrine kingdoms: an urban legacy for Uganda', *Uganda Journal*, 45/1 (1999), 61–78.

Lyon, Ann, 'The place of women in European royal succession in the Middle Ages', *Liverpool Law Review*, 27/3 (2006), 361–93.

Mack, Beverly, 'Royal wives in Kano', in Catherine Coles and Beverly Mack (eds.), *Hausa Women in the Twentieth Century* (Madison, WI, 1991), 109–29.

Macneal, Alina, 'The stone encampment', *Environmental Design*, 11/1–2 (1991), 36–45, http://archnet.org/authorities/2690/publications/4388.

Maczak, Antoni (ed.), *Klientelsysteme im Europa der Frühen Neuzeit* (Munich, 1988).

Mair, Victor H., 'Language and ideology in the written popularizations of the "sacred edict"', in Nathan Johnson and Evelyn S. Rawski (eds.), *Popular Culture in Late Imperial China* (Berkeley, CA, 1985), 325–59.

Malo, David, *Hawaiian Antiquities* (Honolulu, HI, 1903).

Mann, Michael, 'The autonomous power of the state: its origins, mechanisms and results', *European Journal of Sociology / Archives européennes de sociologie*, 25/2 (1984), 185–213.

The Sources of Social Power, vol I: *A History of Power from the Beginning to AD 1760* (Cambridge, 1986).

March, Andrew L., *The Idea of China: Myth and Theory in Geographic Thought* (New York, 1974).

Marcus, Joyce, 'Breaking the glass ceiling: the strategies of royal women in ancient states', in Cecelia F. Klein (ed.), *Gender in Pre-Hispanic America* (Washington, DC, 2001), 305–40.

Marlow, Louis, 'Advice and advice literature', in Fleet et al. (eds.), *Encyclopaedia of Islam, Three*.

Martin, Bradley K., *Under the Loving Care of the Fatherly Leader: North Korea and the Kim Dynasty* (New York, 2006).

Martin, Ralph G., *Seeds of Destruction: Joe Kennedy and his Sons* (New York, 1995).

Martin, Russell E., *A Bride for the Tsar: Bride-Shows and Marriage Politics in Early Modern Russia* (DeKalb, IL, 2012).

'"For the firm maintenance of the dignity and tranquility of the imperial family": law and familial order in the Romanov dynasty', *Russian History*, 37/4 (2010), 389–411.

Marzolph, Ulrich, and Richard van Leeuwen, *The Arabian Nights Encyclopedia*, 2 vols. (Santa Barbara, CA, 2004).

Masters, Bruce, 'Semi-autonomous forces in the Arab provinces', in Faroqhi (ed.), *Cambridge History of Turkey*, III, 186–206.

Matthee, Rudi, 'Gifts and gift-giving in the Safavid period', in *Encyclopaedia Iranica* (2012), http://www.iranicaonline.org/articles/gift-giving-iv.

Persia in Crisis: Safavid Decline and the Fall of Isfahan (London and New York, 2012).

Mazzaoui, Michel M., 'From Tabriz to Qazvin to Isfahan: three phases of Safavid history', *Zeitschrift der Deutschen Morgenländischen Gesellschaft*, supplement 3 (1975), 514–22.

McCaskie, T.C., 'Office, land and subjects in the history of the Manwere Fekuo of Kumase: an essay in the political economy of the Asante state', *Journal of African History*, 21/2 (1980), 189–208.

State and Society in Pre-Colonial Asante (Cambridge, 2003).

McClain, James L., John Merriman, and Ugawa Kaoru (eds.), *Edo and Paris: Urban Life and the State in the Early Modern Era* (Ithaca, NY, and London, 1994).

McDermott, Joseph Peter (ed.), *State and Court Ritual in China* (Cambridge, 1999).

McGowan, Megan, 'Royal succession in earlier medieval Ireland: the fiction of tanistry', *Peritia*, 17–18 (2003), 357–81.

McKitterick, Rosamond, 'A king on the move: the place of an itinerant court in Charlemagne's government', in Duindam et al. (eds.), *Royal Courts*, 145–69.

McMahon, Keith, 'The institution of polygamy in the Chinese imperial palace', *Journal of Asian Studies*, 72/4 (2013), 917–36.

'Women rulers in imperial China', *Nannü: Men, Women and Gender in Early and Imperial China*, 15/2 (2013), 179–218.

Women Shall Not Rule: Imperial Wives and Concubines in China from Han to Liao (Lanham, MD, 2013).

Meier, Mischa, and Meret Strothmann, 'Dynasteia', in Hubert Cancik and Helmuth Schneider (eds.), *Brill's New Pauly: Encyclopedia of the Ancient World*, online edition (Leiden, 2002–).

Méricam-Bourdet, Myrtille, 'Voltaire contre Montesquieu?', *Revue Française d'Histoire des Idées Politiques*, 35/1 (2012), 25–36.

Mettam, Roger, 'Power, status and precedence: rivalries among the provincial elites of Louis XIV's France', *Transactions of the Royal Historical Society*, 38 (1988), 43–62.

Meyer, Eva-Maria, *Japans Kaiserhof in der Edo-Zeit: unter besonderer Berücksichtigung der Jahre 1846 bis 1867* (Münster, 1999).

Meyer, Milton W., *Japan: A Concise History* (Plymouth, 2009).

Michel, Eva, and Maria Luise Sternath (eds.), *Kaiser Maximilian I. und die Kunst der Dürerzeit* (Munich and Vienna, 2012).

Michels, Robert, *Zur Soziologie des Parteiwesens in der modernen Demokratie: Untersuchungen über die oligarchischen Tendenzen des Gruppenlebens* (Leipzig, 1911).

Michon, Cédric, *La crosse et le sceptre: les prélats d'état sous François Ier et Henri VIII* (Paris, 2008).

Millet, Hélène, and Peter Moraw, 'Clerics in the state,' in Reinhard (ed.), *Power Elites and State Building*, 173–88.

Mines, Mattison, and Vijayalakshmi Gourishankar, 'Leadership and individuality in South Asia: the case of the South Indian big-man', *Journal of Asian Studies*, 49/4 (1990), 761–86.

Mitchell, Colin P., 'Am I my brother's keeper? Negotiating corporate sovereignty and divine absolutism in 16th-century Turco-Iranian politics', in Colin P. Mitchell (ed.), *New Perspectives on Safavid Iran: Empire and Society* (Abingdon and New York, 2011).

Moberg, Axel, 'Regierungspromemoria eines ägyptischen Sultans', in Gotthold Weil (ed.), *Festschrift Eduard Sachau zum siebzigsten Geburtstage gewidmet von Freunden und Schülern* (Berlin, 1915), 406–21.

Moertono, Soemarsaid, 'The concept of power in Javanese tradition', *Indonesia Circle: School of Oriental & African Studies: Newsletter*, 2 (1974), 16–17.

State and Statecraft in Old Java: A Study of the Later Mataram Period, 16th to 19th Century (Ithaca, NY, 1963).

Monnet, Pierre, and Jean-Claude Schmitt (eds.), *Autobiographies souveraines* (Paris, 2012).

Monroe, J. Cameron, 'Power by design: architecture and politics in precolonial Dahomey', *Journal of Social Archaeology*, 10/3 (2010), 367–97.

Montefiore, Simon Sebag, *Stalin: The Court of the Red Tsar* (London, 2007).

Moore, Sally Falk, and Barbara G. Myerhoff (eds.), *Secular Ritual* (Assen and Amsterdam, 1977).

Moote, A. Lloyd, *Louis XIII, the Just* (Berkeley, CA, 1989).

Moraw, Peter, 'Der Harem des Kurfürsten Albrecht Achilles von Brandenburg-Ansbach', in Hirschbiegel and Paravicini (eds.), *Das Frauenzimmer*, 439–48.

Morgan, David, *The Mongols* (Cambridge, MA, 1986).

Mormiche, Pascale, *Devenir prince: l'école du pouvoir en France, XVIIe – XVIIIe siècles* (Paris, 2009).

Morris, Craig, 'Enclosures of power: the multiple spaces of Inca administrative palaces', in Evans and Pillsbury (eds.), *Palaces of the Ancient New World*, 299–324.

Mosca, Gaetano, *The Ruling Class* (New York, 1939).

Mounier, Pierre, 'La dynamique des interrelations politiques : le cas du sultanat de Zinder (Niger)', *Cahiers d'études africaines*, 39, 154 (1999) 367–386.

Mulryne, J.R., et al. (eds.), *Europa Triumphans: Court and Civic Festivals in Early Modern Europe*, 2 vols. (London, 2004).

Murdock, George Peter, *Africa: Its Peoples and their Culture History* (New York, 1959).

Murdock, Graeme, '"Freely elected in fear": princely elections and political power in early modern Transylvania', *Journal of Early Modern History*, 7/3 (2003), 213–44.

Murphey, Rhoads, *Exploring Ottoman Sovereignty: Tradition, Image and Practice in the Ottoman Imperial Household, 1400–1800* (London and New York, 2008).

Murphy, Neil, 'Ceremonial entries and the confirmation of urban privileges in France, c. 1350–1550', in Duindam and Dabringhaus (eds.), *Dynastic Centre*, 160–84.

'Royal grace, royal punishment: ceremonial entries and the pardoning of criminals in France, c. 1440–1560', in Duindam et al. (eds.), *Law and Empire*, 293–311.

Murr, Sylvia, 'Le politique "au Mogol" selon Bernier: appareil conceptuel, rhétorique stratégique, philosophie morale', in J. Pouchepadass and H. Stern (eds.), *De la royauté à l' état: anthropologie et histoire du politique dans le monde indien* (Paris, 1991), 239–311.

Musisi, Nakanyike B., 'Women, "elite polygyny," and Buganda state formation', *Signs: Journal of Women in Culture and Society*, 16/4 (1991), 757–86.

Naquin, Susan, *Peking: Temples and City Life, 1400–1900* (Berkeley, CA, 2000).

Nast, Heidi J., 'Women, royalty, and indigo dyeing in northern Nigeria, circa 1500–1807', in Walthall (ed.), *Servants of the Dynasty*, 232–60.

Necipoğlu, Gülru, *Architecture, Ceremonial, and Power: The Topkapi Palace in the Fifteenth and Sixteenth Centuries* (Cambridge, MA, 1991).

'Framing the gaze in Ottoman, Safavid, and Mughal palaces', *Ars Orientalis*, 23 (1993), 303–42.

Ng, Wai-ming, 'Political terminology in the legitimation of the Tokugawa system: a study of "bakufu" and "shōgun"', *Journal of Asian History*, 34 (2000), 135–48.

'Redefining legitimacy in Tokugawa historiography', *Sino-Japanese Studies*, 18 (2011), 1–20.

Nicola, Bruno De, 'Unveiling the Khatuns: some aspects of the role of women in the Mongol empire', PhD thesis, University of Cambridge (2011).

Ning, Chia, 'Qingchao Huangwei Jicheng Zhidu; The Institution of Qing Throne Succession (review)', *China Review International*, 14/1 (2007), 280–8.

Noorduyn, J., 'Majapahit in the fifteenth century', *Bijdragen tot de taal-, land- en volkenkunde*, 134/2 (1978), 207–74.

Norris, H.T., 'Fables and Legends', in Julia Ashtiany et al. (eds.), *Abbasid Belles Lettres* (Cambridge, 1990), 136–45.

Oakley, Francis, *Kingship: The Politics of Enchantment* (Oxford, 2008).

Oberg, K., 'The kingdom of Ankole in Uganda', in Fortes and Evans-Pritchard (eds.), *African Political Systems*, 121–62.

Obeyesekere, Gananath, 'Religion and polity in Theravada Buddhism: continuity and change in a great tradition. A review article', *Comparative Studies in Society and History*, 21/4 (1979), 626–39.

Ocko, Jonathan K., 'I'll take it all the way to Beijing: capital appeals in the Qing', *Journal of Asian Studies*, 47/2 (1988), 291–315.

O'Hanlon, Rosalind, 'Kingdom, household and body: history, gender and imperial service under Akbar', *Modern Asian Studies*, 41/5 (2007), 889–923.

Ooms, Herman, *Charismatic Bureaucrat: A Political Biography of Matsudaira Sadanobu, 1758–1829* (Chicago, IL, 1975).

Oral, Ertugrul, 'Edition of Mehmed Halife, *Tarih-i Gılmani*', PhD thesis, Marmara University (2000).

Oresko, Robert, G.C. Gibbs, and H.M. Scott (eds.), *Royal and Republican Sovereignty in Early Modern Europe: Essays in Memory of Ragnhild Hatton* (Cambridge and New York, 2006).

Osborne, Toby, 'A queen mother in exile: Marie de Medicis in the Spanish Netherlands and England, 1631–41', in Philip Mansel and T. Riotte (eds.), *Monarchy and Exile: The Politics of Legitimacy from Marie de Medicis to Wilhelm II* (Basingstoke and New York, 2011), 17–43.

Ottino, Paul, 'Ancient Malagasy dynastic succession: the Merina example', *History in Africa*, 10 (1983), 247–92.

Owens, Margaret E., *Stages of Dismemberment: The Fragmented Body in Late Medieval and Early Modern Drama* (Newark, NJ, 2005).

Palais, James B., 'Confucianism and the aristocratic/bureaucratic balance in Korea', *Harvard Journal of Asiatic Studies*, 44/2 (1984), 427–68.

Confucian Statecraft and Korean Institutions: Yu Hyŏngwŏn and the Late Chosŏn Dynasty (Seattle, WA, 1996).

Palmer, H.R., 'The kingdom of Gaógha of Leo Africanus. Part II', *Journal of the Royal African Society*, 29/116 (1930), 350–69.

Paravicini, Werner, and Jörg Wettlaufer (eds.), *Der Hof und die Stadt: Konfrontation, Koexistenz und Integration im Verhältnis von Hof und Stadt in Spätmittelalter und Früher Neuzeit*. Residenzenforschung Band 20 (Ostfildern, 2006).

Parfitt, Tom, 'Vladimir Putin goes hunting to "beef-up action man" image', *Guardian*, 1 November 2010.

Pasquet, Sylvie, 'Quand l'empereur de Chine écrivait à son jeune frère, empereur de Birmanie ... Analyse d'une correspondance diplomatique sur "feuilles d'or" (XVIIIᵉ siècle)', *Journal asiatique*, 300/1 (2012), 265–313.

Pazdernik, Charles F., 'Dynasty, idea of, Byzantine', in Roger S. Bagnall et al. (eds.), *The Encyclopedia of Ancient History* (Oxford, 2012), 2243–4.

Pease, Franklin, 'The Inka and political power in the Andes', in Basham (ed.), *Kingship in Asia and Early America*, 243–56.

Pečar, Andreas, *Die Ökonomie der Ehre: der höfische Adel am Kaiserhof Karls VI. (1711–1740)* (Darmstadt, 2003).

Peirce, Leslie P., *The Imperial Harem: Women and Sovereignty in the Ottoman Empire* (Oxford, 1993).

Peksevgen, Şefik, 'Murad III', in Ágoston and Masters (eds.), *Encyclopedia of the Ottoman Empire*, 401–3.

'Sokullu family', in Ágoston and Masters (eds.), *Encyclopedia of the Ottoman Empire*, 534–6.

Pennec, Hervé, and Dimitri Toubkis, 'Reflections on the notions of "empire" and "kingdom" in seventeenth-century Ethiopia: royal power and local power', *Journal of Early Modern History*, 8/3 (2004), 229–58.

Penzer, N.M., *The Harem: An Account of the Institution as it Existed in the Palace of the Turkish Sultans, with a History of the Grand Seraglio from its Foundation to the Present Time* (Philadelphia, PA, 1936).

Perrie, Maureen, *Pretenders and Popular Monarchism in Early Modern Russia: The False Tsars of the Time of Troubles* (Cambridge, 1995).

'"Royal marks": reading the bodies of Russian pretenders, 17th–19th centuries', *Kritika*, 11/3 (2010), 535–61.

Perry, J.R., 'Justice for the underprivileged: the ombudsman tradition of Iran', *Journal of Near Eastern Studies*, 37/3 (1978), 203–15.

Persson, Fabian, 'So that we Swedes are not more swine or goats than they are: space and ceremony at the Swedish court within an international context', in Birgitte Bøggild Johannsen (ed.), *Beyond Scylla and Charybdis: European Courts and Court Residences outside Habsburg and Valois/Bourbon Territories, 1500–1700* (Copenhagen, 2015), 123–36.

Pescheux, Gérard, 'Centre, limite, frontière dans le royaume Asante précolonial', *Journal des africanistes*, 74/1–2 (2004), 180–201.

Peterson, Willard J. (ed.), *The Cambridge History of China*, vol. IX: *The Ch'ing Empire to 1800* (Cambridge, 2002).

Pils, Susanne Claudine, and Jan Paul Niederkorn (eds.), *Ein zweigeteilter Ort? Hof und Stadt in der Frühen Neuzeit* (Innsbruck, 2005).

Pina-Cabral, João de, and Antónia Pedroso de Lima, *Elites: Choice, Leadership and Succession* (Oxford, 2000).

Pines, Yuri, *The Everlasting Empire: The Political Culture of Ancient China and its Imperial Legacy* (Princeton, NJ, 2012).

Pinto-Correia, Clara, *The Ovary of Eve: Egg and Sperm and Preformation* (Chicago, IL, 1998).

Ponsonby-Fane, Richard A.B., *The Imperial House of Japan* (Kyoto, 1959).

Pratt, Keith, and Richard Rutt, *Korea: A Historical and Cultural Dictionary* (Richmond, 1999).

Press, Volker, 'Österreichische Großmachtbildung und Reichsverfassung: zur kaiserlichen Stellung nach 1648', *Mitteilungen des Instituts für Österreichische Geschichtsforschung*, 98 (1990), 131–54.

Press, Volker, and Dietmar Willoweit (eds.), *Liechtenstein – fürstliches Haus und staatliche Ordnung: Geschichtliche Grundlagen und moderne Perspektiven* (Vaduz, Vienna, and Munich, 1987).

Putnam, Robert D., *The Comparative Study of Political Elites* (Englewood Cliffs, NJ, 1976).

Quaritch Wales, H.G., *Siamese State Ceremonies: Their History and Function* (London, 1931).

Qin, Guoshuai, 'In search of divine support: imperial inheritance, political power and Quanzhen Taoism at the court of the Wanli emperor, r. 1573–1620', unpublished paper.

Quigley, Declan (ed.), *The Character of Kingship* (Oxford, 2005).

Radcliffe-Brown, A.R., and D. Forde (eds.), *African Systems of Kinship and Marriage* (London, 1950).

Ranum, Orest A., *The Fronde: A French Revolution, 1648–1652* (New York and London, 1993)

Ras, J.J., 'Geschiedschrijving en de legitimiteit van het koningschap op Java', *Bijdragen tot de Taal-, Land- en Volkenkunde*, 150/3 (1994), 518–38.

Rattray, Robert Sutherland, *Ashanti Law and Constitution* (Oxford, 1929).

Ravina, Mark, *Land and Lordship in Early Modern Japan* (Stanford, CA, 1998).

Rawski, Evelyn S., 'Ch'ing imperial marriage and problems of rulership', in Watson and Ebrey (eds.), *Marriage and Inequality*, 170–204.

The Last Emperors: A Social History of Qing Imperial Institutions (Berkeley, CA, and London, 1998).

Redlich, Oswald, 'Das Tagebuch Esaias Pufendorfs, schwedischen Residenten am Kaiserhofe von 1671 bis 1674', *Mitteilungen des Instituts für Österreichische Geschichtsforschung*, 37 (1917), 541–97.

Reinhard, Wolfgang, 'Die Nase der Kleopatra: Geschichte im Lichte mikropolitischer Forschung. Ein Versuch', *Historische Zeitschrift*, 293/3 (2011), 633–66.

'Staat machen als organisiertes Verbrechen? Die Kriminalität der Mächtigen aus der Perspektive der Geschichte der Staatsgewalt', in C. Prittwitz (ed.), *Kriminalität der Mächtigen* (Baden-Baden, 2008), 174–84.

(ed.), *Power Elites and State Building* (Oxford, 1996).

Reischauer, Robert K., *Early Japanese History, c. 40 B.C. – A.D. 1167)* (Princeton, NJ, 1937).

Rhulman, Robert, 'Traditional heroes in Chinese popular fiction', in Arthur F. Wright (ed.), *The Confucian Persuasion* (Stanford, CA, 1960), 141–76.

Richards, Audrey I., 'African kings and their royal relatives', *Journal of the Royal Anthropological Institute of Great Britain and Ireland*, 91/2 (1961), 135–50.

'The political system of the Bemba tribe – north-eastern Rhodesia', in Fortes and Evans-Pritchard (eds.), *African Political Systems*, 83–120.

'Social mechanisms for the transfer of political rights in some African tribes', *Journal of the Royal Anthropological Institute of Great Britain and Ireland*, 90/2 (1960), 175–90.

'Some types of family structure amongst the Central Bantu', in Radcliffe-Brown and Forde (eds.), *African Systems of Kinship and Marriage*, 246–51.

Richards, J.F. (ed.), *Kingship and Authority in South Asia* (Madison, WI, 1978).

The Mughal Empire (Cambridge, 1995).

Richards, Judith M., '"To promote a woman to beare rule": talking of queens in mid-Tudor England', *Sixteenth Century Journal*, 28/1 (1997), 101–21.

Ringrose, Kathryn M., *The Perfect Servant: Eunuchs and the Social Construction of Gender in Byzantium* (Chicago, IL, 2003).

Rizvi, S.A.A., 'Kingship in Islam: a historical analysis', in Basham (ed.), *Kingship in Asia and Early America*, 29–82.

The Wonder that was India, vol. II: *A Survey of the History and Culture of the Indian Sub-Continent from the Coming of the Muslims to the British Conquest 1200–1700* (London, 1987).

Roberts, J.W. (ed.), *The Oxford Dictionary of the Classical World* (Oxford, 2007).

Robinson, David M. (ed.), *Culture, Courtiers, and Competition: The Ming Court (1368–1644)* (Cambridge, MA, 2008).

Martial Spectacles of the Ming Court (Cambridge, MA, 2013).

'Princely courts of the Ming dynasty', *Ming Studies*, 65 (2012), 1–12.

Rolland, Paul, *Histoire de Tournai* (Tournai and Paris, 1956).

Rollo-Koster, Joëlle, *Raiding Saint Peter: Empty Sees, Violence, and the Initiation of the Great Western Schism (1378)* (Leiden and Boston, MA, 2008).

Rosenthal, Jean-Laurent, and Roy Bin Wong, *Before and Beyond Divergence: The Politics of Economic Change in China and Europe* (Cambridge, MA, and London, 2011).

Rostworowski, María, and Craig Morris, 'The fourfold domain: Inka power and its social foundations', in Frank Salomon and Stuart B. Schwartz (eds.), *The Cambridge History of the Native Peoples of the Americas* (Cambridge, 1999), 769–863.

Rounds, J., 'Dynastic succession and the centralization of power in Tenochtitlan', in George Allen Collier, Renato Rosaldo, and John D. Wirth (eds.), *The Inca and Aztec States, 1400–1800: Anthropology and History* (New York, 1982), 63–89.

Roux, Nicolas Le, *La faveur du roi: mignons et courtisans au temps des derniers Valois (vers 1547 – vers 1589)* (Paris, 2000).

Rowland, Daniel, 'Did Muscovite literary ideology place limits on the power of the tsar (1540s–1660s)?', *Russian Review*, 49 (1990), 125–55.

'Two cultures, one throne room: secular courtiers and orthodox culture in the Golden Hall of the Moscow Kremlin', in Valerie A. Kivelson (ed.), *Orthodox Russia: Belief and Practice under the Tsars* (University Park, PA, 2003), 33–57.

Rowlands, Guy, *The Dynastic State and the Army under Louis XIV: Royal Service and Private Interest, 1661–1701* (Cambridge, 2002).

'Louis XIV, aristocratic power and the elite units of the French army', *French History*, 13/3 (1999), 303–31.

Rüdiger, Axel, *Staatslehre und Staatsbildung: die Staatswissenschaft an der Universität Halle im 18. Jahrhundert* (Tübingen, 2005).

Ruel, Malcolm, 'The structural articulation of generations in Africa', *Cahiers d'études africaines*, 165/1 (2002), 51–82.

Ruff, Julius R., *Violence in Early Modern Europe 1500–1800* (Cambridge, 2001).

Ruskola, Teemu, 'The East Asian legal tradition', in Mauro Bussani and Ugo Mattei (eds.), *The Cambridge Companion to Comparative Law* (Cambridge, 2012), 257–77.

Sahlins, Marshall D., 'Poor man, rich man, big-man, chief: political types in Melanesia and Polynesia', *Comparative Studies in Society and History*, 5/3 (1963), 285–303.

'The stranger-king or, Elementary forms of the politics of life', *Indonesia and the Malay World*, 36/105 (2008), 177–99.

Sansom, George B., 'Early Japanese law and administration', *Transactions of the Asiatic Society of Japan*, 9 (1932), 67–109.

Santucci, James A., 'Aspects of the nature and functions of Vedic kingship', in Basham (ed.), *Kingship in Asia and Early America*, 83–113.

Sariyannis, Marinos, 'The princely virtues as presented in Ottoman political and moral literature', *Turcica*, 63 (2011), 121–44.

Scheidel, Walter, 'Brother–sister and parent–child marriage outside royal families in ancient Egypt and Iran: a challenge to the sociobiological view of incest avoidance?', *Ethology and Sociobiology*, 17/5 (1996), 319–40.

'Monogamy and polygyny in Greece, Rome, and world history', Social Science Research Network (Rochester, NY, 2008), http://papers.ssrn.com/abstract=1214729 (accessed 6 February 2014).

Schiller, Laurence D., 'The royal women of Buganda', *International Journal of African Historical Studies*, 23/3 (1990), 455–73.

Schimmel, Annemarie, *The Empire of the Great Mughals: History, Art and Culture* (London, 2004).

Schlegelmilch, Anna Margarete, *Die Jugendjahre Karls V: Lebenswelt und Erziehung des burgundischen Prinzen* (Cologne, 2011).

Schmugge, Ludwig, and Béatrice Wiggenhauser (ed.), *Illegitimität im Spätmittelalter* (Munich, 1994).

Schneewind, Sarah, *A Tale of Two Melons: Emperor and Subject in Ming China* (Cambridge, MA, 2006).

'Visions and revisions: village policies of the Ming founder in seven phases', *T'oung Pao*, 87/4 (2001), 317–59.

Schneider, David Murray, and Kathleen Gough, *Matrilineal Kinship* (Berkeley, CA, 1962).

Schnettger, Matthias, 'Weibliche Herrschaft in der Frühen Neuzeit: einige Beobachtungen aus verfassungs- und politikgeschichtlicher Sicht', *Zeitenblicke*, 8/2 (2009), http://www.zeitenblicke.de/2009/2/schnettger/dippArticle.pdf.

Schreiner, Peter, *Byzanz 565–1453* (Munich, 2011).

Schumann, Jutta, *Die andere Sonne: Kaiserbild und Medienstrategien im Zeitalter Leopolds I.* (Berlin, 2003).

Scott, Hamish M., *Forming Aristocracy: The Reconfiguration of Europe's Nobilities, c. 1300–1750* (forthcoming).

Scott, James C., *Comparative Political Corruption* (Englewood Cliffs, NJ, 1972).

Screech, Timon, *Shogun's Painted Culture: Fear and Creativity in the Japanese States, 1760–1829* (London, 2000).

Seligmann, C.G., 'Some aspects of the Hamitic problem in the Anglo-Egyptian Sudan', *Journal of the Royal Anthropological Institute of Great Britain and Ireland*, 43 (1913), 593–705.

Sharma, Karuna, 'A visit to the Mughal harem: lives of royal women', *South Asia: Journal of South Asian Studies*, 32/2 (2009), 155–69.

Shillony, Ben-Ami, *Enigma Of The Emperors: Sacred Subservience In Japanese History* (Folkestone, 2005).

Sidney, Henry, 'Sir Henry Sidney's memoir of his government of Ireland. 1583', *Ulster Journal of Archaeology*, 3 (1855), 33–357, and 5 (1857), 299–323.

Sieg, Hans Martin, *Staatsdienst, Staatsdenken und Dienstgesinnung in Brandenburg-Preussen im 18. Jahrhundert (1713–1806): Studien zum Verständnis des Absolutismus* (Berlin, 2003).

Silver, Larry, *Marketing Maximilian: The Visual Ideology of a Holy Roman Emperor* (Princeton, NJ, 2008).

Simms, Katharine, 'Changing patterns of regnal succession in later medieval Ireland', in Lachaud and Penman (eds.), *Making and Breaking the Rules*, 161–72.

Singh, Upinder, 'Governing the state and the self: political philosophy and practice in the edicts of Aśoka', *South Asian Studies*, 28/2 (2012), 131–45.

Sinopoli, Carla M., 'Monumentality and mobility in Mughal capitals', *Asian Perspectives*, 33/2 (1994), 293–308.

Siret, C.J.Ch., *Précis historique du sacre de S.M. Charles X* (Reims, 1826).

Skinner, G.W., 'Introduction: urban development in imperial China', in G.W. Skinner (ed.), *The City in Late Imperial China* (Stanford, CA, 1977).

Slanicka, Simona (ed.), *Bastarde*, WerkstattGeschichte 51 (Essen, 2009).

Smith, Vincent A., *Akbar the Great Mogul 1542–1605* (Oxford, 1917).

Smits, Gregory, 'Ambiguous boundaries: redefining royal authority in the kingdom of Ryukyu', *Harvard Journal of Asiatic Studies*, 60/1 (2000), 89–123.

Smuts, Malcolm, and George Gorse (eds.), *The Politics of Space: Courts in Europe c. 1500–1750* (Rome, 2009).

Sneath, David, *The Headless State: Aristocratic Orders, Kinship Society, and Misrepresentations of Nomadic Inner Asia* (New York, 2007).

Snyder-Reinke, Jeffrey, *Dry Spells: State Rainmaking and Local Governance in Late Imperial China* (Cambridge, MA, 2009).

Southall, Aidan, 'A critique of the typology of states and political systems', in Michael Banton (ed.), *Political Systems and the Distribution of Power* (London, 1965), 113–40.

'The segmentary state in Africa and Asia', *Comparative Studies in Society and History*, 30/1 (1988), 52–82.

Spangler, Jonathan, *The Society of Princes: The Lorraine-Guise and the Conservation of Power and Wealth in Seventeenth-Century France* (Farnham, 2009).

Spawforth, Antony (ed.), *The Court and Court Society in Ancient Monarchies* (Cambridge, 2011).

Spellman, W.M., *Monarchies 1000–2000* (London, 2001).

Spence, Jonathan D., *Emperor of China: Self-Portrait of K'ang-Hsi* (New York, 1974).

'The K'ang-hsi reign', in Peterson (ed.), *Cambridge History of China*, IX, 120–82.

Spielman, John P., *The City & the Crown: Vienna and the Imperial Court 1600–1740* (West Lafayette, IN, 1993).

Sreenivasan, Ramya, 'A South Asianist's response to Lieberman's *Strange Parallels*', *Journal of Asian Studies*, 70/4 (2011), 983–93.

Steenbrink, Karel, 'Groggy bij Garebeg: Nederlanders bij de Javaans-islamitische feesten in Yogyakarta', *Indische Letteren*, 21/1 (2006), 57–69.

Steinhardt, Nancy Shatzman, 'Why were Chang'an and Beijing so different?', *Journal of the Society of Architectural Historians*, 45/4 (1986), 339–57.

Stewart, Alan, *The Cradle King: A Life of James VI & I* (London, 2003).

Stewart, Angus, 'Between Baybars and Qalāwūn: under-age rulers and succession in the early Mamlūk sultanate', *Al-Masaq*, 19/1 (2007), 47–54.

Stewart, Marjorie Helen, 'Kinship and succession to the throne of Bussa', *Ethnology*, 17/2 (1978), 169–82.

Stilwell, Sean, *Slavery and Slaving in African History* (Cambridge, 2014).

Stoeltje, Beverly J., 'Asante queen mothers', *Annals of the New York Academy of Sciences*, 810/1 (1997), 41–71.

Storm, Servaas, 'Why the West grew rich and the rest did not, or how the present shapes our views of the past', *Development and Change*, 44/5 (2013), 1181–206.

Strootman, Rolf, 'Hellenistic court society: The Seleukid imperial court under Antiochos the Great, 223–187 BCE', in Duindam et al. (eds.), *Royal Courts*, 63–89.

Struve, Lynn A., *Voices from the Ming–Qing Cataclysm: China in Tigers' Jaws* (New Haven, CT, 1993).

Subrahmanyam, Sanjay, *Courtly Encounters: Translating Courtliness and Violence in Early Modern Eurasia* (Cambridge, MA, 2012).

From Tagus to the Ganges: Explorations in Connected History (Oxford, 2011).

Supomo, S., 'Some aspects of kingship in ancient Java', in Basham (ed.), *Kingship in Asia and Early America*, 161–77.

Suwannathat-Pian, Kobkua, 'Thrones, claimants, rulers and rules: the problem of succession in the Malay sultanates', *Journal of the Malaysian Branch of the Royal Asiatic Society*, 66/2 (1993), 1–27.

Swann, Julian, *Provincial Power and Absolute Monarchy: The Estates General of Burgundy, 1661–1790* (Cambridge, 2003).

Syros, Vasileios, 'Shadows in heaven and clouds on earth: the emergence of social life and political authority in the early modern Islamic empires', *Viator*, 43/2 (2012), 377–406.

Szonyi, Michael, *Practicing Kinship: Lineage and Descent in Late Imperial China* (Stanford, CA, 2002).

Szuppe, Maria, 'La participation des femmes de la famille royale à l'exercice du pouvoir en Iran safavide au XVIe siècle', *Studia Iranica*, 23/2 (1994), 211–58 (première partie), and 24/1 (1995), 61–122 (seconde partie).

Tacke, Andreas (ed.), *Wir wollen der Liebe Raum geben: Konkubinate geistlicher und weltlicher Fürsten um 1500* (Göttingen, 2006).

Tackett, Timothy, *Becoming a Revolutionary: The Deputies of the French National Assembly and the Emergence of a Revolutionary Culture (1789–1790)* (Princeton, NJ, 1996).

Taft, Frances H., 'Honor and alliance: reconsidering Mughal Rajput marriages', in Karine Schomer, John L. Erdman, and Deryck O. Lodrick (eds.), *The Idea of Rajasthan: Explorations in Regional Identity* (Manohar, 1994), 217–41.

Tambiah, Stanley J., 'The galactic polity: the structure of traditional kingdoms in Southeast Asia', in Stanley A. Freed (ed.), *Anthropology and the Climate of Opinion* (New York, 1977), 69–97.

Tamrat, Taddesse, *Church and State in Ethiopia, 1270–1527* (Oxford, 1972).

Tardits, Claude, *Le royaume bamoum* (Paris, 1980).

(ed.), *Princes & serviteurs du royaume: cinq études de monarchies africaines* (Paris, 1987).

Taylor, C., 'The Salic Law, French queenship, and the defense of women in the late Middle Ages', *French Historical Studies*, 29/4 (2006), 543–64.

Terray, Emmanuel, 'L'économie politique du royaume Abron du Gyaman', *Cahiers d'études africaines*, 22 (1982), 251–75.

'Le royaume Abron du Gyaman', in Tardits (ed.), *Princes & serviteurs du royaume*, 23–58.

Terzioglu, Derin, 'The imperial circumcision festival of 1582: an interpretation', *Muqarnas*, 12 (1995), 84–100.

Tezcan, Baki, 'The debut of Kösem Sultan's political career', *Turcica*, 40 (2008), 347–59.

'The question of regency in Ottoman dynasty: the case of the early reign of Ahmed I', *Archivum Ottomanicum*, 25 (2008), 185–98.

The Second Ottoman Empire: Political and Social Transformation in the Early Modern World (Cambridge, 2010).

Thelander, Dorothy R., 'Mother Goose and her goslings: the France of Louis XIV as seen through the fairy tale', *Journal of Modern History*, 54/3 (1982), 467–96.

Thøfner, Margit, '"Willingly we follow a gentle leader … ": joyous entries into Antwerp', in Duindam and Dabringhaus (eds.), *Dynastic Centre*, 185–202.

Thompson, Elizabeth, 'Public and private in Middle Eastern women's history', *Journal of Women's History*, 15/1 (2003), 52–69.

Thornton, John K., *A Cultural History of the Atlantic World, 1250–1820* (Cambridge, 2012).

'Elite women in the kingdom of Kongo: historical perspectives on women's political power', *Journal of African History*, 47/3 (2006), 437–60.

'Legitimacy and political power: Queen Njinga, 1624–1663', *Journal of African History*, 32/1 (1991), 25–40.

Tilly, Charles, *Trust and Rule* (Cambridge, 2005).

Tin-bor Hui, Victoria, *War and State Formation in Ancient China and Early Modern Europe* (Cambridge, 2005).

Tod, James, *Annals and Antiquities of Rajasthan or the Central and Western Rajput States of India*, 3 vols. (Oxford, 1920).

Torbert, Preston M., *The Ch'ing Imperial Household Department: A Study of its Organization and Principal Functions, 1662–1796* (Cambridge, MA, 1977).

Tordoff, William, 'The Ashanti confederacy', *Journal of African History*, 3/3 (1962), 399–417.

Totman, Conrad D., *Politics in the Tokugawa Bakufu, 1600–1843* (Cambridge, MA, 1967).

Tougher, Shaun, *The Eunuch in Byzantine History and Society* (London, 2008).

Eunuchs in Antiquity and Beyond (London, 2002).

Toynbee, Arnold Joseph, *A Study of History* (various editions).

Trakulhun, Sven, 'The view from the outside: Nicolas Gervaise, Simon de la Loubère and the perception of seventeenth century Siamese government and society', *Journal of the Siam Society*, 85/1–2 (1997), 75–84.

Tremlett, Giles, 'Spain's King Juan Carlos under fire over elephant hunting trip', *Guardian*, 15 April 2012.

Trompf, G.W., *The Idea of Historical Recurrence in Western Thought: From Antiquity to the Reformation* (Berkeley, CA, and London, 1979).

Tsai, Shih-Shan Henry, *The Eunuchs in the Ming Dynasty* (New York, 1996).

Tsukahira, Toshio G., *Feudal Control in Tokugawa Japan: The Sankin Kotai System* (Cambridge, MA, 1966).

Turner, Terence, 'Transformation, hierarchy and transcendence: a reformulation of Van Gennep's model of the structure of *rites de passage*', in Moore and Myerhoff (eds.), *Secular Ritual*, 53–70.

Turner, Victor, 'Variations on the theme of liminality', in Moore and Myerhoff (eds.), *Secular Ritual*, 36–52.

Twitchett, Denis, '*Chen Gui* and other works attributed to Empress Wu Zetian', *Asia Major*, 16/1 (2003), 33–109.

'How to be an emperor: T'ang T'ai-tsung's vision of his role', *Asia Major*, 3rd series, 9 (1996), 1–102.

'The T'ang imperial family', *Asia Major*, 7/2 (1994), 1–61.

Tymowski, Michał, *Early Imperial Formations in Africa and the Segmentation of Power* (Basingstoke, 2011).

Valeri, Valerio, 'Le fonctionnement du système des rangs à Hawaii', *L'Homme*, 12/1 (1972), 29–66.

Vansina, Jan, 'A comparison of African kingdoms', *Africa*, 32 (1962), 324–35.

Kingdoms of the Savanna (Madison, WI, 1966).

Vaporis, Constantine Nomikos, *Tour of Duty: Samurai, Military Service in Edo, and the Culture of Early Modern Japan* (Honolulu, HI, 2008).

Vatin, Nicolas, and Gilles Veinstein, *Le sérail ébranlé: essai sur les morts, dépositions et avènements des sultans ottomans, XVIe–XIXe siècle* (Paris, 2003).

Vec, Miloš, *Zeremonialwissenschaft im Fürstenstaat: Studien zur juristischen und politischen Theorie absolutistischer Herrschaftsrepräsentation* (Cologne and Weimar, 1998).

Völkel, Michaela, *Schloßbesichtigungen in der Frühen Neuzeit: ein Beitrag zur Frage nach der Öffentlichkeit höfischer Repräsentation* (Munich and Berlin, 2007).

Vries, Peer, 'Does wealth entirely depend on inclusive institutions and pluralist politics? A review of Daron Acemoglu and James A. Robinson, *Why Nations Fail*', *Ensayos de Economía*, 43 (2013), 181–202.

'Governing growth: a comparative analysis of the role of the state in the rise of the West', *Journal of World History*, 13 (2002), 67–138.

Wakabayashi, Bob Tadashi, 'In name only: imperial sovereignty in early modern Japan', *Journal of Japanese Studies*, 17/1 (1991), 25–57.

Japanese Loyalism Reconstrued: Yamagata Daini's Ryūshi Shinron of 1759 (Honolulu, HI, 1995).

Wakeman, Jr, Frederic, 'The Dynastic Cycle', in *The Fall of Imperial China* (New York, 1977), 55–70.

Wallech, Steven, et al., *World History: A Concise Thematic Analysis* (Malden, MA, and Oxford, 2012).

Walter, Christopher, 'Raising on a shield in Byzantine Iconography', *Revue des études byzantines*, 33/1 (1975), 133–76.

Walthall, Anne, 'Hiding the shoguns: secrecy and the nature of political authority in Tokugawa Japan', in Bernhard Scheid and Mark Teeuwen (eds.), *The Culture of Secrecy in Japanese Religion* (London, 2013), 332–56.

'Histories official, unofficial and popular: shogunal favourites in the Genroku era', in James C. Baxter and Joshua A. Fogel (eds.), *Writing Histories in Japan: Texts and their Transformations from Ancient Times through the Meiji Era* (Kyoto, 2007), 175–99.

The Weak Body of a Useless Woman: Matsuo Taseko and the Meiji Restoration (Chicago, IL, 1998).

(ed.), *Servants of the Dynasty: Palace Women in World History* (Berkeley, CA, 2008)

Wang, Richard G., *The Ming Prince and Daoism: Institutional Patronage of an Elite* (Oxford, 2012).

Wang, Shuo, 'Qing imperial women: empresses, concubines, and aisin gioro daughters', in Walthall (ed.), *Servants of the Dynasty*, 137–58.

Watanabe-O'Kelly, Helen, '"True and historical descriptions"? European festivals and the printed record', in Duindam and Dabringhaus (eds.), *Dynastic Centre*, 150–9.

Watson, James L., 'Waking the dragon: visions of the Chinese imperial state in local myth', in Stefan Feuchtwang and Hugh Baker (eds.), *An Old State in New Settings: Studies in the Social Anthropology of China in Memory of Maurice Freedman* (Oxford, 1991), 162–77.

Watson, Rubie, and Patricia B. Ebrey (eds.), *Marriage and Inequality in Chinese Society* (Berkeley, CA, 1991).

Webb, Herschel, *The Japanese Imperial Institution in the Tokugawa Period* (New York, 1968).

Weber, Hermann, 'Die Bedeutung der Dynastien für die europäische Geschichte in der Frühen Neuzeit', *Zeitschrift für bayerische Landesgeschichte*, 44 (1981), 5–32.

Weber, Max, *Wirtschaft und Gesellschaft: Grundriss der verstehenden Soziologie* (Tübingen, 1972 [1921]).

'Wissenschaft als Beruf', in *Gesammelte Aufsätze zur Wissenschaftslehre*, vol. I (Tübingen, 1922).

Whitaker, Ian, 'Regal succession among the Dálriata', *Ethnohistory*, 23/4 (1976), 343–63.

Wilkinson, Endymion Porter, *Chinese History: A Manual* (Cambridge, MA, 2013).

Wilks, Ivor, *Asante in the Nineteenth Century: The Structure and Evolution of a Political Order* (Cambridge, 1989).

'Aspects of bureaucratization in Ashanti in the nineteenth century', *Journal of African History*, 7 (1966), 215–32.

'On mentally mapping Greater Asante: a study of time and motion', *Journal of African History*, 33/2 (1992), 175–90.

Will, Pierre-Étienne, 'Views of the realm in crisis: testimonies on imperial audiences in the nineteenth century', *Late Imperial China*, 29/1 (2008), 125–59.

Will, Pierre-Étienne, and R. Bin Wong, *Nourish the People: The State Civilian Granary System in China, 1650–1850* (Ann Arbor, MI, 1991).

Windler, Christian, 'Diplomatic history as a field for cultural analysis: Muslim–Christian relations in Tunis, 1700–1840', *Historical Journal*, 44/1 (2001), 79–106.

Winkelbauer, Thomas, *Fürst und Fürstendiener: Gundaker von Liechtenstein, ein österreichischer Aristokrat des konfessionellen Zeitalters* (Vienna and Munich, 1999).

Wittfogel, Karl August, *Oriental Despotism: A Comparative Study of Total Power* (New Haven, CT, and London, 1957).

Wittfogel, Karl August, and Feng Chia-Sheng, *History of Chinese Society: Liao, 907–1125* (Philadelphia, PA, 1949).

Wood, Andy, *Riot, Rebellion and Popular Politics in Early Modern England* (Basingstoke, 2002).

Wortman, Richard, 'The representation of dynasty and "fundamental laws" in the evolution of Russian monarchy', *Kritika*, 13/2 (2012), 265–300.

Wu, Silas H.L., *Passage to Power: K'ang-Hsi and His Heir Apparent, 1661–1722* (Cambridge, 1979).

Yaya, Isabel, *The Two Faces of Inca History: Dualism in the Narratives and Cosmology of Ancient Cuzco* (Leiden and Boston, MA, 2012).

Yelce, Zeynep Nevin, 'The making of Sultan Süleyman: a study of process/es of image making and reputation management', PhD thesis, Sabanci University (2009).

Yildirim, Riza, 'Inventing a Sufi tradition: the use of the Futuwwa ritual gathering as a model for the Qizilbash Djem', in Curry and Ohlander (eds.), *Sufism and Society*, 165–82.

Yuan, Li, 'The Ming emperors' practice of self-examination and self-blame', *Chinese Studies in History*, 44/3 (2011), 6–30.

Zelin, Madeleine, 'The Yung-Cheng reign', in Peterson (ed.), *Cambridge History of China*, IX, 183–229.

Zens, Robert W., 'Provincial powers: the rise of Ottoman local notables (ayan)', *History Studies*, 3 (2011), 433–47.

Zhu, Jianfei, *Chinese Spatial Strategies: Imperial Beijing, 1420–1911* (London, 2012).

Zilfi, Madeline C., 'The Ottoman ulema', in Faroqhi (ed.), *Cambridge History of Turkey*, III, 207–25.

Zito, Angela, *Of Body and Brush: Grand Sacrifice as Text/Performance in Eighteenth-Century China* (Chicago, IL, 1997).

Zitser, Ernest A., 'Post-Soviet Peter: new histories of the late Muscovite and early imperial Russian court', *Kritika*, 6/2 (2005), 375–92.

    The Transfigured Kingdom: Sacred Parody and Charismatic Authority at the Court of Peter the Great (Ithaca, NY, 2004).

Zmora, Hillay, *Monarchy, Aristocracy, and the State in Europe* (London, 2001).

Zujie, Yuan, 'Dressing for power: rite, costume, and state authority in Ming dynasty China', *Frontiers of History in China*, 2/2 (2007), 181–212.

Index

Lightning Source UK Ltd.
Milton Keynes UK
UKHW022238270421
382751UK00006B/63

9 781107 637580